Embedded Commissioning
of Building Systems

Embedded Commissioning
of Building Systems

Ömer Akın
Tanyel Türkaslan-Bülbül
Sang Hoon Lee
James Garrett
Burcu Akıncı
Daniel Huber
Mario Bergés
Steven Bushby

**ARTECH
HOUSE**

BOSTON | LONDON
artechhouse.com

Library of Congress Cataloging-in-Publication Data
A catalog record for this book is available from the U.S. Library of Congress.

British Library Cataloguing in Publication Data
A catalog record for this book is available from the British Library.

ISBN-13: 978-1-60807-147-0

Cover design by Vicki Kane

© 2012 Artech House
685 Canton Street
Norwood, MA 02060

10 9 8 7 6 5 4 3 2 1   *10066 06 920*

To Mete and Ayça who are full of wonder
and delight ever since their synchronous arrival

Contents

CHAPTER 9

Communication Protocols and Data Accessibility   159

CHAPTER 10

Building Codes   173

CHAPTER 11

Sensors   193

CHAPTER 12

Value-Based Design   207

Preface

It is remarkable that buildings and their infrastructures, for how much they cost, lack comprehensive and reliable metrics that can ensure their expected performance. Although considerable care is put into designing green buildings, once they are put into use there is no systematic and reliable way of evaluating their performance. Many such capital projects, even those that are legendary for breaking new ground in the interests of energy efficiency and environmental impact, have fallen into states of undesirable performance through natural degradation, disrepair, or poor operational practices [1].

Building commissioning and *post-occupancy evaluation* are two of the best known methods that have been used to remedy this problem, albeit with mixed success. In today's digital, green, and consumer-driven marketplace, increasingly, architecture-engineering-construction (AEC) professionals are looking for sophisticated approaches, tools, and systems that can help them conduct building performance verification assessments reliably and effectively.

This book provides a vision for the future of building evaluation in AEC fields through an approach we call *embedded commissioning* (ECx). ECx is an information-based digital technology applied longitudinally to the building life-cycle process. Its purpose is to embed every stage of the capital project delivery (CPD) process, from requirement specification to operation, with interoperable and persistent information (Chapter 2).

Initially, in Part I, we make the case for building evaluation in general and ECx specifically as a general strategy to overcome inefficiencies and failures seen in buildings. Due to evolving client awareness, facility standards, and new digital technologies, these approaches offer the possibility of successfully addressing the most serious challenges in building evaluation engineering.

In the next part, Part II, we place the ECx approach in the context of a variety of tools and technologies currently available and emerging in the AEC sector. We will review major institutional structures that furbish current AEC practices: building information modeling (BIM), product and process modeling, mapping between process and product models, laser technology–based modeling, building code compliance verification, and data access and exchange standards.

In the final part, Part III, we discuss emerging research findings in the areas of sensor networks, value-based design, fields tools and AR/VR methods, just-in-time technologies, and wearable computers. Finally, we conclude with a brief look at visions of new developments beyond the immediate future.

Reference

[1]   Bailey, R., "Unsustainable Promises: Not-So-Green Architecture," *Reason*, May 2002.

Acknowledgments

This book was authored by a team consisting of Burcu Akıncı, Mario Berges, Steven Bushby, James Garrett, Daniel Huber, Sang Hoon Lee, Tanyel Türkaslan-Bülbül, and Ömer Akın, who authored half of the chapters and edited this volume. This team represents affiliations with institutions including Carnegie Mellon University, Penn State University, and Virginia Polytechnic Institute and State University.

The authors owe a debt of gratitude to the individuals, too many in numbers to mention in their entirety here, who helped to make this book the best that it can be. Below we acknowledge some of them.

We gratefully acknowledge that Ms. Aslı Akçamete jointly with Mr. Xuesong Liu wrote the first draft of Chapter 5, the outline of which was developed by Dr. Akıncı. Then, this draft was extensively edited and added to by Dr. Akıncı as well as Ms. Akçamete and Mr. Liu.

We gratefully acknowledge that Mr. Kwang Jun Lee wrote the first draft of Chapter 8, the outline of which was developed by Dr. Akın. Then, this draft was extensively edited and added to by Dr. Akın, as well as Mr. Lee.

We gratefully acknowledge that Mr. Salih Demir wrote the first draft of Chapter 10, the outline of which was developed by Dr. Garrett. Then, this draft was extensively edited and added to by Dr. Garrett, as well as Mr. Demir.

We gratefully acknowledge that Ms. Alejandra Munoz Munoz, Ms. Bhavna Muttreja, and Mr. Vinit Kumar Jain wrote the first draft of the Swiss Re case study in Chapter 12, the outline of which was developed by Dr. Akın. Then, this draft was extensively edited and added to by Dr. Akın, as well as Ms. Munoz Munoz, Ms. Muttreja, and Mr. Jain.

The first draft of all chapters of this book was edited by Ms. Sarah Zeigler and Ms. Bhavna Muttreja, making the task of the editor and the technical editing staff much easier. In addition, Ms. Muttreja and Ms. Zeigler embarked on the arduous tasks of obtaining copyright permissions for the plethora of tables and figures included in the book, and creating the first version of the volume's index.

Last but not least, we thank current and former staff of Artech House, in particular Ms. Lindsey Gendall, Ms. Deirdre Byrne, and Ms. Judi Stone for the professional job that they have done in initiating, facilitating, and bringing to this manuscript a successful conclusion, which we believe will be a seminal book in the field.

This field is best represented by a very large number of academic and industrial colleagues as well as national and international institutions of research such as the National Institute of Standards and Technology, National Science Foundation,

International Agency for Interoperability, and International Energy Agency, with whom we have worked and collaborated over the long years during which much of the research reported on in this book has been conducted and continues to be conducted.

We are deeply grateful for the direct and indirect help that our colleagues, literally located at the four corners of the world, have afforded us in developing the knowledge base that made this book possible. This collaboration is a tribute to the enormously valuable synergy that has been developing during the past few decades between academia and industry, which we hope and trust will continue to flourish in the future.

Ömer Akın
Pittsburgh, PA
September 21, 2011

Part I:
Introduction to Building Evaluation

Like all products of human endeavor, buildings also fail. They fail everyday with consequences that are dire for occupants, their pocketbooks, or the environment. Some of these failures are overt and sudden. Others are unnoticeable and gradual. A spectacular failure of the former kind is the fire at the MGM Grand Hotel and Casino complex in Las Vegas, Nevada, that suffered catastrophic fire damage on November 21, 1980, merely 7 years after it opened its doors to the public.

The cause of the fire was determined to be an electrical short in a deli pie case, due to lack of proper grounding. The fire was spotted by one of the hotel staff who happened to be walking through the area and reported it to others for emergency response. By this time, the fire had already advanced considerably inside the wall around the pie case and its progress into the deli and casino areas had become unavoidable. Due to the many combustible and synthetic finish materials in its path, the fire propelled through the first floor like a bolt of lightning and produced large amounts of "black smoke." Stairwells, elevator shafts, and seismic joints included in the design and construction of the building provided a chimney effect that distributed the toxic gases and smoke from the lower floors to the rest of the 28-story hotel tower. By the time all was said and done, 785 guests were injured and 87 killed. A vast majority of the deaths, more than 60, occurred in the upper floors.

There were four categories of failure in the design, construction, and operations of the MGM: deficient emergency plan, code violations, poor life-safety construction, and unprotected vertical shafts. The hotel did not have an emergency plan, which caused the occupants to find egress paths blocked and elevators, contrary to emergency operational principles, still functioning and full of smoke. In violation of code requirements, the sprinkler system had not been installed consistently throughout the building, most notably in the deli area. This exemption was granted by the fire chief under the assumption that the area would be operated 24 hours/day and there would be constant staff surveillance. The HVAC system lacked sensors to detect the smoke and the ability to shut down in the event of fire, as a consequence of which the building was inundated with deadly smoke by virtue of its own mechanical systems. When operations in the deli changed from a 24-hour schedule to a shorter duration, most of those responsible for the safety of the building became unaware of the impending risk. The building systems were never commissioned to see if they performed at the required level of efficiency or safety.

The life-safety system faults included lack of fire and smoke compartmentalization, noncombustible material use, and ventilation away from occupied spaces. It is estimated that the first two items alone would have accounted for three-quarters of the lives to be saved. Unsealed and unpartitioned vertical shafts included those that were not meant to act as air ducts, such as the seismic joints and elevator and stair towers. These were poorly designed and were not evaluated to account for emergency situations.

In the final analysis, it is quite easy to fall into the trap of labeling this event "just another case of human design error" or "construction failure," like those that have been widely publicized in literature: the Citicorp tower in New York, the John Hancock tower in Boston, the Kansas city Hyatt Regency, and the Tacoma Narrows Bridge. However, such an assumption would most certainly bypass the opportunity to understand the critical relationship between building evaluation and building performance, the main thesis of this book. It is through a critical understanding of such cases that we get to appreciate the important role of building evaluation in general and building commissioning (BCx) specifically. These are critical preventive measures for both catastrophic events and for improving building performance under ordinary circumstances that can translate into enormous energy and environmental savings. We will elaborate further on this point in Chapter 1.

In the case of the MGM fire, regular commissioning of the facility (Chapters 4 and 7), interoperable modeling of building information (Chapter 5), up-to-date as-is drawings of the facility (Chapter 6), live and robust system information communicated through reliable protocols (Chapter 9), proper and persistent code compliance checking (Chapter 10), and installation and upkeep of sensors (Chapter 11) would have all contributed to the prevention of its catastrophic failure.

We also cover additional aspects of persistent building performance evaluation through commissioning in the remaining chapters of this book. In Chapter 8, we describe how product and process information can be automatically interconnected. In Chapter 12, we review a method for estimating the economic value of innovation in capital projects. Finally, in Chapters 13 and 14, we describe the role of virtual reality, augmented reality, and just-in-time technologies used in building operations and maintenance. These pieces of information technology used in the evaluation and monitoring of building performance make up a mosaic representing the overall framework we call *embedded commissioning* (ECx). In Chapter 2, we describe this framework in greater detail, and then place it in its global context in Chapter 3. But first let us consider the motivations that have led us to writing this book, in the first place.

References

[1]   "MGM Fire Investigation Report." Las Vegas, NV: Clark County Fire Department, 1980.
[2]   "Investigation Report on the MGM Grand Hotel Fire; Las Vegas, Nevada, November 21, 1980." Quincy, MA: National Fire Protection Association, 1982.

CHAPTER 1

The Motivation for Building Evaluation

The case of MGM Grand Hotel and Casino fire that we introduced in the introduction to Part I illustrates how building failure can be sudden and catastrophic. However, there are other forms of failure that are slow to develop and not obvious to building occupants. These are the so-called *silent failures* that include systemic as well as component malfunctions, usually due to suboptimal conditions within the systems providing HVAC (heating, ventilation, and air conditioning), emergency egress, universal access, day lighting, healthful environments, and sensory comfort. Their inconspicuous nature often conceals the seriousness with which they degrade occupant health, deplete assets, reduce productivity and comfort, remove opportunities for aesthetic appreciation, and devalue environmental assets. *Building wellness* is an extremely broad topic that requires careful delineation in order to develop pointed and effective strategies for evaluation, monitoring, and improvement of building performance.

In this chapter, we explore some of the important dimensions of this domain in order to define the contents of this book within the larger building wellness context. These include the economic value of buildings, particularly the invisible costs of silent failures such as performance degradation and environmental risks. We will show that while buildings are among the most expensive investments we ever make, their proper documentation and operational parameters are among the least well understood and publicized facts. The variety of methods used to date to document these facts and actively evaluate buildings include both challenges and opportunities. Among these, building commissioning (BCx) provides the greatest potential to improve matters in the area of building evaluation.

1.1 Building Types According to Technology

A consultancy based in England entitled *Building Use Studies* has been conducting surveys and user response studies for several decades under the umbrella of a general question: "What are buildings for?" The answer they provide can be boiled down into three deceptively simple queries [1]. Does a building (1) help or hinder occupants' productivity, (2) provide good value for money as an investment, and (3) minimize environmental impact? Furthermore, the consultancy observed that buildings that work well in all three categories are scarce. Those that do work well or come close enough can be sorted into three major categories.

We call the first one the *close-fit buildings* (CBs). These are buildings that use sophisticated systems and complex technologies to satisfy their missions. These buildings rely on well-informed users, abundant resources, and advanced operations and management (O&M) procedures to closely meet the performance requirements defined at the outset. They use, or need to use, formal and ongoing monitoring and evaluation methods to keep performance efficiency high.

The second category, *loose-fit buildings* (LBs), consists of buildings that are usually low tech and contextually appropriate: "shallow planed, naturally ventilated, smaller, sophisticated in concept, and with robust domestic scale technology" [1]. These can adapt to new uses and expansions of existing uses since the match between spaces and functions is loosely structured and subject to adaptive technologies.

The third category, *experimental buildings* (EBs), is a special set that provides living laboratories for environmental organizations, research centers, and universities. The occupants of these buildings are rarely those other than the designers and constructors of these facilities. In fact, these designers continue to adapt and improve their designs to new needs and experimental objectives throughout the life cycle of these buildings. Throughout this book we will use cases studies that fall into one or another of these three categories to illustrate the methods and tools that will be described.

1.2   Costliest Building Failures

Silent failures can have a significant impact on the value of *capital projects*—buildings and infrastructures—through occupant productivity, value of investment, and environmental impact. More specifically, these failures can cause systemic as well as component malfunctions, often in the use and comfort categories, by disrupting ambient temperature, environment healthfulness, acoustic comfort, daylight, indoor air quality, humidity levels, protection from contaminants, and human productivity. Through the design, construction, operations, and maintenance techniques used in each of the three building categories introduced above offer different remedies for these failures; failures that influence performance variables such as temperature, humidity, ventilation, day lighting, and acoustics.

In a study correlating ambient temperature with productivity measured through performance of standard office tasks, Seppänen et al. [2] showed that productivity is optimal in the range between 21° and 24°C indoor air temperatures. Best performance was observed at 22°C, while almost 9% degradation of performance occurred at 30°C. It is clear from these results, and many others like it [3], that controlling indoor air temperature can add significant value to building and occupant performance.

Another significant indoor air quality issue is moisture and dampness that causes biological and chemical agents to become airborne. There are many causes for this including "water leaks, plumbing system leaks, groundwater entry, damp construction materials, indoor moisture generation, humid outdoor air entry, insufficient dehumidification, water vapor condensation, and floods" [4]. About half of U.S. homes have high levels of dampness or mold present, compared to 45%

of offices and 30% of schools with water leakage, and 27% of schools with roof leakage problems.

High levels of moisture promote mold and mite growth that emits hazardous biological and chemical agents into the air as well as increasing outgassing of chemicals such as formaldehyde from building materials. Through respiratory illnesses, these airborne agents contribute negatively to the health and productivity of occupants in a variety of ways.

Because a substandard supply of fresh air, in schools, offices, and "sick buildings" causes absences from work, respiratory illness, and drops in performance [3], ventilation rates in indoor environments are regarded as an important factor for health and productivity. It has been shown that the minimum standard of 15 cfm/person, when exceeded, can realize dramatic increases in productivity and commensurate decreases in absenteeism [3]. When tested in the 14- to 30-cfm range, the speed and accuracy of work in the office setting can be improved by 0.8% per 10 cfm/person. In the school setting, a 5% to 10% improvement may be attributable to doubling the ventilation rates for conditions at or below the minimum standard of 15 cfm/person.

Both in schools and offices, by doubling the ventilation rate from 25 to 50 cfm/person, absenteeism can be reduced by as much as 30%. Victims of *sick building syndrome*, symptoms of which include irritation of eyes, nose, and throat, headache, fatigue, cough, and tight chest, show anywhere from 10% to 80% fewer symptoms when ventilations levels are above average, up to 40 cfm/person. Dramatically higher levels of respiratory illness (50% to 370%) have been documented in "high-density buildings," including, of all places, nursing homes and health care facilities where fresh air intake is limited by design.

In laboratory conditions, the exposure to low-wavelength (blue) daylight is a significant stimulator of the circadian rhythm of the human body that controls patterns of sleep, work, and many hormonal activities in the body. DLMO (dim light melatonin onset) can be delayed by 30 minutes when students are deprived of exposure to blue light by wearing filtered glasses [5]. There is ample evidence that proper day lighting is a determinant of human performance, not only in the classroom but also at the office and the home [2].

Because its impact on performance reaches far into one's future, one indoor environment that is critical for improving human performance is the classroom. Removing acoustic impediments such as high reverberation and noise levels is central to communication and learning, whether in the classroom or the office environment [6]. To improve acoustical performance conditions, limits on classroom noise and reverberation times have been defined in the American National Standards Institute's standard entitled *Acoustical Performance Criteria, Design Requirements, and Guidelines for Schools* (ANSI S12.60-2002).

1.2.1   Cost of Silent Failures

The quality of the indoor environment of buildings is a significant aspect of occupant health and productivity, which, if not properly handled, also presents an enormous price tag. For instance, a sizable component of respiratory illnesses is asthma resulting from dampness and mold [7]. Studies conducted in homes show that of the 21.8 million people with asthma in the United States, about 4.6 million (around

21%) suffer due to dampness and mold in their indoor environments, primarily in the home. Similarly, severe health problems have been observed in schools, workplaces, and institutional buildings [3].

In the United States, the cost associated with asthma attributable to dampness and mold is estimated to be $3.5 billion, which leaves no room to doubt the seriousness of the economic impact humidity control can have in the area of improving occupant health and productivity. In routine office tasks as opposed to "creative writing or proofreading," when indoor pollutants are removed, an improvement of 4% to 16% in *productivity* (accuracy and speed) is realized [3]. Perception of the indoor air quality also impacts productivity at the rate of 1% improvement for every 10% increase in the number of favorable occupant opinions. Overall productivity-related benefits of indoor air quality are an order of magnitude greater (10 times) than the costs of realizing them.

Through the reduction in respiratory diseases, the "potential annual savings and productivity gains are estimated to be in the range of $6 to $14 billion: $1 to $4 billion from reduced allergies and asthma, $10 to $30 billion from reduced sick building syndrome symptoms, and $20 to $160 billion from direct improvements in worker performance that are unrelated to health" [3]. Altogether the impact of poor indoor environments, whether due to temperature, humidity, ventilation, daylight, health agents, or mental well-being, is in the range of $37 billion to $208 billion.

When we consider the cost to the average user of buildings of all of these factors—respiratory illness, indoor pollution, and productivity gains—the cost/benefit picture for building performance evaluation and improvement is extremely favorable (Table 1.1).

1.2.2 The Most Expensive and Prevalent Market Commodity

What is striking about these findings is that, although these estimates have a wide range, without a doubt, their potential impact is significant. In addition, poor design, operation, and management of buildings have other tangible costs in the wasteful use of energy and the harmful consequences for the environment—two of

Table 1.1 Cost/Benefit of Evaluating and Improving Buildings

Costs	Description
3.5 billion/year	Average annual cost of respiratory illness
$0.39/sq. ft.	Building evaluation cost in close-fit, loose-fit, and experimental buildings
Benefits	*Description*
$38.7 billion/year	Average annual value of increased productivity due to elimination of indoor air pollutants
$0.21/year	Average savings of energy consumption in close-fit, oose-fit, and experimental buildings
Cost Plus Benefit	

1.8 years to amortize the cost of building evaluation (Chapter 2, Section 2.1.2).

Net annual gain of $35.2 billion/year due to air quality improvement.

Source: [3].

the value aspects of buildings defined by Lehman [3]—which we will discuss further in the following sections.

Arguably, the most significant personal expenditure in the United States, both in terms of absolute numbers and percentages, is in the building sector. "We no longer build buildings like we used to, nor do we pay for them in the same way. Buildings today are... life support systems, communication terminals, data manufacturing centers, and much more, they are incredibly expensive tools that must be constantly adjusted to function efficiently. The economics of building has become as complex as its design" [8].

According to the U.S. Department of Labor's Bureau of Labor Statistics, in a report published in March 2010, the average annual expenditures of all consumer units for 2008 was $50,486. Out of this, by far the greatest component is for housing (33.9%), with transportation and food a distant second and third, respectively, at 17% and 12.8% (Table 1.2). Outside of the housing sector, principally the industry, commerce, and transportation sectors, as well as a myriad of others, also contribute significantly to the construction, operation, and maintenance of buildings and their infrastructure. One estimate published in a reference manual, *A Measure of Everything*, places it upwards of 35% of the annual GDP. However we slice it, the importance of buildings in the economic life of the United States comes up paramount.

This is no different in other developed economies all around the globe, so much so that the measure of human development has become synonymous with capital projects. Whether considering the emergence of a nexus for business and commercial investments, as in Dubai in the Near East or Shanghai in China, or the descriptions of ancient civilizations in antique Egypt, Greece, or Rome, the construction of physical infrastructure and buildings is often the most convincing testimonial to superiority of cultures and societies. By the same token, the economic investment in them is undeniably and unavoidably a serious commitment that needs greater scrutiny and clarity.

Table 1.2   Average Annual Expenditures, 2008

Expenditures	Amount	Percentage
Food	$6,443	12.8
Alcoholic beverages	$444	0.9
Housing	$17,109	33.9
Apparel and services	$1,801	3.6
Transportation	$8,604	17.0
Health care	$2,976	5.9
Entertainment	$2,835	5.6
Personal care products and services	$616	1.2
Reading	$116	0.2
Education	$1,046	2.1
Tobacco products and smoking supplies	$317	0.6
Miscellaneous	$840	1.7
Cash contributions	$1,737	3.4
Personal insurance and pensions	$5,605	11.1
Total	$50,486	100

Source: [9]. (Courtesy of U.S. Department of Labor, Bureau of Labor Statistics, 2008.)

1.3   Building Evaluation

While capital projects constitute the largest investment humans ever make, they suffer from an inexplicable neglect of the information transfer needed for their use, care, and proper upkeep. Any modern consumer product in our day comes with supporting literature that usually includes information about the product model, manufacturer, user manual, and warranty, if not an ongoing update for its continued maintenance. One website dedicated to portable, electronic consumer products by manufacturers like Panasonic, Sharp, Casio, Funai, ICOM, Philips, Motorola, Samsung, Kenwood, and Sanyo contains 716 items at its top level. Each item in turn points to an average of 57 different user manual versions, each of which is around 48 PDF pages long. This constitutes a total of 1,958,976 pages and nearly half a billion words.

In contrast, buildings rarely if ever come with a "user manual." Some of their components, like boilers, chillers, and air exchangers, have printed instructions and data embedded in proprietary controls and maintenance software. This is largely because these components are manufactured products in their own right. However, the conference room, hallway, assembly hall, roof, and exterior cladding among many other components of a building, which are assembled from a plethora of different structural, enclosure, MEP (mechanical, electrical, plumbing), finishing, and furnishing components, do not get called out as consumer items. They are not formally described for use, operations, or maintenance. Whereas from the perspective of building economics they constitute the largest investment anyone ever makes, as consumer products the codification of their user information aspects is a foreign concept to capital project delivery (CPD) professionals. How do these professionals get away with it? Four factors are often cited in explaining this deficiency in AEC practices:

1. Buildings are one-off assemblies that do not conform to the ground rules of industrially produced consumer items.
2. Buildings are too complex to describe succinctly and accurately in a single, or even multiple, documents.
3. Buildings have a life of their own; they evolve and are subject to changing use patterns.
4. Writing a manual for one building is not cost effective since it is not likely to apply to any other buildings.

In spite of these explanations, a number of practices specialized to buildings provide significant motivation to change or even reverse current trends. It is expected, if not accepted, in the building sector that the cost and delivery time of buildings are highly unpredictable. Cost overruns are routine. It is not unusual for delivery times to slide and actual completion to be realized much later than the estimated point of occupancy. Contractors and even designers of building systems are hard pressed to predict the precise performance that a finished building will deliver. In the case of close-fit and experimental buildings, this can be ascertained through field measurements, tune-ups of installed systems, and even sophisticated computer simulations of subsystems. But in loose-fit buildings, the vast majority of the building stock, this is much more difficult and continuous monitoring must be used.

There are many stages in the life of a building. The average age of a building in the United States is slightly over 70 years, with significant variation based on the materials used in constructing its structure—wood, masonry, steel, or concrete, in ascending order [10]. Infrastructure, as in the case of roads, bridges, and utilities, is all together a different category, in which both investments and life expectancy are double or even triple those of the building sector. As a result, they are by far the consumer products with the longest life cycle, which to a certain extent justifies the large capital investment in buildings and infrastructure. By the same token, however, these capital investments should command a much more vigorous evaluation and improvement cycle. Finally, building codes, zoning ordinances, contract documents, warranty documents, commissioning reports, and formal evaluation of buildings through post-occupancy evaluation processes should be better structured to make up for the lack of user information (manuals) for buildings.

In spite of all of these motivating factors, the absence of a persistent and inclusive information bridge to connect capital projects with their users results in endemic problems of design, operations, and maintenance that are costly, serious, and rarely observed with other consumer products.

The impetus for change in the AEC industry is also present due to a number of evolving trends, such as stakeholder sophistication, growing performance emphasis, digital information use, and integration of design and operations. As a result, the evolving relationship between users, owners, and CPD professionals has brought to the fore the potential impact of computation and digital information access as a real game changer (Section 1.4). This book is about describing this shift in the landscape of AEC in detail, predicting some of the positive changes that will benefit all building owners and users, sizing up the challenges that await us, and providing nuts and bolts information about some of the important emergent technologies. Before we launch into describing this innovative approach we call embedded commissioning (Chapter 2), let us briefly review the legacy methods that are its precursors: post-occupancy evaluation, building simulation, and building commissioning.

1.3.1   Post-Occupancy Evaluation (POE)

POE is a practice that started in the United States and is primarily recognized by this acronym in the United States and Canada. It is the "the process of evaluating buildings in a systematic and rigorous manner after they have been built and occupied for some time" [11]. It has a broad scope, which is usually customized to fit the project at hand. It can be specifically targeted to a performance issue like day lighting or energy consumption as well as broadly applied to diagnose many potential problems in capital projects. Since its inception through the environmental design movement of the 1960s, it has grown and evolved into a recognized evaluation process in the life cycle of a building.

A typical, broad-scoped POE will involve three stages: problem definition, observation and measurement, and data interpretation and reporting. Some POEs are defined through performance dimensions such as visual, acoustic, thermal, organizational, privacy, lighting, orientation, and maintenance issues. Others are organized around physically situated features of a building, such as lobby waiting areas, dining and cafeterias, patient rooms, classrooms, terraces, and the like. In either approach a set of methods is developed to make observations *in situ* and conduct interviews with primary constituents like the occupants, owners, operators, and design professionals. Some of this data lends itself to only qualitative analysis, as in visual aspects, comfort indicators, privacy, and interaction between occupants, while others can be analyzed quantitatively.

A POE study that exemplifies the best practices in the field was performed for the Philip Merrill Environmental Center by the Center for Environmental Design Research at UC Berkeley [12]. In this study the authors found the following:

- Occupants were highly satisfied with the building as a whole.
- The response to air quality was positive.
- 90% of occupants were satisfied with the day lighting.
- With 80% of the occupants, all psychosocial ratings were positive.
- Occupants expressed a strong sense of pride in the building.
- Acoustical conditions were most negatively rated, primarily due to speech privacy.

Some of these variables are objectively quantifiable like airflow and light levels. Others are subjectively quantifiable like satisfaction with air quality and light levels (Table 1.3).

Recently, research institutions have teamed with government agencies like the General Services Administration to redefine the POE process as *facility performance evaluation* (FPE) [13]. The distinction appears to be in the methodological clarity and rigor that is promoted by FPE. In place of a customized approach, an a priori set of tools and techniques is employed to discover faults and substandard

Table 1.3 POE Performance Measures at the Philip Merrill Environmental Center—Average Scores by Category (N = 71) on a Seven-Point scale of -3 Through +3

General satisfaction—building	2.3
General satisfaction—workspace	2.0
Office layout	1.3
Office furnishings	2.2
Thermal comfort	0.6
Air quality	2.1
Lighting	1.8
Views	1.7
Acoustic quality	1.0
Cleanliness and maintenance	1.5
Attention and concentration	1.0
Awareness and communication	1.1
Interactive behavior	1.3
Functionality	1.7
Acoustic functionality	0.3
Community	1.8
Morale and well-being	1.5

Source: [12].

performance aspects of buildings. Building feasibility analysis (BFA) studies also bear a resemblance to POE and FPE. They are performed on existing facilities to specify the requirements for a replacement facility or to determine the feasibility of a brand new design. While its purpose is somewhat different from POE and FPE, its agenda is similar. In a BFA, the factors to consider include "given building facilities, physical layout of the space, building systems: HVAC, electrical, communication, structural and technical constrains, location, neighborhood, parking facilities, lease terms, demolition and improvement costs necessary to update building, client's budget constraints, building codes, and Americans for Disabilities Act (ADA) compliance requirements. If more than one building is considered, then the comparative analysis between the different sites becomes necessary" [14].

With the enormous number of buildings already in existence in the world, this is a daunting task. Furthermore, most of these buildings contribute the lion's share to energy consumption and carbon emissions. The economic and environmental impact of properly done retrofit and feasibility studies has the potential to be one of the most important areas of building evaluation and performance improvement.

1.3.2 Simulation-Based Evaluation

The rationale for computer simulations for building evaluation arises from the need to accurately estimate, predict, and control the parameters, such as pressure, temperature, energy, and fluid flow rate in HVAC components of a functioning building system, in their dynamic state. This requires that in addition to the attributes of the building system, the building's response to changing external conditions must be accurately modeled. To accomplish this, usually, a steady-state simulation of the system's energy and control flows is required. For more complex cases, including lighting, acoustic, and ventilation flows, finite element analysis simulations can be used.

The use of simulation as an evaluative technique is common in close-fit buildings where advanced technology is used in designing the MEP systems. Otherwise, it becomes almost impossible to connect the dots between the plethora of settings generated by control systems that are governed by proprietary software composed of subcomponents and drive air handling units, heat exchangers, and variable air volume boxes delivering the environmental conditions in a building. Simulations provide the benchmarks against which the measurements obtained from the field can be validated and accurately interpreted (Figure 3.2) [15]. Other applications of building system simulation include self-configuring systems [16], egress patterns [17, 18], biological analogs (Figure 1.1) [19], and productivity modeling [20].

The principal concept of simulation applications is to create sufficiently realistic virtual representations of phenomenon to enable accurate evaluations of how well they would perform in reality, that is, if they were constructed as designed. This approach has the enormous advantage of assessing performance prior to significant capital expenditures and catching mistakes before they happen. This is a growing area of application that will remain an important aspect of building evaluation.

1.3.3 Commissioning Building Energy Systems

Arguably the gold standard of capital project evaluation is building commissioning (BCx). To understand this we have to understand two factors: that the greatest cost and performance gains can be attained by improving energy-consuming subsystems of buildings and their infrastructure, and that, to date, BCx is one of the most systematic, accurate, and advanced building evaluation approaches being applied to the energy consuming subsystems.

Conservative estimates of expenditure related to energy consumption in the AEC sector range between 25% and 36% of all energy expenditures in the United States (Chapter 2). The lower bound corresponds to $300.87 billion per year. The principal categories of consumption that account for this in the residential, manufacturing, and commercial sectors include heating, cooling, ventilation, and lighting. These are similar to levels of energy consumption, and carbon emissions, for that matter, in most if not all developed countries.

BCx is a cost-effective way of determining the inefficient use of energy in HVAC and lighting systems of buildings, related to direct energy savings, greenhouse emissions, occupant comfort, indoor air quality, and reduced operational costs. In Chapter 2, we will expand on these issues and the important role BCx can continue to play in addressing them.

1.4   Emerging Practices and Opportunities

The primary motivation for this book has been the unmistakable importance of building commissioning and information technologies for improving CPD. This

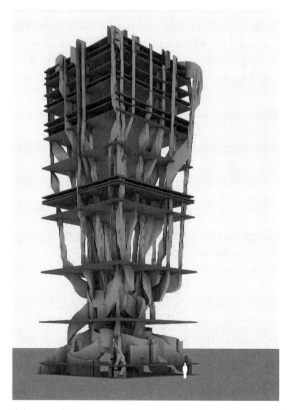

Figure 1.1   A 3D modeling application creating a form based on biological simulations. (Courtesy of Aaron Westre aaron@artificialnatures.com.)

amalgam, embedded commissioning (ECx), at once builds on existing approaches like *Continuous Commissioning*©™ and emerging technologies of computation. Thus, in this book, we will show how some of the critical AEC sector performance problems we described in Section 1.3, in the center of which lies the challenge of reliable information availability, can be addressed and, in fact, solved through the ECx approach.

In the immediate future, due to the emergence of ubiquitous computation and the World Wide Web as a global information repository and access mechanism, capital project information will be digitally based, in order to improve its delivery, operation, maintenance, and usability. Through emerging technologies, storage, access, and modification of just-in-time information about all aspects of buildings and building products will become a reality sooner than we expect.

The tools of this paradigm shift are currently at hand. The information base for the effective design, operation, and maintenance of complex building systems is being standardized and regulated by international organizations like the ISO (International Standards Organization) and IEA (International Energy Agency), and national bodies like the NIBS (National Institute of Building Sciences) in the United States, and SHASE (Society of Heating, Air-conditioning and Sanitary Engineers) in Japan (Chapter 3). Current developments in product and process modeling exemplified in the work done by suborganizations of ISO and research centers examining the mapping of data between them (Chapters 4, 7, and 8) and the emergence of a prevalent practice called BIM (building information modeling) (Chapter 5) have begun to transform the capital project design and delivery fields at a pace unprecedented in the AEC sector.

The gap between as-designed and as-built information, which resides at the nexus of most information-based approaches in advanced CPD, is being bridged by laser-based scanning and automated modeling tools (Chapter 6). Coupled with the advances in communication protocols and data accessibility (Chapter 9), and automated building code checking (Chapter 10), future building evaluation technologies offer opportunities for accuracy, persistence, and effectiveness through improved performance.

This potential is expected to usher in the broad use of a diverse spectrum of sensors and sophisticated sensor networks (Chapter 11). The economic trade-offs between these approaches will have to be measured in tangible ways that can help us engineer the value of innovation against risk (Chapter 12). Digital field tools (Chapter 13) and just-in-time technologies (Chapter 14) are expected to provide the connection between the designer and the field worker that is critical in realizing the value of high-performance buildings and infrastructure.

References

[1]   Lehman, A., "Within These Walls," *Safety and Health Practitioner*, http://www.shponline. co.uk, October 31, 2005.

[2]   Seppänen, O., Fisk, W. J., and Lei, Q.H., "Effect of Temperature on Task Performance in Office Environment," Berkeley, CA: Lawrence Berkeley National Laboratory, Environmental Energy Technologies Division, Indoor Environment Department, July 2006.

[3]   "Impacts of Building Ventilation on Health and Performance," *IAQ-SFRB Indoor Air Quality Scientific Findings Resource Bank*, Lawrence Berkeley National Laboratory, http://www.iaqscience.lbl.gov/vent-summary.html, April 21, 2011.

[4]   "Indoor Dampness, Biological Contaminants and Health," *IAQ-SFRB Indoor Air Quality Scientific Findings Resource Bank*, Lawrence Berkeley National Laboratory, http://www.iaqscience.lbl.gov/vent-summary.html. April 21, 2011.

[5]   Crowley, S. J., et al., "Estimating Dim Light Melatonin Onset (DLMO) Phase in Adolescents Using Summer or School-Year Sleep/Wake Schedules," *Sleep*, Vol. 29, No. 12, 2006, pp. 1632.

[6]   Nabelek, A., and Nabelek, I., "Room Acoustics and Speech Perception," in *Handbook of Clinical Audiology*, J. Katz (Ed.), Baltimore, MD: Williams & Wilkins, 1985, pp. 834–846.

[7]   Fisk, W. J., "Health-Related Costs of Indoor ETS, Dampness, and Mold in the United States and in California," in *Proceedings of Indoor Air Conference 2005*, Beijing, September 4–9, 2005, pp. 308–313.

[8]   Wilson, J., "Foreword," in *Building Economics*, H. E. Marshall and R. T. Ruegg, New York: Van Nostrand Reinhold, 1990.

[9]   U.S. Department of Labor, Bureau of Labor Statistics, "Consumer Expenditures in 2008," Report 1023, Tables A and B, March 2010, p. 2.

[10] O'Connor J., "Survey on Actual Service Lives for North American Buildings," presented at Woodframe Housing Durability and Disaster Issues Conference, Las Vegas, NV, October 2004.

[11] Preiser, W. F. E., Rabinowitz, H. Z., and White, E. T., *Post Occupancy Evaluation*. New York: Van Nostrand Reinhold, 1998.

[12] Heerwagen, J., Zagreus, L., and Zagreus, J. H., "The Human Factors of Sustainable Building Design: Post Occupancy Evaluation of the Philip Merrill Environmental Center," *Indoor Environmental Quality (IEQ) Series*, Berkeley, CA: Center for the Built Environment, Center for Environmental Design Research, UC Berkeley, April 1, 2005.

[13] Zimring, C., Mahbub, R., and Kampschroer, K., "Facility Performance Evaluation (FPE)," website in collaboration with the Public Buildings Service, U.S. General Services Administration, last updated: June 11, 2010.

[14] ITECH, Interior Design Support website, http://web.ku.edu/~itech/index.html, April 21, 2011.

[15] Hensen, J. L. M., "On System Simulation for Building Performance Evaluation," in *Proceedings of the 4th IBPSA World Congress on Building Simulation '95*, Madison, WI, August 1995, pp. 259–267.

[16] Akın, Ö., Akinci, B., and Garrett, J. H., Jr., "Identification of Functional Requirements and Possible Approaches for Self-Configuring Intelligent Building Systems," Interim Progress Report for the Period 07/01/2009–9/30/2009, Carnegie Mellon University, Pittsburgh, PA, submitted to National Institute for Standards and Technology, 2009.

[17] Pan, X., et al., "A Computational Framework to Simulate Human and Social Behaviors for Egress Analysis," presented at Joint International Conference on Computing and Decision Making in Civil and Building Engineering, Montréal, Canada, June 14–16, 2006.

[18] Rahman, A., and Mahmood, A. K., "Agent-Based Simulation Using Prometheus Methodology in Evacuation Planning," in *Proceedings from International Symposium on Information Technology*, Kuala Lumpur, August 26–28, 2008, Vol. 3, pp. 1–8.

[19] Westre A., "Complexity Machine 1: A 3D Modeling Application Implementing Behavioral Simulation," in *Proceedings of the ACADIA 2008: Silicon + Skin: Biological Processes and Computation Conference*, October 16–19, 2008.

[20] Hong, T., Chou, S. K., and Bong, T. Y., "Building Simulation: An Overview of Developments and Information Sources," *Building and Environment*, Vol. 35, No. 4, May 1, 2000, pp. 347–361.

CHAPTER 2

Embedded Commissioning

In Chapter 1, we referred to a set of practices—surrounding and defining the current state of evaluating buildings and their infrastructures—that motivate our work. Building commissioning (BCx), recognized as one of the most effective evaluation methods, is the model around which we will build a new tool-based and analytical application that supports persistent, reliable, robust, and repeatable building evaluation strategies. At the core of our approach is the objective of making information ubiquitous in the AEC domain, thanks to the availability of advanced and ever improving hardware/software tools and applications. Our vision of a universal BCx method for the capital project delivery (CPD) process includes information that is continuously accumulated, accessed, and used through interoperable product and process models.

We call this approach *embedded commissioning* (ECx), referring to the notion that information is embedded in the delivery process in various useful forms, regardless of whether it originates from databases, sensors, people, drawings, or images. This approach subsumes several critical and emergent technologies that are described in detail in Parts II and III of this book: sensors, BIM, BACnet, laser scanning, industry foundation classes (IFCs), process-product modeling, automated building code checking, and AR/VR and JIT technologies.

In this chapter, we get things started by first providing a brief overview of BCx and the important role it plays in building evaluation. Then we describe the setting in which our vision of ECx can flourish based on the current trends that are rapidly reshaping the AEC industry and the CPD process. Finally, we conclude with a description of the ECx framework.

2.1 Commissioning Energy-Consuming Capital Projects

While there are many challenges in the design of capital projects, these are often matched and even exceeded by the challenges in their operations and maintenance. In fact, the most significant cost issue in the building life cycle is in the category of energy consumption and its impact on the environment.

2.1.1   Significance of Energy Consumption in Capital Projects

"In the United States, the building sector (residential and commercial) uses more energy than the transportation sector, and almost as much as the industrial sector. Moreover, the building sector emits more carbon than either the industrial or the transportation sectors. In 1998, the building sector used 36 percent (33.7 quadrillion BTU) of the primary energy and emitted 35 percent (523 million metric tons) of the carbon" [1].

Are these unavoidable economic and environmental costs? What can be done about them? Short of reinventing all end-use systems and replacing them with efficient ones (which will happen on its own in the long run) in the short run, we need to make sure that existing systems are made to function as efficiently as possible. This requires an aggressive agenda for building evaluation and retrofitting, which is a primary motivation for this book

Based on the Energy Information Administration's *Annual Energy Review 2008,* there are four major sectors of consumption: residential, industrial, commercial, and transportation (Figure 2.1).The housing costs we included in Table 1.2 in Chapter 1 are dominated by the "shelter" item, with "utilities" running a significant second, 59.5% versus 21.3%, respectively. End-use consumption by utilities in turn breaks down into four subcategories (Table 2.1).

The total energy consumption for the housing sector, excluding appliances, is 8.33 quadrillion BTUs. To this has to be added to the consumption of energy in the other three sectors, namely, commerce, industry, and transportation. In 2005, the lighting, cooling, ventilating, and space heating in *commercial* buildings totaled 2.42 quadrillion BTUs; and 0.9 quadrillion BTUs in the *manufacturing* sector consumed for HVAC and lighting purposes. Altogether the MEP factor in all sectors, excluding transportation, adds to 11.65 quadrillion BTUs, per year. Then, the cost of energy use in the four sectors, in nominal dollars per million BTUs are 21.56 (residential), 20.64 (commercial), 1.33 (industrial), and 19.11 (transportation). This translates into total expenditures of $226, $167, $227, and $538 billion, respectively.

As a conservative estimate, that is, just including the categories we considered—residential (space heating, water heating, air conditioning), industrial (HVAC, lighting), and commercial (lighting, cooling, ventilation, space heating), in which building professionals are the primary design and operations decision makers—the total expenditure, prorated to the consumption in each category, is $300.87 billion per year. This constitutes 25.9% of the total expenditures in the U.S. economy, per annum. This estimate does not include the building activity in the transportation sector nor a myriad of smaller sectors like office, education, health care, warehouse and storage, lodging, food service, food sales, public assembly, and service. Another source estimates the energy consumption in the housing and the commercial sectors to be 36% of all consumption [2].

2.1.2   Building Commissioning (BCx)

As stated earlier, we consider BCx to be the most advanced method in use for evaluating and reducing energy consumption in buildings for all major sectors of the AEC industry. The term *commissioning* has been borrowed from the naval practice

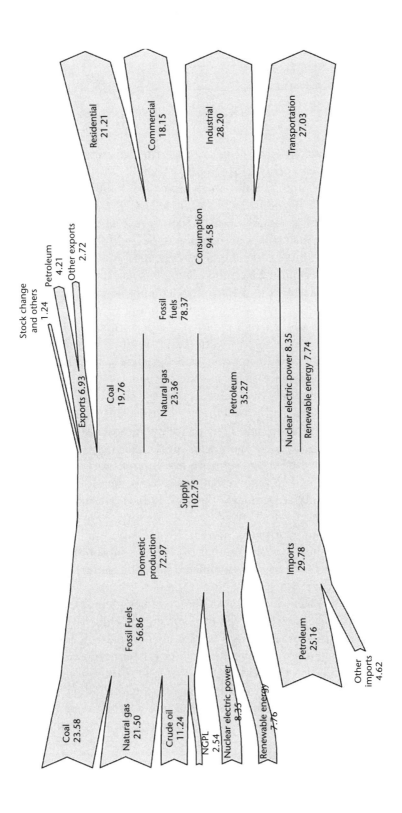

Figure 2.1   Energy flow, 2008 (in quadrillion BTUs). From: Energy Information Administration, *Annual Energy Review 2008*, p. 3.

Table 2.1   Utilities End-Use Consumption, in 2005 [2]

Utilities End-Use Subcategory	Consumption (in Quadrillion BTUs)
Space heating	4.30
Appliances	3.25
Water heating	2.12
Air conditioning	0.88

of testing a new vessel based on standard performance criteria for operations, prior to considering it "seaworthy" [3]. In 1977, Public Works Canada was the first institution to apply commissioning methodology to building. In the United States, formal work on BCx began in 1984, when ASHRAE's Commissioning Guideline Committee published its guidelines. After 1993, several governmental and private organizations started using BCx in their practices. In 1998, the U.S. Green Building Council added BCx to its Leadership in Energy and Environmental Design (LEED) criteria. In 1999, the Building Commissioning Association (BCA) was established.

There are several types of BCx: initial commissioning, retro-commissioning, re-commissioning, and Continuous Commissioning©™. The baseline for all the others, *Initial Cx*, is the act of validating the performance of a building and its subsystems through a structured investigation of all of relevant components and systems. *Retro-Cx* is used to improve and optimize a building's operations and performance when it requires improvement, usually well after the building is occupied. To keep the building operating according to its design requirements, *Re-Cx* reapplies the categories and procedures established in the findings of the initial Cx. Continuous Commissioning©™ is the ongoing process of resolving operating problems, improving comfort, optimizing energy use, and recommending retrofits.

While each of its types takes significantly different formats, the basic tenets of BCx have been adopted in many countries around the globe, including Belgium, Canada, Czech Republic, Denmark, Finland, France, Germany, Greece, Israel, Italy, Japan, the Netherlands, New Zealand, Norway, Peoples Republic of China (Hong Kong), Poland, Portugal, Sweden, Switzerland, and the United Kingdom [4]. In each case, it has been shown that BCx results in significant energy savings.

A survey of 54 BCx projects, completed in seven countries (Belgium, Canada, Germany, Japan, the Netherlands, Norway, and the United States) [5], shows that types of faults that were identified in these studies include problems of air-handling distribution, heating water plant distribution, chilled water plant distribution, thermal energy storage, HVAC system integration, envelope and infiltration, day lighting and lighting controls, thermal units, heat pump systems, domestic hot water systems, and direct expansion split systems. A total of more than 200 measures were recommended by these BCx evaluations including tuning the control loop, changing the reset strategy, modifying the control sequence, modifying the schedule, restaging equipment, modifying the setpoint, calibrating sensors, fixing mechanical faults, rescheduling occupancy, replacing equipment, repairing equipment, and modifying designs.

The benefits observed in these cases include improvements in humidity levels, occupant comfort, system performance, energy performance monitoring, productivity, indoor air quality, and air balance, as well as reductions in operational costs, direct energy expenditures, and greenhouse emissions. Claridge et al. [5] found that the benefits accrued from the use of BCx with new construction ranged from $0.05 to $0.64/sq. ft., while for existing buildings these values were $0.11 to $0.26/sq. ft.

These evaluations were also helpful in uncovering design problems and potential design improvements based on the performance deficiencies observed. Operational, control, and maintenance-related problems accounted for 32% of the total set of problems; 33% dealt with construction and installation; and design accounted for 35% of all faults [5]. This highlights the potentially positive impact building information systems that seamlessly connect the stages of CPD through interoperable information repositories (Section 1.4.4) can have on nipping design problems in the bud, before they cause months if not years of inefficient performance.

Some estimates from other design fields indicate that the early discovery of problems can have significant benefits. If we look at the entire CPD process, nominally it contains six major stages: requirement specification, design, construction, commissioning, operations, and maintenance. This corresponds to the six categories observed in other areas of product delivery such as software products [6]. The pyramid in Figure 2.2 depicts the escalating costs of error discovery and recovery as the stages of delivery are advanced to the subsequent one. From requirement specification to maintenance, the cost escalation is on the order of 200-fold. Thus, discovering problems as early as possible, potentially before or during the design stage, comes with an attractive savings incentive.

Given the magnitude of the impact of the building sector in economic and environmental terms, BCx provides an enormous benefit in both regards. Furthermore, we consider BCx, which is primarily focused on building MEP systems, as a model for other performance areas. In Parts II and III of this book, we will define the current institutional structure of ECx, its evolution in the Information Age, and the specific technologies that will enable this evolution, in detail; but first, let us consider our vision of challenges in the offing that will fuel a model for this evolution.

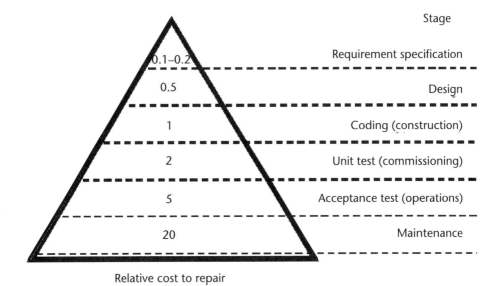

	Stage
0.1–0.2	Requirement specification
0.5	Design
1	Coding (construction)
2	Unit test (commissioning)
5	Acceptance test (operations)
20	Maintenance

Relative cost to repair

Figure 2.2 Cost of repair in phases of design delivery [6].

2.2   Current Challenges and Opportunities in the AEC Sector

Arguably, the AEC industry presents a dynamic and at times unpredictable picture to the outside world. Cost, schedule, and design quality, the three indispensible pillars of CPD, are often compromised beyond the level of acceptability that is standard in other industries. We recognize several key concepts that will shape the emerging new practices: performance basis, stakeholder awareness, and design and operations integration through digital information systems.

2.2.1   Performance Emphasis

Recently, in the interest of improving accuracy and quality in CPD, there has been a shift in requirement specification and evaluation techniques. Prescriptive specifications are being abandoned, or at least augmented, in the interest of using performance-based specifications. This is an active issue in areas such as energy-consuming systems [15], construction methods [16], and construction safety [17], among others. Performance-based building specifications and requirements emphasize functional metrics for design and construction. The means of construction and the ends of design are measured through process or functional descriptions. Solutions, products, or processes are not prescribed. Designers and contractors accomplish desirable performance outcomes in whatever way they deem most suitable. While this can lead to innovation and increased quality, it can also mean that the bottom line can drag design and construction choices to the lowest possible level allowable by performance requirements. Prescribed solutions, on the other hand, can be overdesigned and, by the same token, avoid the least acceptable outcomes.

2.2.2   Stakeholder Awareness

Stakeholders are the owners, users, financiers, and developers of buildings and infrastructure systems. Increasingly, stakeholders are assuming greater responsibility in all phases of building delivery. In the programming phase, when the requirements are specified, they insist on meeting certain performance metrics, for instance, in energy conservation, reduction of carbon emissions, and remediation of indoor air quality. Increasingly, they also consider improving occupant performance requirements.

After the commissioning of buildings and building infrastructures, owners play an increasingly active role in their O&M functions. Large institutional clients usually have their own facilities departments and closely monitor their capital project performance indicators. Frequently, the critical performance issues consist of achieving energy efficiency and carbon emission reduction. However, facilities with critical functions such as laboratories, industrial plants, prisons, hospitals, and transportation hubs face special performance issues like security, uninterrupted operations, egress control, and operations flexibility.

As a result of this heightened awareness, capital project performance measurement and evaluation have become more common, sophisticated, and accessible. Clients and users require—even demand—environments that match and exceed their requirements for high productivity, low cost, environmental sensitivity, and agility of use. They expect buildings and infrastructures to add value through their design and methods of construction (Chapter 12).

2.2.3   Integration of Design and Operations of Capital Projects

A key aspect of the digital realm is to reduce costs and delays stemming from the iterative and repeated creation (and re-creation) of information sets specific to individual phases of CPD. This practice creates spikes in information loss and gathering at the points of transition from one phase to the next (Figure 2.3).

The sawtooth-shaped curve in Figure 2.3 indicates the expenditure of resources in the manual mode, over time. Each sharp increase marks the boundary between one phase of the CPD process grid and a subsequent one. The resources used to develop information are often in formats suitable only to the current phase and do not support work in the subsequent phases. Each time a new phase begins, there is a sharp increase in the committed resources. The smooth curve depicts the resources used in the same CPD process in the digital mode, in which data representation is *interoperable*, that is, transferable with ease from one phase to the next. In this case, resource commitment is significantly less than the manual mode owing to the reuse of data that has been represented in the earlier phases.

These modes of practice present the following trade-offs: either, in the manual mode, pay in smaller amounts but frequently throughout the CPD process; or, in the digital mode, pay a lot up front while paying less and less in each subsequent phase. The digital information base of a project that is truly interoperable can provide feedback as well as feedforward of information, which is just as critical. While the latter ensures efficiency in data acquisition and reduces loss of data that is already acquired, the former is instrumental in fixing faults at the source whether this is in the requirement, design, or construction phase of the CPD.

In Section 2.1.1, we observed that 33% of all faults detected through BCx deal with construction and installation, and design accounts for 35%. In other words,

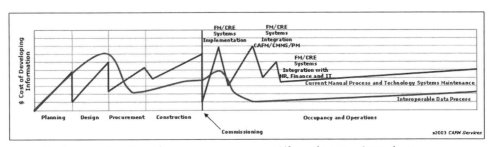

Design-construction phase
(1–5 years)

Life cycle operations phase
(30–100 years)

Owner pays AEC team more $ during design phase to develop BIM and standardize electronic data exchange

Owner saves $$$$$ over operational life of assest ownership by being able to quickly bulk load technology systems, have critical data in electronic format, enabling accurate metrics reporting, benchmarking and transparency

Figure 2.3   Sawtooth model of information acquisition and loss in CPD. (Couresty of Andy Fuhrman, IFMA, previously CAFM services [18].)

68% of faults detected in the operations phase should have been prevented in an earlier phase. Robust information that connects all of the phases can help diagnose and remedy faults through feedback loops.

2.2.4 Building Information Modeling: The Digital Platform for CPD

BIM came to fruition on the heels of the growing interest in modeling and visualization of complex and notable building projects of the 1990s [19]. Assisted by emerging object-based modeling in software engineering and advanced computer hardware, BIM aspires to organize: "all of the information about buildings in a multi-dimensional space, ... containing information on topics as diverse as life-cycle of building delivery, specialized building systems consultants, product and process coordination, cost-schedule-quality measures, ... subsuming a space that is governed by shared product and process representations conforming to broadly accepted standards" [20].

BIM is shaped by three major influences: large data management, intratask collaboration, and smart representations. Capital projects have become very large, with even the most modest versions requiring hundreds of thousands of objects to be modeled. Ease in modeling and communication with other professionals without information loss of such a large repertoire of objects gives impetus to BIM applications, where syntactic, if not semantic, information is embedded with the modeled entity (Chapter 5).

Core CPD operations, like requirement specification, design, costing, scheduling, construction, and operations, benefit from complete and efficient modeling environments. Accurate, complete, and persistent data that is readily computable can enhance all CPD operations and assist in interoperability of information between delivery phases. Just-in-time access to information can reduce errors, costs, and time to completion dramatically.

Finally, BIM allows the inclusion of "intelligence" in data, through self-awareness, identity, and dependencies with respect to other objects. This provides opportunities for "providing persistent, ontological, and data dependent structures in the building information realm. Standards for interoperability, which come in many shades but with one dominant color: Industry Foundation Classes (IFC), provide the platform for data exchange intelligence so essential to BIM" [20].

2.3 Dawning of a New Practice in the AEC Sector: ECx

The core of the CPD process consists of five stages: project programming, design, construction, project commissioning, and project operations (Figure 2.4). In the conventional CPD, the capital *project program* is the input to the design stage. In turn, the output of the *design* stage, or the design, is the input for the *construction* stage. Once the construction is complete, its output, the *building*, becomes the input into the capital project *commissioning* stage. Finally, the commissioned building constitutes the input into the capital *project operations* stage. Each handshake between successive stages is accomplished through a physical entity, namely, the program document, design document, building, and the commissioning report,

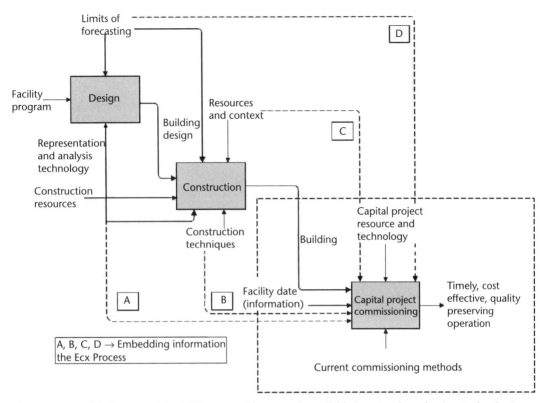

Figure 2.4   IDEF0 diagram of the CPD stages with currently available input and mechanism technologies.

respectively. Each entity embodies information that is inaccessible once the process of using it is complete and is no longer transferrable to a subsequent stage.

For example, the rationale for using artificial turf in a sports facility may be discussed in detail at the outset but all of the reasons and possible consequences do not get documented persistently. Subsequent stages do not have the benefit of such information. The operations manager of the facility may neither understand nor agree with the placement, size, and configuration of drainage chambers from an ease-of-operations standpoint, while their configuration may be determined, by and large, for cost reasons. As a consequence, when it is necessary to know the rationale for a decision made in an earlier stage, decision makers of a subsequent stage either have to guess or spend considerable resources to retrieve or regenerate the information. This is a costly and error-prone process (Figure 2.3).

Embedding information in this process means that there is a persistent data representation bridging every "handshake" between the stages. Furthermore, it also means that information controlling the constraints and mechanisms of each stage (Figure 2.4), like limits of forecasting, representation and analysis of designs, context and resources of construction, construction techniques and materials, capital project management, and building commissioning methods (namely, paths A, B, C, and D), must also be embedded in this representation. All of this would be sufficient to overcome the difficulties endemic to the traditional CPD process, streamlining its process flow, eliminating errors, and controlling the budget—the three pillars of CPD: schedule, quality, and cost.

However, this is easier said than done. To achieve this kind of performance first and foremost we need an ubiquitous representation. BIM provides a limited but competent answer to this question. We also need to achieve standardization in this representation and its mappings from format to format. IFCs provide a partial answer to the first part of this requirement. Process and product model (PPM) mapping outlines a specific solution to the other half of the requirement. Information is dynamic and therefore we need methods and tools for updating and communication of the information encoded through BIM. Laser-based as-is documentation and BACnet, respectively, provide potential answers. Verifying the compliance of designs and construction assemblies to codes and ordinances that govern CPD is critical to avoid *silent failures* as well as those that are not so silent, as in the case of the MGM hotel fire (Part I introduction). Ultimately, to make these projects responsive to change, affordable, and available to fieldwork, we need methods for deploying and networking sensors, accurately estimating the value added by designs, and harnessing augmented reality information just-in-time. This is the framework that we envision for ECx (Figure 2.4).

We believe that the realization of the advances that we began to describe above, and will articulate in detail in the following chapters, is nothing short of being the harbinger of a new age in the AEC industry (Figure 2.5). The vision of such broad innovations must include not just new digital tools and techniques but also advances in AEC practices that utilize these innovations. We envision design and engineering practices that are in the service of a sound economy, environmental conservation, improved value, greater efficiency, and satisfied occupants. CPD is no longer about competence in delivering just conventional services. Engineers and architects have to rise to the challenges of our time and ensure the best economy

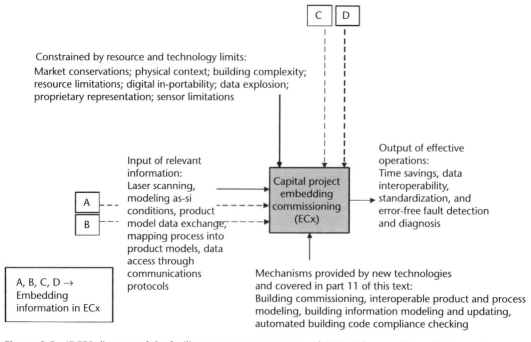

Figure 2.5   IDEF0 diagram of the facility management process of CDP with currently available mechanisms.

by providing the greatest value to stakeholders. Performance needs have to be optimized against first and life-cycle cost of designs. Value must be assessed not just for the bottom line but for other tangible (health, productivity) and intangible (comfort, happiness, recognition) stakeholder benefits. Last but not least, their products must meet the three pillars of the CPD market place: quality, cost, and schedule.

We also envision a computer-based information environment that enhances data acquisition, mining, representation, filtering, processing, transformation, access, fidelity, and communication. In terms of professional and business applications, computers have come of age. Since its early beginnings in the 1960s [20], computer-aided design (CAD) has become the industry standard. Today, with the advent of BIM, we enjoy almost universal acceptance of *object-based* representations of AEC products and processes. IFCs, an outgrowth of the ISO (International Organization for Standardization), have established a sound basis for universal exchange of data with reliable results. Thanks to ubiquitous Internet communication, data mining and shared repositories of information are commonplace. Special applications that can translate among different data formats, compare specifications against designs, and translate among processes and products, are available just for the asking. The remaining problems of standardization, fidelity, and reliability are on their way to being part of the compendium of solutions broadly available.

These developments in the digital realm provide a rich and powerful set of opportunities for engineers and architects to address the challenges of the new and emerging world of the AEC industry. In the following chapters, this book will address specific solutions that match the opportunities we introduced and the challenges we recognized in this part.

References

[1]   Battles, S. J., and Burns, E. M., "Trends in Building-Related Energy and Carbon Emissions: Actual and Alternate Scenarios," presented at Summer Study on Energy Efficiency in Buildings Conference, American Council for an Energy-Efficient Economy, August 21, 2000.

[2]   Energy Information Administration, *Annual Energy Review 2008*, Tables 1.1, 1.2, 1.3, 1.4, 2.1a, Washington, DC: U.S. Department of Energy, p. 3.

[3]   Reilly, J. C., Jr., *Ships of the United States Navy: Christening, Launching and Commissioning*, 2nd ed., Washington, DC: Naval History Division of the Department of the Navy, 1975.

[4]   Akın, Ö., et al., "Flow Charts and Data Models for Initial Commissioning of Advanced and Low Energy Building Systems," Report No. 4, in *Cost-Effective Commissioning of Existing and Low Energy Buildings*, Annex 47 of the International Energy Agency's Energy Conservation in Buildings and Community Systems Program, http://www.iea-annex47.org, 2010.

[5]   Claridge, D., "Commissioning Cost-Benefit and Persistence," Chap. 3 in *Cost-Effective Commissioning of Existing and Low Energy Buildings*, Annex 47 Reports of the International Energy Agency's Energy Conservation in Buildings and Community Systems Program, http://www.iea-annex47.org,2010.

[6]   Kelley, S. W., Hoffman, K. D., and Davis, M. A., "A Typology of Retail Failures and Recoveries," *Journal of Retailing*, Vol. 69, No. 4, 1993, pp. 429–452.

[7]   Beck, P., "The AEC Dilemma: Exploring the Barriers to Change," *Design Intelligence*. Washington, DC: Greenway Communications and Design Futures Council, http://www.di.net/articles/archive/2046, February 1, 2001.

[8]   Teicholz, P., "Labor Productivity Declines in the Construction Industry: Causes and Rem-
        edies," *AECbytes Analysis* (Research, Reviews, Web Publication), No. 4, http://www.
        aecbytes.com/viewpoints.html, April 14, 2004.

[9]   LePatner, B. B., "It's Time to Fix America's Broken Construction Industry," *Engineering
        News-Record*, http://enr.ecnext.com/coms2/article_tebm090429BIMDivisiono, March 12,
        2008.

[10]   Akın, Ö., and Anadol, Z., "Determining the Impact of Computer Aided Design Tools on
        the Building Delivery Process: A Bench Marking Study," in *Proceedings of First Inter-
        national Conference on The Management of Information Technology*, Singapore, August
        1994, pp. 17–20.

[11]   Ballard, G., "The Lean Project Delivery System: An Update," *Lean Construction Jour-
        nal*, 2008, pp. 1–19, http://www.leanconstruction.org/lcj/paper_2008_issue.html, accessed
        April 25, 2011.

[12]   Construction Industry Institute, 3925 West Braker Lane (R4500), Austin, TX, https://www.
        construction-institute.org/scriptcontent/r-teams-list.cfm?section=res, accessed April 25,
        2011.

[13]   Lee, S. H., and Akın, Ö., "Augmented Reality-based Computational Support for Opera-
        tions and Maintenance Fieldwork," *Automation in Construction*, Vol. 20, No. 4, 2011,
        pp. 338–352.

[14]   Beck, P., "The AEC Dilemma: Exploring the Barriers to Change," *Design Intelligence*,
        Washington, DC: Greenway Communications and Design Futures Council, http://www.
        di.net/articles/archive/2046, February 1, 2001.

[15]   Pati, D., Park, C.-S., and Augenbroe, G., "Roles of Building Performance Assessment in
        Stakeholder Dialogue in AEC," *Automation in Construction*, Vol. 15, No. 4, pp. 415–427.

[16]   Lemay, L., "Prescriptive Specification versus Performance Specifications," *Concrete
        Monthly*, http://www.concretemonthly.com/monthly/art.php?884, July 2004.

[17]   *Performance Specifications Strategic Roadmap: A Vision for the Future*, U.S. Department
        of Transportation, Federal Highway Administration, Spring 2004.

[18]   Fuhrman, A., "Pay Now or Pay Later, Diagram Motivating Interoperable and Persistent
        Information Models for the Architecture-Engineering-Construction Industry," Houston,
        TX: International Facility Management Association.

[19]   Eastman, C., et al., *Handbook: A Guide to Building Information Modeling for Owners,
        Managers, Designers, Engineers and Contractors*, Hoboken, NJ: John Wiley and Sons,
        2008.

[20]   Akın, Ö, "Chapter 1: Current Trends and Future Direction in CAD," Chap. 1 in *CAD/GIS
        Integration: Existing and Emerging Solutions*, H. Karimi and B. Akinci (Eds.), New York:
        Taylor & Francis, 2008.

Part II: Elaboration

In Part I, we provided evidence and compelling argument that through systematic and reliable evaluation of capital projects we can ensure the maintenance of the highest levels of performance, throughout the projects' life cycles. In the following chapters, we will show that the methods needed to perform these evaluations are nonexistent in some cases and inadequate in others. Consequently, we will describe a dozen specific techniques that will improve our chances of objectively monitoring performance and enhancing their delivery in capital projects.

Needless to say capital project delivery (CPD) is complex. To construct a comprehensible overview of this process we provide a broad-brush view of the three key phases of CPD: design, construction, and commissioning (Figure 2.4). This figure is drawn in the style of an IDEF0 diagram [1] that shows mutually exclusive process steps interconnected by *input/output* links and further defined by *constraints* and *mechanisms*.

II.1 Programming and Design

The facility program, or design requirement specification [2], is the input that initiates the design process. In fact, in a more inclusive version of the same IDEF0 diagram, this input would constitute the output of a process called *facility programming* that precedes design. The output of design is the customary construction documents including working drawings, shop drawings, and the project manual. Every design is limited by the powers of estimation that the designers have in judging the closeness of the performance expected in the facility program and the performance predictions carried out through visual and quantitative simulations.

Currently, there is a plethora of computer simulation tools that predict performance issues all the way from realistic appearance of rendered designs (Figure 1.1) to precise annual energy consumption values (Figure 3.2). The limitations of these tools, in addition to the budget, timetable, zoning ordinances, building codes, and available construction materials and methods, constitute the *constraints* of the design process. On the other hand, these outcomes are facilitated by the capabilities of various representation and analysis software among many other CPD technologies, such as BIM software [3], standardization tools [4], and communication protocols [5].

II.2   Construction

By definition the input of the construction process includes facility designs. In addition, it also benefits from resources needed to carry out the construction including site conditions, available financing, construction materials, and construction techniques. The construction process is at once enabled (as input) and constrained by the budget, schedule, materials, methods, and even the site conditions. Zoning and building codes impact the construction just as much as they do the design. The mechanisms that enable design, design representation and analysis software, also influence the construction process. In addition, construction is enhanced by new tools that improve as-built representations, digital scheduling and inventory methods, wearable computers, and sensor technology.

II.3   Project Commissioning and Operations

This process is the most persistent one during the CPD life cycle. It includes the upkeep, operations, and maintenance of the facility throughout its life including feedforward into decommissioning (the process step not included in Figure 2.4 for the sake of brevity).

Capital project commissioning includes embedded commissioning (ECx), the topic of this text. The embedding of information in the capital project life cycle is shown in Figure 2.4 by the dotted arrows labeled A, B, C, and D. In other words, through the use of interoperable data, information generated through the constraints and mechanisms of the previous stages (both design and construction) is included seamlessly in the project commissioning process.

The input to the commissioning process by and large consists of the physical facility completed by the construction process. The output is timely, economical, and quality preserving evaluations of capital projects. This is facilitated by the methods and tools of ECx and constrained by the limitations of those aspects of these tools and methods that still need further development.

II.4   Further Elaboration Through Embedded Commissioning

In addition to the constructed building, the input into this process consists of methods we have developed during the past decade to harvest information from physical facilities (Figure 2.5). Many of these methods, including (1) surveying equipment, 3D imaging, laser scanners, cameras, and sensors/methods for modeling as-is conditions (Chapter 6); (2) standards for the exchange of product model data (IFCs) (Chapter 7); (3) embedding commissioning information by mapping process models into product models (Chapter 8); and (4) communication protocols and data accessibility (Chapter 9), also enable ECx in the context of the entire project commissioning process.

The mechanisms that make the commissioning process work include methods such as (1) traditional building commissioning processes (Chapter 3); (2) interoperable product and process modeling (Chapter 4); (3) building information modeling (BIM) and updating (Chapter 5); and (4) automated code compliance checking (Chapter 10). In the following chapters we will elaborate of these aspects of the ECx process highlighted in the original IDEF0 diagram (Figure 2.4), and as expanded on in the input and mechanism sections of Figure 2.5.

Stakeholders and CPD professionals alike, primarily if not exclusively, rely on computer-based representations in order to design, construct, manage, and communicate. Development of specialized software and BIM technology has made the use of digital design nearly ubiquitous (Chapters 4, 5, and 8). Protocols of data exchange enable productive communication (Chapters 6, 7, and 9). Also, building code checking applications offer more reliable and faster verification of requirements (Chapter 10). Finally, sensor and laser technologies make possible the gathering of remote and just-in-time information (Chapters 11, 13, and 14). The benefits expected, and in some areas substantially realized, are increased value, reduced cost, reliable delivery schedules, and improved O&M performance.

References

[1]   *Standard for Integration Definition for Function Modeling (IDEF0)*, Draft Federal Information Processing Standards Publication 183, Computer Systems Laboratory of the National Institute of Standards and Technology (NIST), December 21, 1993.

[2]   Ozkaya, I., and Akın, Ö., "Tool Support for Computer-Aided Requirements Traceability in Architectural Design: The Case of DESIGNTRACK," *Automation in Construction*, Vol. 16, No. 5, 2007, pp. 674–684.

[3]   REVIT, Autodesk, Revit Architecture, http://www.usa.autodesk.com, 2008.

[4]   Froese, T., "Future Directions for IFC-Based Interoperability," *ITcon*, Vol. 8, 2003, pp. 231–246, http://www.itcon.org/2003/17.

[5]   ANSI/ASHRAE, "BACnet: A Data Communication Protocol for Building Automation and Control Networks," ANSI/ASHRAE Standard 135, American Society of Heating, Refrigerating, and Air-Conditioning Engineers, 2010.

CHAPTER 3

Institutional Structure and Practice of Building Commissioning in the Digital Era

3.1 The Global Scope of Building Commissioning

Building commissioning (BCx) has different guises around the globe. In the United States, Canada, Great Britain, and Japan, it is called *commissioning* and is subject to the guidelines of public and private standards organizations like the NRC [1], SHASE [2], CIBSE, ASHRAE, and NIST. In some European countries such as Germany, Sweden, and Norway, the functions of BCx are satisfied through building warranty practices that usually apply to the early years of a building's lifetime. In other European countries, like France, the Netherlands, and the Czech Republic, and Pacific Rim countries, like Hong Kong–China, Singapore, and Korea, the process is a part of the quality assurance requirements usually applied to close-fit and experimental buildings.

The International Energy Agency's Energy Conservation for Building and Community Systems (ECBCS) organization has been conducting international consortia called *Annexes* since 1977 to coordinate standards for energy efficiency in buildings. Several Annexes, notably Annex-40 [3] and Annex-47 [4], have dealt with BCx. Under this framework, BCx systems and components (Table 3.1), automation tools (Table 3.2) and cases illustrating practices in different countries have been documented (Table 3.3).

All of this points to the challenges and opportunities underlying the global efforts to define and standardize BCx in the Information Age that will be addressed in this chapter and the rest of this text. We will do this through the representative countries where these methods and tools for BCx have been developed. They include the Asia Pacific region (Australia, Hong Kong–China, Japan, Korea, Taiwan), the European Union (Belgium, Czech Republic, Finland, France, Germany, The Netherlands, United Kingdom), and North America (Canada, United States). In the next section, we focus on a representative sample of national practices from each of these regions.

Table 3.1 BCx Systems and Components Modeled by the Annex Process

Air-to-air plate heat exchanger	Building zone	Coil heat recovery loop	Cooling coil and control valve
Cooling tower	Fan (variable speed)	Fan and drive train	Fan/duct system–VAV
Heat pipe heat recovery	Heat pump	Heat recovery wheel	Heating coil and control valve
Heating coil and control valve	Humidifier	Mixing box	Mixing box
Terminal unit	Terminal unit control	Vapor compression chiller	VAV terminal units

Courtesy of Annex 40, ECBCS, IEA [3].

3.2 Institutional Structure in Building Commissioning

As we will see in the following sections [5], current BCx applications around the globe illustrate both the "best" and the "no-so-good" practices of data and work-flow management that illustrate the problems we identified in Section 3.1.

3.2.1 European Union Countries

In the European Union, the Energy Performance of Building Directive (EPBD) provides the framework under which energy efficiency procedures and measurements must be conducted for a shared quality assurance process [6]. The directive, while maintaining a shared perspective, recognizes national and regional variations due to local conditions, building age, building type, data availability, technological innovations and legal provisions. The EPBD software calculates U-values, the K-level (average insulation), and the E-level (energy consumption) to help gauge compliance of buildings with energy consumption and indoor air quality standards.

3.2.1.1 BCx Practices in Belgium

Since 2002, the implementation of EPBD in Belgium has facilitated Cx practices during the building performance certification process. In addition to the EPB (Energy Performance of Buildings) and PAE (*Procedure d'Avis Energetique*) software, in the case of passive solar houses and very low energy buildings, PHP passive (PHPP) software is being used (Table 3.4) [7].

   The certification process is fragmented due to the division of labor between the designer (architect) and the energy consultant (engineer) who is qualified to provide passive house design advice, by performing PHPP calculations, and specifications for products and appropriate technologies [7]. It was observed during a workflow analysis of a prototype design application, in which a design was first modeled in SketchUp [8] and then in REVIT [9] (Figure 3.1), that data collection and entry were fragmented and relied on e-mail and telephone transmissions. Data came in natural language format and human operators were required to perform entry, maintenance, and error detection. This led to repeated entries, lack of interoperability with other cases, and inconsistent and unreliable data repositories. The extension of the analysis with IFC modeling showed that a fully data-centric

Table 3.2 BCx Automation Tools Reviewed in ECBCS Annex Process*

BCx Tool	DABO	LCEM	Cite-AHU	EPC	EA and FD	PAT	i-BIG
Country	Canada	Japan	France–USA	Finland	Germany	Norway	Netherlands
Main End Users	BOp MC ES	De CS MC	BOp MC ES	MC	BOp ES	BOp	MC ES BOp
Type Building	Large commercial buildings	Any type	Medium and large commercial buildings	Any type	Whole buildings	–	Any type
HVAC System	AHU VAV	Any type	AHU	Any type	Any type	Heating	AHU
Type of Cx	On-going Cx	Any type	Re-Cx	Ongoing Cx	Ongoing Cx	Re-Cx	Re-Cx
Method	Expert system performance indices	Model based	Expert rules	Statistics and benchmark	Statistics and model based	Model based	Expert rules
Input	-Design data -Operation data -Measured data (control point value: sensor, command, set-point, schedule, etc.)	-Outdoor air conditioning/heat load in each room -Characteristic curve of HVAC component	- OAT, supply, return, mixed, -Outdoor air humidity, return air humidity, enthalpy -Heating coil valve signal, damper control signal	-Building characteristics -Weather data -Meter data -Consumption data	-Measured data -Meta data	-Outdoor air temperature -Indoor air temperature	-Weather data -RT and humidity -Inlet/outlet water of heating and cooling coils -SAT -Schedule of operation -setpoints -Flow rates
Output	-FDD report -Cx report -Points report -Fault MGMT report	-Status and energy consumption -Suggestion of size -Division of capacity of equipment	-Graphic display - Fault reports	–	-Scatterplots -Carpet plots -Boxplots	-2D plots -Fault reports	–
Communication with BEMS	ODBC and BAC-net driver	Manual	OPC	AMR	HDF5 file	–	CSV file
Interoperability	No	No	No	No	No	No	No

See Acronyms and Abbreviations list on page 000.

Source: [5]

Table 3.3 BCx International Demonstration Sites

Building's name	Type				Size (m²)	Phase			Cx type			Tools tested		
	School	Office	Lab & Office	Other		Design	Construction	Operation	Ini Cx	Re Cx	C Cx	Manual	BEMS assisted	Simulation
CA-MET headquarters of the Ministry of Equipment and Transport		✓			15000			✓	✓			✓		
CANMET Energy Technology Centre			✓		3600			✓	✓	✓			✓	
GMS	✓				10000	✓			✓			✓		✓
BSZ	✓				2500			✓	✓			✓	✓	
Munchener Ruckversicherung		✓			9100			✓	✓				✓	✓
Nursery school of Crevecoeur legrand	✓				2700		✓	✓				✓	✓	
Aria, Research building of CSTB			✓		2000			✓	✓			✓	✓	
PB6 headquarters of EDF		✓			63000			✓	✓					✓
Schools of the town of Paris	✓				500-5000			✓			✓		✓	
University Rhone-Alpes	✓				600			✓	✓	✓				✓
Dynamo building of Jyväskylä Polytechnic	✓				10000			✓		✓				✓
Digital building			✓		8300		✓		✓					✓
Cultural Palace				✓	60000		✓		✓			✓	✓	
NH Eurobuilding Hotel (Spain)				✓	50100			✓		✓		✓	✓	
K Building				✓	86000		✓	✓	✓				✓	
Shinkawa building		✓			5400			✓		✓		✓	✓	
Tepco Building		✓			16765		✓	✓	✓			✓	✓	
Yamatake research centre			✓		1692		✓	✓	✓				✓	
O House, residential building				✓	150		✓	✓	✓				✓	✓
Postbank office building			✓		7000			✓			✓		✓	
primary school of Trondheim	✓				1600			✓		✓		✓		
KV Valten		✓			1200		✓		✓	✓				✓
KV Katsan		✓			6300	✓			✓					✓
Kista Entré		✓			46000			✓	✓				✓	✓
Swiss federal institute for forest, snow and landscape			✓		3675			✓		✓		✓		
Wandkorf Bern New stadium and commercial centre				✓	5500	✓			✓			✓		
Government office building of the City of Oakland		✓			6300	✓			✓					✓

Source: [3].

approach [10] allowed for fast, accurate, and reliable date exchange between team members (Figure 3.2) [7].

Table 3.4   EPBD Requirements in the Flemish Region, Belgium [7]

EPBD REQUIREMENTS		Purpose of Building			
Type of Construction		Residential	Office and School	Industry	Other
New building Rebuilding dismantling Partial rebuilding (heated volume >800 m³)	Thermal insulation	Max K45 Max U or Min R	Max K45 Max U or Min R	Max K55 Max U or Min R	Max K45 Max U or Min R
Enlargement (minimum of one residential building)	Energy performance	Max E100	Max E100	—	—
	Indoor climate	Min ventilation Min risk overheating	Min ventilation	Min ventilation	Min ventilation

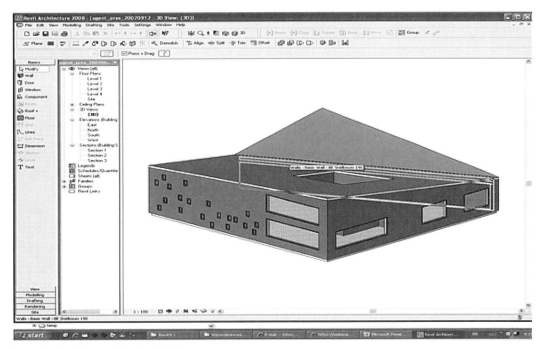

Figure 3.1   BIM model in Revit [7].

3.2.1.2   BCx Practices in the Czech Republic

The practice of regulating energy consumption of buildings is based on estimating demand and consumption of energy in buildings and building zones, based on the "standard use" notion that is determined by "normative conditions of indoor and outdoor environment and operations" [11]. The NKN, the national calculation tool of the Czech Republic, has been developed as a spreadsheet application to facilitate the calculation of heating, cooling, hot water, and lighting system demands and loads, based on appropriate use patterns. The data input into NKN obtained from the sources is listed in Table 3.5.

NKN calculations are streamlined by the use of standard profiles to represent typical cases and contexts. Each profile contains information about the uses, set temperatures, operating periods, lighting standards, climate data, system type, and

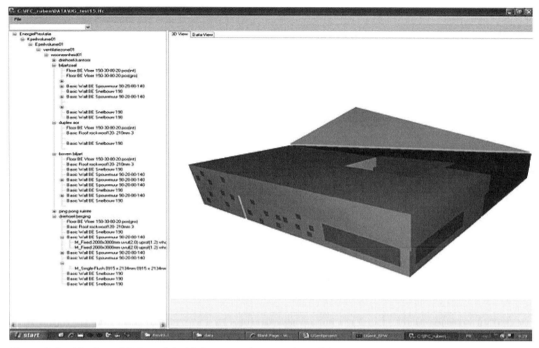

Figure 3.2   3D view of IFC model with integrated EPB analyses [7].

Table 3.5   Input to the NKN [11]

Information	Source
Building geometry, areas, orientation, etc.	Reads from drawings or direct measurement
Climatic data	From the internal database calculation tool
Occupancy profiles for activity areas assigned to each space	For consistency, these come from an internal database; building type and activity are chosen for each zone
Building envelope constructions	Inputs parameters directly ("inference" procedures may be used for energy certification of existing buildings)
HVAC systems	Selects from internal databases or input parameters
Lighting	Selects from internal databases or inputs parameters

efficiencies. Calculating the consumption values is difficult since it can be time consuming to collect the requisite data for it. Therefore, parametric consumption profiles for prototypical cases have been established; see Table 3.6, in which different performance levels are predefined for different building types (A–C for new buildings; D–F for existing ones). Complications arise when different setpoints are established in different buildings of the same type and category [11].

Finer grain profiles are used that specify operation times, heating and cooling setpoints, HVAC input/output air temperatures, heat gain, and lighting settings. To complete this data bank of profiles, both national and international standards and regulations are used. To date, a total of 49 profiles in nine groups of the type shown in Table 3.6 have been identified [11].

Table 3.6   Building Classification Based on Annual Energy Consumption (kWh/m²) [11]

Building type	A	B	C	D	E	F
Family house	< 51	51–97	98–142	143–191	192–240	241–286
Apartment building	<43	43–82	83–120	121–162	163–205	206–245
Hotel, restaurant	< 102	102–200	201–294	295–389	390–488	489–590
Office	< 62	62–123	124–179	180–236	237–293	294–345
Hospital	< 109	109–210	211–310	311–415	416–520	521–625
Education	<47	47–89	90–130	131–174	175-220	221–265
Sport	< 53	53–102	103–145	146–194	195–245	246–297
Shop, market	< 67	67–121	122–183	184-241	242–300	301–362

3.2.1.3   BCx Practices in Germany

The central practice of testing for cost-effective building performance in Germany is based on the Fraunhofer ISE procedure, a four-step, top-down process of building analysis [12]. In this process each step is carried out when available information, measurements, and analysis conform to prerequisite specifications. Flowcharts standardize the steps of this analysis method. To introduce standards of analysis, flowcharts describing each step of the process guide the analyst. At a minimum, the data set indicated in Table 3.7 is considered necessary for a meaningful analysis [12].

Usually, for loose-fit buildings, high-quality measured data is scarce, and the cost of obtaining the data is high (€10,000 to 30,000 per building). Yet the payback on realizing the warranty and the Cx process is significant and often justifies

Table 3.7   Minimal Data Set of Measured Data [12]

Item	Measured Value	Unit	Minimum Time Resolution (per hour)	Remarks
Consumption	Total consumption of fuels	kWh	h	Gas, oil, biomass, etc.
	Total consumption of district heat	kWh	h	
	Total consumption of district cold	kWh	h	
	Total consumption of electricity	kWh	h	
	Total consumption of water	m³	h	
Weather	Outdoor air temperature	°C	h	
	Outdoor rel. Humidity	%	h	
	Global irradiation	W/m²	h	
Indoor conditions	Indoor temperature	°C	h	One or more reference zones
	Indoor relative humidity	°C	h	One or more reference zones
System	Flow/return temperatures of main water circuits	°C	h	In the building, not a district heating system
	Supply air temperature of main AHUs	°C	h	Only if supply air is thermodynamically treated
	Supply air relative humidity of main AHUs	%	h	Only if supply air is humidified/dehumidified

the expenditures. Based on seven case studies conducted in Germany and Finland, and assuming that the cost of data acquisition is €8,000 to €25,000, then BCx saves 10% of the energy consumption. Figure 3.3 shows the payback on yearly energy costs.

The analysis process consists of four steps carried out sequentially: benchmarking (operational rating), certification (asset rating), optimization, and regular inspection [13]. In *benchmarking*, basic stock and consumption data is gathered and baseline performance parameters are established. Stock data consists of minimal building description, and measured data includes utility bills and meter readings. Performance metrics deal with energy consumption signatures, and the outcome of this step is the initial classification of the facility in terms of energy consumption.

Certification deals with an asset rating based on the EPBD. Its outcome is intended to establish a "theoretical benchmark; deep insight; or major energy consumer" of the facility, which is dependent on the national implementation guidelines of the EPBD [12]. *Optimization* analyzes building parameters to set energy-saving measures and optimize performance. Depending on the case, stock data may include a basic data set, simplified HVAC system model data, or more detailed and advanced performance indicators. The measured data consists of a minimal data set (Table 3.7) that is subject to standard analysis through measurement-based or model-based approaches. The outcome of this step is optimized, fault-free system performance for energy savings. *Regular inspection* maintains optimal performance through ongoing monitoring. Data needs are minimal, stock or measured. Energy consumption is the major performance metric that is evaluated, leading to persistent energy savings in the facility throughout its life cycle.

3.2.1.4 BCx Practices in Norway

Norwegian practices follow two documents, one for general purpose commissioning of new buildings and the other for lifetime commissioning. The first one

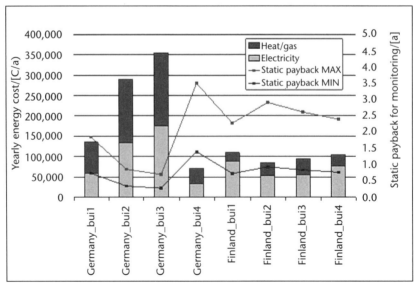

Figure 3.3 Estimated static payback of monitoring in close-fit and experimental buildings [12].

(Standard NS 3935:2005) is called ITB for integrated technical building installations, and is intended for close-fit and experimental building systems. It regulates the coordination of design, Cx of installations, and monitoring of building systems. It covers energy supply and distribution, indoor air quality, safety systems, communications, circulation, water systems, and O&M in new buildings. The Lifetime Commissioning Standard (NS 3451 and 3455) was fashioned after international standards in order to improve communication and interoperability between different agents of the Cx process. This standard recommends a nine-part process, not necessarily sequentially implemented (Table 3.8).

This plan is designed to realize "Owner's Project Requirements (OPR) so that performance verification is possible at an early stage" [14]. In addition, it ensures effective "verification checklists and pre-functional test (PFT) procedures that ensure proper equipment installation and functioning" [14]. However, due to the lack of customization of building types, these requirements do not come with predefined performance metrics. Currently, these procedures are implemented by and large manually [14].

3.2.2   Pacific Rim Countries

3.2.2.1   BCx Practices in Japan

Currently, BCx practices in Japan are guided by the standards issued by SHASE (Society of Heating, Air-Conditioning and Sanitary Engineers). These standards are designed to manage information flow as shown in Figure 3.4. This process has several problems, including manual handling of data, management of large amounts of BEMS data generated automatically, and a lack of interoperability between BCx and database applications. To remedy these problems, the interaction features illustrated in Figure 3.5 have been implemented [15].

First, a CAD application including a common file format for designers and contractors is created. This is defined to incorporate international standards like IFC, Seadec data eXchange Format (SXF), or Green Building XML (gbXML). Second, databases used in BCx operations are modified to store equipment manufacturer's specifications, and operational, sensed data. Relational database management system (RDBMS) and Hierarchical Data Format version 5 (HDF5) technologies are being used to handle the size and complexity of these data formats. Some of this data can be public, such as performance and specification plots of equipment, as opposed to others, like the sensor collected time series data, which is kept private

Table 3.8   Relationship Between Parts and Outputs of the Lifetime Cx Approach [14]

Framework for Lifetime Cx	Design	Construction	Operation
Part 1: Requirements	Part 1.1: Performance requirements in the design phase	Part 1.2: Performance requirements in the construction phase	Part 1.3: Performance requirements in the operation phase
Part 2: Plan	Part 2.1: Plan for commissioning in the design phase	Part 2.2: Plan for commissioning in the construction phase	Part 2.3: Plan for commissioning in the operation phase
Part 3: Common	Performance requirements and description. This is a common document built through all three building phases.		

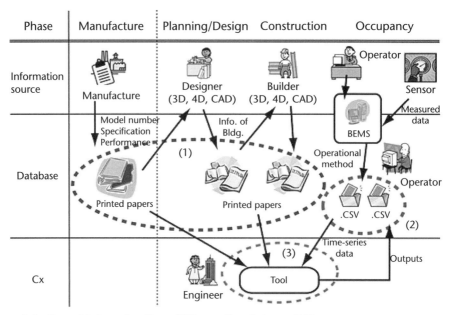

Figure 3.4   Present information flow of BCx practices in Japan [15]

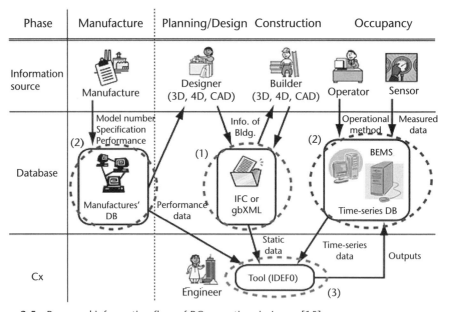

Figure 3.5   Proposed information flow of BCx practices in Japan [15].

[15]. To address some of the problems with manual processing of data, several automation tools have been developed. "Since it is inefficient to read data off of plotted data functions, a tool to build a mathematical model of an HVAC component from its specification curve was developed," using a visual digitizer [15]. This tool displays the specification curve, digitizes the curve when prompted, and calculates model parameters automatically (Figure 3.6).

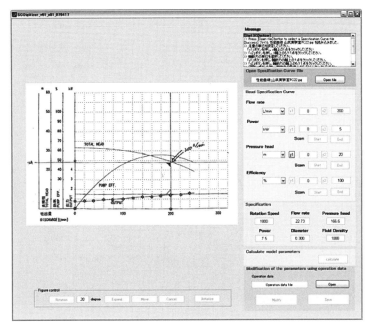

Figure 3.6 Visual digitizer based on HVAC component mathematical model [15].

Another tool that was developed automatically collects operational and sensor data into an SQL database. This application also has the time stamp and missing data interpolation functions built into it. A third tool retrieves stored data from an SQL database and displays it on a graphic user interface field, organized hierarchically [15]. The information flow between these tools and the performance verification process is structured using quasi-formal representations like IDEF0, as depicted in the diagram for the "performance verification of an HVAC system with a ground thermal storage system," in Figure 3.7 [15].

3.2.2.2 BCx Practices in Hong Kong–China

In Hong Kong–China three separate standards documents impact the practice of BCx: HK-BEAM (*Hong Kong Building Environmental Assessment Method*), General Specifications (*General Specification for Air-Conditioning, Refrigeration, Ventilation and Central Monitoring & Control System Installation in Government Buildings of The Hong Kong Special Administrative Region*), and T&C Procedure (*Testing and Commissioning Procedure for Air-Conditioning, Refrigeration, Ventilation and Central Monitoring & Control System Installation in Government Buildings of the Hong Kong Special Administrative Region*).

HK-BEAM is based on the United Kingdom's building research establishment standards (BREEAM). It is the most comprehensive of the three since it applies to all building types and use types, new and old. Its mission is to proactively improve performance in all stages of the delivery process and environmental impact. It covers diverse aspects of CPD including site, material, energy, water, and indoor environmental quality; it also calculates an overall assessment grade for building performance based on these aspects [16].

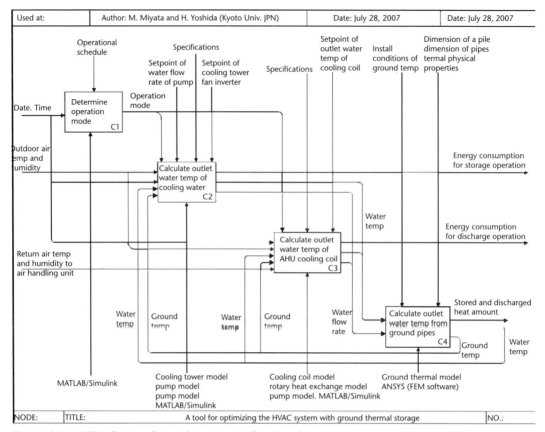

| Used at: | Author: M. Miyata and H. Yoshida (Kyoto Univ. JPN) | Date: July 28, 2007 | Date: July 28, 2007 |

NODE: TITLE: A tool for optimizing the HVAC system with ground thermal storage   NO.:

Figure 3.7 IDEF0 diagram for performance verification of an HVAC system with ground thermal storage [15].

The General Specification "prescribes the technical requirements of materials and equipment, standards of workmanship, requirements on testing and commissioning as well as requirements on document submissions for air-conditioning, refrigeration, ventilation and central monitoring, control system installation and green initiative." While its application in private buildings is not compulsory as it is for government buildings, it is widely used in both categories [16].

The T&C Procedure regulates the minimum requirements for HVAC systems and control system installations through the preliminary testing and inspection of new construction or major alterations. This too is widely used in private and public sectors despite its target being public buildings. These standards follow the same general process structure recommended in Guideline 1-1996 for Cx (Figure 3.8).

To assist in the implementation of these guidelines, a simulation platform for performance testing and optimization of the control strategies has been developed. This platform has been tested in a realistic case (Figure 3.9), demonstrating data communication between independent data repositories and control systems [16].

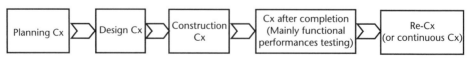

Figure 3.8 Simplified flow diagram for commissioning in Hong Kong–China [16].

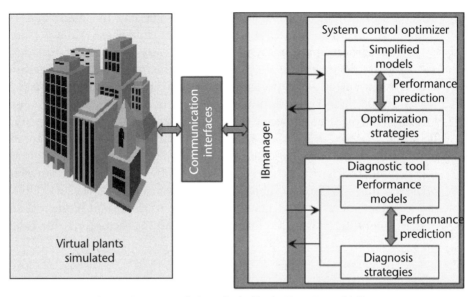

Figure 3.9   Test tool in real-time simulation of a facility in Hong Kong [16].

3.2.3   BCx Standards in United States and Canada

Several key organizations promote guidelines and standards for BCx in the United States and Canada. These include ASHRAE (American Society of Heating, Refrigerating, and Air-Conditioning Engineers), ECBCS (Energy Conservation for Building and Community Systems), PECI (Portland Energy Conservation, Inc.), TAMU (Texas A&M University), CMU (Carnegie Mellon University), NRC (Natural Resources Canada), and US-DOE (U.S. Department of Energy). In the remainder of this chapter, we will describe some of the phases and types of commissioning promoted by these organizations and the tools for automation of the same.

3.2.3.1   Phases and Types of Commissioning Processes

BCx is often treated as a one-time event to verify that all subsystems for HVAC, plumbing, electrical, fire/life safety, and lighting achieve OPR is being delivered to the owner. However, there are multiple phases of CPD during which BCx is needed. Various agency publications, such as ASHRAE Cx guidelines [17], BCx guidelines, and California Cx guidelines [19], define multiple process phases (Table 3.9): predesign,

Table 3.9   Cx Phases by Different Organizations [20]

ASHRAE	*PECI*	*SHASE*	*California Cx Guideline*
Predesign phase	Predesign phase	Predesign phase	Predesign phase
Design phase	Design phase	Design phase	Design phase
		Elaboration phase	
Construction phase	Construction phase	Construction phase	Construction phase
	Acceptance phase		
Occupancy and operation phase	Post-acceptance/ occupancy phase	Operation phase	Occupancy and operation phase

design, construction, and occupancy/operation. The state of California has developed summary descriptions for their Cx guidelines for each phase (Table 3.10).

In the earliest phase, the OPR is expected to define clearly the design intent and program document, develop and update the initial Cx plan, determine related O&M requirements, and prepare the system manual and O&M training documents. In addition to these requirements, there is multiple-stakeholder involvement, including the owner, architect, engineer, contractor, commissioner, and O&M staff. It can be observed in Tables 3.15 and 3.16 that these stakeholders are involved in defining requirement specifications for each phase. A large amount of information is generated, much of which needs to be shared with others or transferred to other phases of the CPD process. The BCx process subsumes all phases of delivery, from predesign to operation and maintenance; due to the broad scope indicated in the above tables four types of Cx have been created for use in the field (Table 3.11).

Table 3.10 Cx Activity and Process Type in Each BCx Phase for State of California

Predesign	Design	Construction	Operation & Maintenance
Select a Cx lead	Design phase meeting (if Predesign meeting did not occur)	Construction phase kick-off meeting	Resolve outstanding Cx issue
Predesign phase Cx meeting	Perform Cx-focused design review	Review submittals, monitor development of shop and coordination drawings	Perform seasonal/deferred testing
Begin developing OPR	Update Cx plan	Review O&M manuals	Perform new warranty-end review
Develop initial Cx plan outline	Develop Cx requirement for the specification	Perform ongoing construction observation	
	Begin planning for verification checklists, functional tests, system manual, and training requirement	Perform verification checks	
		Perform diagnostic monitoring	
		Perform functional testing	
		Develop Cx report and system manual	
		Develop Re-Cx plan	
		Review and verify owner's staff training	

Courtesy of the California Commission Collaborative [19].

Table 3.11 Four Types of Commissioning

Capital Project Delivery (CPD) Process							Operation & Maintenance	
Predesign		Design		Elaboration	Construction		Occupancy & Operation	
Program	Planning	Preliminary design	Working design	Elaboration	Construction	Acceptance	Post-acceptance	Ordinary operation
		Initial Commissioning						Ongoing Cx
		Initial commissioning						Re-Cx
		Missing initial commissioning (or missing documentation on initial commissioning)						Retro-Cx

Courtesy of Annex 40, ECBCS, IEA [3].

Initial Commissioning (I-Cx) is a systematic process applied to production of a new building and/or installation of new systems. Retro-Commissioning (Retro-Cx) is the first time commissioning implemented in an existing building where a documented commissioning process was not previously implemented. Re-Commissioning (Re-Cx) is a commissioning process implemented after I-Cx or Retro-Cx, when the owner hopes to verify, improve and document the performance of building systems. On-Going Commissioning (On-Going Cx) is a commissioning process conducted continually for the purposes of maintaining, improving and optimizing the performance of building systems after I-Cx or Retro-Cx. [3]

A number of product modeling and BCx applications have been developed to fit these BCx types. The primary aim of these tools has been to improve building performance by overcoming paper-based procedures (Table 3.12).

The tools listed in Table 3.12 automate fault detection and diagnostics (FDD) and optimization of HVAC functions. However, most of them focus on the O&M phase only from the point of view of the mechanical and control engineers. This does not help in meeting the information interoperability goal. Although domain-specific modeling for BCx has also been attempted by some of them [21], in general, this effort has demonstrated once again the intractability of this task and the shortcomings of the resulting products. Apart from the enormous amounts of time and resources that are needed for completing this task, the universal product model with all-inclusive coverage remains elusive.

3.2.3.2   Tools for the Automation of the BCx Process

Several of the automation tools listed in Table 3.12 have entered the global marketplace of BCx with the promise of steering the field toward model-based, standardized, and interoperable practices. These include the Design Intent Tool (DIT), Functional Test Data Analysis (FTDA) tool, and Diagnostic Agent for Building Operation (DABO) tool [22].

Design Intent Tool.
Because it is usually a paper-based document, the OPR, a natural point of departure for the BCx process, is usually not properly documented or subjected to data loss. Furthermore, there is no formal way of documenting design intent.

Research by Lawrence Berkeley National Laboratory (LBNL) developed the DIT to help record keeping by building owners, architects, and engineers. Design intent documentation is a channel of communication and contractual obligation between the building owner, architect, engineer, contractor, and commissioning agent. In DIT, the OPR evolves as the project goes through the milestones of programming, design, construction, building occupancy, and operation. The OPR provides the criteria to verify proper installation, operation, and performance of energy-efficiency features [23].

DIT is implemented on MS Access using a macro function to create a database of design intent. Using a visual interface, the owners can set the stage for the design and establish project goals by writing a very brief, high-level mission statement in addition to defining criteria for selecting the design team (Figure 3.10). Using the "Design Intent Document" tab, the user can select the appropriate design

Table 3.12 Recent BCx and Product Modeling Research [20]

	GTPPM	DIT	ECx	VMA	BEMAC	ANNEX
Domain	Precast concrete	BCx	BCx	BCx	HVAC operation	BCx
Purpose	Develop precise concrete product model	Record design intension	Develop PM for BCx	Automated IFC version matching for BCx model	Building performance assessment	-FDD -HVAC optimization
BLC (phase)	Predesign	Design	Whole	Whole	Whole	O&M
User	-Domain expert -Product modeler	-Owner -Architect -HVAC designer	-CxA -Contractor	Modeler	O&M staff CxA	BOp, ES, BI, Bow, MI, CA, CS, MC
Pros for BCx	Derive product model from process model	Easy to install, learn, and use	Interoperable	Interoperable	Interoperable	Automated FDD, HVAC optimization
Cons for BCx	Need the time to collect requirement	Not interoperable	Need time to develop product model	New HVAC modeling concept present in IFC 2.3	Need time to develop product model	Not interoperable Need the time to collect requirement

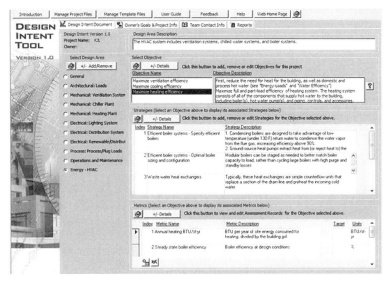

Figure 3.10   Interactive visual interface of the Design Intent Tool. (Courtesy of the Lawrence Berkeley National Laboratory [23].)

area mode. The user can then select or write in the goal descriptions field such as "maximize ventilation/heating/cooling efficiency." Finally, performance metrics corresponding to the objective can be recorded.

Functional Test Data Analysis Tool.
Other applications pursue automated Cx tools that estimate design performance, conduct FDD analysis, optimize HVAC operations, and automate energy consumption estimates. The FTDA, an application developed by LBNL is an application with manual data entry from the building's energy management and control system (EMCS) and temporary instrumentation [24]. Based on an analysis of the performance data generated during the test procedure, the type of fault and location of fault (mixing box, coil, or fan in the AHU) are determined and sorted into five groups (Table 3.13).

To determine the faults for each group listed in Table 3.14, a more precise method of reasoning, such as a knowledge-based expert system (KBES), would be necessary. Because the communication between the EMCS and data analysis is

Table 3.13   Major Faults Sorted into Five Groups by FTDA Tool [24]

Group I	Faults detectable at minimum control signal (e.g., leakage)
Group II	Faults detectable at maximum control signal (e.g., coil fouling, undersized equipment)
Group III	Faults detectable because the target component fails to respond to a change in control signals (e.g., stuck actuator, wiring problems between controller and actuator)
Group IV	Faults occurring across the operating range and detectable from the response of the target components in the middle range of the operation (e.g., hysteresis, sensor offset)
Group V	Faults related to control (e.g., poorly tuned controller, incorrectly implemented sequence of operations)

Table 3.14   Fault Diagnoses in the Mixing Box Functional Performance Test [24]

Fault Group	Cause	Symptoms
Groups I	Leaking outside air damper	$\Delta OAF(u=0)>0$
	Oversized minimum outside air damper	$\Delta OAF(u=0)>0$
Group II	Outside air damper stuck closed or partially closed	OAF (u=0) = OAF (u=10%) = OAF (u=50%)
	Exhaust air damper stuck closed or partially closed	$\Delta OAF(u=50\%)<0$
	Leaking return air damper	$\Delta OAF(u=100\%)<0$
	Return air damper stuck open or partially open	$\Delta OAF(u=100\%)<0$
Group III	Common actuator stuck	OAF (u=0) = OAF (u=10%) = OAF (u=50%) = OAF (u=90%) = OAF (u=100%)
	Actuator wiring or controller output failure	OAF (u=0) = OAF (u=10%) = OAF (u=50%) = OAF (u=90%) = OAF (u=100%)
	Sensor offset/failure	OAF (u=0) = OAF (u=10%) = OAF (u=50%) = OAF (u=90%)= OAF (u=100%)$\neq$ 0
Group IV	Hysteresis in actuator(s) or damper linkage(s)	OAF(u=50% increasing)$\neq$OAF(u=50% decreasing)
	Damper actuator range mismatch	OAF (u=0) = OAF (u=10%) or OAF (u=90%) − OAF (u=100%)
	Excessive nonlinearity	$\Delta OAF(u=50\%)\neq0$
Group V	Poor loop tuning	Oscillation or sluggish response when OAF=10%, 50%, or 90% in closed-loop tests
	Control program error	Failure to meet the setpoints in closed-loop tests

more difficult to automate, mostly due to proprietary communication protocols, a semiautomated application has been developed. This includes not only closed-loop tests that are done under design conditions emphasized in other FPTs, but also open-loop tests applicable to the full range of system operations (Table 3.14).

The user enters the test measurement manually from the EMCS system and the preprocessor checks and converts the data into the appropriate units. This performance data is compared against the predicted data generated from a simulation tool called SPARK [25] for fault diagnosis. This fault diagnosis module uses rule-based reasoning on the symptoms detected. To display controllability issues in the system and support reporting of test results, closed-loop results with time series and open-loop results with X-Y plots of normalized variables are plotted [24]. Since it is hard to set up communication between the FTDA tool and the control device, FPT data is manually submitted for analysis. To establish communication links with the control system, a Cx test shell was developed using the BACnet protocol [26], which will be discussed in detail in Chapter 9.

Diagnostic Agent for Building Operation (DABO) Tool.
Under the auspices of the Canadian Government and National Energy Utilities agencies, DABO achieves both optimization and FDD for automated BCx, and for On-Going and Retro-Cx phases [22]. DABO is a BEMS-assisted Cx tool and a platform to support connection between BEMS data and advanced analytical processes [22]. The DABO analytical process consists of FDD, On-Going Cx (COMM),

energy prediction, and preventive maintenance. To detect unusual system and component behavior, it also addresses the needs of building owners, Cx providers, and building operators. The reasoning algorithms in DABO analyze monitored data, identify faults, calculate performance indices, and facilitate evaluation of energy efficiency improvement. For VAV boxes and AHU systems, DABO has an embedded tool to perform FDD analysis, a stand-alone Cx tool for AHU, and an air distribution system [3]. A third capability developed in DABO is the heating and cooling of hydronic networks applications [4]. FDD and COMM reside on personal computers and analyze incoming data from the BEMS. These behaviors include failures in:

1. Sensors;
2. Linkages and actuators;
3. Controllers—instability;
4. Sequence of operation—nonoptimality.

Based on the abnormal system behavior, the FDD/COMM functionalities diagnose the possible cause and provide the explanation for it. The three levels of analysis for FDD/COMM are at the component, system, and global analysis.

3.2.3.3 Challenges and Opportunities for Computational Embedded Commissioning

Based on these reviews of selected national practices of digital application in the BCx domain, we make several, general observations [5]:

- IDEF (Information DEFinition) methods (http://www.idef.com/idef0.html) provide useful nomenclature for data representations (product models) as well as flowcharts (process models) of a general nature.

- Other more informal flowchart representations used in several of the nationality practices, such as those of North America, Japan, Germany, and Norway, include decision flowcharts. The efficacy of these representations ultimately depends on their ease of usability in the digital medium and their reliability and accuracy in the field.

- Several of the national practices, including those of Belgium and Germany, base their Cx standards on energy auditing, the "green movement," and building occupancy certification procedures. These processes, while not formally linked to Cx regulations and contractual obligations, are explicitly connected to activities that are central to Cx. The use of system selection and performance criteria developed for building performance and certification in contracting Cx authorities and agents needs to be integrated.

- BIM has become a spontaneous and powerful movement to advance information technologies in the CPD sector. It aims to exploit the most advanced intelligence that can be built into computer applications representing building data. The ultimate purpose of this is to make building delivery, performance, and maintenance more efficient, accurate, and productive. To this end, the goal of improving the Cx of both loose-fit and close-fit building systems is consistent with those of BIM. As more advanced data models are developed, standardization of Cx data and process models and interoperability of data between different agents and stages in the CPD process will reach higher levels of acceptance.

- Several data (product) modeling standards including STEP-21, EXPRESS Language of the industry foundation classes (IFCs), Seadec data eXchange Format (SXF), and Green Building XML (gbXML) are suitable for developing new and better applications in the Cx domain.

- Furthermore, sophisticated digital applications are emerging in the Cx field, using Unified Modeling Language (UML) and object-oriented (OO) computing. This demonstrates that mapping between stable and standardized product and process models will offer significant improvements in Cx standards and functionalities (Chapter 8).

- For these advances to become mainstream in the practice of BCx, a steep learning curve among researchers and practitioners is required. Until then, conventional database representations such as ACCESS, RDBMS, and HDF5 will be used to move into formalizing data representations and flowcharts. This will help create mature and robust data banks on which sound UML and OO applications can be constructed.

- Finally, there is a need for further work toward determining the most suitable visualization types and minimum data requirements. Data obtained from sensors and other building automation system (BAS) software can be extremely detailed and overwhelming, especially in the field. Culling useful information from such data is a challenge. Visualization tools developed in digital applications, including carpet plots, data abstraction techniques, and 2D and 3D graphic tools can be effective in assisting Cx agents to quickly process large amounts of BAS data.

3.3   Emerging Requirements for BCx in the Information Age

The transition to the information age presents multiple interrelated and complex challenges that stem from the need for digital connectivity. Industrialized societies have made the transition into this world of information abundance through the Internet and related technologies that provide unimpeded access to data, people, institutions, and sensed information. This phenomenon pervades not only in the social realm (YouTube, Facebook) but also in the business world through business-to-business (B2B) interactions and business to client or consumer (B2C), to employee (B2E), and to government institutions (B2G). In advanced industrialized nations, the overall volume of Internet connections confirms this trend. A similar trend is discerned in emerging industrialized nations, when we consider the rate of connectivity growth (Table 3.15).

As stated in Chapter 1, the AEC industry has been one of the last manufacturing sectors to join the information technology (IT) movement. While its progress is evident in all fronts, including design collaboration [28], ontology libraries [29, 30], data sharing [31], and standardization [32], its achievements pale in comparison to many other manufacturing areas, such as the auto, electronics, and

Table 3.15 World Population and Internet Usage [27]

World Regions	Population (2010 Estimate)	Internet Users as of December 31, 2000	Internet Users' Latest Data	Penetration (% Pop.)	Growth 2000–2010	Users% of Table
Africa	1,013,779,050	4,514,400	110,931,700	10.9%	2,357.3%	5.6%
Asia	3,834,792,852	114,304,000	825,094,396	21.5%	621.8%	42.0%
Europe	813,319,511	105,096,093	475,069,448	58.4%	352.0%	24.2%
Middle East	212,336,924	3,284,800	63,240,946	29.8%	1,825.3%	3.2%
North America	344,124,450	108,096,800	266,224,500	77.4%	146.3%	13.5%
Latin America/ Caribbean	592,556,972	18,068,919	204,689,836	34.5%	1,032.8%	10.4%
Oceania/ Australia	34,700,201	7,620,480	21,263,990	61.3%	179.0%	1.1%
WORLD TOTAL	6,845,609,960	360,985,492	1,966,514,816	28.7%	444.8%	100.0%

appliance sectors, which have already achieved advanced levels of standardization and cradle-to-cradle paperless processing.

One of the reasons for this is that connectivity, particularly in complex product types like those of the AEC industry, brings with it three intractable challenges: standardization, interoperability, and process-product modeling. These challenges determine the success with which data developed by multiple agents within any given stage (*vertical*), and at different stages of the capital project delivery process (*horizontal*), can be seamlessly exchanged. Not overcoming these problems will almost certainly result in serious deficiencies in functionality and cost.

3.3.1 Modeling

The description of building programs, the beginning of most, if not all, design and construction documentation, is written in natural language [21, 33]. Lack of digital data modeling and automation inevitably leads to old and unreliable data, dependency on human-recalled information, and poor documentation [34]. During the past two decades, word processing and spreadsheet software have been adapted to document nongraphical building information. However, although these are digital formats, they are not fully computable [35]. A number of research studies [36–38] have also identified problems with retrieval and delivery of just-in-time (JIT) information that enhances quality, schedule, and budget of CPD significantly. We address these issues in greater detail in Chapters 5, 8, and 14.

3.3.1.1 Product Modeling

A variety of forms are used to manually represent the intent, objectives, and decisions of designers. Most of these are ad hoc and noncomputable in nature. If we are going to succeed in improving the performance of experimental and close-fit, let alone loose-fit buildings, digital tools will be needed to store, update, access, and manage their life-cycle performance assessment.

Developing centralized and universally applicable product models in the digital realm has its own challenges. While it is possible to create inclusive models saturated with data, it is next to impossible to codify and maintain ontologically comprehensive models for all times [39].

Various approaches to creating comprehensive models have been developed in different application domains. For instance, a graphical user interface and multidimensional performance environments that support different stakeholder decision making have been modeled through data warehousing. A decision support tool "that integrates energy-efficient decisions into existing maintenance planning" has been developed in the CLIP EPI-REM environment of Delft University [40]. A concerted effort for standardization of AEC products and processes has been in existence in Finland, through a series of research programs supported by the Finnish Funding Agency for Technology and Innovation (TEKES) and the Finnish construction industry [41]. This effort includes several major research tracks: RATAS, intended to create a research environment for cooperative joint work; SARA, intended to support participating networking business models and IT-based practices into the construction field; and VERA, distributed construction field IT methods and processes for continuous exchange of information between the customer, manufacturer, contractor, and designer without loss of the information spikes depicted in the sawtooth model shown in Figure 2.3.

There are two types of product models: *general* and *domain specific* [42]. Problems with the universal model include the inability of any one model and its computational power to support the range and diversity of design and analysis capabilities required in CPD. The process of developing product models based on the universal model approach is too complex, long, arduous, politically complicated, costly, and ultimately suboptimal [35, 43]. Often it results in a "least common denominator" for all potential capital projects, failing to satisfy anybody's needs [35]. Conversely, in a limited domain, such product models specify only as much of the product data as required for use [35, 44]. A typical problem with such approaches is that product models useful in a given domain, say the BCx process, are hard to standardize due to the lack of standardization in that domain. Since the environment of each building and the configuration of its components are different, the Cx process has to be revised and modified to meet the project requirements of various owners [45].

There is an approach that mediates these two and utilizes information that is both easy for BIM applications to produce and for building analysis applications to consume information. For example, using an XML-based protocol, Green Building XML (gbXML) transfers building model data from BIM to Energy Plus, an energy simulation tool.

Even formal modeling using mathematical representations has been applied to product modeling [46]. Formal models are conducive to semantic and syntactic validation, data combination using ordinary mathematics, and ease of specification through matrix tools used in software engineering. In spite of these advantages, formal modeling has not caught on in the AEC domain. Rather, the standard practice in the field relies on commercial products for BIM applications. A partial list of these vendors is in the left-hand column of Table 3.16.

We will address this topic in greater detail in Chapters 4 and 5. Process modeling is another related topic that we will be addressed in detail in Chapter 8.

Table 3.16   Design Software Vendors Complying with IFC Standards

Software	Compatibility with
AECbytes	IFC
Archimen Group: Active3d	IFC
Arktec: Tricalc	IFC 2x3
Autodesk: AutoCAD, Revit	IFC 2x2; IFC 2x3
Bentley Systems: Bentley Architecture	IFC 2x3.
Cadwork: Cadwork 3D	IFC 2x3
Constructivity: Model Viewer	IFC 2x3; IFC 2x4
Dassault Systems SolidWorks 2011	IFC 2x3
Data Design System: DDS-CAD	IFC 2x3
Datacubist: simplebim	IFC2x3
DDS-CAD file viewer	IFC
Eurostep AB: EMS (Eurostep ModelServer)	IFC 2x3
Gehry Technologies: Digital Project V1R4	IFC 2x3
GRAITEC: Advance Steel, Concrete Design	IFC 2x3.
Graphisoft: ArchiCAD, Archicad 7	IFC 1.51, IFC 2.00, IFC 2x, IFC 2x2, IFC 2x3
InterCAD: AxisVM	IFC 2x3
ITS: SpaceGass, version 10.7 onward	IFC 2x3
Jotne EPM Technology AS: EDM products	IFC models
Kymdata: CADS Planner	IFC 2x3
Nemetschek Allplan; SCIA Eng, VectorWorks	IFC 2x3
Octaga Enterprise and .NET SDK toolkit	IFC models
Progman: MagiCAD	IFC 2x2 and IFC 2x3
pt:CAD/TQS	IFC 2x3
Rhino3d/Grasshopper3d[Geometry Gym	IFC 2x3
Solibri IFC Optimizer, Model Viewer, and Model Checker	IFC file optimizer, file viewer, and model checker
Strusoft: FEM-Design	IFC 2x3
Tekla: Tekla Structures	IFC 2x2; IFC 2x3
Vizelia	IFC 2x3

3.3.1.2   Process Modeling

The building product model has been devised as a means to make the flow of information easier as it interconnects digital processes for CPD activities. Yet, even with comprehensive representations, processing information unambiguously is a difficult challenge [47]. For example, product models based on four-dimensional (PM4D) modeling provide opportunities for making impactful decisions about downstream choices of life-cycle alternatives, design usability inputs, and efficient application of expertise [48]. However, entrenched participants of current technology, culture, and business practices provide hindrances to taking full advantage of PM4D technologies.

As a result, AEC process modeling is recognized as an important frontier in managing workflow and predicting decision consequences [49]. Integrating product models, which formerly dominated the manufacturing domain with process modeling, focus on concurrent engineering in which process and product descriptions are coupled. State of the art in these applications takes natural language–based ontological approaches to represent design activities formally. In the domain-specific modeling area, there have been several successful implementations for structural design, precast concrete construction, and BCx. This involves not only exchanges between different CAD systems but also between heterogeneous combinations like graphics and construction scheduling, material takeoff, and costing. Through these exchanges, several aspects of the CPD process can realize time and cost savings by virtue of automating tedious computational tasks and avoiding data incompatibility errors. These aspects of process modeling and mapping into product models will be described in detail in Chapter 8.

3.3.2 Standardization

Modern manufacturing processes are dependent on versioning and alternative specifications of product components throughout their life cycle [50]. Whereas in other manufacturing sectors standardization is of paramount importance, in the AEC sector, there has been only limited product model standardization through the specification of building components like windows, doors, foundations, and wall assemblies. Although significant focus has been placed on standard 3D models of objects and building components, this has been a distraction, if not an impediment, to the difficult task of achieving true standardization for most if not all aspects of CPD.

This endeavor began at the grassroots level through ad hoc and improvised means of digital data exchange—through web access, DVDs, and CD-ROMs. Yet centralized and widely available standard platforms offer the best opportunity not just for data exchange but also for the subsequent computability of data [51]. The International BuildingSmart Consortium, previously known as the International Alliance for Interoperability (IAI), has dedicated its efforts to standardizing product data exchange formats. This has ultimately led to the creation of industry foundation classes (IFCs), a leading standard for the industry. IFCs "describe an object model with *concepts* (classes or terms), *relations* (as direct association or objectified relationships), and *attributes* (or properties)" [52]. Based on IFCs, a multitude of design software systems have developed strategies for design collaboration and optimization toward better building performance [53] (Table 3.16).

However, from the point of view of a specific user of such universal models of standardization, often the models contain excessive information that increases processing overhead. For example, in an IFC-STEP file, a fan coil unit drawn in the AutoCAD Revit MEP application has 793 entity instances, a majority of which is taken up by geometric information, which is the least critical information in BCx. Only 88 out of 793 entity instances represent functional properties of the fan coil unit, while 705 instances are for geometric properties. IFC representations have responded to the increasing requirements of complex CPD processes by modeling AEC information in the third and fourth dimensions; however, some of the consultancy information best shown in 2D and related annotations have been left behind. As a result, an application of IAI called XM-4 has been developed to address this problem [54].

Bentley systems have proposed to exchange AEC-specific business-to-business information that is nongraphic through aecXML technology. The aecXML technology exchanges entities in building delivery processes without explicitly modeling the building. Taking advantage of the overlap between IFC and aecXML in representing nongraphic data, once a graphic representation is completed in IFC, the representation can be extended to other areas such as project management and cost estimation [55]. As a result, aecXML has become a part of BuildingSmart.

While IFCs offer the best chance the AEC industry has for a centralized standard for seamless exchange of data, it needs to be extended significantly to meet the diverse requirements of interoperability in the AEC industry and the BCx area [56]. These include broader scope of information types, project types, exchange mechanisms, formalized transactions, model-based functionality, and project management integration strategies. In Chapter 7, we will cover the opportunities presented by data modeling standards, which are diverse and internationally located. These standards enable the sharing of building information in order to improve productivity in design, construction, and maintenance operations.

3.3.3   Interoperability

According to Froese [56] interoperability is the transferability of "a *building product model* data … with all of the relevant applications, throughout the life cycle of a facility or a building, by using a *common logical structure*." Interoperability is intended to serve the seamless flow of information throughout the CPD process and building life cycle (Chapter 5).

Earlier we stated that a complete representation of the building's design and construction is difficult to accomplish. Each stakeholder involved in the building delivery processes has the incentive to be interested only in a subset of BIM data. In spite of the fact that it has been a long-time goal of the myriad of tools, systems, and research projects [57–59], the ultimate success of seamless information exchange, both horizontally and vertically, has been elusive.

For example, through the INTEROP NoE EC project guidelines, an ontological approach, nonstandard proprietary representations have been transformed into representations with fidelity of data standardization, information interoperability, and semantic consistency. To facilitate such interactions, the viability of linguistic models to support interoperability has been explored. A language called PSL (Process Specification Language) has been developed in order to translate proprietary data into a neutral-standard information representation and facilitate efficient and accurate communication between related AEC sectors [10, 60]. Another ontological approach is the ISO 15531 "MANDATE" (MANufacturing management DATa Exchange) to facilitate interoperability. MANDATE makes use of system theory to provide a general overview of manufacturing-management data modeling and standardized information exchange between software applications. MANDATE, which is written in EXPRESS, the exchange language of STEP, has been instrumental in improving the costs, schedules, and quality of manufactured products through data management [10].

Multiprong efforts are being made at LBNL to implement tools and systems that assist interoperability. University College Cork developed a framework named BEMAC (Building Energy Monitoring Analyzing and Controlling) that is aimed at improving building operations by tracking performance metrics throughout the CPD [61]. They use the BIM technologies supported by IFC standards as the basis for interoperability (Figure 3.11). A C++ programming language–based application

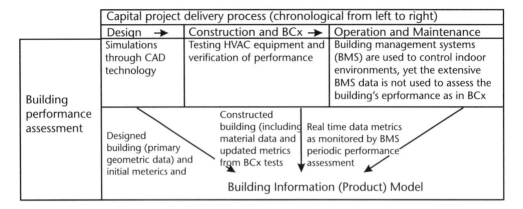

Figure 3.11 Building performance assessment and building performance management methods used to track CPD process metrics [61].

is used to input BIM data obtained from building sensors (Chapter 11). The same application is also used to communicate with various analytical/design tool packages.

Concurrent engineering is one of the research avenues that has brought to the fore the need for interoperability. Ma et al. [62] have shown how a "unified and consistent semantic scheme" for knowledge engineering can support interoperable exchange between the design, manufacturing, operations, and maintenance phases of product life cycles. Similarly, Kulvatunyou et al. [63] use semantic data modeling that is "coherent and scalable" to support interoperability and achieve cost reductions in data integration. Fan and Garcia [64] also merge engineering data with enterprise knowledge in order to obtain standards that can help seamless access to knowledge-based engineering applications within the product life cycle. Alternatively, the Design Analysis Integration (DAI) initiative [35] has been developing a workbench for the integration of design and analysis through mapping simulation tools into existing building models (IFCs), in order to overcome data-centric approaches to interoperability.

Software systems and tools developed for the BCx field (Table 3.2) do not fare any better than the general interoperability approaches. In fact, information developed in the beginning and middle stages of the BCx process fails to transfer to the later stages. Some of the efforts that have addressed this problem include those that support design collaboration, optimize building performance, and provide interoperability support through open standards such as IFC [32] and aecXML [65–67]. Feng and Song [68] in NIST observe that there is a lack of interoperability of information in various CPD planning stages. They developed activity and object models for conceptual design in early product design processes for integrating design and manufacturing engineering. Several other studies addressing the problem of interoperability [69] also recognize the need for seamless collaboration between consulting experts and successive delivery stages. While they acknowledge the potential of IFC standards to address these problems, they also note the shortcomings inherent in the IFC approach: loss of semantic content, inadequate coverage of domain-specific applications and excessive information that hinders functionality.

3.3.4   Cost of Interoperability

Lack of interoperability has its cost that far exceeds the cost of implementing and maintaining these capabilities. A research project by the National Institute of Standards and Technology (NIST) has documented the additional costs incurred by the building owner as a result of inadequate interoperability (Figure 3.12) [59]. The cost of inadequate interoperability in the O&M phase is the highest ($9 billion) compared to other phases. Interoperability of BCx data can help facilitate preventive maintenance amounting to substantial savings.

On the other hand, estimating the cost of interoperability in the entire AEC sector is difficult. The industry lacks standards and is distributed, diverse, and poorly documented. However, there are comparable manufacturing industries in which the cost of interoperability has been estimated with reasonable accuracy. The automotive industry, although less unruly than the construction sector, is also large (9% of goods, 4% of employment in all of manufacturing; and 5% of all consumption expenditures (p. 1-1) [70], widely distributed in the lower tiers of the production cycle (first-tier suppliers: in the hundreds, some large some small; subtier suppliers: in the thousands, mostly small), and utilizes CAD tools that are similar to those of the AEC sector [70].

Multiple CAD/CAM systems used in the automobile supply chain are classified into three tiers: original equipment manufacturers, first-tier suppliers, and sub-tier suppliers (p. 3-3) [70]. In the top tier CATIA, Unigraphics, CADDS, and I-DEAS are used. The representations developed in this system are then passed on to the second tier where CADDS, I-DEAS, Intergraph, pro/ENGINEER, CATIA, and Unigraphics are used. In turn, their representations are interlinked with those in the third tier, namely, CADKEY, ARIES, Applicon, ANVIL, AutoCAD, Pro/ENGINEER, I-DEAS, PDGS, HP, Intergraph, EUCLID, and CATIA [70]. More significantly, the sources of interoperability costs include a series of maintenance issues: redundant systems, multiple point-to-point translations, errors in translation, undetected translation errors, time lost due to manual entry of data, and translation problems (p. 1-6) [70]. Once errors have been detected, there are several costly

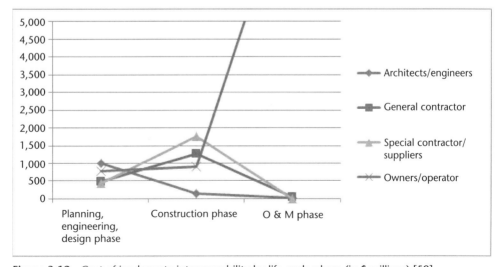

Figure 3.12   Cost of inadequate interoperability by life-cycle phase (in $ millions) [59].

courses of action such as reattempting to transfer, repairing the errors, or entering data from scratch. All of these factors contribute to the cost of inoperability.

In the automotive sector the sources of costs incurred due to interoperability also are diverse [70]. Based on the *cost component* approach, there are avoidance costs, mitigating costs, and delay costs. Using an *aggregate cost* approach, the total costs consist of estimates of interoperability and "discounted present value" of delay costs [71] (Table 3.18). Both estimates agree that the total cost of interoperability is around a billion dollars a year. Adjusted to 2010 values, this is $2,786,972.000, which is more than 1% of the total sector expenditures. Based on the cost component approach, the estimate of avoidance cost is $52,799,000/year, mitigating costs are $907,645,000/year, and delay costs are $90,000,000/year, adding up to a total of $1,050,444,000/year [70].

In other CAD/CAM-related sectors, solutions to interoperability problems advocate either *standardization* into a single system of exchange, providing tools for *point-to-point translation*, or *manual data entry* or neutral *data translation* [13, 71].

> By far, the largest portion of interoperability costs is due to the need to repair or replace unusable data files—approximately $248 million per year is spent on correcting or recreating unusable data. On the average, rework requires an average of 4.9 hours per data exchange. With over 450,000 PDEs per year, this rework is extremely expensive in terms of engineering labor time. ... Suppliers and tooling companies also incur significant mitigating costs. Suppliers incur over $204 million per year for reworking data files. [70]

In the aggregate cost approach, direct interoperability costs are $925,602,000/year, plus delayed profit losses amounting to $90,000,000/year, together representing a total of $1,015,602,000 annual loss due to interoperability problems [70].

These challenges, namely, modeling, standardization, and interoperability and recent developments in several national practices around the globe, shed light on current trends. Data is volatile by nature. Depending on the phase of building delivery, the actors involved in each phase, applicable standards, emerging technologies, and corporate and institutional practices, the data needed for commissioning close-fit or loose-fit buildings can be very different. Therefore, the parameters of Cx data, users, and practices need to be standardized; representations that can carry data from one phase of building delivery to the next, and minimizing of data loss, need to be developed. Current efforts in the area of BIM need to be tapped into and parallel models and software applications for Cx are needed. Challenges of cost, function, and payback in using digital BCx tools need further research. Finally, historic data records for BCx need to be captured.

References

[1]   *Energy Efficiency Planning and Management Guide*, Office of Energy Efficiency, Natural Resources Canada, 2002.

[2]   Society of Heating, Air-Conditioning and Sanitary Engineers of Japan, 2006, http://www.shasej.org/English, last accessed November 12, 2009.

[3]   International Energy Agency, *Annex 40: Commissioning of Building HVAC Systems for Improving Energy Performance*, 2004, http://www.commissioning-hvac.org, accessed February 17, 2009.

[4]   International Energy Agency, *Annex 47: Cost Effective Commissioning of Existing and Low Energy Buildings*, 2008, http://cetc-varennes.nrcan.gc.ca/fichier/37285/Fyler_work_program_e_final.pdf, accessed March 21, 2008.

[5]   Akın, Ö., et al., "Flow Charts and Data Models for Initial Commissioning of Advanced and Low Energy Building Systems," Report No. 4, in *Cost-Effective Commissioning of Existing and Low Energy Buildings*, Annex 47 of the International Energy Agency's Energy Conservation in Buildings and Community Systems Program, http://www.iea-annex47.org, 2010.

[6]   European Commission, "Green Paper: Towards a European Strategy for the Security of Energy Supply," contribution of Energie-Cités (adopted by the General Meeting, London Borough of Southwark, 5th April), *Practical Guide to Contract Procedures for EC External Actions*, 2000.

[7]   Versele, A., "Belgium," in "Flow Charts and Data Models for Initial Commissioning of Advanced and Low Energy Building Systems," O. Akin (Ed.), Report No. 4, in *Cost-Effective Commissioning of Existing and Low Energy Buildings*, Annex 47 of the International Energy Agency's Energy Conservation in Buildings and Community Systems Program, http://www.iea-annex47.org, 2010.

[8]   SketchUp, Google, *SketchUp*, http://www.sketchup.com, 2008.

[9]   REVIT, Autodesk, *Revit Architecture*, http://usa.autodesk.com, 2008.

[10]   Cutting-Decelle, A. F., et al., "ISO 15531 MANDATE: A Product-Process-Resource Based Approach for Managing Modularity in Production Management," *Concurrent Engineering: Research and Applications*, Vol. 15, No. 2, 2007, pp. 217–235.

[11]   Kabele, K., "Calculation of EPBD Energy Performance Certification in the Czech Republic," in *Proceedings of Indoor Climate of Buildings 2007*, Bratislava: Slovenska spolocnost pro techniku prostredia, ISBN 978-80-89216-18-5, 2007, pp. 197–211.

[12]   Neumann, C., and Jacob, D., *Guidelines for the Evaluation of Building Performance*, Report for the Framework of the IEE Project Building EQ: Tools and Methods for Linking EPDB and Continuous Commissioning, Freiburg, Germany: Fraunhofer Institute for Solar Energy Systems, http://www.buildingeq.eu, 2008.

[13]   Mazzarella, L., et al., "Description of European Prototype Tool for Evaluation of Building Performance and the National Tools," in *Intelligent Energy*, Europe (IEE) Publication Agreement No. EIE/06/038/SI2.448300, supported by the European Commission. This report was prepared as a deliverable of Workpackage 5 of Building EQ, May 2009, http://www.buildingeq.eu.

[14]   Djuric, N., "Norway," in "Flow Charts and Data Models for Initial Commissioning of Advanced and Low Energy Building Systems," O. Akin (Ed.), Report No. 4, in *Cost-Effective Commissioning of Existing and Low Energy Buildings*, Annex 47 of the International Energy Agency's Energy Conservation in Buildings and Community Systems Program, http://www.iea-annex47.org, 2010.,

[15]   Yoshida, H., "Japan," in "Flow Charts and Data Models for Initial Commissioning of Advanced and Low Energy Building Systems," O. Akin (Ed.), Report No. 4, in *Cost-Effective Commissioning of Existing and Low Energy Buildings*, Annex 47 of the International Energy Agency's Energy Conservation in Buildings and Community Systems Program, http://www.iea-annex47.org, 2010.

[16]   Wang, S., "China (Hong Kong)," in "Flow Charts and Data Models for Initial Commissioning of Advanced and Low Energy Building Systems," O. Akin (Ed.), Report No. 4, in *Cost-Effective Commissioning of Existing and Low Energy Buildings*, Annex 47 of the International Energy Agency's Energy Conservation in Buildings and Community Systems Program, http://www.iea-annex47.org, 2010.

[17]   "The HVAC Commissioning Process," Atlanta, GA: American Society of Heating, Refrigerating, and Air-Conditioning Engineers, 1996.

[18]   PECI, "Building Commissioning Guidelines," Bonneville Power Administration, U.S. Department of Energy, 1992.

[19]   CCC, "California Commissioning Guide: New Buildings," 2006, http://www.cacx.org/resources/documents/CA_Commissioning_Guide_New.pdf, last accessed November 11, 2009.

[20]   Lee, K. J., *Functionalizing Product and Process Models for Embedded Commissioning of Buildings*, Unpublished PhD proposal, School of Architecture, Carnegie Mellon University, Pittsburgh, PA, 15217, USA, 2010

[21]   Türkaslan-Bulbul, M. T., "Process and Product Modeling for Computational Support of Building Commissioning," Ph.D. Dissertation, Carnegie Mellon University, Pittsburgh, PA, 2006.

[22]   Choiniere, D., "DABO: A BEMS Assisted On-Going Commissioning Tool," in *Proceedings of National Conference on Building Commissioning*, Newport Beach, CA, 2008.

[23]   Lawrence Berkeley National Laboratory, "Design Intent Tool," 2008, http://ateam.lbl.gov/DesignIntent/home.html, last accessed November 1, 2009.

[24]   Xu, P., Haves, P., and Kim, M. "A Semi-Automated Functional Test Data Analysis Tool," in *Proceedings of National Conference on Building Commissioning*, New York, NY, 2005.

[25]   SPARK, "Simulation Problem Analysis and Research Kernel," 2005, http://simulationresearch.lbl.gov, last accessed Oct 10, 2008.

[26]   Xu, P., Haves, P. and Kim, M., "A Semi-Automated Functional Test Data Analysis Tool," in *Proceedings of National Conference on Building Commissioning*, New York, NY, 2005.

[27]   Internet World Stats, *Usage and Population*, June 30, 2010, http://www.internetworldstats.com/stats.htm. Copyright © 2000–2010, Miniwatts Marketing Group. All rights reserved worldwide.

[28]   Nahm, Y. E., and Ishikawa, H. "Integrated Product and Process Modeling for Collaborative Design Environment," *Concurrent Engineering*, Vol. 12, No. 5, http://cer.sagepub.com/content/12/1/5, 2004.

[29]   McCallum, A., Wang, X. and Mohanty, N. "Joint Group and Topic Discovery from Relations and Text," *Statistical Network Analysis: Models, Issues and New Directions*, Lecture Notes in Computer Science 4503, 2007, pp. 28–44.

[30]   Katranuschkov, P., Gehre, A., and Scherer, R. J., *Reusable Process Patterns for Collaborative Work Environments in AEC*, Dresden, Germany: Institute of Construction Informatics. Funded by the FP6 project InteliGrid (IST-004664) of the European Commission and Project ArKoS (Project No. 01ISC35C) of the German Ministry of Education and Research (BMBF), 2008.

[31]   East, C. M., Lee, G. and Sacks, R. "Deriving a Product Model from Process Models," in *Proceedings of ISPE/CE2002*, Cranfield University, UK, 2002.

[32]   EuroSTEP Inc., "4D Application Development: MS Project—IFC Mapping Specification," Released June 29, 2001.

[33]   O'Sullivan, D. T. J., Keane, M. M, and Kelliher, D., "Improving Building Operation by Tracking Performance Metrics Throughout the Building Lifecycle (BLC)," *Energy and Buildings*, Vol. 36, No. 11, 2004, pp. 1075–1090.

[34]   Lee, S.H., "Computational Fieldwork Support for Efficient Operation and Maintenance of Mechanical, Electrical and Plumbing Systems," Ph.D. Dissertation, Carnegie Mellon University, Pittsburgh, PA, 2009.

[35]   Augenbroe, G., et al., "An Interoperability Workbench for Design Analysis Integration," *Energy and Buildings*, Vol. 36, No. 8, 2004, pp. 737–748.

[36]   Clayton, M. J., Johnson, R. E., and Song, Y., *Operations Documents: Addressing the Information Needs of Facility Managers*, 1999, http://itc.scix.net/data/works/att/w78-1999-2441.content.pdf, last accessed January 16, 2007.

[37]   Lui, L. Y., et al., "Capturing As-Built Project Information for Facility Management," in *Proceedings of First Congress Held in Conjunction with A/E/C Systems ASCE*, Washington, DC, 1994, pp. 614–612.

[38]   PECI, "O&M Best Practices Series: Operation and Maintenance Assessments," 1999, http://www.energystar.gov/ia/business/assessment.pdf, last accessed December 16, 2008.

[39]   Türkaslan-Bülbül, M.T., and Akın, Ö, "Computational Support for Building Evaluation: Embedded Commissioning Model," *Automation in Construction*, Vol. 15, pp. 438–447.

[40]   Gürsel, I., Sarıyıldız, S., Stouffs, R., and Akın, Ö., "Contextual Ontology Support as External Knowledge Representation for Building Information Modeling," in *Proceedings of the 13th International CAAD Futures Conference*, T. Tidafi and T. Dorta (Eds.), Montréal:,Les Presses de l'Université de Montréal, ISBN: 978-2-7606-2177-0, 2009.

[41]   Penilla, H. "The State of the Art of Finnish Building Product Modeling Methodology," in *Computer Aided Architectural Design Futures*, B. Martens and A. Brown (Eds.), Vienna: Springer Verlag, 2005, pp. 225–239.

[42]   Ito, K., "General Product Model and Domain Specific Product Model in the A/E/C Industry," in *Proceedings of Computing in Civil Engineering/Proceedings of the Second Congress Held in Conjunction with A/E/C Systems '95*, Vol. 1, 1996, pp. 13–16.

[43]   Spearpoint, M. J, "Integrating the IFC Building Product Model with Fire Zone Models," 2003, http://ir.canterbury.ac.nz/bitstream/10092/486/1/12589008_Integrating%20the%20IFC%20building%20product%20model%20with%20zone%20fire%20simulation%20software.pdf, last accessed September 20, 2010.

[44]   Spearpoint, M. J, "Integrating the IFC Building Product Model with Fire Zone Models," 2003, http://ir.canterbury.ac.nz/bitstream/10092/486/1/12589008_Integrating%20the%20IFC%20building%20product%20model%20with%20zone%20fire%20simulation%20software.pdf, last accessed September 20, 2010.

[45]   Akın, Ö, et al., "Product and Process Modeling for Functional Performance Testing in Low-Energy Building Embedded Commissioning Cases," in *Proceedings of the ICEBO Conference*, San Francisco, CA, November 2007.

[46]   Chadha, H., Baugh, J., and Wing, J., "Formal Specification of AEC Product Models," in *Computing in Civil Engineering, Proceedings of the 1st Congress*, American Society of Civil Engineers, 1994, pp. 571–578.

[47]   Horvath, L., and Rudas, I. J., "Product Modeling Beyond Information," in *Proceedings of Applied Computational Intelligence and Informatics, SACI '09, 5th International Symposium*, May 28–29, 2009, pp. 177–182.

[48]   Kam, C., et al., "The Product Model and Fourth Dimension Project," *ITcon*, Vol. 8, 2003, pp. 137–166, http://www.itcon.org/2003/11.

[49]   Bletzinger, K. U., and Lähr, A., "Prediction of Interdisciplinary Consequences for Decisions in AEC Design Processes," *ITcon,* Vol. 11, 2006, p. 529, http://www.itcon.org/2006/38/g.

[50]   Tarandi, V., "Editorial: IFC—Product Models for the AEC Arena," *ITcon*, Vol. 8, 2003, pp. 135–137, http://www.itcon.org.

[51]   Owolabi, A., Anumba, C. J., and El-Hamalawi, A. "Architecture for implementing IFC-Based Online Construction Product Libraries," *ITcon*, Vol. 8, 2003, pp. 201–218, http://www.itcon.org/2003/15.

[52]   Lima, C., et al., " A Historical Perspective on the Evolution of Controlled Vocabularies in Europe," in *Proceedings of the CIB W102 3rd International Conference 2007*, Fraunhofer IRB Verlag, Stuttgart, Germany, 2007.

[53]   "Industry Foundation Classes," *Wikipedia*, http://en.wikipedia.org/wiki/Industry_Foundation_Classes, last modified May 27, 2011.

[54]   Kim I, Liebich, T., and Kim, S. S. "Development of a Two Dimensional Model Space Extension for IAI/IFC2.X2nd Model," *ITcon*, Vol. 8, 2003, pp. 219–230, http://www.itcon.org/2003/16.

[55]   Froese, T., et al., "Industry Foundation Classes for Project Management—A Trial Implementation," *ITcon*, Vol. 4, November 1999, pp. 17–36, http://www.itcon.org/1999/2.

[56]   Froese, T., "Future Directions for IFC-Based Interoperability," *ITcon*, Vol. 8, 2003, pp. 231–246, http://www.itcon.org/2003/17.

[57]   Gallaher, M. P., et al., "Cost Analysis of Inadequate Interoperability in the US Capital Facilities Industry," National Institute of Standards and Technology, Gaithersburg, MD, 2004.

[58]   IAI, "International Alliance for Interoperability," 2004, http://www.iai-na.org, last accessed December 11, 2004.

[59]   Yang, Q. Z., and Zhang, Y. "Semantic Interoperability in Building Design: Methods and Tools," *Computer Aided Design*, Vol. 38, No. 10, 2006, pp. 1099–1112.

[60]   Das, B., et al., "Towards the Understanding of the Requirements of a Communication Language to Support Process Interoperation in Cross-Disciplinary Supply Chains," *International Journal of Computer Integrated Manufacturing*, Vol. 20, No. 4, June 2007.

[61]   O'Sullivan, D. T. J., et al., "Improving Building Operation by Tracking Performance Metrics Throughout the Building Lifecycle (BLC)," *Energy and Buildings*, Vol. 36, No. 11, 2004, pp. 1075–1090.

[62]   Ma, Z. J., Wang, S.W., and Pau, W. K., "Secondary Loop Chilled Water in Super High-Rise," *ASHRAE Journal*, Vol. 50, No. 5, 2008, pp. 42–52.

[63]   Kulvatunyou, B., et al., "Development Life Cycle for Semantically Coherent Data Exchange Specification," *Concurrent Engineering*, Vol. 16, No. 4, 2008, p. 279. http://cer.sagepub.com/content/16/4/279.

[64]   Fan, I. S., and Garcia, P. B., "International Standard Development for Knowledge Based Engineering Services for Product Lifecycle Management," *Concurrent Engineering*, Vol. 16, No. 4, 2008, p. 271, http://cer.sagepub.com/content/16/4/271.

[65]   AEX, "Automating Information Equipment Exchange," 2004, http://www.fiatech.org/projects/idim/aex.htm, last accessed December 12, 2004.

[66]   CIMSteel, "Computer Integrated Manufacturing for Constructional Steelwork," 2004, http://www.cae.civil.leeds.ac.uk/past/cimsteel/cimsteel.htm, last accessed December 12, 2004.

[67]   COMBINE, "Computer Models for the Building Industry in Europe," http://erg.ucd.ie/combine.html, last accessed December 12, 2004.

[68]   Feng, S. C., and Song, E. Y. "Information Modeling of Conceptual Design Integrated with Process Planning," in *Proceedings of Symposia on Design for Manufacturability*, 2000 International Mechanical Engineering Congress and Exposition, Orlando, FL, 2000.

[69]   Sacksa, R., et al., "The Rosewood Experiment—Building Information Modeling and Interoperability for Architectural Precast Facades," *Automation in Construction*, Vol. 19, No. 4, July 2010, pp. 419–432.

[70]   Brunnermeier, S. B., and Martin, S. A., *Interoperability Cost Analysis of the U.S. Automotive Supply Chain*, Final Report: RTI Project Number 7007-03, prepared at Research Triangle Institute, Center for Economics Research, Research Triangle Park, 3040 Cornwallis Road, Post Office Box 12194, North Carolina 27709-2194 USA, for Gregory Tassey, National Institute of Standards and Technology, Bldg. 101, Room A1013, Gaithersburg, MD 20899-1060, 1999.

[71]   Doty, R., "Open Systems: The Next STEP," *Action Line*, January/February, 1994, pp. 30–33.

CHAPTER 4

Product and Process Models for Building Commissioning

4.1 The Need for Product and Process Models in Building Commissioning

Building features fulfill performance categories that need to be evaluated for conformance to a variety of requirements. However, evaluation procedures in the architecture-engineering-construction (AEC) sector are complex. Furthermore, the multifaceted nature of the capital project delivery (CPD) process presents an obstacle for defining measurement methods toward a general-purpose evaluation objective. This leads to practices that use isolated measurements with discrete objectives. To improve building quality and value throughout its life cycle, evaluation should be a persistent part of the operations and maintenance of CPD [1–3]. Persistent evaluation can be achieved through a systematic and standardized approach. The need for building evaluation and the significance of Embedded Commissioning (ECx) has been discussed in Chapters 1 and 2.

As for any other aspect of building evaluation, the building commissioning (BCx) process needs to become systematic and standardized [3, 4]. Related practices and evaluation techniques need to be standardized among various BCx providers. This is important for two reasons: First, having standard data in the domain will provide a universal basis for equipment design, maintenance, and assessment. Second, it will provide seamless information flow, ease of interoperability, and facilitate communication among stakeholders including manufacturers, designers, and maintenance staff [2]. The importance of standardization and interoperability in the AEC sector is clearly defined in the literature [6–11] and elaborated on in Chapter 3.

In this context, it is important to have reliable standards for ECx data, test procedures, and methods. For example, while testing an air-handling unit (AHU) fan, BCx providers should apply standard inspection protocols like verifying that a fan is installed, operational, and oriented in the correct airflow direction. In practice, procedures and methods used for a specific equipment test may have to differ depending on who is performing the test, for what purpose, the type of building, and whether it is done before or after the building is occupied [11].

It is possible to make building evaluations continuous starting with the early design and programming phases to the decommissioning of the facility, and to provide the much needed building performance assessment to the owner, designer, construction manager, O&M personnel, and occupant [2, 14]. Studies of current practice show that BCx is often treated as a one-time operation, and building information produced during this process is not fed into facility management procedures after the building is occupied [13]. In Chapter 8, we will discuss in detail the relationship between the ECx process and product models that can overcome this deficiency.

Existing BCx practice lacks the structure to manage information exchange between BCx processes and those of the building life cycle. An accurate assessment of building systems through BCx provides the necessary support for the linear progression of design, construction, occupancy, and decommissioning. To improve performance and functioning of the building throughout its life cycle, every phase can be supported with ongoing measurements and evaluations and with the guidance coming from continuous evaluation for downstream decisions (Figure 2.1) [16–18].

In this chapter, we describe a product and process model (PPM) based approach that has been developed to address these needs [4]. The objective of developing the ECx-PPM has been to explore formal systems and operations that can facilitate information standardization efforts. We implemented this approach in two steps (Figure 4.1). The goal of the first step was to develop a better understanding of

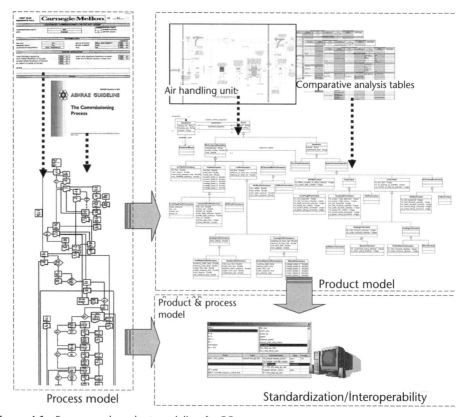

Figure 4.1   Process and product modeling for ECx.

how BCx works. The ECx process model was created to represent an illustrative BCx scenario. A detailed description of the illustrative scenario can be found in [2, 21]. More detail on the process is also given in [4]. In this chapter, our focus is specifically on the ECx process model. We describe the general layout and the flow of the BCx tasks. Guidelines from the American Society of Heating, Refrigerating and Air-Conditioning Engineers (ASHRAE) [23, 24] are used as the main source for the scenario. Then, an observed BCx process is compared and incorporated into the ideal scenario to identify the general layout of BCx operations and how they are practiced in the real world.

The second step of the ECx-PPM approach involves creating an ontological framework for representing the specific BCx information through an object-based data model (Chapter 8). ECx tasks and documents identified in the process model are used as a source in this step for identifying specific ECx documents. Because a very large amount of information is generated during the ECx process, we limited our exploration to the object model of a singular building component: an air-handling unit (AHU). To generate a robust structure that can easily be expanded to include every component in a building system, we developed a modular configuration for the ECx data model.

4.2   Capturing the Building Commissioning Process in a Flowchart

In the ASHRAE guidelines [24–26] the BCx process is defined as a comprehensive progression of specifications, tests, and measurements. So far, ASHRAE has published three guidelines on commissioning. The first guideline was published in 1989 [20] and later superseded by a more comprehensive version, Guideline 1-1996. The second [21] and third [19] guidelines were published in 2005 and 2007, respectively. The focus of the first guideline is specifically on HVAC commissioning, whereas Guideline 0-2005 has a larger scope and defines the process from a more general perspective for the commissioning of all building systems. The most recent guideline, Guideline 1.1-2007, complements Guideline 1-1996 by focusing on the HVAC domain and providing details on the technical requirements of HVAC Cx. All three guidelines are specification-oriented documents that give in-depth and thorough descriptions on how to perform BCx tasks. Sample documents for reporting are provided together with testing procedures and data collection sheets.

In addition, example documentation and guidelines for BCx have been published by private companies that provide such services as well as local and state agencies that standardize BCx practices under their jurisdiction. It would serve the uninitiated reader to quickly review some of the sample documents and procedures recommended by these entities, before reading through the detailed description of ASHRAE's guidelines, which exemplify the "best practices" in the field, that we provide in this chapter. In Table 4.1 we provide some links to notable private and public web resources that exemplify BCx practices.

Our ECx process model aims to take the standard process descriptions in the ASHRAE guidelines and elaborate on them further by defining every task, document, and decision point. Since the scope of PPM covers AHU commissioning,

Table 4.1 BCx Resource References for the Uninitiated Reader

Organization	Description	URL
ASHRAE (American Society of Heating, Refrigerating and Air-Conditioning Engineers)	Guideline 0-2005 and total building commissioning	http://www.techstreet.com/standards/ashrae/guideline_0_2005?product_id=1619765
CCC (California Commissioning Collaborative)	Existing building commissioning toolkit, templates, and sample documents	http://www.cacx.org/resources/rcxtools/templates_samples.html
EEI (Engineering Economics Inc.)	Provides energy-related engineering services to building owners and managers. Building commissioning, retro-commissioning, facility assessments, MEP consulting	http://www.eeiengineers.com/about.asp
EnerNOC	Energy management applications for utilities, commercial, institutional, and industrial customers	http://www.enernoc.com/landing/efficiencysmart.php?src=ga_MBCxad48&gclid=CIqD-a-RhqoCFYpd5Qodq3Z4og
New York State Energy Research and Development Authority	Sample of existing building commissioning plan and existing building commissioning statement of work	http://www.nyserda.org/programs/pdfs/cmsampleretrocxplan.pdf
OOCFM (VA–Office of Construction and Facilities Management)	Whole building commissioning process manual, Department of Veteran's Affairs	http://www.cfm.va.gov
PECI (Portland Energy Conservation, Inc.)	Commissioning Resource Center, commissioning and technical services resource library	http://www.peci.org/resources/commissioning.html
RCx Building Diagnostics	Local PA and NYC engineers and consultants dedicated to the holistic improvement of existing building stock; retro-commissioning experts	http://www.rcxbd.com/retrocommissioning/?gclid=CKGKyKGQhqoCFcJo4Azdi0W5zQ
NIBS (National Institute of Building Sciences)	Building commissioning guidelines by WBDG Project Management Committee	http://www.wbdg.org/project/buildingcomm.php

we specifically focused on Guideline 1-1996 and Guideline 1.1-2007. Our ECx process model representation is intended to visually capture the crucial steps in HVAC-Cx and shows the general flow of BCx while illustrating the relationships between different tasks and decision points. In this representation, it is also possible to observe how the information is transferred and modified from one party to another while the changes are tracked and recorded in log files.

To map the differences between an ideal scenario and real world practice, we compared the Process Model with an observed BCx example [17], Then we organized a flowchart similar to a design-bid-construct process, capturing the Process model contained in ASHRAE's BCx description that consists of five main phases: predesign, design, construction, acceptance, and post-acceptance (Figures 4.2 through 4.6) [32, 33].

All BCx procedures, including those that pertain to the HVAC-BCx process, can be explained in relation to these phases. This process model distinguishes tasks from documents. BCx tasks that are explained in the ASHRAE guideline [19] are represented in the flowchart in Figures 4.2 through 4.6, and the professional performing each task is denoted in the "action" box. All inputs and outputs of tasks are identified and relationships between documents are differentiated, such as "part-of" and "transformation relations" (Figure 4.7). This helps to keep track of changes in the BCx documentation. Every document is represented as the output of a certain task. We also distinguished between decision points and roles of decision makers. Accept or reject conditions are identified for decisions. In the process model, every procedure is divided into simple actions. This helped in identifying and representing some key steps for HVAC Cx.

4.2.1   Process Model Terminology

The terms used in the process model, as discussed next, map into the descriptions of the BCx process in the ASHRAE guideline [19]:

Actors
> *Owner*: A person or company, who owns the property, hires the commissioning authority, and has the right to decide building-related issues.
>
> *Commissioning authority*: The person chosen to implement the overall commissioning process. The commissioning authority can be a company or an agent that is specialized in this practice and has the necessary experience in the AEC industry.
>
> *Design professional*: The person or company hired by the owner responsible for the design of the building.
>
> *Construction manager*: The designated person, company, or agent who is responsible for managing the overall construction process.

Documents
> *Basis of design*: The information that is essential to realize the design intent, such as targeted cost, climate conditions, design considerations, codes, and regulations.

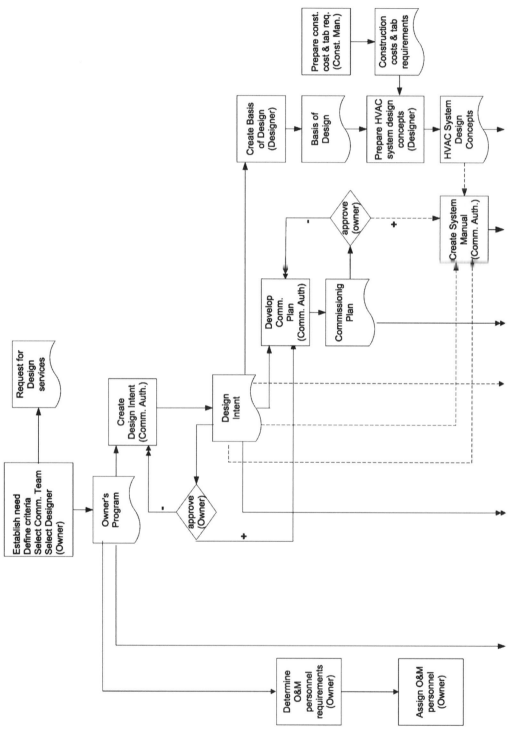

Figure 4.2 Predesign phase BCx process model.

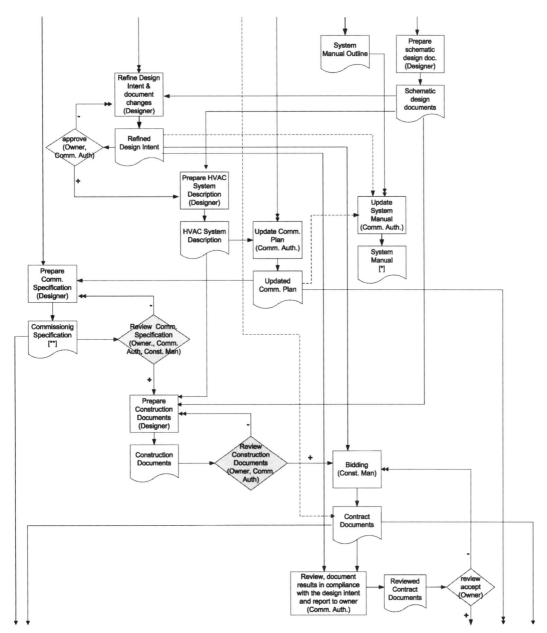

Figure 4.3 Design phase BCx process model.

Certificate of readiness: A document that is used to certify that all systems are verified, functional performance testing (FPT) (Chapter 8) and other acceptance procedures have been successfully competed, and the building is ready for occupation.

Commissioning plan: A document that is developed to define the specifics of the BCx process. It starts as a rough draft during the predesign and early design phases and grows in detail as the project is developed.

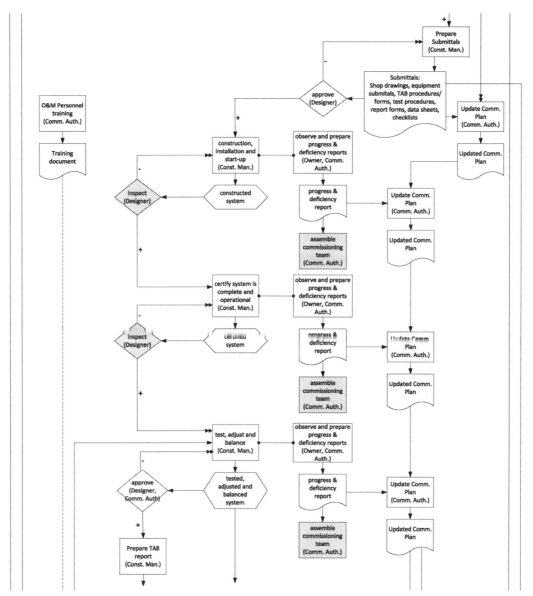

Figure 4.4   Construction phase BCx process model.

Commissioning report: The log document for keeping track of the outcome of the BCx inspections.

Commissioning specification: The contract document that is developed in the design phase to explain the terms of the BCx process, including what will be covered in the evaluation.

Design intent: A document explaining the owner's vision in necessary detail about how the building performs, including concepts and intended use that guide the BCx principles.

Owner's program: A document for describing the expected use and operation of the facility.

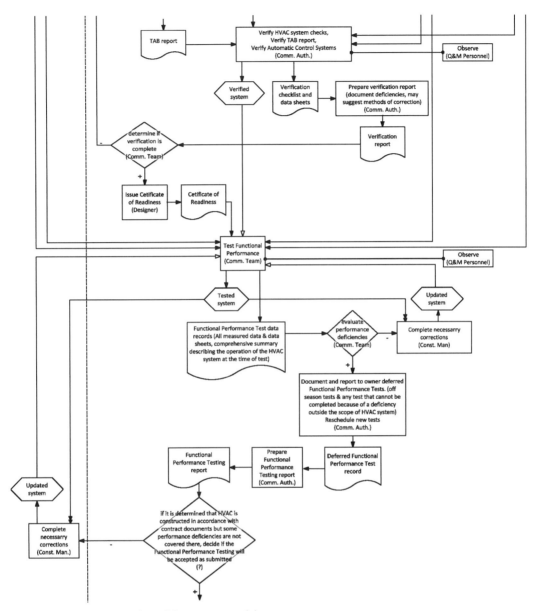

Figure 4.5   Acceptance phase BCx process model.

Systems manual: A manual created by compiling documents prepared during the BCx process that can be used as an operation and maintenance manual.

Operations

Functional performance testing (FPT): The inspection done to measure the overall performance of building systems.

Verification: The process of testing each piece of building equipment and verifying that all systems and subsystems function properly as described in the contract documents.

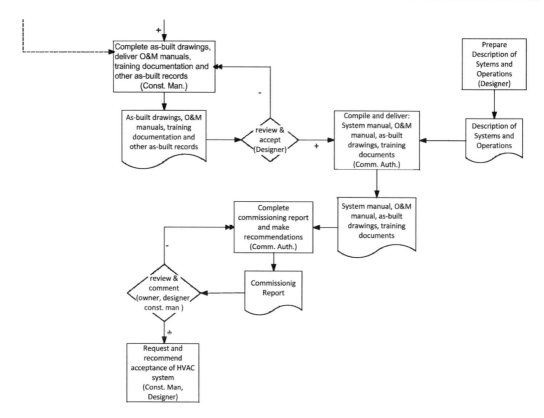

Figure 4.6   Post-acceptance phase process model.

4.2.2   BCx Process Description

In this section, we include a brief description of the BCx process as denoted in the process model (refer to Figures 4.2 to 4.6) [4].

4.2.2.1   Predesign Phase

Predesign phase BCx operations start with the establishment of the need and end when the necessary HVAC system design concepts have been formalized. The overall target in this phase is generating the first group of information that will be used as a guide during the design of the system and the system performance criteria. At the beginning of this phase, the owner picks the commissioning authority in order to facilitate the involvement of the BCx team in the early design decisions. Then owner's program is developed by the owner to describe the preliminary design principles. The owner's program is used as a basis for starting other documents such as the initial design intent document, which is created by the commissioning agent and approved by the owner. Design intent evolves through the BCx process and is used to keep track of every project alteration. Then, from the design intent document, the designer produces the basis of design and the commissioning agent produces the commissioning plan. Both of these documents need to be consistent with the design intent document and should be reviewed and updated as the design intent goes through changes during the project's life cycle.

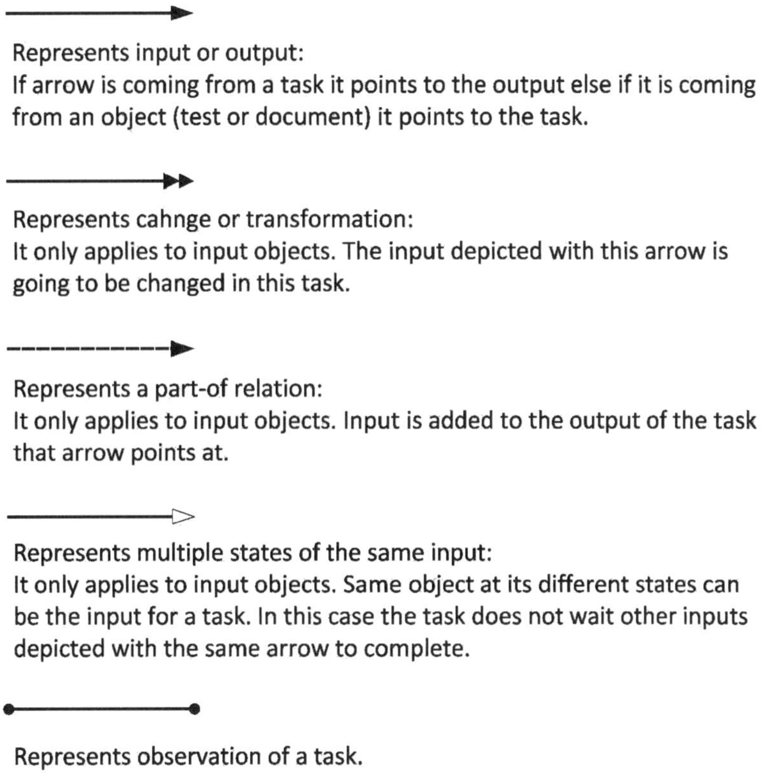

Represents input or output:
If arrow is coming from a task it points to the output else if it is coming
from an object (test or document) it points to the task.

Represents cahnge or transformation:
It only applies to input objects. The input depicted with this arrow is
going to be changed in this task.

Represents a part-of relation:
It only applies to input objects. Input is added to the output of the task
that arrow points at.

Represents multiple states of the same input:
It only applies to input objects. Same object at its different states can
be the input for a task. In this case the task does not wait other inputs
depicted with the same arrow to complete.

Represents observation of a task.

Figure 4.7 Process model "association" descriptions.

The basis of design document then becomes a foundation for developing the
HVAC system design concepts document, together with the construction cost and
the testing, adjusting, and balancing (TAB) requirements, both of which are prepared by the construction manager. This document includes the conceptual designs
for the HVAC system. The last document generated in this phase is the system
manual as a compilation of all BCx-related documents.

4.2.2.2 Design Phase

The design phase starts with the designer who prepares the schematic design documents in compliance with the design concepts set forth in the predesign phase, and
ends with the owner's approval of the contract documents. Other tasks involved in
this phase are refining the design intent document according to new schematic design, generating the HVAC system description, and formalizing the commissioning
specifications. In this phase, the commissioning agent is responsible for updating
the commissioning plan to reflect the latest changes to the system design. Approval
of commissioning specifications by the owner is an important decision point in this
step and it requires the involvement of the commissioning agent and the construction manager. After this step the construction documents are generated by the designer and approved by the owner and the commissioning agent. At the end of this
phase, the construction manager prepares the contract documents for bidding, and

with the review and consent of all parties on these documents, the preconstruction tasks are considered to be completed.

4.2.2.3   Construction Phase

At the beginning of the construction phase, the construction manager develops the project submittals and secures the approval of the designer. This phase has three main tasks that are all completed by the construction manager: (1) construction, installation, and start-up of the HVAC system; (2) certifying that the system is complete and operational; and (3) TAB operations. The designer inspects the constructed system at every stage and gives a final approval to the construction manager after the TAB is completed. This phase ends when the construction manager submits the TAB report to the commissioning agent for FPT. The commissioning agent's main responsibility during the construction is observing and preparing progress and deficiency reports. The commissioning plan is also updated to reflect all as-built information in the evaluation procedures.

4.2.2.4   Acceptance Phase

In comparison to the previous phases of BCx, the acceptance phase is completed in a very short time. However most of the testing, measurement, and evaluation of the HVAC system is conducted in this stage. The commissioning agent performs two main tasks in this phase: completion of a prefunctional checklist (PFC) and functional performance testing (FPT). PFC starts after the TAB report is received. The commissioning plan and the contract documents are the main sources of this task together with other BCx documents created in the previous phases. The result of the verification checks are recorded in data sheets and the commissioning agent generates the verification report to document the outcome. If this report is satisfactory, it is certified by the designer with the certificate of readiness document. After that, the FPT starts and the commissioning agent populates the results into FPT data sheets. Before generating the FPT report, the commissioning agent needs to await the completion of all deferred tests. If there are any deficiencies in the HVAC system that are not in accordance with the design intent or contract documents, the construction manager needs to make the necessary arrangements for fixing the problems. The tests need to be repeated to verify every fix and system update.

4.2.2.5   Post-Acceptance Phase

The post-acceptance phase tasks primarily involve finalizing the documentation and generating system description for operations. The first task is completing as-built documents, operation and maintenance manuals, and training materials. After these have been accepted by the designer, the commissioning agent compiles and delivers the system manual and develops a comprehensive commissioning report. This report is reviewed and accepted by the owner, the designer and the construction manager. The BCx process flow is culminated by the construction manager and designer by requesting and recommending the acceptance of the HVAC system from the owner.

4.2.3   Significance of the ECx Model

The ECx process model we developed is significant for various reasons. First it puts all ECx-related activities in the context of the CPD process. This allows one to easily follow how ECx supports and gets feedback from the predesign, design, and construction activities. Next, it provides a visual yet detailed representation of ECx that is not contained in BCx manuals and guidelines. The visual representation of the ECx-PPM allows us to see how building information flows between different parties and different tasks, how this information is recorded in various documents, and what quantity of information is needed for making specific decisions. One can follow the interactions between tasks and identify loops, parallel actions, and any missing elements between phases. From the perspective of generating a product model for ECx, the process model is also fundamental for identifying the type of data that is required for ECx tasks.

4.3   Capturing Embedded Commissioning Information in the Product Model

The ECx product model is developed in two steps: defining and classifying the data and developing the data model structure. The specific focus of the product model we use for illustration purposes is the AHU Cx.

4.3.1   Identifying BCx Data

As illustrated by the ECx process model, BCx information generated throughout the phases of the CPD process, from predesign to post-acceptance, is accumulated in several documents such as the commissioning plan, system manual, and PFC and FPT reports. In our observations of commissioning practice, we note that these reports can have significant differences based on the time BCx is performed, the commissioning agent completing these tasks, and the motivation of the owner for ordering it [4].

BCx guidelines are also produced by different organizations or government agencies, such as ASHRAE [24–26], NIST [24], IEA [25], and others [43, 44]. These guidelines agree on a general outline for HVAC Cx; however, the specific BCx data identified in these resources can show variances on different cases. The ECx product model addresses this issue with a formal ontology framework that can promote standardization, interoperability, and efficiency in ECx, using a generic, normalized data set (Chapter 8).

The process of identifying the normalized data set that we use in the ECx product model has two main steps. First, since they contain different data types, we select as many different types of sources as possible. Then, we identify a structured way to compile this data into a standard representation.

In this illustrative example, we collected HVAC-Cx data from four source types [22]: (1) commissioning reports and PFC and FPT records collected from practicing companies; (2) codes, regulations, and guidelines from institutions, such as ASHRAE [25, 26] and NIST [24]; (3) HVAC equipment specifications from manufacturers, such as Trane and Carrier; and (4) body of research from groups like

Portland Energy Conservation, Inc. (PECI) [49, 50] and Lawrence Berkeley National Laboratory (LBNL) [30] that practice in this domain. To compile the data from these four groups, we used comparative analysis tables (CATs) [22]. Because of the eclectic nature of the data, CATs are useful in identifying different terms referring to the same concept, such as "Fan Capacity" and "Airflow (cfm)," or sorting out the ambiguities that come with natural language, like one data point referring to the two features of a piece of equipment. One source may record data as "supply fan belt properly installed" when referring to "proper V belt alignment" as well as to "proper V belt tension." Separate CATs were developed for nine basic AHU components, including air filters, fans, coils, sensors, humidifiers, ducts, dampers, pumps, VAV boxes, and economizers. The organization of a CAT requires placing of the same attributes from different sources in the same row. Each source has its own column and if a source does not have matching data for a specific attribute that cell is left empty.

4.3.2   Developing the Product Model

After creating the generic and normalized data set for BCx, we developed a formal model that encapsulates this data. To determine the requirements of a product model that can represent standardized ECx information, we need to identify the general characteristics of ECx information [2]. The first characteristic of ECx information is its generality. It is not specific to the commissioning operations and can be generated and exchanged between various parties for different purposes. Because our premise for creating a data model is to achieve interoperability, we include not just technical attributes, but information that can be used for reasoning purposes, in the case of automated tests and accurate representation of the domain knowledge. For example, for the modeling of a humidifier we need to include "entering air relative humidity" and "leaving air relative humidity" to the attribute sets since this information is crucial during the prefunctional checklists (PFC) and FPT procedures (Chapter 8). During the PFC procedure the "unique identification number" of the humidifier is validated, which normally has no impact on its performance. However, this information needs to be included in the data model because it is elemental in identifying the humidifier in the overall system and allows us to keep track of the history of the equipment.

Another characteristic of the ECx information is its fragmented but synthetic nature—every piece comes together to create a whole. This requires developing a systems-based approach to modeling. An AHU is a complex piece of equipment that can take many different forms depending on which subcomponent types are used during its design. When evaluating the performance of an AHU, the commissioning agent needs to verify the functional performance of every equipment type separately, including the fan, heating coil, and cooling coil. At the same time, the relationships between these components need to be checked, like the connection of the return duct to the return fan or the location of a temperature sensor in relation to a heating coil.

The next level of checks needs to be performed at the AHU level. The overall performance of the AHU as an individual component should be verified for different purposes such as the manual shutdown and start-up operations or smoke management systems. To accurately represent the relationships between different pieces that create an AHU, we need to include the topological information in the ECx data model. This information is crucial for inspecting connections between different component types and verifying operation sequences.

The final characteristic of the ECx information that we need to consider in the ECx data model is that it grows in detail as it evolves between different phases. As we see in the ECx process model, the commissioning agent creates the initial ECx documentation including the commissioning plan and system manual in the predesign phase. As the project progresses through the design, construction, and acceptance phases, these documents are updated and populated with detailed information In the design phase, the only AHU information needed for ECx planning is an approximate value for equipment capacity. However, during the acceptance phase the commissioning agent needs to know all of the specifications for every equipment type in that particular AHU including centrifugal pump power, humidifier entering/leaving air relative humidity, and coil temperature stratification. If we compare the predesign ECx data with the post-acceptance phase ECx data, we see that the early information is mostly related to the overall system description, whereas the later information is saturated in detail and increased in quantity.

In conclusion, we observe that the ECx product model needs to represent not only technical attributes but all of the information pertaining to the domain knowledge. It also needs to have a modular structure so that the relationships and associations between different equipment types can be flexibly modeled. Finally, it needs to have a hierarchical structure in which the data range from abstract to concrete forms.

The ECx data model was developed in four versions by gradually adding new equipment information (Figure 4.8). The first stage focused on modeling only two pieces of equipment: air filter and fan. This stage provides the general outline of the model but the model structure is not yet determined. The second stage expands the model by adding the coil and the air terminal box, thus defining the model core. This is the vehicle for achieving modularity in data representation. In this stage, the aim is to create a flexible structure so that the model can be expanded without redoing everything from scratch. In the third stage, the model is expanded by adding the remaining equipment data. While the model structure stays the same, throughout this process, the model content is improved (Table 4.2). A general overview of the data model is explained in [4]. In this section we give specifics about how data is organized in the ECx product model.

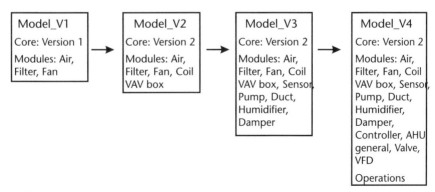

Figure 4.8   ECx product model versions.

Table 4.2 Expansion of the ECx Data Model in numbers

	Version 1	Version 2	Version 3	Version 4
Number of classes (C)	21	37	75	81
Number of attributes (A)	49	106	182	425
Number of operations (O)	0	0	0	23
A/C	2.33	2.86	2.42	5.24

The ECx data model structure is organized around evaluation criteria and testing of the HVAC equipment. Two main inspection operations take place in the acceptance phase: FPT and PFC. During PFC, the commissioning agent verifies the TAB report and performs a context-based inspection. This evaluation is qualitative in nature and includes queries such as "Is the inlet ductwork properly attached?" The outcome is binary and can be recorded in check sheets. FPT is more comprehensive and involves actual measurements and operational sequence verification. The commissioning agent develops test layouts and evaluation protocols in accordance with the design documents and verifies if the constructed system performs as specified. The outcome of this inspection is quantitative and it should be compared with the values in design criteria.

The model has an event-based structure because we observed that, in the BCx test documents collected from practicing companies, the AHU component tests are separate events [22]. The fan system context inspection and coil system context inspection can be carried out separately on different dates. The ECx data model is structured to allow defining three discrete events for every component of AHU.

The information in the ECx data model is organized in modules around a main core. From the definition of an AHU given previously, we know that it is composed of different equipment types. The core of the model is created to represent the ECx information that is common to all equipment types. Then, the ECx information that is specific to an equipment type is encapsulated in modules. This modular structure provides flexibility to the product model because modules can be added, removed, or modified without changing its general structure.

In fact, these features served us well in creating the different versions of the ECx model, where the content of each version was substantially different from that of the previous ones. This was achieved without significantly altering the structure of previous versions and by simply adding new data types through the modular structure of the product model (Chapter 8).

The data in the core and modules are arranged in a hierarchical manner from general to specific. This mimics the temporal changes in data from the early to later phases of the BCx process. The hierarchical arrangement allows for encapsulation of the abstract and the specific information separately. The root of this hierarchy represents higher level objects such as Event and Equipment classes and the leaf nodes represent specific equipment classes, such as VaneAxialFanPerformance and VaneAxialFanContext, discussed and shown later in Figures 4.12 and 4.13.

Figure 4.9 shows the overall model representation. The Equipment class at the top of the model encapsulates unique attributes that are common to every equipment type. These attributes are not required for measuring the performance of the equipment but they are needed for the traceability of ECx information. The component association allows us to define a new piece of equipment that is composed

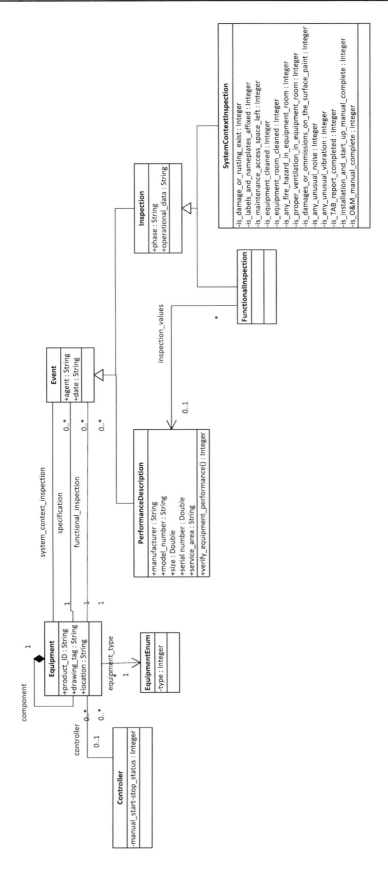

Figure 4.9   ECx data model structure.

of other pieces of equipment, such as the AHU. This property gives us the ability to create a "system of systems" using this model. There is a hierarchical relationship between the Event class and the PerformanceDescription and Inspection classes. This relationship allows the PerformanceDescription and Inspection classes to inherit the attributes in the Event class. There is a similar relationship between the Inspection class and FunctionalInspection and SytemContextInspection classes.

Figures 4.10 and 4.11 show how individual equipment classes are modeled according to performance- and context-related attributes. The ECx process requires three separate sets of data for specification, system context inspection, and functional inspection events, but since specification and functional inspection events use same type of data, equipment are modeled according to their performance and context attributes (Figure 4.11).

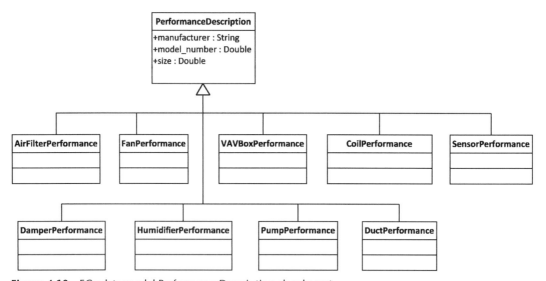

Figure 4.10 ECx data model PerformanceDescription class layout.

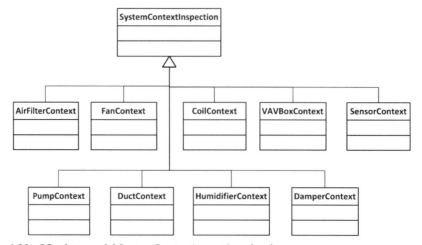

Figure 4.11 ECx data model SystemContextInspection class layout.

The individual modeling of an HVAC equipment type as a leaf node is shown in Figures 4.12 and 4.13 for the fan example. The hierarchical structure of the larger model continues in the leaf nodes as well. The VaneAxialFanPerformance and the CentrifugalFanPerformance classes are children of the FanPerformance class and they inherit all of its attributes. The same relationship exists between the VaneAxialFanContext and the CentrifugalFanContext classes and the FanContext class. Since the FanPerformance and the FanContext classes are children to the PerformanceDescription and the SystemContextInspection classes, the hierarchy reaches to the top Event class.

We developed the data model through a model-based-approach aimed at standardizing and automating the ECx process. This approach has been implemented in two steps. First, the ECx process model is developed as a detailed visual representation of BCx operations and an analysis of how BCx tasks, documents, and decision points are related. This information is later fed into data model development in order to identify the characteristics of BCx data. Next, specific ECx data, distilled from CAT, are used to develop the ECx data model.

Although the ECx process model covers the entire commissioning process for a new construction, the ECx product model focuses only on the AHU. This model can be expanded to an ontology representing all HVAC-Cx-related information. From the standardization and interoperability perspectives, having both process and product models has clear benefits. On the other hand, capturing, storing, and

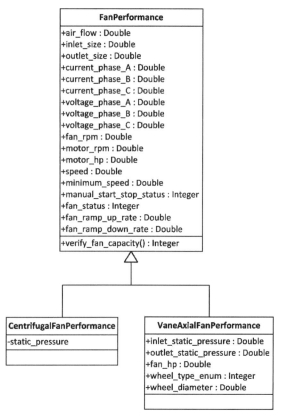

Figure 4.12 FanPerformance class hierarchy.

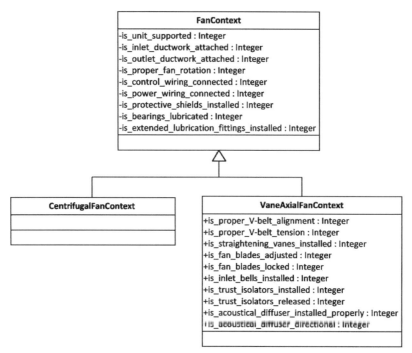

Figure 4.13   FanContext description hierarchy.

retrieving such large amounts of data presents specific challenges. In Part III, we will discuss some technology options that present a potential for automated building evaluation.

References

[1]   Türkaslan-Bülbül, M. T., et al., "Overview of Design Evaluation Towards a Comprehensive Computational Approach," in *Proceedings of E-Activities and Intelligent Support in Design and the Built Environment, 9th EuropIA International Conference*, Istanbul, Turkey, 2003.

[2]   Türkaslan-Bülbül, M.T., and Akın, Ö., "Computational Support for Building Evaluation: Embedded Commissioning Model," *Automation in Construction*, Vol. 15, 2006, pp. 438–447.

[3]   Liu, M., Claridge, D. E., and Turner, W. D. *Continuous Commissioning Guidebook: Maximizing Building Energy Efficiency and Comfort*, Federal Energy Management Program, U.S. Department of Energy, 2002.

[4]   Türkaslan-Bülbül, M. T., "Process and Product Modeling for Computational Support of Building Commissioning," Ph.D. Dissertation, Carnegie Mellon University, Pittsburgh, PA, 2006.

[5]   Gallaher, M. P., et al., "Cost Analysis of Inadequate Interoperability in the US Capital Facilities Industry," Gaithersburg, MD: National Institute of Standards and Technology, 2004.

[6]   Yang, Q. Z., and Zhang, Y., "Semantic Interoperability in Building Design: Methods and Tools," *Computer Aided Design*, Vol. 38, No. 10, 2006, pp. 1099–111

[7]   Eastman, C. M., *Building Product Models: Computer Environments Supporting Design and Construction*, Boca Raton, FL: CRC Press, 1999.

[8]   Owolabi, A., Anumba, C. J., and El-Hamalawi, A., "Architecture for Implementing IFC-Based Online Construction Product Libraries," *ITcon*, Vol. 8, 2003, pp. 201–218, http://www.itcon.org/2003/15.

[9]   Koivu, T. J., "Future of Product Modeling and Knowledge Sharing in the FM/AEC Industry." *ITcon*, Vol. 7, 2002, pp. 139–156.

[10]   Penilla, H., "The State of the Art of Finnish Building Product Modeling Methodology," in *Computer Aided Architectural Design Futures*, B. Martens and A. Brown (Eds.), Vienna: Springer Verlag, 2005, pp. 225–239.

[11]   Hagler Bailly Consulting, Inc. "Building Commissioning: Survey of Attitudes and Practices in Wisconsin," Report #172-1, Madison, WI: Energy Center of Wisconsin, 1998.

[12]   Claridge, D. E., et al., "Is Commissioning Once Enough?" *Energy Engineering*, Vol. 101, No. 4, June–July 2004.

[13]   Piette, M. A., Kinney, S., and Haves, P., "Analysis of an Information Monitoring and Diagnostic System to Improve Building Operations," *Energy and Buildings* Vol. 33, No. 8, 2001, pp. 783–791.

[14]   Brambley, M. R., and Katipamula, S., "Automating Commissioning Activities: Update with Examples," in *Proceedings of the 11th National Conference on Building Commissioning*, Portland, OR, May 20–22, 2003, Portland Energy Conservation Inc.

[15]   Claridge, D. E., et al., "Campus-Wide Continuous Commissioning SM of University Buildings," in *Proceedings of the 2000 ACEEE Summer Study*, Washington, DC: American Council for an Energy Efficient Economy, 2000.

[16]   Katipamula, S., Brambley, M. R., and Luskay, L., "Automated Proactive Techniques for Commissioning Air-Handling Units." *ASME Journal of Solar Energy Engineering*, Vol. 125, No. 1, 2003, pp. 282–291.

[17]   Akın, Ö.. et al., "Comparison of ASHRAE Guidelines with Building Commissioning Practice," in *Proceedings of National Conference on Building Commissioning*, Palm Springs, CA, 2003.

[18]   "The HVAC Commissioning Process," Atlanta, GA: American Society of Heating, Refrigerating, and Air-Conditioning Engineers, 1996.

[19]   *HVAC&R Technical Requirements for the Commissioning Process*, ASHRAE Guideline 1.1-2007, Atlanta, GA: American Society of Heating, Refrigerating, and Air-Conditioning Engineers, 2007.

[20]   "The HVAC Commissioning Process," Atlanta, GA: ASHRAE American Society of Heating, Refrigerating, and Air-Conditioning Engineers, 1996.

[21]   "The Commissioning Process," Atlanta, GA: ASHRAE American Society of Heating, Refrigerating, & Air-Conditioning Engineers, 2005.

[22]   Türkaslan-Bülbül, M.T., and Akın, Ö., "Formal Models for Embedded Commissioning," in *Proceedings of the International Conference for Enhanced Building Operations*, Pittsburgh, PA, 2005.

[23]   Akın, Ö., et al., "Embedded Commissioning for Building Design," in *Proceedings of European Conference on Product and Process Modeling in the Building and Construction Industry*, Istanbul, Turkey, 2004.

[24]   Kao, J. Y., *HVAC Functional Inspection and Testing Guide*, Gaithersburg, MD: National Institute of Standards and Technology (NIST), U.S. Department of Commerce, 1992.

[25]   "Cost-Effective Commissioning for Existing and Low Energy Buildings," *Annex 47 IAE*, 2005, http://www.iea-annex47.org, last accessed April 2011.

[26]   Haasl, T., and Sharp, T., "A Practical Guide for Commissioning Existing Buildings," Report ORNL/TM-1999/34, prepared by Portland Energy Conservation, Inc., and Oak Ridge National Laboratory for the Office of Building Technology, State and Community Programs U.S. Department of Energy.

[27]   *Model Commissioning Plan and Guide Commissioning Specifications*, NTIS: # DE9700456, Gaithersburg, MD: National Institute of Standards and Technology, 1997.

[28]   PECI, "Building Commissioning Guidelines," Bonneville Power Administration, U.S. Department of Energy, 1992.

[29]   PECI, "O&M Best Practices Series: Operation and Maintenance Assessments," 1999, http://www.energystar.gov/ia/business/assessment.pdf, last accessed in April 2011.

[30]   LBNL, "Design Intent Tool," 2008, http://ateam.lbl.gov/DesignIntent/home.html, last accessed in April 2011.

CHAPTER 5

Building Information Modeling: Current Practices in Building Evaluation Models and Updates

5.1 Introduction

Building information modeling (BIM), "a modeling technology and associated set of processes to produce, communicate and analyze building models" [1], has been changing the capital project delivery (CPD) processes significantly. BIM provides a common way to store information that is created by different stakeholders in a data-rich, parametric, and digital representation [1]. It also provides semantically rich information for building elements that can be accessed automatically by software applications [2]. Many analyses tools, enabled by BIM and its information-rich models, are being heavily used in the architecture-engineering-construction/facility management (AEC/FM) industries to support a diverse set of process, analysis, and decision methods throughout a project's life cycle.

Today, most architects, engineers, contractors, and owners realize the potential benefits of utilizing semantically rich information for managing infrastructure systems. Many federal owners in the United States, such as the Government Services Association (GSA), U.S. Army Corps of Engineers (USACE), and Veterans Administration [3–5]; state agencies, such as the Wisconsin Division of State Facilities and Texas Facilities Commission [6]; and institutions, such as Penn State University and Indiana University [7, 8], have developed integrated project delivery guidelines and contracts that incorporate BIM into the CPD processes. In addition, organizations like the Association for General Contractors (AGC) and the American Institute of Architects (AIA) have also developed BIM guidelines that promote BIM's adoption into their respective sectors. The National Institute for Building Sciences (NIBS) has been undertaking a major effort to target the development of a national building information modeling standard [9]. Under this effort, NIBS oversees important initiatives like the creation of industry foundation classes [10] to enable transfer of rich information and interoperability between different software systems, and Construction Operation Building Information Exchange (COBIE), which targets the capture of facility information throughout building's life cycle [10, 11]. These efforts have significantly increased the adoption of building information modeling by the AEC/FM industry.

BIM was initially considered to provide a competitive advantage for AEC/FM firms, but later became a necessity for improving the existing business processes of capital project design, construction, and operations. Today, it supports early design decisions and the communication of the conceptual design to stakeholders. It allows fast comparison of design options as the parametric capabilities, which come with BIM-enabled design tools that make design modifications easier. In addition, it enables collaboration and communication among project team members and stakeholders and supports functional analyses of buildings through detailed 3D visualization capabilities [1]. BIM also supports simulations for energy, emergency egress and lighting, comparison of alternatives for energy efficient buildings, and evaluation of LEED certification requirements. Upon design completion, it provides an intelligent model that can be automatically evaluated. As automatic building code verification becomes available through efforts such as SMARTcodes [12], BIM's potential impact during the CPD process will become even more prominent (Chapter 10).

During the construction phase, many documented case studies highlight the benefits of BIM in supporting mechanical, electrical, and plumbing (MEP) coordination [13–15]. These studies highlight significant improvement in coordinating the construction trades, which reduces the number of field-generated change orders drastically through the integration of model-based clash detection. Furthermore, the coordinated models can be trusted for their accuracy. The parties involved in their generation utilize them for prefabrication of building components, allowing for smoother construction and field installation and waste reduction. Likewise, BIM is utilized for generating shop drawings during construction. Other ways in which BIM supports timely delivery and cost control during construction includes 4D scheduling and simulation and model-based estimation. Though currently underutilized, 4D scheduling is gaining importance, especially in complicated projects, to identify spatial conflicts, to identify logic errors in the schedule, and to facilitate communicating construction plans to tradespeople. It is used as a visual means to perform constructability analyses. Model-based estimation helps engineers avoid errors in the quantity takeoff process with significant time savings in the generation and monitoring of cost estimates.

Spatial conflicts are common. Structural, mechanical, and lighting engineers all compete for the often limited space available in the plenum. Unless there is conflict detection software, light fixtures, ducts, and beams can physically collide or interfere with each other's performance, as in the case of the light fixture heating the air carried in the duct. Furthermore, installation of the fixtures, if not scheduled after the ducts, or vice versa, depending on their physical configuration, can create serious installation problems and labor scheduling problems. BIM software can be "smart" enough to detect these sequencing conflicts in the 4D and alert fieldworkers to them. Often the logic underlying these scheduling conflicts is impossible to detect through algorithmic processes. In these cases in particular, designers and contractors can detect the problems visually when the BIM system is equipped with sophisticated 4D visual display tools.

Other than time and cost controls, BIM has the potential to be used along with data captured by reality capture technologies, such as laser scanners, for quality control purposes during construction. Laser scanning can be performed regularly to compare the progress with respect to the design model and construction schedules as well as to check and document existing as-built conditions (Chapter 6).

Because post-construction is the longest phase in a building's life cycle, utilization of BIM during this phase promises the greatest benefits. During the handover of the building to facility operators, building information models can be submitted as part of as-built documentation. Such models can then be populated with facility asset and operations-related data, such as equipment manuals. Availability of integrated information is valuable for the facility operators and managers by improving their access to relevant information depicting up-to-date representation. For instance, fieldworkers can benefit greatly from pulling up on their portable devices 3D views of invisible items like pipes, ducts, and other equipment concealed behind walls, floors, or ceilings. Since building information models subsume semantic information that enables spatial and topological analyses, like identity, type, manufacture, and configuration of building components, they can support fault diagnosis (Chapter 8) and emergency response activities [1, 16]. A plumber would not need to break a wall apart, for example, only to discover that the specialty for the fix belongs to steamfitters.

The information contained in as-built information models can be used to directly populate the data needed in facility management tools, such a computerized maintenance management systems (CMMS) and computer-aided facilities management systems (CAFM) [17, 18]. Through BIM integrated facility management tools, it is possible to significantly reduce the reentry of facility information since the information would be contained in the as-built information model.

To utilize BIM throughout a building's life cycle, these models must be continuously updated to include information needed by different stakeholders and to reflect the changes to facilities. New processes and standards being accepted by the AEC/FM industry are aimed at enabling information capture and transfer between life-cycle phases. One of the greatest impediments to efficient fault diagnosis and repair of building systems is the lack of reliable information of existing conditions. While the location of a piece of equipment, an actuator, a valve, or an electrical panel may be an easy search for the design engineer, the fieldworker looking for them may spend precious minutes, in an emergency, or hours locating them.

BIM usage during preconstruction, construction, and post-construction phases is expected to support methods of facility evaluation for ECx throughout the building life cycle. Next, we consider these aspects of BIM and conclude with a discussion of the challenges and opportunities associated with updating building information models.

5.2   Utilization of BIM in Evaluating Facilities During Preconstruction

Surveys of the AEC/FM industry highlight that BIM is commonly used during the design/preconstruction phase of facilities. In 2009, 60% of architects used BIM for building design. More than half of them also used BIM for analysis including for code compliance checking and energy evaluation [19]. The design phase, and hence decisions made during this phase, impact the overall performance of a facility significantly. This is evidenced by the life-cycle cost escalation due to modification of design decisions [20, 21]. Therefore, the results of the analyses performed in the design phase can significantly affect building function and performance (Figure 5.1).

Two types of building evaluation methods, namely, energy analysis and building code compliance checking, that are applied during the design phase are associated with BCx. BIM is instrumental in streamlining these methods of analysis.

5.2.1   Using BIM for Energy Analysis During Design

Data from the U.S. Department of Energy (DoE) and the U.S. Energy Information Administration (EIA) showed that in 2008, buildings accounted for 41% of the total energy consumption and 38% of carbon dioxide emissions in the United States [22, 23] (Figure 5.2).

HVAC systems and lighting systems together account for about 60% of all energy usage in buildings. However, research shows that roughly 10% to 20% of the energy used by the HVAC systems and 20% to 30% of the energy consumed by the lighting systems are wasted due to decisions made during the design of these systems [24, 25]. For example, ASHRAE estimated that replacing manual switches with occupancy sensors can result in an average energy savings of about 30% for lighting systems [26]. Clarke also estimated that if energy simulation is used to model alternative designs of HVAC systems in newly designed buildings, energy consumption may be reduced by about 25% [27].

Energy analysis of building design is a process of evaluating the energy efficiency of alternative design options, such as glazing and building envelope materials, types of lighting control systems, and HVAC system configurations [20, 27]. To evaluate different design configurations quantitatively, architects and engineers simulate building energy usage and estimate the energy consumption for alternative

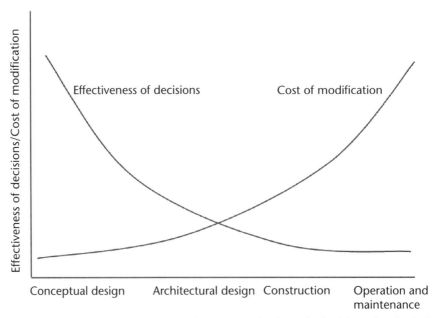

Figure 5.1   Cost and effectiveness of the decisions made through the life cycle of a building (adapted from [20]).

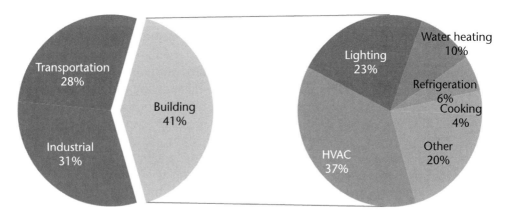

Figure 5.2 Decomposition of energy usage in buildings (adapted from [23]): (a) the contributions of different sectors to the energy usage; (b) the contributions of different building systems and activities to the energy usage within buildings.

options [28]. The building energy simulation tools, developed roughly about four decades ago, offer hundreds of recent tools for this purpose [27]. These tools can be divided into two major categories: tools that perform conceptual design simulation and tools that perform detailed design simulation. For example, DOE-2 is a tool for simulating the energy consumption of a conceptual building design and, therefore, does not require detailed information about the configuration of lighting and HVAC systems; users do not need to model the detailed components, they need only select the type of HVAC systems [29]. DOE-2 is useful for the conceptual design when the detailed configuration of the system design is not yet available. On the other hand, EnergyPlus, developed by the DoE, is designed for simulating energy usage based on detailed design information [30]. This software provides accurate results by simulating total building energy consumption with detailed configuration information for the lighting and HVAC systems.

With increasing energy awareness, energy analysis is a critical process of building design. A major barrier to the widespread application of energy simulation tools is the complexity of the required data as input [31–34]. Architects and structural, mechanical, and electrical engineers are involved in the design process and utilize different design, modeling, and simulation tools. While the energy modeling tools available to them need data from each of their respective domains, they can only handle certain types of domain-specific data formats and use limited libraries containing only generic options for building systems [35].

Due to the resulting lack of interoperability between different specialty software systems, BIM is the proposed candidate to overcome barriers created by limited components libraries [36–40]. The information required by the building energy simulation tools, such as building spatial layouts, materials of building elements, functions of the spaces, and components of the building systems, can be acquired from BIM so that users do not need to reinterpret domain-specific models or documents or input the information needed through time-consuming means.

Several approaches exist in current industry practice for utilizing BIM to facilitate the building energy simulation process. Green Building XML (gbXML) is an open schema for BIM and focuses on representing information for energy simulation of facilities [41]. It represents material and geometric information about building elements, configuration of the building systems, and space load information. Autodesk Ecotect software is a conceptual energy simulation and analysis tool with the ability to import information using BIM formats, such as IFC and gbXML [42, 43]. While such applications are emerging, many of the better known energy simulation systems have yet to actively interface with BIM completely utilization of BIM generated information [37]. A major barrier for this is existing BIM standard schemata, such as those in IFC that do not contain information related to detailed configurations of lighting and HVAC systems [44, 45]. For instance, IFC schema mainly represent the material and geometric information of the ducts and equipment in the HVAC systems, while the configuration of the HVAC control systems, such as the controller and data interfaces, is not covered. With the increased development and usage of such standards, this impediment will be significantly reduced, and BIM will contain most, if not all, of the information needed to perform energy simulations. Dong et al. proposed an extension for gbXML schema to provide information for lighting simulation applications [45]. In the latest version of IFC schema, about 40 new classes, such as IfcAirTerminal, IfcSpaceHeater, and IfcTank, have been added to support the representation of HVAC systems [10].

5.2.2 Using BIM in Building Code Compliance Checking

Building codes are rules that guide the design and construction of buildings so that acceptable levels of performance can be realized. They are usually published by federal, state, and local government agencies, such as the California Code of Regulations (CCR), and international industry organizations, such as the International Code Council (ICC) and ASHRAE. Every design must be checked and verified against violation of applicable codes and ordinances. Provisions of codes specify the minimum requirements for building elements including structural safety, space accessibility, and energy efficiency. After a building design is completed, the design documents are submitted to building officials for assessment of their compliance with relevant codes and ordinances. If in conformance, a permit for construction is granted; otherwise, the design is returned to the designers for modification. Chapter 10 describes in detail the nature of building codes and the processes associated with code generation, maintenance, and conformance assessment.

In current industry practices, compliance checking is conducted manually, using text-based descriptions. This tedious and error-prone process relies on building officials' knowledge and interpretation of codes, which may contain conflicting provisions and inconsistencies. As a result, the permitting process is time consuming, error prone, and nonreplicable [46, 47]. To overcome these problems, automated approaches have been widely researched.

With the increased utilization of BIM in the AEC/FM industry and its ability to provide semantically rich design information, two major industry-driven efforts in code compliance checking have emerged: SMARTcodes [12] and CORENET [48].

SMARTcodes is an automated code checking platform, developed by the ICC. It has two main components: computer-interpretable building codes and an automated code checking engine [12]. The rules defined in the codes are described digitally, facilitating interpretation by the code checking engine and evaluation of a given design depicted in a semantically rich way. The SMARTcodes platform assumes that the building design is documented in BIM so that the computerized approach can access and interpret the information in relevant building codes.

CORENET is an automated, web-based electronic permitting system utilized by Singapore's Building and Construction Authority [48]. This system also utilizes IFC-based model files for automated code checking and is leading the effort in demonstrating the feasibility of automated code checking and e-permitting based on computer-interpretable representations such as those supported in BIM.

In addition to these two major industry-driven initiatives, several other software systems check BIM representations against codes including Solibri Model Checker [49]. This tool takes an IFC-based building information model as its input and performs validity compliance of a BIM model with respect to user-defined rules as well as rules available in the system library, to identify modeling errors and components that violate the given rule sets [46].

5.3   Using BIM in Evaluating Facilities During Construction

The success of construction projects is based on how they satisfy time, cost, and quality constraints. Construction project teams using BIM often meet and exceed the requirements of these constraints. For example, BIM allows streamlining of the cost estimating process and provides more time to evaluate design alternatives (e.g., [1, 50]). Design-based BIM can be further augmented by creating 4D simulations to identify whether there are inconsistencies and time-space conflicts in project schedules; and to evaluate alternative construction methods and sequences. To proactively coordinate and manage the trades, information models generated by different specialty trades are evaluated for clash detection, prior to construction. Finally, as-designed information models augmented by data from data capture technologies, such as 3D imaging, help in quality control by assessing compliance with construction tolerances written into the construction specifications.

Several cost estimating systems that support these processes, including Timberline Precision Estimating and Vico Estimator, take these models as input and perform automated quantity takeoffs. Similarly, parametric modeling environments like Revit provide quantity takeoff capabilities. Automated quantity takeoff streamlines the cost-estimating process and enables architects and engineers to perform what-if analyses in a more reliable and efficient manner. Similarly, many software systems perform 4D simulation, such as Synchro 4D and Bentley ConstrucSim, to streamline the linking schedules with 3D models and the simulation of the construction process for spatiotemporal analyses used for identifying problems in the schedule and time-space conflicts. Finally, several software systems, such as Navisworks and Solibri, utilize federated building information models generated by specialty trades to streamline clash detection and construction process analysis and coordination.

The documented benefits of BIM include improved cost estimation, scheduling, and quality control support. Examples include increased efficiency, and accuracy for estimating, proactive management, and communication of schedules and active quality control at construction sites (e.g., [1, 13, 50–52]). Closely related to the general theme of ECx, the following sections describe these topics in greater detail such as how BIM helps coordinate different building trades and assists with the quality control of the construction process, thus ensuring that building systems meet their design intent.

5.3.1 Using BIM for Coordination of Building Systems and Specialty Trades

A major benefit of BIM is the coordination of designs generated by architects, engineers, and specialty trades to identify clashes prior to fieldwork. Identifying problems in the schedule and time-space conflicts prevents undocumented design changes and costly fixes caused by clashes that used to be identified only in the field. Such changes can result in inconsistencies between design and as-built documents that may invalidate the original design intent. This has significant implications for ECx.

Without BIM, clash detection consists of overlaying one 2D drawing over another to identify possible inconsistencies. This manual approach is cumbersome and error prone. Potentially, it results in unidentified clashes. BIM-based tools enable automatic clash identification through geometry and semantic rule-based analysis. They enable identification of both hard-clashes, in which two components spatially conflict with each other, and soft-clashes, in which there is physical intrusion into the work and access spaces needed to construct or operate a building component.

Studies have documented possible savings associated with proactive coordination of specialty trades through automated clash detection. A major metric used in these studies is the comparison of costly field-generated requests for information (RFI) versus those generated during coordination. Another advantage is that once the design information is coordinated, the models can be trusted and components can be prefabricated. Case studies show that these benefits translate into savings of both time and money (e.g., [13, 15, 53]).

One of the limitations of current BIM-based coordination is that the accuracy and the effectiveness of coordination depend on models with the appropriate level of detail provided by specialty trades. If key components are absent from these models, then clashes associated with such components will be missed [13, 54]. On the other hand, if too much detail is provided, then there will be many false positives, which can overwhelm data management. As BIM-based coordination becomes more widely adopted, companies will develop their own policies and processes regarding the desirable levels of detail in models and effective clash management strategies.

5.3.2 Use of BIM and 3D Imaging Techniques for Construction Quality Control

A coordinated BIM depicts an accurate construction scope and a baseline for quality control. 3D imaging, such as laser scanners, enables capturing and documenting the as-is field conditions spatially (Chapter 6). Such technologies coupled with BIM provide an opportunity for thorough quality control and assessment of as-built conditions [51, 55]. Through assessment, it is possible to identify discrepancies between as-built and as-designed conditions, and evaluate whether discrepancies constitute defects. In addition, capturing as-built conditions during construction provides accurate dimensions for engineered-to-order components and ensures that they match work done at the job site. Chapter 6 further details the capture of as-built conditions using 3D imaging technologies.

5.4   Using BIM in Evaluating Facilities Throughout Their Life Cycle

Building operation accounts for about 60% of the total costs throughout a building's life cycle. A major portion of this cost arises from expenses associated with energy usage during building systems operations and the materials and equipment needed for their maintenance and repair [56–58]. Previous research, however, shows that current operation phase practices have inefficiencies and are not always effective. First, unnecessary energy is consumed by building systems due to the defective components' inability to diagnose faults effectively. About 20% to 30% of energy used by HVAC systems is wasted due to faults such as misplaced sensors (Chapter 11), malfunctioning controllers, and controlled devices (Chapter 8), as well as the improper implementation and execution of control logic [24, 59–61]. Computerized analysis of system components is needed to automatically diagnose these faults and reduce energy waste [60–66].

Second, most of the maintenance work performed in current practice is reactive, costing three to four times more than planned work [67–69]. Planning of maintenance activities requires improved facility information and analysis, like as-built information models and maintenance histories [70]. Three types of building analyses can be performed to service facilities that are streamlined by BIM.

5.4.1   Utilization of BIM for Traditional Commissioning Activities

Currently, BCx is performed mainly through manual inspection, testing, and analysis. Previous research has concluded that manual commissioning suffers from the limited time and resources to undertake testing, a shortage of skilled personnel, and the difficulty of defining performance criteria using prescriptive metrics [71–73]. Therefore, a computerized approach is needed to automate the current commissioning process and fully realize ECx [74, 75] (Chapters 2, 4, and 8).

Correct commissioning protocols require various types of information about building elements and building system configurations, performance measurements of system components, and benchmark values for the performance requirements [61]. Researchers have proposed approaches for using building automation systems to acquire performance measurements for automated BCx (Chapter 3). Choiniere [76] used building energy management systems to acquire measurements, such as indoor temperature and occupancy, that supported a rule-based automated commissioning application [76]. BIM represents semantic information about building elements and enables computerized approaches to automatically access and reason about building information. Previous studies have applied BIM to storing and providing the required information for automated BCx. Türkaslan-Bülbül and Akın [77] developed an information model based on BIM that represents the information requirements for embedded commissioning [77]. Wang and his collaborators analyzed the capability of IFC schema for representing the information requirements for ECx and proposed a potential extension for IFC schema [78]. O'Donnell et al. [80] proposed an architecture for an integrated framework that not only accesses existing BIM information, but also maintains the commissioning rules and measurements to achieve automation in BCx. Ahmed et al. [79] proposed an approach that integrates data from information models and sensor networks into a data warehouse to support automated and Continuous Cx© [79].

A major barrier inhibiting the use of BIM in BCx is the lack of formal representations of building system information and measurement of data within BIM schemata [80]. Existing approaches focus on framework architecture and not representation deficiencies. Therefore, current research is directed at extending BIM schemata to include needed information representations to satisfy the information requirements of automated BCx and to evolve into ECx (Chapter 8).

5.4.2   Using BIM for Fault Diagnosis of Building Systems

Building automation systems typically consist of sensors, controllers, actuators, and controlled devices [81]. Control is achieved by configuring these components and implementing the control logic. The designed control systems malfunction if a component fails to behave as designed. However, due to rising indoor environment requirements, an increasing number of software and hardware components are being used in building automation systems (BASs). As BASs become increasingly complex, it becomes increasingly challenging for operators to manually diagnose building system conditions [62, 82, 83]. Fault detection and diagnosis (FDD) methods have been studied and developed to address some of the challenges associated with manual operation and maintenance of BASs. Both laboratory and real-world experiments have been conducted to validate the energy-saving capabilities of existing computer-aided FDD approaches [59, 84, 85]. One limitation of computerized FDD approaches is that they are mainly developed within academia. Very few are deployed in real-world applications [86]. Deployment requires a thorough knowledge of BAS parameters, such as condition measures of the building environment, the configuration of the BAS, and physical properties of the building elements. Due to the proprietary nature of this information, it is difficult for system operators to acquire and reformat the information to support various FDD requirements [62].

BIM contains information, including properties of building elements and BAS components, that helps in the deployment of BAS and corresponding computer-aided FDD approaches. Currently, only a few proposals utilize BIM in automated FDD for BAS. One such an approach by Provan et al. [16] uses BIM to generate a simulation model of the HVAC systems and to acquire sensor information to collect the needed measurements from the BAS.

The major challenge in this approach is that BIM schemata for holistic representation of the information requirements for existing FDD approaches, like schemata that represent information on fault types and faulty components, have not yet been developed.

5.4.3   Using BIM in Planning of Maintenance Tasks

The performance of maintenance tasks is critical for ensuring the continuous, correct functioning of buildings [87]. However, maintenance tasks that are reactive cost three to four times more than planned maintenance [67–69]. Reactive maintenance only fixes the symptoms instead of the root cause of problems [70].

Increasing the number of planned maintenance tasks, therefore, will reduce the costs of building maintenance. Various products are available for computer-aided facilities management (CAFM), computerized maintenance management systems (CMMS), and integrated workplace management system (IWMS). These products provide users with the necessary functions for planning preventive maintenance tasks. For example, FM:Systems is a suite of software applications for CAFM. The FM:Interact application enables users to schedule preventive maintenance work orders for equipment [88]. Similar software applications include Maximo [89], ArchiBus [90], and Tririga [91].

One limitation of these software applications is that they predominantly provide the template for the user to manually input the required information but do not support automated planning of maintenance tasks, except for the scheduling of recurring preventive maintenance. Planning of maintenance tasks requires as-is building information and the performance history of building elements and systems (Chapter 6). Planning preventive maintenance requires having access to the specifications of existing equipment and information about their loads [92]. Therefore, automated planning requires that the software application be able to access and reason about this information. BIM provides semantic-rich information about building elements and has the potential to support the planning of maintenance tasks.

Existing software applications, such as ArchiBus and FM:Systems, can import information from BIM-based design software like Autodesk Revit [93]. However, the information imported is limited and these approaches still do not support automated maintenance planning. Currently, the utilization of BIM for supporting maintenance tasks is still an evolving field with only a few approaches proposed for utilizing BIM for maintenance tasks planning. For example, Hao et al. [94] proposed an approach that integrates BIM with condition monitoring systems and CAFM to develop a decision support framework for planning preventive maintenance and condition-based maintenance [94]. Akçamete et al. [70] discussed the potential of using BIM to store the performance history of the building elements so that the information can be used to identify spatial/topological breakdown patterns and to evaluate conditions for supporting decisions related to maintenance planning [70]. Chapters 13 and 14 introduce several emerging areas of field applications in facility operations and maintenance: augmented reality, wearable computers, and just-in-time technologies.

5.5   Evolution of BIM and the Need for Information Updating

As buildings evolve, building information models must evolve to correspond to changing representational requirements. Due to its creative nature, the parameters of a design are unpredictable. Moreover, constructability issues, costs, and quality constraints require design changes even during the detailed design and construction phases of CPD. In each phase, the stakeholders require information from previous phases and from various parties, necessitating the transfer of information from one phase to another. However, every stakeholder has different building information needs in terms of the level of representation and the level of detail in a building information model. As the information evolves, it becomes more detailed. Providing the details of system O&M manuals creates additional challenges to streamlining the progression of the information throughout the capital project life cycle.

The solutions proposed for this problem promote adding information to the information model, when created by its creator [11, 95]. However, because different parties need to input data into the same model, this raises problems of information ownership, accountability, creation, and maintenance authority allocation.

Studies suggest placing a new CPD approach to resolve these issues, under the title of integrated project delivery (IPD). IPD aims to optimize stakeholder collaboration between all participants at every phase by encouraging early contribution of knowledge and experience through the proactive involvement of key participants [96].

Currently, building information is transferred manually from one phase to another. The transferred documents generally include only the necessary information for the users of the successor phase. Since the information is not captured and transferred automatically, it requires re-creation by each stakeholder. In a study conducted at NIST, recollecting and transferring information adds redundant costs to projects, estimated to be about $65 million a year [97]. On the other hand, if redundant tasks were not performed, then new problems would arise due to the unavailability of necessary information. Through the integration of BIM during all stages of a capital project's life cycle, it is possible to keep the model up to date and adequate for each phase.

Construction Operations Building Information Exchange (COBIE) is a standard that was developed to capture building information during design, construction, and commissioning, to enable the handover of the information to the operations phase [11]. Because it enables different parties to input information for which they are responsible, it is a structured way to capture information essential for operations in a common database that persists throughout design and construction. As a result, building information is ready and complete at the time of the handover to the next phase of CPD. This information can be input into the facility management database or be automatically transferred to more specialized facility management tools. Similarly, the Specifiers' Properties Information Exchange (SPie) project assists manufacturers in exporting product data in an open format used by designers, specifiers, builders, owners, and operators [95].

Even though the information transfer to facility operators can be streamlined through these efforts, there still remains the challenge of keeping the information up to date in an information model during the service life of a facility because facilities continually change during occupancy. In addition to major renovations initiated by users, changes in building functionality and daily maintenance and repair activities also result in facility modifications. Information related to these changes must be recorded to update the facility information [98]. Therefore, it is extremely important to maintain an information model and update it throughout a facility's service life.

In conclusion, BIM has a critical role in supporting a variety of tasks in relation to ECx throughout the life cycle of facilities. These include, but are not limited to, energy analysis, building code compliance checking, clash detection, trade coordination, quality control during construction, traditional commissioning activities, fault detection and diagnosis, and planning of maintenance tasks during facility operations. While the added values of BIM to these functions are well documented, a few major challenges still remain in ensuring that BIM is a reliable source of information to support these tasks. The primary challenge is that the information model necessitates frequent updates. In addition, the level of information detail provided by BIM must evolve with the facility life cycle and must support corresponding decisions and tasks. These challenges must be addressed to maximize the usefulness of BIM in supporting ECx tasks.

References

[1]   Eastman, C., et al., *BIM Handbook A Guide to Building Information Modeling for Owners, Managers, Designers, Engineers, and Contractors*, Hoboken, NJ: John Wiley & Sons, 2008.

[2]   Borrmann, A., and E. Rank, *Query Support for BIMs using Semantic and Spatial Conditions*, Handbook of Research on Building Information Modeling and Construction Informatics: Concepts and Technologies, IGI Global, 2010.

[3]   GSA, *3D-4D Building Information Modeling*, 2010, available from http://www.gsa.gov/portal/content/105075, accessed February 21, 2011.

[4]   USACE, *USACE BIM Roadmap*, 2011, available from https://cadbim.usace.army.mil/MyFiles%5C1%5C2%5C1%5CERDC-TR-06-10,%20supplement%202.pdf, accessed February 11, 2011.

[5]   VA, *The VA BIM Guide*, 2010, available from http://www.cfm.va.gov/til/bim/BIMGuide/, accessed February 11, 2011.

[6]   DSF, *State of Wisconsin BIM Guidelines and Standards*, 2009, available from http://www.doa.state.wi.us/dsf/masterspec_view_new.asp?catid=61&locid=4, accessed February 11, 2011.

[7]   CIC Research Group, *BIM Project Execution Planning Guide*, Department of Architectural Engineering, The Pennsylvania State University, 2009, available from http://www.engr.psu.edu/ae/cic/bimex/download.aspx, accessed February 11, 2011.

[8]   BIM, *Indiana University BIM Standards*, 2010, available from http://www.indiana.edu/~uao/iubim.html, accessed February 11, 2011.

[9]   NBIMS. *National BIM Standard Version 1—Part 1: Overview, Principles, and Methodologies*, 2010, available from http://www.wbdg.org/pdfs/NBIMSv1_p1.pdf, accessed February 11, 2011.

[10]   IAI-Tech, *IFC2x Edition 4 Release Candidate 2 Specification*, 2011, available from http://www.iai-tech.org/ifc/IFC2x4/rc2/html/index.htm, accessed February 27, 2011.

[11]   East, E. W., *Construction Operations Building Information Exchange*, 2010, available from http://www.wbdg.org/resources/cobie.php.

[12]   Nisbet, N., Wix, J., and Conover, D., "The Future of Virtual Construction and Regulation Checking," in *Virtual Futures for Design, Const. and Procuremenet*, P. S. Brandon and T. Kocatürk (Eds.), New York: Wiley-Blackwell, 2008, pp. 241–251.

[13]   Khanzode, A., Fischer, M., and Reed, D., "Benefits and Lessons Learned of Implementing Building Virtual Design and Construction (VDC) Technologies for Coordination of Mechanical, Electrical, and Plumbing (MEP) Systems on a Large Healthcare Project," *Journal of Information Technology in Construction (ITCON)*, Vol. 13, 2008, pp. 324–342.

[14]   Kunz, J., and Fischer, M., "Virtual Design and Construction: Themes, Case Studies and Implementation Suggestions," CIFE Technical Reports, Stanford, CA: Center for Integrated Facility Engineering, 2007.

[15]   Tocci, *ROI for VDC*, 2011, available from http://www.tocci.com/index.php?option=com_content&view=article&id=160&Itemid=168, accessed February 11, 2011.

[16]   Provan, G., et al., "Using BIM Data for Generating and Updating Diagnostic Models," in *Proceedings of the Twelfth International Conference on Civil, Structural and Environmental Engineering Computing*, Stirlingshire, Scotland, 2009.

[17]   EcoDomus website, http://www.ecodomus.com, accessed February 21, 2011.

[18]   Onuma System website, http://www.onuma.com/index.php, accessed February 27, 2011.

[19]   "Green BIM—How Building Information Modeling is Contributing to Green Design and Construction," *SmartMarket Report*, McGraw-Hill Construction, 2010.

[20]   Al-Homoud, M. S., "Computer-Aided Building Energy Analysis Techniques," *Building and Environment*, Vol. 36, No. 4, 2001, pp. 421–433.

[21]   Cornford, S. L., Feather, M. S., and Jenkins, J. S., "Intertwining Risk Insights and Design Decisions," in *Proceedings of the 8th International Conference on Probabilistic Safety Assessment and Management*, New Orleans, LA, 2006.

[22]   *Building Energy Data Book*, Washington, DC: Energy Efficiency and Renewable Energy, Buildings Technologies Program, U.S. Department of Energy, 2008.

[23]   *The 2007 Commercial Building Energy Consumption Survey (CBECS)*, Washington, DC: U.S. Energy Information Administration, 2008.

[24]   Roth, K. W., et al., *The Energy Impact of Commercial Building Controls and Performance Diagnostics: Market Characterization, Energy Impact of Building Faults and Energy Savings Potential*, 2005, Cambridge, MA: TIAX:.

[25]   Bourgeois, D., Reinhart, C., and Macdonald, I., "Adding Advanced Behavioural Models in Whole Building Energy Simulation: A Study on the Total Energy Impact of Manual and Automated Lighting Control," *Energy and Buildings*, Vol. 38, No. 7, 2006 pp. 814–823.

[26]   *ASHRAE/IESNA Standard 90.1-2004, Energy Standard for Buildings Except Low-Rise Residential Buildings*, Atlanta, GA: American Society of Heating, Refrigerating, and Air-Conditioning Engineers, 2004.

[27]   Clarke, J., *Energy Simulation in Building Design*, Woburn, MA: Butterworth-Heinemann, 2001.

[28]   Crawley, D., et al., "Contrasting the Capabilities of Building Energy Performance Simulation Programs," *Building and Environment*, Vol. 43, No. 4, 2008, pp. 661–673.

[29]   DOE2 website, http://www.doe2.com, accessed January 3, 2011.

[30]   Crawley, D. B., et al., "EnergyPlus: Creating a New-Generation Building Energy Simulation Program," *Energy and Buildings*, Vol. 33, No. 4, 2001, pp. 319–331.

[31]   Papamichael, K., and Pal, V., "Barriers in Developing and Using Simulation-Based Decision-Support Software," in *ACEEE 2002 Summer Study on Energy Efficiency in Buildings*. Pacific Grove, CA, 2002.

[32]   Hong, T., Chou, S. K., and Bong, T. Y., "Building Simulation: An Overview of Developments and Information Sources," *Building and Environment*, Vol. 35, No. 4, 2000, pp. 347–361.

[33]   Bazjanac, V., "Acquisition of Building Geometry in the Simulation of Energy Performance," *Building Simulation*, 2001, pp. 305–311.

[34]   Augenbroe, G., "Trends in Building Simulation," *Building and Environment*, Vol. 37, Nos. 8–9, 2002, pp. 891–902.

[35]   Punjabi, S., and Miranda, V., "Development of an Integrated Building Design Information Interface," in *Ninth International IBPSA Conference*, Montréal, Canada, 2005, pp. 969–976.

[36]   Laine, T., et al., "Benefits of Building Information Models in Energy Analysis," in *Proceedings of Clima 2007 Well-Being Indoors*, 2007.

[37]   Azhar, S., Brown, J., and Farooqui, R., "BIM-Based Sustainability Analysis: An Evaluation of Building Performance Analysis Software," in *Proceedings of the 45th ASC Annual Conference*, Gainesville, FL, 2009.

[38]   Bazjanac, V., and Maile, T., *IFC HVAC Interface to EnergyPlus—A Case of Expanded Interoperability for Energy Simulation*. Berkeley, CA: Lawrence Berkeley National Laboratory, 2004.

[39]   Howell, I., and Batcheler, B., "Building Information Modeling Two Years Later—Huge Potential, Some Success and Several Limitations," *The Laiserin Letter*, Vol. 22, 2005.

[40]   van Treeck, C., Romberg, R., and Rank, E. "Simulation Based on the Product Model Standard IFC," in *Proceedings of Building Simulation*, Eindhoven, Netherlands, 2003.

[41]   gbXML website, http://www.gbxml.org, accessed January 3, 2011.

[42]   Autodesk Ecotect Analysis website, http://usa.autodesk.com/adsk/servlet/pc/index?id=126 02821&siteID=123112, accessed February 20, 2011.

[43]   Thuesen, N., Kirkegaard, P. H., and Jensen, R. L., "Evaluation of BIM and Ecotect for Conceptual Architectural Design Analysis," in *Proceedings of the International Conference on Computing in Civil and Building Engineering*, Nottingham, UK: Nottingham University Press, 2010.

[44]   Glazer, J., "Common Data Definitions for HVAC&R Industry Applications," *ASHRAE Transactions*, Vol. 115, 2009, pp. 531–544.

[45]   Dong, B., et al., "A Comparative Study of the IFC and gbXML Informational Infrastructures for Data Exchange in Computational Design Support Environments," in *Proceedings Building Simulation 2007*, Vol. 1, 2007, pp. 1530–1537.

[46]   Han, C. S., Kunz, J. C. and Law, K. H., "A Hybrid Prescriptive/Performance Based Approach to Automated Building Code Checking," in *Fifth Congress in Computing in Civil Engineering*. Boston, MA, 1998.

[47]   Lee, J. M., "Automated Checking of Building Requirements on Circulation over a Range of Design Phases," Atlanta: Georgia Institute of Technology, 2010.

[48]   Sing, T. F. and Zhong, Q. "Construction and Real Estate NETwork (CORENET)," *Facilities*, Vol. 19, No. 11/12, 2001, pp. 419–428.

[49]   Solibri Model Checker website, http://www.solibri.com/solibri-model-checker.html, accessed February 20, 2011..

[50]   Shen, Z., and Issa, R. "Quantitative Evaluation of the BIM-Assisted Construction Detailed Cost Estimates," *Journal of Information Technology in Construction (ITcon),* Vol. 15, 2010, pp. 234–257.

[51]   Akinci, B., et al., "A Formalism for Utilization of Sensor Systems and Integrated Project Models for Active Construction Quality Control," *Automation in Construction*, Vol. 15, No. 2, 2006, pp. 124–138.

[52]   Issa, R. R. A., Flood, I., and O'Brien, W. J., *4D CAD and Visualization in Construction: Developments and Applications*, Taylor & Francis, 2003.

[53]   Staub-French, S., and Khanzode, A., "3D and 4D Modeling for Design and Construction Coordination: Issues and Lessons Learned," *ITcon*, Vol. 12, 2007, pp. 381–407.

[54]   Leite, F., et al., "Analysis of modeling effort and impact of different levels of detail in building information models," *Automation in Construction*, 2011. In Press.

[55]   Bosche, F., and Haas, C. T., Automated Retrieval of Project Three-Dimensional CAD Objects in Range Point Clouds To Support Automated Dimensional QA/QC," *Information Technologies in Construction*, Vol. 13, 2008, pp. 71–85.

[56]   Liu, L., et al., "Capturing As-Built Project Information for Facility Management," in *OMPUT, CIV ENG,* New York: ASCE, Vol. 1, 1994, pp. 614–621.

[57]   Clayton, M., Johnson, R., and Song, Y., "Operations Documents: Addressing the Information Needs of Facility Managers," *Durability of Building Materials and Components*, Vol. 8, No. 4, 1999p. 2441–2451.

[58]   Teicholz, E., "Bridging the AEC/FM Technology Gap," *IFMA Facility Management Journal,*. March–April 2004.

[59]   Mansson, L.-G., and McIntyre, D. "Controlling and Regulating Heating, Cooling and Ventilation Methods and Examples," in *IEA Annex 16 & 17 Technical Synthesis Report*, International Energy Agency, 1997.

[60]   Liddament, M. W., *Technical Synthesis Report: Real Time Simulation of HVAC Systems for Building Optimisation, Fault Detection and Diagnostics*, Coventry, UK: ESSU, 1999.

[61]   Liu, M., Claridge, D., and Turner, W. *Continuous Commissioning Guidebook: Maximizing Building Energy Efficiency and Comfort*, Washington, DC: Federal Energy Management Program, U.S. Department of Energy, 2002.

[62]   Katipamula, S., and Brambley, M. "Methods for Fault Detection, Diagnostics, and Prognostics for Building Systems—A Review, Part I," *HVAC&R Research*, Vol. 11, No. 1, 2005, pp. 3–25.

[64]   IEA, "Commissioning Tools for Improved Energy Performance," No. 40, International Energy Agency, 2004.

[65]   House, J., and Kelly. G. "An Overview of Building Diagnostics," in *National Conference on Building Commissioning*. 2000.

[66]   Castro, N. "Commissioning of Building HVAC Systems for Improved Energy Performance," in *Proceedings of the Fourth International Conference for Enhanced Building Operations*. Paris, France, 2004.

[67]   Mobley, R. K., "Corrective Maintenance," in *Maintenance Engineering Handbook*, L. R. Higgins and D. J. Wikoff (Eds.), New York: McGraw-Hill, 2008, pp. 2.3–2.6.

[68]   Franklin, S., "Redefining Maintenance—Delivering Reliability," in *Maintenance Engineering Handbook*, L. R. Higgins and D. J. Wikoff (Eds.), New York: McGraw-Hill, 2008, pp. 1.3–1.8.

[69]   Sullivan, G. P., Pugh, R., and Melendez, A. P., *Operations and Maintenance Best Practices—A Guide to Achieving Operational Efficiency*, Richland, WA: Pacific Northwest National Laboratory, 2002.

[70]   Akcamete, A., Akinci, B., and Garrett, Jr., J. H., "Potential Utilization of Building Information Models for Planning Maintenance Activities," in *Proceedings of the International Conference on Computing in Civil and Building Engineering*, Nottingham, UK: Nottingham University Press, 2010.

[71]   Salsbury, T., and Diamond, R., "Automated Testing of HVAC Systems for Commissioning," in *PECI Commissioning Conference*, Portland, OR, 1999.

[72]   Castro, N. S., and Vaezi-Nejad, H., "CITE-AHU, an Automated Commissioning Tool for Air-Handling Units," in *National Conference on Building Commissioning*, 2005.

[73]   Brambley, M. R., and Katipamula, S., "Automated Commissioning for Lower-Cost, Widely Deployed Building Commissioning of the Future," in *Web Based Enterprise Energy and Building Automation Systems*, B. L. Capehart and L. C. Capehart (Eds.), The Fairmont Press, 2007, pp. 145–156.

[74]   Katipamula, S., Brambley, M., and Luskay, L., "Automated Proactive Techniques for Commissioning Air-Handling Units," *Journal of Solar Energy Engineering*, Vol. 125, 2003, pp. 282–291.

[75]   Vaezi-Nejad, H., Salsbury, T., and Choiniere, D., "Using Building Control System for Commissioning," in *International Conference for Enhanced Building Operation*, Paris, France, 2004.

[76]   Choiniere, D., "DABO: A BEMS Assisted On-Going Commissioning Tool," in *Asia-Pacific Conference on Building Commissioning (APCBC) Workshop*, Kyoto, Japan, 2008.

[77]   Turkaslan-Bulbul, M. T., and Akin, O. "Computational Support for Building Evaluation: Embedded Commissioning Model," *Automation in Construction*, Vol. 15, No. 4, 2006, pp. 438–447.

[78]   Wang, H., et al., "Feasibility and Fidelity of Data Exchange Through IFC for Building Commissioning," in *ICEBO 2005*, Pittsburgh, PA, USA, 2005.

[79]   Ahmed, A., et al., "Multi-Dimensional Building Performance Data Management for Continuous Commissioning," *Advanced Engineering Informatics*, Vol. 24, 2010, pp. 466–475.

[80]   O'Donnell, J., et al., "BuildingPI: A Future Tool for Building Life Cycle Analysis," in *Proceedings of the SimBuild 2004 Conference*, Boulder, CO, 2004, Citeseer.

[81]   *2009 ASHRAE Handbook—Fundamentals*, Atlanta, GA: American Society of Heating, Refrigerating and Air-Conditioning Engineers, 2009.

[82]   Jagpal, R., "Computer Aided Evaluation of HVAC System Performance: Technical Synthesis Report," 2006.

[83]   Lee, W., House, J., and Kyong, N., "Subsystem Level Fault Diagnosis OF A Building's Air-Handling Unit Using General Regression Neural Networks," *Applied Energy*, Vol. 77, No. 2, 2004, pp. 153–170.

[84]   Schein, J., and Bushby, S., "A Simulation Study of a Hierarchical, Rule-Based Method for System-Level Fault Detection and Diagnostics in HVAC Systems," NISTIR 7216, 2005.

[85]   Wang, S., Zhou, Q., and Xiao, F., "A System-Level Fault Detection AND Diagnosis Strategy for HVAC Systems Involving Sensor Faults," *Energy and Buildings*, Vol. 42, No. 4, 2009, pp. 477–490.

[86]   Liang, J., and Du, R., "Model-Based Fault Detection and Diagnosis of HVAC Systems Using Support Vector Machine Method," *International Journal of Refrigeration*, Vol. 30, No. 6, 2007, pp. 1104–1114.

[87]   Chanter, B., and Swallow, P., *Building Maintenance Management*, Oxford, UK: Wiley-Blackwell, 2007.

[88]   FM:Systems website, http://www.fmsystems.com, accessed February 21, 2011.

[89]   IBM Maximo Asset Management Software website, http://www-01.ibm. com/software/tivoli/products/maximo-asset-mgmt, accessed February 21, 2011.

[90]   ArchiBus website, http://www.archibus.com, accessed February 21, 2011.

[91]   Tririga website, http://www.tririga.com/home, accessed February 21, 2011.

[92]   Horner, R., El-Haram, M., and Munns, A., "Building Maintenance Strategy: A New Management Approach," *Journal of Quality in Maintenance Engineering*, Vol. 3, No. 4, 1997, pp. 273–280.

[93]   Autodesk Revit website, http://usa.autodesk. com/adsk/servlet/pc/index?id=3781831&siteID=123112, accessed February 21, 2011.

[94]   Hao, Q., et al., "A Decision Support System for Integrating Corrective Maintenance, Preventive Maintenance, and Condition-Based Maintenance," in *Construction Research Congress 2010: Innovation for Reshaping Construction Practice*, Banff, Alberta, Canada, 2010, ASCE.

[95]   BuildingSMART website, http://www.buildingsmartalliance.org/index.php/projects, accessed February 11, 2011.

[96]   AIA. *IPD Guide*, available from http://images.autodesk. com/adsk/files/ipd_definition_doc_final_with_supplemental_info.pdf, accessed February 11, 2011.

[97]   Gallaher, M., et al., "Cost Analysis of Inadequate Interoperability in the U.S. Capital Facilities Industry," in NIST GCR 04-867, National Institute of Standards & Technology , 2004.

[98]   Akcamete, A., Akinci, B., and Garrett, Jr., J. H., "Motivation for Computational Support for Updating Building Information Models (BIMs)," in *2009 ASCE International Workshop on Computing in Civil Engineering*. Austin, TX, 2009, ASCE.

CHAPTER 6

As-Is Modeling: Capturing Existing Spatial Conditions Using Laser Scanners

6.1 Introduction

Capturing as-is conditions during construction and facility operations is paramount to having an accurate understanding of facility performance and comparing it to performance expectations. Laser scanning, with its capability of rapid generation of 3D, dense point clouds, is gaining wide acceptance in the architecture-engineering-construction/facility management (AEC/FM) industry. Through periodic deployment of laser scanners throughout the life cycle of a facility, it is possible to capture the as-built conditions and record how the shape of a facility or infrastructure element changes over time [1, 2]. It is then possible to assess a facility's deterioration and identify when the current conditions are no longer aligned with the expected conditions and when to intervene [2]. Laser scanning also provides an opportunity to create as-is models of facilities already in use and, hence, provides a baseline on the form of a facility used for commissioning activities. This chapter overviews laser scanning technology and the associated processes to convert laser scanner data into an as-is building information model (BIM).

6.1.1 Sensors and Methods for Capturing As-Is Conditions

A number of measuring devices are commonly used to document as-is conditions. The list includes physical tape measures, laser trackers, total stations, laser scanners, and cameras. Each measuring device has unique capabilities, advantages, and disadvantages (Table 6.1). Tape measures, laser trackers, and total stations are well suited for fewer measurements. For example, a total station can precisely measure the position of a key point on a pipe flange to ensure that it is correctly positioned to connect to a flange on a prefabricated assembly. Unfortunately, the slow speed of these devices limits the density of measurements that can be cost effectively obtained. Modeling as-is conditions of an entire facility with such small numbers of points requires numerous assumptions about the geometry of unmeasured regions.

The introduction of laser scanners into the AEC/FM industry is changing the fundamental process by which as-is conditions are documented and is greatly

Table 6.1 Common Devices Used for Measuring As-Is Conditions and Their Advantages and Disadvantages

Measurement Device	Advantages	Disadvantages
Tape measure	Low cost, can measure curved surfaces	Slow, low accuracy
Laser tracker	Very high accuracy	Slow, limited range
Total station	High accuracy	Slow, relatively high cost
Laser scanner	Moderately high accuracy, fast	High cost
Camera	Low cost	Moderate accuracy, scale ambiguity

enhancing the accuracy and level of detail at which a facility can be modeled. Laser scanners rapidly and accurately measure a dense array of points in 3D space, capturing the shape of all surfaces visible to the scanner (Figure 6.1). The 3D points produced by a laser scanner are known as a *scan* or a *point cloud*. Although all of the aforementioned measuring technologies may be used in a given project, this chapter focuses primarily on workflows involving the use of laser scanners.

6.1.2 The Scan-to-BIM Workflow

It is possible to conduct many types of analysis directly using point clouds obtained from a laser scanner. Virtual measurements can determine the distance between individual points. The point cloud can be overlaid with an existing CAD model or BIM to test for intersecting surfaces—a process known as *clash detection*. The difference between points and a design model can identify construction mistakes or deviations from the design [1].

Figure 6.1 A scan (or point cloud) created by a laser scanner.

Despite the myriad applications of point cloud data, this type of analysis is ultimately limited because the point cloud model represents the facility at a raw, unintelligent level. For example, the model does not specify which points belong to a wall and which ones belong to the floor. The model does not indicate where a pipe originates or where it leads. The burden of interpretation falls on the user, which leads to labor-intensive analysis processes and raises a barrier against straightforward usage by nonexperts.

The limitations on the use of point cloud data suggest that there is a substantial benefit to abstracting the raw point cloud data to a higher level by converting the data into a BIM. Building information models are information-rich, object-oriented representations of a facility. A BIM represents a facility in terms of components, such as walls, floors, and windows, with geometry to describe their shape. The components also include metadata that describes the behavior of components and their relationships to one another. This metadata endows components with intelligence. For example, a wall "knows" when it is connected to another wall, and a window is "aware" that it is embedded within a wall.

A BIM is useful for many purposes, including facility management (e.g., to plan space usage and maintenance), simulation (e.g., to model the effects of a building fire), construction planning (e.g., for planning a renovation project), and visualization (e.g., for a virtual walkthrough of a facility). The process of transforming laser scan data into a BIM is known as the *points-to-BIM* or *scan-to-BIM process* [3].

The scan-to-BIM workflow typically involves four steps: data collection, data registration, modeling, and verification. In the data collection step, laser scans are obtained from locations throughout the facility. Scanning locations are selected to ensure that surfaces are imaged with sufficient coverage and accuracy to support project requirements. Next, the individual scans are aligned in a common coordinate system through a process known as data registration. In the modeling step, the BIM is created by estimating the geometry, identity, and other relevant properties of each component, and by adding relationships among components. Finally, the BIM is verified to ensure that it was constructed to the accuracy requirements of the project.

The next several sections describe this scan-to-BIM workflow in detail. The workflow and supporting details are based on the experiences of the authors and on interviews with key personnel in government and industry (Ron Aarts, interview, April 1, 2011; Landon "Alfie" Cross, interview, April 1, 2011; Eric Hoffman, personal communication, March 23, 2011; Jason Hosch, interview, March 23, 2011; Dale Stenning, interview, March 23, 2011; Peggy Yee, interview, March 31, 2011).

6.1.3   As-Is Modeling Needs and Requirements

Documentation of as-is conditions is applicable to several environment types within the AEC/FM domain, each with unique characteristics and requirements. The main divisions include architecture (e.g., buildings); process plants (e.g., chemical plants or refineries); mechanical, electrical, and piping (MEP); and transportation infrastructure (e.g., bridges). Architectural models usually include structural components, such as walls, ceilings, floors, windows, doorways, beams, columns, and stairways. Plant models typically include pipes, flanges, valves, manufactured equipment, and structural steel. Models for MEP projects are similar to plant models, but are usually part of a building rather than a process plant. These models involve pipes, ductwork, wiring trays, mounting brackets, and specialized components, such as lights and sprinkler heads. Infrastructure models, such as bridges, may include concrete components, like columns and piers, as well as steel assemblies.

The necessary level of detail and accuracy for a model varies by project and anticipated downstream needs for the data. Process plant models generally involve key points, known as tie points, where pipes or structural steel must meet exactly. For such tie points, scan data may be augmented by measurements from total stations or laser trackers. An architectural BIM may require a high level of detail if the model is for renovation planning or historical preservation. On the other hand, less accuracy may be needed for space usage planning or energy simulations.

6.1.4 Comparison with As-Designed Modeling

The concept of BIM was originally developed to support design and construction of facilities [4]. A BIM that documents as-is conditions differs significantly from a design or construction BIM. Most importantly, an as-is BIM is challenged to represent the actual, and generally imperfect, conditions of a facility, rather than the idealized conditions of a virtual design model. Real-world walls are rarely perfectly flat or plumb, and they rarely meet at 90-degree angles, even for perfectly square corners. The imperfections of reality can be difficult, because modelers must, on a case-by-case basis, decide whether to include such imperfections in the model or to approximate a component by its idealized counterpart.

Because an as-is BIM is an abstraction of the associated underlying point cloud, a number of aspects of the abstraction process are unique to an as-is BIM [5]. Recording and visualizing these features can provide downstream users with a more complete picture of the as-is BIM. The geometry and position of modeled components is uncertain due to accumulated uncertainties in the scanning, registration, and modeling procedures. Some surfaces may be occluded in the scan data, due to self-occlusions (e.g., the back side of a pipe) or due to other objects in the environment (e.g., furniture blocking a wall). Depending on the scanner position, surfaces may be measured at different densities, which affect the size of features that can be accurately modeled. Finally, having access to the underlying point data associated with a BIM component can be helpful when the accuracy of the original data is needed. In the example shown in Figure 6.2, the wall surface (boxed region) in part (a) is analyzed according to these characteristics: (b) data density (in points per square meter), (c) occlusion regions (black = occluded, gray = unoccluded), (d) data uncertainty, and (e) deviation from the ideal planar wall (in meters).

6.2 Preparation and Data Collection

The first step in the scan-to-BIM process is obtaining the scans. Scanning a facility is the culmination of an extensive preparation process that includes choosing the appropriate scanner technology, planning the scan locations, setup and survey of registration targets, and, finally, scanning.

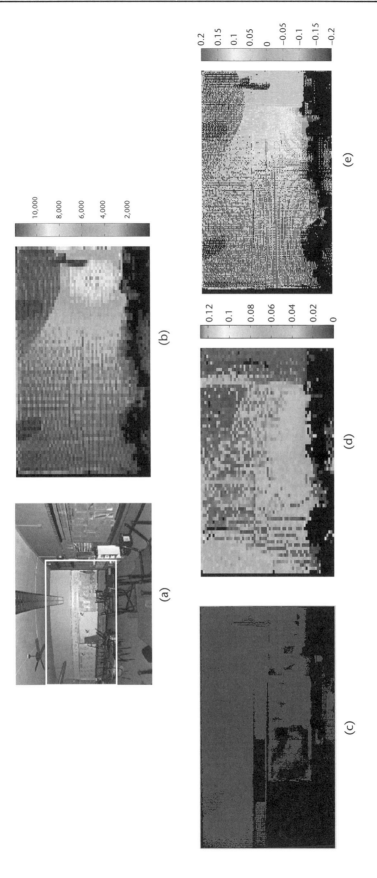

Figure 6.2 The wall surface in (a) is analyzed according to (b) data density, (c) occlusion regions, (d) data uncertainty, and (e) deviation from the ideal planar wall.

6.2.1　Laser Scanner Technology

Laser scanners determine 3D position by measuring the distance and direction to visible surfaces. A typical scanner design uses a laser emitter/receiver that rotates about two orthogonal axes, with one axis spinning rapidly and one axis spinning slowly. With two axes of rotation working together, one can achieve nearly full coverage over the sphere of possible viewing directions. It is also possible to mount a single axis laser scanner on a vehicle for mobile scanning of transportation infrastructure elements, such as bridges and tunnels. In this case, the laser rotates around an axis parallel to the direction of vehicle travel, producing a fan-shaped pattern of measurements to the sides and above the vehicle.

The range measurement produced by a laser scanner is usually accomplished by one of two technologies. The first approach is pulsed time of flight (PToF). In this method, a short-duration pulse of laser light is emitted, the time required for the light to reflect off of a target surface and return to the sensor is measured, and the distance is computed based on the measured "time of flight" and the speed of light. The second common laser scanner technology is amplitude modulated continuous waveform (AMCW). In this method, a continuous laser beam with varying amplitude—typically a sine wave pattern—is emitted. The distance to the target surface is estimated by measuring the phase difference between the reflected signal and the currently emitted waveform, a function of range.

Each scanning technology has strengths and weaknesses. Pulsed scanners are generally slower than phase-based scanners, sampling at rates of tens of thousands of points per second as compared to hundreds of thousands to nearly a million points per second for phase-based scanners. Pulsed scanners can measure longer ranges than a phase-based scanner. Currently, commercially available pulsed scanners operate at ranges up to 3,000m, whereas phase-based scanners have ranges only up to 153m. Phase-based scanner range measurements are subject to an ambiguity interval—the range at which a complete wavelength of phase offset occurs. Objects beyond this distance cannot be measured accurately because the range measurement restarts at zero at the ambiguity interval distance. As an example, if the ambiguity interval is 50m, then an object at 51m would actually be reported as being 1m away. For this reason, phase-based scanners are more frequently used for indoor applications rather than outdoors, because it is possible to ensure that no observable surfaces lie beyond the ambiguity interval distance.

Laser scanners are not perfect range-measuring devices and have limitations not explicitly expressed by device manufacturers. Some types of surfaces are difficult or impossible for laser scanners to measure. Dark-colored surfaces absorb nearly all laser light, resulting in either an uncertain range estimate or no measurement at all. Shiny surfaces reflect most of the incident light away from the scanner, making it difficult to determine the range to the surface. Often, the laser beam will hit another, nonshiny surface, and the reflected light will produce a phantom surface in the scene at a distance beyond the shiny surface. This problem commonly occurs, for example, with water, mirrors, and reflectors on commercial light fixtures. Figure 6.3b shows an example where a mirror in a bathroom (highlighted box) creates a wall surface that extends beyond the boundary of the room, as indicated in the side view. Shiny surfaces and retroreflectors can also cause unexpectedly large magnitudes of reflected light, which can saturate the receiver and cause range errors that persist for a significant number of future measurements.

Transparent surfaces, such as glass and plastic, are also difficult to scan, and, depending on various factors, the surface may act like a mirror, resulting in a virtual surface as described above, or the laser may pass through and measure a surface beyond. In either case, the transparent surface is not usually imaged. Different colored surfaces can also introduce errors into the range measurement due to color-based range biases [6].

The geometry of the scene itself can cause measurement errors. Concave corners in the scene enable reflections along multiple paths, which can bias the range estimate. At depth discontinuities in the scene, the laser spot can span two surfaces simultaneously, leading to the "mixed-pixel" effect (Figure 6.3a) [7]. In this example, mixed pixels create phantom points at the boundary between two walls (top). The close-up (bottom) shows three curved lines of mixed pixels from the region within the hightlighted box. Depending on the underlying scanner technology, the reported range of mixed pixels may be located between the two surfaces, or it may lie in front of the front surface or behind the back surface. Mixed pixels can give the impression of false surfaces, especially in regions with small, highly detailed geometry, for example, along occluding edges of moldings high up on a

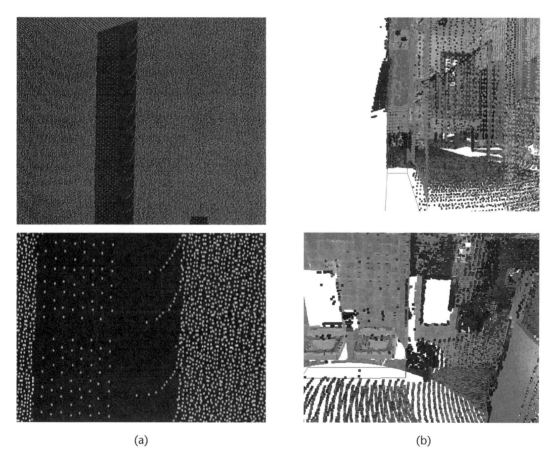

(a)   (b)

Figure 6.3 Laser scanners difficulties: (a) mixed pixels create phantom points at object boundaries; (b) reflections in a mirror create a wall surface extending beyond the room boundary.

building's exterior façade. The combined effects of mixed pixels and the sparseness of laser scanner measurements leads to edge loss at depth discontinuities [8]. The amount of edge loss can be significant with respect to the accuracy goals of as-is BIM projects. For example, depending on the viewing angle, scans of a bridge from a distance of 10m can result in edge loss of between 1 and 10 cm [8]. Awareness of these sensing limitations is crucial because of their potential direct impact on creating accurate models of existing conditions.

6.2.2   Scan Planning

Once the appropriate scanner technology is chosen, the next step is to create a scan plan. A scan plan indicates the expected positions where the scanner and registration targets will be placed during data collection. This is typically accomplished using blueprints of the facility, if available, or hand-drawn layouts, as well as pictures or videos of a walkthrough of the facility obtained during field reconnaissance. A good scan plan will ensure that the relevant components are scanned with adequate coverage to enable modelers to correctly construct the BIM. Additionally, logistics, such as site access, safety, and design of special-purpose setups for scanning challenging locations, are addressed prior to data collection.

6.2.3   Scanning

On arrival to the site, registration targets are set up at locations throughout the facility (Figure 6.4a). Some or all of these targets will be surveyed using, for example, a total station, to establish a set of known 3D control points, known as a control network. Additional surveying may be conducted to link the control network to known surveying monuments to allow georeferencing of the project data (i.e., put the data into a global coordinate reference frame).

A variety of target types are available, each with different advantages and disadvantages (Figure 6.4b). The simplest and least expensive type of target is printed on paper, and often consists of a two-square by two-square checkerboard. Such targets can only be observed from limited viewing directions. This problem can be addressed with paddle-style targets, which may use a checkerboard pattern or concentric circles. Paddles may be reoriented to face the current scanner location without moving the 3D position of the target center. Spheres are a third type of commonly used target. The benefit of spheres is that they can be viewed from any direction without reorientation. Targets may be augmented with a number or code to help identify the targets during processing.

A challenge of modeling large facilities is accurately relating the data from different rooms, different floors, and from inside and outside of the facility. This problem can be addressed by surveying points visible through windows and doorways and in stairwells and elevator shafts.

Once the control network is in place, scanning can commence. At each location specified in the scan plan, the scanner is set up and a scan is collected. The exact scan location is often modified somewhat based on the judgment and experience of the scanning team. The visible registration targets are normally scanned again at a higher resolution to maximize the accuracy of target position estimates. Because

(a)   (b)

Figure 6.4   (a) Target placement and (b) target types—paper checkerboard, (c) paddle, and (d) sphere (top to bottom). (Sphere target image courtesy of Kin Yen, AHMCT Research Center, University of California, Davis.)

returning to the site to scan again can be costly, the scans may be registered in the field to verify that the necessary coverage has been achieved.

Some environments and types of components prove difficult to scan. Pipes, ducts, and other components for an MEP project are often hidden above drop ceilings. To scan those elements, some or all of the ceiling tiles must be removed to provide direct visibility of the desired region. Special-purpose rigs can raise the scanner above the ceiling, in which case, just one or a few tiles need to be removed (Eric Hoffman, personal communication, March 23, 2011). The challenge in this case is to accurately relate the above-ceiling data to that taken below the ceiling. Elevator shafts are also challenging to scan, since most scanners are designed to operate on horizontal surfaces. Special-purpose rigs may be built to appropriately position the scanner for vertical shafts. On the exterior of a facility, high ledges and details of the façade may be occluded from ground level. Often, permission can be obtained to use neighboring buildings to achieve the necessary vantage point to observe such structures.

6.3   Registration and Data Cleanup

The registration process aligns all of the scans in a single, project-wide coordinate system. The most common registration approach is to align individual scans to the surveyed control network. Depending on the target type, visualization of two to four targets is required to register with the control network. Using five or more targets typically increases registration accuracy. Targets are identified within the scan either manually or using an automated target detection algorithm. Fitting algorithms will precisely find the 3D position of the control point on the target (e.g., sphere center or checkerboard center). The detected targets are then matched to their corresponding targets in the control network. Once the correspondences have been established, the optimal rigid body transformation (i.e., rotation and translation) that registers the scan to the control network can be computed directly. Figure 6.5 shows five registered scans, each using a different color.

For some projects, it is necessary to manually remove undesirable data from the scans. Manual deletion of clutter objects, such as trees, can simplify the modeling process. Data from moving objects, such as passing cars or people, can also be detected and removed. The scans may be filtered to remove uncertain data or artifacts like mixed pixels or reflections.

6.4 Modeling

The modeling process converts a registered point cloud into a BIM, which provides a semantically rich information repository as described in Chapter 5. Typically, generating a BIM from point cloud data involves three tasks: (1) modeling the geometry of each component, (2) assigning object identity and metadata to the component, and (3) establishing spatial and functional relationships among components. The components that need modeling vary with the type of project and level of detail requirements. For example, typical components for an architectural project include walls, slabs, windows, doors, and roofs.

Figure 6.5 Five registered scans. (Image courtesy of Intelisum, Inc.)

In the geometric modeling task, a simplified representation of the component is created based on the 3D measurements on that component's surfaces. Usually, the desired BIM representation is a solid, volumetric object model. For example, a wall may be modeled as a rectangular parallelepiped (box shape). The wall surface observed from two adjacent rooms is used to determine the thickness of the wall. However, some or all portions of the surface may be unobserved. For instance, the wall surface adjacent to a void will only be observable from one side. In such cases, the modeler must make assumptions about the unobserved data using domain knowledge or information specific to the project.

Although numerous techniques for modeling the components of a BIM exist, the methods can be broadly divided into two categories: sectioning and surface fitting. The sectioning method uses 2D cross sections to create the model, whereas the surface-fitting method uses optimization algorithms to fit geometric primitives to the data.

In the sectioning method (Figure 6.6a), 2D cross sections of the data are generated by projecting the points from a thin slice through the point cloud onto a plane. The lines and curves in the cross section serve as a guide for positioning and sizing components. Once the 2D outline of a component is set, it can be converted to 3D by lofting (i.e., extending the outline along a path). This method can be used to model walls from a plan view cross section, to model complex molding shapes, or to model pipe assemblies. A disadvantage of the sectioning method is that it only uses some of the available data for modeling a component. One way to address this limitation is to use multiple cross sections for modeling. For example, to model a column, cross sections at three different heights can identify whether the column is plumb or has unacceptable shape variations (Jason Hosch, interview, March 23, 2011).

In contrast to the sectioning approach, the surface-fitting method uses all of the available data. With the surface-fitting method, the modeler selects a point or a patch of points and specifies a specific geometric primitive to fit to this patch (Figure 6.6b). For example, the modeler may select a patch of points on a wall surface, and the software will fit a plane to the selected data. Automated tools can extend the patch beyond the initially selected data, making it easier to model large surfaces. For planar surfaces, the boundaries may be inaccurately detected or may not be observable at all. Intersections of adjacent components can be used to clean up edge and corner estimates.

A library of known objects or standard components can be used to improve the modeling process. For example, if a cylinder is fitted to a pipe, a library of standard pipe diameters can be used to limit the pipe model to a feasible choice. As new automated and semiautomated tools for modeling are developed, the process of segmenting and modeling components becomes increasingly easier.

Identifying the appropriate object category may be performed simultaneously with modeling or as a separate process. Some software packages require specifying the object type being modeled before the modeling of that component can begin. In other cases, the object category may be automatically determined by the geometry. For example, a component is modeled as a particular flange picked from a model library. Components may be further annotated with metadata, such as the part number of a manufactured component or the surface material.

Finally, the BIM must be annotated with information about relationships between components and groups of components. Many relationships are automatically

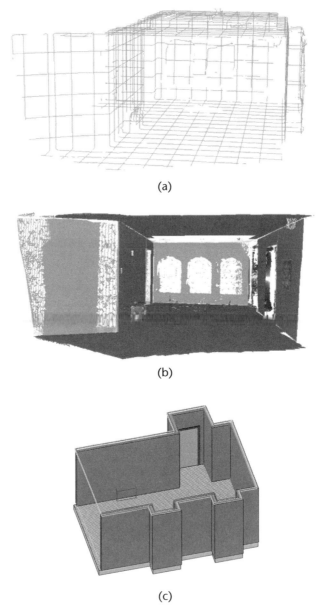

Figure 6.6 Two common modeling techniques are sectioning and surface fitting: (a) sectioning; (b) surface fitting; (c) resulting BIM, in Autodesk Revit (adapted from [3]).

generated during the modeling process. For example, modeling software may create "attachment" relationships by automatically joining one wall to another whenever its end approaches close to another wall.

6.4.1 Interoperability Issues

While several standards exist to depict BIM, as described in Chapter 7, there is no standard format for storing or transferring working process information associated with point clouds. Different products are best suited for different aspects of the problem. A service provider may need to transfer data between 10 or more products throughout the scan-to-BIM workflow (Jason Hosch, interview, March 23, 2011; Dale Stenning, interview, March 23, 2011). Each time data is transferred, there is a potential for information loss or miscommunication between software packages.

This lack of interoperability introduces inefficiencies in the scan-to-BIM work-flow. A modeler may be forced to perform redundant processes to re-create the necessary information in the software where it is needed. For example, it is common to initially create a 3D model using a non-BIM modeling program, such as AutoCAD or Polyworks, export the 3D model to a BIM-capable program like Revit, and finally re-create the model from scratch using the imported model as a template. However, BIM-capable programs do not, as yet, have the ability to convert existing 3D models into intelligent BIM components. As the software for the scan-to-BIM process matures, and as the techniques become more standardized, the limitations of interoperability should decrease.

6.5   Quality Assurance

Once created, the BIM must be checked to ensure that it accurately reflects existing conditions—a process known as quality assurance (QA). Ideally, QA should be conducted by a different contractor from the one(s) performing the scanning and modeling steps of the scan-to-BIM process to ensure that the analysis is an objective one. Although it is important to verify the correctness of all aspects of the BIM, the primary focus of QA has centered on verifying the geometric accuracy of the model. Occasionally, components are modeled with an incorrect shape or position or are omitted entirely.

Errors may be introduced at any step in the scan-to-BIM process. In the data collection step, errors may arise from incorrect calibration of the scanner or from scan data artifacts, such as those described in Section 2.1. In the registration step, the registration results can be degraded by a poor-quality control network, errors in localizing targets in scan data, or mistakes in matching detected targets to their corresponding targets in the network. However, the modeling step allows the greatest potential for the introduction of errors, since the process is subjective and primarily manual. Modelers must decide what to model and at what level of detail. They are constrained by the representations allowed by the particular software being used to create the model. Furthermore, they are limited by the capabilities of the modeling tools available within the software. Modeling errors can be divided into four categories: (1) failing to model a component entirely, (2) modeling a component using incorrect geometry, (3) modeling a component using incorrect positioning, and (4) using the wrong component type to model a component. Several methods can be used to conduct QA of an as-is BIM. These methods include visual inspection, clash detection, physical inspection, and deviation analysis.

In the visual inspection method, an inspector overlays the modeled BIM with the original point cloud data and visually checks that the BIM and the point cloud are in agreement. Errors in the model appear because the point cloud will jut out from the model in an unexpected manner. Although the approach is easy to implement, it is, by nature, subjective. The inspector may overlook obvious modeling errors where the point cloud is hidden inside a BIM component.

Clash detection is sometimes used as a more objective alternative to visual inspection. Clash detection was originally designed to test whether a design model for an upgrade or modification would interfere with existing structures in a facility. If a model is constructed correctly, substantially all of the model should clash with the underlying point cloud, and nonclashing regions are potential modeling errors. Because clash detection was not designed for QA, it can be cumbersome to use for this purpose. Not only is it difficult to see nonclashing regions, but, because clash detection is usually implemented as a binary clash/nonclash decision, the method provides no information about the magnitude of the difference between the model and point cloud.

Physical inspection involves comparing measurements on the actual facility to virtual measurements of the corresponding locations on the BIM. If the measurements are conducted randomly, statistical methods can estimate the probability that the model is accurate to a specified tolerance [9]. Alternately, deterministic measurements can be used to spot check structures that are considered difficult to model. Physical inspection is attractive because it offers direct comparison between the model and the original structure. Due to the time needed to make the measurements, the method only achieves limited coverage, and critical modeling errors may be overlooked.

Finally, it is possible to detect errors by overlaying the model and point cloud and analyzing the differences between them. Because the model is intended to represent the point cloud, any significant differences between the model and the point cloud are potential modeling errors. These differences may be visualized by deviation maps computed for surfaces in the BIM [10]. In Figure 6.7, deviation regions marked "1" are windows that were not modeled at all, region 2 is an indentation

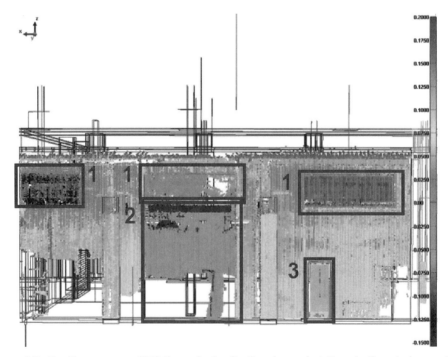

Figure 6.7 Quality assurance (QA) through visualization: large deviations in the window regions (1), at a setback (2), and a door (3) (adapted from [10]).

that was modeled at an incorrect setback, and region 3 is a door that was modeled at the wrong location. A deviation map, if "thresholded," is essentially the inverse of clash detection. The patterns in the deviation maps can be used to identify regions needing further analysis for modeling errors.

The deviation map concept is applicable to pairs of overlapping point clouds as well. In this case, the patterns can identify calibration errors or registration problems. Advantages of the deviation analysis method include providing objective measures of the differences (unlike visual inspection), offering fine-grained visualization of deviation patterns (unlike clash detection), and achieving complete coverage of a facility (unlike physical inspection). The primary limitation is the need to filter out deviations caused by clutter in the environment, which requires a QA inspector to carefully check models in cluttered regions. Although this method is not yet commonplace for as-is QA inspections, the same basic idea has been used in the inspection of manufactured parts. Several software packages for creating and analyzing 3D models already support the creation of deviation maps to a limited extent [11].

6.6   The Future of As-Is Modeling

The demand for as-is modeling is steadily rising as stakeholders develop a better understanding of the benefits of the BIM approach to AEC/FM projects. The U.S. General Services Administration (GSA), which owns and operates all federal building facilities, initiated a national 3D-4D BIM program in 2003. The GSA sought to determine whether adopting BIM practices would reduce costs and increase it ability to manage its assets effectively (Peggy Yee, interview, March 31, 2011). Initial studies were sufficiently compelling that the GSA mandated that, from 2007 onward, major projects would be required to use building information models to support spatial program validation. The GSA has conducted studies to evaluate the use of building information models for facility management, energy performance analysis, support for renovations, and historical preservation (Peggy Yee, interview, March 31, 2011). The lessons learned have been distilled into a series of BIM guides published by the GSA [12].

Other organizations are championing the use of as-is BIM as well. For example, Intel uses laser scanners and surveying methods to capture and model their wafer fabrication facilities (Jason Hosch, interview, March 23, 2011; Dale Stenning, interview, March 23, 2011). In the chip manufacturing industry, the time required to construct or upgrade a facility can have a significant impact on profitability. Intel uses building information models to assist in scheduling and synchronizing construction activities. First, an as-is model of an existing building is created, including the precise locations of the supply lines that will be connected to the equipment. In parallel, the equipment is prefabricated off-site. When the equipment is ready for installation, the measurements of the BIM ensure that the connections will match up correctly. Not only does this process save time and money in construction, but because assemblies can be manufactured off-site, it is easier to maintain the cleanliness required of a clean-room environment.

In response to the increased demand for as-is building information models, the hardware and software processes for capturing existing conditions of facilities are evolving at a rapid pace. Each new generation of laser scanners improves performance along metrics (e.g., range, accuracy, and speed), reduces the price, or a combination of both. For example, the maximum range of phase-based scanners has increased by a factor of almost 4 in the past 10 years. Meanwhile, the measurement speed has increased to nearly 1 million points per second, and the price for scanners has dropped by as much as 75% during this time. As the performance improves and the price drops, the benefits of using laser scanners for as-is modeling will increase, and the applications for which the devices are practical should become more widespread.

Other hardware devices and configurations are also making inroads in industry. Outdoor mobile scanning, which was a nearly nonexistent field 3 years ago, is experiencing significant growth. Mounted on vehicles, these sensors scan roads, bridges, tunnels, and other transportation infrastructure elements. More recently, indoor mobile scanning systems, such as the Trimble Indoor Mobile Mapping Solution, have been introduced [13]. These devices have the potential to revolutionize the indoor scanning marketplace. Laser scanners are mounted on mobile platforms that are either tele-operated or autonomously navigate throughout a facility. A 3D model is constructed as the sensor travels using a method known as simultaneous localization and mapping (SLAM), along with inertial sensors and other motion estimation methods, to localize the platform. Although the accuracy of the resulting maps is not yet high enough to replace fixed-position laser scanning for most BIM applications, the data can be collected in a fraction of the time. One can expect that improvements in the accuracy of the mobile maps may lead to these devices overtaking fixed-position laser scanners in the not-too-distant future.

Software products have been continuously improving their support for modeling as-is conditions. A few years ago, support for the large point clouds produced by laser scanners was rare, which restricted as-is modeling to a few specialized products. Since then, major CAD, BIM, and architectural modeling software programs have introduced support for point clouds, either directly or through third-party plug-ins.

Tools and techniques to automate or partially automate the as-is modeling process are now beginning to appear in commercial software products. Semiautomated pipe modeling, in particular, has experienced significant progress toward automation. One interface allows the user to select a portion of a pipe and then the software fits a cylinder to the data and attempts to follow the pipe along its axis. With another interface, the user clicks on two points on the axis of the pipe, and the software automatically determines the best fitting pipe along that axis. Fully automated approaches detect all cylindrically shaped regions in a scene and fit cylinders to those detected regions [14]. Similar techniques allow modeling of structural steel components.

Automation for architectural modeling is also improving. BIM creation software uses "snapping" capabilities to dynamically fit planar components to data as the user interactively constructs the model [15]. Modeling algorithms by ClearEdge [14] automatically detect planar patches in data. Research on more advanced automatic modeling capabilities is under way. It is possible to extract approximate floor plans from point cloud data by projecting cross sections onto the ground plane and fitting lines to the resulting 2D data [16]. A number of researchers have developed façade modeling pipelines that are capable of modeling building exteriors, including detecting and modeling windows and doors [17, 18]. Full 3D modeling of building interiors can be accomplished by reasoning about planar patches extracted from the data.

Many of these methods take advantage of context to recognize the more challenging components [19–21]. Context can be beneficial in situations where objects are difficult to identify on their own. By considering the relationship with other nearby surfaces, which may be more easily identified, these difficult components can be accurately recognized (Figure 6.8).

Two challenges facing automated modeling of interiors are the problems of clutter and occlusion. Any object in the environment that is not intended to be modeled is considered clutter, and these clutter objects frequently occlude the surfaces of interest. Not only must automated algorithms successfully differentiate clutter from the surfaces of interest, they must also be able to infer properties of the surfaces that are occluded. One approach to this problem is to explicitly reason about the causes and effects of occlusions when analyzing and modeling components [22].

If significant progress toward automation of the creation of as-is building information models can be accomplished, it will open the door for their use in applications that are currently not cost effective. For example, it may one day be commonplace for robots to roam construction sites, constantly monitoring the progress

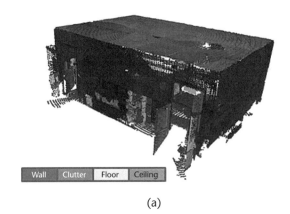

(a)

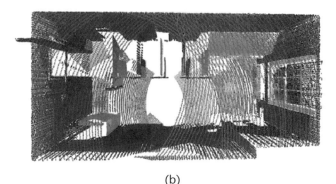

(b)

Figure 6.8 Walls, floors, ceilings, and clutter objects were automatically segmented and recognized from point cloud data.

and dynamically creating as-built models on a daily basis. Similar methods could easily and quickly document the as-is conditions of any existing building.

Methods of capturing as-is conditions of a facility provide a great resource for embedded commissioning (ECx) as well as traditional forms of commissioning (Chapter 3). While currently, most commissioning activities revolve around assessing the behavior of building systems, not knowing the forms of such systems could potentially result in misleading assessments. Laser scanners and the corresponding as-is models, as described in this chapter, provide accurate information about the geometric and spatial aspects of a facility, much needed in assessing its performance. It is expected that as the usage of laser scanning becomes more pervasive, it will be possible to capture the spatial changes occurring in a facility promptly and accurately to further support ECx.

References

[1]   Akinci, B., et al., "A Formalism for Utilization of Sensor Systems and Integrated Project Models for Active Construction Quality Control," *Automation in Construction,* Vol. 15, No. 2, February 2006, pp. 124–138.

[2]   Tang, P., Akinci, B., and Garrett, J. H., "Laser Scanning for Bridge Inspection and Management," in *Proceedings of the International Association for Bridge and Structural Engineering (IABSE) Symposium*, Weimar, Germany, 2007.

[3]   Tang, P., et al., "Automatic Reconstruction of As-built Building Information Models from Laser-Scanned Point Clouds: A Review of Related Techniques," *Automation in Construction,* Vol. 19, No. 7, November 2010, pp. 829–843.

[4]   Eastman, C., et al., *BIM Handbook: A Guide to Building Information Modeling for Owners, Managers, Designers, Engineers and Contractors*, New York: Wiley, 2008.

[5]   Anil, E., Akinci, B., and Huber, D., "Representation Requirements of As-is Building Information Models Generated from Laser Scanned Point Cloud Data," in *Proceedings of the International Symposium on Automation and Robotics in Construction (ISARC)*, Seoul, Korea, June 2011.

[6]   Cheok, G., Leigh, S., and Rukhin, A., "Calibration Experiments of a Laser Scanner," NISTIR 6922, Gaithersburg, MD: Building and Fire Research Laboratory, National Institute of Standards and Technology, September 2002.

[7]   Hebert, M., and Krotkov, E., "3-D Measurements from Imaging Laser Radars: How Good Are They?" *Image and Vision Computing,* Vol. 10, No. 3, 1992, pp. 170–178.

[8]   Tang, P., Akinci, B., and Huber, D., "Quantification of Edge Loss of Laser Scanned Data at Spatial Discontinuities," *Automation in Construction,* Vol. 18, No. 8, December 2009, pp. 1070–1083.

[9]   Cheok, G. S., Filliben, J. J., and Lytle, A. M., "Guidelines for Accepting 2D Building Plans," NISTIR-7638, Gaithersburg, MD: National Institute of Standards, 2009.

[10]   Anil, E., et al., "Assessment of Quality of As-is Building Information Models Generated from Point Clouds Using Deviation Analysis," in *Proceedings of the SPIE Vol. 7864A, Electronics Imaging Science and Technology Conference (IS&T), 3D Imaging Metrology*, San Francisco, CA, January 2011.

[11]   Polyworks, Innovmetric Software, http://www.innovmetric.com.

[12]   GSA BIM Guide Series, http://www.gsa.gov/bim.

[13]   Trimble Indoor Mobile Mapping Solution, http://www.trimble.com/Indoor-Mobile-Mapping-Solution/Indoor-Mapping.aspx.

[14]   ClearEdge 3D, Inc., http://www.clearedge3d.com.

[15]   Revit   Architecture,   Autodesk,   Inc.,   http://usa.autodesk.com/adsk/servlet/index?id=3781831&siteID=123112.

[16]   Okorn, B., et al., "Toward Automated Modeling of Floor Plans," in *Proceedings of the Symposium on 3D Data Processing, Visualization and Transmission*, Paris, France, May 2010.

[17]   Böhm, J., Becker, S., and Haala, N., "Model Refinement by Integrated Processing of Laser Scanning and Photogrammetry," in *Proceedings of 3D Virtual Reconstruction and Visualization of Complex Architectures (3D-Arch)*, Zurich, Switzerland, 2007.

[18]   Pu, S., and Vosselman, G., "Extracting Windows from Terrestrial Laser Scanning," in *ISPRS Workshop on Laser Scanning*, 2007, pp. 320–325.

[19]   Cantzler, H., Fisher, R. B., and Devy, M., "Improving Architectural 3D Reconstruction by Plane and Edge Constraining," in *Proceedings of the British Machine Vision Conference*, 2002, pp. 663–672.

[20]   Nüchter, A., and Hertzberg, J., "Towards Semantic Maps for Mobile Robots," *Journal of Robotics and Autonomous Systems*, Vol. 56, No. 11, November 2008, pp. 915–926.

[21]   Xiong, X., and Huber, D., "Using Context to Create Semantic 3D Models of Indoor Environments," in *Proceedings of the British Machine Vision Conference (BMVC)*, 2010.

[22]   Adan, A., and Huber, D., "3D Reconstruction of Interior Wall Surfaces Under Occlusion and Clutter," in *Proceedings of 3D Imaging, Modeling, Processing, Visualization and Transmission (3DIMPVT)*, Hangzhou, China, May 2011.

CHAPTER 7

Standards: IFC and STEP

Architecture-engineering-construction (AEC) information encapsulated in building product models plays a significant role in capturing the domain knowledge and supporting interoperability between various software tools in the building industry (Chapters 3 and 4).

Capturing domain knowledge is the overarching target of the AEC industry's standardization efforts. One of the earliest initiatives in this area comes from the Construction Specification Institute (CSI). CSI was established in 1948 by a group of government specification writers in order to provide quality construction information during the post–World War II construction boom [1]. CSI created *MasterFormat* to classify all construction-related information provided through a list of titles with unique identification numbers. The latest version of *MasterFormat*, developed in 2004, contains 50 divisions expanded from 16 in the earlier versions [2]. In addition to *MasterFormat*, CSI also generated *GreenFormat* and *UniFormat*. *GreenFormat* consists of a taxonomy for manufacturers to classify the sustainability properties of their products [3]. Similarly, *UniFormat* is a classification system for early capital project delivery (CPD) information such as design criteria and cost estimates [4].

After the introduction of computer applications in the AEC domain, the need for capturing domain knowledge and standardization gained a new emphasis. In comparison to manufactured goods, buildings are unique constructs with individual features, and the scale of the end product prevents the AEC domain from creating a prototype to test realistically against design requirements (Chapters 1 and 2). Consequently, because computer-aided design (CAD) tools allow quick and realistic visualization of design features, the industry became one of the early adopters of CAD tools. Once CAD tools reached a level of maturity, with Autodesk's AutoCAD and Bentley's Microstation, other CPD operations began relying on computer-based tools, particularly for procurement and delivery. Because it is elemental to have interoperability among different tools and provide data exchange at different levels of the CPD process, standardization gained more importance. The current trend in the industry reflects this need through a shift from CAD-based tools to building information model (BIM) based tools. The domain knowledge that can be captured by various data modeling and standardization initiatives is likely to justify the "I" in BIM.

As discussed earlier, BCx is crucial for providing quality and efficiency in the CPD process. In this chapter, we look at the standardization efforts in AEC through various information modeling initiatives and discuss how specific ECx-related approaches can be incorporated in these initiatives. Our focus will be on developing a better understanding of how these initiatives are organized, what the specific steps are for developing information models, and whether ECx is adequately considered. We will also evaluate existing models as a point of departure for developing a framework for representing ECx information more comprehensively than current practice allows.

Two of the major efforts in collecting and modeling building information for data exchange and interoperability are the ongoing development of the STandard for Exchange of Product Model Data (STEP) [5] and industry foundation classes (IFCs). STEP was developed by International Organization for Standardization (ISO) Technical Committee TC 184. Its reference code is ISO 10303. The IFC project was started by the International Alliance for Interoperability (IAI) [6] and is currently being developed and maintained by the buildingSMART Alliance. buildingSMART is also the developer of ifcXML, which represents AEC information in XML (eXtensible Markup Language) schemata [7]. Similar to ifcXML, AEX (Automating Equipment Information Exchange) is another standard developed by FIATECH utilizing XML technology [8]. Unlike the first three models, which target the entire AEC domain, AEX focuses only on HVAC equipment.

In addition to these models, CIS/2 (CIMSteel Integration Standards, Release 2) is another important modeling effort in the AEC domain. It is an internationally accepted standard for digital data exchange of technical, engineering information across the entire steel frameworks life cycle [9]. In the following sections we present an overview of these initiatives.

7.1   Standard for Exchange of Product Model Data (STEP)

The overall idea behind STEP is to generate a mechanism that describes a complete and unequivocal definition of a product, independent of any specific computer platform, throughout its life cycle [10–12]. This initiative was started by the ISO in 1984 and is formally known as ISO 10303. STEP is the successor to the U.S. standard IGES (Initial Graphics Exchange Specification) that, in turn, was started in 1979 by a group of CAD vendors with the support of the National Institute of Standards and Technology (NIST) and the U.S. Department of Defense (DoD) [11]. Under ISO, the group that is responsible for the development of STEP is Technical Committee (TC) 184, Sub-Committee (SC) 4.

For anyone who is involved in product design and delivery, it is important to have seamless product information flow between upstream and downstream decisions and among different stakeholders such as manufacturers, contractors, suppliers, and customers. Because different parties often use different computer systems that are specifically designed for their needs, data transfer is an essential requirement for the procurement of quality products. STEP tries to achieve standardization during these data transfers through a neutral computer-interpretable representation of industrial products.

STEP is the most ambitious effort in the product modeling area. It not only focuses on the AEC industry but also covers all CAD/CAM and product information management systems, including electronics, ship building, and process plants.

It is intended to cover industrial automation standards for all product data representation and exchange issues. STEP's approach to product modeling is modular. Instead of defining a large model with subsets of specific domain views, STEP defines various partial models, called *application protocols*, which are expected to become larger domain-specific models. The overall structure of STEP is based on five groups, which cover all phases of process modeling (Chapter 4) [13]:

1. The *description methods group* defines modeling languages, such as EXPRESS, NIAM, and IDEF1x. EXPRESS is a formal language that defines how the product data will be represented. EXPRESS is similar to the Unified Modeling Language (UML) for facilitating software implementations and providing consistency and precision in the representation of various product data.

2. The *integrated resources group* develops reusable model subsets that are used for model definitions, such as geometry and material properties.

3. The *application protocols group* focuses on specific model parts developed for particular application domains, such as ship design, electrotechnical plants, or structural frames for steel construction. STEP's scope is broad enough to cover several hundred application protocols to support many industrial products and processes.

4. The *implementations methods group* covers the methods that can be used as a source for STEP implementations. So far, the STEP Physical File (SPF) and Standard Data Access Interface (SDAI) have been implemented. STEP 21 is a widely used data exchange form of STEP. It has an ASCII structure that is easy to read and write with one instance per line. ISO 10303-21 describes the encoding mechanism of any EXPRESS schema. The file extensions are .stp or .step to show that the data in the file conforms to STEP application protocols (Figures 7.1 and 7.2).

5. *Conformance testing* group defines and generates the tests that verify whether an implementation is properly executed and in line with STEP specifications.

STEP is one of the most comprehensive product modeling approaches that involves not only capturing the knowledge but also defining the modeling language, the format of information exchange files, protocols for data exchange, and model conformance mechanisms. On the other hand, because it is a large-scale effort with limited funding, it takes longer to fully complete every feature. Some of the application protocols such as configuration controlled design, core data for automotive design processes, explicit drafting and associative drafting, the model is mature enough to be used as a data exchange alternative for a variety of transactions.

7.1.1   AP225 Building Elements Using Explicit Shape Representation (ISO 10303-225:1999)

Application protocol (AP) 225 in ISO 10303 specifically targets the standardization of the information related to building elements. AP 225 became an industry standard in 1999 [14–16]. The information that is specified in this protocol pertains to the building element "shape, property, and spatial arrangement requirements" ([5],

```
1   ISO-10303-21;
2   HEADER:
3   FILE_DESCRIPTION (('ArchiCAD generated IFC file.'), '2:1'):
4   FILE_NAME ('BC.IFC', '2003-06-02T20:26:34', ('Architect'), ('Building Designer Office'), 'PreProc - IFC Toolbox Version 2.0
5   FILE_SCHEMA (('IFC20_BC'));
6   ENDSEC;
7   DATA;
8   #1 = IFCBCEVENT('TESTAGENT', '10-01-2003', 'PHASE 1', 'POINT A');
9   #2 = IFCBCEQUIPMENT('TESTID', 'TESTTag', 'TESTLocation', (#1, #8), (#1), (#1));
10  #3 = IFCBCCENTRIFUGALFAN('TESTBCFan', 'TestTag', 'Office', (#1), (#7), ());
11  #7 = IFCBCSYSTEMCONTEXTINSPECTIONEVENT('SYSAGENT', '05-01-2003', 'PHASE 2', 'POINT B', #5);
12  #5 = IFCBCSYSTEMCONTEXTDESCRIPTION();
13
14  #8 = IFCBCEVENT('TESTAGENT', '05-01-2003', 'PHASE 1', 'POINT A');
15
16  #11 = IFCBCEVENT('AGENTB', '05-11-2003', 'PHASE 2', 'POINT B');
17  #12 = IFCBCEQUIPMENT('TESTID', 'TESTTag', 'TESTLocation', (#1, #8), (#1), (#1));
18  #13 = IFCBCCENTRIFUGALFAN('TESTBCFan', 'TestTag', 'Office', (#18), (#7), ());
19  #17 = IFCBCSYSTEMCONTEXTINSPECTIONEVENT('SYSAGENT', '01-01-2004', 'PHASE 2', 'POINT B', #5);
20  #15 = IFCBCSYSTEMCONTEXTDESCRIPTION();
21
22  #18 = IFCBCEVENT('TESTAGENT', '12-01-2004','PHASE 3','POINT C');
23
24  ENDSEC;
25  REV_DATA;
26  //#10 = IFCBCCENTRIGUGALFANCONTEXT(.T., .F., .F., .T., .T., .T.);
27  //#20 = IFCBCCENTRIGUGALFANCONTEXT(.T., .F., .F., .T., .T., .T.);
28  ENDSEC;
29  END-ISO-10303-21;
30
```

Figure 7.1   Example STEP 21 file.

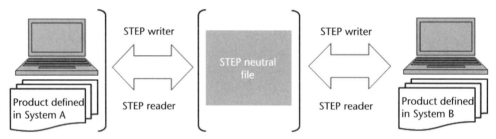

Figure 7.2   STEP 21 file exchange between two systems.

p. 68). This covers information that is related to every phase of the CPD process, including commissioning. The information requirements specified support of the following activities:

- "concurrent design processes or building design iterations
- integration of building structure with building systems designs to enable design analysis
- building design visualization
- specifications for construction and maintenance
- analysis and review to check for physical clashes of the building structural elements with piping or air conditioning elements."

From the perspective of ECx, the scope of AP 225 is broad enough to represent many of the equipment and building system evaluation processes. Table 7.1 summarizes the scope of AP225 as it is defined in the ISO STEP handbook, version 3 [10]:

Table 7.1   Scope of AP 225

Within Scope	Out of Scope
3D geometric information	2D representation
Spatial configuration	Building standards description
Structural information	Parameter-based implicit representation
Nonstructural enclosure information	Information required for structural or thermal analysis
Geometric and spatial information of building services (HVAC, etc.)	Information related to the building component assembly
Geometric and spatial information of building fixtures (furniture, etc.)	Maintenance information
Description of spaces	Any alteration information
Site information	Bill of quantities
Building component properties (material, etc.)	
Building component classification (acoustics, cost, egress, etc.)	
Building component changes	
Approval information related to building components	
As-built information	

Since the scope of AP 225 is large, subsets have been defined for robustness of the model that allow partial implementation by software developers. These subsets are defined by conformance classes. Conformance classes allow a user to know which subsets of an AP are implemented in a software application that has AP 225. So far, AP 225 includes 14 different conformance classes at three levels of geometric information.

An application protocol goes through various stages to become an ISO 10303 standard. In the preparatory stage, an approved work item (AWI) is selected and a proposal for a technical specification (AWI TS) is approved. A committee draft (CD) is created in the committee stage and it becomes a draft technical report (DTR) through amendment and corrigendum. During the enquiry stage, a final proposed draft international standardized profile (FPDISP) is developed and it goes to the approval stage. Once the final draft international standard (FDIS) has been approved, it becomes an international standard and labeled an ISO, during the publication stage.

7.2   Industry Foundation Classes (IFC)

The IFC is an object-based building data modeling standard that was started by IAI, an international assembly of industry members and researchers founded in 1995 [15–17]. The group later reorganized itself as the buildingSMART initiative under the National Institute of Building Services (NIBS) [18]. NIBS is a nonprofit, nongovernmental organization where representatives of government, industry, and regulatory agencies come together for the identification and resolution of problems for the delivery of safe, affordable buildings throughout the United States. NIBS collaborated with the American Institute of Architects (AIA) and the Construction Specifications Institute (CSI) for the development of the U.S. national CAD standards (NCS) [19]. The fourth version of NCS was released in 2008. The scope of NCS includes CAD layer guidelines and uniform drawing system and plotting guidelines. NIBS is aiming to generate a similar standard for BIM through the build-ingSMART initiative. The first version of the U.S. national BIM standards was re-leased in 2007 and gives an overview of the principles and methods of the initiative [18].

The IFC approach supports interoperability between discipline-specific ap-plications that are used during the CPD process. Its focus is to capture all data pertaining to any building feature or infrastructure system from early conception to decommissioning. IFC exclusively aims at providing information exchange be-tween model-based tools in the construction and facility management industries. This effort is supported by major BIM-based software developers

IAI made its first IFC model public in 1997. This version was updated and grew in size via regular releases of new versions. IFC 2x4 release candidate was announced in 2010 as the 13th version of the model. Although IFC is an industry standard, it is closely tied to STEP open standard AP 225. EXPRESS is used as a modeling language in IFC; and STEP 21 is used as the file format for information exchange. Whereas AP 225 is mostly limited by the geometric information of the building elements, IFC targets all building-related information during each phase.

7.2.1   IFC Development Process

The development of a new release of IFC contains nine steps [20]:

1. *Definition of user requirements:* This step selects one or more industry processes that are going to be modeled. It is important to be able to break down these processes into manageable parts that can be modeled within the time frame of scheduled IFC releases. Every task in the selected process is described in detail using wording familiar to professionals.

2. *Definition of domain processes:* This step creates a process model that shows the sequence of tasks defined in step 1 in order to complete an indus-trial process. This process model is used as the basis of defining the object model scope. IDEF0 is used as the modeling language.

3. *Test by usage scenarios:* This step puts the textual description within the scope of the CPD process. It gives assertions, defines relationships, and identifies numerical constraints that are used during modeling.

4. *Specification of domain model:* This step is carried out in two stages: (1) forming a set of assertions about task descriptions, process models, and usage scenarios; and (2) creating a formal data model for all classes and relationships handled by the processes. A set of assertions defines a usage scenario through simple sentences that can be used for identifying classes, relationships, cardinality of relationships, direction of relationships, attri-butes, and rules. Next, these assertions are turned into a formal model us-ing the EXPRESS modeling language. In this step, responsibility for version development passes from the domain team to the technical team.

5. *Integration into current release of IFC:* This step synthesizes newly created elements with the existing model. Developers need to identify entities that are already included in the IFC model, entities that are common between

domains, entities that are similar between domains (to see if it is possible to create common entities), and truly new entities.

6. *Review of new release of IFC*: In this step, IFC developments are reviewed by industry experts, information modelers, and software developers. Critical issues raised are stored in the IFC Issue Resolution Database. The IFC Specification Task Force decides to accept or reject these issues.

7. *Final documentation*: This step publishes the final IFC release through a series of documents like the *IFC End User Guide* or *IFC Object Model Architecture Guide*.

8, 9. The *conformance class definition* and *implementation support* steps are specifically targeted for software developers. In these steps implementation-related problems are addressed.

7.2.2 IFC Model Architecture

In IFC, building components are represented as entities. Each entity has a variety of attributes that are used to store the information specific to the instances of that entity such as location, color, dimensions, and material. Physical building elements like doors, windows, and columns, alongside abstract concepts like spaces, activities, schedules, and costs, are represented in the model. The final version of an IFC model can include 759 entities on equal number of building components or concepts [21].

To identify properties of entities, IFC uses a hierarchical entity structure. Each entity is represented by a class. For instance, the IfcWall class is defined as a subtype of the IfcBuildingElement class. Similarly, IfcBuildingElement is a subtype of IfcElement class. IfcElement's super-type is IfcProduct class and its super-type is IfcObject. At the last level, the super-type of the Object entity that is the Root Entity (IfcRoot) resides. Root Entity is the parent of all entities and it is at the top of the entity hierarchy. In this order, attributes are associated with each type of entity, and the entity inherits the attributes of all of its parent entities. For example some of the properties of the Wall Entity, such as location, ID, and material, are common to all building entities. So they can be defined by the parent entity (IfcElement) and inherited by all child entities [22].

In IFC, it is also possible to represent relationships between different entity types. For example, the IfcRelAggregates class is defined to represent the aggregation relationship. With this entity we can bring all structural elements such as columns and beams together to create a building's structural frame. Similarly, we can use the IfcRelSequence entity to define the progressions through the predecessor and successor relationships between tasks of a construction schedule. Specific relationship descriptions are one of the strengths of IFC since they help to build reasoning mechanisms. For example, when the height of a window is changed in a model, the associated windows, walls, and mullions will be modified as well.

IFC's main architecture is designed in four layers: *resource, core, interoperability,* and *domain* (Figure 7.3). These layers represent levels in the hierarchical model structure that we described earlier, in the IfcWall example. Each level has diverse categories that are composed of individual entities. If we look at the wall example again, we see that the IfcWall class is in the shared building elements category, and

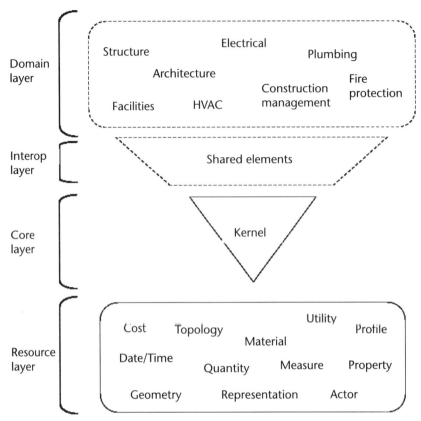

Figure 7.3 IFC model architecture.

the shared building elements category is in the interoperability layer. Layers also allow the model to have an association hierarchy between different groups of entities. For example, an entity in the interoperability layer can only be related to the entities in the same or lower level. Having multiple categories at every layer leads to a modular architecture, which in turn makes the growth of the model possible. Modularity also creates a clear distinction between the entities of different AEC disciplines and enables easy maintenance of the model.

Now, let us consider brief descriptions of these layers starting with the lowest:

- *Resource layer:* This layer contains entity categories that function as resources for defining entities in the upper layers. These are generic properties that are not specific to buildings but used for defining entity attributes, such as geometry, material, and cost. Several resource definitions are based on STEP descriptions.

- *Core layer:* This layer gives the most abstract definitions in the model. All of the entities in the interoperability and domain layers extend from the conceptual descriptions in this layer. The three main categories in this class are kernel, product extension, and process extension.

- *Interoperability layer:* Entity categories in this layer are the building components and properties that are shared between multiple AEC applications. Most of the common building entities would be defined in this layer. These include wall, beam, furniture type, occupant, flow controller, and sound properties.

- *Domain layer:* At this layer, the entities have the most detailed representation. The domain layer is at the top of the model architecture and the categories are defined as specific domains such as HVAC, electrical, and construction management. This is the highest level of the IFC model. It represents the entity definitions that are specific to individual domains like HVAC, electrical, architecture, construction management, and facilities management.

7.2.3   ifcXML

IFC-XML is an XML format defined by ISO 10303-28 ("STEP-XML"), part 28. The latest version, ifcXML2x3, was released in 2007 to support IFC 2x3 [23]. ifcXML is an effort to establish rules and policies for managing and developing XML schemata that are going to be used as industry standards for e-commerce or AEC web applications. In these applications, software interoperability is primarily based on the format of the messages exchanged among software tools. Messages contain tagged data in standard XML technology. XML schemata are used to validate these files according to a previously defined data format that is agreed on by industry members. Instead of exchanging geometric object descriptions between systems, ifcXML is designed to support business-to-business transactions. The goal is to create a well-defined business process on the Internet by bringing users, producers, and consumers together for the benefit of a common data format, enabling information flow during different phases of the CPD process. Due to IFC's comprehensive structure, ifcXML has a larger file size. If a project's complete information is saved in ifcXML, the file size will be at least doubled. ifcXML is beneficial for encapsulating only a portion of a project, which allows it to reach a broader community of applications for the built environment and related resources [24].

7.3   Automating Information Exchange (AEX) Project

Although not directly related to the building delivery process, we will briefly consider AEX as an industry standard development effort for engineered equipment. The AEX project is developed by Fully Integrated and Automated Technology (FIATECH) [25]. FIATECH is a nonprofit research organization with members from academia, industry, and government agencies. To provide economic benefit to the industry, this project defines and standardizes the information exchange specifications for the engineered equipment life cycle, including design, delivery, operation, and maintenance. FIATECH defines AEX as being complementary to STEP, ISO 15926 (Industrial automation systems and integration—integration of life-cycle data for process plants including oil and gas production facilities) and IFC.

FIATECH is aware of the interoperability problem that exists in the current capital facility industry, where large amounts of information accumulate during the programming, design, construction, operation, and maintenance phases of capital projects. Most of this information is in the digital domain, and produced and used by incompatible software systems. AEX addresses this problem by defining a common protocol that is accepted by all stakeholders.

Similar to the ifcXML, Extensible Markup Language (XML) is used for developing Capital Facilities Industry Extensible Markup Language (cfiXML) schema. The first phase of the project is completed by delivering XML specifications for centrifugal pumps and shell and tube heat exchangers. In the third edition, which was released in 2009, this work is extended to support additional types of equipment and pilot implementations that are developed by participating software and equipment suppliers.

7.3.1   cfiXML Schema Development Process

In an AEX project, 20 information transactions are defined in the in the life cycle of engineered equipment [26]. From the point of view of economic benefits, five of these transactions are identified as having high importance: *request for quote, quote, purchase order, as-built,* and *bill of materials.* The main criteria in the selection process is the usage context that cuts across organizational boundaries between owner, engineer, and supplier. Centrifugal pumps and shell and tube exchangers were selected as initial equipment types based on the interest expressed by AEX sponsors.

After defining transaction scenarios, FIATECH conducted a survey on what type of processes and software tools generate and use equipment information over the CPD process. In this survey, two key document types that are used to transmit information between software packages were identified: equipment datasheet and equipment list or bill of materials. Two software information flow diagrams have been prepared to show the selected types of software and engineering information transmittal communication documents.

7.3.2   cfiXML Schema Structure

XML schema provide the rules for the structure and content of an XML document. Development of cfiXML schemata is based on defining equipment type properties and validating the information in XML files. Overall, XML schemata are effective in formulating complex groups of data with rich information content. Although engineering information is suitable for object-oriented data modeling, defining equipment types and physical properties of materials has an inherently complex structure. Accordingly, cfiXML schemata are object-oriented representations of engineering information through different XML namespaces, and schema files on a variety of topics. This schema structure is organized into four basic types [27]:

- *Core data type:* Schema to define additions to basic data types to cover all engineering information for an equipment type;
- *Core engineering object:* Schema to define common engineering information that is used in more than one engineering domain;
- *Subject engineering object:* Schema to define individual equipment information;
- *Collection container:* Schema to define data exchange documents.

7.4   CIS/2 and the CIMsteel Integration Standards

CIS/2 is the information standard in the construction steel domain. The initial work for this standard started as AP 230, a STEP application protocol. But later AP 230 was instigated and the industry used it as a base for the development of CIMsteel. CIMsteel began in 1987 as a collaborative European research endeavor [28, 29, 31]. Since 1998, it has operated under the Eureka framework. The project focuses on building-type steel-framed structures in order "to improve the efficiency and effectiveness of the European Construction Steelwork industry both through harmonization of design codes and specifications, and through the introduction of Computer Integrated Manufacturing techniques for design, analysis, detailing, scheduling, fabrication, erection and management functions" [31].

CIMsteel's purpose is to build an integrated work pattern in the steel industry by utilizing information technology. By making use of the digital environment, they create internationally accepted standards for technical data exchange. CIMsteel integration standards (CISs) are the output of this approach, which provides flexibility for sharing engineering information across the steel framework design and delivery life cycle. CISs are a set of data exchange standards for structural steel frame specifications. Engineering software application vendors use these standards for implementing data exchange. According to a proposed scenario, engineering information can be exported in a logical and standardized data exchange file format that conforms to Part 21 of STEP. CIMsteel Standards act in accordance with STEP technology.

7.4.1   CIMsteel Development Process

CIMsteel integration standards are supported by the Logical Product Model (LPM). The product data used in LPM covers engineering information for a specific steel framework, generated in the design phase. Similar to other models defined earlier, LPM is built with entities, attributes representing the characteristics of these entities, and associations between entities. [36, 37] Information is transferred in the form of data exchange files between CIS-compatible applications and, thus, between the project participants. In addition to this, LPM is divided into smaller implementable subgroups that are referred to as Data Exchange Protocols (DEPs). DEPs allow CIS to have a modular structure based on the domain, defining what types of data should be exchanged [31]. The protocols include analysis, member design, connection design, and detailing. Each DEP addresses a particular type of information transfer. For example, DEP1 deals with structural analysis–related data, whereas DEP4 covers structural steelwork detailing. The LPM is used to define the relationship between all four protocols, such as retaining the integrity of a single beam that is subdivided into parts for analysis purposes.

7.4.2   CIS/2

CIS/2 was started in 1999. CIS/2 is an expanded version of CIMsteel and it covers the structural steel fabrication aspects that are left out of the CIMsteel LPM. Similar to IFC, CIS/2 is closely associated with STEP and it adopts some of the integrated resource libraries, such as Fundamentals of Product Description and Support, Parts 42, 43 and 45. The main product model of CIS/2 has been formally developed using the EXPRESS language [32].

7.5 Analysis of the Presented State of the Art

In this chapter we looked at some of the major standardization efforts in the AEC domain for interoperability. We started with STEP, which has initiated product modeling ventures in a variety of areas and provided essential modeling tools and techniques. Then, we covered IFC and ifcXML, which are ongoing efforts maintained by buildingSMART and form the backbone of BIM-based tools in the industry. We also looked at AEX and CIS/2 as two other standardization schemes that specifically target individual domains. This list can be extended considerably by adding other data standards that are in the process of development, such as Building and Construction XML (bcXML), Green Building XML (gbXML), Open Building Information Xchange (oBIX), and Construction Operations Building Information Exchange (COBIE). These standards are still in the early phases of industry approval and acceptance.

A number of these AEC information standardization attempts confirm that there is a clear need and room for improvement in this area that will surely advance the CPD process. On the other hand, there are also risks in having many standards, which can lead to conflicting requirements and defeat the purpose of standardization. They can also create confusion in making advances for data exchange and interoperability. From the software development perspective, in order to have fully interoperable tools, a single, universally approved standard is needed. But the challenges in AEC information standardization are that data is intrinsically complex, and the capital facility development process is ill defined. Based on the analysis of the models we reviewed, we can assert the following:

An object-oriented approach is utilized in all models to represent the building-related information. Building elements are defined as entities or classes, and their properties become the attributes in these classes. Expandability of the standard for future additions is one of the most critical topics and we observe this in all models with multiple versions. To address this issue, all models have a modular structure where the data representation is divided into smaller subsets. The scope of these models is one of the most important determinants of how many versions a model will have. The organization of the data is mostly hierarchical where general and domain specific data are separated. The information that is used by other entities is separated into resource levels and linked to other units.

During the model development process, IFC, AEX, and CIMSteel follow a process-oriented method. They first define the industry process from which the domain information is going to be extracted. None of these models specifically focuses on building evaluation or ECx processes. But they are all capable of modeling HVAC-related data and can be used to carry and transfer partial HVAC information.

References

[1]   Construction Specification Institute, http://www.csinet.org/, last accessed April 2011.

[2]   MasterFormat, http://www.csinet.org/masterformat, last accessed April 2011.

[3]   GreenFormat, http://www.csinet.org/greenformat, last accessed April 2011.

[4]   UniFormat, http://www.csinet.org/uniformat, last accessed April 2011.

[5]   *STEP Application Handbook*, ISO 10303, Version 3, North Charleston, SC: SCRA, 2006.

[6]   IAI International Alliance for Interoperability, http://www.iai-tech.org, last accessed April 2011.

[7]   IAI International Alliance for Interoperability, http://www.iai-tech.org, last accessed April 2011.

[8]   FIATECH Consortium, http://www.fiatech.org, last accessed April 2011.

[9]   CIS/2 CIMSteel Integration Standards, Release 2, http://www.cis2.org, last accessed April 2011.

[10]   *STEP Application Handbook*, ISO 10303, Version 3, North Charleston, SC: SCRA, 2006.

[11]   Pratt, M. J., "Introduction to ISO 10303—STEP Standard for Product Data Exchange," *Transactions of the ASME*, Vol. 1, March 2001, pp. 102–103.

[12]   Patil, L., Dutta, D., and Sriram, R., "Ontology-Based Exchange of Product Data Semantics," *IEEE Transactions on Automation Science and Engineering*, Vol. 2, No. 3, July 2005, pp. 213–225. doi: 10.1109/TASE.2005.849087.

[13]   Eastman, C. M., *Building Product Models: Computer Environments Supporting Design and Construction*, Boca Raton, FL: CRC Press, 1999.

[14]   STEP Tools AP 225: Building Elements, http://www.steptools.com/support/stdev_docs/express/ap225/, last accessed April 2011.

[15]   Froese, T. M., "Industry Foundation Class Modeling for Estimating and Scheduling," in *Durability of Building Materials and Components 8*, M. A. Lacasse and D. J. Vanier (Eds.), Ottawa: Institute for Research in Construction, 1999, pp. 2825–2835.

[16]   Yu, K., Froese, T., and Grobler, F., "International Alliance For Interoperability: IFCs," in *Computing in Civil Engineering: Proceedings of the International Computing Congress*, Boston, MA, 1998, ASCE, pp. 395–406.

[17]   Froese, T., Grobler, F., and Yu, K., "Development of Data Standards for Construction—An IAI Perspective," in *The Life-Cycle of Construction IT Innovations-Technology Transfer from research to practice, Proceedings of the W78 Conference*, B.-C. Björk and A. Jägbeck (Eds.), Stockholm, Sweden, June 3–5, 1998, KTH, pp. 233–244.

[18]   Building Smart Alliance, http://www.buildingsmartalliance.org, last accessed April 2011.

[19]   National CAD Standards, www.buildingsmartalliance.org/ncs, last accessed April 2011.

[20]   Liebich, T., and Wix, J., "Highlights of the Development Process of Industry Foundation Classes," in *Durability of Building Materials and Components 8*, M. A. Lacasse and D. J. Vanier (Eds.), Ottawa: Institute for Research in Construction, 1999, pp. 2758–2775.

[21]   IFC Specification, http://buildingsmart-tech.org/specifications/ifc_specification, last accessed April 2011.

[22]   Khemlani, L. "A Look Under the Hood," AECBytes Feature, http://www.aecbytes.com/feature/2004/IFCmodel.html, last accessed April 2011.

[23]   ifcXML, http://buildingsmart-tech.org/downloads/ifcxml, last accessed April 2011.

[24]   Nisbet, N., and Liebich, T., "ifcXML Implementation Guide," International Alliance for Interoperability Modeling Support Group, Version 2.0, June 2007.

[25]   FIATECH Consortium, http://www.fiatech.org, last accessed April 2011.

[26]   Teague, T. L., Palmer, M. E., and Jacson, R. H. F., "XML for Capital Facilities," *Journal of Leadership and Management in Engineering*, Vol. 3, No. 2, April 2003, pp. 82–85.

[27]   AEX Automated Equipment Information Exchange, http://fiatech.org/aex.html, last accessed April 2011.

[28]   Crowley, A. J., and Watson, A. S., "CIMsteel Integration Standards," Release 2, Vols. 1–6, Ascot, UK: Steel Construction Institute, 2000.

[29]   Reed, K. A., "The Role of the CIMSteel Integration Standards in Automating the Erection and Surveying of Structural Steelwork," *Proceedings of ISARC,* September 2002.

[30]   Lipman, R. R., "Mapping Between the CIMSteel Integration Standards and Industry Foundation Classes Product Models for Structural Steel," presented at International Conference on Computing in Civil and Building Engineering, Montreal, Canada, June 14–16, 2006.

[31]   CIS/2 CIMSteel Integration Standards, Release 2, http://www.cis2.org, last accessed April 2011.

[32]   CIMsteel Project website, http://www.engineering.leeds.ac.uk/civil/research/cae/past/cimsteel/cimsteel.htm, last accessed April 2011.

CHAPTER 8

Mapping Between Process Product Models: Challenges and Opportunities

In Chapter 3, we described a set of motivations and practices applicable to the area of building commissioning (BCx). The leading challenges we identified were standardization, interoperability, and process and product modeling. In Chapter 4, we described the need for process and product models used in BCx and how to codify these models in computable form. In Chapters 5 and 6, we described BIM as a repository of as-designed and as-built data, respectively. In Chapter 7, we introduced data representation standards for diverse AEC practices and international standardization efforts like STEP-IFC [1]. In Chapter 9, we will introduce standard protocols, such as BACnet [2], that enable accurate and efficient data accessibility in distributed data networks. And in Chapter 10 we will deal with the challenges of automatic code compliance checking using BIM. This sets the stage for addressing data mapping between process and product models (PPM), an emerging technology in AEC fields, including diverse applications like structural design, prefabrication, and BCx. In this chapter, we cover these emerging novel technologies. This is essential for fostering greater domain functionality for BCx, while assisting with standardization and interoperability for a variety of capital project delivery (CPD) applications.

8.1 Derivation of Product Models from Process Models

Formal or digital modeling of data in the AEC sector is both essential for improved CPD and unavoidable in the heightened information technology context of AEC participants (Section 3.2). Efforts to standardize data and make information available across proprietary software applications have led to a plethora of tools and research programs that deal with product and process models, sometimes separately and at other times in tandem (Section 3.2.1).

When clients buy a product, the process that leads up to the finished product, as ephemeral as it is, determines the quality, budget, and schedule of the product. Thus, modeling both the process and the product data must be done in tandem (Chapter 5). Concurrent engineering practices at Sony and Honda also confirm that product delivery models need to control the "triad comprising product, process and [design]," in order to ensure deployment of feedback to designers about the capabilities and features that will best serve product delivery (Figure 8.1).

Major performance improvements in quality, schedule, and cost of CPD require the seamless bridging of process and product models, an emerging area in AEC research.

As in most manufacturing industries and the AEC sector, the BCx product delivery process is complex [3]. Initially, a design or partial design emerges from customer requirements. Typically, ready-made or custom-designed component providers that are geographically, chronologically, and technologically distributed are involved. This can cause considerable schedule, budgetary, and design quality compromises (Section 3.2.4).

The discontinuity between requirement specification and design is the basis for making a similar case for computationally supported interoperability models of processes and products in the AEC domain [4, 5]. By formal modeling of design specifications and linking of them to PPM-based design approaches, broadly used standards like IFC (Chapter 7) can be applied to processes that improve quality in CPD [4]. IFC classes can be used to fully integrate AEC data and processes so that critical data formats like design, budget, and timetable can be bidirectionally linked. Adapters between several applications, such as *Architectural Desktop*, *Microsoft Project*, and *Timberline Precision*, have been developed to demonstrate this point-to-point mapping of data (Chapter 5) [6].

Evidence in the literature indicates that, due to frequent changes observed in the BCx process, product models required in these processes are difficult to standardize. To enhance quality and management practices in buildings, studies have been carried out to define the relationship between process and product models [7–11]. During design and process planning stages, Feng and Song [12] observed inadequate information integration and interoperability. With the goal of integrating design and manufacturing engineering in conceptual design, they developed activity and object models.

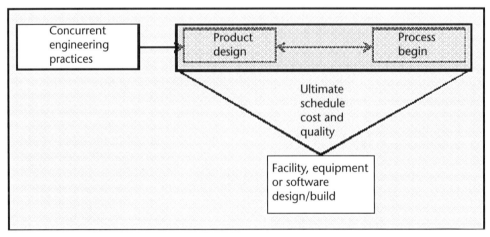

Figure 8.1 Ultimate cost and quality [3].

8.2   Three PPM Mapping Application Domains

Against this background of research accomplishments and challenges yet to be overcome, we consider sustained work in three PPM mapping efforts in three specific AEC domains: steel, precast, and ECx, respectively.

8.2.1   PPM Mapping in the Steel Construction Domain

One of the early applications of data standardization in the PPM area has been in the steel industry. In demonstrating the effectiveness of PPM integration, concurrent engineering (CE) has been used to develop a comprehensive approach to the domain of steelwork. Based on a detailed analysis of the *waterfall* model of the design process, the following steps have been identified: "inception and project definition; outline design; structural engineering and analysis, construction specifications; cost management; procurement and supply; fabrication, assembly and erection; and facility management (FM)" [11]. Opportunities for CE between these stages have been explored through a computer-based application (ProMICE). This tool was also instrumental in demonstrating interoperability between the construction industries in Britain and France [11].

As opposed to traditional approaches, modeling needs of CE can also be addressed through the use of IFC standards and Uniform Modeling Language (UML) methods (Section 3.2.2). In particular, IFC provides a core that accepts model extensions for process-based applications and their subdomains. The IAI ST-4 project, one such extension, integrates the structural analysis models with structural information management processes [13]. Use cases, a UML method, and application scenarios for each exchange process, exchange view, and application type have been developed. Different roles involving the structural design, design checking, and detail design are specified through these scenarios, as well as data exchanges between architects and building operations managers [13].

One of the latest developments in PPM mapping for the steel design construction domain is that of CIS/2 (CIMsteel Integration Standard, Release 2). This is a widely accepted product model used for data exchange and productivity improvements [14, 15]. Functionalities of CIS/2 include project definition (geographical location, buildings, zoning, contracts), design (structural members, member types, stairs-ramps-floors), analysis (elastic, dynamic, solid modeling, dynamic loading, spherical coordinates), detailing (parts, features, joints), and data management (data sharing, version control). The broad scope of CIS/2 has enabled mapping between PPM data in project delivery through a variety of translator bridging applications and data types [14]. One of these, the PMR-based translator enables interactions between process and product models.

8.2.2   PPM Mapping in the Precast Construction Domain

In the precast industry, based on IFC standards, data exchange models are used to facilitate interaction between architects, mechanical engineers, and precast system designers [16]. To exchange information between different design consultants, IMPACT was developed to integrate the Swedish construction industry's classification system (BSAB, Byggandets Samordning AB) with IFC standards. Cost estimation and scheduling programs have been incorporated through this exchange.

In the United States, based on process-model-derived data in the precast concrete industry, Lee [17] developed methods for deriving product models from process requirements. This work established the logic and the procedures for supporting a formal method for derivation and normalization of product model data. Working with 14 precast producers in North America, Lee analyzed the processes and information flow for precast concrete design and fabrication. The method that emerged, GT-PPM (Georgia Tech Process to Product Modeling), consists of two modules: Requirements Collection and Modeling (RCM) and Logical Product Modeling (LPM) [17, 18].

RCM begins with multiple process models that represent diverse use-case-based information. Using a context-free-grammar (CFG) originally introduced by Chomsky [19], researchers defined semantic mechanisms, like information constructs (IC), that are formally defined information items representing domain semantics. The LPM process incorporates five steps: (1) union information constructs, (2) decompose information constructs into entities, (3) detect and merge semantically equivalent entities, (4) detect and merge semantically equivalent attributes, and (5) resolve conflicts between attributes of a super-type and its inherited attributes. As a result, specified information items are collected, integrated, normalized, and refined into a formal product model, all semiautomatically [20].

Strengths of the GT-PPM concept (Figure 8.2) include the specification of information needed in a process by domain experts and the availability of a logical and dynamic consistency checking. Through this technique, *nym* (synonym or homonym) issues are detected and product model ambiguities are resolved. Because the data model is defined in EXPRESS, GT-PPM is able to read it as an information menu.

Utilizing a linguistic approach through CFG, GT-PPM defines precast concrete product information through syntactic rules. Instead of relying on the Backus Naur form (BNF), a context-free grammar notation [21], bracket notation is used to express constituent tree structures. Figure 8.3 shows an example that describes the data "when a beam was cast." It is based on syntactic rules used in precast concrete manufacturing (e.g., IC[P[DP[building]]M[MA[name]]]).

8.2.3 PPM Mapping in the Building Commissioning Domain

Although many standardization and interoperability problems are addressed by AEC industry-wide specifications, such as IFC and aecXML, effective mapping between process and product models in the BCx field continues to be a challenge. One reason for this is the need for nongraphic building information in ECx, as opposed to the preponderance of geometric information modeled by most standards. Another problem is the frequent changes in BCx practices that make it difficult to develop common standards.

In spite of this, efforts to develop standards for the entire BCx domain persist. Türkaslan-Bulbul [22] developed a product model for computational support. She attempted to include the broadest scope of data representation by starting with the ASHRAE Commissioning Guideline 0-2005 [23] and then adding to this data harvested from a diverse set of other repositories (Chapter 4). This is the motivation

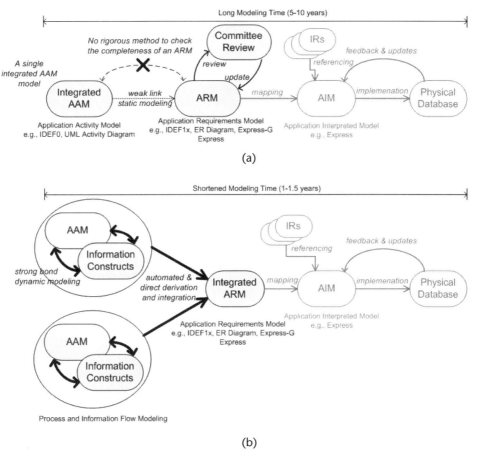

Figure 8.2   (a) Traditional and (b) proposed product data modeling in GT-PPM. (Reprinted from with permission from Elsevier [20].)

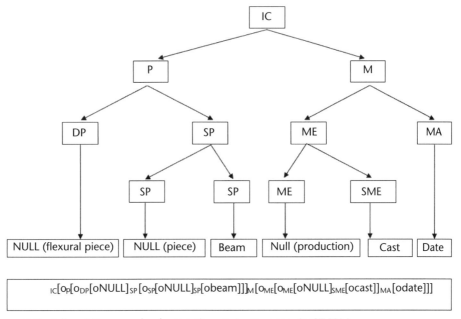

Figure 8.3   A linguistic example of a constituent structure tree in GT-PPM.

for the embedded commissioning (ECx) approach intended to *embed* comprehensive product data in the building life-cycle process to sustain interoperability.

To complement this work, Wang et al. [24] developed a domain-specific, semi-automated model matching method to support data exchange in ECx (Figure 8.4). The Version Matching Approach (VMA) automatically detects version-based differences between standards, say, between IFC 2.0 and IFC 2x. Once identified, the differences can be used to update given data sets into the desired format.

A central problem with this approach is the amount of effort and time required to develop representations that are functionally "complete." To ensure correctness, modeling of this kind is done by domain experts and requires an iterative review process. Nominally, this takes 5 to 10 years of development time [20]. Even then, the next application that comes along is likely to have entities that are not covered by the current standard model [22].

In ECx, processes are formally described using BNF notation to convert natural language prefunctional checklist (PFC) and functional performance test (FPT) protocols into computable code. Thus, as-needed product models can be derived from given process descriptions, thereby eliminating the difficulties of developing singular universal product models, and saving time and avoiding human error. The PPM mapping application developed in the ECx project (ECx-PPM) [25] aims to:

- Define and identify standard ECx product modeling requirements and data types.
- Develop strategies to streamline ECx data modeling and mapping between PPM.
- Develop and test these strategies through a proof of concept prototype implementation.

The ECx-PPM's system architecture (Figure 8.5) combines several existing technologies (Schema Matcher, Schema Parser, Schema) with several new applications (ECx Output Manager, BCx Report, User Input Manager, FPT parser, ECX-PPM,

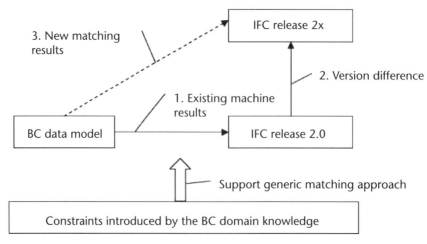

Figure 8.4 Overall data model matching process (Reprinted from with permission from Springer [24]).

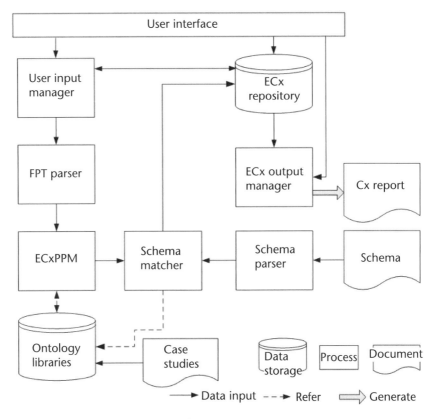

Figure 8.5   General system architecture of ECx-PPM.

Ontology Libraries) designed to create an interactive computational environment for developing product models from process descriptions.

8.3   A Generalized Framework for PPM Mapping

In spite of the recent research efforts in the steel, precast, and BCx fields that convincingly demonstrate advances in PPM mapping (Section 8.2), a proper parsing of the generic issues and challenges in this area has not been developed. PPM mapping needs to address several problems that can be organized along two axes: representation (Table 8.1, top row) and process types (Table 8.1, left column) [11, 15, 17, 18].

PPM specifications are intended to conform to central, shared standards like IFC. From the standpoint of coverage, PPM mapping is like a search engine matching string values against indexed values. Accuracy problems are related to interoperability between proprietary representations of digital applications (vertical) and CPD phases (horizontal). Owing to customized representations prevalent in the proprietary realm, mapping between them require the use of formal syntactic languages like CFG. Fidelity problems are related to ontological consistency maintenance across role, type, and cardinal representation.

Three technologies are critical in making this mapping between PPM possible: natural language processing, building ontology applications, and just-in-time accessibility. For this, a complete process and product ontology library is needed. In

Table 8.1 Challenges in Mapping between Process and Product Model

M-PPM Problems	Coverage Standardization – shared process and product representations	Accuracy Interoperability – vertical and horizontal information transfer across representations	Fidelity Ontology–role, type, and cardinality maintenance across representations
Process specification	Central, shared (IFC, etc.)	Local and proprietary	Ontology input
Mapping between PPM	Index matching	Structural, linguistic (BNF, etc.)	Ontology matching
Product specification	Central, shared (IFC, etc.)	Local and just-in-time	Ontology output

each of the PPM mapping approaches we reviewed above, all three of these components and their relationships are present. Now, let us consider them individually.

8.3.1 Natural Language Processing

Process descriptions that are needed to derive product models in the precast concrete, steel fabrication, or BCx sectors are obtained from industry-wide protocols, owner project requirements, and system manuals. These are natural language documents from which information can be automatically extracted. There are three primary computational linguistics approaches that can be used to extract meaningful semantic and syntactic information from descriptive building information: Treebank, PTB, and CFG.

The Treebank approach is applied in string data prevalent domains like training parsers for newspapers, journals, novels, and technical manuals. To achieve correct parsing, each sentence is annotated with semantic and syntactic tags enabling automatic interpretation and sorting. Terminal nodes are tagged with grammatical categories such as noun, verb, and adjective. Nonterminal nodes in a tree are represented by parts-of-speech tags like NP (noun phrase) and VP (verb phrase).

The Penn Treebank (PTB) approach developed by the University of Pennsylvania is the most widely used Treebank application [26]. Penn Treebank II uses additional tags, such as nouns being further categorized as NN (noun, singular or mass), NNS (noun, plural), NNP (proper noun, singular), and NNPS (proper noun, plural). Stanford Language Process Group's Part-Of-Speech (POS) Tagger also uses PTB. The POS Tagger is able to "read" and parse text input in natural language format and output the text in categories representing common forms of speech like verb, noun, adverb, article, adjective, and pronoun.

Chomsky [19] proposed the CFG notation as a model for describing natural languages, which is used in the GT-PPM project (Figure 8.3). CFG notation creates a formal hierarchy of left-hand/right-hand rules that can nest arbitrarily deep layers of "clauses" within one another. Thus complex syntaxes consisting of clauses made up of "primitive" symbols can be constructed. These syntaxes, often represented in BNF notation, can be used to define well-formed language domains.

8.3.2 Ontology Building in the AEC Industry

An ontology is a "formal explicit specification of a shared conceptualization" of domain knowledge [27]. By assembling information into concept hierarchies, axioms, and semantic relationships, ontology applications enable processes that categorize domain knowledge items into unambiguously interrelated concepts [28]. "Core themes" that are connected to information processing, communication, and shared constructs reside at top levels of ontology applications, whereas "support themes" reside in the lower levels [29].

Ontology applications can help define and retrieve the data type/relationship automatically from the process descriptions. Through this functionality they support semantic agreement and facilitate interoperability in a given domain-specific area. They support shared understanding between humans and software applications by reusing formally represented knowledge [15].

The AEC and FM industries have studied the sharing and communicating of information in formal ways. Among all others, the engineering and construction domain has expended the most effort in this direction. Due to the distributed and virtual work environments that are becoming commonplace, it is of greater importance, today, more than any other time, to represent data with ontological accuracy [30]. To date, ontology-based approaches have been applied principally to the integration of geometric component models in 3D space [31].

While elements from disparate representations may have common attributes, human interaction is still required to disambiguate semantic ambiguities. In terms of power versus generality trade-offs, there are benefits to domain-specific versus shared ontology applications. To create shared as well as domain-specific ontology applications, specialized languages like Knowledge Interchange Format (KIF) are needed [32]. KIF is a feature-based application derived from detailed analyses of domain software.

Development of ontology-like resources for the construction sector is more active in Europe than in the United States. The eConstruct project developed the taxonomy bcBuildingDefinitions in order to demonstrate the power of bcXML. The LexiCon, initiated by researchers working on this subject in The Netherlands, offers a vocabulary for the construction industry. There are additional vocabulary resources in the building and construction industries such as BARbi (Norway, reference data library) and the Standard Dictionary for Construction (French, vocabulary) [33]. E-COGNOS, a project that establishes and deploys domain ontology applications for knowledge management in the AEC/FM sector, helps develop consistent knowledge management within collaborative environments. The main advantage of e-COGNOS is the ability to incorporate an iterative approach with reliable sources such as IFC, bcXML, and BS6100 (Glossary of Building and Civil Engineering Terms, British Standard Institution) [33] (Table 8.2).

Unlike the controlled vocabularies in Europe, there have been attempts in North America to bring classification within a single, multifaceted approach. The OmniClass Construction Classification system is one of these [33]. However, OmniClass uses a text-based classification whereas e-COGNOS is a Java-based knowledge management system that is customizable.

8.3.3   Just-in-Time Information

While decades old, the principle of just-in-time (JIT) information customized to the point of the task at hand, is gaining new popularity (Chapter 14). One reason is the

Table 8.2   Comparative Analysis Table of Ontology Developed in AEC Industry

	eConstruct bcBuilding Definitions	*e-COGNOS*	*LexiCon*	*BARbi*	*Standard Dictionary for Construction*
Domain	Building and construction industry	Construction	Construction	Building and construction industry	Supply chain of the construction
Category	Taxonomy	Ontology	Vocabulary	Reference data library	Vocabulary
Pros	Demonstrate the power of bcXML	15,000 concepts covering different domains; customizable	mySQL used for concurrent access by multiple developers	IFC, STEP-AP is included as resource	Unify the vocabulary in supply chain
Cons	Only 3,000 terms specifically related to doors	Need JAVA for e-COGNOS in e-CKMI	Not customizable		Only French version available

explosion of information caused by ubiquitous digital information. Hence, it is not a surprise that JIT remains a core challenge for web applications:

> "Just-in-Time" information describes content provided to users at a specific time, place, and in a particular way to enable them to complete a transaction or learn more about the content they are browsing. Although many websites spend a great deal of time and money implementing JIT information to lower service costs and keep their customers happy, there are a number of challenges they need to overcome. One of the largest of these is the diverse user base with a variety of behaviors, expertise, literacy levels, and broad range of content needs. [34]

An effective demonstration of value-adding, "lean" information content in IT comes from the area of first responders. In a cognitive load experiment, the performance of seasoned first responders diminished as the amount of information and resources provided to them was increased beyond the norm [35].

Providing JIT information and lean knowledge for product life-cycle management requires multilayered, ontology-based frameworks [36]. This can help in creating, editing, visualizing, and inferring new, relevant data with the help of inference engines that process multiple knowledge types. For decades, the JIT supply of materials and labor at the workplace has revolutionized management in the manufacturing industry. Current advances in the AEC sector have made similar benefits possible at the construction site for housing providers [37] and in general. "By eliminating waste on site, controlling the movement of inventory coming into the site and within the site, and controlling the usage of mechanized plant and equipment, smooth work flow can be achieved" [38].

Since as-built information is notoriously unreliable (Chapter 6) [39], web technologies have been used to provide JIT information to improve facility management through HTML files that are custom composed at the field. Through this application, four objectives have been realized: (1) Determine building information needed, (2) improve the format for delivering building information, (3) store and deliver facility information through the web, and (4) determine suitable mechanisms of documenting building information [40]. Lee [41] also demonstrated that O&M fieldwork can be significantly enhanced through advanced visualization.

We will cover JIT and related technologies for the O&M field in greater detail in Chapter 14.

8.4   A Detailed Case Study of PPM Mapping in Embedded Commissioning

PPM mapping in ECx begins with natural language parsing (*FPT Parser* in Figure 8.5). The FPT Parser analyzes natural language formatted protocols of ECx that include a PFC and FPT. These industry-defined protocols are imported by the User Input Manager (Figure 8.5) and are mapped into BNF notation. Then, the protocols are parsed by the FPT Parser, paragraph by paragraph, and sentence by sentence, and followed by decomposition into a series of procedures. Each action in the "unit of behavior" (UOB) is parsed further into a word level, a lexicographic representation expressed in IDEF3 diagram format (Figure 8.6).

An ontology-based approach is used to categorize parsed items and define hierarchical relationships between them. The FPT Parser verifies the parsed items through the process model-ontology library in order to derive the corresponding product model. In this representation, further semantic interoperability needs to be achieved, by mapping it into standards like IFC. For this derivation, the LPM (Logical Product Modeling) approach of GT-PPM is adopted. After accessing and applying LPM in the ontology library, the parsed ECx item from the FPT Parser follows the ontological entities of the IFC-HVAC schema to structure the product model.

According to ECx's ontology schemata, items are defined either as *classes* or *attributes* (Figure 8.7). Synonyms are checked and matched against corresponding concept(s) and then placed in a hierarchical structure. For example, the FPT item "participants" is a synonym of the item "actor" in the IFC standard. Since these two items are predefined as synonyms, they are automatically matched. This item does not involve multiple levels in the ontology hierarchy, therefore no adjustments in the library and its hierarchy are required. If no match were to be found, the unmatched item would be returned to the user for manual processing, which entails selection of an item from potential matches or an entirely new input into the ontology library.

Next, to improve the interoperability of ECx representations, the verified item is matched with a standard schema, as in IFC [1] or AEX [42] schemata. In this matching step of ECx, since there are no common schemata shared by all standards, a single standard based on IFC schemata is used. The final step in the ECx-PPM process is to save the product model in the ECx repository for later use. This product model can be retrieved by the input/output (I/O) manager to record ECx data and generate a BCx report. I/O utilities of the BEMAC (Building Energy Monitoring, Analyzing and Communication) framework [43] are used to input and output data in ECx.

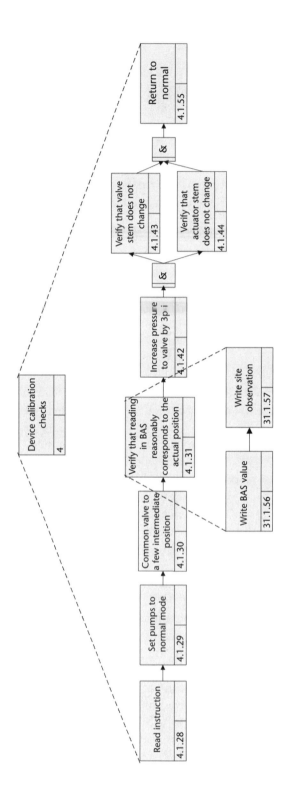

Figure 8.6   Decomposition of UOB Device Calibration Checks in IDEF3 notation.

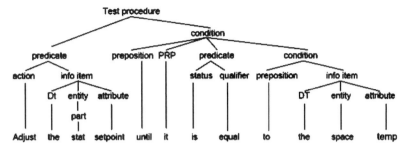

Figure 8.7 Constituent tree of a fan-coil unit functional performance test statement.

8.4.1 Natural Language Parsing in ECx PPM Mapping

BNF notation [44] is used in ECx-PPM to construct formal representations of lexicon; and syntax is used to capture semantic information present in the natural language protocols of PFC and FPT. Table 8.3 illustrates a BNF developed for formal representation of an FPT protocol .

The descriptions of FPT protocols consist of a list of "Test_procedures":

"a. With boilers in normal mode and ON, increase space setpoint 20Fof TU-_____ (interlocked to the fin tube). If OSAT is not > 40F, overwrite it to be > 40F. Overwrite space temp to be 3F below main setpoint (cooling) _____F and observe in BAS that there is heating deck flow and cooling flow goes to minimum. Observe that the fin tube or radiant panels remain OFF.

b. Change the space temp. to be 5F below main setpoint (cooling) _____F and observe the radiant panels or fin tubes remain OFF.

c. Change the OSAT to be < 40F. Observe that the radiant panels or fin tubes start heating. Return all parameters to normal." [45]

These are followed by a list of corresponding "Expected_results" [45]:

"a. TU goes into heating mode. Fin tube HCV's remain closed.

b. TU remains in heating mode. Fin tube HCV's remain closed.

c. TU remains in heating mode. Fin tube HCV's open [45]."

"Test_procedures" consists of an "Action" that changes the value of equipment attributes. This can involve a "Condition" to set a situation of "Action" or a "Qualifier" to supplement the "Action." The "Expected_result" verifies the

Table 8.3 Functional Performance Tests in BNF Notation [25]

ProcessModel ::= {Test_Procedure} {Expected_Result}

Test_Procedure ::= [oCondition],<,>, <Action>, Predicate, [oQualifier] , <.>

Expected_Result ::= [oAction], Predicate, [oCondition]

Condition ::= <Preposition>|<if>|<When>, Predicate

Predicate ::= [oEquipment], [oStatus], {AVP}

AVP ::= {<Attribute>}, <Value>

{ }-repetitive; [o]-conditional; <>-terminal node

expected "Value" of "Attributes" of the equipment based on the "Test_procedures." This involves an "Action" to check the result of a test or a "Condition" to satisfy a certain situation.

For example, when the first sentence in the fin-tube FPT is parsed, the system recognizes the term based on BNF notation and assigns it to a category (Figure 8.8). Then, the system checks for errors, which are indicated by a change in font color or style. To correct this, the user manually adds the omitted phrase into the lexicon. As shown in Table 8.4, the final result is an ECx term dictionary for the FPT protocol based on BNF notation.

Next, the user organizes the dictionary by adding a synonym or description for each item. Since the intentions and semantics of those who interactively develop these terms vary, the possibility of creating inconsistent entries exists. For the ontology to be interoperable it must provide universal agreement over definitions, relationships between terms, and meanings underlying them To address this problem, we extended e-COGNOS to become part of the ECx functionality. However, even with e-COGNOS, which assists users to achieve a broad consensus in ontology building, potential inconsistencies are avoided only if the domain experts and users are diligent in using the tool as intended.

A computable ECx lexicon can be developed from a predefined FPT protocol through this process. The ECx authority or the stakeholder can build his or her own FPT protocol based on a primitive lexicon. On the other hand, an FPT in IDEF3 notation can be retrieved from the system library, and then modified using this lexicon.

The steps in this process are to first select an attribute that the user wants to commission and a requirement value for that attribute. The second step is to select an element and a corresponding action. For the expected results, the ECx authority

1st Sentence	With boilers in normal mode and ON, increase space setpoint 20F of TU									

Test Procedure	Preposition	Element	Attribute	Value	Punctuation	Action	Element	Attribute	Value	Qualifier
1st Sentence	with	boiler		normal mode	,	increase		space setpoint	20F	

1st Sentence	With boilers in normal mode and ON, increase space setpoint 20F of TU									

Test Procedure	Preposition	Element	Attribute	Value	Punctuation	Action	Element	Attribute	Value	Qualifier
1st Sentence	with	boiler		normal mode	,	increase	Test Unit	space setpoint	20F	
				ON						

Figure 8.8 The process of parsing and building a lexicon.

Table 8.4 The ECx Term Dictionary for the Fin-Tube FPT [25]

Equipment	Status	Action	Attribute	Value	Punctuation	Proposition
Boiler	goes into	increase	space setpoint	ON	, (comma)	with
Test unit	should change	overwrite	OSAT	20F	. (period)	only after
Fin tube	shut off	observe	main setpoint	normal mode		below
Redundant panel		change		OFF		after
Heating coil valve						

or the stakeholder chooses the expected value for the attributes. Conversely, the user may select elements from each category of an ECx term dictionary. Since the structure of each category would have been predefined in BNF notation, the process of composing sentences manually tends to be syntactically correct. In the event that ill-formed statements are constructed by users, these are interactively corrected to match the normative FPT syntax (Figure 8.9). The steps required to model the ECx process in this manner are illustrated in Figure 8.10.

8.4.2   Ontology Development in ECx PPM Mapping

First a glossary that is a precursor to ontology is developed. This is compiled from PFC and FPT protocols obtained from well-established sources like the Portland Energy Conservation, Inc. [45], ASHRAE guidelines [23], and the BCx handbook [46]. From this glossary, the ontology for ECx applications is derived. In this process, for the purposes of interoperability, consensus among AEC/FM stakeholders must be achieved [15].

E-COGNOS as the base ontology for ECx-PPM application provides a distinct advantage, in this regard, due to its extensibility through the addition of new concepts and relationships. Other advantages of the e-COGNOS ontology include compatibility with not only bcXML taxonomy but also with IFC. In fact, the IFC 2.x kernel structure [1] serves as e-COGNOS's backbone. In ECx-PPM, Protégé is used in order to save and export ontology data through different formats such as Resource Description Framework (RDF)/XML Web Ontology Language (OWL)/XML, CLIPS, and Turtle.

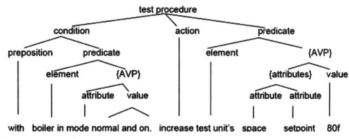

Figure 8.9   The structure of an FPT statement using BNF notation.

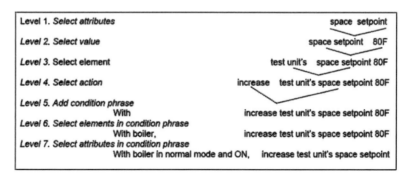

Figure 8.10   The process of building an ECx procedure from scratch using an ECx term dictionary [25].

8.4.3   Schema Matcher and Schema Parser in ECx PPM Mapping

In ECx-PPM, HVAC component modeling is done in the IFC schemata format. This is considered to be the best fit with the general ECx process (Figure 8.11). The *type* concept can express the OPR by defining a normal design condition that is usually determined in the early phase of ECx. The *occurrence* concept, which shows placement, connectivity of other elements and systems, and interaction with its environment, can represent the status of installation that is checked by PFC immediately after construction is completed. The *performance history* concept in the HVAC component schema is useful for storing FPT information in the IFC format.

In modeling an HVAC component in ECx-PPM, each PFC or FPT protocol is matched to one *type, occurrence,* and *performance history* concept. For example, a model verification of pump PFC checks the *type* of pump installed as to manufacturer, model, serial number, volts, and GPM. Installation checks of the pump ensure that pumps are in place, while the *occurrence* concept in IFC checks that grouted vibration isolation devices are installed properly and the devices are functional [45]:

"*Check [Equipment Tag]*:

General Installation

Equipment tag and nameplate permanently affixed

Pumps in place and properly grouted

Installation of balancing devices allow balancing to be completed following NEBB or AABC procedures & contract documents

Test and balance report reviewed for pump flows, head, elec.

Pump environment clean

Adequate access for maintenance

Vibration isolation devices installed and functional

Factory alignment correct (checked by installer)

Field alignment, if required, completed (checked by installer)

Seismic anchoring installed per spec

Temperature, pressure, and flow gages and sensors installed per spec.

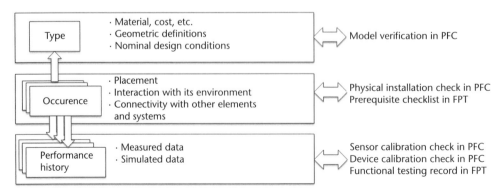

Figure 8.11   HVAC component modeling concept in the IFC 2X2 data model [25].

Required valves installed & in right direction

No visible leaks

Pump lubricated (checked by installer)

Piping (in vicinity of pump)

Pipe fittings complete and pipes properly supported

Air vents, expansion tanks, air separators installed per spec.

Piping type and flow direction properly labeled"

FPT protocol for the functional testing of a fan-coil unit and to record its performance the following steps must be taken [45]:

"Test Procedure (including special conditions)

1. Adjust the stat set point until it is equal to the space temperature.
2. Adjust the stat set point until it is 4F below the space temperature.
3. Return all changed control parameters and conditions to their pre-test values.

Expected and Actual Response to these procedures include the following [45]:

1. __Fan starts. __ Heating coil valve opens; __Warm air delivered.
2. Fan stops. Heating coil valve closes.
3. Check off in Section 2 above when completed."

This type of information can be captured through the *performance history* concept in IFC-HVAC modeling. However, IFCs represent only 30% of the parsed ECx information, while the HVAC modeling in IFC (*concept, type, occurrence,* and *performance history*) is generally compatible with the entire ECx process [24, 47].

To remedy this apparent shortcoming of coverage by IFC schema, in ECx-PPM, the *Property Set* object is used to represent detailed properties of HVAC components. The IFC parser and BC-IFC matcher developed and updated for current use by Wang et al. [24] have been adapted to the ECx-PPM application environment. After deriving the HVAC product model, in order to associate it with PFC and FPT protocol information, they are encoded in EXPRESS-G. For instance, the left box in Figure 8.12 is a fan-coil unit product model derived from the steps of a PFC protocol; and the right box shows the property set needed to capture the information about *fan type, flow moving device fan,* and *fan performance history.*

In addition, *IfcProject* and *IfcProcess* are used to represent the project information and the commissioning process, respectively. The relationship between project, process, and the commissioned equipment is defined by using the IFC Relationship entity. Approval regarding the ECx process is represented by *IFCApproval* connected by *IFCRelAssociatesApproval.*

8.5   Opportunities for PPM Mapping in ECx

In this chapter, we have been primarily concerned with the mapping of data between process and product representations in the interoperable world of shared

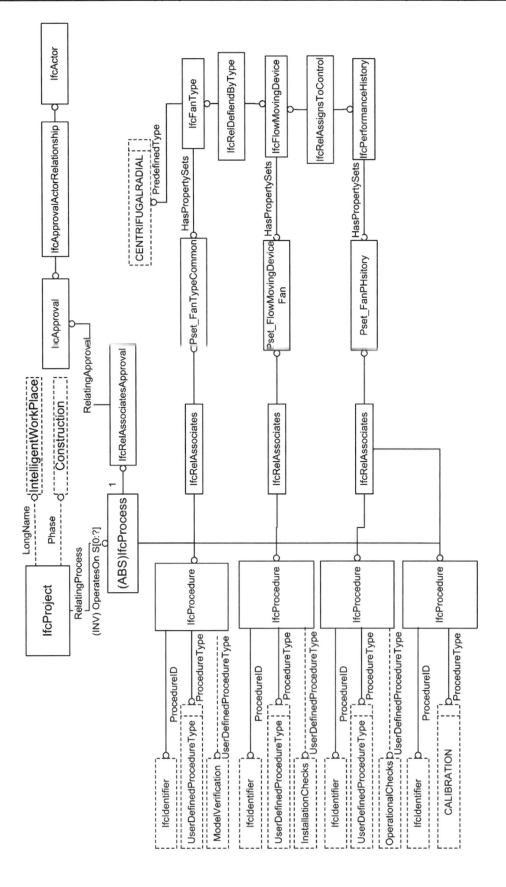

Figure 8.12 IFC model implementation for a part of FCU PFC with EXPRESS-G.

standards, like IFC and AEX (Chapter 4). Because building "universal" product models suitable to every occasion has serious drawbacks—including unaffordable modeling time and resources, volatility, rapid obsolescence, and excessive information content of modeled objects—JIT modeling of products mapped from process descriptions (or protocols) can lead to significant improvements. This can help reduce the costs of product model building, deployment, and training of their users. Furthermore, such an approach is immune to changes in AEC practices, and will make design and field operations lean, accurate, and efficient.

In this chapter, we reviewed the viability of this approach, particularly through an in-depth discussion of PPM mapping in ECx, and a breadth of applications in other CPD domains like steel and precast concrete systems design. In doing so, we demonstrated the level to which ECx data exchanges can be achieved, with reliability and interoperability, through standards like IFC. Without an accurate understanding of the coverage provided by current standards (Chapter 7), interoperability in ECx can never be achieved. Evaluating the coverage of data provided by IFC standards and supplementing them to reach full coverage will facilitate the widespread use of these standards to manage ECx information effectively.

The ECx research described in detail, in this chapter and in Chapter 7, proposes extensions to the IFC standard in the form of new, predefined property sets for HVAC equipment modeling. This will undoubtedly enrich IFC standards and also facilitate the global interoperability required to support the required data exchange applications for ECx.

Finally, in this chapter, we reported on the formal representation of ECx information about *type, occurrence*, and *performance history* of HVAC systems. This information will help in the development of guidelines in the proper use of IFC schemata that represent ECx data. Through this, developers can understand how to use IFC standards in the HVAC domain efficiently and encourage software companies to implement their IFC-compatible releases in the domain of building commissioning.

References

[1]   STEP: STandard for Exchange of Product Model Data, http://www.apaa.org/step.html.

[2]   Castro, N. S., Galler, M. A., and Bushby, S. T., "A Test Shell for Developing Automated Commissioning Tools for BACnet Systems," in *Proceedings of National Conference on Building Commissioning*, Las Vegas, NV, February 23–26, 2003.

[3]   Whitney, D., , "State of the Art in the United States of CAD Methodologies for Product Development," Final Report Under Grants from Office of Naval Research and the National Science Foundation, Cambridge, MA: MIT, Center for Technology, Policy and Industrial Development, October 1995.

[4]   Kiviniemi, A., "Requirements Management Interface to Building Product Models," dissertation submitted to Department of Civil and Environmental Engineering and the Committee of Graduate Studies, Stanford University, Stanford, CA, March 2005.

[5]   Özkaya, I., and Akin, Ö, "Tool Support for Computer-Aided Requirement Traceability in Architectural Design: The Case of DesignTrack," *Automation in Construction*, Vol. 16, No. 5, 2007, pp. 674–684.

[6]   Halfawy, M., and Froese, T., "Integration of Data and Processes of AEC Projects Using the Industry Foundation Classes," Report No. NRCC-48131; also published in *Proceedings of the 6th Construction Specialty Conference*, Toronto, Ontario, June 2–4, 2005, pp. 1–10.

[7]   Lehne, M. G., and Wollert, J., "Integrated Process and Product Modeling in Shipbuilding Industry—Why and How," *Netherlands*, 1992, pp. 289–303.

[8]   Cutting-Decelle, A. F., et al., "The Application of PSL to Product Design Across Construction and Manufacturing," *Concurrent Engineering*, Vol. 11, No. 1, March 2003, pp. 65–75.

[9]   Tesfagaber, G., et al., "Semantic Process Modeling for Applications Integration in AEC," *American Society of Civil Engineers*, 2002, pp. 318–335.

[10]   Lee, C. H., Sause, R., and Hong, N. K., "Overview of Entity-Based Integrated Design Product and Process Models," in *Civil-Comp* Press, Edinburgh, UK, 1996, pp. 185–197.

[11]   Anumba, C. J., et al., "Integrating Concurrent Engineering Concepts in a Steelwork Construction Project," *Concurrent Engineering: Research and Applications*, Vol. 8, No. 3, 2000, pp. 199–212.

[12]   Feng, S. C., and Song, E. Y., "Information Modeling of Conceptual Design Integrated with Process Planning," in *Proceedings of Symposia on Design for Manufacturability, The 2000 International Mechanical Engineering Congress and Exposition*, Orlando, FL, 2000.

[13]   Weise, M., et al., "Structural Analysis Extension of the IFC Modeling Framework," *ITcon*, Vol. 8, 2003, pp. 181–200.

[14]   Crowley, A. J., and Watson, A. S., "CIMsteel Integration Standards, Release 2," Ascot, UK: Steel Construction Institute, 2000.

[15]   Eastman, C., et al., "Deployment of an AEC Industry Sector Product Model," *Computer-Aided Design*, Vol. 37, No. 12, October 2005, pp. 1214–1228.

[16]   Rönneblad, A., and Olofsson, T., "Application of IFC in Design and Production of Precast Concrete Constructions," *ITcon*, Vol. 8, 2003, pp.167–180.

[17]   Lee, G., "A New Formal and Analytical Process to Product Modeling (PPM) Method and Its Application to the Precast Concrete Industry," Atlanta, GA: Georgia Institute of Technology, 2004.

[18]   Lee, G., et al., "Grammatical Rules for Specifying Information for Automated Product Data Modeling," *Advanced Engineering Informatics*, Vol. 20, No. 2, April 2006, pp. 155–170.

[19]   Chomsky, N., "Three Models for the Description of Language," *IEEE Trans. on Information Theory*, Vol. 2, No. 3, September 1956.

[20]   Lee, G., Eastman, C. M., and Sacks, R., "Eliciting Information for Product Modeling Using Process Modeling," *Data & Knowledge Engineering*, Vol. 62, No. 2, August 2007, pp. 292–307.

[21]   Backus, J. W., "The Syntax and Semantics of the Proposed International Algebraic Language of the Zurich ACM-GAMM Conference," in *Proceedings of the International Conference on Information Processing*, UNESCO, 1959, pp. 125–132.

[22]   Türkaslan-Bulbul, M. T., "Process and Product Modeling for Computational Support of Building Commissioning," Ph.D. Dissertation, Carnegie Mellon University, Pittsburgh, PA, 2006.

[23]   *ASHRAE Standards Committee Guideline 0-2005—The Commissioning Process*, Atlanta, GA: American Society of Heating, Refrigerating and Air-Conditioning Engineers, 2005.

[24]   Wang, H., et al., "Towards Domain-Oriented Semi-Automated Model Matching for Supporting Data Exchange," in *Proceedings of the 10th International Conference on Computing in Civil and Building Engineering*, Weimar, Germany, 2004.

[25]   Akın, Ö., et al., "Product and Process Modeling for Functional Performance Testing in Low-Energy Building Embedded Commissioning Case," in *Proceedings of ICEBO, 2007*, San Francisco, CA, November 1–2, 2007.

[26]   McCallum, A., "Joint Inference for Natural Language Processing," in *Proceedings of the Joint Inference for Natural Language Processing*, held at CoNLL, 2009.

[27]   Gruber, T., "A Translation Approach to Portable Ontology Specifications," Technical Report KSL 92-71, Knowledge System Laboratory, 1993.

[28]   El-Diraby, T. E., and Kashif, K. F., "Distributed Ontology Architecture for Knowledge Management in Highway Construction," *Journal of Construction Engineering and Management*, Vol. 131, No. 5, 2005.

[29]   Turk, Z., "Construction Informatics: Definition and Ontology," *Advanced Engineering Informatics*, Vol. 20, No. 2, April 2006, pp. 187–199.

[30]   Dutra, M., et al., "A Generic and Synchronous Ontology-Based Architecture for Collaborative Design," *Concurrent Engineering*, Vol. 18, No. 1, March 2010, pp. 65–74.

[31]   Park, M., and Fishwick, P. A., "Integrating Dynamic and Geometry Model Components through Ontology-Based Inference," *Simulation*, Vol. 81, No. 12, December 2005, pp. 795–813.

[32]   Dartigues, C., et al., "CAD/CAPP Integration Using Feature Ontology," *Concurrent Engineering*, Vol. 15, 2007, p. 237.

[33]   Lima, C., et al., "A Historical Perspective on the Evolution of Controlled Vocabularies in Europe," in *Proceedings of the CIB W102 3rd International Conference*, Frauenhofer IRB Verlag, Stuttgart, Germany, 2007.

[34]   Guerra, J. A., and Cianchette, C., "Just-in-Time Information: A Layered Approach to Information Design," *Insight*, Avenue A, Razorfish, December 2006.

[35]   Omodei, M. M., et al., "More Is Better?: Problems of Self-Regulation in Naturalistic Decision Settings," in *How Professionals Make Decisions*, R. Montgomery, R. Lipshitz, and B. Brehmer (Eds.), Psychology Press, 2005.

[36]   Lee, J.-H., and Suh, H.-W., "Ontology-Based Multi-Layered Knowledge Framework for Product Lifecycle Management," *Concurrent Engineering*, Vol. 16, No. 4, December 2008, pp. 301–311.

[37]   Bates, M., et al., "JIT in UK House-Building: Feasibility for Partial Implementation Using CAPM," in *Proceedings of the Second International Pan Pacific Conference on Construction Industry Development*, Singapore, October 27–29, 1999.

[38]   Pheng, L. S., and Hui, M. S., "The Application of JIT Philosophy to Construction: A Case Study in Site Layout," *Construction Management & Economics*, Vol. 17, No. 5, September 1999, pp. 657–668.

[39]   Liu, L. Y., et al., "Capturing As-Built Project Information for Facility Management," in *Proceedings of the First Congress held in conjunction with A/E/C Systems*, Washington, DC, 1994, pp. 614–612, ASCE.

[40]   Song, Y., Clayton, M. J., and Johnson, R. E., "Anticipating Reuse: Documenting Buildings for Operations Using Web Technology," *Automation in Construction*, Vol. 11, No. 2, February 2002, pp. 185–197.

[41]   Lee, S. H., "Computational Fieldwork Support for Efficient Operation and Maintenance of Mechanical, Electrical and Plumbing Systems," Ph.D. Dissertation, Carnegie Mellon University, Pittsburgh, PA, 2009.

[42]   AEX, "Automating Information Equipment Exchange," December 12, 2004, http://www.fiatech.org/projects/idim/aex.htm.

[43]   O'Sullivan, D. T. J., et al., "Improving Building Operation by Tracking Performance Metrics Throughout the Building Lifecycle (BLC)," *Energy and Buildings*, Vol. 36, No. 11, 2004, pp. 1075–1090.

[44]   Knuth, D. E., "Backus Normal Form vs. Backus Naur Form," *Communications of the ACM 7*, Vol. 12, 1964, pp. 735–736.

[45]   "Building Commissioning Guidelines," Portland Energy Conservation, 1992, http://www.peci.org/resources/commissioning.html.

[46]   *Building Commissioning: The Key to Quality Assurance. Commissioning Retrofits and Existing Buildings: Overview, Process and Case Studies*, Rebuild America, U.S. Department of Energy and Portland Energy Conservation, Inc., 1998.

[47]   Türkaslan-Bulbul, T., and Akin, O., "Computational Support for Building Evaluation: Embedded Commissioning Model," *Automation in Construction*, Vol. 15, No. 4, July 2006, pp. 438–447.

CHAPTER 9

Communication Protocols and Data Accessibility

9.1   Context

Modern building automation systems (BASs) are an integral part of building system operations and play a critical role in temperature and humidity control, ventilation, lighting control, and life-safety systems. They are also the principal tool for managing the energy efficiency of building operations. Building automation systems are becoming more sophisticated and complex. As the nation moves toward a future "smart grid" electrical generation and distribution system, building automation will play an even more important role. Onsite electrical generation and management of building electrical loads to reduce peaks and to better match the dynamics of intermittent generation from renewable energy sources, such as wind and solar photovoltaics, will make buildings a critical partner in the national electric grid instead of being a load at the end of a wire.

Past experience has shown that, for a variety of reasons, these systems have not lived up to their potential in buildings, a problem that building commissioning (BCx) can help to address [1, 2]. As part of the functional performance testing (FPT) phase of a BCx process, BASs provide a rich set of measurement data and tools that can be used to analyze the performance of a building's mechanical equipment and associated controls. Thus, BASs are important both as targets of BCx activities and as tools to assist them.

BASs will have a key role, particularly, in the realization of embedded commissioning processes. The communication protocol standards that enable the interconnection and interoperation of the equipment and controls of building systems provide a way to make the functionality of the component's network visible and accessible. As this functionality expands to include embedded information and processes linked to BCx, communication protocols will be one of the key ways to access and execute this functionality.

9.1.1   What Are Communication Protocols and Why Do They Exist?

Modern building automation and control systems use what is known as *direct digital control* technology. This terminology is derived from the evolution of building control systems. Historically, pumps, fans, dampers, boilers, and other building mechanical equipment were controlled manually, by pneumatic systems, and eventually by systems that combined central computers with remotely connected signal multiplexing devices. The development and mass production of microprocessors provided an economical way to distribute the computing power throughout the building. These distributed systems have microprocessor-based controllers that control the mechanical equipment directly, as opposed to remotely from a central location. They also use digital processing to implement the control algorithms instead of earlier analog systems. Hence the name, direct digital control (DDC).

Although the functionality of DDC systems is distributed, there is a need for the individual controllers to interact and exchange information in order to efficiently manage building systems and automate functions such as occupancy scheduling, nighttime setback, optimization of subsystem components, and other energy efficiency measures. This interaction and information exchange is accomplished by linking the distributed controllers together in a communication network. Today's building automation systems are specialized computer networks that share many of the characteristics of other kinds of computer networks used for information technology applications.

A communication protocol is a set of rules that govern how computers or microprocessors exchange information. This set of rules governs all of the details of information exchange between connected devices, including the physical characteristics of the network, regulating access to the network, and information content and encoding of the messages (Table 9.1). A computer communication protocol is similar to a language. The protocol rules are analogous to vocabulary, alphabet, spelling, punctuation, and grammar rules that enable and govern the use of a language.

9.1.2   Standardization of Communication Protocols

Within this context, a standard is defined to be a written document that establishes uniform engineering or technical criteria, methods, processes, or practices set by an authority or by general consensus. There are many national and international organizations that are linked in a formal system to develop standards. The standards developed by these groups can be thought of as *de jure* standards because they result from formally recognized due process procedures. Other standards become recognized by virtue of their widespread use even though they may have been developed by an individual or organization for commercial benefit. These are often called *de facto* standards. Sometimes a company or trade group will promote something as a "standard" even though it has neither of these features. In effect this is an effort, through marketing, to create a new *de facto* standard. Blurring of these distinctions is usually intentional and motivated by self-interest. Here, unless stated otherwise, "standard" means something that has been adopted by a recognized national or international authority.

Table 9.1   Types of Protocol Rules and Descriptive Examples

Type of Protocol Rules	Descriptive Examples
Physical characteristics of the network	The message transmission medium (wire type or wireless transmission frequencies)
	Network length or wireless transmission distance limitations
	Size and arrangement of physical connecters
	Electrical or optical signals used to indicate 1's and 0's
	Transmission speed (the number of bits per second)
	Physical network topology
Regulating access to and use of the network medium	Addressing to identify individual or groups of communication partners
	Constraints on the maximum number of connected devices
	Bit patterns that denote the beginning and end of a message
	Rules to indicate when a device can transmit a message
	Constraints on message length
	Rules for segmentation and reassembly of long messages
	Rules for acknowledging the receipt of a message
Defining the information content of the messages	Definition of allowed message types
	Message encoding/decoding rules
	Error detection and message retransmission

When system manufacturers began making DDC products, there were no standard communication protocols for building automation and control applications. Out of necessity each company came up with its own protocol. For competitive reasons these protocols have been proprietary. Products made by one company could not readily be connected to and exchange information with products made by a different company. The result was that building owners became "captive customers," forced to rely on a single vendor for building control products or take drastic steps like replacing the entire system when an upgrade or change was needed, or segregating the building control system into isolated partitions.

In the mid-1980s, building owners became so frustrated by the operational constraints imposed by proprietary protocols—and a well-founded belief that a lack of competition raised prices—that they forced a movement to develop industry standards. This led to the development of a standard called BACnet® [3, 4], which is now well recognized and widely used around the world.

Although BACnet has been a worldwide commercial success and its importance in building automation is still growing, it is not the only communication protocol used in the industry. There are other communication protocol standards that have some use in building applications even though that is not the primary application for which they were developed. There are also many examples of legacy proprietary protocols that are still in use. The most important protocols used in building automation applications are described later in this chapter.

In any given year newly constructed buildings represent a very small portion of the total building stock (about 1% in the United States). Buildings generally last much longer than the mechanical equipment and control technologies that are used in them. Building renovations and equipment upgrades usually happen in a piecemeal fashion. For these reasons, building owners often need to manage several generations of equipment and technology at the same time. Accomplishing this task sometimes requires the use of communication protocol translators or gateways.

9.1.3 Protocol Gateways or Translators

A communication protocol translator is called a *gateway*. "Protocol translation, like language translation, is an imperfect art. Concepts that are easily and clearly expressed in one language or protocol may be difficult or even impossible to translate into another" [5]. Sometimes a concept is represented in a much more detailed and nuanced way in one protocol than the other. These factors are a significant challenge to gateway designers who must consider the unintended consequences of missing or misinterpreted information. The usual result is a reduction in scope to the simplest and clearest information that can be translated, thereby significantly limiting the connectivity.

Gateways are sometimes confused with routers, which are also used to connect different networks. A router is a simpler device than a gateway. A router's job is to forward a message to the next network in the path between the source and the destination device. This can involve changes in networking technologies that affect addressing, packet format, electrical signals, transmission speed, error detection, and other communication details but it does not involve translating the message because the application messages are the same on both networks, as illustrated in Figure 9.1. The content of the message does not change even though the addressing, signaling, and framing change. In a gateway the data must also be translated [5].

To make the distinction between a router and a gateway clear, consider "sending a letter through an interoffice mail system or through the postal service. The same letter can be sent either way, although the type of envelope, the necessary addressing information" and the transport details are different. "Using this analogy, a router removes the letter from the interoffice envelope, puts it in a postal service envelope, addresses the envelope, and sends it on its way. The content of the letter

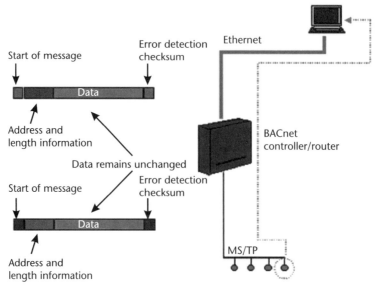

Figure 9.1 A BACnet router connecting an Ethernet LAN to an MS/TP LAN.

itself remains unchanged" [5]. A gateway performs all of the functions of a router but, in addition, must translate the letter from, say, English to Mandarin [5].

Although gateways are sometimes necessary and beneficial, they always add complexity and can be a source of significant problems. Table 9.2 summarizes the benefits and limitations of using gateways. From a BCx perspective gateways present two distinct challenges. The first is ensuring that a specification is written in a very tight and enforceable way before the system is procured. The second challenge is developing and administering an FPT protocol to verify that the gateway meets all of the details of the specification. A more detailed discussion of gateways for building automation applications can be found in [5].

9.2   An Overview of Communication Protocols Commonly Used in Building Automation

9.2.1   BACnet®

The name BACnet is shorthand for Building Automation and Control networks. It is the only communication protocol standard in the world that was developed specifically for commercial building control applications. It was originally published as an American national standard by the American Society of Heating, Refrigerating, and Air-Conditioning Engineers (ASHRAE) in 1995. Since that time, it has been adopted as a European standard, a world standard, and a national standard in more than 30 countries around the world [3, 4]. It has also been adopted in the United States as part of the suite of standards that will enable a future smart grid [6]. Open-source implementations and protocol analyzer tools are also available [7].

The BACnet standard was designed to evolve with technological advances. ASHRAE maintains a standing committee of building control experts from around the world that oversees maintenance of the standard. Coordination of revisions to the ASHRAE standard with the international versions is done through ISO Technical Committee 205, Building Environment Design. ASHRAE also maintains a companion standard that defines product tests for conformance to BACnet that is also adopted and used throughout the world [8, 9].

BACnet interest groups have formed in various countries around the world to provide education and promote the use of this technology [10]. There is an internationally recognized testing and certification program for BACnet products [11].

Table 9.2   Summary of Gateway Benefits and Limitations [5]

Gateway Benefits	Gateway Limitations
Provides connectivity that may otherwise be impossible	Limited capacity and expandability
	Limited ability to translate dissimilar concepts
May expand options for competitive bidding	Configuration and programming of devices through the gateway is generally not possible
Provides a point of isolation between two largely independent systems	Failure results in communication loss between all devices on opposite sides of the gateway
Permits interconnectivity of legacy systems with newer products	Possible time delay or the return of cashed data that is old
	More difficult to troubleshoot problems

All major manufacturers of building automation systems in the world make and sell BACnet products [12]. Increasingly, manufacturers of building equipment and components make their products with embedded BACnet controls for integration into a larger building system. The growth in the number of BACnet vendors over time is shown in Figure 9.2.

The key design feature of BACnet is that the content of the information to be exchanged is distinct from the mechanisms used to deliver the information. BACnet defines an object-oriented model of the information that needs to be exchanged. Each object has a set of attributes or properties that describe the key information that is to be made visible over the network. BACnet defines a rich set of data objects that includes analog inputs and outputs, binary inputs and outputs, trends, schedules, control loops, life-safety system components, electrical load control, and many others.

From the perspective of the communication network, a BACnet device is a collection of BACnet objects. The object model is combined with a set of application services or messages that enable the properties of these objects to be read or manipulated, indicating and responding to building system alarms and events and various types of system configuration and maintenance. The modular, object-oriented design allows the features and capabilities of BACnet to be extended in a backward-compatible way through the definition of new objects and, when needed, additional application services. BACnet object building blocks can be combined to represent a device as simple as a temperature sensor or as complex as an industrial chiller.

In principle, BACnet messages can be conveyed over any communication network. In practice, the standard defines a specific set of networking technologies that offer a range of cost and performance trade-offs. It also provides a way to

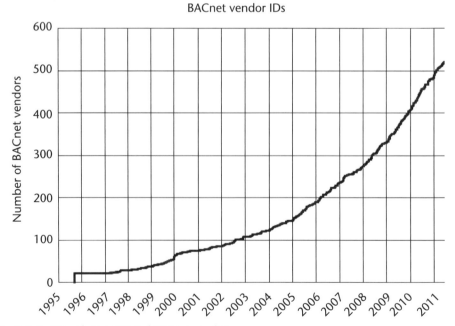

Figure 9.2 Growth in registered BACnet vendors.

interconnect them into a single system. In a typical BACnet system, a high-speed backbone connects operator workstations with supervisory controllers that also function as routers to lower cost networks that link sensors and application-specific controllers. The most commonly used backbone network is called BACnet/IP, which, as the name suggests, is a way to convey BACnet messages across an Internet Protocol network. BACnet also offers web service capabilities and sophisticated security features.

This collection of capabilities enables BACnet to be used in very small and simple building applications but also allows the interconnection of multiple large buildings colocated in a campus environment or geographically distributed around the world. Real-world examples of both exist and require the sort of functionality provided by BACnet.

9.2.2 Modbus

Modbus is an example of a *de facto* communication protocol standard. It was originally developed in 1979 by a company called Modicon, which is today a part of Schneider Electric. Modicon was founded by an entrepreneur named Richard Morley (the name Modicon is derived from Morley Digital Controls), who was an early pioneer in digital control systems. A decade later, Dick Morley became an early member and contributor to the ASHRAE BACnet committee.

Modbus was developed as a simple master–slave protocol to link programmable logic controllers (PLCs) used in industrial applications such as factory machinery control and assembly lines. PLCs are designed to operate reliably and safely in conditions harsher than typical building control applications and include features such as the ability to operate in extended temperature ranges, immunity to electrical noise, resistance to vibration and impacts, and circuitry designed to operate safely in explosion hazard environments. PLCs are also used in "hard-real-time" applications where response to an input condition must be within a bounded time or unintended operations will result.

Modbus is one of the most widely used protocols in industrial manufacturing. It is also used in supervisory control and data acquisition (SCADA) systems for applications such as electrical power generation, water treatment, and oil refining. Its widespread use, even though its origin was a public specification produced by a single company, makes it a clear *de facto* standard.

Modbus is a character-based, multi-drop serial protocol originally designed for use over simple twisted-pair point-to-point (RS-232) or multi-drop (RS-485) networks [13, 14]. More modern extensions include the use of other networking technology and Modbus TCP/IP (Transmission Control Protocol/Internet Protocol), which provides a way to convey Modbus messages over IP networks. A message consists of the receiver's address, a simple function code, a data block, and an error check value. There are 255 possible function codes but not all devices support all codes.

Modbus defines several types of data registers that are mapped on a device in ways specific to the application. The protocol provides a way to read values from and in some cases write values to these registers. The application meaning of the data is not defined by the standard. Modbus is supported by an industry organization called the Modbus Association [15]. The specification and various tools and sample implementations are freely available.

Modbus has very limited application in building automation. Because of its simplicity and widespread use, it is primarily used as a way to create a gateway for integrating a specific product into a building's automation system based on BACnet or some other protocol.

9.2.3 LonTalk

LonTalk is a communication protocol developed for local operating networks by the Echelon Corporation in the 1990s. In order for the technology to benefit from the economies of mass production, its concept is to provide a simple protocol that can be implemented on a custom, microprocessor chip that would be applicable to a wide range of control applications. The chip that implemented the upper layers of the protocol stack could be combined with a range of transceivers to accommodate different physical media including twisted-pair wiring, power line carrier, and infrared. Originally, the technology required the use of a specific microprocessor chip called a *neuron*. Over time, the hardware options expanded. Also, over time, a tunneling mechanism was developed to convey LonTalk messages over IP networks in order to link small local networks into a larger system.

The LonTalk protocol was formally adopted as an American national standard by the Electronics Industries Association for home automation applications and today, the standard is maintained by the Consumer Electronics Association (CEA). The CEA 709 series of standards defines the basic protocol [16] and the physical media–specific options [17–19]. CEA 852 defines the associated IP tunneling protocol [20]. In Europe, the CEA 709 standards have been adopted with name and scope changes as the EN 14908 series for building automation applications. The CEA 709 standards are one of several local-area networking options supported in the BACnet standard although this option has not been a commercial success.

The term *LonTalk* is often confused with the similar terms *LonMark* and *Lon-Works*. The LonTalk protocol is a generic networking protocol that is independent of any particular application. Information is exchanged through the use of a concept called shared network variable types (SNVT). LonMark International is a global industry association that promotes the use of LonTalk technology and develops implementer's agreements that define profiles of SNVTs for use in that particular application domain. LonWorks is a marketing name used to represent the set of microprocessor chips, development tools, and product configuration tools used to commercialize the LonTalk technology.

LonWorks technology is used in a wide range of commercial and industrial control application areas including automotive, electrical machinery, food processing, materials handling, conveying and tracking systems, oil and gas, paper and pulp, semiconductor electronics, wastewater treatment, street lighting, electric metering, and building automation. The LonTalk protocol is included as part of the suite of standards that will enable a future smart grid [6].

In the building automation system market, all of the companies who developed LonTalk products have since added a BACnet product line to remain competitive in the face of growing demand for BACnet products. Although this suggests the growing strength of BACnet, it does not necessarily indicate an end to the use of LonTalk in the building automation market. The widespread use of LonTalk products in other industries suggest that it will be viable to maintain building automaton product lines as long as there is a market demand for them.

9.2.4   KNX

KNX is a communication protocol for home and building electronic systems that was derived in the late 1990s from a combination of three predecessor protocols used in Europe for home automation applications. Those protocols are Batibus, primarily used in France, Italy, and Spain; the European Installations Bus (EIB), primarily used in German-speaking and northern European countries; and European Home Systems (EHS), primarily used by manufacturers of white goods. The KNX protocol is based on the communication stack of EIB, which was expanded to include physical layers derived from the other protocols. It includes options for wired twisted-pair, power line carrier, infrared, and an Ethernet-based IP option. The most commonly used physical layer is the wired twisted-pair.

The KNX specification is made up of multiple parts, which were published by the KNX Association in 2002. Over time, the KNX specification and its enhancements have been formally adopted as standards. The basic protocol stack and the various media options were adopted as European standards in the CENELEC EN 50090 series [21]. In 2006 these CENELEC standards were adopted as world standards in the ISO/IEC 14543-3 series [22]. In Europe a variation of the KNX standards was adopted specifically for building automation applications by CEN as the EN 13321 series of standards.

The KNX technology is primarily used in Europe for home applications including lighting control, blind and shutter control, security, and HVAC control. The standards have also been adopted in Canada and China. There is a fuzzy boundary between control technology used in homes and small commercial buildings, and KNX can be found in both. In 2004, the KNX Association, in cooperation with the ASHRAE BACnet committee, developed a gateway mapping specification to enable integration of KNX devices with a BACnet building automation system.

The KNX Association is an industry support group that has affiliated national groups in many European countries. The association has a technical board that oversees maintenance of the protocol and also an independent testing and certification process for KNX products. The association also has a marketing board for promoting use of the technology.

9.3   Design Phase Commissioning Considerations for BACnet Systems

Commissioning is a quality-oriented process that ideally begins at the inception of a construction process and continues through construction and into the operation of the building. A summary of international commissioning practices is contained in the work of the International Energy Agency Annexes 40 and 47 reviewed in Chapter 3. An early part of that process is documenting the owner's requirements and ensuring that clear specifications are created that match those requirements.

Requirements and specifications for building automation systems are a part of this process.

A good control specification contains many items that are independent of the communication protocol used. These include expectations of the comfort requirements that are to be maintained, the control strategies and sequences of operation, the type and location of sensors, alarm requirements, strategies for implementing electrical demand reductions during peak periods, operator workstation graphics and features, various types of reports on operations, and archiving of operational data.

Other aspects of a good control specification are protocol specific. Specifying the use of an international standard like BACnet enables future extensions and the integration of multiple building systems and even multiple buildings. It also provides a path for managing the evolution of building control technology over the lifetime of the building that does not require removing current systems every time something new is added. These advantages do not happen by accident. Careful planning and the oversight that a thorough commissioning process provides are required. Table 9.3 summarizes the key items that should be carefully specified for the commissioning of BACnet systems. Other resources for developing high-quality BACnet specifications are available [23–25].

If it is known or expected that multiple buildings will be integrated together or that there will be multiple phases in a building's renovation, it can be helpful to combine key aspects of the control system requirements into an integration plan that is included by reference in all of the project specifications. This can help ensure the consistency needed over time and with multiple vendors.

Table 9.3   Key Items for Inclusion in a BACnet Specification

BACnet Feature	Description of need
Object naming conventions	The industry widely uses the concept of a "point" to represent a piece of information. BACnet implements points as objects that have a text name. A single naming convention should be created and used throughout a system. The vendor will make one up if it is not provided and it will almost certainly not match the expectations of the building operating personnel.
Descriptions	Every BACnet object has a Description property, which is a placeholder for textual information about that object. This is a great way to document details that will be needed throughout the life of the system. Unless guidance is provided about how to configure these descriptions they will be left blank.
Network numbering	BACnet systems are typically made up of several interconnected networks with unique numbers. The network number is part of the addressing scheme. A plan for allocating these numbers is needed to ensure that they are unique. This is much like managing address space in an IP network.
IP infrastructure	The most common high-speed backbone for a BACnet system is BACnet/IP. This can be a network dedicated to building control or it can be a network shared with IT functions in the building. Shared IT networks require coordination with IT staff to ensure that building control needs and security considerations are met.
Documentation of system configuration	BACnet enables competitive expansions to an existing system. In order for a new vendor to integrate with an existing system, the details of object names, network numbering, and the location of key information that must be shared needs to be documented. This information is also critical for system maintenance over time.

9.4   Functional Performance Testing of BACnet Systems

As mentioned in the introduction to this chapter, the data collection and analysis capabilities of building automation systems are important tools in the FPT phase of BCx. It is also important to do FPT of the BACnet system itself. The point of this testing is to verify that requirements outlined in Table 9.3 have been met and to ensure that some common misconfiguration pitfalls have been avoided. The workstation interface provided with the system can be used to verify the proper implementation of naming conventions and descriptions by reading the relevant properties.

Independent tools that can observe and interact with the control system can help find other common configuration errors. These errors include improper references to data points used in the control logic, duplicate-numbered or misnumbered Device Object identifiers, improper network numbering, and misconfiguration of broadcast management tables. It takes training to learn how to identify these problems but in general they are uncovered by looking at the message traffic to find error messages, repeated attempts to locate a device, an object that does not respond, or unexpected bursts of message traffic. Some useful tools to use for this work are shown in Table 9.4.

9.5   A Growing Role for Building System Communication Protocols in ECx

There is a growing trend for homes and buildings to become more energy efficient, to the point of becoming net-zero energy buildings, meaning that over a year's time they generate as much energy as they consume. Home and building systems are also becoming increasingly automated. Occupants demand more comfortable conditions and there is increasing awareness of health issues related to indoor environmental quality. These drivers will make microprocessor-based controllers and the communication protocols that enable them to be networked even more important in the future. The ability of protocols like BACnet to evolve with both

Table 9.4   Control Vendor Independent Tools for Examining and Debugging BACnet Networks

Tool	Source	Description
Wireshark	SourceForge	A free open-source protocol analyzer that includes BACnet message display and decoding capabilities.
Visual Test Shell	SourceForge	A free open-source tool designed for testing BACnet products. It can transmit custom BACnet messages, run test scripts, and contains a protocol analyzer.
BACnet Explorer	Cimetrics Technology	A commercial tool for exploring and documenting the configuration of BACnet systems. It has the ability to automatically discover networks and devices, building a tree of the network system. It also has the ability to read and write properties of BACnet objects.
BAS-o-matic	Cimetrics Technology	A commercial BACnet protocol analyzer.
BACbeat	Polarsoft Corporation	A commercial BACnet protocol analyzer and analysis tool. It includes the ability to read and write properties of BACnet objects.

increasing expectations and advancing computer technology will prove to be critically important.

As intelligence becomes increasingly embedded in automated systems, their role in the ECx process will grow. These systems already provide a primary means for BCx agents to see and understand the performance of building systems. The performance expectations of the future will only be met if BCx processes become part of this embedded intelligence and automated assistance becomes a part of the ECx process.

Historically, building codes standards have primarily been about public safety. They ensure that buildings do not fall down in storms and have reasonable fire protection features. Future code requirements will also establish minimum performance requirements for energy efficiency and environmental quality. They may even require minimum standards for building automation and ECx.

References

[1]   NSTC, *Federal Research and Development Agenda for Net-Zero Energy, High-Performance Green Buildings*, Report of the Subcommittee on Buildings and Technology Research and Development, National Science and Technology Council Committee on Technology, 2008.

[2]   DOE, "Energy Impact of Commercial Building Controls and Performance Diagnostics: Market Characterization, Energy Impact of Building Faults and Energy Savings Potential," Report No. D0180, prepared for the DOE Building Technologies Program, 2005.

[3]   ANSI/ASHRAE, *BACnet: A Data Communication Protocol for Building Automation and Control Networks*, ANSI/ASHRAE Standard 135, American Society of Heating, Refrigerating, and Air-Conditioning Engineers, 2010.

[4]   EN/ISO, *Building Automation and Control Systems—Part 5: Data Communication Protocol*, EN/ISO 16484-5, International Organization for Standardization, 2010.

[5]   Bushby, S. T., "Communication Gateways: Friend or Foe?" *ASHRAE Journal*, Vol. 40, No. 4, 1998, pp. 50–53.

[6]   NIST, "Framework and Roadmap for Smart Grid Interoperability Standards," Release 1.0, Special Publication 1108, National Institute of Standards and Technology, U.S. Department of Commerce, 2010.

[7]   BACnet, "Open Source BACnet Projects," http://www.bacnet.org/Developer/index.html, 2011.

[8]   ANSI/ASHRAE, *Method of Test for Conformance to BACnet*, ANSI/ASHRAE Standard 135.1, American Society of Heating, Refrigerating, and Air-Conditioning Engineers, 2009.

[9]   EN/ISO, *Building Automation and Control Systems—Part 6: Data Communication Conformance Testing*, EN/ISO 16484-6, 2009.

[10]   SSPC 135, "BACnet Interest Groups," http://www.bacnet.org/Contact/Groups.htm, 2011.

[11]   BACnet International, "BACnet Product Testing," http://www.bacnetinternational.net/btl, 2011.

[12]   SSPC 135, "BACnet Vendor IDs," http://www.bacnet.org/VendorID/index.html, 2011

[13]   EIA/TIA, *Interface Between Data Terminal Equipment and Data Circuit-Terminating Equipment Employing Serial Binary Data Interchange*, EIA/TIA Standard 232-E, Electronic Industries Association, 1991.

[14]   EIA/TIA, *Electrical Characteristics of Generators and Receivers for Use in Balanced Digital Multipoint Systems*, EIA/TIA Standard 485, Electronic Industries Association, 2003.

[15]   Modbus Association, http://www.modbus.org, 2011.

[16]   ANSI/CEA, *Control Network Protocol Specification*, ANSI/CEA Standard 709.1-C, Consumer Electronics Association, 2010

[17]   ANSI/CEA, *Fiber-Optic Channel Specification*, ANSI/CEA Standard 709.4, Consumer Electronics Association, 1999.

[18]   ANSI/CEA, *Free-Topology Twisted-Pair Channel Specification*, ANSI/CEA Standard 709.3 R2004, Consumer Electronics Association, 2004.

[19]   ANSI/CEA, *Control Network Power Line (PL) Channel Specification*, ANSI/CEA Standard 709.2-A R2006, Consumer Electronics Association, 2006.

[20]   ANSI/CEA, *Enhanced Protocol for Tunneling Component Network Protocols over Internet Protocol Channels*, ANSI/CEA Standard CEA-852.1, Consumer Electronics Association, 2010.

[21]   CEN, "Home and Building Electronic Systems (HBES)," EN 50090, Committee for European Normalization, 2003.

[22]   ISO/IEC, *Information Technology—Home Electronic Systems (HES) Architecture—Part 3-1: Communication Layers—Application Layer for Network Based Control of HES Class 1*, ISO/IEC 14543-3, International Organization for Standardization, 2006.

[23]   Bushby, S. T., Newman, H. M., and Applebaum, M. A., *GSA Guide to Specifying Interoperable Building Automation and Control Systems Using ANSI/ASHRAE Standard 135-1995*, BACnet, NISTIR 6392, National Institute of Standards and Technology, 1999.

[24]   Haakenstad, L. K., "How to Specify BACnet-Based Systems Engineered Systems," *ASHRAE Journal*, Vol. 14, No. 6, pp. 46–55, 1997.

[25]   Tom, S., "A Simple Way to Specify BACnet, BACnet Today," *Supplement to ASHRAE Journal*, Vol. 47, No. 11, pp. B27–31, 34, 2005.

CHAPTER 10

Building Codes

10.1   Introduction to Building Codes and Standards

Building codes and standards specify a minimal set of requirements for buildings to ensure that building designs achieve an acceptable level of safety and quality. Regulatory agencies, which adopt model codes or create their own codes, do so to protect public health and safety and sustain the welfare of the general public by regulating and controlling the design, construction, and use of buildings within their jurisdiction.

The idea of controlling the construction of structures by creating governmental regulations is not a recent phenomenon. Codes evolved from the very early ages of humanity. The body of knowledge in building codes is usually a product of experience gained from disasters and afterthoughts of a tragedy. One of the earliest examples of community-wide requirements was observed in the ancient Babylonian Empire in the Code of Hammurabi, which held home builders liable: "If a builder build[s] a house for someone, and does not construct it properly, and the house which he built fall[s] in and kill[s] its owner, then that builder shall be put to death" [1].

Widespread loss of life from natural disasters, such as earthquakes, tsunamis, floods, and hurricanes, and human-made hazards, such as fire and poor design, have led affected communities to research, standardize, and enforce best practices to reduce the impacts of such disasters and hazards. Even though it is not possible to eliminate all of the risks associated with buildings, pervasive utilization of standards can potentially reduce the risks to an acceptable level.

In the first section of this chapter we present some basic knowledge about building codes and standards. The processes in which the codes and standards are created and used are then described in Section 10.2. Some of the earlier efforts related to the computerization of the codes and standards are discussed in Section 10.3, and more recent approaches are described in Section 10.4. We conclude this chapter by describing the remaining challenges related to the digitization of codes and standards.

10.1.1   Nature of Codes

Building code documents consist of several parts that focus on different elements of structures. The main body of the documents has a hierarchical nature (e.g., decomposed into sections, subsections, clauses, and subclauses) reflecting the classification of building elements within the code context. Such structuring enables the reader to identify and parse more easily the specific and relevant parts of the document. However, to do so efficiently requires a familiarization period. Apart from the main body of the code documents, there are sections for clarifying the meanings of domain terms and abbreviations, as well as sections describing informative references and appendices of more detailed information. The terminology definition sections are of great importance during this familiarization period since users of building codes may not necessarily be familiar with the domain terminology. The magnitude of terminology and the level of detail of the definitions may still be limited for some of the users with less knowledge of the building domain.

As building research progresses, there is a need to update some parts of the building codes according to the new research findings and emerging building technologies. Hence, building codes have a dynamic nature and are subject to frequent changes via addendums or newer versions. Building codes are not self-sufficient documents [2]. Kılıççöte and Garrett classify the knowledge not explicitly expressed in the building codes into three groups: knowledge about the world, knowledge about the domain, and knowledge accumulated in other domain documents, including other building codes. The first group is the information every person is supposed to know, which is usually referred as "common sense," for example, concepts of time and space. The second group is the specialized information that is relevant in the building domain. For example, understanding energy-efficiency codes requires knowledge about what components make up a "building envelope" and how "thermal bridges" in the building envelope affect the energy performance of the building. The last group is the regulatory information that is not included in the building code itself, but to which there are references, such as references to other building codes and standards. In addition to the primary content of the building codes, supplements, guidelines, and amendments are also an important part of this kind of regulatory information.

10.1.2   Purpose of Codes

Implementation of building codes yields several advantages. First of all, they protect the health, safety, and welfare of the public by ensuring an acceptable level of safety and quality of buildings. While choosing a building for occupancy, a majority of buyers are likely to have neither the knowledge necessary to comprehensively evaluate the design and the future building performance, nor the willingness to hire a consultant possessing such knowledge to conduct the evaluation. Redundant efforts would result in unnecessary costs if each potential buyer of a building were to perform this kind of analysis. Building codes provide a degree of risk reduction, and thus increased confidence, to buyers in terms of the safety and quality of buildings. They provide some degree of expected building performance by the construction industry for all buildings and components within those buildings. Such expectations also enable the members of the construction supply chain to conduct business with each other more effectively.

There is also a liability perspective to building codes. Public and private entities, as well as individuals, can be held accountable when they allow an unsafe situation to persist. Injured individuals will have grounds to file a liability claim against the negligent parties who created a situation that resulted in injury and loss of life or property. Hence, if these entities or individuals adopt and adhere to a standard set of building codes, they will be deemed as being aware of and following known best practices, which may help avoid claims of liability for injuries sustained during building failure.

Adoption of the building codes that reflect the state of the art of research and practice is necessary, but not sufficient, to achieve the full value of these codes. They have little value when not enforced by qualified, trained, and certified plan reviewers and building inspectors. Hence, the building permitting departments in most municipalities have the responsibility of ensuring that the building codes they adopt are current and of enforcing adherence to those codes within their jurisdiction.

10.1.3   Types of Codes and Code Organizations

Some countries separate the development and maintenance of codes and standards from their enactment. In this case, national code and standards organizations develop and maintain codes, and local authorities (such as municipal building departments) adopt and enforce compliance with adopted codes and standards. In the United States, the American Society of Heating, Refrigerating and Air-Conditioning Engineers (ASHRAE) and the International Code Council (ICC) are examples of national organizations committed to developing and maintaining national codes and standards, referred to as *model building codes*. Model building codes are recommended baseline documents made available to local building authorities with jurisdiction for code enforcement and the authority to formally adopt and modify model codes for use in that jurisdiction. States are free to adopt model codes fully or partially, make amendments to model codes, or develop their own codes. In many cases, counties and cities within these states are able to further amend the codes they adopt. Considering the large number of jurisdictions in the United States, uniformity of codes throughout the nation is important to eliminate redundant time and effort spent on development and maintenance of the codes and on the education and training of the building inspectors, plan reviewers, designers, and other code users. For a more detailed discussion of the taxonomy of building regulations, we refer the reader to the work of Kılıççöte [37, 38, 40].

To promote innovation and use of new research and technology, there has been a recent move toward performance-based requirements as opposed to the traditional procedural and prescriptive language of codes. Rather than expressing the objectives of a given requirement within a code, many existing building codes usually either require compliance with outlined procedures in the design of a component or prescribe specific details and dimensions on products and approved processes. This approach significantly increases the volume of the building code documents, restricts change and innovation in design, and requires frequent updates to code documents. Performance-based requirements, however, specify a set of performance objectives that all buildings must meet. They do not specify how the required level of performance should be achieved and thus do not hamper the proposed solution. They also require a more sophisticated conformance assessment process compared to traditional processes and involve advanced knowledge and skill. Building designers have to demonstrate achievement of the desired level of performance and prove that the design satisfies the objectives specified in the building code.

10.2 Processes for Creation and Use of Building Codes and Standards

Many of the construction companies and related businesses, such as insurance, material procurement, and urban planning companies, are involved in the creation of, and are affected by, construction regulations. We discuss how construction regulations are created in Section 10.2.1 and how they are used in Section 10.2.2.

10.2.1 The Processes Used to Create Building Codes and Standards

As building research makes new advances possible, code and standard writing organizations try to reflect the state of the art of that research within the requirements of their codes and standards. They eliminate outdated and unnecessary requirements and add new requirements deemed necessary based on relevant and valid research findings and emerging building technologies. Collaboration with all the users of a code or standard is important to achieve a practical, usable, fair, high-quality, coordinated, and widely accepted and used set of requirements. Hence, these organizations usually follow an open and consensus-based development process enabling all interested parties to contribute to the requirements by offering their insights and expertise (see Figure 10.1). Since construction regulations impact construction and construction-oriented businesses, a wide variety of industry practitioners and groups of building researchers are involved in the code and standards development process.

The first major step in a code development process is research. If there was no research experience behind regulations, codes and standards would be mostly static documents. However, researchers, industry practitioners, and governmental institutions continuously strive to increase the quality and safety of the built environment by conducting and supporting building research and improving the building regulations accordingly. Federal and state agencies and industry organizations promote and support building-related research that will potentially improve the knowledge of buildings systems' performance, failures, and improvements. On the

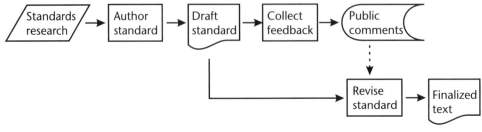

Figure 10.1 Code and standard development process.

other hand, the role of industry practitioners is to contribute and give feedback to the code development process by applying their knowledge and practical experience in using and maintaining these systems. Gathering feedback from all the users of a code is fundamentally important for ensuring the inclusiveness and usability of the building code or standard.

The second major step is authoring of codes and standards, which is done by code and standards organizations. Authorities with jurisdiction to author their own codes and standards may do so instead of using model codes. The code and standards authoring organizations consist of technical committees that specialize in different subdomains of codes and standards. The deliberations of the technical committees are usually open to the public, but the organizations will usually apply restrictions about voting membership and ability to approve changes to the code. Authoring committees are typically responsible for a certain subdomain, which is typically addressed by a major section in a code. All industry stakeholders are invited to propose new requirements for the technical committees to consider for adoption into the code. After the committees finish writing their respective sections, all the sections are compiled into a full draft, which is then published to elicit public review and commentary.

The final major step is for receiving feedback and revision, in which comments from industry professionals on the published draft version of the code document are sought. After they publish the draft version, code writing organizations typically conduct a public hearing after allowing for some amount of review time [3]. The proposed changes are presented for debate and discussion and during the hearing a balanced discussion among representative stakeholders is sought. Then the technical authoring committees decide and make transparent recommendations by considering all views that emerge during the hearing. After the hearing for public review is complete, the results are published in a timely fashion. Finally, a final action hearing is conducted, where the voting members of the technical committees make their final decisions before promulgating the code. In doing so, the technical committees review the proposed changes as well as the recommendations from the public hearings. Following the action hearings, the proposed changes are incorporated into the new editions of codes and standards, which are then published for adoption and use by the numerous U.S. jurisdictions that regulate buildings.

10.2.2   The Processes in Which These Codes and Standards Are Used

A building code becomes the regulatory law of a state when the authority with jurisdiction formally adopts and enacts it. At that point, the code becomes an integral part of the permitting, certification, and inspection process. Designers, building officials, building inspectors, and other potential users of the building code must be trained following the adoption of a new model code or a new version of an existing model code. The diversity, complexity, volume, and dynamic nature of building codes add significant challenges to user training.

The major groups of users are designers and capital project reviewing building officials. Typical questions posed by these groups are "Which regulations and which specific provisions apply to the building design we are reviewing?" and "Does the building design comply with the applicable regulations?" [4] Delivering correct and timely answers to these questions, usually called *conformance assessment*, becomes a challenge given the aforementioned dynamic nature of codes and standards. Apart from the plan review for building permitting, periodically building officials also inspect the construction of permitted buildings and issue occupancy permits after verification of code compliance during the final inspection.

The building code requirements usually enter into the building design process as hard constraints, although some codes also allow trade-offs. Considering code-related constraints, as well as other constraints, such as design specifications, designers make detailed decisions about the aspects of their design and then apply to authorities with jurisdiction to obtain a review of proposed building designs and building permits. Building officials perform conformance assessment against the applicable code and then issue building permits upon demonstration of compliance with all applicable requirements in that code. Unfortunately, this process is usually iterative and time consuming due to the complex nature of codes and standards [5–7]. The requirements expressed in the natural language versions typically contain ambiguities leading to differing interpretations. Some requirements may be completely missed due to manual checking procedures based on text versions of codes and standards. Hence, what may be considered compliant by a designer may be considered noncompliant by the building officials. These problems cause delays in the permitting process and sometimes result in safety hazards. To address this issue, a great deal of research and development has been carried out on the creation and use of building codes via computer-based approaches.

Because both codes and building commissioning (BCx) protocols ensure that building systems function as intended, building codes also have an impact on BCx. Codes are mandated by governmental organizations to address the building design phase, whereas the BCx process is initiated by building owners to ensure that the design complies with building system function objectives. A building owner works with a BCx authority to prepare commissioning protocols and to document the owner's project requirements. The detailed procedures of functional performance tests (FPT) in commissioning are derived from sources similar to those in codes of practice, including research specifying performance expectations for buildings, standards, guidelines [8, 9], and manuals describing system start-up procedures and operations. Hence, logical conditions from code provisions (and possibly other sources) appear in BCx protocols. Some codes require tests to be conducted, the results of which are checked by building officials before the approval of occupancy. These tests typically become part of BCx-FPT protocols.

10.3 History of Computer-Based Approaches for Code Creation and Use

To improve building code creation and implementation, computer-based approaches have been explored to provide computerized support to the developers, maintainers, and users of the codes. Several attempts were made by academic researchers to improve manual code-related processes, such as finding and retrieving codes and traversing between codes [4, 10 –12]. Earlier code retrieval approaches were based on hypertext modeling of codes, which enables the traversal among codes represented on the same digital platform.

With the advent of the World Wide Web, researchers moved toward Hypertext Markup Language (HTML) to enable users to search and retrieve relevant parts of building codes using domain-independent Internet search engines. These search engines are based on indexing the web content using keywords/phrases, such as the "bag of words" approach [13], which is necessary considering the large volumes of text communicated through the web. This approach provides a shallow understanding of the text and is insufficient for accurately answering queries from code users, including what requirements are relevant and whether those relevant requirements are satisfied. For example, a search engine would require a keyword-based query, like "building, energy efficiency, Pennsylvania" for the query: "What are the energy efficiency requirements for my building in Pennsylvania?" Using this set of keywords to search for a set of relevant code documents would likely result in a set of documents containing many requirements irrelevant to the intended query (false positives) and missing many documents with relevant requirements that contain terms like "building envelope" or "U-value" rather than "energy efficiency." Domain-specific taxonomies and more advanced search methods that provide a deeper understanding of the text are currently being used to improve the code requirement retrieval process. [14]

To streamline the policy-making process and increase the awareness and the participation of the public, the U.S. government established a program called electronic rulemaking and began publishing proposed regulations. This has allowed the public to comment electronically via a governmental website (http://regulations.gov). Although the electronic rulemaking process substantially decreased the previous amount of paperwork and increased public involvement, it presents technical and political challenges to policy makers who need to analyze large volumes of information from a diverse set of industry stakeholders. With the help of the National Science Foundation's (NSF) Digital Government Research Program (http://digitalgovernment.org), researchers have been investigating novel information technology approaches to help policy makers address these challenges and help their decision-making process. These novel approaches include categorization of public comments representing different opinions and stakeholders, and summarization of these public comments through information retrieval and natural language processing techniques [14–16].

Both code requirement retrieval and electronic rulemaking have been introduced to accelerate the manual processes associated with code usage while eliminating needless effort from code authors or users. However, they did not fundamentally change the manner in which codes are created or used. Ideally, computers should understand the code content and facilitate semiautomation of the human participatory procedures in code creation and use. Currently, natural language understanding algorithms do not provide error-free interpretation of requirements expressed in natural language–based codes. To achieve the required level of intelligence in the automation of regulatory processes, there is a need for formally representing the code content in a computer-interpretable form.

Formal representation of code requirements has been investigated for more than 40 years and different approaches have been explored to support a number of digital functionalities, such as automated conformance evaluation systems and automated e-approvals of building designs. So far we have briefly presented some of the earlier approaches that laid the foundation for more advanced approaches;

in the following subsections, in particular, in Section 10.4, we will present more recent approaches. In the absence of comprehensive taxonomies that classify building codes, a task rarely if ever attempted owing to the diversity of location, purpose, nationality, and scope of building codes, we present the six categories discussed below as an introductory taxonomy of building codes: procedural programming based, decision table based, object oriented, logic programming based, context oriented, and standards modeling language.

10.3.1   Procedural Programming–Based Approaches

Though still widely used, the earliest computerized building regulations were implemented by hardcoding the procedures of the manual conformance evaluation process into design software. In this approach, design software developers typically read the text-based regulations and tried to capture correctly the intent of the provisions. They then embedded their interpretation of code requirements in programs supporting building design using conventional programming languages, such as C and Fortran. Some of the earlier efforts that implemented procedural programming for computerization of building regulations have been reviewed by Vanier [17].

One of the advantages of procedural programming is its expressiveness. It can handle a variety of complex reasoning procedures that frequently appear in the conformance checking process, such as provisions modifying the applicability status of other provisions. However, an important concern with this approach is that when building codes become coupled with design software, a significant amount of reprogramming effort is required to update the code, a frequent occurrence. Given the dynamic nature of codes, often the design software becomes susceptible to code changes. Therefore, embedded code requirements typically go unverified by code and standard organizations due to the complexity of procedurally representing code requirements and the programming language syntax.

10.3.2   Decision Table–Based Approaches

The problems of coupled representation of codes with software led researchers to investigate generalized code processors that separate the digital representation of code requirements from reasoning with code requirements [18]. With the advent of generalized code processing algorithms, the design software became resistant to changes in codes. The idea of decoupling was first investigated by Fenves [19] and applied to the American Institute of Steel Construction (AISC) Specification [20] by transforming the code requirements into a tabular format called a *decision table* (DT). A DT consists of a condition stub, which addresses the determination of applicability, and an action stub, which is used to determine a set of actions to perform the requirements of the provision.

DTs enabled precise representations of code requirements that are easy to comprehend and validate. Mapping the requirements into a tabular form made it possible to easily check the consistency and completeness of the represented requirements by observing missing columns in the DT (when no action was specified for a given set of conditions), conflicting columns in the DT (when two conflicting actions were given for the same set of conditions), or redundant columns in the DT (when the same action was listed for two related columns of conditions). Sets of possible conditions, for which the users are unguided for code compliance, reveal gaps in policy making.

Since it would require a complex maintenance effort, it is not practical to have a singular, comprehensive DT corresponding to a complete code document. The number of conditions in a code increases exponentially with the number of condition variables. In turn, these increase monotonically with the number of provisions to be represented. Hence, one must create an organization scheme for intertable relations and smaller tables. Typically a table is needed for each cluster of requirements on a specific topic [21 , 22]. Follow-up studies were conducted to find such organizational networks and to develop an environment to assist authors in creating regulation models, called the Standards Analysis, Synthesis and Expression (SASE) system [23]. These studies led to substantial changes in versions of the AISC Specification on Allowable Stress Design (ASD) requirements.

10.3.3 Object-Oriented Approaches

Although the procedural and DT-based approaches were useful and had an impact on the industry, they still required a significant amount of effort to represent the conditions and requirements of codes in DT. As researchers and software developers began to develop domain models and design patterns [24] that captured the characteristics of the application domain and created easily understood and maintained software, object-oriented programming became a dominant solution.

Garrett and Hakim [25] developed an object-oriented model of building code concepts that filled the representational gap between codes and design software. Effective use of objects for regulation and building concepts increased the reusability of code models and streamlined effort in handling updates and new code versions. While the approach was built on the inheritance concept, resulting in an unmanageable bushy classification hierarchy of code concepts, their work inspired subsequent research efforts [26].

10.3.4 Logic Programming–Based Approaches

Application of mathematical logic to software programming, called logic programming, had a significant impact on code modeling research. Logic programming has a declarative nature that is similar to the Standard Query Language (SQL) used with relational databases. These applications are suitable for cases where the users have no interest in the procedure used to generate an answer to their question; they just want the answer. For instance, is the building envelope compliant with applicable energy-efficiency code requirements? Logic programming compilers apply generalized search strategies on a given set of facts and rules. If the rules represent energy-efficiency code requirements and the facts are the specifics of the building envelope, then the generalized search strategies of logic programming determine whether a set of facts satisfy the rules. Although the search strategy employed may be suboptimal for all specific cases compared to optimized procedures, elimination of the need to define these specific procedures for each code requirement is a significant benefit.

The first-order predicate logic approach was applied to modeling code requirements by several researchers [27–29]. Once the code requirements have been translated into logical statements, inferences can be made on the conformance of buildings to these requirements using first-order logic inference engines (automated theorem proverbs). Yabuki and Law [30] extended the first generation of logical representations by making the logic representations object oriented, which naturally exhibits the same problems as the pure object-oriented approach. Apart from first-order logic, expert system shells were also investigated [6, 31 , 32].

A drawback of the logic-based, object-oriented systems is that nonmonotonic reasoning is required in some parts of codes. An example requirement that mandates such reasoning would be the following energy-efficiency requirement from ASHRAE's energy efficiency standard for buildings: "Doors that are more than one-half glass are considered fenestration" (ASHRAE 90.1 2007) [33]. In this example, a fenestrated part of an object classified as an instance of the Door class is supposed to be reclassified as an instance of the Fenestration class. In logic-based approaches, asserted facts cannot be reclassified as a different fact and instantiated objects cannot be instantiated as an instance of a different class.

Another drawback of these systems is model instability caused by the representations of both the product and code being coupled and a change in the product description requiring changes in the model of the code, and vice versa. Hakim and Garrett [34] suggested a description logic–based [35] and product-oriented model of a code that solves these two problems. Description logic is an object-centered logical reasoning system (as opposed to being class centered) in which the system creates objects without restrictions of class definitions and classifies them as an instance of a class when they satisfy defined membership conditions (when a door needs to be reclassified as fenestration). Description logic provides a significant amount of flexibility and is still widely used today, as in the implementation of the OWL Web Ontology Language (http://www.w3.org/TR/owl-features) of the semantic web [36].

10.3.5 Context-Oriented Approach

Object-oriented systems rely on multiple inheritance for the creation of derived objects from source objects, resulting in deep object hierarchies. These hierarchies increase the difficulty of modeling a specific building because a significant amount of knowledge about the code must be known prior to instantiating the correct object in the model. To address this issue, Kılıççöte et al. [37] devised a new method, called *context orientation*, that requires minimal added effort by the user to maintain object hierarchies. When the user inputs a set of contexts defining an object, objects derived from existing objects, called "Contexts," are produced automatically by the compiler.

Although existing context-oriented systems are limited to using generalization-specialization hierarchies, the approach is also applicable to other relationships and sophisticated mappings, like holonym-meronym (also called member/group or aggregation) relationships. For example, compilers should determine instances that are members of the "Building Envelope" context without explicitly creating an object representing Building Envelopes, when the set of exterior building elements, such as "Roof," "Foundation," and "Exterior Wall," are all specified to be members of the context for Building Envelope.

10.3.6   Standards Modeling Language

The systems presented thus far are limited in terms of the level of semantics that can be explicitly represented. In addition to expressiveness, Kılıççöte and Garrett [38] presented the need for isomorphic representations, approximating a one-to-one mapping between the structure of the model and the actual structure of the code (Figure 10.2). The similarity and abstraction of the domain is also important for software engineering and it is studied as a software design pattern, called *low representational gap* [24, 36, 39]. The initial code representing systems were also limited because the representation required pieces from different parts of the code to be incorporated into the same representational unit, such as all requirements related to the U-value of a window being represented in a DT (Figure 10.3). It is not only difficult to validate that no parts of a regulation have been missed, but also difficult to determine which parts of the model require changes when the text is updated.

Kılıççöte and Garrett [40] developed an isomorphic and context-oriented domain-specific language, called the Standards Modeling Language (SML), for creating formal models of the first and higher order logic found in building regulations. SML is basically a semantic network that treats parts of a code and its requirements and term definitions as nodes and edges. This structure allows for the use of semantic network reasoning mechanisms, such as graph algorithms.

SML was defined to explicitly represent isomorphically parts of a code; for instance, the SML representation followed the exact same order and structure as the code text, and was also a part of a larger framework, the Standards Processing Framework (SPF). SPF was also composed of the Agent Description Language (ADL) [40], which provides design systems with interfaces to a variety of reasoning agents, some of which represent higher order logical constructs, and an application programming interface, the Standards Usage Language (SUL) [40]. The SPF captures both first-order and higher order logical constructs within an isomorphic

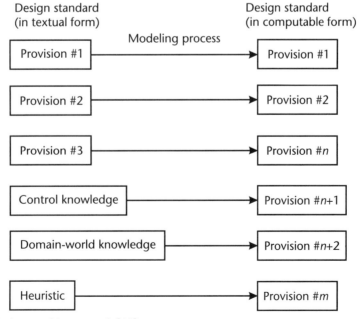

Figure 10.2 Isomorphic approach [40].

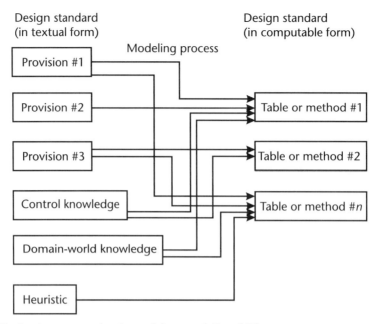

Figure 10.3 Previous approaches to modeling regulations [40].

representation of the code, and then reasons with this representation, checking conformance of a modeled building to the represented code. At that time, there was no standard building model to check for conformance to a code model in SML. Neither further development nor deployment of the SPF-based approach was completed [2].

10.4 More Recent Approaches for Supporting Code Creation and Use

More recently, a complementary and promising research activity on building information modeling has provided standardized product descriptions for buildings, such as the industry foundation classes (IFCs) by buildingSMART [41] and the open Green Building XML (gbXML, Chapter 7). Prior to such efforts, approaches for computerization of building codes suffered from the lack of a standardized building representation utility. Most of the code models were limited in application to only the building model on which they were based. Standardized building descriptions have enabled computer-aided engineering researchers to investigate these problems separately. We will describe some of these approaches in the following subsections.

10.4.1 SMARTcodes Approach

The approaches presented thus far do not incorporate a simple enough syntax that can be easily used by anyone modeling a portion of a code. This is a major deterrent for code and standards organizations trying to validate and understand these approaches. The SMARTcodes project [42] was initiated by the ICC to enable the authors of regulations to create, test, and maintain the models of their authored regulations.

The SMARTcodes group observed that the suitability of code text is a starting point for modeling code content. Thus the model can be built by annotating relevant portions of the text using semantic pens to indicate which text is an instance of which code concept classes. Compliance evaluation occurs in two steps: (1) determining an applicable set of building components and (2) evaluating compliance with the requirements of the applicable set. The classes are chosen accordingly: the Applicability, Selection, and Exception classes for the first step, and the Requirement class for the latter step. The Applicability class is used to annotate the set of applicable building components. The Selection class is used to define a more appropriate group from within the applicable set. The Exception class is the opposite of the Applicability class because it handles conditions of an object's exemption from the relevant code requirement. Requirements are mandated on the set of building components that are applicable, selected, and not exempted.

All of the semantic classes are treated as logical expressions consisting of four parts: (1) a reference to a term in the underlying dictionary, (2) the specification of a property of the reference term, (3) a comparator, and (4) a value with a specified unit. These logical expressions specify a condition evaluated against a building model and the system determines the set of building components that pass the condition. For example, "Buildings located in climate zone 1" can be modeled using the applicability pen and the condition would refer to the term "Building," its property "Climate Zone," the comparator "=" and the value "1." When the condition is applied to a building in Climate Zone 1, all components of the building pass.

Within the current approach implemented in the SMARTcodes system, the mappings of the dictionary terms to the building model are hardcoded into the system, and hence the code requirement representation is not completely explicit. When additions of new dictionary terms are needed, the program code must be updated.

10.4.2   Other Approaches

Other efforts relevant to computerization of building regulations require mentioning. CORENET is the web-based conformance evaluation and electronic permitting system of Singapore's Building and Construction Authority [43]. The system allows the users to submit IFC-based building models and apply for electronic permits when the building conforms to the applicable building codes. CORENET was one of the leading, innovative systems that demonstrated the feasibility of electronic evaluation and permitting, though it lacks explicit code representation (Chapter 5). DesignCheck is an Australian automated compliance checking system, where the Australia Disabled Access Code is encoded as rules using the EXPRESS language. A geometry engine and semantic interpretation are used to check for code compliance of either individual object types or an entire building. It also offers multiple viewing options for interactive reporting [44]. Han et al. [45] proposed a performance-based approach for conformance evaluation of accessibility regulations using simulation of motion planning algorithms in client/server architecture. Lee [46] developed a domain-specific rule-based language for building circulation rules, called Building Environment Rule and Analysis (BERA).

10.4.3   An Approach Based on OWL

We have been evaluating the past approaches for computerization of building regulations and eliciting requirements to create computable models of building regulations. These major requirements, many of which have been illustrated in the preceding sections of this chapter, include:

- Understandability and testability by the authors of code models;
- Isomorphism (i.e., low representational gap) between code text and code model;
- Ability to leverage standardized building descriptions;
- Explicitness (i.e., separation of code representation and processing);
- Context orientation (i.e., no need to create deep and bushy object hierarchies);
- Expressiveness (i.e., the ability of the code representation and reasoning mechanisms to handle the higher level semantics contained in the codes).

Demir et al. [39] proposed an OWL-based approach for representing and reasoning with codes inspired from software design patterns; this suggests separation of the vocabulary term descriptions, and the mappings of these terms, from code to standardized building representations. We propose the use of OWL to simplify code representation with the application of the design patterns, such as low coupling and high cohesion, and increase the explicitness and expressiveness.

10.5   Remaining Challenges and Opportunities

While developing a representation for codes and standards, the organizations responsible for creating, testing, maintaining, and publishing these documents must be considered [39]. The organizations must understand and test representations before publishing code documents for use by designers. They also must maintain the correctness and coverage of the computer-processable versions of codes and vocabulary as the code is updated and expanded. This is an important requirement, which suggests the need for a simple syntax for the vocabulary and code requirement representations. However, there is a trade-off between the simplicity of the syntax and the expressiveness of the representation. As the syntax becomes simpler, the representation becomes less powerful. Hence, organizations require assistance maintaining the models of their regulations by providing advanced computerized tools to support the creation, editing, assessment, and verification of the models of codes (note that this set of needs is consistent with the original goals of SASE) [23].

With such formal models of regulations made possible by these editing tools, a variety of analyses and uses of these models can be performed. Such models could be reasoned with to create abstractions of the codes that could be used in the early stages of planning, design, and ECx. This is similar to what Garrett demonstrated with the SPEX system [47], which reasoned with a formal model of a code to create a detailed design optimization problem that when solved resulted in a code-compliant detailed design of structural components. To apply this concept to earlier stages of the design process, abstractions of the detailed provisions in a code need to be created and reasoned with. In later stages of the ECx process, these formal models of regulations will be explored to automatically create FPT from the represented logic found in regulations and design specifications. Finally, to understand these regulations for the different parts of the facility and the implications of making changes to the facility or to changes in the applicable regulations, such formal models of regulations can constitute the basis for effective code reasoning. Thus, formal models of these regulations are critical for delivering computer support for a large number of activities in the life-cycle phases of a facility, including ECx.

References

[1]   King, L. W., *The Code of Hammurabi,* NuVision Publications, 2007.

[2]   Kılıççöte, H., and Garrett, J. H., Jr., "Obstacles to the Development of Computable Models of Design Standards," *Modeling of Buildings Through Their Life-Cycle, Proceedings of the CIB*, Publication 180, August 1995, pp. 31–39.

[3]   International Code Council, *Code Development Process: An Introduction to the Development of International Construction and Fire Codes*, International Code Council, http://www.iccsafe.org/AboutICC/Documents/GovtConsensusProcess.pdf.

[4]   Turk, Z., and Vanier, D. J., "Tools and Models for the Electronic Delivery of Building Codes and Standards," *Modeling of Buildings Through Their Life-Cycle*, M. A. Fischer, K. H. Law, and B. Luiten (Eds.), CIB W78 Workshop, Stanford, CA, 1995.

[5]   Fenves, S. J., et al., "Computer Representations of Design Standards and Building Codes: A U.S. Perspective," *International Journal of Construction Information Technology*, Vol. 3, No.1, 1995, pp. 13–34.

[6]   Delis, E. A., and Delis, A., "Automatic Fire-Code Checking Using Expert-System Technology," *Journal of Computing in Civil Engineering*, Vol. 9, No. 2, 1995, pp. 141–156.

[7]   Han, C. S., Kunz, J. C., and Law, K. H., "A Client/Server Framework for On-Line Building Code Checking," *Journal of Computing in Civil Engineering*, Vol. 12, No. 4, 1997, pp. 181–194.

[8]   *ASHRAE Standards Committee Guideline 0-2005—The Commissioning Process*, Atlanta, GA: American Society of Heating, Refrigerating and Air-Conditioning Engineers, 2005..

[9]   *ASHRAE Guideline 1.1-2007—The HVAC Commissioning Process: HVAC&R Technical Requirements for the Commissioning Process*, Atlanta, GA: American Society of Heating, Ventilating and Air-Conditioning Engineers, 2007.

[10] Cornick, S. M., "HyperCode: The Building Code as a Hyperdocument," *Engineering with Computers,* Vol. 7, No. 1, 1991, pp. 37–46.

[11] Yabuki, N., and Law, K. H., "Hyperdocument Model for Design Standards Documentation," *Journal of Computing in Civil Engineering*, Vol. 7, No. 2, 1993, pp. 218–237.

[12] Neilson, A. I., "A Dependency Network Generator for Standards Processing," *Computers & Structures*, Vol. 67, No. 5, 1998, pp. 357–366.

[13] Jurafsky, D., and Martin, J. H., *Speech and Language Processing*, Upper Saddle River, NJ: Prentice Hall, 2008.

[14] Lau, G. T., Law, K. H., and Wiederhold, G., "Legal Information Retrieval and Application to E-Rulemaking," in *Proceedings of the 10th International Conference on Artificial Intelligence and Law*, New York, 2005, pp. 146–154.

[15] Yang, H., and Callan, J., "Near-Duplicate Detection for E-Rulemaking," in *Proceedings of the National Conference on Digital Government Research*, pp. 78–86, Digital Government Society of North America, 2005.

[16] Coglianese, C., "E-Rulemaking: Information Technology and the Regulatory Process," *Administrative Law Review*, Vol. 56, 2004, pp. 353–402.

[17]   Vanier, D. J., "Computerized Building Regulations," in *Proceedings International Conference on Municipal Code Administration*, Winnipeg, Canada, 1989.

[18]   Rehak, D. R., and Lopez, L. A., "Computer-Aided Engineering Problems and Prospects," Civil Engineering Systems Laboratory Research Series No. 8, Urbana-Champaign, IL: University of Illinois, 1981.

[19]   Fenves, S. J., "Tabular Decision Logic for Structural Design," *Journal of the Structural Division*, Vol. 92, No. 6, 1966, pp. 473–490.

[20]   Fenves, S. J., Gaylord, E. H., and Goel, S. K., "Decision Table Formulation of the 1969 AISC Specification," Civil Engineering Studies Structural Research Series No. 347, Urbana-Champaign, IL: University of Illinois, 1969.

[21]   Nyman, D. J., and Fenves, S. J., "Organizational Model for Design Specifications," *Journal of the Structural Division*, Vol. 101, No. 4, 1975, pp. 697–716.

[22]   Harris, J. R., and Wright, R. N., "Organization of Building Standards: Systematic Techniques for Scope and Arrangement," National Bureau of Standards Building Science Series 136, 1980.

[23]   Fenves, S. J., et al., "Introduction to SASE: Standards Analysis, Synthesis, and Expressions," National Bureau of Standards Report No. NBSIR 87-3513, 1987.

[24]   Larman, C., *Applying UML and Patterns*, Upper Saddle River, NJ: Prentice Hall, 2005.

[25]   Garrett, J. H., Jr., and Hakim, M. M., "An Object-Oriented Model of Engineering Design Standards," *Journal of Computing in Civil Engineering*, Vol. 6, No. 3, 1992, pp. 323–347.

[26]   Condamin, E., et al., "Context-Oriented Modeling of Eurocodes," in *Proceedings European Conference on Product and Process Modelling in the Building Industry*, Dresden, Germany, 1994.

[27]   Jain, D., Law, K. H., and Krawinkler, H. "On Processing Standards with Predicate Calculus," in *Proceedings 6th Conference on Computing in Civil Engineering*, Atlanta, GA, 1989.

[28]   Rasdorf, W. J., and Lakmazaheri, S., "Logic-Based Approach for Modeling Organization of Design Standards," *Journal of Computing in Civil Engineering*, Vol. 4, No. 2, 1990, pp. 102–123.

[29]   Kerrigan, S., and Law, K., "Logic-Based Regulation Compliance-Assistance," in *Proceedings of 9th International Conference on Artificial Intelligence and Law*, Edinburgh, Scotland, 2003.

[30]   Yabuki, N., and Law, K. H., "An Object-Logic Model for the Representation and Processing of Design Standards," *Engineering with Computers*, Vol. 9, No. 3, 1993, pp. 133–159.

[31]   Rasdorf, W. J., and Wang, T. E., "Generic Design Standards Processing in an Expert System Environment," *Journal of Computing in Civil Engineering*, Vol. 2, No. 1, 1988, pp. 68–87.

[32]   Heikkila, E. J., and Blewett, E. J., "Using Expert Systems to Check Compliance with Municipal Building Codes," *Journal of the American Planning Association*, Vol. 58, No. 1, 1992, pp. 72–80.

[33]   *Standard 90.1—Energy Standard for Buildings Except Low-Rise Residential Buildings*, Atlanta, GA: American Society of Heating, Ventilating and Air-Conditioning Engineers, 2007.

[34]   Hakim, M. M., and Garrett, J. H., Jr., "A Description Logic Approach for Representing Engineering Design Standards," *Engineering with Computers*, Vol. 9, No. 2, 1993, pp. 108–124.

[35]   Brachman, R., and Schmolze, J., "An Overview of the KL-ONE Knowledge Representation System," *Cognitive Science*, Vol. 9, No. 2, 1985, pp. 171–216.

[36]   Berners-Lee, T., Hendler, J. and Lassila, O., "The Semantic Web," *Scientific American* Magazine, 2001, http://www.scientificamerican.com/article.cfm?id=the-semantic-web, last accessed February 11, 2011.

[37]   Kılıççöte, H., "The Context-Oriented Model: An Improved Modeling Approach for Representing and Processing Design Standards," M.Sc. Thesis, Carnegie Mellon University, Pittsburgh, PA, 1994.

[38] Kılıççöte, H., and Garrett, J. H., Jr., "Standards Modeling Language," *Journal of Computing in Civil Engineering,* Vol. 12, No. 3, 1998, pp. 129–135.

[39] Demir, S., et al., "A Semantic Web-Based Approach for Representing and Reasoning with Vocabulary for Computer-Based Standards Processing," in *Proceedings International Conference on Civil and Building Engineering,* Nottingham, UK, 2010.

[40] Kılıççöte, H., and Garrett, J. H., Jr., "Standards Usage Language," *Journal of Computing in Civil Engineering*, Vol. 15, No. 2, 2001, pp. 118–128.

[41] IFC, "Industry Foundation Classes (IFC) Release 2x3," Online Specifications, 2000, http://www.iai-tech.org/ifc/IFC2x3/TC1/html/index.htm, last accesssed February 11, 2011.

[42] Nisbet, N., Wix, J., and Conover, D., "The Future of Virtual Construction and Regulation Checking," in *Virtual Futures for Design, Construction and Procurement*, P. Brandon and T. Kocatürk (Eds.), New York: Wiley-Blackwell, 2008, pp. 241–251.

[43] Sing, T. F., and Zhong, Q., "COnstruction and Real Estate NETwork (CORENET)," *Facilities*, Vol. 19, No. 11–12, 2001, pp. 419–428.

[44] Ding, L., et al., "Automating Code Checking for Building Designs—Designcheck," in *Proceedings 2nd International Conference of the CRC for Construction Innovation*, Gold Coast, Australia, 2006.

[45] Han, C. S., et al., "A Performance-Based Approach to Wheelchair Accessible Route Analysis," *Advanced Engineering Informatics*, Vol. 16, No. 1, 2002, pp. 53–71.

[46] Lee, J. K., "Building Environment Rule and Analysis Language," Ph.D. Thesis, College of Architecture, Georgia Institute of Technology, Atlanta, GA, 2011.

[47] Garrett, J. H., Jr., and Fenves, S. J., "Knowledge-Based Standard-Independent Member Design," *Journal of Structural Engineering*, Vol. 115, No. 6, pp. 1396–1411, June 1989.

Part III:
The Future

In Part II we described a set of methods and tools that, during the facility management phase of capital project delivery, enable the effective operation of the embedded commissioning (ECx) process (see Figure 2.5). These methods and tools impact the process through inputs and mechanisms that feed into the operations of ECx. In this part, we will consider some of the methods and tools that are good candidates for making ECx an even more effective aspect of capital project evaluation in the near future. These include sensors, value-based design evaluation, field tools, AR/VR technology applications, and just-in-time technologies including wearable computers.

Sensors, which were first deployed in capital facilities decades ago, have come of age. The potential impact of sensors in monitoring and improving performance of facilities is not just limited to the functionalities provided by singular sensors; those that reside in systematically installed networks of sensors will have an impact also. This complements the network of local device controls that have microprocessors, actuators, sensors, and communicating capabilities (Chapter 9). These networks enable us to obtain relevant information and effective intervention in facilities to achieve high levels of performance. This can be realized both locally, through one or a small number of sensors dedicated to singular, physical features or pieces of equipment, and globally, compiling information from a large number of equipment and facility subsystems, based on integrated sensor networks (Chapter 11).

Furthermore, design-added value (DAV) analysis is used to assess the value created solely through the power of innovation and design of new and advanced technologies—and not just by throwing money and influence behind capital projects (Chapter 12). Through such methods of value prediction we can make the correct decisions that will enable the success of innovative technologies in the marketplace. DAV analysis helps not only in objectively estimating the value of innovation that is effective, but also in weeding out that which is likely to waste resources and energy. A well-known example of such ill-conceived value assessment underlies the substitution of ethanol—a less economical and environmentally beneficial fuel than gasoline—for gasoline [1].

Emerging technologies in the field of computing have all but completely transformed the way we represent, communicate, and process information in every conceivable realm of daily life. It will not be long before all of what we do in the AEC sector will become digital as well (Chapters 5 through 10). Two of the critical areas of development in this direction are (1) field tools and AR/VR technology applications (Chapter 13) and (2) just-in-time technologies including wearable computers (Chapter 14).

Through the use of AR/VR technology, the ECx process will make use of hard-copy documentation obsolete. All ECx activities will be completed at the site, eliminating time-consuming travel from field to shop or office in order to test or readjust equipment or control settings. Information needed for reporting and updates will be embedded in devices and systems for later retrieval. These developments will make the ECx process more efficient, robust, and accurate.

Technologies enabling JIT applications and wearable computation are developing faster than any other. Thanks to the popularity of handheld devices used for communication and data transfer in the social realm, hardware is becoming smaller, lighter, and cheaper by orders of magnitude compared to similar devices developed only 3 or 4 years ago. Tablets and cameras are embedded in garments and light accessories that make seamless communication and data transfer at the field a realistic expectation. It is highly likely that a specialized wearable computing system that supports JIT data will revolutionize how we conduct ECx in the near future. In the chapters in this part (Chapters 11 through 15), we will describe in detail these emerging new methods and tools that are applicable in the ECx domain.

Reference

[1]   Harasanyi, D., "Ethanol Is a Waste of Energy," *Denver Post*, April 23, 2007, http://www.denverpost.com/ci_5728436#ixzz1NIWHte54.

CHAPTER 11

Sensors

11.1 Context

The embedded commissioning (ECx) process, the main topic of this book, requires and generates large amounts of digital data. As explained in Chapters 2 and 9, the vast majority of this data comes from monitoring and control systems distributed within facilities. Recent advances in computing, in general, and in sensor networks in particular, have made the development of inexpensive and powerful remote monitoring technologies possible [1]. Wireless sensor nodes like the ones shown in Figure 11.1, are now commonplace, and will only decrease in size and improve in performance with time. This trend is likely to continue for years to come [2], and one of the applications gaining considerable traction in recent times is the use of these technologies in the facility management and operations (FM&O) industry. In this chapter, we discuss the research trends, future opportunities, and challenges associated with the inevitably ubiquitous presence of sensors in buildings, and their application to ECx.

To help set the context, we first describe three important concepts related to sensors and their role in modern buildings: their ubiquity, how this may lead to an *Internet of Things*, and the peculiarities of data streams (as opposed to data sets). Note that we use the term *sensors* here to describe any device that can measure a physical quantity and convert it into a digital signal. In other words, we assume that sensors include analog-to-digital converters (ADC) as well. While some prefer to use *transducer* as a generic term for both sensors and actuators, we will include actuators—devices that can convert an electrical signal into a physical phenomenon—in our definition of sensors.

11.1.1 Ubiquitous sensors

Sensors allow us to conveniently capture the vast majority of the data needed in the ECx process. As sensing technologies continue to mature, and their price decreases even more, they will become an integral part of most buildings. This is already the case, to a certain extent, in close-fit and experimental buildings, as discussed in Chapter 9. Today's applications of sensors in buildings include:

Figure 11.1 Sensor nodes from the FireFly wireless sensor networking platform. (Courtesy of Anthony Rowes, http://www.nanork.org/wiki/firely-basic-sensor-driver.)

- Monitoring of resource usage at different points in the building's electrical, water, and gas distribution systems;
- Measurements of environmental parameters such as temperature, illuminance, and relative humidity for different areas or building components;
- Continuous monitoring of the performance of different building system components, primarily in HVAC systems;
- Surveillance and security systems to monitor and control access to different areas in a building.

In the near future, sensors are expected to be the dominant source of digital data generated in the world, far exceeding the human-generated content through social media [3]. Buildings will likely be important contributors to this trend. Due to their long life span, however, the CPD industry has been slow to adopt these new technologies (Chapter 1). On the other hand, other industries with products having a shorter life span have been aggressively integrating sensors and actuators in their design. For instance, a modern jet plane can generate terabytes of data during its flights, and modern cars are equipped with hundreds of sensors that provide critical information to assist in their regular operation. Hence, we can expect future buildings to follow a similar path.

11.1.2 The Internet of Things

When considering these trends, the envisioned future is one where large portions of the physical world can be remotely monitored and controlled in real time. For buildings, this means better information and finer control of the design, construction, and operation phases and the opportunity to develop more adaptive technologies that can sense their environment and plan their actions accordingly. This vision has inspired many ideas in different fields and generated new terms to describe them: the Internet of Things [4], the Semantic Web [5], and cyber-physical systems [6], to name a few. Depending on the context, these terms may be used to refer to different concepts. Their definition is not always clear and researchers utilize them differently. For clarity, we will define the *Internet of Things* as the application of information and communication technologies to allow remote monitoring and control of the physical infrastructure or buildings systems through the Internet.

Current technologies could easily allow us to provide every instrumentation system on the planet with a connection to the Internet. In this sense, the Internet of Things may already be a reality. However, as described in more detail in the sections that follow, the problems currently being addressed in this area go beyond provisioning these devices with an Internet connection.

In essence, the problem is how to enable all instrumentation systems to communicate with each other in an automated, secure, scalable, and privacy-preserving fashion while retaining the semantics of the exchanged information. For instance, if measurements from a temperature sensor inside a ventilation duct of a building are being published to the Internet in some form, how can a fault detection and diagnosis (FDD) algorithm automatically discover and make use of this data to facilitate the commissioning process? Technologies for doing this are sometimes referred to as machine-to-machine (M2M) technologies [7], and rely heavily on rich semantic descriptions of the information being exchanged in computer networks. We explore these issues in later sections of this chapter.

11.1.3   Streaming Data

When dealing with sensor data for buildings, data streams are more common and in many cases more appropriate than data sets. A *data stream* is a "sequence of data items that can be read once by an algorithm, in the prescribed sequence" [8]. It is the preferred model when dealing with large volumes of data, or in applications that naturally generate vast amounts of data continuously. This is in contrast to *data sets*, which are stored sequences that are typically processed in batches.

A significant number of the existing algorithms for analyzing and interpreting building systems data have been developed to work on data sets. However, with the increasing availability of sensor data in recent years, the research community has focused on developing novel approaches to deal with streaming data. Even when an application may not require real-time responses that are based on historical data, the sheer volume of data that is available could require a data stream model for efficient processing. This will have even greater validity in the future. For instance, while the majority of the buildings today rely on a utility-installed electricity meter that provides monthly values of consumption, some modern smart-meters can report power measurements as fast as every 10 sec (0.01 Hz), and off-the shelf power quality meters can easily increase this by a hundred- or thousand-fold (10 Hz). One month of 10-Hz measurements may result in 1 GB[1] of data for a single building. Figure 11.2 shows 20-Hz power measurements for a single-family house for a period of approximately 5 min. At this resolution, changes caused by individual appliances are appreciable. When plug-level meters become more common, larger data sets will be generated in this domain. Figure 11.3 shows an example of this. Data sets could thus grow in size very easily, making stream data processing more attractive.

---

1.   Assuming five simultaneous power quality metrics, each represented with 64-bit precision.

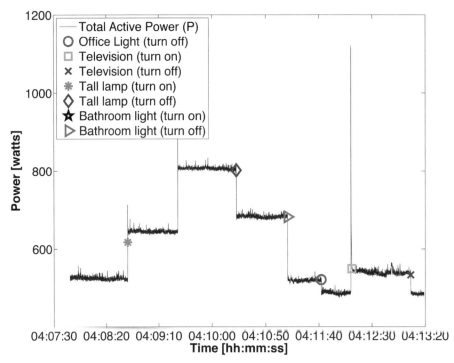

Figure 11.2 Electric power measurements at 20 Hz for a single-family home. (Courtesy of Mario Berges.)

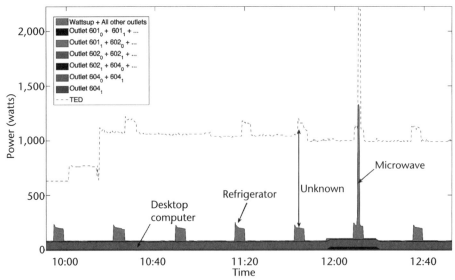

Figure 11.3 Total power consumption of a house as measured by a whole-house meter (TED) and plug-level meters. (Courtesy of Mario Berges.)

11.1.4   Opportunities for Embedded Commissioning

In the context of the building industry, as we have been describing, ECx opportunities will be abundant. Although the majority of the ECx opportunities for sensors would appear to lie in the operational phase, the same can be said about the other phases. Akin et al. [9] define eight building life-cycle phases, which we group by sensor-specific opportunities that exist in each and provide a short illustrative example for each group:

- *Requirement and design specifications:* Historical data from sensors can help refine specifications. Once sensor data becomes ubiquitous, it will be possible to analyze the actual performance of different building components and processes under various conditions and for extended periods of time. Specifying sensor placement and function in the design stage is one of the innovations that ECx will usher in. Depending on their downstream functions—local harvesting of data, goal-directed broadcasting through communication protocols, or automatic fault detection and diagnosis—sensors will be placed and networked strategically. Opportunistic inclusion of device-specific sensors like those in laptops needs to be considered as a creative aspect of this process.

- *Facility construction:* One of the primary functions of ECx during or at the conclusion of construction is to make sure that sensors are properly installed (PFC) and calibrated to make valid readings (FPT). Naturally, sensors can be used to monitor and control the construction progress. Although still in its infancy, this sector is poised to introduce a variety of reality-capture technologies for automating processes and making them more efficient. This includes automated equipment and inventory tracking and productivity monitoring (Chapter 5).

- *Facility management:* The main advantage in the future of facility operations will come from the development of intelligent systems that continuously monitor and control facility operations, assist fieldworkers in identifying subsystems and their performance parameters, detecting malfunctions, diagnosing faults, and actuating change in the settings of equipment components (Chapter 13).

- *Facility occupation, re-occupancy, and decommissioning:* Sensors can assist in verifying the performance of building systems in each of these stages. Sensors can be adapted to the new uses that facilities may acquire over time as well as to changes in the composition or behavior of its occupants.

- *Materials recycling:* Sensors, some of which may be embedded in the materials that make up the facility, can provide information about the condition and status of building components as well as the history of their operation. This information can help determine their remaining lifetime.

11.2 Going Beyond Specific Protocols and Formats

As seen in previous chapters, especially in Chapter 9, there are many emerging data exchange and communication standards for sensors. The plurality of standards, many of which are not interoperable, is one of the major challenges that the industry will need to face in the following years. In some situations, this problem can force people to deploy new sensors instead of reusing the existing ones, as depicted in Figure 11.4. As with any other problem for which there are competing solutions, it is difficult to predict which of these standards will dominate the industry in the near future. Perhaps the two main problems for which a standard solution would benefit the ECx process relate to data communication and data modeling. The former refers to communication protocols, or the way in which computers communicate with each other to exchange data, while the latter refers to the ways in which the information is represented in the data packets that are being exchanged. In this last one we include issues related to semantics, integration, representation, and storage of data.

11.2.1 Abstraction Layers for Communication

Given the uncertainty that exists about the future of standards, a number of efforts are aimed at utilizing existing, tried-and-true technologies to develop solutions that are not tied to any of the emerging, untested standards. For example, some propose to use the existing Internet Protocol (IP) infrastructure and provide hardware and/ or software translators (gateways) that can interface with technologies that would otherwise not be able to communicate with each other. In other words, instead of standardizing the low-level sensor network communication, these projects focus on abstracting these and providing applications with a common platform to access all of these resources, in much the same way that a computer's operating system provides a hardware abstraction layer for its applications, or the way in which IP is able to support the various devices that make up the Internet. This type of protocol-agnostic solution is likely to continue to gain traction in the near future.

The abstraction layers need to be able to not only translate the low-level communication protocols, but also translate the data representation formats. For the

Figure 11.4 Two anemometers on the roof of a research building, with different communication protocols. (Courtesy of Mario Berges.)

communication protocols, there are a number of competing standards in the facilities industry. In addition to the ones discussed in Chapter 9, given that the devices that are used have tight constraints on their resources and may be based on the IEEE 802.15.4 *de jure* standard [10], a large portion of the new standards are for low-rate and/or low-power wireless networks. These standards are used for communicating with certain electrical meters, light fixtures, and electrical appliances, and include ZigBee [11], WirelessHART,[2] 6LoWPAN [12] and Z-Wave.[3]

Rather than indicating a problem, the long list of standards for low-level communication confirms the industry's interest in sensor systems. Moreover, the challenges that remain to be solved in this domain are not necessarily technical. Solutions for efficiently communicating with millions of devices distributed across large facilities, or the globe, are already available. Hence, if all interested parties agree on a communication protocol, it would be technically possible to create a single communication layer through which all different sensor systems in buildings can be accessed. The same cannot be said, however, about the automated interpretation of and reasoning about the data that is being exchanged.

Exchanging machine-interpretable messages requires a previously agreed-on understanding between the different parties involved in the communication, and this is what communication protocols provide. However, the description of the data being exchanged is generally limited to covering only the requirements of the specific applications for which the communication protocol is being used. For example, BACnet can be used to describe certain properties of a thermostat installed inside a room (Chapter 9), but it cannot be easily used to describe other relevant contextual information such as the materials making up the walls of a room, the sensor's location in the room, or the specific variable air volume (VAV) box in the HVAC system that it controls. To stress the difficulties of creating metadata that is relevant to all intended uses, this problem has been described as the "tragedy of meta information" [13].

A number of efforts are under way to introduce this semantic information in a standard and extensible way. However, just as with communication protocols, the plurality of such emerging standards currently forces researchers to employ abstraction layers that include translators and automated data integration approaches. We will review two of these in the following section.

In the near future the FM&O industry is likely to experience a solidification and maturation of communication protocols, allowing easy access to different sensor systems present in buildings, a trend that can already be seen in close-fit and experimental buildings. Due to the projected growth in the number of sensors, measured values will be easily exchanged and continuous monitoring of the majority of the building components will be feasible. Nevertheless, performing automated reasoning using these measurements is a challenge that requires more research, especially when merging contextual information from disparate sources is required.

11.2.2 Metadata Encapsulation

State-of-the art standards being proposed to describe sensors, and their measurements, include the Sensor Model Language (SensorML), by the Open Geospatial Consortium (OGC), and the Transducer Markup Language (TransducerML), all

---

2.   http://www.hartcomm.org/protocol/wihart/wireless_overview.html.
3.   http://www.z-wavealliance.org/modules/AllianceStart.

by the same organization. These efforts are part of OGC's Sensor Web Enablement (SWE) suite of standards to enable the discovery, exchange, and process of sensors and their observations. SensorML and TransducerML can be used to describe sensors through models that are specified in each standard and Extensible Markup Language (XML) schemas for encoding. In SensorML, everything is modeled as a process, and thus it is better suited for describing the process models and process chains associated with sensors, whereas TransducerML focuses more on describing the system as being measured or controlled and the measurements themselves. It is also better suited for handling streaming data. However, it appears that OGC plans to stop the development of TransducerML [14] and favor SensorML. To better understand the models and XML elements defined in SensorML, consider Table 11.1, which presents elements of a *Detector* along with a brief description for each, while Table 11.2 shows elements of a *System*. These are two of the sections for every *ProcessModel* class. A *Detector* is defined as an atomic part of a composite measurement system that can detect a state. Similarly, a *System* is defined as a composite model of a group or array of components, which can include detectors, actuators, or subsystems [15].

In contrast to other more popular standards in the industry, such as the IEEE 1451 standards family, the SWE suite was designed to provide a way to describe higher level concepts beyond basic sensor functionalities. Some researchers are also investigating ways to leverage the advantage of both of these families of standards [16]. Nevertheless, despite years of existence, none of these standards have become the *de facto* standard for any industry. For instance, the earliest standard in the IEEE 1451 family dates back to 1997. This may largely be due to the limited involvement that device manufacturers have in their development. For a more detailed review of the existing standards, their limitations, and their future, see [14, 17].

11.3   Issues Regarding Scalability

So far we have described the benefits of a densely sensed environment for ECx, and have reasoned that while there are important challenges related to the use and

Table 11.1   Elements of a SensorML Detector

XML Element	Description and Notes
metadata	Optional section for information not described in the other required ones. The metadata is described inside <identification> elements and uses terms defined by a Universal Resource Name (URN).
referenceFrame	Optional description of temporal and spatial coordinate reference systems.
inputs	Required section. Used to describe the type of phenomena that the detector measures. Inputs are described inside <InputList> elements and using URNs.
outputs	Similar to inputs.
parameters	Required section to describe parameters of the ProcessModel.
ParameterList	List of parameters, each described separately inside an XML element such as steadyStateResponse, frequencyResponse, error, etc.
method	Description of the process methodology by which one can transform input values to output values using the parameters. Typically points to a Universal Resource Identifier (URI) that contains the methodology.

Table 11.2 Elements of a SensorML System

XML Element
description
identification
classification
contact
documentation
referenceFrame
inputs
outputs
processes
connections
positions
interfaces

creation of metadata, the underlying communication technologies required for this vision already exist. Next, we explore if solving these metadata challenges would be sufficient to achieve sensor-enabled ECx processes. In other words, if it were possible for a heterogeneous collection of sensors and computers to establish communication with each other and understand the semantic meaning of the data being exchanged, would that be all that is necessary?

The answer, although not completely evident at first, is a resounding "no." It may be possible to support a number of ECx activities with this limited set of functionalities, but to ensure that these solutions can scale up to the levels where they become meaningful for the industry (including collection of buildings, city-size facilities, microgrids) and minimize unintended consequences, there are two remaining issues that must be addressed: (1) choosing an appropriate system architecture and (2) ensuring privacy, security, and tight access control policies. The first is the topic of this section, while the second is discussed in the next section.

When designing the architecture for a distributed instrumentation system such as the one we are envisioning, the following considerations need to be made: (1) the ability to support a large number of devices and users is of paramount importance, (2) extensions made by a particular application to satisfy new requirements should ideally benefit the entire community, (3) the architecture should be flexible enough to allow for the implementation of different computation paradigms, and (4) it also needs to be able to change over time.

The architecture evolving from this is largely dependent on the requirements of the emerging application, especially the timescales of interest and the timeliness with which the data is required. In the ECx processes, a wide range of timescales is of interest. However, architectures for handling long and medium timescales are very common in modern systems. On the other hand, the rapid timescale is better managed through a push-based or event-driven architecture, and the new landscape of sensors in buildings will require the use of this approach.

11.3.1 Event-Driven Architecture

An event-driven architecture (EDA) is a software design paradigm that relies on asynchronous communication between the software components and "deals directly with the production detection, analysis of and reaction to, various events" [18]. Events take different meanings depending on the application, but are typically pieces of information about the change of state of a particular process or resource. Applications built using this architecture utilize a publish/subscribe model where each software component subscribes to and/or produces event streams. Events are pushed through these streams, instead of having to be requested by the subscribers, thus minimizing communication overhead. Figure 11.5 illustrates these concepts.

Although event-driven programming is a well-established area that has been applied to various problems including financial transaction systems, it has only recently been adopted by the building automation systems community. The area of most active research in this topic is known as complex event processing [19] and deals with the online analysis of patterns and statistical properties of a large collection of events.

11.4   Privacy, Security, and Access Control

Given the physical nature of the information collected and exchanged by these sensor systems, one naturally has to be concerned about security and privacy issues. Privacy mechanisms range from technological solutions, such as encryption, to informal user policies and fairly simple strategies like proper labeling of devices. Devices placed in public areas should clearly display what information they are capturing and where further information about them can be obtained. The future privacy solutions for this field, however, will most likely come from other areas like mobile computing and social networks that are currently undergoing major transformations to properly preserve the privacy of their users. Similarly, encryption mechanisms for these types of applications are well established and what remains to be solved is how to perform analysis on encrypted data in a privacy-preserving fashion.

Proper access control mechanisms are also incredibly important for all cyber-physical systems. In particular, access to actuators should be strictly controlled to prevent intentional attacks or unintentional accidents. The relevance of these issues

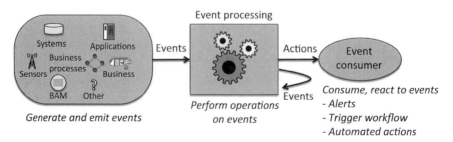

Figure 11.5   General even processing flow. (Adapted from http://www.ibm.com/developerworks/websphere/tutorials/0909_wang/Section2.html, based on copyright granted from Irene Wang and Leo Liu.)

was recently illustrated in a recent computer virus incident that received worldwide media coverage. The Stuxnet computer worm [20] targeted industrial systems and managed to affect operation in nuclear facilities in Iran. The future of sensor systems in the building industry will depend on being able to minimize these risks to a point in which the benefits outweigh them.

11.5 Future Prospects

Future systems that deal with these problems are already being developed and utilized in research laboratories around the world. Multiple projects have created architectures that benefit ECx—by enabling resource reuse and collaborative Internet-scale sensing. For instance, in Global Sensor Networks (GSN) [21], the authors propose a service-oriented architecture in which sensors can be queried using commands in the style of Structured Query Language (SQL) and using web services. A peer-to-peer architecture is used for efficiently indexing data. Simple sensor syndication [22] creates a publish/subscribe model for sensor data using Really Simple Syndication (RSS) feeds. A small server located at a sensor gateway preprocesses sensor data and can be configured to publish particular events of interest. This system does not address issues of access control or resource management, which are important if wide adoption of the technology is sought. In [23], the authors present a system for making sensor data shareable and searchable over the Internet. The system is designed primarily for searching sensor data. It does not focus on management of sensors between different users with different access control rights. The same is true for the system presented in [24].

Multiple research groups have worked on collaborative sensing services like SenseWeb [25] from Microsoft Research, SensorWeb [26], and Sensorpedia.[4] These systems are targeted toward visualizing and sharing data with end users. They currently appear to have little support for managing actuators.

11.5.1 Sensor Andrew

We finish this chapter with a description of one of the many research projects that is focused on developing solutions to the problems we have explored so far. In particular, this project is relevant because it was designed to provide support for all transducers (sensors and actuators), leveraging existing technology from Internet chat messaging services. Sensor Andrew is a research project at Carnegie Mellon University that aims to develop an infrastructure for Internet-scale sensing and actuation across a wide range of heterogeneous devices designed to facilitate application development [27]. The goal of Sensor Andrew is to enable a variety of ubiquitous large-scale monitoring and control applications in a way that is extensible, easy to use and secure, while maintaining privacy. Sensing devices that are used range from cameras and battery-operated wireless sensor nodes to energy-monitoring devices wired into building power supplies.

As discussed earlier, supporting multiple applications and heterogeneous devices requires a standardized communication medium capable of scaling to tens of

---

4.   http://www.sensorpedia.com.

thousands of sources. For this, the core Sensor Andrew architecture is built around the eXtensible Messaging and Presence Protocol (XMPP) [28]. Sensors are modeled as event nodes in an event-driven architecture. Sensor Andrew also allows for easy integration of new sensors as well as support for legacy systems. A data-handling web application, shown in the architecture diagram of Figure 11.6, provides registration, discovery, and data-logging facilities for each device.

A facility manager or building commissioner can easily register the instrumentation systems present in the facility through a web application, as shown in Figure 11.7. If a software adapter, such as a gateway translator, is available for the device

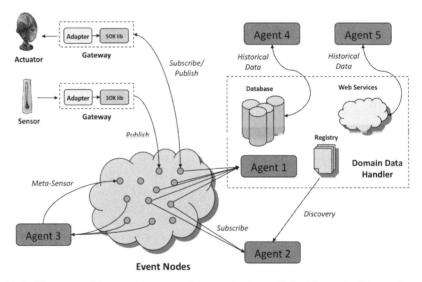

Figure 11.6   The event-driven architecture of Sensor Andrew. (© IBM Journal of Research and Development, 2011, [27].)

Figure 11.7   Sensor Andrew's web portal for metadata registration. (*Source:* http://sensor.andrew. cmu.edu/.)

being registered, it can be downloaded from the same interface. Applications that are developed under the Sensor Andrew framework can leverage data from any device on the network, given that the event-driven architecture abstracts all the low-level protocols (Chapter 13). The project is still in its initial phase, but results from this and similar efforts will probably dictate the future of sensor interoperability in buildings.

References

[1]   Guralnik, V., and Srivastava, J., "Event Detection from Time Series Data," in *Proceedings of the Fifth ACM SIGKDD International Conference on Knowledge Discovery and Data Mining*, San Diego, CA, 1999, pp. 33–42.

[2]   Freedonia Group Inc., "Sensors to 2014—Demand and Sales Forecasts, Market Share, Market Size, Market Leaders," 2010, p. 373.

[3]   Gantz, J. F., Chute, C., and Corporation, I. D., "The Diverse and Exploding Digital Universe: An Updated Forecast of Worldwide Information Growth Through 2011," 2008.

[4]   Gershenfeld, N., Krikorian, R., and Cohen, D., "The Internet of Things," *Scientific American*, Vol. 291, No. 4, 2004, pp. 76–81.

[5]   Berners-Lee, T., Hendler J., and Lassila, O., "The Semantic Web," *Scientific American*, Vol. 284, No. 5, 2001, pp. 28–37.

[6]   Lee, E. A., "Cyber Physical Systems: Design Challenges," in *Object Oriented Real-Time Distributed Computing (ISORC), 2008 11th IEEE International Symposium*, 2008, pp. 363–369.

[7]   Lawton, G., "Machine-to-Machine Technology Gears Up for Growth," *Computer*, Vol. 37, No. 9, 2004, pp. 12–15.

[8]   Henzinger, M. R., Raghavan, P., and Rajagopalan, S., "External Memory Algorithms," 1999, pp. 107–118.

[9]   Akın, Ö., et al., "Embedded Commissioning for Building Design," in *Proceedings of ICEBO-2004 Conference*, Paris, France, 2004, pp. 14–18.

[10] Gutierrez, J. A., et al., "IEEE 802.15.4: A Developing Standard for Low-Power Low-Cost Wireless Personal Area Networks," *IEEE Network*, Vol. 15, No. 5, October 2001, pp. 12–19.

[11] ZigBee Alliance, "ZigBee Specification," http://www.zigbee.org/Products/DownloadZigBeeTechnicalDocuments.aspx, last accessed on June 14, 2010.

[12] Mulligan, G., "The 6LoWPAN Architecture," in *Proceedings of the 4th Workshop on Embedded Networked Sensors*, 2007, pp. 78–82.

[13] Havlik, D., and Schimak, G., *The Tragedy of Meta Information*, Vienna, Austria: European Geosciences Union, 2010.

[14] Bröring, A., et al., "New Generation Sensor Web Enablement," *Sensors*, Vol. 11, No. 3, 2011, pp. 2652–2699.

[15] Robin, V., "SensorML Tutorial 1," 2006.

[16] Peizhao, H., Robinson, R., and Indulska, J., "Sensor Standards: Overview and Experiences," in *Proceedings of the 3rd International Conference on Intelligent Sensors, Sensor Networks and Information*, Melbourne, Australia, 2007, pp. 485–490.

[17] Chen, C., and Helal, S., "Sifting Through the Jungle of Sensor Standards," *IEEE Pervasive Computing*, Vol. 7, No. 4, 2008, pp. 84–88.

[18] "JASON, Data Analysis Challenges," McLean, VA: The MITRE Corporation, 2008.

[19] Etzion, O., "Complex Event Processing," *Proceedings of the IEEE International Conference on Web Services*, 2004, p. 30.

[20]   Chen, T., "Stuxnet, the Real Start of Cyber Warfare?" *IEEE Network*, Vol. 24, No. 6, 2010, pp. 2–3.

[21]   Aberer, K., Hauswirth, M., and Salehi, A., "Global Sensor Networks," School of Computer and Communication Sciences, Ecole Polytechnique Federale de Lausanne, 2006.

[22]   Colagrosso, M., Simmons, W., and Graham, M., "Simple Sensor Syndication," in *Proceedings of the 4th International Conference on Embedded Networked Sensor Systems*, Boulder, CO, 2006, pp. 377–378.

[23]   Reddy, S., et al., "Sensor-Internet Share and Search—Enabling Collaboration of Citizen Scientists," in *Proceedings of the ACM Workshop on Data Sharing and Interoperability on the World Wide Sensor Web*, Cambridge, MA, 2007, pp. 11–16.

[24]   Priyantha, N B., et al., "Tiny Web Services: Design and Implementation of Interoperable and Evolvable Sensor Networks," in *Proceedings of the 6th ACM Conference on Embedded Network Sensor Systems*, Raleigh, NC, 2008, pp. 253–266.

[25]   Santanche A., et al., "SenseWeb: Browsing the Physical World in Real Time," in *Demo Abstract*, Nashville, TN, 2006, pp. 547–548.

[26]   Sheth, A., Henson, C., and Sahoo, S. S., "Semantic Sensor Web," *IEEE Internet Computing*, Vol. 12, No. 4, 2008, pp. 78–83.

[27]   Rowe, A., et al., "Sensor Andrew: Large-Scale Campus-Wide Sensing and Actuation," *IBM Journal of Research and Development*, Vol. 55, No. 1.2, 2011, pp. 6:1–6:14.

[28]   XMPP Standards Foundation, http://xmpp.org, last accessed on February 22, 2010.

CHAPTER 12

Value-Based Design

A deep-rooted motivation for this book is *innovation* in the operations and evaluation of capital projects. Every important innovation comes with extraordinary costs. Sensor-based operations, product and process modeling, data interoperability, standardization of BCx, automatic code compliance, BAS communication protocols, augmented reality applications, and wearable computing all have a higher price tag than installations without them. The only reason these innovations are ever realized—if they are—is due to the added value they create [1]. Therefore, we would be remiss if we did not devote at a minimum a chapter to the exploration of yet another innovation, one that estimates the value added by innovative design. We call this *design added value* or DAV analysis [2].

12.1 Innovation in the AEC Industries

AEC industries are ripe for innovation. Arguably they present a dynamic and at times an unpredictable picture to external observers. Cost, schedule, and design quality, the three indispensible pillars of capital project delivery (CPD), are often compromised beyond standards of acceptability in other industry sectors [3]. The capital project industry is also recognized for its inability to realize these improvements [4, 5]. Microlevel studies on change order costs in institutional construction projects place the added cost at 8% to 10% of total cost [6].

Several players in the construction sector have risen to the occasion with new research leading to management strategies to improve CPD performance (Chapter 2), like lean construction [7], Construction Industry Institute sponsored research [8], and fieldworkers' productivity research [9]. According to Beck, current AEC practices may be responsible for 25% in field inefficiencies through practices like: "incomplete and poorly coordinated contract documents, use of shop drawings and Request For Information (RFI), change orders, outdated manufacturer specifications, value engineering, quality control of drawings, and fixing and documenting problems" [10]. This indicates a dire need for innovation both in the products and processes of CPD and how we evaluate them. In this chapter, we focus solely on the measurement of the value of innovation in the AEC industries.

12.1.1 Value in Design

The simplest definition of design added value (DAV) is the prediction of the value that design adds to capital projects, either *post facto* (measured after completion), or *pre facto* (predicted during design). Taking an example from industrial design, consider the new iPad by Apple for which third-party vendors have designed touch-and-view screen covers. Most of these covers are leather or vinyl pouches that snuggly fit the iPad 2. The *smart*-est cover in the market, developed by Apple, is one that attaches to and detaches from the front of the device magnetically with ease. It turns the iPad 2 on and off through a sensor and folds to prop the lightweight device on its long or short side, which facilitates two different angles, one for viewing and the other for typing. The product description states, "The Smart Cover and iPad 2 were made for each other. Literally, built-in magnets draw the Smart Cover to iPad for a perfect fit that not only protects, but also wakes up, stands up, and brightens up your iPad" (http://www.apple.com/ipad/smart-cover). The costs for materials and fabrication of this cover are at most marginally higher, if at all, than the conventional leather or vinyl pouches. However, its slim, practical, and multifunctional aspects make it, as the ad goes, "not just smart ... genius." We call this *value added through design* or DAV.

The same principle also applies to capital projects, which is illustrated by countless buildings of note, such as Frank Lloyd Wright's Fallingwater, the Sydney Opera House, the Guggenheim at Bilbao, the Brooklyn Bridge, and the Crystal Palace. Their design-features—the cantilevered structure of Fallingwater, the modular iron and glass skin of the Crystal Palace, and the curved, titanium-clad form of the Guggenheim, to mention a few—have made them not only legendary, but also priceless. Even though these are expensive buildings, value-adding design, not mindless cash expenditures, rendered them of great value to their owners, users, and the general public. The following sections describe DAV analysis, a method just as valuable as other innovative technologies being applied in ECx. DAV is illustrated with examples and a description of its methods.

12.1.2 Value Engineering

Because the conventional value engineering method aims to reduce costs by eliminating "unnecessary" design features that support secondary functions, it provides a suitable bookend for DAV analysis, which aims to assign value to features of secondary functions, thus realizing exceptional value (Figure 12.1).

"Value engineering is the systematic application of recognized techniques which identify the function of a product or service, establish a monetary value for

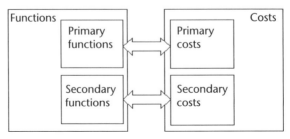

Figure 12.1   The two-part value engineering model [11].

that function and provide the necessary reliability for it at the lowest overall cost" [11]. It applies to two central concepts: function and cost. It aims to minimize cost without sacrificing functionality. In value engineering, functionality, whether indispensible or incidental to the core purposes of a facility, is the primary objective of any design or facility. Hence, the functions of the facility are analyzed in detail with close attention paid to distinguishing primary and secondary functions. Next, the costs of the design components that correspond to these functions are estimated. By eliminating the components solely responsible for providing inessential secondary functions, the overall cost of the facility can be reduced without adversely affecting the components that serve primary functionality (Figure 12.1).

In value-based design (VBD), there is a third critical ingredient: the design feature. What is tacit in value engineering (VE), that is, the physical design features and components, are explicit in VBD (Figure 12.2). Here, the same VE analysis is performed and the value-adding potential of design components, called design features, is estimated. In VBD, some design features are eliminated through VE, because they are not shown to be of any or of sufficient benefit to the project. However, these features may in fact add to the project value in unexpected ways. Such value is emergent in many creative design proposals; thus, it is justifiable for the two-part VE model to be extended to the three-part DAV analysis model (Figure 12.2).

Observing the universe of value in CPD through the lens of VE has important implications for DAV analysis. DAV resides in the *flexible* and *selling* functions and their corresponding features. Flexible functions can be altered without adversely affecting the permanent or principal functions; and selling functions can make the product more attractive, beyond that provided by the principal functions [11]. While VE isolates and minimizes costs of flexible and selling functions, DAV elevates their value by predicting their potential value-adding qualities. The DAV "engineer" must look for the value of selling features and the promising design options for flexible functions.

12.2   Design Added Value Engineering

DAV analysis shows how design adds value to the CPD process in both quantitative and qualitative terms. Naturally, the field of economics is a principal ally in this mission. No stranger to the building and facility life-cycle fields, real estate

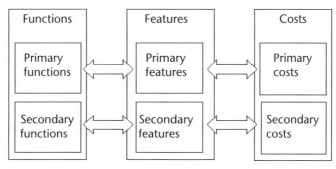

Figure 12.2   The three-part value-based design model.

economics, design economics, and building economics have been applied to frame this knowledge area. The underlying premise of these approaches is to ensure that the economic value aspects of AEC projects, such as investment and revenue, are managed effectively.

Often the value added to buildings by design goes unnoticed until after most, if not all, financial decisions have been undertaken. This has several deleterious effects that can be remedied through DAV. In conventional analysis, the economic impact of innovative design features cannot be estimated. If unrealized without proper evaluation, the result would be opportunity loss. Conversely, if realized, they may lead to "gold plating." In either scenario, monetary loss is compounded by loss of reputation and innovation opportunity.

Since there is no widely accepted methodology for carrying out DAV analyses, estimates of potential value could be inaccurate. Developers and financiers assume risks to counteract the lack of methods for recognizing the importance of design features. To demonstrate positive DAV, they use private funds (P. Johnson's Glass House [12]), inflating the expected value of these design features (the Millennium Dome [13]), and forcing clients to accept their designs on faith (F. L. Wright's Fallingwater [14]). These practices, even with positive DAV, can damage the CPD process.

We consider DAV decisions as instances of rational choice theory [15] subject to the perceptual and subjective effects of bounded rationality [16] and heuristics [17]. Thus, we start by defining the value (V) added by design features as the probability (ρ) of creating the feature times its utility (μ):

$$V = \rho * \mu \qquad (12.1)$$

The economic utility of commodities like buildings relies on two quantifiable factors: the *discount value* and *gain on investment* [18]. Discount value is the estimate of deductions due to depreciation and maintenance costs that occur over time. Gain on investment is the profit expected in the marketplace. Design features are intended to increase the value of a capital project and are subject to depreciation and maintenance costs. These two factors form the negative and positive components of μ.

When deciding to invest in a design feature the following decision alternatives exist: (1) spending $\$X$ to build a facility without design features, where the discount value is $-\$x$ and the gain on investment $+\$x$, versus (2) spending $\$Y$ to build a facility without design features where the discount value is $-\$y$ and the gain on investment $+\$y$. This requires "qualitative economics" modeling to manage the differential $\$Y - \$X$. Bon, in his seminal work *Building as an Economic Process* [18], outlines the approach adaptable to this problem. Value of real estate economics is assessed as the interaction between the *use value* and the *exchange value* of real property. Use value is the value of real property assessed as a function of the benefit provided to the occupants or users of a facility, compared to the market value, which is determined by market forces such as supply and demand. Bon [18] defines the value of alternative choices in building construction decisions through the interaction of *discounted costs* to *net present value* (NPV) of buildings (Figure 12.3).

As the gain on investment of a capital project increases over time, the discount value of alternate design features declines over the same period of time. The

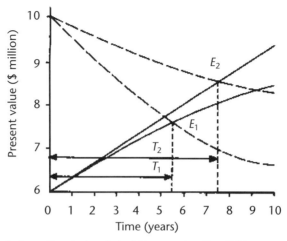

Figure 12.3 Value of alternative choices in building construction [18].

intersection of two curves, in Figure 12.3, marks the indifference points (E_1 or E_2). There would be no incentive to invest in the alternative feature past the point of indifference. Considering design features as alternative features in which to invest, this applied NPV calculation can estimate their life-cycle value. Assessing the value of a design feature is further complicated due to the potential difference between exchange and ascribed use value.

12.2.1 An Illustrative Example of a DAV Case: Fallingwater

Fallingwater is the legendary house designed by Frank L. Wright for Edgar Kauffman on Bear Run Creek, near Pittsburgh, Pennsylvania. Its exceptional design features (the most visited private architectural site in the United States) and market value (in seven figures) make this building exemplary for illustrating DAV analysis. The market value of a building like Fallingwater cannot be assessed merely by its rental or sale value. Instead, its value must be estimated through its use as a "museum." Therefore, we must account for its role as an exemplar for students of architecture, as the impetus for countless other capital projects, and as a structural design invention, not to mention its revenues as a site of visitation (Figure 12.4). The original owner of the house, Edgar J. Kaufmann, is quoted (addressing the architect Mr. F. L. Wright): "My money has bought me great many fine things in life, but none of them have brought me greater joy than the house you built for me on Bear Run" [19].

Fallingwater is arguably the icon of American architecture that ushered in several significant modern design principles, like breaking the "box," employing material characteristics such as decoration, and harmonizing natural and human-made entities. These were achieved with the help of eliminating window mullions at corners of rooms, using vertical chimney elements to counterbalance horizontal cantilevers, and creating the hearth of the fireplace from stone ledges that form the cascading terraces of the site. Each of these features adds value through design. The lack of practical methods for measuring their true value prevented their recognition as assets at the time of their construction. This led to serious conflicts between

(a)

(b)

Figure 12.4 Fallingwater's celebrated views from the (a) outside and (b) inside; (c) composition with horizontal and vertical elements and (d) corners without mullions (Courtesy of Ömer Akın).

the architect and client, initially threatening the project's completion and, later, its longevity. They were realized only through the momentum created by the personal

(c)   (d)

Figure 12.4   (continued)

stature of Fallingwater's architect and the equally remarkable staying power of its owner.

In the end, stakeholders besides the architect and the client were also affected by Fallingwater, including the *host city and region* (the regional economy of the "Bear Run" area), the *cultural milieu* (architectural industry), *related professions* (media and commercial products), and *commerce* (tourism and retail). In DAV cases in which the owner is a public entity, additional constituents of interest may be relevant, such as the political establishment, public institutions, and the electorate.

These stakeholders are subject to potential benefits and harms that influence their interests through different levels of impact: immediate, medium, and long term. In Fallingwater, the immediate level of impact encompasses impacts during the first year after realization of its design features. The medium level of impact comprises the next 2 to 4 years of the building's existence. The long-term impact covers its remaining lifetime. Hence DAV analysis is conducted in a multidimensional space (Figure 12.5) consisting of design features, stakeholders pertaining to each feature along the three levels of impact, and the costs and benefits estimates of their utility.

The design features of Fallingwater—the cantilever structure, horizontal bands of windows, stone chimneys, retaining wall anchoring the building over the waterfall, and open corners of rooms—represent potential benefits and costs to all stakeholders. The benefits may impact each stakeholder's finances, reputation, career,

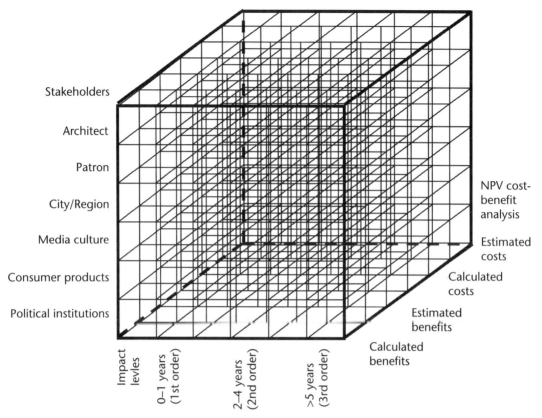

Figure 12.5 Multidimensional space of DAV parameters per design feature.

and overall goals differently. The challenge is to accurately estimate these *benefits*, determine if they can be included in the early stages of the design decision process, and determine if their impact on subsequent design decisions can be measured. Similarly, one should estimate the same with associated *costs*.

This DAV analysis is considered to be *post facto* because the building has already been constructed and commissioned, and it does not assist the CPD process during the consideration or design of potentially value-adding features. Impacting the success of a capital project in earnest, the potential costs and benefits must be assessed *pre facto* at the time of the requirement specification or at the architectural programming phase.

12.2.2   DAV Cost/Benefit Analysis

12.2.2.1   *Costs*

During their inception, construction, or use, all design features entail some cost. Mudge [11] decomposes CPD costs into two major categories: first costs and use costs. *First costs* are further divided into profit and cost of goods. In turn, cost of goods is divided into selling, general administration, and manufacturing goods, which consists of conversion and material costs, and is alternatively parsed into overhead costs that consist of field service and miscellaneous, indirect labor, and indirect material costs and prime costs. These are equivalent to direct labor and material costs. *Use costs* are divided into maintenance and operating costs (include shipping, receiving, installation, etc.). Operating, or life-cycle, costs are usually related to HVAC, lighting, indoor air quality, and productivity factors. Since this is a significant component in the life of a building, it is treated as a separate item in a *cost/benefit with risk* (C-BR) analysis. Utility costs, maintenance costs, liability/insurance costs, promotional costs, and the like are part of the operating costs category.

Costs of capital projects are well documented, but these are generally confidential records that holders of this information consider private or proprietary. Sometimes the figures published or made available are difficult to classify into these categories. Interpolation of given cost figures and projections based on benchmarks obtained from similar capital projects may be useful in estimating the costs in a DAV analysis. Depending on the level of confidence ascribed to these estimates, a *risk* component should be assigned to each cost or benefit.

In DAV analysis, in addition to these standard categories, there are other potential costs to consider. A missed deadline or a rejected design may lead to additional work, while an unevaluated or undervalued design feature presents a more serious problem for the entire project, and even the CPD industry. Without an effective means to realize innovation, the entire industry would come to a standstill. It is also important to acknowledge that realizing these innovative design features requires that associated costs must be reduced to acceptable levels.

The odds of affordable innovation improve with the designer's years of experience, self-selection of clients, and improvements in innovation methods. Furthermore, the CPD schedule is equally as important as quality and cost aspects of design. Delays in completion can be estimated as direct costs and opportunity costs. In some extreme cases, the inherent difficulties in realizing innovation lead to fatal design errors (Kansas City Hyatt Regency, [20]) or lengthy fault detection, diagnosis, and retrofit processes (John Hancock Tower, [21]).

12.2.2.2 Benefits

Each innovative design feature that requires an investment of time and resources must be assessed for its potential DAV outcome. This includes benefits to stakeholders: professionals, patrons, local institutions, culture, media, commercial establishments, and political institutions (Figure 12.5). These benefits may equate to new commissions, invitations to exhibitions, publications, improved property value, improved reputation, improved tourism, new investments, and the appreciation of nearby properties. While all of these are important factors for DAV analysis, the metrics and tools available to measure qualitative (such as reputation, user satisfaction, and publicity) as well as quantitative factors (such as appreciation of market value, sales receipts, number of patrons, and number of new jobs) are inadequate. Often the data necessary to make these estimates have not been accurately recorded. Even when they are, it may be difficult to access original data sources. More often than not, creative information elicitation techniques must be used to make reliable estimates, as discussed later in this chapter.

12.2.2.3   Risks

Whenever innovative design features are included in a design, there are serious risks of failure. Investors and capital project assessors, who control investment decisions, are reluctant to approve unproven features. Even when design features are cleared for implementation, the expectation is that their benefits need to be realized in the short term. To implement them, an extraordinary investment of resources, often disproportionate with the payoffs, may be required. Risk analysis can provide a way to estimate the likelihood of implementation and expected returns on investment. These expected benefits and the probabilities of realization provide the essential decision parameters, or *independent* variables, that must be accounted for while deciding on other *dependent* variables, such as decision to build, completion time, and fees for services.

The concept of risk in decision making is less associated with the notion of hazard and more with the probability of an event occurring. Will wearable computers be cost effective? Will the cost of energy used by the project be sustainable over the amortization period? Will the sensor network be reliable? Will the project reach the anticipated level of notoriety and success? Given alternative designs choices, these are the potential risks, the probabilities of which need to be estimated.

12.2.2.4   Cost/Benefit Analysis with Risk

For a given design feature and stakeholder, we formulate the net effect of cost plus benefit as follows:

$$\{\alpha(\text{B}, t) \, \text{B}(t) - \beta \, (\text{C}, t) \, \text{C}(t)\} \tag{12.2}$$

where t is time, and α and β are coefficients of conversion into a common unit, for benefit (B), and cost (C), respectively. The entire term is equal to μ in (12.1).

Risk, or likelihood of events, can be measured as a function of past instances. In DAV analysis the probabilities we need to estimate are benchmarks based on past instances, which may occur infrequently. In most cases, innovative designs are one-off projects with a very scarce number of precedents. They require a specialized reasoning such as Bayesian logic that defines probability, based on previous observations, as the degree to which a proposition is believed to be true. Starting with such an estimate, one can continuously update this "degree of truth," or probability, in the light of new events that are relevant to that truth. Bayes' theorem formulates the conditional and marginal probabilities of current, say X, and future, say Y, stochastic events as follows [22]:

$$\text{``P}(X|Y) = \text{P}(Y|X) * \text{P}(X)/\text{P}(Y) \tag{12.3}$$

where $\text{P}(X)$ is the marginal probability of X; $\text{P}(X|Y)$ is the conditional probability of X, given Y;

$\text{P}(Y|X)$ is the conditional probability of Y given X; and $\text{P}(Y)$ is the marginal probability of Y."

Similar to the formulation in (12.3) based on the cost and benefit of a design feature, one can represent the DAV with risk as follows:

$$\{\alpha(B, t)\, B(t) - \beta(C, t)\, C(t) \mid \gamma\, (R, t)\, R(t)\} \qquad (12.4)$$

where γ is the coefficient of conversion of risk (R) into a common unit with benefit and cost for a given design feature and stakeholder. Further, the objective function of C-BR analysis for DAV aims at resolving:

$$\max\{\Sigma_{k,l}\, [\Sigma_{j,i}\, ((B_d - C_d) \mid R_d)]\} \qquad (12.5)$$

where B_d are the benefits subject to risk R of a decision d; C_d are the costs subject to the same risks; R_d represents the risk factor involved in a decision d; k and l define the range of costs; and i and j define the range of benefits that could result from the decisions.

Thus, choosing a design feature intends to improve the total gain achieved after the deduction of costs. This formulation makes an obvious assumption rarely available in complex decision situations: the scalability of all risks, costs, and benefits along the same measurement dimension. The measure of risk of dissatisfaction in a client meeting is very different from that of payments withheld due to change orders. Likewise the cost of human life for insurance companies is not the same as that of loss of reputation or life. Thus, at a minimum, the formulation in (12.4) must be amended to include correction factors:

$$\max\{\Sigma_{j}\, [\Sigma_{l}\, ((\alpha B_d - \beta C_d) \mid \Phi R_d)]\} \qquad (12.6)$$

where, α, β, and Φ are correction functions to map B_d, C_d, and R_d, into a common cardinal scale. In reality, of course this remedy is purely a theoretical one that makes an allowance for the possibility of achieving such a mapping rather than ensuring that such mappings are always feasible.

The general strategies in completing a C-BR include, but are not limited to, three methods: zero-risk, as-low-as-reasonably-achievable (ALARA), best-available-control-technology (BACT), and full C-BR analysis. Zero-risk analysis is suitable when there are no options likely to lead to a proposition K, that is $P(K) = 0$. These are events commonly considered to be "impossible," such as the sun not rising, gravity not attracting, or taxes not being collected. ALARA is defined as the risks involved in all "reasonable" occurrences, such as designing a structural span within "normal" physical and monetary limits, arriving at your flight destination, or having lunch. BACT, on the other hand, applies to cases where the risks are governed by the "best" option commercially available at reasonable cost. Options outside of these strategies are subject to full C-BR analysis where one must explicitly account for the values of risks, costs, and benefits.

Another way to define the scope of C-BR analysis is to view it in terms of certainty. When the probability of a given event is so small that it is negligible or so high that it is unavoidable, we say that there is "certainty." When the value of risk is somewhere in between, there is uncertainty. Uncertainty implies risk. Risk must be accommodated. This involves reducing or eliminating uncertainty and risk through the acquisition of new information. The context of the risk—that is, the perception of those subject to risk, the criticality of the problem at hand, and the availability of information—is a key determinant to increasing certainty. Some individuals and institutions are so risk averse that even the smallest risk must be eliminated (Figure 12.6a), whereas others are risk prone and ignore uncertainty until the consequence becomes unavoidable (Figure 12.6b).

A key decision in C-BR analysis for DAV is how much effort (or resources) should be dedicated to risk mitigation. Sometimes, critical problems lead to risk prone behavior, like commissioning the Crystal Palace to Joseph Paxton, a mere 9 months before the 1851 World's Fair was to open [23] or changing the design of its elliptical superstructure in order to realize the Sydney Opera House [24]. At other times, it leads to risk averse behavior like the demolition of the Pruitt-Igoe public housing buildings [25] or retrofitting the structure of the Citicorp Tower in New York [26].

12.2.2.5 Net Present Value in DAV Analysis

The true value of a DAV feature must take into account the net present value (NPV) of a design feature in C-BR terms:

$$NPV = \Sigma_{t=0}, T\, D(t)\, \{[(\alpha(B, t)\, B(t) - \beta(C, t)\, C(t)] \,|\, \gamma\,(R, t)\, R(t)\} \qquad (12.7)$$

where B, C, R − {benefit, cost, risk}; B(t), C(t), R(t) − {benefit, cost, risk} at time t; α(B, t), β (C, t), γ (R, t) = factors to convert their values onto a common scale; D(t) = discount value of {benefit, cost subject to risk} adjusted for time t, i.e., the value of a benefit B1(t) may be less at a future time t' by a factor of D($t − t'$); D(t) 1/(1 + r)($t − t'$). This formulation should also account for multiple stakeholders. Thus, (12.7) needs to be adjusted to represent multiple costs/benefits/risks, each one for a different stakeholder, say i, j, k, and so on:

$$NPV = \Sigma t = 0, T\, \{\Sigma j\, \Sigma i\, Dj(t)\, \{[(\alpha j\, (Bji, t)\, Bji(t) - \beta j\, (Cji, t)\, Cji(t)] \,|\, \gamma j\, (Rji, t)\, Rji(t)\} \quad (12.8)$$

When there are multiple dimensions of risk with constant costs and benefits, the difference between their respective NPVs can be estimated by simply calculating the difference between the two values: NPV1 − NPV2. In Table 12.1, we simulate these terms for Fallingwater through ordinal values (on a scale of −3 to +3) to approximate potential values from real data. The cumulative average is the mean of the values in each column. This weighted average is estimated as a cumulative product of the number of years for each order (short, medium, or long term) times its value divided by the total number of years.

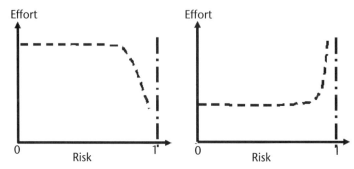

Figure 12.6   (a) Risk averse behavior; (b) risk prone behavior.

Table 12.1   Fallingwater's C-BR Estimate for DAV Analysis Using an Ordinal Scale of −3 to +3

CATEGORY (i, j, k, …)	(t1) First-Order Measure of (B − C)|R	(t2) Second-Order Measure of (B − C)|R	(t3) Third-Order Measure of (B − C)|R	Weighted Average of (B − C)|R During 1936–2010
Architect	0.0	1.0	2.5	2.4
Patron	1.0	1.0	2.5	2.4
Host city and region	−1.0	0.0	1.0	0.9
Culture industry and media	1.0	3.0	3.0	2.8
Linked products for sale	0.0	1.0	2.0	1.8
Political establishment	0.0	0.0	0.0	0.0
CUMULATIVE AVERAGE	0.67	1.0	1.83	1.72

The normative sequence of tasks to undertake a DAV analysis of a given design feature includes:

1. Define objectives and goals of the DAV analysis for all stakeholders.
2. Identify design features that are assumed to impact the DAV for each stakeholder.
3. Measure (or estimate through benchmarks in the case of an analysis) costs and associated risks in the realization of design features
4. Measure (or estimate through benchmarks in the case of a *pre facto* analysis) benefits and associated risks of realizing the design features.
5. Sort costs and benefits into qualitative and quantitative categories.
6. Add costs and benefits with similar units of measurement; aggregate all into one summary end result.
7. Repeat steps 3 through 6 for each stakeholder category.
8. Summarize and communicate results to all stakeholders.

12.3   A Detailed Example of DAV Analysis: Swiss Re Tower, London

12.3.1   Introduction

The Swiss Re Tower, designed as the headquarters of the Swiss Reinsurance Company, is situated at the historic core and financial district of the city of London. Designed by the architect Foster and Partners, it is one of the most distinguished and controversial office skyscraper designs in London. Officially named 30 St Mary Axe, and popularly called the "Gherkin," the Swiss Re Tower adds a distinctive identity to the skyline of the city due to its form (Figure 12.7). In addition, this award-winning building reflects Foster's ideals about quality of workplace and Swiss Reinsurance Company's core values of sustainability [27].

The history of the Swiss Re Tower project begins early in the 1990s when the company decided to unite its five London offices in one building at the heart of the insurance district of London in order to incentivize interaction, interexchange of ideas, and creativity [27]. Nevertheless, the process was not straightforward and the project did not become a reality until 13 years later, in 2003. The main facts of the final project are summarized in Table 12.2.

Figure 12.7 The Swiss Re Tower at 30 St Mary Axe. (Courtesy of Wikimedia Commons.)

Table 12.2 Main Facts of Swiss Re Tower

Category	*Fact*
Type	Office skyscraper [27]
Location	The city of London [27]
Design	November 1997–July 1999 (21 months) [27]
Construction	2000–2003 (33 months) [28]
Occupancy	Late 2003 [27]
Opened	May 2004 [27]
Site area	5,667 m^2 (1.4 acres) [28]
Gross floor area	74,300 m^2 [28]
Office space floor area	46,450 m^2 [28]
Retail space floor area	1,400 m^2 [28]
Costs	$215 million [29]

The first constraint of the project, and perhaps the main problem, was the site. The company wanted to use a site on St Mary Axe Street, part of a Victorian redevelopment area occupied by historic medieval and first half nineteenth-century buildings [27]. In April 1992, the city of London suffered an Irish Republican Army attack at 30 St Mary Axe, killing three people and damaging several buildings, among which was the historic Baltic Exchange (BE) Company Building [27]. Since 1987 the BE had been on the Grade II list of the Statutory List of Buildings of Special Architectural or Historic Interest. After the attack, the City Corporation of

London and the English Heritage organization ruled that any future development on the site should restore the hall and rebuild the BE façade [27].

When the burden of the historical designation reduced the market value of the property, Trafalgar House bought the site for a mere £12.5 million and started to develop a building for Swiss Re. One year after, the City Corporation allowed Trafalgar House to explore the option of a "ground scraper" scheme that incorporated the BE façade. In 1996, the English Heritage Head Paul Drury reported that the BE building was in worse condition than expected and a restoration would be a replication rather than a reconstruction. The demolition of the BE building was allowed in return for a high-quality development by a high-status architect—which makes this project a perfect candidate for DAV analysis. Two other factors supported this decision: (1) to keep the "square mile" area as a center of the financial and services activities of London and (2) to develop areas outside of the corridors that protect the view of important historic buildings [27].

Another constraint on the project was to meet the City Corporation and English Heritage's height and shape restrictions. After several missteps, consensus around a final scheme emerged in 1999. The design evolved from a scheme that called for a 100-m-high building to one that was 180m high that was proposed—surprisingly—by the city authorities and their advisers, who argued that a higher building would eliminate the "bulky" appearance of the design. In July 1999, the final solution was presented to the City Corporation Planning Authority for approval [27].

There was a confluence of requirements for this project from several fronts: client, architect, and city planning authorities and their advisers. In the end, these requirements could be summarized under the categories listed in Table 12.3.

12.3.2   DAV Parameters: Stakeholders

We identified 11 stakeholders for the Swiss Re Tower. Planning authorities, authorities' advisers, and citizen organizations played an important role in the development of the final project design. The design process went through 21 months of negotiations and proposals dealing mostly with the height and shape of the building. Another important stakeholder group was the media, which generated the "spin" and "buzz" that made the building well recognized among conservationists and the general public. All stakeholders were interested in the general impact of the building on the economics, stature, productivity, and environmental quality surrounding its site.

Table 12.3   Final Project Requirements

Forty-story building, one basement, second building for services [27]

Icon for city of London [27]

Baltic Exchange site [27]

360-degrees views [27]

500,000 sq. ft. of office space [27]

200,000 sq. ft. for lease (higher rental space) [44]

40% to 50% energy Class A performance specifications

First sustainable building in London [27]

Awards [31]

Light wells (interaction between floors) [27]

12.3.3   DAV Analysis of the Swiss Re Tower

Based on a review of the planning, design, and execution decisions of the Swiss Re Tower, we identified five potential DAV features in its design: its 3D curved shape, the use of a diagrid structure, the cladding system, the light wells, and the use of building information modeling (BIM). To demonstrate the methods used in our DAV analysis, we will address the first two features in detail. We selected these features because with them we can maximize our coverage of the building's impact on the stakeholders. The shape is a prime determinant of the building's impact over the urban environment and the building's overall cost/benefit picture.

12.3.3.1   DAV Feature: Building Form

The development of the Swiss Re Tower's form is the result of a synthesis based on a number of criteria that were a direct response to the particular site and client requirements. [28] The form was achieved in two ways: First, it was based on a radial plan with a circular perimeter; second, its diameter was different for each floor, that is, it widens as it rises from its base and then tapers towards its peak. This allowed the floors at the middle of the tower to offer more floor space [30].

The radial plan of the tower responds to the constraints of the site: less space on the ground level and the desire to build less of a footprint on the ground floor in order to maximize external public space (Figure 12.8) [31, 32]. The diameter of the tower is reduced at street level, which opens up the areas in front of adjacent buildings. The tapering profile allows the reduction in floor diameter towards the top of the building, culminating in the glazed domed roof that enhances but does not dominate the London skyline [28]. The shape also appears more slender than a rectangular block of equivalent size and allows less of the sky to be obstructed [30, 31].

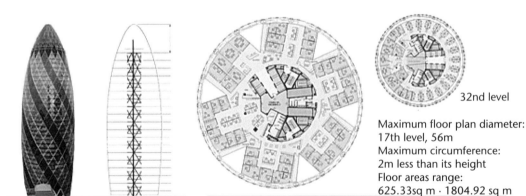

Swiss Re tower's tapering profile   Typical floor plan: 18th level

32nd level

Maximum floor plan diameter:
17th level, 56m
Maximum circumference:
2m less than its height
Floor areas range:
625.33sq m · 1804.92 sq m

Figure 12.8   Tapered form of the Swiss Re Tower. It is widest in the middle. (Courtesy of Foster and Partners [27]).

This unusual form was not only beneficial to the project because of its unusual appearance, but it also achieved the following:

- *Reduced the amount of wind deflected to the ground*: Due to its aerodynamic tapering profile, there is a reduction in the amount of wind deflected to the ground as compared with rectilinear towers of similar size. This helps to maintain pedestrian comfort and safety at street level and in the plaza [31].

- *Maximized the plaza space on the ground level.*

- *Minimized the wind loads on the structure and cladding*: The building form encourages wind to flow around its face, which helps to minimize the wind loads on the structure and cladding [27].

- *Assisted the natural ventilation*: External wind pressure differentials are generated by the building's aerodynamic form and this helps in assisting the natural ventilation through the light wells and thus reduces the requirement for conventional air conditioning. This reduced the costs incurred for air conditioning, heating, and lighting [33].

- *Enhanced the public environment at street level*: The plaza space created by the radial plan opens up new views across the site to the frontages of the adjacent buildings and allows good access to and around the new development [28].

- *Allowed less heat loss and less solar gain*: The circular building form of the Swiss Re Tower requires up to 25% less surface area than a rectilinear building, which means less area for heat loss in the winter or solar gain in the summer in addition to reduced construction costs [27, 32].

- *Provided better physical and visual interconnectivity*: Each floor plate of the tower is rotated by 5 degrees with respect to the floors above and below (creating a light well), this provides better physical and visual interconnectivity for the users on each floor in addition to providing natural ventilation.

Cost/Benefit Analysis: Building Form.
We estimated the benefit and cost picture of the building's form in quantitative and qualitative terms, with respect to its stakeholders: architect/engineers (Norman Fosters and Partners), client (Swiss Re, reinsurance company), city and country (city of London, Britain), and culture and media (exhibitions, books, publications, movies). Table 12.4 elaborates on these aspects of the analysis.

Building Form Benchmarking.
To measure and compare the form and shape of Swiss Re Tower with other buildings, we used a benchmarking tool developed by the Construction Industry Council (CIC), the Design Quality Index (DQI). It is used to measure the quality of a building. This benchmarking tool includes simple measures of space usage, construction, engineering, and sustainability. It identifies three aspects of design

Table 12.4 Cost and Benefit Aspects of Building Form for Each Stakeholder Category

	BENEFITS		COSTS	
Constituent	Qualitative	Quantitative	Qualitative	Quantitative
Norman Fosters and Partners	Awarded the Royal Institute of British Architects' (RIBA) Stirling Prize in October 2004 [27] Identified as one of the seven next wonders of the world by U.S. edition of *Conde Nast Traveler*, April 2005 [27] Design: Helps in maintaining pedestrian comfort and safety at the base of the building because wind is not deflected to ground level Minimizes wind loads on structure and cladding Improves wind conditions in the vicinity (as per wind tunnel tests)	Maximizes area on the ground for public spaces (as compared to square plan geometry); 13% increase (= 4,994 m^2) Maximizes natural light: reduction in heating, lighting, and ventilation costs = £82,278.336 ($129,000) per year [34] Development of new software to cope with the complexities of the design (structural and parametric), reduction in construction costs: NPV = $5,376,414.80 (2% to 5%) refer Aggregated Evaluation section Requires up to 25% less surface area than a rectilinear building, resulting in less heat loss in the winter and less solar gain in the summer [27]	Criticism about the shape (not pleasing and does not fit in urban space around) [27]	Costs incurred and time spent during planning and feasibility stage (August 1996 to July 1999) Cost of conducting wind tunnel tests and aerodynamic studies
Swiss Re	Rebranded Swiss Re, the reinsurance business company [27]	Revenue generated from renting the office space Swiss Re Tower rents: Bottom floors: NPV = £65 ($102)/sq. ft./annum Upper floors: NPV = £70.1 ($110)/sq. ft./annum		Cost of circular slabs = £4,981,663.50
City of London	Rebranded the city of London and has become a symbol of London [27] Changed the perception of tall buildings in London [27] The building outline now appears in a variety of images such as logos, promotional posters, artwork, posters, and publicity materials referring to London	Gave rise to the approval of a large number of interesting high building projects in London [27] Price escalation of land in the vicinity	Criticism about the shape, (not pleasing and does not fit in urban space around) [27]	

Table 12.4   continued

	BENEFITS		COSTS	
Constituent	Qualitative	Quantitative	Qualitative	Quantitative
Culture and Media	Recognition in exhibitions even before its completion, Great Expectations, at New York City's Grand Central Station in 2001 [27] Intensive media coverage of the building from the time the design was unveiled [27] Appeared on the cover of magazines (*Time Out*'s 2005 guide to London, *Architecture Today*, *Architectural Review*), newspapers (*The Guardian*), and journals (RIBA journal, Italian design journal *Domus*, *Wall Street Journal*) [27] Number of lectures, writings, books, articles, citations published on Swiss Re	Revenue generated by exhibitions, books, publications Revenue generated from movies: appeared as the setting in movies like *Match Point*, *Basic Instinct II*, and *Bridget Jones* [27] Revenue generated by documentary film *Building the Gherkin*, a documentary about the design and construction process [27]		

quality—*functionality*, *build quality*, and *impact*—and subdivides them into elements to allow for quality comparisons [35, 36]. It is possible to compare generic forms of buildings, using a five-point scale, on the elements of the DQI process, as is done in Table 12.5. [36]

The general implication of this analysis is that the conventional, rectilinear form is the safest and most economical in most situations, but more complex forms may come close to this benchmark. As complexity increases, the risk also increases; however, the value of iconic buildings can be of a different order altogether as we will see in the cost assessments of Swiss Re [36].

Conclusion: Building Form.

Comparing the net present values of the costs and benefits, the benefits of the form of the Swiss Re Tower far outrank its costs. The distinctive form not only rebranded the Swiss Re company but also the city of London. It has become a landmark in its own right and also led to the approval of a large number of interesting high-rise projects in London. Its outline now appears in a variety of books, magazines, journals, and publicity material referring to London.

12.3.3.2   DAV Analysis of the Diagrid System

The steel diagrid is the triangulated curved perimeter structural framing system used in the construction of the Swiss Re. It serves as a rigid frame for the structure,

Table 12.5 Comparison of Building Forms Using the DQI Process [36]

Aspect	Rectilinear	2D Circular Curve	2D Spline	3D Curve	3D Spline
Example	John Hancock Tower (Chicago, USA)	Commerz-bank Tower (Frankfurt, Germany)	Willis Faber & Dumas office building (Ipswich, UK)	Swiss Re Tower (London)	Guggenheim Bilbao (Spain)
Use	3	2–4	2–4	2–4	2–4
Space	3	2	3	3	2–4
Performance	3	2–4	2–4	2–4	2–4
Construction	4	2–4	2	2	1
Engineering	4	3	2–4	2	1
Character and innovation	2	3	3	4	5
Urban integration	3	2	2	2–4	2–4
Internal environment	3	3	2	1–3	1–3
Form and material	4	3	2	2	1
TOTAL	29	25±2	24±4	24±4	22±5

apart from providing stability to the tower and vertical support for the slabs. It is a self-reliant structure, such that its service core that can take any loading. It also eliminates the need for perimeter columns as well as columns within the building [28].

The diagrid is composed of straight circular steel sections that are connected by steel nodes/junctions at the intersecting points between the sections, and at points where the geometry of the tower changes. The steel sections form two-story high A-frames, which are placed end to end to form a frame that reads as a pattern of diamonds. The diameter of the A-frame columns varies from 508 mm on the lower floors to 273 mm toward the 36th and 37th floors [28].

Each A-frame measures 9m at its base. The diagonal struts consisting of steel tubes are connected by a horizontal tie 250 mm in diameter. The wide flanged radial floor beams, 540-mm-deep plate girders, span 14m between the diagrid and the central core. Adjacent beams are arranged on plan at 10 degrees so that the slab has a maximum span of 4.5m at the façade. The floor is a composite deck slab creating a horizontal diaphragm that assists in distributing the wind loads [37].

Each of the nodes is 2m high and contains three steel plates, which are welded together at varying angles to address the changing geometry of the structure, avoiding the need to fabricate individual end details to suit each location. Steel subcontractor Victor Buyck–Hollandia Joint Venture (VB-H) developed the detailed node design to meet a number of defined performance criteria, including these:

- Loading combinations involving primary structural actions, local floor eccentricities, and cladding loads;
- Robustness tying requirements;
- Movement and restraint requirements between the diagrid structure and the floor slab;
- Erection tolerances and fit within the cladding geometry [28].

At every other floor in line with the nodes, perimeter hoops encircle the building, counteracting horizontal spread of the structure and binding the whole together. The hoops also turn the diagrid into a very stiff triangulated shell, which provides excellent stability for the tower [28]. The diagrid construction happened on two stories at a time. However, specialized steel construction was required on the top three floors of the building (the 38th, 39th, and 40th floors), which has the domed structure. The dome is 22m tall and has eight horizontal hoops of diminishing diameter. The steelwork required for the dome was partially fabricated in Austria, and the segments were first assembled at ground level after which the final structure was welded at the top. Some of the steel used in the project was from the remains of the Baltic Exchange building that used to exist on the site [28]. Parametric modeling was used to resolve the complex geometry of the diagrid and determine the sizes of the steel frame.

One of the main advantages of the diagrid system is the inherent ability of the members to resist compression and tension, creating a need for less steel in the building. This structural system has been used in many other projects such as the Hong Kong and Shanghai Bank in Hong Kong, the Greater London Authority in London, and Hearst Tower in New York [38]. The amount of steel and details of all of the members used in the building are summarized in Table 12.6.

Cost Benefit Analysis: Diagrid Structure.
The benefit and cost picture of the building's diagrid structure was estimated in quantitative and qualitative terms, from the vantage point of its architect, client/user, city and region, contractors (Skanska Construction), and structural engineer/steel fabricators (ARUP, Victor Buyck–Hollandia Joint Venture Ltd., and Waagner-Biro). Table 12.7 shows the results.

An assessment of the advantages and disadvantages of the diagrid system over other structural types is given in Table 12.8.

Conclusions: Diagrid Structure.
It can be concluded that a diagrid structure is a structurally efficient system compared to other structural types for heights greater than 40 stories, with fabrication of nodes being the only disadvantage. The material savings in using the diagrid system as opposed to a braced-tube structure is substantial (Table 12.9).

Table 12.6   Steel Used in the Swiss Re Tower [28]

Description	*Number and/or Weight*
Total amount of steel used	8,358 tons
Diagrid (29% of total steel)	2,423 tons
Total number of primary steel pieces	8,348
Total length	35 km
Diagrid column size (ground–level 2)	508 mm, 40 mm thick
Diagrid column size (level 36–38)	273 mm, 12.5 mm thick
Number of nodes	360
Top dome—rectangular hollow sections 110 × 150 mm welded	

Table 12.7   Cost and Benefit Aspects of the Diagrid System [28]

	BENEFITS		COSTS	
Constituent	Qualitative	Quantitative	Qualitative	Quantitative
Contractor	Rigid structural frame Core can be designed as an open-plan steel structure Foundation loads reduced Window panes and cladding customized to the frame, use of plane glass Interior columns are not required [39]	Structural efficiency gained by adding to building stiffness by 40% [39] An increase in area of 185 m^2 for a typical floor	Training of construction crew to build structure Coordination issues as different parts of the structure were fabricated and shipped from outside of London	Added cost and time that went into training crew
Structural engineer/steel fabricators	The structure allowed for cutting down use of steel by 20% [28] Parametric modeling made process of fabrication and construction simpler and faster	Cost savings of £85,606 Construction cost savings of approximate £2.76 million (2% of total construction cost) by using BIM	Complex constructability of nodes and dome structure: time and effort increased Steel sections needed to be enveloped in fire protection and encased in aluminum cladding [40] Difficulty in designing corresponding parallelogram-shaped curtain wall units to be clad over structure Nodes had to be fabricated in Netherlands and Belgium [28]	Cost incurred and time spent during planning and feasibility stage (August 1996 to July 1999) Cost of conducting wind tunnel tests and aerodynamic studies
Architect	Allowed for irregular design of floor plates Helped realize the complex building form Expertise in building the structure resulting in minimum errors	Time and cost savings		
Client/user	Immense recognition for high-profile design Column-free interior spaces Natural light and ventilation	Calculated in building form Calculated for building form	BIM required for form and structure Experienced structural engineers and fabricators had to be employed	Fabricating nodes and transportation (from Netherlands, Belgium and Austria) = £1,000,000 Fire proofing cost = £55.7/m^2 [41] Building information modeling
City and region	Iconic design Wide use of diagrid in other structures			

Table 12.8   Advantages and Disadvantages of the Diagrid System [42]

Type of Structure	Material	Efficient Height Limit	Advantages	Disadvantages
Framed tube	Steel	80	Resists lateral loads	Shear lag hinders true tubular behavior
Braced tube	Steel	100	Resists lateral shear, wider column spacing possible, reduced shear lag	Bracings obstruct view
Bundled tube	Steel	110	Reduced shear lag	Interior planning limitations
Diagrid	Steel	100	Efficiently resists lateral shear	Complicated joints
Diagrid	Concrete	60		Expensive formwork and slow construction
Space truss structure	Steel or concrete	150	Efficiently resists lateral shear	May obstruct view
Superframe	Steel	160	Could produce super tall buildings	Building form depends on structural system
Exoskeleton	Steel	100	Interior floor never obstructed by perimeter columns	Thermal expansion and contraction

Table 12.9   Assessment of Material Savings of Diagrid System Compared to a Braced-Tube Structure [39]

Building Story Height	Braced-Tube Steel Mass	Diagrid Steel Mass	Material Usage Difference Between Braced Tube and Diagrid (%)
40 stories	989	821	20.5
50 stories	2,128	1,855	14.7
60 stories	4,113	3,822	7.6
70 stories	7,222	6,882	5.9
80 stories	11,848	11,574	2.4
90 stories	18,545	18,412	0.7
100 stories	27,287	27,703	−1.5

In terms of material savings, use of the diagrid system saves between 2% and 20% of material for buildings up to 80 stories high when compared with a conventional braced-tube steel structure.

12.3.4   Economic Analysis of the Swiss Re Tower

12.3.4.1   Exchange Value

Sale Value of Land.
In 1994 the Exchange Baltic Company sold the land and the old building to Trafalgar House at a price of £12 million [27]. The low price was due to the restrictions attached to the site requiring restoration of historic structures. In 1998, Swiss Re compromised the purchase of the site from Trafalgar House. The media reported a sale price in the range of £80 to £100 million [27]. This new high value of the site reflects the changes in the restrictions regarding the restoration of the damaged BE

Building. Subsequently, the Swiss Re was sold to the German property firm IVG Immobilien and U.K. investment firm Evans Randall for £600 million.

Rental Value.
The bottom floors of the Swiss Re Tower rent for £55/sq. ft. per annum, while the upper floors, totaling 50,000 sq. ft., go for £60/sq. ft. per annum [43]. When fully occupied the total yield of the building ranges between £54 and £72/sq. ft. per annum [44, 45]. The average office rental rate, at the time of our research, in London, was £54 to £72/sq. ft. per annum [45], which breaks down into base rent of £35 to £45/sq. ft. per annum, added rates of £12 to £18/sq. ft. per annum, and services at £7 to £9/sq. ft. per annum. Comparing the Swiss Re to other comparable office towers in Table 12.10, we find that its exchange value is considerably higher.

12.3.4.2   Use Value

Regarding the use value of the Swiss Re Tower, we found both negative and positive aspects. Negative aspects include the discomfort of tenants because of the lack of confidentiality created by the open design. As a consequence partitions were added in some floors, affecting the natural ventilation system [27]. The only tenant that uses the natural ventilation system is the Swiss Re Company. Another adjustment made by the tenants of the building was the lowering of the temperature control from 26° to 24°C, increasing the energy consumption for cooling. Positive aspects about the use value of the Swiss Re Tower are the morale-boosting effect over the workers that the famous building provides. More than 25,000 individuals have visited the restaurant and enjoyed the 360-degree views that the upper floors provide [27].

12.3.4.3   Aggregated DAV Evaluation

Due to the innovative structural system of the Swiss Re Tower, a savings of £85,606 was realized from material, labor, and fabrications processes. Given the inflation rate of 2.65 between 2001 and 2009 [46], this represents a NPV savings of £105,529.97 or $166,758.46. Total construction cost savings due to innovations in the construction systems of the tower equal £2,760,000 [47]. Given the same inflation rate, this represents a NPV savings of £3,402,363.51 or $5,376,414.80.

Energy savings, a critical factor for our undertaking in this book, was estimated based on the "typical prestige air-conditioned office building" consumption

Table 12.10   Summary of the Comparison of Swiss Re with Other Towers

Conversion: 1 m^2 = 10.7 sq. ft.	Rental Price	Average Rental Price Location	Ratio of Rental Price to Average Price	Over Price per Sq. Ft.	Ratio of Office Space Area to Site Area
Swiss Re (London)	$ 10.78	$9.42	1.14	$1.40-$3.73	8.19
Agbar Tower (Spain)	$ 3.97	$2.3	1.69	$1.77	0.6
Hearst Tower (New York City)	$6.04	$5.75	1.04	$0.24	21.7

rate of 568 kW/m^2 per year. The "good practice" target consumption, based on this standard, is 348 kW/m^2 per year. Swiss Re Tower energy consumption turned out to be 215 kW/m^2 per year due to the cladding design and because natural ventilation is used 40% of the year [48]. Using the aforementioned inflation correction, this represents a NPV savings of £82,278.336 or $129,000/year.

On the other hand, the O&M functions gave rise to substantial costs. Maintenance costs for the Swiss Re Tower equal £4,402,200 per annum (inflation corrected = £5,039,270). There were added maintenance costs due to the special forms and structure: £251,963.50 or $398,152.72 [49].

The total DAV calculation for the Swiss Re Tower based on its form and structural system was estimated with the following assumptions:

- The net cost of finishing and fire protection for the diagrid system could not be quantified.

- Revenues from use of the building or its image in publications, movies, and so on have not been included.

- Additional costs and benefits resulting from other features such as the glass cladding and maintenance, sustainable design features, and so on, have not been included.

With these caveats the aggregate cost/benefit value of the DAV features of the Swiss Re Tower equals $5,341,010.54 to $5,452,501.04 (Table 12.11).

12.4   Methods of DAV Engineering

Let us now review some of the key methods used in the completion of a DAV analysis. These include archival documentation of parameters, carryover from precedents, scaling ordinal probabilities, sensitivity analysis, indifference curves, and elicitation methods.

Table 12.11   Aggregate DAV Cost/Benefit Picture for the Swiss Re Tower Based on Its Form and Diagrid Structure Features

Category	Benefits–Risks	Costs–Risks
Energy savings	$129,000	
Structural system	$166,758.46	
Construction cost (parametric modeling)	$5,376,414.80	
Increase in rental value	$66,990–$178,480	
Added maintenance costs (due to structure and form)		$398,152.72
TOTAL	$5,739,163.26–$5,850,653.76	$398,152.72
NET BENEFITS (form and diagrid structure)	$5,341,010.54–$5,452,501.04	
Savings/m^2 (rentable area = 47,850/m^2)	($111.62–$113.95)/m^2	

12.4.1 Archival Documentation of Parameters

This approach is used when there is an abundance of data available on the DAV parameters of a capital project. These parameters include, but are not limited to, project size, scope, client, site, architect, cost, schedule, and facility program. At a minimum, the archival records should include information on the costs, benefits, and risks taken in realizing the design features. This approach is particularly effective for *post facto* analysis. The normative procedure for this method includes documentation of the following:

- *Features:* List all features, match features with corresponding functions distinguishing DAV functions from non-DAV ones, such as *work* versus *sell* functions and *basic* versus *secondary* functions.
- *Stakeholders:* List all stakeholders that have been affected by the features of this facility. At a minimum, include six levels: design professional, user (client), city or region, culture and media, commercial, and political.
- *Costs and benefits subject to risks at three levels of impact:* Estimate the costs and benefits, both subject to probability of occurrence (risk), at the immediate (first year), medium (first 4 years), and long term (life = yrk) impact levels, as delta (differential) obtained by comparing against a benchmark.

In Section 12.3, we described two DAV features for the Swiss Re Tower: building form and the diagrid structural system. Such documentations should answer questions such as these: What is included in a feature and what is excluded? Is the feature just a planar element or should adjacent volumes be included? Does it include structural components and architectural finishes? Is it mutually exclusive from the other features? These questions receive different answers depending on the frame within which they are viewed. Viewed through the lens of DAV, a feature is seen as the difference between having an added value or not. In its absence, the value estimate reverts to the benchmark or a conventional solution, such as a precast wall element in place of aluminum and glass cladding.

Features result in costs and benefits that affect the various stakeholders differently. While the features described earlier matter a great deal to the designer, architect Foster and Associates, his cohorts and employees, or the users and the general public who assess the Swiss Re every day, many of them assign entirely different meanings to its features—like the overall form and the skin. To each of these stakeholders, the diagrid structure and the light shafts and natural ventilation it provides may represent excellence in green design, an interesting form, or a comparative advantage over other towers. These differences must be recorded in documenting the stakeholders.

Normally cost and benefit items are indicated as singular aggregate amounts. Since the ultimate impact of a DAV feature may not be evident immediately, it is useful to disaggregate this for different levels of impact: short term, medium term, and long term. Whereas, in the first few years, due to the negative NPV caused by the massive initial investment, the C-BR estimates of the Swiss Re's DAV features will fall in the negative column, over the 10-year duration, due to the productivity gains of day lighting and natural ventilation, their combined effect turns out to be positive.

12.4.2   Carryover from Precedents

When reliable data is not available for all features of the DAV analysis, data can be carried over from suitable precedents after proper recalibration of value estimates. This method requires that the precedents at hand actually contain data that correspond to the categories missing in the case being analyzed. The dimensions along which the DAV project must resemble the precedent include project size, scope, client, site, architect, costs, schedules, and facility program. At a minimum, the precedent must have well-documented design features, costs of realizing these features, and benefits realized because of these features. Judged qualitatively, the similarity between them must be reasonably close—within approximately 10%. When these conditions are met, the procedure outlined in Section 12.3.1 can be applied.

12.4.3   Qualitative and Intervariable Estimates

Other obstacles in adapting C-BR to DAV analysis include mapping costs and benefits onto a common scale, quantifying ordinal evaluations, and sensitivity analysis. Ordinal scales can be instrumental in finding commonality between unlike value measurements. For example, by mapping these measurements onto a five-point ordinal scale of high, medium-high, medium, medium-low, and low, we can assign a corresponding cardinal value to each of these points, say 0.95, 0.75, 0.50, 0.25, and 0.05, respectively; thus we can aggregate the two parametric dimensions of cost and benefit, using a qualitative calculus.

The weakness of this approach is that the five-point scale used may create untenable sensitivities. What would happen if we assign 0.9 to high and 0.1 to low? Would the aggregated C-BR value for these two dimensions be significantly different? This is the topic of sensitivity analysis. Sensitivity analysis is the study of how uncertainty in the output of a model (in quantitative or qualitative terms) can be attributed to uncertainties hidden in the inputs to the model.

> A quantitative model is defined by a series of equations, input factors, parameters, and variables aimed to characterize the process being investigated. Input is subject to many sources of uncertainty including errors of measurement, absence of information and poor or partial understanding of the driving forces and mechanisms. This uncertainty imposes a limit on our confidence in the response or output of the model. [50]

In models involving many input variables, sensitivity analysis is an essential ingredient of model building and quality assurance.

12.4.4   DAV Elicitation Methods

As discussed in Section 12.4.1, a *post facto* analysis, in which we estimate the costs, benefits, and risks associated with DAV features for all stakeholders at different levels of impact, is relatively straightforward. What about designs, however, that are still on the drawing board or the planning stage? How does one estimate these parameters for DAV analysis? In fact, isn't it even more critical to have accurate estimates of these parameters at a time when the investment in their DAV features is under consideration? The decisions made *pre facto*, during the early design stages, may make or break the viability of these designs. Next, we outline several survey techniques—interview, brainstorming, prototyping, cognitive walkthrough, and ethnographic observation—that can be used to estimate DAV parameters not only after the fact but also before a design is finalized or implemented.

12.4.4.1 Structured Interview

A structured interview consists of a set of questions asked in a given order and typically conducted face to face. While it follows the general outline of the predefined list of questions, it has the advantage of allowing the interviewer to pursue important issues that may come up during the course of the interview. It provides the best means for getting to the crux of what is needed in a design problem. For instance, the requirement specifications of potential DAV features can be directly gathered from the users or clients. While a structured interview is best suited to documenting requirement specifications and establishing a customer profile, it can assist the other steps in DAV elicitation, such as assessing the user environment, potential design features, resources needed to realize these features, and risk management.

In conducting a structured interview, care must be taken to minimize duration; certainly no longer than 1.5 hours. If necessary the interview can be broken up into shorter segments. Conducting interviews with multiple participants on the same topic is subject to the "law" of information accumulation (Figure 12.9). As subsequent participants are interviewed, new information emerges alongside redundant information. In this process, the amount of repeat information increases as new information decreases (Chapter 4).

12.4.4.2 Brainstorming

Brainstorming is the perfect technique for discovering solutions or ideas that do not meet the eye at first. Among the steps of the DAV elicitation process the two that are most suitable for brainstorming are assessing design features and managing DAV risks.

Brainstorming is best conducted with adherence to a handful of golden rules: Generate as many ideas as possible, allow imaginations to soar, permit no criticism or debate while generating ideas, and mutate and combine ideas by piggybacking on previously stated ones. To initiate a brainstorming session, the first step is to state the objectives of the session to the participants. Next the participants are urged to maintain informality and use their own words. A scribe keeps accurate

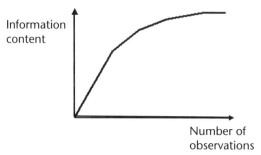

Figure 12.9 Law of elicited information accumulation.

notes of keywords that represent ideas generated. Finally, the session should not exceed 1 or 1.5 hours, at most.

Once ideas have been generated, they are then edited and organized into a coherent format. First the list of keywords and clusters of keywords associated through piggybacking are pruned into a shorter list. Here judgment is required to separate ideas into three categories: unworkable ideas, workable ideas, and exceptional ideas (albeit generated without regard for feasibility). During this stage there should be further elaboration of the key ideas and features. Finally, these ideas must meet the filter of reality. One of the best ways to reduce the scope is to prioritize the keywords. Creating hierarchical priority schema is a vast area of research. Most approaches are based on pairwise comparison of options by predefined and prioritized criteria such as the analytical hierarchy method [51].

12.4.4.3   Prototyping

Prototyping is an approach that is best suited for assessing design feature possibilities in a capital project. It involves the development of an advance model or representation of the project that allows for visualization and estimates of performance. Prototyping is also helpful in correcting known design pitfalls by revealing them. "Yes, but" responses from potential users to the prototype imply indecision about the priorities associated with design features. "Undiscovered ruins" are emergent features that are hard to identify until a simulation of the design is created as a prototype. And "design biases" can be identified through the creation of visionary prototypes.

Prototypes come in several forms [52]. Some are focused on the *user interface* aspects of a design, such as the digital tools. Others may be more interested in *performance issues*, such as minimizing energy use in a light fixture. Some prototypes are *evolutionary*, where work continues on the prototype to enhance it until it closely approximates the final product. Alternatively, a prototype may be designed to be a *throwaway*. It is used once and then an entirely different prototype is developed thereafter. Finally, prototypes can be *vertical*, deeply exploring all aspects of a limited section of a large project, say the lobby of a hotel design, or the cleanrooms in a lab building. They can also encompass a *broad* coverage of all major parts of a project, highlighting the interrelationships between these parts rather than the minute details of each feature.

12.4.4.4   Cognitive Walkthrough

A versatile elicitation method is the cognitive walkthrough. The cognitive walkthrough can be used to assess the overall problem, recap the problem for the client or user toward a shared understanding, and assess the resources needed to realize design features. Cognitive walkthroughs are completed by domain experts, individuals most familiar with the building type or technology. They are invited to examine a legacy design or a prototype expressly developed for the problem at hand. A predefined script is followed to assess the system or design under investigation with the purpose of developing a specific, feature-by-feature evaluation. The cognitive walkthrough must be managed carefully by someone experienced in facilitating workshops. The proceedings of the walkthrough must be recorded and later analyzed for evidence to support evaluative inferences.

12.4.4.5   Ethnographic Observation

This is the most elaborate and resource intense of all elicitation methods in DAV analysis. It is most suitable for understanding the user environment and its limits in their entirety. Ethnographic observation is a structured and systematic way of codifying user behavior as it occurs in its natural context. It uses the actual events and interactions in a facility rather than creating simulations or prototypes, which are abstractions of real conditions. In addition to being naturalistic, ethnographic observations are also unobtrusive. They do not interfere with the behaviors they codify. To achieve these goals, ethnographic observation techniques involve extensive data recording either through video documentation or other recording means. Yet they are not limited to such recordings because the process is a multigranulated approach that includes a variety of sources of data: physical products and tools used, written records, databases, and traces of human behavior.

12.5   Analyzing the Value of Designs

In his foreword to the book titled *Building Economics: Theory and Practice*, Wilson wrote [1]:

> The challenge is often how to determine the true costs and the true benefits of alternative decisions. For example, what is the economic value in electric lighting savings and productivity increases of providing daylight to workplace environments? Or, what is the value of saving historic structures? Alternately, what is the cost of a building integrated photovoltaic system, given that it may replace a conventional roof? The following three overarching principles associated with ensuring cost-effective construction reflect the need to accurately define costs, benefits, and basic economic assumptions:
>
> · *Utilize Cost Management and Value Engineering Throughout the Planning, Design, and Development Process*: As most projects are authorized or funded without a means of increasing budgets, it is essential that the project requirements are set by considering life-cycle costs.
>
> · Use Economic Analysis to Evaluate Design Alternatives: In addition to first costs, facility investment decisions typically include projected cost impacts of, energy/utility use, operation and maintenance and future system replacements.
>
> · *Consider Non-Monetary Benefits such as Aesthetics, Historic Preservation, Security, and Safety*: Most economic models require analysts to place a dollar value on all aspects of a design to generate final results. Nevertheless it is difficult to accurately value certain non-monetary building attributes, such as formality (for example, of a federal courthouse) or energy security. In some cases, these non-monetary issues are used as tiebreakers to quantitative analyses. In other instances, non-monetary issues can override quantitatively available cost comparisons. These cost-effectiveness principles serve as driving objectives for

cost management practices in the planning, design, construction, and operation of facilities that balance cost, scope, and quality.

Wilson illustrates both the difficulty and importance of value assessment for making sound CPD decisions. He points out the importance of recognizing at once the value of photovoltaic technology and saving historic structures, while they may have conflicting end goals. It is essential for us to be able to place the relative value of divergent CPD goals on the same scale and sort out the hype from real value. Also we have to appreciate how an asset can be valuable for one group of stakeholders, but may be a liability for others. Unfortunately, we have at best crude tools to help make such decisions. Value engineering, cynically relabeled "devalue engineering," provides a chainsaw when a scalpel is needed.

The approach that we have described and illustrated in this chapter, value-based design, will go a long way toward filling the gaps in our CPD decision-making tool case. We believe that design added value (DAV) analysis will enable designers to choose the most value-effective building technologies for the efficient use of energy in building and infrastructure systems.

References

[1]   Wilson, R., "Foreword," in *Building Economics: Theory and Practice*, R.T. Ruegg and H.E. Marshall, New York: Van Nostrand Reinhold, 1990.

[2]   Akın, Ö., "Current Trends and Future Direction in CAD," Chap. 1 in H. Karimi and B. Akinci (Eds.), *CAD/GIS Integration: Existing and Emerging Solutions*, New York: Taylor & Francis, 2008

[3]   Beck, P., "The AEC Dilemma: Exploring the Barriers to Change," in *Proceedings of Design Intelligence, Greenway Communications and Design Futures Council*, Washington, DC, February 1, 2001, http://www.di.net/articles/archive/2046.

[4]   Teicholz, P., "Labor Productivity Declines in the Construction Industry: Causes and Remedies," *AECbytes Analysis, Research, Reviews*, Vol. 4, 2004, http://www.aecbytes.com/viewpoints.html.

[5]   LePatner, B. B., "It's Time to Fix America's Broken Construction Industry," *Engineering News-Record*, McGraw-Hill Construction, March 12, 2008, http://enr.ecnext.com/coms2/article_tebm090429BIMDivisiono.

[6]   Akın, Ö, and Anadol Z., "Determining the Impact of CADrafting on the Building Process," *International Journal of Construction Information Technology*, Nos. 1–8, Spring 1993.

[7]   Ballard, G., "The Lean Project Delivery System: An Update," *Lean Construction Journal*, Issue 1, 2008, pp. 1–19, http://www.leanconstruction.org/lcj/paper_2008_issue.html.

[8]   CII, *Applicability of CII Best Practices by Industry Sector and Project Type*, Austin, TX: Construction Industry Institute, 2009, https://www.construction-institute.org/scriptcontent/r-teams-list.cfm?section=res.

[9]   Lee, S. H, and Akin O., "Augmented Reality-Based Computational Support for Operations and Maintenance Fieldwork," *Automation in Construction*, 2010.

[10] Beck, P., "The AEC Dilemma: Exploring the Barriers to Change," in *Proceedings of Design Intelligence, Greenway Communications and Design Futures Council*, Washington, DC, February 1, 2001, http://www.di.net/articles/archive/2046.

[11] Mudge, A., *Value Engineering*, New York: J. Pohl Associates, 1989.

[12] Friedman, A.T., *Women and the Making of the Modern House*, New Haven, CT: Yale University Press, 2006.

[13]   Page, J., "My Crown of Thorns," *London: The Guardian*, 2000. http://www.guardian. co.uk/uk/2000/may/04/dome.millennium1, last accessed April 18, 2011.

[14]   Toker, F., *Fallingwater Rising*, New York: Alfred A Knopf, 2003.

[15]   von Neumann, J., and Morgenstern O., *Theory of Games and Economic Behavior*, 3rd ed., Princeton, NJ: Princeton University Press, 1953.

[16]   Simon, H.A., *Models of Man: Social and Rational*, New York: Wiley, 1957.

[17]   Kahneman, D., and Tversky A., "Prospect Theory: An Analysis of Decision Under Risk" *Econometrica*, Vol. 47, 1979, pp. 263–291.

[18]   Bon, R., *Building as an Economic Process*, Upper Saddle River, NJ: Prentice Hall,1989.

[19]   Millar, C. J., *Frank Lloyd Wright Letters to Clients The Press,* Fresno: California State University, 1986.

[20]   Pfrang, E.O., and Marshall R., "Collapse of the Kansas City Hyatt Regency Walkways," *Civil Engineering—ASCE*, Vol. 52, No. 7, 1982, pp. 65–69.

[21]   Schwartz, T. A., "Glass and Metal Curtain-Wall Fundamentals," *APT Bulletin*, Vol. 32, No. 1, 2001, pp. 37–45.

[22]   "Bayes' Theorem," *Stanford Encyclopedia of Philosophy,* June 28, 2003; rev. September 30, 2003, http://plato.stanford.edu/entries/bayes-theorem.

[23]   Hobhouse, C., *1851 and the Crystal Palace*, London: John Murray, 1950.

[24]   Messent, D., *Opera House Act One*, Sydney, Australia: David Messent Photography, 1997.

[25]   Bauman, J. F., *From Tenements to the Taylor Homes: In Search of an Urban Housing Policy in Twentieth-Century America*. University Park: Pennsylvania State University Press, 2000.

[26]   Delatte, N., *Beyond Failure: Forensic Case Studies for Civil Engineers*, Reston, VA: ASCE Press, 2009, pp.333–345.

[27]   Powell, K., *30 St Mary Axe: A Tower for London*. London/New York: Merrell Publishers, 2006.

[28]   Munro, D., "Swiss Re's Building, London," 2004 Nyheter om Stalbyggnad, NR3. 36–43. http://www.epab.bme.hu/microstation/FreeForm/Examples/SwissRe.pdf, accessed November 27, 2010.

[29]   Morrin, N. "Sustainable Landmark for Swiss Re in London," May 2008, http://skanska-sustainability-case-studies.com/index.php/Sustainable-Landmark-for-Swiss-Re-in-London.html, accessed November 29, 2010.

[30]   Bridwell, S. G., "Swiss re by Norman Foster," *Studio 489,* 200, http://web.utk.edu/~archinfo/a489_f02/Phase1.html, accessed October 2010.

[31]   Fosterandpartners.com, "Awards by Project," 2010, http://www.fosterandpartners.com/Data/Awards/S.aspx, accessed October 2010.

[32]   Shen, Y., "Green Design and the City, Buildings: The Gherkin, London," October 15, 2009, http://www.greendesignetc.net/Buildings_09/Building_Shen_Yuming_paper.pdf, accessed November 2010.

[33]   Fedun, W., *30 St. Mary Axe by Foster and Partners*, 2005, http://www.daapspace.daap.uc.edu/~larsongr/Larsonline/SkyCaseStu_files/SwissRe.pdf.

[34]   Lawrence, H. O., and Samuel, H. W., "Purchasing Power of Money in the United States from 1774 to 2010," *Measuring Worth*, 2009.

[35]   "Design Quality Indicator," 2010, http://dqi.org.uk., accessed November 2010.

[36]   Howard, R., "CAD, Curved Surfaces and Building Quality." *Journal of Information Technology in Construction*, Vol. 11, 2006, pp. 427–436.

[37]   "Architecture Steel Stahl Acier, Swiss Re London," 2010, European Convention for Constructional Steelwork, http://www.steelconstruct.com.

[38]   McCain, I., "DiaGrid: Structural Efficiency & Increasing Popularity," 2009, http://www.dsg.fgg.uni-lj.si/dubaj2009/index.php?limitstart=20, accessed November 2010.

[39]   Moon, K., Connor, J. J., and Fernandez, J. E., "Diagrid Structural Systems for Tall Buildings: Characteristics and Methodology for Preliminary Design," *Structural Design of Tall and Special Buildings,* Vol. 16.2, 2007, pp. 205–230.

[40]   Victaulic.com, http://www.victaulic.com/content/fireprotectionsection.htm, accessed November 27, 2010.

[41]   Langdon, D., *Spon's Architects' and Builders' Price Book,* 130th ed., New York: Spon Press, 2005.

[42]   Ali, M. M., and Moon, K., "Structural Developments in Tall Buildings: Current Trends and Future Prospects," *Architectural Science Review,* Vol. 50.3, 2007, pp. 205–223.

[43]   Rossiter, J. "The Gherkin Up for Sale for £600m," *This Is Money,* September 15, 2006, http://www.thisismoney.co.uk/markets/article.html?in_article_id=412713&in_page_id=3, accessed November 25, 2010.

[44]   Reinke, S. C., "Forms Follow Finances: Twisted, Turned, Tall," in *Public #3 Work Life,* J. Calder (Ed.), Woods Bagot, http://www.woodsbagot.com/en/Documents/Public3.pdf.

[45]   Find a London Office, http://www.findalondonoffice.co.uk/toolbox/rental-guide.

[46]   Williamson, S. H., "Seven Ways to Compute the Relative Value of a U.S. Dollar Amount, 1774 to present," *Measuring Worth,* 2009, http://www.measuringworth.com/calculators/inflation/result.php, accessed April 2010.

[47]   Reinhardt, J., "Computer-Aided Construction Management," guest speaker at Course 12-611, Carnegie Mellon University, Pittsburgh, PA, November 30, 2010.

[48]   Buchanan, P., "The Tower: An Anachronism Awaiting Rebirth," *Harvard Design Magazine,* 2007, http://www.gsd.harvard.edu/research/publications/hdm/ back/26_Buchanan.pdf, Accessed November 2010.

[49]   "Table 1—Importance of Maintenance and Operational Costs (Based on 2002–3 Typical Cost Figures by BMI)," *Whole Life Costing, Consulting Excellence,* 2004, http://www.constructingexcellence.org.uk, accessed November 2010.

[50]   "Sensitivity Analysis," Wikipedia the Free Encyclopedia, http://en.wikipedia.org/wiki/Sensitivity_analysis, last modified on May 25, 2011.

[51]   Saaty, T., *The Analytic Hierarchy Process: Planning, Priority Setting, Resource Allocation,* New York: McGraw-Hill, 1980.

[52]   Davis, A. M., "Software Prototyping," in *Advances in Computers,* Vol. 40, M. C. Yovits (Ed.), New York: Academic Press, 1995, pp. 39–42

CHAPTER 13

Field Tools and Augmented Reality Technology

This chapter describes computational field tools and the use of augmented reality (AR) technology to support embedded commissioning (ECx) activities at the job site. First, computational field applications currently available are briefly summarized. Then, the use of AR technology as a means to provide data associated with commissioning activities is discussed in detail.

13.1 Need for Computational Field Tools

Because the term *commissioning* refers to ensuring that the target equipment is properly installed and that the performance of the equipment meets its specifications, ECx activities require diverse types of data, including 2D/3D geometric models, equipment specifications, and sensor-driven performance data such as temperature, humidity, and flow rate readings (Part II). Traditionally, commissioning teams carry 2D blueprint drawings and specifications documents in hardcopy formats to the site. More specifically, during verification activities, the commissioning team determines if the equipment is installed properly at the right location and if the equipment satisfies the required performance and design specifications.

In the verification process, the commissioning team use drawings and specification documents. During the performance tests, the commissioning team determines if the equipment performs as specified by comparing performance data from sensors against specification documents and data obtained from calibrated sensors to see if a piece of equipment and its sensors are performing as intended. This traditional way of using information is inconvenient and inefficient. To facilitate information-related activities as well as the overall ECx process, computational field tools and IT technologies such as AR are helpful for collecting, manipulating, and visualizing data and for inspecting the overall performance of the entire system.

13.2 Existing Commissioning Tools

Several field tools are currently being used to support commissioning field activities. Examples include ENFORMA® Building Diagnostics (EBD), CITE-AHU, PACRAT

(Performance And Continuous Re-commissioning Analysis Tool), and Whole Building Diagnostician (WBD).

EBD [1] can continuously diagnose equipment and provide meaningful information about the status of the equipment by utilizing data obtained from the building automation system (BAS) that controls the equipment (Chapter 9). In particular, EBD monitors energy-related performance data and reports any inefficiencies and their impacts. The input data for EBD includes operating schedules of the target facility, the facility's HVAC systems information, and performance data from sensors. EBD generates various kinds of plots (e.g., time series) using the performance-related data of building systems, including the actual performance data, setpoints, and energy load profiles. With the data, EBD helps identify potential operations and maintenance problems, resulting in both time and cost savings in terms of developing and executing diagnosis plans. Therefore, EBD is a useful tool for performance tests during the commissioning process because it can reveal inefficient performance on the part of the target equipment.

CITE-AHU [2] is another automated commissioning support tool specialized for air-handling units during retro-commissioning processes (Chapter 2). Through automation, it aims to save time and reduce the skill levels needed for ECx. APAR (AHU Performance Assessment Rules), a set of expert rules designed to assess the performance of AHUs, helps commissioning teams make better decisions. APAR uses operational data, like occupancy information of facilities, setpoints, performance data from deployed sensors, and design data such as specifications, obtained from existing sensors in the building energy management system (BEMS). The tool helps commissioning teams review control logic and sensor placement plans and accuracy, review and verify actual equipment installation in the field, capture equipment-specific information such as the operator's knowledge and operation history, and verify measurements using data from the BEMS. The tool also assists with functional tests such as open-loop tests and closed-loop tests to verify the performance of AHUs by automatically executing various testing scenarios during occupied and unoccupied periods. When testing systems in occupied periods, performance data from the BEMS may be used. The tool provides interfaces to document effectively the ECx results and automatically save the documents in an HTML format.

Similarly, PACRAT [3], a data-mining tool, aims to diagnose building systems, identify poor performance, and provide the operator with the problem and corresponding energy waste data. PACRAT's core functions are monitoring and verifying building systems, efficient data management, visualization, and documentation. PACRAT can also identify and prioritize problems, energy waste, and causes for the waste such as inefficient unoccupied period operation and inadequate setpoints. It suggests solutions; diagnoses malfunctioning system components, incorrectly calibrated sensors, and unstable control; performs customizable analyses; and provides enterprise, historical, and interoperability data for various automation systems and energy consumption patterns.

For more accurate diagnoses, PACRAT uses NCDC (National Climatic Data Center) weather data. PACRAT calculates and documents various statistical data such as highs, lows, and averages of sensed data, system loads and space load profiles, energy consumption and costs, and efficiencies of components. PACRAT also provides various visualization functions such as zooming, panning, time slicing, and plots, such as candle plots, pie charts, 3D surface and scatterplots, time-series plots, and histograms. Furthermore, it can access data recorded from computerized energy management and control systems (EMCS) or data logging systems (DLS). It also integrates data from different sources, such as metering systems and data loggers.

Finally, WBD [4] is another diagnostic software system that automatically diagnoses operation problems with equipment, especially HVAC systems. In particular, the Whole Building Energy Module of the WBD monitors the energy consumption of a building and allows the operator to detect noticeable changes, while the Outdoor Air/Economizer Diagnostic Module monitors and detects problems with air-handling units focusing on controlling outside air and economizer operation. The WBD provides results in graphical formats with color coding so the building operator can easily recognize the problem. Furthermore, it allows the user to hierarchically explore causes of problems and provides helpful information on repair. The WBD is module based, so it can be extended by adding new modules.

13.3   Key System Components

Core components of these computational diagnostic systems are input and output devices, control modules, and data (Figure 13.1). The input device acquires the user's inputs and collects data from various sources such as deployed sensors, data loggers, and other building automation systems. The control modules then manipulate the data according to the user's input command. With the results shown on the output device, the commissioner determines whether the target equipment performs as specified. The control modules can provide helpful functions to support the commissioner's decision-making process.

Recently, building automation systems (BASs) have been used to monitor and control building systems. They provide user-friendly intuitive interfaces so the user easily understands the building systems, their conditions, and their performance values. With a BAS, the user relatively easily understands the building system and

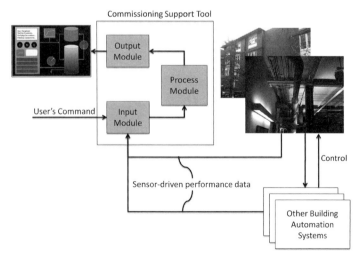

Figure 13.1   Core components of diagnostic systems and their data exchange.

can access performance-related data such as setpoints and current sensor values as well as data trends. Once the BAS has been commissioned, it becomes a tool to gauge system performance successfully throughout the entire commissioning process, especially during execution of ECx processes.

13.4   Limitations of Conventional Field Tools

Contemporary diagnostic field tools can facilitate the ECx process, especially when conducting functional performance tests (FPTs), by enabling commissioning teams to access with ease data related to the performance and condition of equipment and facilities. As described earlier, some tools detect problems and provide possible causes and solutions, a helpful function for the commissioning team to verify whether the target equipment performs as intended.

However, there is a further opportunity to facilitate the ECx process. In traditional commissioning, the commissioning team frequently carries hardcopy documents to the site. Blueprints and equipment specification documents are substantial and weighty. Locating proper data from the documents and mapping the drawings to the actual equipment is no simple task, especially for a commissioning team unfamiliar with the particular site. These inefficiencies result in wasted time because they are non-value-adding activities.

Diagrams of the target equipment and associated pieces of equipment are helpful, but they require additional processes to locate the actual equipment. It may be even more difficult to find equipment hidden within other building elements such as walls, ceilings, and floors. Three-dimensional CAD models can provide better perception of the system for the commissioning team to understand and locate equipment, yet that process is also inefficient due to the additional time and effort needed to interpret these documents and match them against the field equipment.

Furthermore, to commission even just one piece of equipment, the diverse data types mentioned earlier are required. Existing field tools can support only a portion of the entire set of commissioning tasks. For instance, the tools described earlier focus on mainly diagnosing equipment performance. CAD drawings and applications are needed to determine if the target equipment is installed as specified in the drawings. To digitize the ECx process, the commissioning team will use applications that allow generation of commissioning templates, open documents, and connections to other building systems.

13.5   Augmented Reality Technology for Commissioning-Support Field Tools

To overcome the limitations and improve the efficiencies of commissioning processes at the site, augmented reality (AR) technology can be adapted as a user interface of commissioning-support field tools. Augmented reality is a technology that recognizes objects in a video stream captured from a camera and superimposes computer-generated data associated with the object onto the actual physical objects in real time. Head-mounted display (HMD) devices are one of the most popular output devices for AR technology. The user wears the device and views the processed data through its display units.

The technology is used for diverse application areas including interactive books, navigation tools, and sports broadcasting systems. Some systems require substantial computing power, whereas other applications can be executed on average desktops, laptops, and even smartphones. For instance, Junaio [5] developed by Metaio, Inc., is an AR-based mobile application that recognizes the user's location and the direction of his or her smartphone and can provide a variety of location-specific data such as local 3D maps, information on local landmark buildings, and the location of ATMs.

From the perspective of software development, AR technology, especially for smartphones, is in the early development phase, although several development platforms and programming libraries are currently available. The ARToolKit [6], its variants, and its successors comprise one of the most popular AR application development toolkits. It provides computer vision–based software libraries to detect predefined visual markers and to superimpose computer-generated geometric data. It can also import various geometry types such as OBJ and VRML using additional open-source libraries.

In the AEC/FM industry, several research projects have been conducted to develop and evaluate the effectiveness and potential contributions of the technology. For instance, Dunston and Wang [7] developed an AR application to identify design conflicts. Khoury and Kamat [8] developed a mechanism and an application for the mechanism to track the user's location, with precision, and assist decision-making processes in construction, inspection, maintenance, and emergencies.

As described earlier, the potential for improvement in facilitating ECx processes by integrating various types of data and providing the data in a unified interface exists. When the target equipment is automatically identified, information-seeking activities can be minimized. The AR technology fits well within these requirements. AR-based applications are object centered, in that all functions begin with object recognition. By adding modules for interaction with other databases, AR-based applications can effectively deliver data associated only with the target equipment.

13.6   System Architecture of an AR System

Figure 13.2 depicts the system architecture of an AR-based commissioning field tool. The object detection module analyzes a video stream fed from the camera and sends the unique ID of the detected pieces of equipment to the process module. The process module then retrieves data associated with the detected equipment using that ID. The module also utilizes the user's inputs to manipulate the data accordingly. Because different kinds of building data are stored in separate systems, modules corresponding to each data type are required for seamless data exchange. The data is then finally displayed through the output device such as a HMD.

Furthermore, the ECx report module provides an interface to open and customize templates used for commissioning the particular target equipment and reporting the results. The data obtained from the BIM database and the BAS database may be used for documentation. Images captured from the video stream can also be included in the report.

For the successful use of AR technology, the AR-based field tool should have the ability to manage all of the various types of data needed to support diverse ECx activities, especially at the site where accessing data is more difficult and inconvenient. Three-dimensional geometric models of facilities and pieces of equipment are constructed in CAD applications and specifications of facilities and equipment are stored and maintained in various documents in electronic formats (Chapter 5). The BIM approach can manage these diverse types of data and appropriate schemas of building models can transfer BIM data, including the Green Building XML (gbXML) and ifcXML schemas. The BIMserver [9], for instance, is an open-source building information model server that allows project participants to query and selectively retrieve building data from the central database server. The server also enables multiple users to work collaboratively and merge their work into a central database. File formats it supports include IFC 2X3, IFCXML 2X3, WebGL, KMZ (Google Earth file format), and CityGML.

Contemporary BAS manages performance-related data of the building systems they control and supports data exchange in real time. The AR-based field tools should communicate with sensors, data loggers, and BASs in real time so the commissioning team can verify that the target equipment and facility are performing as specified. To interact with BASs and retrieve performance data, on the other hand, BACnet, LonTalk, and Zigbee are popular example protocols and specifications.

13.7   An Example AR-Based Information Support System

Augmented reality is an emerging technology that requires additional research and development to support ECx activities. Recently, researchers in the AEC/FM industry have paid attention to this technology and related research efforts. AR systems have been developed to support diverse activities within the AEC/FM industry. For example, Lee and Akin [10] developed a prototype application of an AR-based information support field tool. The tool saves time when information is being sought and thus facilitates diagnosis and inspection field activities. The core structure of the field tool is similar to the architecture of Figure 13.2. It recognizes equipment and facilities and displays geometric models, performance data, and brief specifications of the detected object.

Lee tested the field tool in a research and educational facility at Carnegie Mellon University. Figure 13.3 shows a typical office unit of the facility in which a mullion heating/cooling system is used to cool the space in summer and heat the space in winter. Discerning the heating and cooling system from other elements such as walls (architectural elements) and columns and beams (structural elements) is difficult. The elements of the HVAC system such as pipes and valves located under the plenum, shown in the red box in Figure 13.3, are difficult for the commissioning team to locate and to conduct FPT as well as prefunctional checklists (PFCs).

Figures 13.4 and 13.5 show the results of how the AR-based tool supports commissioning activities. In this verification test, the tool identifies the predefined marker attached to the window, displays the name of the identified equipment, and superimposes 3D models of the mullion components of the particular facility. The model was constructed using Autodesk 3D Studio MAX and then loaded into the prototype application in the VRML file format. The user can then choose to

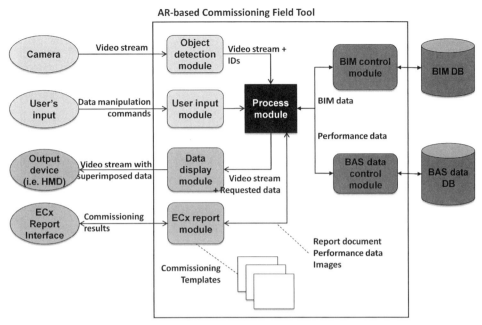

Figure 13.2   System architecture of an AR-based commissioning field tool.

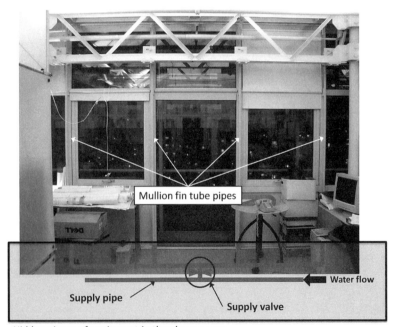

Figure 13.3   A research and educational facility for testing the AR-based field tool.

display detailed specifications of the equipment and associated performance data obtained from sensors. As shown in Figure 13.5, two colors distinguish equipment components hidden under the floor from those exposed above the floor so the user can intuitively understand the models and match them to the actual equipment.

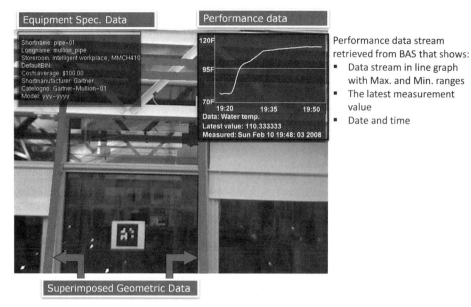

Figure 13.4 Upper portion of the facility superimposed with data.

Figure 13.5 Lower portion of the facility superimposed with data.

Although the precision of the model superimposition requires further improvement, the result is accurate enough for the user to locate equipment.

13.8 Benefits of AR Technology

The two essential benefits of AR technology are (1) automatic recognition of objects and (2) the ability to superimpose computer-generated data onto the objects in real time. When coupled with database systems for information retrieval, the user can automatically retrieve information associated only with the target objects. This technology can thus facilitate activities to obtain diverse kinds of data, especially data related to field activities.

Lee and Akin [10] evaluated the potential improvement in facilitation of information-related field activities during daily O&M, including locating equipment/facilities and obtaining equipment performance data and facilities condition data by using the AR-based information support. Information-related field activities during commissioning processes are similar to those of O&M activities. Example activities include locating the target equipment and surrounding equipment associated with the target equipment, and obtaining performance data from sensors. These activities are indispensable when conducting verification and performance tests during the commissioning process. Hence, the results of Lee's experiment show the potential for efficiency improvement in ECx processes.

To identify inefficiencies in traditional O&M field activities due to difficulty seeking information at the site, Lee and Akin [11] shadowed actual fieldworkers and identified inefficiencies in field activities that could be remedied through proper information support. On average, the O&M fieldworkers spent 12+% of their total time seeking information to conduct core activities such as diagnosis, repair, and inspection of equipment. The results further show that the potential improvement reaches up to 20+% time savings when transit time is included.

Lee and Akin [11] tested their AR-based information support field tool described earlier through a series of experiments conducted with O&M fieldworkers. They found that the tool saves time during information-seeking activities, resulting in improved overall efficiency. The data and information provided to the fieldworkers during the experiment can be categorized into three type: fundamental building information such as geometries and specifications, real-time equipment performance data and facility condition data, and maintenance data such as spare parts information and maintenance history. The results show that the AR-based field tool demonstrates potential time savings of about 50% when it locates equipment and facilities and an 8% time savings when obtaining sensor-driven performance data. The difference is due to the fact that current BASs already provide convenient web browser–based interfaces so that the users can easily access the system and retrieve electronic data in real time. In this particular test environment, the time savings of 8% was obtained from eliminating additional transit time, because the fieldworkers usually visited the local O&M staff's office with requests for data.

In addition to time savings, the use of data in a fully electronic format eliminates the burden of carrying weighty hardcopy documents, which can make field navigation safer, particularly in hazardous settings such as bridges, highways, and high-tension electrical structures. Use of wearable computers, discussed in Chapter 14, may well enhance the benefits of AR technology.

13.9   Representative Commissioning Procedures Using AR Technology

Finally, we describe two representative ECx procedures using the AR-based information support tool. An example procedure for conducting verification tests with an AR-based information support tool would follow this outline:

1. The commissioner selects the "Verification Test" option and opens a verification test template designed for the target equipment.
2. The commissioner points the field tool at the target equipment.

3. The tool detects the target equipment.
4. The tool retrieves the geometric model of the equipment from the BIM server.
5. The tool superimposes the geometric model based on the user's location and direction data onto the video stream captured through the attached camera.
6. The commissioner verifies that the equipment is installed as specified in the as-designed 3D model.
7. The commissioner selects "Specifications."
8. The tool retrieves the specification data of the equipment from the BIM server.
9. The tool displays the specification data on an equipment specification template.
10. The commissioner determines if the actual equipment installed is the correct model specified.
11. The commissioner documents the results of the verification tests using the provided verification template. They can add pictures captured through the camera and superimposed 3D model.
12. The commissioner saves the report to the central commissioning report database.

In addition, an example procedure for conducting performance tests with the tool would include the following:

1. The commissioner selects the "Performance Tests" option and opens a performance test template designed for the target equipment.
2. The commissioner points the field tool at the target equipment.
3. The field tool detects the target equipment from the video stream captured through the attached camera.
4. The field tool retrieves the geometric model of the equipment from the BIM server.
5. The tool superimposes the geometric model based on the user's location and direction data onto the video stream captured through the attached camera.
6. The commissioner selects the "Performance Data" option.
7. The tool displays a list of performance-related data sources.
8. The commissioner selects sensors.
9. The tool displays current measurement and, if exists, the setpoint for each sensor.
10. The commissioner determines if the equipment is performing as specified with different inputs.
11. The commissioner selects the "Report" option.
12. The commissioner documents the results of the performance tests using the provided template. He or she can add measured data and input commands.
13. The commissioner saves the report to the central commissioning report database.

The essential differences between these two processes and traditional workflows are, first, there is no need for hardcopy documents because all documents are electronic; second, ideally all ECx activities can be completed on location without the need to move to other locations for obtaining data, because the commissioner can access all the data remotely at the location in real time. Finally, the report generated is linked to the target equipment for subsequent retrieval.

References

[1]   ENFORMA Building Diagnostics, http://www.pierpartnershipdemonstrations.com/documents/EnformaBrochure_BOMv3.pdf .

[2]   Castro, N. S., and Vaezi-Nejad, H., "CITE-AHU, An Automated Commissioning Tool for Air-Handling Units," in *Proceedings of the National Conference on Building Commissioning,* 2005.

[3]   PACRAT, http://www.facilitydynamics.com/Pacwho.pdf.

[4]   Whole Building Diagnostician, http://availabletechnologies.pnnl.gov/technology.asp?id=60.

[5]   Junaio, http://www.junaio.com.

[6]   ARToolKit, http://www.hitl.washington.edu/artoolkit.

[7]   Dunston, P. S., and Wang X., "Mixed Reality-Based Visualization Interfaces for Architecture, Engineering, and Construction Industry," *Journal of Construction Engineering and Management,* Vol. 131, No. 12, 2005, pp. 1301–1309.

[8]   Khoury, H. M., and Kamat, V. R., "High-Precision Identification of Contextual Information in Location-Aware Engineering Applications," *Advanced Engineering Informatics,* Vol. 23, No. 4, 2009, pp. 483–496.

[9]   BIMserver, http://bimserver.org.

[10]   Lee, S., and Akin, Ö., "Augmented Reality-Based Computational Support for Operations and Maintenance Fieldwork," *Automation in Construction,* Vol. 20, No. 4, 2011, pp. 338–352.

[11]   Lee, S., and Akin, Ö., "Shadowing Tradespeople: Inefficiency in Maintenance Fieldwork." *Automation in Construction*, Vol. 18, No. 5, 2009, pp. 536–546.

CHAPTER 14

JIT Technology and Wearable Computers

This chapter discusses the just-in-time (JIT) technology and wearable computers to support embedded commissioning (ECx) activities in the field. JIT technology, already popular in many manufacturing industries such as the assembly systems of Toyota and Dell Computer Corporation, reduces waste and improves productivity. As many case studies have shown the benefits of the JIT concept, more companies in diverse industries have tried to adapt the concept. Wearable computers, on the other hand, have been developed to support fieldworker activities computationally when the user's hands and eyes must engage with the physical environment [1]. Users wear devices that understand the user's gestures and/or take direct inputs and then respond accordingly. In general, these technologies are helpful when the user needs to use his or her body freely while interacting with computing systems and when only limited computing resources are available in the field.

Currently, almost all building design and construction data are created and maintained in electronic formats throughout the data's life cycle. It is, thus, natural to maximize the use of the electronic data throughout the entire ECx processes to improve the efficiency and accuracy of each subtask. However, in traditional practice, the commissioning team still uses hardcopy documents frequently during their field tests and then re-inputs the results to their computing systems when they return to the office. To provide effective computing systems for the ECx process at the job site, the JIT concept and wearable computing technology are discussed in this chapter.

14.1 Just-in-Time Technology

14.1.1 Introduction

Traditionally, companies predicted future demands for their products and kept inventories well stocked. During manufacturing, companies tried to use the minimum amount of resources to maximize their efficiency while reducing costs. However, it is not easy to accurately predict future demands, so companies often ended up maintaining large inventories to keep their production lines running, resulting in extra costs.

The types of inventories can be categorized into three groups: raw materials, work-in-process, and finished products. Keeping inventories of raw materials allows the company to prepare for delays in material deliveries so that the production line does not have to be stopped. Keeping inventories for work-in-process allows the company to continue running the main production line in the event that any particular parts cannot be produced due to unforeseen accidents. Finally, keeping inventories of the finished products allows the company to respond properly to unforeseen additional demands from customers. Therefore, the main objective of maintaining these inventories is to create buffers to respond to unanticipated events. However, keeping inventories on hand increases costs due to larger inventory spaces required and the additional resources required to maintain them.

As a business term, *just in time* (JIT) [1] refers to a strategy for product management in which materials, parts, and subassemblies are delivered from the vendor just when they are needed in the manufacturing process. In other words, companies purchase, produce, or ship materials and parts only as needed to meet actual demand. The objective of the JIT strategy is to eliminate or minimize product inventories from the supply chain and, consequently, associated costs. When a company uses the JIT concept, it purchases enough materials, parts, and subassemblies to last for only that day of production. Products are then shipped immediately to customers. Consequently, no inventories are needed in this environment, because raw materials are purchased just in time and products are manufactured just in time to be shipped to customers. In successful implementations, such as with Toyota, companies that use the JIT concept have significantly reduced their inventories, resulting in saving costs and more efficient manufacturing.

The JIT concept works as follows: The consumers order products. The product company orders the precise number of parts for its subassembly lines in order to satisfy the needs of the final product assembly. In turn, the subassembly lines order the exact amount of raw materials from the companies that supply the materials needed by the subassembly companies. In this way, the raw materials needed by all links in the chain of part fabrication and delivery are delivered to the appropriate levels of production just in time. In the same fashion, the subassembled parts are delivered to the final assembly line just in time. The final products are delivered to the customers immediately. In this manufacturing process, under ideal conditions, no inventories are necessary.

Benefits of the JIT concept include the following:

- *Better flow of raw materials, parts, and subassemblies:* Because the size of raw materials to be delivered is smaller than that in traditional methods, thanks to simplified inventory flow and inventory management, the JIT method can diminish delays of material delivery.
- *Saved expense of inventory maintenance:* Because fewer inventories are required, less expense is incurred maintaining inventories.
- *Saved space from reduced inventories:* Fewer raw materials, parts, and subassemblies are stacked in storage, therefore less space is needed.

14.1.2 The JIT Concept of Information Support for Commissioning Processes

When the JIT concept is applied to the field of computational information support for the ECx process, electronic data corresponds to the raw material, parts, or subassemblies of the capital project delivery (CPD) sector. The manufacturing process in information technology corresponds to the manipulation of data so that the user can use the data JIT during ECx.

Recently, mobile computing systems, especially web-based systems, have become popular for supporting activities in the field. Portable devices such as rugged tablet PCs with electronic building data as well as templates for specific ECx tasks can be used in the field to eliminate hardcopy documents entirely. The ECx results recorded and documented by the field tool at the site are then directly saved to the central database, saving time and reducing errors (Figure 14.1).

The challenge with computational field systems is that portable computers such as rugged tablet PCs and smartphones, for instance, must have powerful graphics performance and large memory caches to visualize complex 3D geometric models. They should also have ample storage space given sizable building models. Although contemporary laptops have limited computing resources, they still provide reasonable computing resources both in their screen sizes and battery capacities. Smartphones are much lighter with longer lasting batteries than laptops. They also provide fieldworkers with better usability. However, 3D graphics performance is weaker, since they focus on lightweight and easy-to-use tools. Furthermore, software applications for smartphones are limited. ECx systems that are currently available focus on providing a set of templates through web-based interfaces so that the commissioning team only needs to mark, select, and write brief comments on laptops and smartphones for maximum usability and efficiency. From this perspective, these portable devices are a good hardware solution as an ECx field tool if properly supported.

The JIT concept can prove to be an effective solution for better use of building data with the limited computing resources available in ECx fieldwork conditions. Recently, as network infrastructures such as Wi-Fi and mobile telecommunication services have become available and reasonably fast enough to transfer the proper amount of ECx data, anyone can access the network and obtain data needed at the site. Furthermore, it is now possible to maintain electronic data in a central database and/or distributed databases and retrieve necessary data at the site, especially in cloud computing environments, as shown in Figure 14.1. Thus, instead of the field tool carrying large quantities of data, the data necessary at the precise place and time can be delivered just in time. Conceptually the field tool only needs to handle data relevant to the particular user's location and present activities. Therefore, the JIT concept allows the commissioning team to overcome the limitations of

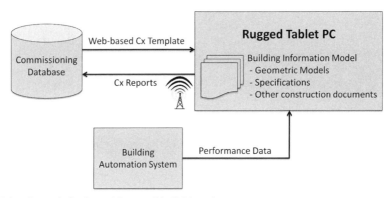

Figure 14.1   Commissioning with portable field tools.

computing resources available in field tools and allows use of the latest versions of data, since each piece of data is delivered JIT. This is crucial in collaborative work environments.

14.1.3   Core Technologies for the JIT Approach

The core technologies for JIT data delivery include user location tracking, context awareness, networking for real-time data exchange, and computer graphics that can manage 3D BIM models and other construction documents. The user location tracking allows the system to identify pieces of equipment at the user's current position. Context awareness further narrows down the list of equipment to only those associated with the specific activities.

Figure 14.2 depicts the core components of a computing system with the JIT concept. First, the object tracking module tracks the commissioner's location in real time. The location data is then used by the ECx data control module and the BIM data control module to retrieve equipment and facility data, such as their respective geometric models and specifications. The ECx data control module manipulates the data retrieved from the ECx database. Finally the data is provided to the commissioner through the output device.

The user location tracking module uses various tracking technologies depending on the condition of the working environment, including GPS (Global Positioning System), Wi-Fi, RFID, and ZigBee technologies. GPS is one of the most common tracking technologies in outdoor environments, while Wi-Fi is more promising for indoor environments.

Once the user's current location has been tracked, based on the direction of the user's eye fixation, the BIM control module continuously retrieves BIM data for equipment and facilities from the BIM database in real time. The module employs

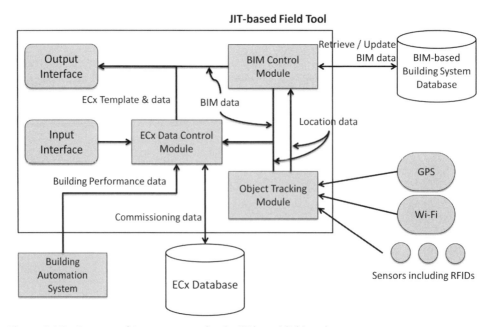

Figure 14.2   System architecture example of a JIT-based field tool.

two different data sources to determine what equipment and facility data should be retrieved. In the first method the module uses the commissioner's location data to identify equipment around the area from the BIM database. In the second method the object tracking module detects pieces of equipment directly from their IDs such as RFID tags. The BIM control module then uses the IDs to retrieve data from the BIM database. The retrieved data are then sent to the ECx data control module for further manipulation.

The ECx data control module is the core module that—on the commissioner's command—manipulates data in response to the command and displays the results on the output device. Three different types of data are supplied to the module: equipment and facility data from the BIM database, equipment performance data from the building automation system (BAS), and commissioning data on templates.

Various input and output devices can be used, including wearable computers, which are discussed in detail in the next section. As previously discussed, AR technology may prove one of the most suitable solutions. This technology properly visualizes 3D models of the target building system where only a portion of the entire model is transferred to the field tool. Thus, a proper real-time rendering of the model is generated based on the user's location.

14.1.4   Just-in-Time Data Delivery

For the JIT concept to become a reality, computational infrastructures that support real-time data exchange must be realized. Contemporary hardware infrastructures are powerful enough to support real-time data transfer between data servers and client field tools. For performance data, BASs provide sensor-driven data in real time for the user to see the performance and the condition of the building system. BAS also alerts the operators with proper signals when it detects any abnormal behavior in the building system.

For geometric models and specifications of architectural elements, a database server such as the BIMserver [2] can provide necessary data to the commissioning team at the site. The BIMserver enables the user to manage the building information in a central database and exchange BIM data in various file formats such as IFC 2x3, KMZ, and WebGL. The commissioning team members can query, merge, and selectively retrieve the building information. Additionally, wireless communication services allow smartphone users to view video streams in real time.

Therefore, during the commissioning process, once the user's location is detected and target equipment as well as other relevant equipment and facilities have been identified, the field tool collects fundamental data to aid the user in performing ECx activities. As the user proceeds with the ECx process, the field tool retrieves JIT data toward the next activity.

14.2   Wearable Computers

A wearable computer is a computational device that a user wears when he or she conducts field activities. The fundamental objectives of a wearable computer are to allow users to use both hands, eliminating the need to carry portable computers; to provide an intuitive user interface that has been specially designed to support the particular field activity in which the user is engaged; and to improve the user's productivity and safety. In this section, we discuss the needs and benefits of wearable computers for field ECx activities.

14.2.1   Need for Wearable Computers in Commissioning Activities

We now consider wearable computers as a means to maximize the effectiveness of computing environments developed for the ECx processes from the human/computer interaction (HCI) perspective. As noted earlier, construction sites may be dangerous especially when handling documents and devices, even laptops. Application of electronic data can partially improve the safety of the site and efficiency of ECx activities through superior software applications. In addition, wearable computers can provide viable solutions for this through superior hardware products as well as hardcoded software.

14.2.2   Wearable Computers Being Developed for Inspection

The following two example projects demonstrate different types of wearable computers that have been designed to address traditional paper-based inspection practices. Sunkpho et al. [3, 4] developed a wearable computer for bridge inspectors, named the Mobile Inspection Assistance (MIA) device. The device provides field inspectors with mobile devices and a software application to facilitate bridge inspection tasks by reducing a significant amount of paperwork and redundant data entry in their inspection report database. The inspectors directly input their inspection results using various types of input means such as speech and stylus pens in an inspector-friendly user interface. Consequently, the device allows the inspector to spend more time on the actual inspection.

The application for this type of wearable computers is easily extended by simply replacing the software application because the hardware devices were initially developed for more general applications (Figure 14.3). Boronowsky et al. [5] also address the problems of inefficient, troublesome paper-based documentation and repeated input into their computer system. As a solution, they developed a wearable computing device, named Winspect, for inspecting steel plants. Unlike MIA, Winspect enables the user to navigate, select, and input data via the user's gestures,

 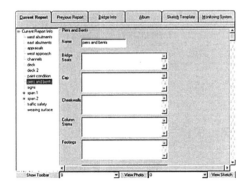

Figure 14.3   Hardware components (*left*) and software application (*right*) for MIA (*Journal of Infrastructure Systems* by American Society of Civil Engineers. Reproduced with permission of the Society, in the format journal via Copyright Clearance Center).

allowing the user free use of the hands and the ability to perform inspections in the rough working environment wearing an input glove. This device, however, was developed for the specific application area by analyzing the behaviors of the target users, and its application area is thus less extensible.

Figures 14.4 through 14.7 show example hardware sets of wearable computers that use the AR technology as their output devices and sample screenshots of their output images produced and projected through their head-mounted displays (HMDs). Their core components include a camera to capture video stream, an

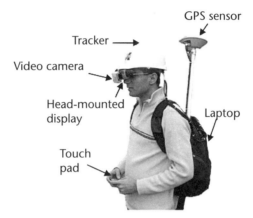

Figure 14.4   The AR-based wearable computer for the construction industry. (Reprinted with permission from Elsevier [6].

Figure 14.5   Screenshots of images through the wearable computer. (Reprinted with permission from Elsevier [6].)

Figure 14.6 A prototype of the mobile augmented reality system. (Reprinted with permission from Elsevier [7].)

Figure 14.7 Output imaged through the see-through display of the MARS device. (Reprinted with permission from Elsevier [7].)

HMD, input devices for the user's direct commands such as a wearable keyboard and a touch pad, a GPS unit to track the user's location, an orientation tracker for tracking the user's orientation, a battery, and a laptop or the like to control these components [6, 7].

The sample systems shown in Figure 14.4 through 14.7 were developed to support various applications areas. For instance, the system developed by Behzadan et al. [6] allows the user to explore a virtual model of a building in order to, for example, check the design and constructability of the building. The MARS [7] superimposes useful information for easier navigation by providing information filtering, a user interface component properly designed based on the information to be displayed and tracking accuracy, and view management techniques.

14.2.3   Key Components of Wearable Computers and Their Challenges

As shown in Figures 14.4 and 14.6, the core components of wearable computers include a processing unit, storage units, a power unit, input devices such as a keyboard, a camera, a microphone, a motion-capturing device, and output devices such as see-through glasses, various types of screens, and speakers. Due to the challenges for each component of wearable computers, their widespread use is still emerging.

An appropriate processing unit is essential for managing 3D geometric models and for controlling diverse input/output interfaces and data exchange between the client application and the database server. Commonly, heavy computing demands and the corresponding power requirements result in heavy power consumption. The use of an appropriate processor is essential for successful wearable computing systems. Naturally, an appropriate amount of power should be available to other devices, especially to the processing units while scheduled field activities are being completed. The size and weight of batteries is an important factor because the user wears them the entire time the wearable computer is being used and the battery is one of the heaviest components. While their size presents a problem for wearable computers, storage units with proper capacity are fundamental for storing data locally to prepare for unexpected network problems.

Input and output devices are the key components of a wearable computer. When developing interfaces for a wearable computer, the most critical factors include size, weight, and ergonomic design. Naturally, reducing the size and weight of devices is important because the user wears all component devices. Ergonomic design provides more comfort to the user, resulting in an improvement in usability. However, because fieldworkers frequently wear gloves or protective equipment, the components of input device such as buttons should be large enough to mitigate potential user mistakes. This also applies to the design of software applications. Input devices for wearable computers include a simplified keyboard that is specialized to the particular tasks, a glove that recognizes the user's gestures, and a device specially developed for specific tasks. Output devices frequently considered for wearable computers include a small-sized screen and goggles.

If the user requires access to a remote database, the wireless networking module of the wearable computer should allow access to database servers and data retrieval. For the JIT approach, this communication should occur in real time. Furthermore, as some components of a wearable computing system are distributed on the user's body, wireless communication among components can minimize cumbersome wiring and provide the user with more comfort. For example, if the user wears input devices on the hands such as gloves or on a wrist, wires to link the central processing module and the input devices may limit the movement of the user's arm. Another similar example would be a head-mounted display as an output device with a camera mounted on the user's helmet.

From the perspective of software applications, the application should be developed such that it minimizes power consumption and has a large, simple interface for reasoning similar to hardware interfaces.

Overall, ECx tasks at the site include diverse field inspection and measurement activities. Some equipment has limited accessibility and requires special accommodations to support ECx activities. To effectively support ECx field activities in harsh environments, wearable computers should be carefully designed to specifically support the particular working environment. For instance, the voice recognition function is harder to implement in noisy environments. Because mechanical rooms are commonly noisy, voice recognition may not be an appropriate feature for this environment. In this case noise filtering capability gains particular significance.

14.3 An Application Scenario Using the JIT Technology and Wearable Computers

So far, we have learned that wearable computers can help the ECx commissioner conduct key activities at a job site by providing an intuitive user-friendly interface. Given the limitations of the hardware devices discussed earlier, the JIT concept is a good solution for providing the massive amounts of data needed for commissioning activities. The following is a sequence of activities for a performance test using a wearable computer equipped with a glove as an input device and an AR-based HMD as an output device with JIT data access:

1. The wearable computer detects the current location of the commissioner.
2. The wearable computer retrieves a list of equipment and facility names in the area from the building information database.
3. The wearable computer displays the list of equipment in the area.
4. The commissioner browses the list and selects the target equipment by performing a series of gestures.
5. The wearable computer retrieves the equipment-related data and visualizes the data by superimposing the data through the HMD. While displaying the data, the wearable computer continues to retrieve data from adjacent equipment. When the commissioners change their direction of eye fixation, the HMD superimposes data about the equipment that is now being viewed by the commissioner. This process continues until the device is turned off.
6. The commissioner opens a template for a performance test.
7. The commissioner selects "Set-Point" and inputs a value by scrolling and selecting the value with the glove.
8. The commissioner selects a sensor with gesture inputs to ensure the equipment performs accordingly.
9. The wearable computer retrieves current measured data from the BAS and displays the data stream on the HMD.
10. The commissioner documents the results on the template using the input glove.
11. The commissioner turns on speech mode and speaks his comments.
12. The wearable computer records the speech and converts it into text.
13. The commissioner saves the record as well as the text.
14. The wearable computer saves the new report on the local storage space as well as the central commissioning report database.

This scenario is developed to reflect the use of a wearable computer and JIT data exchange approach, based on the example in the previous chapter. Therefore, the overall sequence of the activities is similar, but the methods in this scenario to input the commissioner's commands and display the outputs are specifically described to emphasize the implementation of these technologies. However, in spite of the dramatic benefits expected, to date, owing to the newness of this technology, little field experience or statistics are available to back up these claims. Their efficacy will be verified only in due time. In spite of the speculative nature of our predictions, the promise of emerging developments in this area should not go unnoticed.

Hardware devices are becoming smaller, thinner, and thus light enough to carry with ease. Many tablet PCs have embedded cameras that provide video streams and a touchscreen that allows the user to input commands using their fingers. The components of a wearable computer can seamlessly communicate with each other wirelessly using, for instance, the Bluetooth protocol as well as with other systems using the Internet. Therefore, it is likely to expect a wearable computing system specialized to support ECx activities at job sites in the near future.

References

[1]   "Wearable Computer," *Wikipedia*, http://en.wikipedia.org/wiki/Wearable_computer.

[2]   BIMserver, http://bimserver.org.

[3]   Sunkpho, J., Garrett, J., and McNeil, S., "A Framework for Field Inspection Support Systems Applied to Bridge Inspection," in *Proceedings of the 7th International Conference on the Applications of Advanced Technologies in Transportation*, Cambridge MA, August 5–7, pp. 417–424.

[4]   Sunkpho, J., Garrett, J. H., Jr., and McNeil, S., "XML-Based Inspection Modeling for Developing Field Inspection Support Systems," *Journal of Infrastructure Systems*, Vol. 11, No. 3, 2005, pp. 190–200.

[5]   Boronowsky, M., et al., "Winspect: A Case Study for Wearable Computing-Supported Inspection Tasks," in *Proceedings of the 5th International Symposium on Wearable Computers*, 2001.

[6]   Behzadan, A. H., Timm, B. W., and Kamat, V. R., "General Purpose Modular Hardware and Software Framework for Mobile Outdoor Augmented Reality Applications in Engineering," *Advanced Engineering Informatics*, No. 22, 2008, pp. 90–105.

[7]   Höllerer, T., et al., "User Interface Management Techniques for Collaborative Mobile Augmented Reality," *Computers and Graphics*, Vol. 25, No. 5, 2001, pp. 799–810.

CHAPTER 15

Future of Embedded Commissioning: What Is Possible in 20 Years?

In the preceding 14 chapters, we described the basic tenets, methods, and tools of embedded commissioning (ECx) and how we envision it will transform capital project delivery (CPD) and evaluation in the years to come. The primary strategy has been to create an entirely new approach to building evaluation by merging building commissioning methods and information technologies into a new framework of methods called ECx. We began describing this framework through three successive preface sections that also served as an introduction to each of the three parts of this book. Figures 2.4, 2.5, and III.1 are integrated into a single IDEF0 diagram in Figure 15.1 to help the reader visualize the ingredients of this framework and their relationships.

Perhaps more ambitious than any of the preceding ones, the task of this chapter is to envision, based on the ECx framework (Figure 15.1), what should be possible in 20 years' time. First we explore a vision for what is possible in the physical world of capital projects. Then we envision the future of the world of facility management. We follow this with a detailed view of the future state of ECx. Next, we shift our focus to visions of information technology futures—product models and digital infrastructures. Finally, we consider a vision of the world of the owners/users of facilities and the marketplace of capital projects.

15.1 What Is Possible in the Physical World of Capital Projects?

Buildings and building infrastructures have come a long way. Historically, building technology has caused significant shifts in the way buildings are constructed. Innovations realized during the Renaissance (16th and 18th centuries), Neo-Classicism (18th and 19th centuries), Modernism (19th and 20th centuries), or Post-Modernism (20th century) periods were all based on sociocultural shifts enabled by new technology. For instance, the increase of glazing in the Renaissance façade, the flexibility of interior planning achieved through the pattern books of Neo-Classicism, the industrial mass production of buildings achieved during the Modern Era, and the diversity of use and technology admitted into the production of buildings during Post-Modernism are all shifts in the CPD process ushered in by revolutionary technologies of the past [1]. Today, by virtue of the merging of building and information

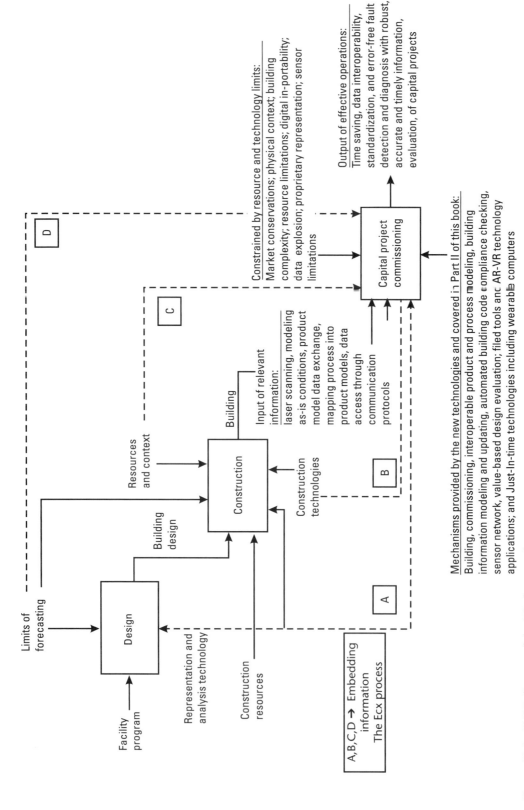

Figure 15.1 IDEF0 diagram of the ECx framework.

technologies, including the personal computer, the Internet, handheld and wearable computers, sensors, BIM, BACnet, IFC, and intelligent computer applications that harvest, mine, and package relevant information, we are at the cusp of a new and powerful shift in the way we build and evaluate capital projects.

In a mere two decades from now, we will be able to "dial up" information about manufacturer specifications of equipment and building parts, specific building histories, codes and ordinances applicable to specific situations, and integrated CAD-GIS databases [2], at will, from handheld and wearable devices. In addition, buildings will possess intelligence and initiate self-intervention automatically or through human contact.

We envision that buildings will be equipped with sensors, actuators, gateways, and reasoning mechanisms to be able to send precise alerts when systems fall to undesirable efficiency or performance levels. Live performance tracking that is remotely adjustable through PDAs or wearable devices will screen false positives and highlight critical fault detection and diagnosis (FDD) results. FDD will be achieved through collaboration among self-regulating building systems and facility management and operations staff. Minor fixes will be carried out by self-correcting actuators and sophisticated, decentralized control systems. On the web, interoperable and standardized communication connections to updated manufacturer specifications and pricing information will facilitate identification, procurement, repair, and replacement of systems.

15.2   Envisioning the Future of the World of Facility Management

The field of facility management will become a true collaboration between man and machine. Sensors in building system components will send alerts to a facility manager when components fatigue or fail. In states of emergency, sensors will directly contact emergency response personnel, before the condition becomes critical. Sensors will become an integral part of building materials and will alert occupants to moisture, termites, and other forms of undesirable penetration in the cladding system [3]. Systems for close-fit buildings will automatically adjust exterior skin to optimize daylight, temperature differentials, and moisture and sound insulation properties. Controls systems will be linked to geographic databases gathering live weather data, self-adjusting systems settings based on local conditions, operational parameters, maintenance histories, and user needs.

Although many of these technologies are available even today, their seamless interconnection is the Achilles heel of current facility management practices. In a case study we conducted in an institutional setting, we discovered useful behind-the-scenes information about emergency management practices. In December 2007, a water main burst open, submerging documents, furniture, and desktops in waist-deep water and threatened to do the same to the electrical panels servicing entire wings of an eight-story-high institutional building. As the clock ticked the facility management personnel scrambled to locate the main water valve that could control the pipe rupture. More than 4 hours and several false attempts at fixing the problem later, it was discovered that the faulty water main was merely passing through the building in question, to service a neighboring building, not the current one. Consequently, it was not included in the CAD files of the building but was present only in the GIS files that included the entire campus plan. This case high-lights the lack of coordination that exists in BIM documentation.

In a similar near-catastrophic water-main break case, the same campus experienced the potential impact of incomplete information, this time in the city water authority's documentation. Several hours passed before facility managers could locate the city employee who knew the location of the valve that he had installed months ago in a retrofit job and never recorded on the blueprints.

We envision a world in which JIT information, such as specifications about newly installed equipment and the locations of all pipes and maintenance items (servicing both local and global destinations), is marked *in situ* with the help of sensors, RFID tags, and other information capture-and-store devices. Handheld devices including cell phones will be used to grab information from a myriad of radio-frequency threads already present in the space around us.

15.3 A Vision of the Future State of ECx

In principle, ECx is a simple process. It compares the *required* performance of a capital project against its *actual* performance. If the desirable temperature setpoint for an indoor space is 68°F throughout the calendar year, then we should measure the temperature in that space and check it against the setpoint value. Complications arise because of difficulties like these:

- Is there an appropriate room to use in the facility of interest?
- What is the best way to measure the ambient temperature in a room?
- During which time(s) should these measurement(s) be taken?
- How can we verify that the setpoint value is satisfied?
- How can we validate that the measured value is adequate for occupant comfort or productivity?

Once these questions have been satisfied we still face further problems of what to do when the measured and expected values do not agree.

- What magnitude of difference between these values signifies agreement or disagreement?
- If there is disagreement, which value is incorrect?
- If the expected value is incorrect, how can we obtain a correct value?
- If the measured value is off, where in the system is the fault?
- If a fault is detected, how can we correct the system defect?

15.3.1 Locating Rooms and Equipment

Questions of location may seem trivial, but given the complexity of modern facilities, finding a particular location or a piece of equipment can be tricky. The reasons behind this include rapid change of equipment and rooms, and the lack of proper updates of information about facilities. In one of our shadowing experiments of an electrician in an institutional setting, we discovered that physically locating an electrical box that is behind other equipment and painted black for architectural reasons can take up to 5 hours (Chapter 13) [4].

We envision a world in which capital projects are accurately modeled in BIM systems that are interoperable with facility maintenance information and documents. These data banks are updated with as-built and as-modified data in a timely and accurate manner (Chapters 5 and 6) [5]. With the help of JIT information access systems and wearable computers, ECx agents will be able to locate facilities and equipment with ease and accuracy.

15.3.2   Measuring Ambient Temperature

Setpoint information recorded in an HVAC control system is at best approximate. Sometimes it specifies the time frame during which this must be observed. Even then the location of the measurement is dependent on the thermostat location, sensor availability, and the schedule of these readings. Due to variations in time and location, the spot measurements could vary drastically from the "average" or "representative" value gathered by the thermostat.

We envision a world in which rooms are equipped with multiple sensors, some of which would be in garments (laptops also have this capability) [6], where the location and time of data gathered would be most relevant to user needs. Multiple sensors would collect data distributed over periods of time most indicative of the needs of users of the space. Automated data harvesting and distilling algorithms would summarize not only the most appropriate temperature readings but also point to anomalies and variances that matter. With the help of advanced HCI methods, this information can be conveyed to the ECx tools succinctly, accurately, and just in time.

15.3.3   Verifying the Setpoint Value

System controls, in which setpoint data reside, include complex equipment and software components. Furthermore these mechanisms are proprietary, which means that we cannot view, scrutinize, or interfere with their inner workings. In short, the ability to verify the set values for all kinds of variables including temperature, humidity, and change-actuation to the system components as well as to the controls parameters is not available to us.

We envision a world in which proprietary mechanisms can map their internal parameters and procedures to a neutral, standard, and universally shared representation that can assist us in verifying the correctness and reasons for set values, without having to waste valuable time and budgetary resources of the ECx process (Chapter 9) [7].

15.3.4   Validating User Acceptability of Measured Values

User requirements are volatile. This is due both to changes experienced by the individual, such as illness, adjustment to diurnal and calendar variations, physiological and psychological state, and to intraindividual variations, such as age, sex, nationality, race, and education. These changes can mean significant comfort and productivity deficits or gains depending on the availability of the ambient environment (Chapter 1) [8]. Therefore, validating the acceptability of ambient environments cannot be decided on the basis of simple comparisons between as-designed and as-measured values. It also requires the consideration of relevant and up-to-date (even live) input from users.

We envision a future in which users are connected to the ECx process through updated design intent (Chapter 4) documents that are embedded in the process by virtue of interoperable and standardized data representations and tools.

15.3.5   What Are the Thresholds for Value Comparison?

In this brand new world of ECx, where updated information is broadly available, we still need human judgment and interpretation of data to decide what is significant. To a brain surgeon, the precision of the electron microscope-driven laser scalpel needs to be measured in micromillimeters, whereas the precision of kicking the ball through the space defined by the goal posts in a football game (or match) would be measured in yards, feet, or inches at best. How do we determine what variance from set values or desirable performance criteria is within an acceptable range?

In doing the fieldwork to determine how to construct correct product and process models for building commissioning (BCx), we encountered a similar phenomenon (Chapter 7). BCx reports prepared for the purpose of satisfying LEED (Leadership in Energy and Environmental Design) criteria, usually in loose-fit buildings, use a much more lenient criterion for satisfying required performance values than those prepared to assess the performance of critical functions in experimental and close-fit buildings (Chapter 1). For instance, in the former case, a wide variance (order of magnitude difference) in the wattage required in the HVAC system is waved off by the BCx agent, assuming that the amperage in the system will make up for this anomaly. In the latter category, the BCx report for a close-fit building, a medical laboratory, introduced us to several hundred new performance measurement criteria not used in the former category.

We envision a future in which data and criteria of evaluation for comparable buildings, live and appropriately packaged, are readily available to fieldworkers and ECx agents. A web-wide B2B database (Chapter 2) can accommodate comprehensive commissioning guidelines created by owners and users. Interactive checklists for different sustainability quality points would be maintained and relevant modeling software applications with version updates would be within reach of a palm device via the Internet.

15.3.6   How Do We Know Which Value Is Correct?

In some cases, the as-measured value is off due to equipment malfunction. But, too often, users neglect to update control settings and maintain equipment as required by the protocols designed to operate facilities in the most effective way (i.e., the most economical and suitable way for user needs). Therefore, human judgment and intervention are required. This process is assisted by a plethora of software applications that perform automated fault detection and diagnosis (FDD) (Chapter 8), facilitate BCx (Chapter 13), and even do some self-configuring [9].

Therefore, it is not a stretch to imagine a world in which we would have systems possessing sufficient "wisdom" to discriminate between false positives and eminent, catastrophic failures. In one case, we discovered that a loose-fit building that was commissioned for LEED purposes had a power outage that led to a meltdown due to the overheating of the liquid in its heat-exchange equipment. The entire equipment, which was a six-figure installation, had to be replaced. This logical consequence can be reasoned out by knowledge-based expert system (KBES) driven ECx applications. False positives may be more difficult to weed out of such a system since sensor readings can be volatile, subject to miscalibration, and over-responsive to local conditions. Therefore, we envision a future in which sensors systems eliminate local factors when necessary and perform self-reasoning and calibration.

15.3.7   What Does It Mean to Discover Errand As-Measured Value?

In one BCx case study that we undertook, we found that there was no difference in the performance of the system when we changed the settings of a valve in a fin-tube radiant heating system (Chapter 9). Does this mean that the valve was faulty? Or was there something wrong with the control settings? Was there something else interfering with the functions of the valve, which could be in perfect shape? It turned out that the actuator of the valve had malfunctioned years ago and it was removed for repair or replacement, neither of which materialized. There was no record of its removal other than the memories of maintenance and operations personnel of the time, who were no longer with the institution. This case illustrates the diversity of reasons that can be the cause of a malfunction or error. Therefore, misdiagnosis is common and the role of human judgment in FDD is critical.

The universal solution for correctly interpreting the meaning and significance of the misalignment of as-designed versus as-measured values is communication. ECx agents conducting field measurements need a complete and correct record of maintenance histories, access to robust and reliable BIM models, best practices in FDD, and plenty of comparable cases at their fingertips. We emphasized the tools and methods particularly applicable to these tasks in Part III and Chapters 13 and 14.

15.3.8   If a Fault Detection Is Confirmed, What Can We Do About It?

Interventions to correct diagnosed faults range from doing nothing, to readjustment or calibration of the existing system, to readjustment and correction of operating protocols and their implementation, to minor equipment repair and replacement, and, finally, to major equipment or subsystem repair or replacement. Many factors impact the selection of one of these options including available funding, schedule, use type, severity of fault, resource savings, and owner/user motivation.

Once again in our vision of the future, we revert to good communication with experts, sound human/computer interface systems, and accessibility to relevant information sources. JIT modeling linked to a database of "all-buildings" updated by manufacturers can help hone in to best practices in reconfiguring building systems, pricing, and new technologies entering the market.

15.4   Visions of Information Technology Futures

The critical technologies that will make all of this possible are digital modeling of AEC products and processes and the digital infrastructures that will make access, retrieval, and storage of information ubiquitous. Current trends indicate that in short order all new buildings, including the ones that were built in the past few decades, will have interoperable representations of their as-built drawings, project manuals, management and operation plans, repair histories, and manufacturer's specifications. Creation and updating of all of this information will be coordinated with planners, architects, engineers, and other relevant consultants of capital projects. Information will be embedded in their life-cycle process for ongoing evaluation to meet optimal performance and energy conservation goals. This process, which we call embedded commissioning (ECx), will be enforced by licensing and certification agencies that finance capital projects, such as the U.S. Green Building Council, U.S. General Services Administration, U.S. Army Corps of Engineers, and U.S. Postal Service.

These advances will not be realized unless several technological and organizational developments in the area of standardization have been realized first. Standards of interoperability must be agreed on and adhered to by major software and hardware houses like Microsoft, Google, IBM, Intel, and Autodesk that control the development and deployment of BIM software and AEC databases including GIS and infrastructure information. We also expect that agencies significantly contributing to the development of effective building standards like the U.S. National Institute of Standards and Technology will play a critical role in this process.

15.5   A Vision of the World of Facilities, Owners/Users, and Capital Project Marketplace

Just as the CPD process and its participants operate with entirely different tools, technologies, and procedures, the owners and operators of facilities also have to adapt to this process. This is not a simple, passive adaptation. Owners and operators of capital projects have to enable this innovation through their input and continuous participation. This future world will have not only online and live data about the history of facilities and operation/maintenance manuals, it must also have an interactive repository of best practices and troubleshooting queries for equipment and building parts. The owners/users are both receivers of and contributors to this information base. As they sort out their operation, maintenance, and ECx issues, the distributed web of information repositories will capture this information and store it so that, in the future, others will be able to use it. It will provide for less fragmentation of information, increase cooperation, and be linked through standardized modeling software applications. This requires the existence of a very large database of ECx groups with sustainable practices, distributed in the digital cloud, and accessible from laptops and handheld devices. A popular ontology of AEC terms, used and supplemented by users, will support this cloud utility.

An online survey utility will have access to different scenarios in order to determine the type of ECx protocol applicable to a given capital project for owners. The latest sensor, laser, modeling, and self-corrective technologies will be available to owners and users of capital projects. Users and their O&M personnel will be able to access, online, standard training and certification programs for ECx. O&M requests with links to location and relevant systems within the facility will be linked to efficient interactive troubleshooting applications. With the simple pointing of a device to a RFID tag, or sensor, in the problem area, the users will be able to access the relevant database for uploading useful information and downloading current changes in the form of pictures and models of the local condition.

Urgent requests will be broadcast to roaming facility staff through mobile devices, and nonurgent requests will be queued by an interactive tracking utility to monitor the progress of each request. Different aspects of the facility will be accessed for humidity-temperature penetration and termite infestation through sensors and sensor-embedded cladding materials. Through this process, building owners and users will become convinced of the value of embedded commissioning. Groups like LEED, ASHRAE, NIST, and SHASE will provide presentations, examples of successful case studies, access to entities outside of the building industry, comparative analyses by consultants to government and private agencies, tax incentives for life-cycle ECx, and energy-saving opportunities.

Although throughout this book we have emphasized the challenges alongside the opportunities that will propel embedded commissioning to the forefront of digital CPD processes, we remain optimistic. Without a doubt, a future enhanced by improved quality, schedule, and budget management of capital projects awaits those members of the architecture-engineering-construction sector, who are willing and excited about embracing information technologies and all that they have to offer.

References

[1]   Akın, Ö., "Keynote Address: I Am Not Rem Koolhaas," in *Proceedings of the Design Communication Conference*, Architecture Department, Southern Polytechnic, Atlanta, GA, March 25–29, 2009.

[2]   Akın. Ö, "CAD and GIS Integration: Challenges and Opportunities," in *CAD and GIS Integration*, H. A. Karimi and B. Akinci (Eds.), Boca Raton, FL: CRC Press, 2010.

[3]   Yang, B., et al., "Compliant and Low-Cost Humidity Nanosensors Using Nanoporous Polymer Membranes," *Sensors and Actuators B*, Vol. 114, (006, pp. 254–262.

[4]   Lee, S., and Akin, Ö., "Shadowing Tradespeople: Inefficiency in Maintenance Fieldwork," *Automation in Construction*, Vol. 18, No. 5, 2009, pp. 536–546.

[5]   Böhm, J., Becker, S., and Haala, N., "Model Refinement by Integrated Processing of Laser Scanning and Photogrammetry," in *Proceedings of 3D Virtual Reconstruction and Visualization of Complex Architectures (3D-Arch)*, Zurich, Switzerland, 2007.

[6]   Rowe, A., et al., "Sensor Andrew: Large-Scale Campus-Wide Sensing and Actuation," *IBM Journal of Research and Development*, Vol. 55, No. 1, pp. 6:1–6:14.

[7]   *BACnet: A Data Communication Protocol for Building Automation and Control Networks*, ANSI/ASHRAE Standard 135, American Society of Heating, Refrigerating, and Air-Conditioning Engineers, 2010.

[8]   Fisk, W. J., "Health and Productivity Gains from Better Indoor Environments and Their Relationship with Building Energy Efficiency," in *Annual Review of Energy and the Environment*, Vol. 25, November 2000, pp. 537–566.

[9]   Akinci, B., Garrett, J., and Akin, Ö., "Identification of Functional Requirements and Possible Approaches for Self-Configuring Intelligent Building Systems," NIST Grant 60NANB8D8140, final report submitted to Steven Bushby, National Institute for Standards and Technology.

Abbreviations and Acronyms

Term	Definition	Chapter
ABCCC	automated building code compliance checking	C-2
ACCESS	Microsoft's Database Software	C-3
ADA	Americans with Disabilities Act	C-1
ADC	analog-to-digital converters	C-11
ADL	Agent Description Language	C-10
AEC	architecture-engineering-construction	Preface, C-1, C-4, C-5, C-6, C-7,
AEC/FM	architecture-engineering-construction/facility management	C-5, C-6
aecXML	Architecture-engineering-construction eXtensible Markup Language	C-3, C-8
AEX	Automating Equipment Information Exchange	C-7, C-8
AEX	Automating Information Exchange	C-7
AGC	Association for General Contractors	C-5
AHU	air-handling unit	C-4
AIA	American Institute of Architects	C-5, C-7
AISC	American Institute of Steel Construction	C-10
ALARA	as-low-as-reasonably-achievable	C-12
AMCW	amplitude-modulated continuous waveform	C-6
AP	application protocol	C-7
APAR	AHU performance assessment rules	C-13
AR	augmented reality	C-13
ASD	AISC Specification on Allowable Stress Design	C-10
ASHRAE	American Society of Heating, Refrigerating and Air-Conditioning Engineers	C-3, C-4, C-5, C-9, C-10,
AWI	approved work item	C-7
B2B	business to business	C-3
B2C	business to client or consumer	C-3
B2E	business to employee	C-3
B2E	business to employee	
B2G	business to government institutions	C-3
BACnet	Data Communication Protocol for Building Automation and Control Networks	C-3, C-8, C-9, C-11, C-13
BACT	best-available-control technology	C-12
BARbi	Norway, reference data library	C-8
BAS	building automation system	C-3, C-5, C-9, C-13, C-14

BCA	Building Commissioning Association	C-2
BCx	building commissioning	C-1, C-2, C-3, C-4, C-8, C-9, C-15
bcXML	Building and Construction XML	C-7
BEMAC	building energy monitoring analyzing and controlling	C-3, C-8
BEMS	building energy management system	C-3
BEMS	building energy management system	C-13
BERA	building environment rule and analysis	C-10
BFA	building feasibility analysis	C-1
BIDS™	Building Investment Decision Support	C-12
BIM	Building Information Modeling	Preface, P-I, C-1, C-2, C-3, C-5, C-7, C-13
BNF	Backus-Naur form	C-8
BREEAM	United Kingdom's building research establishment standards	C-3
BREEAM	Building Research Establishment's Environmental Assessment Method	C-3
BSA	buildingSmart Alliance	C-7, C-10
BSAB	Byggandets Samordning AB	C-8
BTUs	British thermal units	C-2
building EQ	Building energy quotient	C-3
CAD	computer-aided design	C-2, C-7
CAFM	computer-aided facilities management	C-5
CAT	comparative analysis tables	C-4
CB	close-fit buildings	C-1
C-BR	cost/benefit with risk	C-12
CC	Continuous Commissioning©™	C-2
CCR	California Code of Regulations	C-5
CD	committee draft	C-7
CE	concurrent engineering	C-8
CEA	Consumer Electronics Association	C-9
CEN	Centre European de Normalization - European Committee for Standardization	C-9
CFG	context-free grammar	C-8
cfiXML	capital facilities industry extensible markup language	C-7
CIBSE	Chartered Institution of Building Services Engineers	C-3
CII	Construction Industry Institute	C-12
CIS	CIMsteel Integration Standards	C-7
CIS/2	CIMsteel Integration Standard, Release 2	C-7, C-8
CITE-AHU	automated commissioning tool for air-handling units	C-13
CLIPS	C Language Integrated Production System	C-8
CMMS	computerized maintenance management systems	C-5
CMU	Carnegie Mellon University	C-3, C-12
COBIE	Construction Operation Building Information Exchange	C-5, C-7
COMM	ongoing commissioning	C-3
CPD	capital project delivery	Preface, C-2, C-3, C-4, C-5, C-7, C-8. C-12. C-13, C-14
CSI	Construction Specification Institute	C-7

CSN	SN Czech technical standards.	C-3
CSV	comma-separated values	C-3
Cx	building commissioning	C-2. C-3. C-4
CxA	building commissioning agent	C-3
DABO	diagnostic agent for building operation	C-3
DAI	design analysis integration	C-3
DAV	Design added value	P-II, C-12
DDC	direct digital control	C-9
DEP	data exchange protocols	C-7
DIT	design intent tool	C-3
DLMO	dim light melatonin onset	C-1
DLS	data logging systems	C-13
DoD	U.S. Department of Defense	C-7
DoE	U.S. Department of Energy	C-5
DT	decision table	C-10
DTR	draft technical report	C-7
EB	experimental buildings	C-1
EBD	ENFORMA® building diagnostics	C-13
ECBCS	energy conservation for building and community systems	C-3
ECx	embedded commissioning	Preface, C-2, C-4, C-5, C-6, C-8, P-II, C-11, C-13, C-14, C-15
ECx-PPM	PPM mapping application	C-8
EDA	event-driven architecture	C-11
EESB	energy efficiency standard for buildings	C-10
EHS	European home systems	C-9
EIA	U.S. Energy Information Administration	C-5
EIB	European Installations Bus	C-9
E-level	energy consumption	C-3
EMCS	energy management and control system	C-3, C-13
EPB	energy performance of buildings	C-3
EPBD	energy performance of building directive	C-3
EXPRESS	exchange language if IFC	C-3, C-7, C-8, C-10
FDD	fault detection and diagnosis	C-3, C-11, C-15
FDIS	Final Draft International Standard	C-7
FIATECH	fully integrated and automated technology	C-7
FM	facility management	C-8
FM&O	facility management and operations	C-11
FPDISP	Final Proposed Draft International Standardized Profile	C-7
FPE	facility performance evaluation	C-1
FPT	functional performance test	C-3, C-4, C-8, C-9, C-10, C-13
FTDA	functional test data analysis	C-3
gbXML	Green Building eXtensible Markup Language	C-5, C-10
GIS	geographic information systems	C-15
GPS	Global Positioning System	C-14
GSA	U.S. General Services Association	C-5, C-6, C-7, C-10, C-13

GSN	global sensor networks	C-11
GT-PPM	Georgia Tech process to product modeling	C-8
HCI	Human/computer interaction	C-14
HDF5	Hierarchical Data Format, Version 5	C-3
HK-BEAM	Hong Kong Building Environmental Assessment Method	C-3
HKSAR	Hong Kong Special Administrative Region	C-3
HMD	head-mounted display	C-13
HTML	Hypertext Markup Language	C-10
HVAC	heating, ventilation and air conditioning	C-1, C-2, C-4, C-11
I/O	input/output	C-8
IAI	International Alliance for Interoperability	C-7
IC	information constructs	C-8
ICC	International Code Council	C-5, C-10
ICC	International Commerce Center, Hong Kong	C-3
I-Cx	initial commissioning	C-3
IDEF	information definition	C-2, C-3
IEA	International Energy Agency	C-1, C-3, C-4
IEE	Intelligent Energy–Europe	C-3
IFC	Industry Foundation Classes	C-2, C-3, C-7, C-10
IfcElement	IFC parent entity	C-7
IfcRoot	IFC root entity	C-7
ifcXML	XML format defined by ISO 10303-28	C-7, C-13
IGES	Initial Graphics Exchange Specification	C-7
IP	Internet Protocol	C-11
IPD	integrated project delivery	C-5
ISE	Institute for Solar Energy Systems	C-3
ISO	International Organization for Standardization	C-1, C-2, C-7
IT	information technology	C-3
ITB	integrated technical building	C-3
IWMS	integrated workplace management system	C-5
JIT	just in time	C-3, C-8, P-II, C-14, C-15
KBE	knowledge-based engineering	C-3
KBES	knowledge-based expert system	C-3, C-15
KIF	Knowledge Interchange Format	C-8
K-level	average insulation	C-3
KMZ	Google Earth file format	C-13
kWh	kilowatts per jour	C-3
LB	loose-fit buildings	C-1
LBNL	Lawrence Berkeley National Laboratory	C-3, C-4
LCS	Lifetime Commissioning Standard	C-3
LEED	Leadership in Energy and Environmental Design	C-2, C-15
LonMark	international organization promoting energy efficiency through standards	C-9
LPM	Logical Product Modeling	C-7, C-8
M2M	machine-to-machine	C-11
MANDATE	ISO MANufacturing management DATa Exchange	C-3
MEP	mechanical, electrical, and plumbing	C-3, C-5, C-6

MIA	mobile inspection assistance	C-14
NCDC	National Climatic Data Center	C-13
NCS	U.S. National CAD Standards	C-7
NIBS	National Institute for Building Sciences	C-1, C-5, C-7
NIST	National Institute of Standards and Technology	C-3, C-4, C-7
NKN	Czech national calculation tool	C-3
NN	noun, singular or mass	C-8
NNP	proper noun, singular	C-8
NNPS	proper noun, plural	C-8
NNS	noun, plural	C-8
NP	noun phrase	C-8
NPV	net present value	C-12
NRC	Natural Resources Canada	C-3, C-8
NS	Norway standard	C-3
NSF	National Science Foundation	C-10
O&M	operations and maintenance	C-3, C-8, C-13
oBIX	Open Building Information Xchange	C-7
OGC	Open Geospatial Consortium	C-11
OO	object oriented	C-3
OPR	owner's project requirements	C-3
OS	operating system	C-11
OWL	Web Ontology Language	C-8, C-10
PACRAT	Performance And Continuous Re-commissioning Analysis Tool	C-13
PAE	Procedure d'Avis Energetique	C-3
PECI	Portland Energy Conservation, Inc.	C-3, C-4
PFC	prefunctional checklist	C-3, C-4, C-8, C-13
PHPP	PHP passive	C-3
PLCs	programmable logic controllers	C-9
PM4D	product models based on four dimensions	C-3
POE	post-occupancy evaluation	C-1
POS	part-of-speech	C-8
PPM	product and process model	C-2, C-4, C-8
ProMICE	computer-based application to explore between CE stages	C-8
PSL	process specification language	C-3
PTB	Penn Treebank	C-8
QA	quality assurance	C-6
RCM	requirements collection and modeling	C-8
RDBMS	relational database management system	C-3
RDF	resource description framework	C-8
ReC	Re-Commissioning	C-2, C-3
Retro-Cx	Retro-Commissioning	C-2, C-3
REVIT	Autodesk BIM product	C-3
RFI	request for information	C-2
RSS	Really Simple Syndication	C-11
SASE	standards analysis, synthesis and expression	C-10
SC	subcommittee	C-7
SCADA	supervisory control and data acquisition	C-9

SDAI	Standard Data Access Interface	C-7
SensorML	Sensor Model Language	C-11
SHASE	Society of Heating, Air-Conditioning and Sanitary Engineers	C-1, C-3
SLAM	simultaneous localization and mapping	C-6
SMARTcodes	international energy conservation code by the International Code Council	C-5
SML	Standards Modeling Language	C-10
SNVT	shared network variable types	C-9
SPF	standards processing framework	C-10
SPF	STEP physical file	C-7
SPie	Specifiers' Properties Information Exchange	C-5
SQL	Standard Query Language	C-10
SQL	Structured Query Language	C-11
STEP	Standard for the exchange of product model data	C-2, C-7
SUL	standards usage language	C-10
SWE	sensor web enablement	C-11
SXF	Seadec data eXchange Format	C-3
TAB	testing, adjusting, and balancing	C-4
TAMU	Texas A&M University	C-3
TC 184	ISO Technical Committee	C-7
TCP/IP	Transmission Control Protocol/Internet Protocol	C-9
TEKES	Finnish Funding Agency for Technology and Innovation	C-3
TML	Transducer Markup Language	C-11
UI	user interface	C-14
UML	Unified Modeling Language	C-3, C-7, C-8,
UOB	unit of behavior	C-8
USACE	U.S. Army Corps of Engineers	C-5
US-DOE	U.S. Department of Energy	C-3
U-values	insulation quotient	C-3
VA	Veterans Administration	C-5
VAV	variable air volume	C-11
VBD	value-based design	C-12
VE	value engineering	C-12
VMA	version matching approach	C-8
VP	verb phrase	C-8
WBD	Whole Building Diagnostician	C-13
WWW	World Wide Web	C-10
XML	eXtensible Markup Language	C-7, C-8, C-11
XMPP	eXtensible Messaging and Presence Protocol	C-11

About the Author

Ömer Akın, professor, School of Architecture, Carnegie Mellon University, is a frequently published researcher in the areas of design cognition and computation. His books include Representation and Architecture (1982), Psychology of Architectural Design (1986, 1989) Generative CAD Systems (2005), and A Cartesian Approach to Design Rationality (2006).

Upon completing his bachelors and masters degrees in architecture at the Faculty of Architecture, Middle East Technical University in 1970, he obtained a Fulbright Scholarship for graduate studies in the United States. Subsequently, he earned a master of architecture in environmental systems from Virginia Polytechnic Institute and State University in 1972, and a Ph.D. in architecture from Carnegie Mellon University in 1979.

He has been teaching at Carnegie Mellon University since 1978. He served as the head of the Department of Architecture from 1981 to 1988; and the director of the graduate programs from 1989 to 2000.

His research interests include design cognition, computer-aided design generation, case-based instruction, ethical decision making, design of virtual worlds, building commissioning, and automated requirement management.

Over the past two decades, he has received numerous research grants from external sources, including the National Science Foundation and the National Institute of Standards and Technology. In addition to those in the School of Architecture, he has also conducted research with associates in the Psychology, Civil and Environmental Engineering, School of Urban & Public Affairs, and Computer Science departments.

He is a registered architect in the Commonwealth of Pennsylvania and the Republic of Turkey. He has a small, selective practice. He has designed and built residential, commercial, and office buildings in the United States, Turkey, and the Middle East. Currently, he is the architect of record for the Turkish Nationality Room for the Cathedral of Learning at the University of Pittsburgh.

Index

American
Democratic
Theory

American
Democratic
Theory

PLURALISM
AND ITS CRITICS

William Alton Kelso

 Contributions in Political Science, Number 1

GREENWOOD PRESS
WESTPORT, CONNECTICUT • LONDON, ENGLAND

Library of Congress Cataloging in Publication Data

Kelso, William Alton.
    American democratic theory.

    (Contributions in political science ; no. 1, ISSN 0147-1066)
    Includes bibliographical references.
    1. Democracy. 2. Pluralism (Social sciences). 3. Political participa-
tion—United States. 4. United States—Politics and government—
1945-   . I. Title. II. Series: Contributions in political science ; no. 1.
JC423.K379   321.8   77-83894
ISBN 0-8371-9825-9

Library of Congress Catalog Card Number: 77-83894
ISBN: 0-8371-9825-9
ISSN: 0147-1066

First published in 1978

Greenwood Press, Inc.
51 Riverside Avenue, Westport, Connecticut 06880

Printed in the United States of America

10 9 8 7 6 5 4 3 2 1

Acknowledgments

Chapter 2 is adapted from William Kelso, "Public Pluralism: A New Defense of an Old Doctrine," *Social Science*, Winter 1977, Vol. 52, No. 1, pp. 16-30, and is reprinted with permission of the publisher.

Part of chapter 6 is from William Kelso, "Organizing the Poor: Reexamining the OEO Data," *The Bureaucrat*, October 1977, Vol. 6, No. 3, and is reprinted with permission of the publisher.

Table 1 is from Robert Dahl, *A Preface to Democratic Theory*. Copyright © 1956 by The University of Chicago. Used with permission of the University of Chicago Press.

Table 3 is adapted from *Public Finance* by Richard Musgrave and Peggy Musgrave. Copyright © 1973 by McGraw-Hill, Inc. Used with permission of McGraw-Hill Book Company.

To **Linda**

Contents

Preface

My reasons for writing a book on
democratic theory are essentially threefold. First of all, this piece
is intended as a defense of a pluralistic form of democracy. In
recent years textbooks on American government and more specialized monographs on democratic theory have been extremely hostile
to pluralistic forms of politics. Many of the criticisms seem unwarranted for they fail to distinguish among different types of pluralism
and they often overlook considerable evidence that pluralistic
patterns of participation can work well if properly structured.
While many readers will undoubtedly reject a number of my conclusions, this book will serve some purpose if it causes them to
reconsider the merits of pluralistic government.

Besides defending an often maligned form of government, this
book also attempts to identify and analyze the major assumptions
underlying competing theories of democracy. In many cases the
debate over democratic theory seems muddled because commentators use the same label to refer to what are analytically different
forms of government. Quite frequently, people mistakenly equate
pluralistic democracy with polyarchal, or elitist, forms of democratic rule even though the two systems of government entail radically different conceptions of what democracy means. As a means
of clarifying some of this confusion, this study analytically identifies and then compares four types of democratic theory: (a) polyarchy, which sees the essence of democracy as competition among
political elites, (b) pluralism, which conceives of democratic government as a twofold process involving competition among elites
and bargaining among interest groups, (c) populism, which equates
democracy with maximizing the power of the majority to decide
substantive political issues, and (d) participatory democracy,

which views democratic government as a form of community decision making in which all citizens can actively participate on a day-to-day basis.

Finally, this book is an attempt to synthesize recent findings in the fields of voting behavior, participation, decision making, and public administration. More often than not, specialized studies in these fields have larger ramifications for democratic theory that have never been fully discussed or developed. As the discipline of political science has become more specialized, there has been a tendency for scholars to ignore the larger consequences of their own work. While this study is a normative defense of one type of democratic theory, it also attempts to offer a new perspective for analyzing and understanding recent developments in the various subfields of political science.

In preparing this manuscript I have received generous help from numerous friends and colleagues whom I would like to thank. I am especially endebted to Booth Fowler, my graduate advisor at the University of Wisconsin, who originally got me interested in the subject of democratic theory. As innumerable other students will testify, he is a very gifted teacher. His encouragement as well as his numerous critical comments greatly improved the quality of this manuscript. Nobutaka Ike also read the book in its entirety and made many helpful suggestions. David Colburn, Manning Dauer, Mark Kann, Brian Peckham, Richard Scher, and Dan Siminoski provided much needed assistance and encouragement during the actual writing. Thanks are also due to Molly Loughlin and Adrienne Turner, who cheerfully typed the completed manuscript. Finally, I should like to thank my wife, Linda, who is in reality almost a coauthor of this book. She patiently read and reread the various drafts of the manuscript, pointing out instances where the logic of an argument seemed weak or the evidence substantiating a point appeared inadequate. Her excellent editing also improved the clarity and readability of the book. And, as a respite from democratic theory, she willingly spent many an evening at the movies with me. While such behavior delayed the completion of the work, it greatly improved the morale of the author.

William Alton Kelso

PART I

Alternative Types of Democratic Theory

Chapter

1

Introduction

This study is primarily a response to recent attacks on a pluralistic theory of democracy. In the 1950s and 1960s, scholars like Robert Dahl and David Truman articulated and defended a model of politics that viewed democracy as a two-fold process involving competition among political elites and bargaining among interest groups. As the term *pluralism* implies, the underlying assumption of the doctrine was that political power is and ought to be wielded by a number of groups rather than any single set of interests. In recent years, however, this model of democracy has been subject to intense attack from a wide spectrum of critics. Robert Paul Wolff, among others, has insisted that the disparity in power and resources between established and marginal groups is so great in a pluralistic system that there is little genuine possibility of initiating reform from below. [1] In contrast, critics like Theodore Lowi have argued that a pluralistic dispersion of political power makes it impossible for public officials to deal with pressing social issues in any sort of centralized, purposeful fashion. [2] Still other commentators, like Michael Harrington, have charged that pluralism so caters to the needs of special interest groups that the welfare of the larger public suffers as a result. [3]

The critics not only disagree on their diagnosis of pluralism's problems but also are at odds as to the measures necessary to remedy its alleged defects. In the debate over how the political system should be structured, three rivals to pluralism have been proposed.

First, participatory democrats like Robert Paul Wolff, Alan Alt-shuler, and Milton Kotler have advocated the creation of small units of government that will allow people to participate more intensely in the day-to-day affairs of the community.[4] Traditional communitarian democrats like Wolff have justified decentralization of political power on the grounds that the individual will be likely to develop his capabilities to their fullest only when he has an opportunity to participate in the deliberation of important social issues. They believe that regardless of the instrumental advantages a person may secure, he will emotionally and morally benefit from immersing himself in the social affairs of his community. More recently, advocates of community control like Altshuler and Kotler have also argued that political decentralization is necessary in order to increase the ability of minority members to shape their own lives. In their view, unless a centralized political system devolves more power to local neighborhoods, blacks and other minority groups will lack the leverage to control those policies which directly affect their communities.

On the other hand, polyarchal democrats like Theodore Lowi, Robert Crain, and Joseph Schumpeter have called for the concentration of power in the hands of political elites.[5] Lowi in particular maintains that a pluralistic system of decision making so fragments political power that it renders the government incapable of dealing quickly and comprehensively with the numerous problems that beset it. Other polyarchists like Schumpeter contend that consolidation of authority is necessary because the vast majority of citizens are incapable of rational, competent behavior in the political realm. Rejecting the notion of intensive citizen participation, they insist that democratic government entails the right of the public to hold its elites accountable for their actions. In the polyarchal view, government officials can be made to exercise their enhanced power in a beneficent and responsible fashion so long as there are periodic elections in which the public can hold them accountable for their behavior.

Thirdly, populist democrats like Michael Harrington have called both for increasing participation from the bottom up and for strengthening government power from the top down.[6] Populists contend that policy should be determined by a majority of citizens rather than a handful of elites or a small coterie of interest groups, and they therefore advocate periodic referendums as the major means of arriving at public decisions. But because they believe that the pluralistic interplay of groups can often frustrate the wishes of the majority, they maintain that referendum voting should be accompanied by a consolidation of government authority. If the political system is to be made responsive to the needs of the majority, the state must have sufficient power to block small minorities that seek to thwart the wishes of the larger public.

The Need for a Comparative Focus

In order to respond to the above criticisms, this book will look in a more analytical fashion at both the alleged defects of pluralism and the limitations of competing theories of democracy. Unfortunately, many critics have failed to examine the strengths and weaknesses of pluralism from this sort of comparative perspective. When opponents maintain that an interest-group theory of democracy works to the disadvantage of minority groups, they overlook the fact that marginal interests have often fared less well under alternative forms of decision making. Similarly, when commentators insist that a pluralistic system of power makes it impossible to get anything done, they fail to take account of the evidence indicating that pluralistic forms of decision making lead to more policy innovations than do either more centralized or more decentralized patterns of policy making. All too often critics have faulted pluralism for one reason or another but have neglected to show how polyarchy or populism or participatory democracy would rectify the defects they attribute to an interest-group theory of politics.

Recent attacks on pluralism are also deficient because they often fail to distinguish among different varieties of the doctrine. While many commentators assume that there is a single form of pluralistic democracy, I wish to suggest that there are several different analytic types and that many of the complaints leveled against pluralism are actually problems that trouble only certain varieties of the theory.[7] The type of interest-group democracy that I shall call *laissez-faire pluralism* posits a self-regulating political system made up of a multitude of private interests that bargain among themselves and check one another's advances. The advocates of this model—including Robert Dahl, David Truman, and Charles Lind-blom—contend that powerful interest groups will precipitate the emergence of countervailing groups to restrain the monopolistic exercise of power by any single element in society. They also argue that interest-group competition will lead to rational and innovative policy making, since a mulititude of participants can compensate for the limitations in knowledge and ability of any single decision maker. Like its counterpart in economics, laissez-faire pluralism regards competition as the mechanism that maintains the system in working order without any need for outside regulation.

An alternative form of pluralism, which I shall call *corporate pluralism*, minimizes the benefits that accrue from the clash of interests and instead stresses the importance of cooperation be-tween interest groups and government agencies. This model, which is embodied in programs like the NRA of the New Deal, envisions a political system broken down into a series of autonomous fief-doms presided over by small coteries of interest groups. In each separate domain, government authorities have conferred the ability to make public decisions upon private groups, thereby blurring the boundaries between private interests and public power. The basic assumption is that enhanced decision making will result when the public and private sectors cooperate in resolving problems common to both.

Finally, it is possible to identify a third type of interest-group democracy, which I shall call *public pluralism*. It is this third type of the doctrine that I will defend in this study as the most viable alternative among all the competing models of democracy. The efforts of the Johnson administration to organize the poor under OEO and to coordinate federal policies under the Model Cities program are forms of organizational behavior most closely approx-imating this variety of pluralism. Like its laissez-faire counterpart, public pluralism regards competition among groups as the mecha-nism that will produce the optimal set of public policies. But be-cause various elements in society lack the resources to organize or to gain access to government decision makers, and because interest groups and agencies often agree to refrain from competing with one another in specific policy areas, public pluralism calls upon the government to undertake measures that will guarantee that the political arena remains competitive. More specifically, it envisions public supervision of the bargaining process, increased centralization of the decision-making arena on both regional and national levels, and stepped-up government action to organize marginal elements in society that lack the resources for bargaining effectively with competing interest groups. In this latter sense public pluralism is similar to corporate pluralism, for it seeks to erase the distinction between public and private authority; but in calling for public agencies to share their resources with private groups, it seeks to foster competition rather than to discourage it.

The Issue of Participation

In defending pluralism against rival theories of democracy, this study will focus on two perennial issues of democratic theory, the scope and limits of popular participation and the consequences of such participation for public decision making. The reason for focusing on these two problems is that on the most basic level democracy has been defined in terms of popular participation in government decision making. Beyond this general level, however, alternative theories of democracy have very different conceptions of what popular participation should involve. While all forms of democratic theory see the public as playing a crucial role in politics, they disagree on three fundamental issues: (1) what the scope of the public's power should be, (2) how the public should be defined and how it should express its views, and (3) what purpose should be served by popular participation in politics.

Polyarchal democrats have usually wanted to confine the public's involvement in politics to choosing among competing elites at election time. By contrast, pluralists and populists have argued that the citizenry should have a voice in deciding many of the substantive issues confronting the political system, while participatory democrats have gone even further and insisted that the public should participate in all the daily decisions that face the political community. Pluralists, populists, and participatory democrats contend that elitist versions of democracy underestimate the citizenry's ability to make informed decisions in crucial policy matters. Despite their common agreement that the public should play a prominent role in politics, these three versions of democracy have often strongly disagreed over who constitutes the public and how it should express its sentiments on important issues. Pluralists have tended to conceive of the relevant constituency as the numerous issue publics that make up society, while populists have envisaged the people as the numerical majority existing on any one particular issue and participatory democrats have insisted that the public includes all members of the community. In addition, both populists and pluralists have differed over how policy decisions should be formulated. While populists have wanted to rely on referendums to decide major issues confronting the political system, pluralists have maintained that public welfare can be maximized if decisions are made through political bargaining. Finally, alternative theories of democracy often have very different conceptions of the benefits that accrue to the individual from becoming involved in political affairs. Polyarchists, populists, and pluralists have usually tended to visualize political participation as a utilitarian device for realizing the interests of the public. In contrast, participatory democrats have argued that participation fosters the intellectual and emotional development of the individual and that it should therefore be viewed as an end in and of itself and not as a means for the accomplishment of other substantive ends.

To demonstrate that the pluralist theory of participation is preferable to the above alternatives, this study will argue with opposing democratic theories on both empirical and normative grounds. If, as populists insist, the wishes of the majority ought to prevail, it will be essential to look at the empirical evidence to see whether a majority interest actually exists on most issues. And if it is possible to identify a majoritarian position, it will then be imperative to debate on normative grounds whether the intensity of interests or the majority of interests should be the determining factor in arriving at public decisions. Likewise, to respond to the claim of participatory democrats that pluralism fails to provide adequate opportunities for individual participation, it will be necessary to determine whether there is adequate empirical evidence for the assumption that people are able to sustain an intense involvement in communitarian politics.

The Issue of Decision Making

After comparing their contrasting views of participation, this book will examine how alternative theories of democracy attempt to deal with the problem of decision making. In many respects participation and decision making are corollary problems, for individuals participate in politics in order to influence the content of public decisions. However, as the modern state has assumed increasing responsibility for the welfare of its citizens, the question has arisen whether popular participation and rational, innovative policy making are compatible goals. Many commentators have argued that the complexities of social planning require a trade-off between citizen involvement and effective policy making. Since so many of the attacks on pluralism have focused on the subject of decision making, it is essential that we examine this issue in more detail. More specifically, it will be necessary to study alternative forms of democratic theory in terms of (1) what kinds of decision-making procedures will be most effective in generating rational policy solutions and (2) what kinds of institutional or administrative procedures will be most likely to succeed in translating publicly determined goals into operating policy. While polyarchists like Lowi maintain that effective, long-range policies will be developed only when political elites have sufficient power to act in a decisive, comprehensive manner, I will argue that public pluralism's adversary style of decision making constitutes a more effective method of social planning since bargaining and competition among a multitude of groups and agencies can offset the limitations in knowledge and ability of any single set of decision makers. Likewise, while advocates of community control like Kotler contend that decentralized, neighborhood forms of government will maximize responsiveness to constituent needs, I will argue that a pluralistic style of policy making can better meet public demands since it can deal with complex issues, like pollution, which transcend the boundaries and the problem-solving capabilities of local jurisdictions.

Besides analyzing pluralism's doubts about both highly centralized and highly decentralized forms of decision making, I will also show how pluralism questions the rationality and effectiveness of bureaucratic behavior. Polyarchal democrats like Lowi tend to see bureaucracies in Weberian terms as rational instruments for neutrally implementing predetermined social goals, but students of the administrative process have long argued that bureaucratic behavior can often be inefficient and even pathological in nature. By drawing on the work of Mathew Holden and Philip Selznick, among others, I hope to demonstrate how the political constituents of organizations often inhibit agencies from translating publicly determined goals into operating policy.[8] Likewise, I hope to show how a system of public pluralism can mitigate this type of bureaucratic goal displacement by encouraging agencies and interest groups to monitor one another's activities.

Finally, in a related fashion, I wish to question Lowi's argument that government bureaus should be granted only limited discretion in the implementation of their organizational responsibilities. Lowi maintains that because of our pluralistic system of administration, in which government agencies have considerable leeway in interpreting their obligations, the public has lost faith in the legitimacy and inherent justice of our political institutions. As I shall argue in more detail, it is questionable whether Lowi's explanation for the existence of widespread cynicism about government institutions is completely accurate. And even more importantly, I shall show there is considerable evidence to indicate that if Lowi's call for "juridical democracy" were ever implemented and government bureaus were forced to behave in a highly legalistic, nondiscretionary manner, the ability of public officials to act effectively might be drastically curtailed. In pursuit of what he believes is a just administrative state, Lowi has proposed administrative reforms that may severely hamper the successful delivery of public services.

However, before taking up these issues, it is necessary to deal in more detail with the doctrine of pluralism itself. Although many critics talk as if there were a single form of interest-group democracy, it is possible to identify several different analytic types. Chapter 2 will therefore be devoted to the delineation of three different models of pluralism. In parts II and III I will defend pluralism against rival theories of democracy, arguing that a public form of pluralism can meet many of the objections raised by alternative theories of democracy.

NOTES

1. Robert Paul Wolff, Barrington Moore, Jr., and Herbert Marcuse, *A Critique of Pure Tolerance*, pp. 3-53.
2. Theodore J. Lowi, *The End of Liberalism*.
3. Michael Harrington, *Toward a Democratic Left*.
4. Alan Altshuler, *Community Control*; Milton Kotler, *Neighborhood Government*; Wolff, Moore, and Marcuse, *Critique of Pure Tolerance*.
5. Lowi, *End of Liberalism*; Robert L. Crain, Elihu Katz, and Donald Rosenthal, *The Politics of Community Conflict*; Joseph A. Schumpeter, *Capitalism, Socialism and Democracy*.
6. Harrington, *Toward a Democratic Left*; See also Jack Newfield and Jeff Greenfield, *A Populist Manifesto*.
7. It should be stressed that this book is not intended to be a history of pluralism. In delineating three types of pluralistic government I have focused primarily on the works of contemporary American political scientists and ignored the writings of English pluralists at the turn of the century. In the early 1900s Frederick Maitland and John Neville Figgis and later Harold Laski, R. H. Tawney, and G. D. H. Cole formulated the doctrine of pluralism as an attack on continental idealism and British liberalism. They rejected both the Hegelian notion that the modern state has a virtual monopoly on legitimate authority and the nineteenth-century liberal belief that the individual exists in a social vacuum. Since these concerns have been of only peripheral interest to American pluralists, I have refrained from dealing with the above authors. For similar reasons I have spent no space discussing Arthur Bentley's classic work, *The Process of Government*. While many people might be inclined to call him a pluralist, his interests were very different from those explored in this book. Rather than offering an empirical description of American politics or a normative defense of a style of decision making, Bentley was primarily concerned with fashioning a tool to analyze political phenomena. Revolting against the "formalism" of the political thought of his day, he proposed the use of group analysis as a means of capturing the very process of governmental activity. While he maintained that group analysis was a useful device to apply to political behavior, he did not necessarily conclude that the interplay of groups was either empirically important or normatively desirable in resolving policy disputes.
8. Mathew Holden "Imperialism in Bureaucracy," pp. 943-51; Philip Selznick, *TVA and the Grass Roots*.

Chapter

2

Three Types of Pluralism

In recent years the debate over pluralistic democracy has elicited intense comment from detractors as well as defenders of the doctrine. While supporters of a group theory of democracy contend that the interplay of interests enhances individual freedom and promotes rational decision making, critics claim that it retards comprehensive planning and works to the disadvantage of marginal interests in society. The purpose of this chapter is to argue that the debate has often been somewhat beside the point since the antagonists have failed to realize that there are distinct varieties of pluralism. The pattern of policy making that Robert Dahl and David Truman have described as pluralism has little in common with that form of politics Theodore Lowi has called "interest group liberalism" or Grant McConnell has termed "a group theory of politics." Because of their failure to recognize the existence of different kinds of interest-group democracy, many commentators have not always realized that their criticisms may apply only to specific forms of the doctrine. As we shall soon see, it is analytically possible to identify three distinct varieties: laissez-faire, corporate, and public pluralism. These alternative types make not only very different empirical assumptions about the openness of the present political system, but also very different normative assumptions about the most desirable pattern of group interaction.

Laissez-faire Pluralism

The form of pluralism I have labeled laissez-faire finds its clearest expression in the works of Robert Dahl, David Truman, Wallace Sayre, Herbert Kaufman, Edward Banfield, Charles Lindblom, and William Kornhauser. [1] Despite some variations in their respective views, these authors conceive of democracy as essentially a twofold process involving competition among political elites and bargaining among interest groups. They insist that whenever members of the public are concerned about a particular issue, they can bring about political change either directly through the process of group bargaining or indirectly through the mechanism of elections. Laissez-faire pluralists reject the argument that the political system is dominated by a single ruling elite and instead insist that it is responsive to a variety of interests with divergent policy preferences. Like their laissez-faire counterparts in economics, they view the political arena as a competitive marketplace in which any entrepreneur can gain entry to merchandise his views. Politics is seen as an open, fluid process in which responsibility for formulating decisions is shared by a diverse array of groups and public officials who constantly bargain and negotiate with one another.

According to Dahl, whose case study of New Haven politics constitutes the classic example of the laissez-faire model, this openness represents the major distinguishing characteristic of the American political system.

When one looks at American political institutions in their entirety and compares them with institutions in other democracies, what stands out as a salient feature is the extraordinary variety of opportunities these institutions provide for an organized minority to block, modify, or delay a policy which the minority opposes. Consequently, it is a rarity for any coalition to carry out its policies without having to bargain, negotiate, and compromise with its opponents. [2]

In New Haven, the process of bargaining and negotiation has made it possible for such diverse groups as wealthy businessmen, old-time patricians, and working-class ethnics to wield considerable control over those policies which happen to concern them. [3] Since these groups have a variety of resources at their disposal as well as a number of points at which to influence policy, they cannot be denied access to the bargaining table for any prolonged period of time. Given the decentralized nature of the decision-making process, no single party can succeed in permanently excluding interests that hold opposing views. If a group feels intensely about an issue and is skillful in using its resources, it can win a favorable hearing of its demands even though it may not wield any preponderant strength in terms of wealth, social standing, or the like. [4]

Secondly, laissez-faire pluralists contend that the political system is self-regulating and self-correcting. If particular groups do start to accumulate excessive amounts of power, countervailing forces are likely to become active, which will check or limit their actions. Dahl argues that the phenomenon of unused resources, or what he terms "political slack," constitutes the chief brake on the decision-making process. [5] Since all groups possess some sort of resources, whether they be numbers, skill, or wealth, and since on most occasions groups do not expend all of their available assets to influence the deliberations of the political system, they have a certain amount of political slack on which they can draw when they perceive a threat to their interests. If a group starts to abuse its power or to deny access to other interests, opposing groups can tap previously unused resources in order to counterbalance these developments.

While Dahl speaks of political slack, Truman regards the phenomenon of "potential groups" as the chief restraint on monopoly power. Truman points out that individuals who are concerned with a particular issue do not necessarily need to use their resources overtly in order to wield influence. Established interests that recognize that their actions may elicit hostile reactions from other parties often seek to moderate their demands in order to minimize political opposition to their programs.

The power of unorganized interests lies in the possibility that, if these wide, weak interests are too flagrantly ignored, they may be stimulated to organize for aggressive counteraction. In a society permitting wide freedom of association, access to power is not confined to the organized groups in the population. [6]

In a slightly different vein, Sayre and Kaufman argue that the self-regulating nature of the political system derives from the existence of multiple decision-making points.[7] In their case study of politics in New York City, they show how the decentralized nature of the city's government structure prevents any one group from monopolizing the political arena. Because there are so many points at which groups can voice their opinions, interests that lose out at one center of decision making can often seek redress of their grievances at another location.

Thirdly, because laissez-faire pluralists see the political system as both open and self-regulating, they believe that the power of the state to guide and regulate the political process is problematic at best. In a fluid political system in which decisions are reached through continual negotiation and compromise, the power of all parties, including that of political elites, is necessarily limited. Truman views government officials as playing primarily a mediative role, reconciling conflicting group demands when particular interests are unable to resolve their differences by themselves.[8] In contrast, Banfield recognizes that political officials can institute change if they want to, but he argues that they often feel the cost is too high. Banfield's case study of Chicago graphically illustrates the constraints political leaders face under a highly pluralistic system of decision making: "In a system in which the political head must continually 'pay' to overcome formal decentralization and to acquire the authority he needs, the stock of influence in his possession cannot all be 'spent' as he might wish."[9] Thus instead of supervising the policy-making arena and orchestrating support for particular issues, leaders like Mayor Daley often choose to play a passive role. "When there is disagreement . . . the rational strategy for the political head usually is to do nothing."[10]

However, if government officials are especially skillful at what Dahl calls "pyramiding resources,"[11] they may be able to initiate significant change. In a laissez-faire system, elites like Mayor Lee of New Haven may be able to have a significant impact on their community by employing previously unused resources. But even when government officials are prominent actors in the political arena and not just mediators or passive bystanders, their power is based more on their personal skills as negotiators than on the institutional authority of their office. Mayor Lee succeeded in initiating an extensive urban redevelopment program in New Haven, but he was able to do so because "he was a negotiator rather than a hierarchical executive."[12]

He rarely commanded. He negotiated, cajoled, exhorted, beguiled, charmed, pressed, appealed, reasoned, promised, insisted, demanded, even threatened, but he most needed support and acquiescence from other leaders who simply could not be commanded. Because the mayor could not command, he had to bargain.[13]

While the above authors have developed a model that is primarily an empirical theory of politics, their work is not without normative significance. The defenders of laissez-faire pluralism can easily be seen as the inheritors of eighteenth- and nineteenth-century liberalism's interest in the rights and liberties of the individual. Like James Madison before them, they recognize that in a large and diverse society men are prone to infringe on the liberties of those who espouse conflicting values. But as an article of faith, most laissez-faire pluralists insist that the presence of multiple centers of power will be sufficient to deter any party from abusing the rights of others. Instead of attacking what Madison called the cause of faction—the very diversity of human goals—they seek to control its consequences by dividing power among numerous groups. As Dahl argues, when "one center of power is set against another, power itself will be tamed, civilized, controlled and limited to decent human purposes, while coercion, the most evil form of power, will be reduced to a minimum."[14]

By dispersing power among many parties laissez-faire pluralists believe they will not only inhibit the misuse of government power but also retard the development of coercive mass movements. As William Kornhauser has shown in an important defense of pluralistic democracy, when individuals have no ties to secondary associations, they often lack standards for evaluating the appeals of various mass movements.[15] In such a state of anomie or normlessness, they are more likely to be receptive to movements with authoritarian characteristics. However, if people have an opportunity to participate in a rich and diverse group life, they acquire alternative sources of information and standards for assessing various points of view. A plurality of groups that can shield the individual from the machinations of the government can also protect him from the pressures of an intolerant majority.

Although many laissez-faire pluralists endorse the responsiveness of the political system because it enhances liberal values, they often raise troublesome questions about the rationality of pluralism as a form of decision making. Truman recognizes that the dispersal of political power among many groups protects individual freedom, but he nonetheless suggests that widespread participation might lead to what he calls "morbific" politics, a state in which the political system cannot act quickly enough to deal with pressing problems.[16] Even though Truman is supportive of a pluralistic system of politics, he suggests that it might have offsetting costs. But other laissez-faire pluralists—like Dahl, Banfield, and Kornhauser—overlook or ignore questions dealing with the policy consequences of a pluralistic system of decision making. The fact that it tames the use of power, whether by the government or by the mass public, seems to them reason enough to normatively defend the existence of multiple decision makers.

However, in what constitutes a major revision of laissez-faire pluralism, Charles Lindblom has criticized his fellow pluralists for failing to see that a system of multiple decision makers bargaining and competing with one another fosters the formulation of informed and creative policy decisions.[17] Lindblom argues that a laissez-faire form of pluralism not only enhances individual freedom but also results in better policy making. First of all, a competitive, pluralistic style of politics simplifies the burdens a political system has to bear in deciding among alternative policy choices. The interaction among a variety of parties—or what he prefers to call "partisan mutual adjustment"—is often a convenient device for identifying problems and acquiring reliable information on issues. Lindblom insists that the ability of any one individual to anticipate and plan for the contingencies associated with a set of programs is limited. While centralized planners may desire to analyze all possible ramifications surrounding a problem, the burden of weighing the evidence bearing on complex issues may prompt them to screen out important bits of information. The attempt to engage in long-range, comprehensive planning is thus likely to be frustrated by the complexity of events. However, a competitive, pluralistic form of decision making avoids these difficulties, since it "imposes on no one the heroic demands for information, intellectual competence, time, energy, and money that are required for an overview of interrelationships among decisions."[18] When decisions are made through the give-and-take of partisan mutual adjustment, numerous groups have responsibility for defending and analyzing a limited set of values.

Moreover, as Lindblom notes, in partisan mutual adjustment there are "powerful motives for groups to mobilize information and analysis on the relations among possible decisions."[19] When decisions are made in a competitive fashion, each party has a vested interest in finding information that will advance the policies it prefers while discrediting the programs it opposes. Thus any attempt by a group to suppress information harmful to a particular course of action is likely to be uncovered by opposing interests. While no one participant is motivated to undertake a comprehensive view of a problem, the bargaining and competition among numerous interests will develop more information bearing on the issue than will more centralized and unified forms of decision making. As in the operation of Adam Smith's marketplace, the "invisible hand" of group competition helps to transform limited, parochial views into much broader, public benefits.

Besides stimulating the production of more information, partisan mutual adjustment can also help soften the consequences of political disagreement. The give-and-take of the bargaining process at times results in various parties' reformulating or modifying their values and therefore helps to narrow, rather than widen, policy differences among groups. Through the process of bargaining and negotiation, individuals often come to a more precise definition of what goals they hope to achieve, since the rank ordering they would attach to particular values may not become clear to them until they are faced with making concrete choices. What at first may appear to be a serious point of disagreement may disappear when a plurality of interests must negotiate over the shape of a particular policy.[20]

While Lindblom often stresses aspects that other laissez-faire pluralists have ignored, taken together their work nonetheless adds up to a unified theory of pluralism. The terms vary from "political slack" to "multiple decision making points," from "the noncumulative distribution of resources" to "potential groups," but they suggest a common theme: whether we look at the operations of local politics or the federal government, we see an open and self-regulating political system. The competitive nature of the political marketplace inhibits the rise of monopolistic power, while the openness of the polity in turn promotes the advancement of both individual freedom and rational policy making. This division of power among many groups curtails the ability of the government or a majority to infringe on individual liberties while enhancing the capability of the political system to identify and respond to pressing social issues. When groups share responsibility for deciding issues, they have not only ample incentives for generating data on important issues confronting the polity but also sufficient reason for containing the worst consequences of partisan disagreement.

Corporate Pluralism

Although the laissez-faire model is the dominant view of pluralism in the academic literature today, analytically it is possible to identify another form, which I have chosen to call corporate pluralism. Its clearest description—albeit a hostile one—is found in Lowi's notion of interest group liberalism and McConnell's group theory of politics. [21] Empirically most laissez-faire pluralists have derived their model of interest-group interaction from the realm of urban politics, but Lowi and McConnell have examined the behavior of federal agencies and their clientele groups and argue that the notion of an open, competitive political arena does not apply. While laissez-faire pluralists envision a self-correcting system in which the invisible hand of political bargaining inevitably restrains the concentration of power, Lowi and McConnell see the fragmentation of the polity into a series of small, autonomous fiefdoms, all of which are independent of one another. Under a corporate form of pluralism, no single party has the ability to monopolize all decisions, but certain groups have been able to acquire controlling power within individual policy areas. Regardless of the political slack in the system or the existence of potential groups, various parties have been able to isolate their detractors and enjoy the luxury of making decisions without negotiating or bargaining with their competitors. Any self-correcting pressures that may once have been present in the political system have been overwhelmed by the organized power of selective interest groups.

The reasons for the breakdown of the laissez-faire model are varied, but critics like Lowi and McConnell usually point to three factors: (1) the capture of government power by interest groups, (2) the efforts of interest groups and agencies to narrow the size of the policy making arena, and (3) the tacit agreement among certain interests to refrain from competing with one another. By any criterion, the willingness of government officials to relinquish their power to interest groups has been the most distinctive characteristic of corporate pluralism. While laissez-faire pluralists have tended to view government officials as either neutral mediators of the group process or merely another party competing with private groups for political power, McConnell and others have recognized that public officials often become captured by constituents who use the authority of the state to enhance their own well-being. The process leads to a blurring of the distinction that laissez-faire pluralists have implicitly, if not explicitly, made between private interests and public authority. Private groups come to exercise the regulatory and rule-making powers that were once the exclusive responsibility of public officials, while public officials, having parcelled out their authority, become mere legitimizing agents, sanctioning the decisions agreed upon by private interests.* McConnell points to the

---

*While it is important to distinguish corporate pluralism from its laissez-faire counterpart, at the same time we must be careful not to confuse it with the doctrine of corporativism. Some of the examples of corporate pluralism, such as the NRA of the New Deal, have often been mistakenly called instances of corporativism. On a superficial level there is some degree of similarity, for both corporate pluralism as practiced in the United States and corporativism as practiced in fascist Italy involve a fusion of public and private authority. But aside from that similarity there are immense differences between the two approaches to government. In a corporativistic political system the government either sets up allegedly private groups or acquires control of private groups in order to advance its own specific objectives.

War Industries Board of World War I as a classic example involving this kind of surrender of government authority. The board was responsible for drawing up wartime mobilization plans for private industry, but instead of requiring business to implement government-decreed objectives, it allowed private industry to assume responsibility for setting prices and establishing production quotas. [22] A similar willingness to relinquish power to private groups underlay the National Recovery Administration of the New Deal, which sought to combat the economic disruption of the 1930s by encouraging business to draw up codes of fair competition regulating sales and production. As with the War Industries Board, the guiding assumption was that policy should be made through the cooperation and mutual agreement of business and government rather than through the competition of the economic and political arenas. [23]

Besides capturing government authority, interest groups have also managed to exercise semi-monopoly power by narrowing down and isolating the decision-making process. Established groups realize that the smaller the decision-making arena is, the easier it becomes for a few parties to shut out opposing interests and undermine the competitive nature of the political marketplace. As the decision-making sphere contracts, the advantages enjoyed by the most powerful interest become magnified, while the resources available to the least influential group become increasingly vulnerable. [24] Interest groups have often invoked the rhetoric of grassroots democracy in order to achieve this kind of narrowing of the decision-making arena. Farm groups have utilized such tactics to establish ten separate self-governing systems within the Department

---

In corporate pluralism, however, the situation is much more complex. Instead of the government attempting to assume exclusive control over the actions of private groups, it relinquishes much of its power to private groups seeking to advance their own special interests. Even when there is a common problem that government and private interest groups wish to resolve, public officials often turn their authority over to various interests to tackle the issue. Corporate pluralism involves the private capture of public agencies and the establishment of semipublic monopolies, while corporativism involves public domination of private groups. See W. Y. Elliot, *The Pragmatic Revolt in Politics,* for a theoretical discussion of the doctrine of corporativism.

of Agriculture, ranging from the soil conservation districts to the various price support districts. As Lowi has shown, each program is run as an independent fiefdom, with little or no interaction among them. [25] But even more importantly, on issues like price supports, commodity growers are able to exercise veto power over any policy recommendations public officials may wish to make. Rather than merely sharing power with government personnel, they have acquired full legal authority to approve or reject any changes that affect their interests.

Other groups, such as professional educators, have achieved similar objectives by calling for the depoliticization of certain policy areas. As Marilyn Gittell argues, once issues are removed from politics, it becomes much more difficult for groups with influence in the larger political realm to wield any appreciable degree of power in isolated decision-making arenas. Gittell's study of the New York school system describes how professional educators sought to limit the influence of local politicians and community groups by taking "politics out of education" and how this attempt served merely to remove educational policy from the influence of groups, like minorities, who relied on alliances with political officials to achieve their goals. By making school policy independent of the city commission, the educational bureaucracy succeeded in undercutting those opposing groups which might have been able to challenge its decisions in a larger political setting. [26]

If interest groups have not been able to capture public authority or narrow down the policy-making arena, they have often sought to build monopolistic empires through tacit agreements and collusion. As a case in point, McConnell notes that in the 1940s when Congress considered measures for controlling the Missouri River, the Army Corps of Engineers and its clientele groups of construction firms and navigation companies called for the construction of extensive flood levies, while the Bureau of Land Reclamation and its agricultural supporters were more interested in promoting the development of dams and irrigation canals. Rather than pointing out the deficiencies in each other's programs, the two agencies agreed to refrain from criticizing one another and recommended the implementation of both proposals. In place of partisan mutual adjustment, the two agencies agreed to restrain their competitive impulses in return for mutual noninterference in each other's domains. [27]

Whether we look at the country's past efforts to mobilize for war or to recover from a depression, or at its present efforts to manage agriculture, formulate educational policy, or regulate our rivers, there emerges a pattern of interest-group activity differing significantly from the laissez-faire picture of politics. As is true of the economic marketplace, a competitive political market is neither self-maintaining nor self-correcting. By either persuading political officials to surrender their decision-making power to various interests, or by narrowing down the size of the decision-making arena, or by implicitly or explicitly agreeing not to compete with one another, a variety of groups have been able to exert semi-monopolistic dominance over certain policy areas. Through deft use of the above tactics, many organized interests have succeeded in restraining the countervailing forces which laissez-faire pluralists have posited as the main deterrent to excessive monopoly power.

While McConnell and Lowi are extremely critical of what we have called corporate pluralism, the doctrine is not without its defenders. It is possible to piece together a normative defense of the corporate model from a variety of sources, including the writings of individuals like Herbert Hoover and Raymond Moley or the pronouncements of various interest groups. [28] Despite the rather unsystematic nature of these sources, certain themes reappear constantly. For instance, unlike laissez-faire pluralists, who see numerous benefits accruing to society from competition among interest groups, corporate pluralists attach value to making decisions in a cooperative, rather than a competitive, fashion. Both Hoover, an enthusiastic supporter of the War Industries Board, and Moley, a strong advocate of the National Recovery Administration, maintained that the nation's social problems could be solved through cooperative action between government and business. Neither Hoover nor Moley believed there were any significant differences in the goals that government and business sought to achieve and they therefore did not see any need to pit organizations against one another. Unlike laissez-faire pluralists, who have argued that competition is necessary to tame the misuse of power, corporate pluralists have contended that in turning power over to private groups, government officials need not worry that public authority will be used for parochial or illicit ends. As Hoover once argued, "there is a wide difference between the whole social conception of capital combinations against public interest and cooperative action between individuals which may be profoundly in the public interest."[29] Unfortunately, however, corporate pluralists have not always been clear as to how one distinguishes between beneficial and harmful monopolies.[30] While the overriding importance of winning a war or ending a depression has perhaps resulted in a certain degree of convergence among most interests in society, it has nonetheless left a host of other problems unresolved. Especially on more mundane issues like agriculture or education, the most desirable course of action to follow often resists easy definition.

Corporate pluralists have also contended that competition is an inherently wasteful and disorderly process of decision making. In a laissez-faire system, where there is competition among a variety of groups and agencies, government programs often overlap one another. Instead of a unified, coherent attack on a particular issue, there is likely to be considerable duplication of effort in the formulation of various programs. In addition, as the number of parties involved in a particular policy increases, problems of coordination arise and energy has to be expended to resolve divergences of opinion. However, as Hoover and many others have often argued, when decisions are made in self-contained centers, the problems of duplication and coordination are greatly diminished. By establishing independent centers of decision making, public authorities and the private groups they rely on for guidance can develop uniform standards for regulating each separate policy area.

Finally, many of the defenders of a corporate form of pluralism have insisted that the establishment of semi-monopolistic decision-making centers is necessary to guarantee the professional handling of important social issues. For example, the Interior Department has often justified the surrender of government oil policy to the Petroleum Council, a semiprivate group, on purely technical grounds. The problem of developing and processing natural resources is so complex that the agency has sought to tap the expertise of those companies directly involved in the production of the country's basic energy resources. Many professional groups have sought to restrict the decision-making arena for very similar reasons, arguing that the complexity of issues like education or welfare requires the establishment of independent, nonpartisan commissions to supervise these programs. In the corporate view, not all semipublic monopolies are undesirable: when issues are technical or complex in nature, professionals or technicians should have the decisive voice in setting policy.

Public Pluralism

Finally, it is analytically possible to identify a third form, which I call public pluralism. This doctrine, which will be defended in the remainder of this book, differs from its predecessors in that it is essentially a prescriptive model of decision making. Whereas both laissez-faire and corporate pluralists attempt to describe the give-and-take of American politics as well as to normatively justify the variety of politics they have empirically identified, I wish to advance public pluralism as a reform-oriented model of decision making for regulating the interplay of interests in society.

Public pluralism recognizes, as does corporate pluralism, that the competitive nature of the political marketplace may break down, but it does not share corporate pluralism's approbation of this phenomenon. In any society as diverse and heterogeneous as the United States, there are bound to be disagreements over both the methods and the goals that the political system seeks to realize. The hope of corporate pluralists to formulate public policy in a cooperative, rather than a competitive, fashion is thus likely to prove illusory. But even more importantly, by insisting that decisions be made in a cooperative fashion, corporate pluralism may inadvertently create a political system that ignores important segments of the population and represses dissenting views.[31] Likewise, its stress on efficiency and technical expertise raises this problem: efficient for what purposes or ends? If a variety of groups must constantly bargain with one another and settle their differences through negotiation, it is true that the process may involve a great deal of time and may even result in a duplication of effort; but a process that may be uneconomical in saving time may be very economical in insuring that many different interests have an opportunity to make their voices heard. Finally, a corporate form of decision making that emphasizes technical expertise may overlook the fact that a large number of policies are not technical at all. Even if issues like education involve questions of a highly specialized nature, we must recognize that most problems have a normative, as well as a technical, aspect to them. While the most successful reading method may be a technical decision that professional educators should determine, the larger purposes schools should serve or the amount of resources they should have at their disposal are political or normative questions that no one group should have the exclusive power to decide. Allocating resources among different segments of society is a political, and not a technical, process.

The doctrine of public pluralism thus represents a reaction to the establishment of cooperative, semi-independent centers of decision making. Like its laissez-faire counterpart, the public variety of pluralism believes that it is imperative to divide power among numerous groups and to pit one interest against another. But in embracing laissez-faire's normative faith in the beneficial results of partisan mutual adjustment, it does not necessarily accept laissez-faire's contention that the present political system represents an empirical fulfillment of the competitive model. On the contrary, the doctrine of public pluralism identifies three defects in the laissez-faire picture of American politics.

First, it recognizes, as laissez-faire pluralists often do not, that many constituencies, especially marginal groups like the poor or amorphous groups like consumers, lack either the resources or the incentives to defend their interests effectively against opposing elements in society. While Truman often seems to suggest that potential groups will become activated when their wishes are thwarted, the less than successful record of many marginal elements seems to suggest otherwise. Secondly, as we have already seen, public pluralism realizes that various interests often avoid competition with one another either by capturing government authority or by insulating part of the political process from outside pressure. Lindblom's argument that partisan mutual adjustment may enhance the ability of the political system to recognize pressing social issues is based on the assumption that agencies and their clientele groups actually bargain and compete with one another. Unfortunately, as Lowi and McConnell have shown, many groups have been able to shut out their rivals and formulate policy monopolistically in specific areas. Thirdly, as Truman himself points out, a laissez-faire system faces the additional problem of not being able to respond quickly enough to pressing social issues. While Lindblom makes a convincing case that the clash of competing groups will simplify the decison-making process, he fails to show that this same system can resolve problems with any degree of dispatch. A pattern of policy making that is rational in Lindblom's sense of exposing all facets of a problem may be ineffective in the sense that it cannot act expeditiously to resolve issues. Naturally, as more parties participate in the decision-making arena, it becomes increasingly more time consuming to forge acceptable agreements among all concerned interests.

Public pluralism seeks to deal with the above problems through a system of regulated interest-group activity. The operating assumption of the doctrine is that many of the values espoused by laissez-faire pluralism can in effect be achieved if the president and the executive branch adopt a dual policy of organizing marginal elements from the bottom up and regulating the give-and-take among interests from the top down. Even if many groups are not organized or engage in collusion or restraint of trade, judicious government action may mitigate, if not eliminate altogether, the worst defects of an unregulated form of pluralistic government.

Public pluralism thus differs from Lindblom's version in that it rejects a pure or free-market, bargaining style of decision making. Instead it relies heavily on central direction and management to insure that the competitive nature of the political arena remains intact. [32] On those occasions when the political marketplace is no longer self-correcting, it insists that public officials facilitate the process of group competition by playing what must first appear as three mutually antagonistic roles. First, the government can act as an advocate, defending and even organizing interests like the poor or consumers who presently lack political clout. In stimulating previously dormant elements to become more active, government bureaus can assist various potential groups to contest the actions of agencies or groups that are pursuing objectives detrimental to their interests. Such a course of action will necessarily lead to a blurring of the distinction between public and private power, but instead of fostering the development of semi-monopolies, as occurs under a corporate form of pluralism, it will serve to enhance the competitive nature of the political process. Rather than relinquishing their authority to semi-monopolies, public officials will assist potential groups to become mobilized so that the rise of concentrated power can be averted.

Secondly, in order to prevent newly activated groups from being denied access to the bargaining table, the executive branch must also assume the role of political custodian, structuring and arranging the formulation of policy decisions so that interest groups are forced to compete with one another. Just as the government has acquired responsibility in the economic arena for breaking up monopolies, so it must seek to restrain any concentration of power that threatens the openness of the political marketplace. When it appears that the competitive nature of the political system is threatened, the president or central government bureaus, such as the Office of Management and Budget, must intervene to hinder the development of semiclosed centers of decision making.

Finally, in order to focus the bargaining process among different groups, the executive branch must assume responsibility for one additional role, that of political manager. Besides fostering competition among different interests, elected public officials such as the president must at the same time act as arbitrators, mediating disputes and choosing among the proposals of contending groups. Under public pluralism, the numerous interests in society will have to compete against one another not only for specific advantages, as they would under a laissez-faire system, but also for the attention and approval of political elites and their staff agencies. In contrast to a laissez-faire system of politics, in which the power of public officials like Mayor Lee is dependent primarily on their personal negotiating skills, a public form of pluralism seeks to augment the institutional, and not merely the personal, power of elected officials so that they have the capacity to direct the outcome of the group process. If elites acquire these additional responsibilities, they will be in a position to significantly alter the environment in which groups and their allies interact by vetoing logrolling arrangements that attempt to shut out other interests in society. Similarly, if government officials acquire the power to manage negotiations among interest groups, they may be able to insure that the political system does not become mired down in endless bargaining. Under a decentralized system in which groups must negotiate with many different parties, gradual and even time-consuming incremental changes in policy can give way to fruitless periods of interminable bargaining; but under a centrally coordinated style of decision making, political officials and their staff agencies will be in a position to mediate disputes and force the settlement of issues.

Admittedly, initiating such political changes is bound to be a difficult task, but we must realize that the fragmentation of the political marketplace and the freezing out of weaker competition were often accomplished not in the face of government opposition but with the tacit, if not open, consent of many government agencies and officials. In contrast, if various agencies choose to play advocate, custodial, and managerial roles, the breakdown of the bargaining process can possibly be contained. The visible hand of government regulation may be able to achieve what laissez-faire's self-corrective, invisible hand of bargaining promised but failed to deliver.

While public pluralism is primarily a set of prescriptive principles for regulating the interplay of interest groups and agencies, the doctrine is not without historical precedent. On a variety of occasions the federal government has attempted to initiate policies that are certainly consistent with a public form of pluralism. For example, in establishing his war on poverty, President Johnson created a variety of government bureaus to perform an advocate role for those segments of society which were unorganized at the time. OEO programs such as Community Action and Vista have sought to mobilize the poor to apply pressure on units of government that are insensitive to the plight of low-income individuals. [33]

The actions of the Johnson administration are by no means unusual, for at various points in time federal officials have sought to organize other groups that seemed incapable of effectively defending their interests against opposing groups. For instance, the formation of the Chamber of Commerce was in large part initiated by Charles Nagel, Secretary of Commerce and Labor under President

Taft. At Nagel's invitation, representatives from a number of local
business associations met at the Department of Commerce and
Labor in 1912 and drew up a plan for a nationwide organization
whose main purpose was to counteract the anti-business stance of
militant Progressives. [34] Similarly, the creation of the Farm Bureau,
the most powerful agricultural pressure group in the United States
today, was a result of government attempts to disseminate information about improved agricultural methods. What began in 1914
as an effort to improve traditional farming practices eventually
resulted in the formation of local, state, and national bureaus that
became powerful lobby groups for agricultural interests. [35] The rise
of industrial unions in the United States likewise owed its success
to government advocacy of union demands. While the AFL met
with substantial success in organizing craft unions, the CIO never
made much headway in organizing industrial workers until the
government forced business to recognize and bargain with unions
under section 7a of the National Industrial Recovery Act. Above
all, however, it was the creation of the National Labor Relations
Board under the Wagner Act that greatly strengthened the ability
of mass industrial unions to extract concessions from business. [36]

    If the efforts of the government to act as an advocate for pre-
viously unorganized interests perhaps date further back in time,
there are nonetheless many instances in which the government has
played a custodial role in politics. On the one hand, political officials have often attempted to stimulate competition directly by
assigning overlapping jurisdictions and incomplete grants of authority to various agencies. Perhaps the most dramatic example of
such action can be found during the Second New Deal of the Roosevelt administration when FDR made it a point to blur the mandate
given to various government agencies. In contrast to the corporate
spirit of the First New Deal, in which private groups and agencies
were allowed to establish self-contained centers of decision making,
Roosevelt pursued an administrative policy of setting one agency
against another. By assigning overlapping responsibilities to various government bureaus and by issuing only incomplete grants of
authority to competing government officials, Roosevelt made it
impossible for any one agency or interest to establish a monopoly
over a particular issue. [37] Besides attempting to foster competition

by such direct means, the federal government has also tried to stimulate competition indirectly by breaking down isolated patterns of decision making and expanding the policy-making arena. For instance, the Nixon administration indirectly increased the competitive pressures on bureaus and their clientele groups by standardizing the regional boundaries of most federal agencies. Prior to 1971 the regional offices and jurisdictions of many agencies were not conterminous with one another and the resultant haphazard, unstandardized nature of each agency's field operations enabled them to avoid direct comparisons of their respective programs by Congress or the OMB.

Finally, the efforts of Presidents Kennedy, Johnson, and Nixon to strengthen institutions like the Office of Management and Budget on a national level and to encourage the spread of planning on supra- and sub-state levels may serve to enhance the managerial role of government. Nixon increased the OMB's staff and sought to expand its activities so that it could more effectively guide and regulate the interplay of agencies and interests seeking divergent and often conflicting goals. While many members of his administration who supported such attempts to concentrate power in the hands of central staff organizations may have done so in the hopes of limiting, rather than expanding, the interplay of pluralistic groups and agencies, the power of these institutions need not be used for that purpose. The strengthening of bureaus like OMB may prove to be more successful in regulating the partisan mutual adjustment among various segments of society than in supplanting agency and group bargaining with more centralized direction.

However, it must be admitted that recent efforts by the federal government to oversee and regulate the interplay of agencies and groups on a suprastate level are still in a state of evolution. Since President Johnson's administration, a variety of organizational arrangements have been employed on a suprastate level to provide some central direction to the myriad number of regional programs presently being administered.[38] For example, Johnson tried designating certain agencies like HUD as "convener," or lead, agencies that were to be responsible for resolving differences among various government bureaus in particular regions. However, this institutional arrangement encountered difficulties in achieving its objectives. Because HUD has special interests of its own to advance, many other government agencies have been unwilling to accept it as a convener agency with the power to choose among alternative requests. Since 1971 the federal government has relied on collections of federal agencies known as regional councils to establish policy priorities for different sections of the country. Unlike lead agencies, regional councils initially lacked central directors to control and guide their deliberations, but in recent years the makeup of these bodies has been considerably revamped to correct this oversight. The president has insisted that political appointees, rather than civil servants, represent each agency on the councils, and he has also designated one agency representative as his chairperson of each council. Similarly, in the last several years, the chief executive has increased the OMB's power over the members of the councils so that it might steer these regional units of government in a more purposive direction. [39]

There have also been attempts on a substate level to develop administrative machinery that will foster competition as well as focus the bargaining process among different interests in society. In the 1964 Housing Act, or Model Cities program, Congress stipulated that all requests from municipalities for federal funds be reviewed and cleared by local area-wide review boards. Similarly, in 1968 the OMB issued its A-95 review guidelines, which spelled out the procedures communities had to follow if they wished to satisfy federal requirements for central review of policy. In response to this federal pressure, most municipalities have joined councils of government, or COGs, which serve as A-95 review boards for evaluating local government applications for federal funds. Whether COGs and regional councils are the final institutional arrangements that will be adopted is difficult to say, but these recent efforts of the Johnson and Nixon administrations indicate that the government is experimenting with ways of managing the give-and-take of the political system more effectively.

A question that must be asked, however, is whether such kinds of measures will result in a viable form of pluralistic decision making. Merely because the federal government has or is presently experimenting with programs that are consistent with an advocate, custodial, or managerial role is no guarantee that such programs have been or will be successful. It stands to reason that established groups who have isolated themselves from the demands of partisan mutual adjustment are likely to resist government efforts to organize the poor or to foster more competition in the political arena. Nevertheless, as we shall see, the record of the programs we have been reviewing holds out some promise of eventual success. (Chapter 6 will look in more detail at the literature on OEO and suggest that the poverty program often did improve the conditions of the poor in a significant fashion.) However, the results of government efforts to supervise the bargaining process on supra- and sub-state levels presently appear to be too inconclusive for us to judge their effectiveness. Because government attempts to develop lead agencies or COGs are still in a process of evolution it is difficult to speculate what their future role will be.

Nonetheless, it is possible to identify certain conditions that must be present before the doctrine of public pluralism has a chance to work. Obviously, the attitude of the president toward our reformed style of pluralistic decision making will be crucial. Unless the chief executive and his staff are willing to act as advocates and to build an alliance between their offices at the top and the poor at the bottom, it will be difficult for these groups to exercise any leverage in the political system. As Nixon so aptly demonstrated, when the president is not supportive of government programs to organize marginal groups, efforts to expand the number of participants in the decision-making arena may falter. If there is going to be a true redistribution of political power to groups on the lower rungs of society, the federal government must throw its prestige and resources behind those seeking to become mobilized.

Similarly, if we wish to see the government foster competition and mediate among the divergent interests in society, we would need to elect a president who is highly interested in administrative matters and able to tolerate disagreement and conflict. As many observers have noted, if the administrative reforms discussed earlier are going to work, the president or the OMB need to put pressure on regional councils and COGs to play a custodial and managerial role in the decision-making process. Public pluralism is not a self-executing set of decision-making rules. On the contrary, it requires the executive branch to devote a considerable amount of time to

structuring the policy-making arena so that every concerned interest has the opportunity to point out the deficiencies or benefits of
programs that affect it. However, as Richard Neustadt has shown,
presidents often vary in their interest in administrative matters and
their tolerance of institutional arrangements where disagreement is
prevalent. [40] But such an aversion may often reflect more an intellectual blind spot to the benefits of a guided style of pluralistic
decision making than any deep-seated hostility to a more open,
yet contentious, form of policy making.

In either case, it would be naive to assume that a public form of
pluralism could or would be implemented with no difficulty what-
soever. Moreover, it should be pointed out that the reforms suggested here are not a panacea leading instantaneously to a more
just and equitable society. As we have already seen, many interest
groups and agencies who have transformed a laissez-faire form of
pluralism into a corporate style of decision making are likely to
resist any change in the status quo. Yet if many of the government
activities of the late 1960s—such as Community Action Programs,
lead agencies, and COGs—are given a new lease on life, the benefits
of a competitive, pluralistic style of decision making may still be
realized and the establishment of semi-independent, noncompeti-
tive centers of decision making arrested. But to accomplish such an
objective, these agencies will require time to gain political strength
and maturity and will need the support of a chief executive who
favors more public participation as well as more central guidance
of the policy making process.

NOTES

1. In the course of his academic career Robert Dahl has espoused a
variety of positions. In *Who Governs?* and *Pluralistic Democracy in the
United States* he proposes what we have called a laissez-faire system of
pluralism. In contrast, in *A Preface to Democratic Theory* he seems to
advocate a polyarchal view of democracy, while more recently in *After the
Revolution* he has argued that the most appropriate form of democracy
depends on the level of government. See also Wallace Sayre and Herbert
Kaufman, *Governing New York City*; David Truman, *The Governmental
Process*; Edward C. Banfield, *Political Influence*; Charles Lindblom, *The
Intelligence of Democracy*; David Braybrooke and Charles Lindblom, *A

Strategy of Decision Making; Charles Lindblom, "The Science of Muddling Through," pp. 79-88; William Kornhauser, *The Politics of Mass Society.*

2. Dahl,*Pluralistic Democracy,* p. 326.

3. Dahl, *Who Governs?,* pp. 89-168.

4. See chap. 6 for a more detailed treatment of the explanations laissez-faire pluralists give for the openness of the political system.

5. Dahl, *Who Governs?,* p. 310.

6. Truman, *Governmental Process,* p. 114.

7. Sayre and Kaufman, *Governing New York City,* p. 710.

8. Truman, *Governmental Process,* pp. 45-63, 352-437.

9. Banfield, *Political Influence,* p. 241.

10. Ibid., p. 252.

11. Dahl, *Who Governs?,* p. 308.

12. Ibid., p. 209.

13. Ibid., p. 204.

14. Dahl, *Pluralistic Democracy,* p. 24.

15. Kornhauser, *Politics of Mass Society,* pp. 65-75.

16. Truman, *Governmental Process,* pp. 516-24.

17. Lindblom has developed this thesis in a variety of places but the best statements are found in *The Intelligence of Democracy* and "The Science of Muddling Through."

18. Lindblom, *Intelligence of Democracy,* p. 171.

19. Ibid., p. 174.

20. Ibid., pp. 206-25.

21. Theodore J. Lowi, *The End of Liberalism;* Theodore J. Lowi, "The Public Philosophy: Interest Group Liberalism"; Grant McConnell, *Private Power and American Democracy.*

22. McConnell, *Private Power and American Democracy,* p. 64.

23. Hugh Johnson, *The Blue Eagle.*

24. McConnell, *Private Power and American Democracy,* pp. 91-110.

25. Lowi, *End of Liberalism,* pp. 102-15.

26. Marilyn Gittell, *Participants and Participation.*

27. McConnell, *Private Power and American Democracy,* p. 224.

28. U. S. Department of Commerce, *Annual Report of the Secretary of Commerce, 1922;* Raymond Moley, *The First New Deal.*

29. U. S Department of Commerce, *Annual Report of the Secretary,* p. 29.

30. See McConnell, *Private Power and American Democracy,* pp. 66-69, for a further discussion of Hoover's outlook on cooperation.

31. See Arthur M. Schlesinger, Jr., *The Age of Roosevelt,* Vol II: *The Coming of the New Deal,* pp. 165-75, for a description of how NRA worked to the benefit of large corporations.

32. See Alexander George's excellent article on foreign affairs, "The Case for Multiple Advocacy," pp. 751-86, for another treatment of possible government roles. His analysis of foreign policy has greatly influenced my conception of public pluralism.
33. See James L. Sundquist, *Making Federalism Work*, for a history of the Johnson OEO and Model Cities programs.
34. Truman, *Governmental Process*, pp. 66-74.
35. Philip Selznick, *TVA and the Grass Roots*.
36. See Schlesinger, *Age of Roosevelt*, Vol. II, pp. 385-422.
37. Ibid., p. 535.
38. Harold Seidman, *Politics, Position, and Power*, pp. 164-94.
39. Martha Derthick, *Between State and Nation*, pp. 157-81.
40. Richard Neustadt, *Presidential Power*.

PART II

The Issue of
Participation

Having delineated three types of
pluralistic democracy, we must now place the doctrine within the
larger context of democratic theory. To properly evaluate the
advantages or drawbacks of an interest-group model of politics, it
is imperative to examine it from a comparative perspective, since
the merits of a theory can never be fully appreciated or discounted
until they have been measured against the advantages of competing
theories of democracy. While pluralism may appear to confront
serious difficulties in the abstract, its limitations may be rather
insignificant in the light of the problems that trouble other models
of democratic government.

The following six chapters will compare how pluralism and
alternative theories of democracy define the role that the public
should play in the decision-making process. Even though democracy has always been defined in terms of popular participation in
government policy making, few studies have attempted to examine
the ways in which different theories view the nature of this participation. To remedy this deficiency, chapter 3 will discuss what the
scope of the electorate's power should be. In particular, I will
critically analyze the argument advanced by polyarchal democrats
that the public's role in politics should be confined to choosing
among competing political elites. I will try to demonstrate that
the polyarchal position is based on a misreading of the empirical
evidence about the citizenry's political capabilities. After arguing

that the public should play an important role in politics, chapter 4 will try to analyze how we should define who the public is, an issue providing one of the major points of contention between pluralists and populists. While pluralists believe that the relevant constituency consists of the interest groups that make up society, populists have tended to define the relevant public in terms of the sentiments of the majority. I will argue that the majority is in many cases a mythical entity, that on numerous issues it is difficult to identify anything resembling a majoritarian position. In chapter 5 I will take a more critical look at the pluralist view of the public, analyzing the argument often made against pluralism that very few people actually belong to interest groups. Chapter 6 will look at the charge that pluralism ignores the interests of marginal groups in society. If pluralism insists that the public is made up of what Philip Converse calls "interest publics," it is necessary to analyze whether all interests in society are fairly represented. Chapter 7 will deal with the contention made by Henry Kariel and others that interest groups often become unresponsive to the needs of their own members. If we wish to argue that the public not only is, but should be, made up of numerous interest groups, we must show that organized groups will not necessarily become elitist in nature.

Be reexamining my threefold typology of pluralism, I hope to demonstrate how public pluralism is better equipped to deal with these difficulties than its laissez-faire or corporate counterparts. Having attempted to show in chapters 3 and 4 how pluralism is preferable to polyarchal or populist forms of democracy, I will argue in chapters 5, 6, and 7 that public pluralism is superior to alternative varieties of pluralistic democracy. Finally, in chapter 8 I will examine the purpose that is served by popular participation in politics. Participatory democrats have often attacked pluralists for failing to realize that political involvement can be an ennobling process that contributes to the self-development of the individual. However, by examining the available evidence, I hope to show that intensive participation may not have uniformly beneficial consequences.

Chapter

3

Pluralism Vs. Polyarchy:
The Scope of Public Participation

Over the past several decades an increasing number of political scientists have come to advocate what is now known as an elitist or polyarchal form of democracy. Joseph Schumpeter, who formulated the classical statement of polyarchal democracy, has argued that elite rule is necessary because "the typical citizen drops down to a lower level of mental performance as soon as he enters the political field."[1] In a similar vein Giovanni Sartori has maintained that polyarchal government is a means of restraining the "mediocrity" he fears to be an inevitable part of mass participation in politics.[2] Still other polyarchists, such as Herbert McClosky, have embraced such a theory of democracy because they fear that a politically active public may pose a threat to civil liberties,[3] while others, like Theodore Lowi, have argued that a strong and insulated political elite is necessary in order to develop long-range plans capable of dealing effectively with such pressing problems as poverty and urban redevelopment.[4]

Admittedly, individual polyarchists often do not share all the same assumptions nor support elite rule for identical reasons, but it is nonetheless possible to piece together from their work a model of democracy that revolves around two sets of concerns: the political ineptitude of the masses and the capabilities of elites. On the one hand, it is assumed that the masses at best are apathetic or ill-informed and at worst are guilty of genuinely undemocratic attitudes and behavior. On the other hand, it is implied that elites display a greater concern for democratic modes of conduct and have the rationality and expertise to engage in effective social planning. Hence it is argued that day-to-day political affairs should be left to the purview of government officials while members of the public should involve themselves in politics only to the extent of choosing among elites at election time. In the polyarchal view democratic government involves electoral accountability rather than extensive citizen participation: democracy is preserved so long as there are mechanisms, like elections, that allow the public to hold its leaders accountable and there are competing political elites from which the electorate can choose. While the public lacks the capability to assume full control over politics, it is to retain the residual power to check or restrain its leaders through the process of competitive elections. Or as Harold Lasswell once argued:

Government is always government by the few, whether in the name of the few, the one, or the many. But this fact does not settle the question of the degree of democracy . . . since a society may be democratic and express itself through a small leadership. The key question turns on accountability. [5]

The objective of this chapter is to ascertain whether polyarchists are on solid ground in attempting to equate democracy with electoral accountability. I will maintain that the polyarchal model is based on assumptions about (1) the public, (2) elites, and (3) the mechanism of elections that are unwarranted from both empirical and theoretical standpoints. Research on public opinion and voting behavior indicates that the electorate is not as ill-informed or as anti-civil libertarian as polyarchists often make it out to be. Moreover, the available empirical evidence suggests that political elites have been overrated as social planners and as defenders of democratic norms. I will argue that polyarchists have underestimated the feasibility and desirability of public participation in the policy-making process and will attempt to show that the most suitable vehicle for such participation lies in the realm of interest-group activity.

Polyarchy's View of the Public

If we look in detail at polyarchy's view of the public, it immediately becomes apparent that elitist democrats make two very different and even contradictory assumptions about the ability of the electorate. On the one hand, polyarchists like Schumpeter and Sartori argue that the public is not rational enough to express a preference on the issues; on the other hand, they imply that the electorate is rational and informed when it must choose among competing political elites. However, if voters are actually as ill-informed or as irrational as Schumpeter and Sartori claim, it is unclear how they can be knowledgeable enough to hold their officials accountable for their actions. The doctrine of electoral accountability assumes an alert and informed electorate who will reward or punish political officials according to their conduct in office. It thus appears that the justification many polyarchists have advanced for limiting the public's role to choosing among competing political elites at the same time undermines the very effectiveness of their call for electoral accountability. However, since many polyarchists do insist that voters can rationally hold elected officials responsible for their actions, it is necessary to inquire why the public's insight must be limited to that one act alone. If people are capable of choosing among alternative sets of elites, it certainly seems possible that they might be able to play an informed role in deciding specific policy issues.

To escape from this seeming paradox, a polyarchal democrat could argue that it might be easier for individuals to assess the performance of their elected officials than it would be to express a reasoned preference on a particular policy question. However, this line of reasoning is also open to criticism. While it is certainly more time-consuming to become involved in the policy-making process, an individual might find it intellectually less demanding to participate in the formulation of a specific set of policies than he would to assess the behavior of his elected representatives. To evaluate the record of a political official, a person would have to (1) have some knowledge of the issues he felt were salient public problems, (2) know what stand the competing political elites took on each issue, and (3) decide if his own policy preferences were in harmony or disagreement with the actions taken by his representatives. In contrast, if an individual wanted to contribute to the formulation of public policy, he would have to meet only the first condition stated above.

But leaving aside for the moment the logical problems inherent in a polyarchal theory of democracy, we need to ask if the empirical evidence supports polyarchy's pessimistic view of the public's abilities. To know whether an electoral accountability model of democracy is feasible in American politics requires an examination of the voluminous literature on voting and public attitudes for evidence of voter interest and concern about issues. As every student of American government undoubtedly knows, the early research on voting behavior was decidedly pessimistic about the capabilities of the average citizen to be aware of—let alone understand—the issues being debated in the public arena.[6] *The American Voter,* one of the best-known voting studies to emerge from the 1950s, argued that the public's awareness of political issues was generally minimal and that even when voters could state an opinion on a particular policy, they were often unable to identify the stand taken by either of the two contesting parties. On sixteen different issues, the authors found that only 18 to 36 percent of the public could (1) offer a definite opinion as to what policy should be pursued, (2) perceive what actions the government was undertaking, and (3) identify differences on issues between parties.[7] In measuring the degree of conceptualization among the public, Campbell et al. argued that less than 15 percent of the electorate could be defined as ideologues or near ideologues.[8] A large segment of the population seemed to vote for reasons totally unrelated to the performance of the candidate in office.

Although confirming polyarchy's rather pessimistic view of the public's awareness of issues, studies like *The American Voter* seemed to undermine the polyarchal assumption that the electorate could effectively hold its officials accountable for their actions. The early research on voting behavior seemed to support two rather uncomplimentary propositions about the public: first, the average voter rarely appeared to engage in policy voting; secondly, his lack of interest in political issues seemed to be a result of his own shortcomings. The typical voter was depicted as an individual who was neither informed nor concerned about any matters of political consequence.

However, additional research has indicated that the public may be more rational than studies like *The American Voter* have led us to believe. In particular, there are two approaches to voting behavior that have portrayed the American electorate in a much more favorable light. The first of these, which we shall call the *Downsian model*, contends that the voter's lack of concern with issues may be a result, not of his own shortcomings, but of the tweedledum-tweedledee nature of our party system. Since Republicans and Democrats often advocate similar stands on major issues, it may be difficult for the electorate to cast their votes for policy reasons. Or as Anthony Downs has argued in his seminal work *An Economic Theory of Democracy*, it may be "rational" for an individual to vote for frivolous and non-issue-related reasons if there are no meaningful differences between electoral contestants. [9] If candidates refuse to advocate divergent policies, the public will not be able to reward or punish elected officials for their position on the issues even if it is capable of doing so.

Furthermore, if contestants deliberately seek to confuse their stands on controversial questions, it should be expected that the public will be unable to identify the position of the different parties. The extent to which policy voting occurs in an election may be determined more by the campaign strategy of the candidates than by the competence or rationality of the voter. For confirming evidence we need only look at John Field's and Ronald Anderson's study of the 1956 and 1964 elections. They found that the number of people who voted for ideological reasons rose from 9 percent in 1956 to 24 percent in 1964, when Barry Goldwater offered the American public a radical alternative to the policies being pursued by Lyndon Johnson. [10] Similarly, Benjamin Page and Richard Brody discovered in a study of the 1968 election that the electorate was more likely to take into consideration an individual's position on a highly salient issue like Viet Nam when there were candidates like George Wallace and Eugene McCarthy who differed radically on their policies toward the war. [11] And more recently Norman Nie, Sidney Verba, and John Petrocik found in a survey of American voting behavior between 1952 and 1972 that the public has grown more interested in policy questions, and they indicated that "the new role of issues in the elections since 1964 is, in good part, a reaction to the nature of the candidates offered."[12] "The political behavior of the electorate is not determined solely by psychological and sociological forces," they concluded, "but also by the issues of the day and by the way in which candidates present those issues."[13]

A second approach to public attitudes, which we shall call the *issue-specific model* of voting, argues that the public is interested and concerned about issues but that the relevant area of policy varies from one individual to the next. Gerald Pomper among others has argued that the electorate should be viewed in terms of a series of "issue publics":

Sophisticated understanding of issues is not widespread, but there are different "issue publics" scattered throughout the electorate. Whereas few voters have an interest in and understanding of the entire range of issues, many do have an interest and understanding of a small number of issues. If we examine these separate "issue publics," rather than concentrating on the total electorate we find considerable sophistication and a direct relationship between policy views and the vote.[14]

Unfortunately most previous studies of voting behavior have been unable to detect the presence of these many issue publics because they have relied on closed-end questions to elicit information from the electorate. As David RePass has argued, closed-end questions often fail to identify people's concern with issues because they do not necessarily mention the problems that the public itself considers to be most important.[15] However, when open-end questions are used, allowing the individual to personally state the issues he feels are salient, citizens appear to have definite, informed opinions on a variety of matters. In the data from the 1960 and 1964 elections, when the Survey Research Center began asking open-end questions, RePass found that different segments of the population cited over twenty-eight issues as important political problems that they felt needed attention. Rather than being apathetic, the public seemed very concerned about a great variety of issues, even though the area of concern varied from one citizen to the next.[16]

Although the Downsian and the issue-specific models of public behavior differ radically in their interpretations of the empirical data, both imply that under certain conditions the public is indeed highly concerned and informed about policy issues. While the authors associated with the two approaches have not explicitly dealt with this problem, their studies suggest (1) that polyarchy's negative assessment of the public is unwarranted and (2) that electoral accountability may not be the most suitable mechanism for the public to express its concern with issues. Contrary to the view of many polyarchists, the political apathy of the average citizen may merely reflect the fact that most elections fail to offer meaningful policy choices. The average person will demonstrate an informed concern with issues if he is given the opportunity to discuss those particular policy areas which he finds personally relevant. However, there is no guarantee that he would engage in policy voting even if candidates were to begin advocating conflicting stands on the issues. Since most individuals are interested in certain select policy areas, it is possible that they might not ever find candidates for office who would take a stand on those particular issues which happen to be significant to them. As Sidney Verba and Norman Nie have argued, "given the fact that [a person's] own agenda is quite individual, and may contain many and varied issues, it is unreasonable to expect that there will be a voting choice tailored to his own particular policy preferences at the moment."[17] Thus, it is only natural that citizens will appear uninterested or uninformed under a system that seeks to limit popular participation to the act of voting. The quality of an individual's participation will depend to a large extent on whether or not he has meaningful opportunities for political involvement.

For this reason a pluralistic, rather than polyarchal, form of democracy may provide the best mechanism for the public to express its preferences. As indicated above, individuals have the potential to act in an informed and constructive manner if their concerns with particular issues are treated in a rational fashion. But because citizens are often interested in only a limited range of policies, group bargaining is preferable to elite competition as a vehicle for them to express their sentiments. In contrast to a polyarchal form of democracy in which individuals must choose among competing elites on the basis of issues that elites elect to discuss, a pluralistic style of decision making enables citizens to participate on only those issues which happen to interest them. Naturally, to the extent that pluralism relies on elections, it too will be plagued by the lack of meaningful policy choice characteristic of a polyarchal form of democracy. However, in a pluralistic system elections are supplemented by group bargaining; an individual who is concerned about a particular policy outcome can participate in the lobbying activities of the relevant interest group instead of having to wait until he can find a candidate for office who takes the desired stand on the issue. By expanding the public's role in politics, pluralism increases an individual's opportunities to participate rationally since it allows him to focus his time and energy on those issues he personally feels are the most salient.

The polyarchist's assertion that the public is hostile to democratic or civil libertarian norms can also be questioned. Elitist democrats like Herbert McClosky argue that a majority of citizens in this country are not supportive of basic civil liberties and that the preservation of democracy therefore depends on keeping the public's involvement in politics at a minimum. [18] In comparing a national sample of political influentials and nearly fifteen hundred adults in the general population, McClosky finds that elites display considerably more commitment to civil rights than do the public at large. While there seems to be a general consensus on abstract statements of principle, only political elites appear willing to defend civil liberties on a concrete, individual level. The importance of these findings, at least to McClosky, is obvious:

The evidence suggests that it is the articulate class rather than the public who serve as the major repositories of the public conscience and as the carriers of the Creed. Responsibility for keeping the system falls most heavily upon them. [19]

In McClosky's mind political apathy serves a useful function. Since the public is hostile to important civil liberties, it is desirable that they do not participate actively in the affairs of the community.

While the above findings are certainly no cause for rejoicing, they need not be interpreted in the pessimistic light that McClosky views them. First of all, it is unclear from McClosky's figures whether his results reflect well-ingrained beliefs among the public at large or whether they can more easily be explained by situational factors. In the 1950s many political leaders of high standing sanctioned political witch-hunts that jeopardized important civil liberties. Richard Hamilton has argued:

> It seems likely that . . . [public] response involved little more than an acceptance of the official "sounds of alarm" and of the official position about a need for new "rules of the game." If this was the case, then the . . . [public's] response would not indicate "authoritarianism" but instead would indicate acceptance of the leads provided by governments and private "opinion leaders."[20]

As in the case of voting behavior, the alleged faults of the average citizen may very easily be traced to the irresponsible behavior of public officials. The political appeals of government leaders who sanctioned the disregard of civil liberties may have stimulated and reinforced public attitudes that were hostile to the country's basic creed of individual rights.

But even if we ignore for the moment the causes of popular attitudes toward basic individual liberties, the consequences of such attitudes for the functioning of the political system need not be those suggested by McClosky. It is important to realize that his sample is based on a mass-society model of politics that compares only political elites and an undifferentiated public. While McClosky institutes controls for education and high-status occupations, he does not attempt to determine if people who belong to secondary associations are as anti-civil libertarian as those who do not. On the basis of a variety of studies, including those of William Kornhauser, Philip Hastings, and James Coleman, we know that individuals who are well integrated into a network of group affiliations are not likely to support mass movements hostile to liberal values.[21] Philip Hastings noted in a study of Pittsfield, Massachusetts, that social isolation often leads individuals to be apathetic and uncommitted to established institutions.[22] Likewise, James Coleman has observed that when lower-status people are drawn into community affairs, they often show no respect for the constitutional rights of individuals who espouse unpopular or controversial points of view, but he pointed out that such behavior is merely a reflection of the fact that these individuals are often more isolated and less experienced with community forms of activities.[23] Because McClosky insists on comparing only the elites with the masses, we cannot determine if his data would reconfirm the findings of Kornhauser et al. This issue is an important one because it is possible that polyarchal democrats have greatly exaggerated the threat to civil liberties posed by citizen involvement in politics. If people who belong to groups are more civil libertarian in their outlook than those who do not, there is no reason to fear public participation so long as citizens participate in a group-oriented fashion.

But even if by chance citizens who oppose civil liberties happen to participate in politics, they may still prove to be ineffectual in undermining the individual rights of others. The larger and more heterogeneous the political system, the more unlikely it is that a majority of citizens could ever become organized enough to be able to restrain the activities of groups who subscribe to unpopular beliefs. As James Madison noted many years ago:

Extend the sphere and you take in a greater variety of parties and interests; you make it less probable that a majority of the whole will have common motive to invade the rights of other citizens; or if such a common motive exists, it will be more difficult for all who feel it to discover their own strength and to act in unison with each other.[24]

Similarly, when the policy-making arena is large, we are apt to see those citizens who are hostile to civil liberties becoming fragmented into many diverse issue publics with unrelated, if not opposing, concerns. While McClosky may have statistically identified a large number of individuals who would curtail basic rights, in practice this portion of the population may never be able to act in a concerted fashion to achieve its objectives.

However, even if people who are less than sympathetic with expanding individual rights ever do become organized and the groups they belong to fail to moderate their anti-civil libertarian attitudes, they still may not undermine public respect for individual liberties. While McClosky seems to imply that all forms of participation may lead to a serious erosion of our basic freedoms, it is possible that only unrestrained and unchecked forms of participation constitute a threat to liberal values. As mentioned earlier, pluralists recognize that not all persons may choose to respect the rules of the political game, including the right of individuals to espouse unpopular beliefs. But like James Madison before them, pluralists wish to control the consequences, rather than the causes, of factions. [25] It is better to control and check the manner in which anti-civil libertarians participate than to discourage them from participating in politics altogether. As long as there are restraints on the wishes of any one element in society, the dangers of public involvement in politics are likely to be minimal. When political elites and interest groups share responsibility for making decisions, it is difficult for any one element in society to override and curtail the liberties of other groups who advocate opposing goals. The political competition built into a pluralistic form of democracy is a means of insuring that citizen participation never gives way to popular misuse of power.

Polyarchy's View of Elites

While polyarchy's conception of the public seems excessively negative, its view of political elites appears overly optimistic. First of all, it is possible to take issue with the polyarchist's argument that elites display a greater commitment to democratic modes of conduct than do members of the general public. As noted above, McClosky detects more support for civil liberties among political leaders than among ordinary citizens, but his findings refer primarily to liberal—rather than to democratic—values, e.g., respect for due process or protection of free speech. Since these are values that elites themselves are more likely to exercise, it is not surprising that elites should believe more firmly in them. However, there is no indication in McClosky's study that political leaders value democratic norms, such as popular participation, more highly than do members of the public at large.

It should also be noted that political elites may not be as civil libertarian as McClosky makes them out to be. By relying only on attitudinal data, McClosky cannot adequately judge the potential threat to civil liberties posed by either leaders or the masses. If we look only at the attitudinal evidence that McClosky presents, elites do appear to be somewhat more supportive of civil liberties than do ordinary citizens. But upon consideration of the degree of influence that both parties exercise, the situation appears very different. If we weight the percentage of each party who appear hostile to civil liberties by the amount of influence they actually wield, then elites may pose as great a threat to the constitutional creed as do the masses. Public officials tend to be less authoritarian than ordinary citizens, but those who do have reservations about certain individual rights actually possess the power to curtail the enjoyment of civil liberties by their very position in society.

Finally, if we leave aside the above theoretical point and reexamine the actual evidence that McClosky presents, we find that a substantial number of political elites appear uncommitted to the protection of civil liberties. While his figures for the masses are disappointing, his data on political elites can be described only as less than encouraging. McClosky notes that over 42.5 percent of the general public is willing to flout the rules of the game and take the law into their own hands if they believe the situation warrants it, but at the same time he finds that over one-fourth, or 26.1 percent, of political elites have expressed similar views. Thirty percent of the masses state that they would disregard general rules of honesty and integrity on certain occasions, but over 12 percent of the elites echo similar sentiments. [26] However, one does not have to rely on McClosky's figures alone to know that political officials are often willing to abuse civil liberties. While McClosky argues that elites are the major carriers of the creed, episodes like the McCarthy era and Watergate indicate that political elites may also attempt to subvert the principles of that creed. Since the end of World War II the greatest threats to civil liberties have not been the outcome of mass movements but, on the contrary, have resulted from political leaders' abusing their legitimate authority.

The incidents of elite misconduct cited above serve to demonstrate the need for a pluralistic, rather than a polyarchal, form of democracy. Political elites as well as the mass public may at times constitute a genuine threat to important liberal values. [27] Although a large percentage of leaders may genuinely desire to protect individual liberties, McClosky's data also point to numerous political elites who appear uncommitted to the protection of civil rights. Under a pluralistic form of democracy a sharing of political power between public officials and a diverse number of private groups serves to prevent the potential misuse of authority by either party. A rich group life not only protects citizens against the misappropriation of government power by political elites but also helps filter out public requests that might jeopardize important civil liberties. In contrast, under a polyarchal form of democracy, we must place our faith solely in the good intentions of our political leaders.

Besides arguing that political officials are more likely to protect civil rights, some polyarchists have insisted that a unified set of elites is necessary in order to develop effective, long-range plans for solving our social problems. Theodore Lowi among others has often stressed the importance of consolidating public authority so that government elites will have not only the ability to develop rational, comprehensive plans but also the power to act in a decisive, expeditious manner.* However, for both theoretical and empirical reasons it is possible to argue that centralized decision making will achieve neither of these objectives. First of all, the idea of long-range synoptic planning has come in for widespread criticism. As Edward Banfield has noted, students of urban politics have lost much of their confidence in the feasibility, as well as the desirability, of master planning. [28] In retrospect, despite the best of intentions, many so-called master plans often failed to account for the diverse array of needs of a complex, heterogeneous society. The rather poor record of this type of synoptic planning suggests that polyarchists have place too much faith in the expertise of political elites.

---

*It should be stressed that Lowi's attack on pluralism is twofold. Besides arguing that more centralized planning is necessary in order to overcome pluralism's fragmentation of the decision-making arena, Lowi also insists that the law should be more strictly enforced and that less discretion should be granted to administrative agencies. He contends that pluralism's bargaining style of decision making results in bad planning and that its discretionary style of decision making leads to the breakdown of justice. While the discussion that follows outlines some of the difficulties with his views on decision making, I shall look in greater detail at Lowi's call for juridical democracy and limited agency discretion in chapters 9 and 10.

While polyarchists contend that a few experts have the capacity to rationally reorder their environment, it is possible to argue, as do Herbert Simon and Charles Lindblom, that individuals are characterized by bounded, rather than limitless, rationality. [29] In a study of organizational decision making, Simon notes that there are repeated examples of persons who are unable to anticipate—let alone plan for—all the consequences of their actions. [30] As Simon and Lindblom suggest, political elites have informed yet partial views of the problems they must deal with, just as voters have informed yet limited knowledge of the issues before them. Consequently pluralists insist, in contrast to polyarchists, that the expertise of political elites is inadequate for viable social planning and that popular participation in government decision making is essential if the needs of those affected by public policy are to be successfully met. When political officials are not directly affected by the policies they propose, they are not always able to fully understand the impact of their decisions; but by multiplying the number of decision makers, we may overcome the shortcomings of any one individual policy maker. Although a few political elites might overlook certain problems inherent in a new policy, a variety of groups debating a specific course of action are less likely to ignore any difficulties that might afflict a new program. If each affected interest can articulate and defend its own position on a specific issue, the pluralistic interplay of groups will insure that all pertinent information and values are exposed and fully debated.

Finally, it is possible to object to the assumption implicit in many elitist theories of democracy that people's needs can be objectively determined. As Hanna Pitkin has noted, most representative theories of democracy, including polyarchy, maintain that public officials can discern what the objective interests of their constituents actually are. [31] It is not necessary for the public to participate directly in the shaping of policy because their elected officials can represent their true interests for them. However, as Charles Lindblom has convincingly argued, individuals often do not achieve a clear conception of the objectives they hope to realize until they are forced to articulate them. [32] A person's preferences for one set of values over another usually grow out of and reflect the concrete decisions that he is forced to make. Consequently, when government officials try to act in the best interests of their constituents without consulting them, they run the risk of trampling on the public's subjectively determined needs.

Herbert Gans's sensitive study of the Italian community in Boston provides an excellent illustration of the types of misunderstandings that arise when decisions are made in this kind of manner. Gans describes how city planners decided to redevelop a ghetto because they believed that the Italian community had to be unhappy with its run-down neighborhoods. However, the outward appearance of the neighborhood may have been shabby by suburban standards, but the residents were nostalgically attached to the homes in which they had grown up. Because the city's planners had merely assumed in an a priori fashion that the residents would be happy to trade their old homes for new ones, they inadvertently overlooked the neighborhood's concern with other values. In this way the alleged ghetto came to be torn down for purposes of redevelopment even though the people who resided there would have preferred to leave the neighborhood as it was. [33]

Whenever power is placed exclusively in the hands of political or technical elites, the problem that troubled Gans's "urban villagers" is likely to reappear in other situations. People's needs are not static in nature; they change and grow depending on the situations that are confronted. While individuals may want better housing in the abstract, they may not want it at the cost of breaking up their old neighborhood. The relative importance people attach to different values, as found in the above situation, is not likely to become apparent until individuals are faced with making concrete decisions. People's preferences for different sets of values are likely to become crystallized only when they can participate in the formulation of those specific policies which directly affect them. However, when competing political officials have the sole responsibility for deciding policy, we must trust their alleged expertise to determine the "objective" needs of their constituents.

The Notion of Accountability

Having considered polyarchy's negative evaluation of the public and its positive assessment of political elites, we now need to examine in more detail the final piece of this theory of democracy: the notion of electoral accountability. Even though many polyarchists like Schumpeter and Sartori believe that the public is apathetic and ignorant about politics, they insist that the electorate should have the right to hold its officials responsible for their actions. The question we need to ask is whether the conditions that satisfy an accountability theory of democracy are actually present in American politics. Two prerequisites for electoral accountability have already been established: the voters must perceive policy differences between the candidates, and they must vote for one set of elites over another on the basis of the stands the two candidates take. There are, however, two additional yet related conditions that must be satisfied for a polyarchal model of democracy to be effective: political incumbents must encounter serious competition at election time, and opposing candidates for the same office must differ attitudinally on the issues. Unless candidates face serious challenges on the policy positions they have taken, there is no reason why they should be responsible to anyone. If elected representatives know that they are automatically going to be returned to office, there will be little incentive for them to consider the wishes of the electorate.

An examination of the evidence indicates that these two conditions are not always found in American politics. For instance, in a study of city governments Kenneth Prewitt has noted that a significant number of public officials are in effect drafted for office. Once elected, city commissioners are rarely retired from public life by the action of the voters. Over a ten-year period in his sample of cities four out of five incumbent councilmen were successful in their bid for reelection. It seemed that men entered and left public office according to their own self-defined schedules and not at the whim of the electorate. This lack of competition, Prewitt observed, seriously undercut the doctrine of electoral accountability. Since most councilmen never had to worry about major electoral competition, there was no reason for them to be sensitive to the needs of their constituents. In fact, most councilmen came to view their position as an outlet for discharging their social responsibilities rather than a vehicle for representing the public's needs. [34]

The data on Congress are more mixed but still not conducive to a polyarchal theory of democracy. John L. Sullivan and Robert E. O'Connor found in a study of the 1966 congressional races that there were significant attitudinal differences between the contenders for each House seat. They likewise discovered that the differences were not confined to the election campaign alone; the winning candidates usually voted as their pre-election positions indicated they would. However, despite the fact that most congressional candidates differed on their policy stands, few challengers ever managed to unseat incumbents. In fact, when Sullivan and O'Connor attempted to determine how many congressional races were competitive as well as offered a policy choice, they found that only 73 out of 435 seats met both these requirements.[35] In a similar vein, David H. Leuthold has discovered that during the years 1924 to 1956, 90 percent of the congressmen who sought reelection were returned by the voters.[36] And more recently, R. W. Apple has noted that in 1968, 98 percent of all incumbents running for the House were reelected, while in 1970 and 1972 the figure was 96 percent. Most of the changes that occurred in the House had taken place in districts where there was no incumbent. It thus appeared that once a person was elected to Congress, he rarely had to worry about being retired by the voters.[37]

Sullivan and O'Connor have also argued that attitudinal differences between congressional candidates may provide little or no incentive for representatives to be sensitive to the needs of their constituents. They note there is evidence that the issues that divide the public are not necessarily the same issues on which congressional candidates disagree. While there are significant differences between the candidates on various policy matters, the candidates do not necessarily argue over problems that the electorate itself finds highly salient.[38] The ever recurring elections thus provide few incentives for congressmen to be sensitive to the wishes of their districts since the debate between contesting candidates may have little relevance for the public at large.

For confirming evidence of this point we need only look at Warren Miller's and Donald Stokes's study of public opinion and congressional voting patterns. If congressional elections led representatives to be sensitive to the needs of their constituents, Miller and Stokes did not detect it. Except for the issue of race relations, they found little or no relationship between the votes of specific congressmen and the attitudes of the public within their districts. And even on the race issue the correlation between constituent opinion and representative roll-call votes was just 0.6, which in turn explained only 36 percent of the fluctuation in a congressman's voting pattern.[39] Moreover, there is evidence that congressmen themselves do not necessarily visualize their role as one of representing the views of their constituents. Donald Matthews has found that senators who aspire to be insiders are often more sensitive to the needs of their colleagues and to the protocol or folkways of the upper chamber than they are to the wishes of voters back home.[40] And more recently, Richard Fenno has argued that members of the House pursue a variety of roles, some of which (e.g., achieving influence within the House) deemphasize the importance of being responsive to constituent opinion.[41]

If congressional races do not necessarily provide meaningful opportunities for voters to hold their representatives accountable for their actions, the same can be said of presidential elections. For instance, as noted earlier, Page and Brody found that in 1968 Richard Nixon and Hubert Humphrey did not offer any meaningful choice to the American public on the issue of Viet Nam.[42] Instead of being able to hold one set of elites accountable for their actions, the public was faced with the unattractive position of choosing between two candidates who espoused foreign policy programs that were basically indistinguishable from one another. It should also be noted that voters have no way of holding their president accountable during his second term of office. If by law second-term incumbents are barred from running for reelection, presidents no longer face the prospect of electoral competition and thus have no real incentive to be responsive to the wishes of the constituents who elected them. Unless a person is able to run for reelection, electoral accountability breaks down.

The above studies of elections on the local, congressional, and presidential levels thus raise serious questions about the possibility of polyarchal democracy in America. It appears that on different levels of government the American political system does not meet the conditions that need to be satisfied for an accountability theory of democracy to work: on numerous occasions political elites do not encounter serious opposition, nor do they always face opponents who disagree with them on the issues.

It could be argued, however, that this form of criticism is basically unfair. A polyarchist could agree that there is presently very little meaningful competition between political elites, but he might argue that the situation can be corrected. After all, the advocates of the "responsible party doctrine" have always believed that our party system can be altered to provide for meaningful, issue-related competition between electoral contestants. However, as indicated before, it is difficult to believe that this situation is ever likely to occur. Even if we had two responsible parties, there is no guarantee that they would take a stand on the diverse number of issues that interest different segments of the public. While two programmatic parties might vigorously contest one another on a few key policies, there is no reason why they would be likely to take definite and contrasting stands on the numerous and often particularistic issues that concern the average citizen. The policy areas that political elites consider important are not necessarily the same ones that interest members of the public.

Even if political parties did formulate positions on a great variety of issues, the theoretical problems with an accountability theory of democracy would still remain. As soon as two political parties take contrasting stands on two or more issues, there is no theoretical way of insuring that the electorate can hold a party responsible for all of its actions. There is no logical relationship that necessarily links different political issues together. A person could favor public welfare legislation yet either approve or disapprove of U.S. policy towards Israel. Similarly, an individual could favor federal aid for education yet be opposed to federally sponsored health insurance. Thus if a political party takes a stand on two logically unrelated issues and a person does not agree with both of those positions, he is unable to hold that party accountable for all of its actions. Given the lack of logical connection among different policy areas, there is no way that competition between political elites can provide the individual with a clear-cut choice on all issues.

In fact, Robert Dahl has shown that if the public must choose between two candidates who differ on three issues, it is possible that a resounding majority of the voters might elect a candidate all of whose policies are the first choice of only a minority of the electorate. Suppose, as Dahl has demonstrated, that voters must choose between two candidates on the basis of three issues (see table 1).[43] Imagine that we are looking at the preferences of three distinct groups in society who make up 75 percent of the voters.

Table 1

	Candidate A prefers alternative	Supported by	Candidate B prefers alternative	Supported by
Foreign policy	u	25% of voters	v	75% of voters
Farm policy	w	25% of voters	x	75% of voters
Fiscal policy	y	25% of voters	z	75% of voters

Suppose that the first group of people regards foreign affairs as most important and consequently rank orders the different policies according to the following scheme: u, x, z, w, y. Even though they do not care for his farm and fiscal programs, these people will nonetheless vote for candidate A because they like his stand on foreign affairs. If the second group considers farm policy as most important and orders its preferences w, z, v, u, y, they will also choose candidate A even though they do not favor his position on foreign and fiscal affairs. Finally, if the preferences of the third group are arranged in an analogous fashion, we can see how candidate A might win 75 percent of the vote even though 75 percent of the voters opposed one or more of his positions on the issues.[44]

Polyarchy Reexamined

Thus while polyarchists believe that competition between elites insures public accountability, there are a variety of empirical and theoretical reasons for thinking otherwise. The polyarchal model of electoral competition is theoretically too blunt an instrument to provide meaningful accountability. In any election in which there are only two possible options, it is theoretically impossible for the candidates to offer a meaningful and clear-cut choice on a diverse number of issues. But even if electoral contests could insure that officials would act in a responsible fashion, there is no reason why the public's role in politics must be confined to that of choosing among competing elites. The public appears concerned and competent enough to have earned the right to participate in the actual formulation of policy. When the citizenry reacts in an uninformed or un-civil libertarian fashion, it is often in response to the muddled campaign appeals of political elites or to attacks on individual rights by prominent government officials. In contrast to the claim of polyarchal democrats that we need elite rule to protect the political system from the inadequacies of the public, it is necessary to realize that leaders themselves have often been responsible for the unenlightened behavior of the public in the first place. Instead of concentrating authority in the hands of a few elites, it seems far more desirable to parcel power out among a diverse array of groups. The more power is diffused and shared by many parties, the harder it becomes for any one element in society, whether it be elites or the public, to curtail the civil liberties of others. Similarly, when a multiplicity of parties is involved in formulating policy, insightful and well thought out plans are more likely to emerge than when a privileged few have sole responsibility for shaping government programs. In their desire to reduce democracy to the notion of electoral accountability, polyarchal democrats have failed to appreciate the beneficial effects of citizen involvement in the decision-making process.

NOTES

1. Joseph A. Schumpeter, *Capitalism, Socialism and Democracy*, p. 262.

2. Giovanni Sartori, *Democratic Theory*, pp. 96-124.

3. Herbert McClosky, "Consensus and Ideology in American Politics," pp. 361-82.

4. Theodore Lowi, *The End of Liberalism*.

5. Harold Lasswell, Daniel Lerner, and C. Easton Rothwell, *The Comparative Study of Elites*, p. 7.

6. See, among others, Paul Lazarsfeld, Bernard Berelson, and Hazel Gaudet, *The People's Choice*; Bernard Berelson, Paul Lazarsfeld, and

William McPhee, *Voting;* Angus Campbell, Gerald Gurin, and Warren Miller, *The Voter Decides;* Angus Campbell, Philip Converse, Warren Miller, and Donald Stokes, *The American Voter;* and Angus Campbell, Philip Converse, Warren Miller, and Donald Stokes, *Elections and the Political Order.*

7. Campbell et al., *The American Voter,* pp. 168-87.

8. Ibid., pp. 188-215.

9. Anthony Downs, *An Economic Theory of Democracy,* pp. 96-114.

10. John O. Field and Ronald E. Anderson, "Ideology in the Public's Conceptualization of the 1964 Election," pp. 380-93.

11. Benjamin Page and Richard Brody, "Policy Voting and the Electoral Process: The Viet Nam War Issue," pp. 979-96.

12. Norman Nie, Sidney Verba, and John Petrocik, *The Changing American Voter,* p. 318.

13. Ibid., p. 319.

14. Gerald M. Pomper, *Elections in America,* pp. 94-95.

15. David E. RePass, "Issue Salience and Party Choice," pp. 389-400.

16. Recent studies by Philip Converse, Norman Luttbeg, Joel Aberbach, and Jack Walker likewise seem to confirm Pomper's and RePass's argument that the political system is made up of numerous issue publics. However, Converse has argued that once we drop below the most educated 10 percent of the American populace, the various issue publics lack well-integrated or well-constrained belief systems. But Norman Luttbeg, Joel Aberbach, and Jack Walker have suggested otherwise. In a study of two Oregon communities, Luttbeg found that while the content of people's belief systems varies from one individual to another, the coherence and organization of their beliefs is comparable to that of elites. And more recently, Aberbach and Walker have discovered a very narrow, yet highly sophisticated, belief system on the race issue among the black population of Detroit. The members of this issue public are not among the most educated 10 percent of the American population, but they apparently have a well-informed and well-constrained belief system on matters related to race relations. See Philip E. Converse, "The Nature of Belief Systems in Mass Publics"; Norman Luttbeg, "The Structure of Beliefs among Leaders and the Public," pp. 398-409; Joel Aberbach and Jack Walker, "The Meaning of Black Power: A Comparison of White and Black Interpretations of a Political Slogan," pp. 367-88.

17. Sidney Verba and Norman Nie, *Participation in America,* p. 106.

18. McClosky, "Consensus and Ideology in American Politics," pp. 361-82.

19. Ibid., p. 376.

20. Richard Hamilton, *Class and Politics in the United States*, p. 448.

21. William Kornhauser, *The Politics of Mass Society*, pp. 60-70; James Coleman, *Community Conflict;* Philip Hastings, "The Nonvoter in 1952: A Study of Pittsfield, Massachusetts," pp. 301-12; Philip Hastings, "The Voter and Nonvoter," pp. 302-07.

22. Hastings, "The Nonvoter in 1952," pp. 301-12.

23. Coleman, *Community Conflict*, pp. 21-22.

24. James Madison, "Federalist 10," p. 83.

25. Ibid., pp. 77-84.

26. McClosky, "Consensus and Ideology in American Politics," p. 367.

27. See Kornhauser, *Politics of Mass Society*, pp. 21-39, for an elaboration of this point.

28. Edward C. Banfield and James Q. Wilson, *City Politics*, pp. 188-92.

29. Herbert A. Simon and James G. March, *Organizations;* Charles Lindblom, *The Intelligence of Democracy.*

30. Simon and March, *Organizations*, pp. 137-69.

31. Hanna F. Pitkin, *The Concept of Representation*, pp. 190-207.

32. Lindblom, *Intelligence of Democracy*, p. 206.

33. Herbert J. Gans, *The Urban Villagers.*

34. Kenneth Prewitt, "Political Ambitions, Volunteerism, and Electoral Accountability," pp. 5-18.

35. John L. Sullivan and Robert E. O'Connor, "Electoral Choice and Popular Control of Public Policy: The Case of the 1966 House Elections," pp. 1256-68.

36. David Leuthold, *Electioneering in a Democracy*, p. 127.

37. R. W. Apple, Jr., "The GOP Fears November Will Be No Grand Old Picnic."

38. Sullivan and O'Connor, "Electoral Choice and Popular Control of Public Policy," p. 1258. See also Steve Brown and Richard Taylor, "Objectivity and Subjectivity in Concept Formation: Problems of Perspective, Partition, and Frames of Reference."

39. Warren E. Miller and Donald E. Stokes, "Constituency Influence in Congress."

40. Donald R. Matthews, *U.S. Senators and Their World*, pp. 92-118, 218-42.

41. Richard F. Fenno, *Congressmen in Committee*, pp. 1-15.

42. Page and Brody, "Policy Voting and the Electoral Process," pp. 979-96.

43. Robert Dahl, *A Preface to Democratic Theory*, p. 128.

44. Ibid.

Chapter
4

Pluralism Vs. Populism:
Defining Who the People Are

To assert that the "people" should play an important role in the formulation of policy leaves many questions unanswered. If we want to build a theory of democracy around the idea of citizen participation, we must define who constitutes the relevant public, and we also must specify what form popular participation should take.

In place of a unified, homogeneous public with relatively constant preferences, pluralists see a wealth of different associations with varying interests and contrasting policy preferences. Pluralists contend that society is composed of myriad groups of people, many of whom might be called issue publics, that is, groups of individuals who are concerned about only a limited range of issues. The degree to which these interest publics are organized and active in the political arena may vary from one group to the next. An interest public may be a loosely knit group of people who are troubled about a particular problem in their local neighborhood, or it may be a well-organized and powerful interest, like the United Auto Workers, which actively seeks to improve the material well-being of its members. Alternatively, an interest public may be what S. E. Finer calls a "promotional group," an organization like Common Cause, which seeks to realize general and ideological goals above and beyond the concrete, material interests of its members. [1]

Because of this very diversity of the American populace, pluralists maintain that group bargaining is the most feasible method for the average citizen to influence the shape of government policy. Besides fostering the development of rational plans on a macro-level, the give-and-take of a pluralistic style of decision making results in policies that maximize welfare on a micro-level. When individuals have the opportunity to bargain with one another on specific policies, they can compromise their position on issues that do not interest them in return for specific benefits that they value highly. In the resulting exchange relationship, individuals may be able to hammer out compromises best satisfying the needs of all concerned.

While pluralists favor group bargaining as the most desirable method of formulating government programs, populist democrats like Michael Harrington have often argued that the interplay of groups works to the benefit of special interests rather than the citizenry at large.* They have insisted that the public consists not of interest groups but of the sentiments of the majority who make up society. Because of these fundamental differences in outlook between populism and pluralism, it is imperative that we examine the tenets of the populist model in more detail. It is necessary to raise certain questions about a number of the empirical, normative,

---

*While historically a great number of people have called themselves populists, today it is difficult to find many proponents of populist government. Some writers, such as Jack Newfield and Jeff Greenfield, authors of *A Populist Manifesto,* are really not concerned about substantive questions of democratic theory. Instead, like many other so-called populists, they are more interested in discussing specific policy proposals, such as tax relief, which they think will bring about a more socially just society. But these kinds of issues, which certainly need to be debated, should more properly be discussed in a book that analyzes public policy or one that deals with questions of social justice. A book on democratic theory—as opposed to a study of social justice—must focus on procedural questions concerning how policy should be decided and not just on substantive questions concerning what programs ought to be implemented. We need to know how the adoption of certain patterns of policy making, or inputs, will affect the outputs of that political system. In this regard Michael Harrington's book *Toward a Democratic Left* is a useful contribution to both the democratic and the social-justice components of populist government. It should be noted, however, that Harrington is a socialist as well as a populist. He wishes not only to increase the power of the majority but also to transform our capitalist economic system into a socialist one. Because it is beyond the scope of this study we shall not attempt a direct evaluation of his normative position as a

and theoretical assumptions that populism makes concerning the nature of the public and how it should participate.

Although populists have often chosen to emphasize very different concerns, certain key assumptions that characterize the doctrine today can be identified. First, populists insist that the public be given the opportunity to participate actively in the determination of government policy. In their view, democratic participation requires that the majority of the public, and not simply one portion of it, have the final say in the determination of government programs. Secondly, populists believe that participation should take the form of referendum voting. They reject the give-and-take of interest-group bargaining, arguing that if the majority of citizens can vote on specific policy issues, they will be able to thwart the efforts of more limited groups to dictate policy to the larger community. Thirdly, populists generally seek to remove all external checks on the ability of the majority to legislate its will.[2] While it is conceivable for a populist to argue that the power of the public should be limited to certain areas in order to prevent the majority from encroaching on individual liberties, most populists have called for unlimited majoritarian rule. If the principles of popular sovereignty and political equality are to prevail, the majority itself

---

socialist. Moreover, Harrington himself insists that *Toward a Democratic Left* can be analyzed solely on its political prescriptions. "It is not at all necessary," he notes in that book, "to agree with the socialist philosophy which I outlined in *The Accidental Century* in order to favor these ideas here" (p. 17). Nevertheless there are undoubtedly die-hard Marxists who will refuse to accept Harrington's statement that it is possible to debate the desirability of different forms of democratic government independent of economics. Such Marxists are likely to argue that institutional arrangements, alternative forms of decision making, or even politics, for that matter, have no independent influence on the way society allocates its resources. Serious socialists such as Harrington refuse to embrace this kind of economic determinism. While abstaining from directly analyzing Harrington's normative economic views, I shall attempt to assess whether his political prescriptions are likely to result in substantial socioeconomic reforms. As we shall see in this chapter and more specifically at the end of chapter 6, the evidence indicates that majoritarian, or populist, rule and significant political and economic change do not always go hand in hand. In this sense political institutions may be a major influence shaping our economic institutions.

must be the sole judge of the scope of its political power. Hence populists maintain that the only limits on the public's ability to act should be the result of its own actions. And last, populists stress the affirmative role that a powerful state can play in initiating new programs and policies. Populists like Harrington want not only to liberate the public from the pernicious influence of interests groups but also to develop the government into an instrument that can respond vigorously and effectively to the wishes of the larger community. As Harrington dramatically puts it, if one argues that this nation "is so heterogeneous that it must operate by deals between a myriad of factions then American history is tragic, for it does not permit the people to make the sweeping innovations upon which the survival—which is to say the deepening—of democracy depends."[3] In the populist creed today, the strengthening of government power is seen as complementing, rather than detracting from, popular participation.

Empirical Objections to Populism

The argument that majoritarian rule should supplant pluralistic bargaining among groups assumes empirically that the public has some clear ordering of values it wishes to realize. It is possible for the interplay of groups to frustrate the wishes of the general citizenry only if there is a clearly identifiable majoritarian position on most issues. However, the notion that the electorate has a well-defined set of priorities is at times highly dubious. On an abstract level of political values it might be possible to identify the existence of a general consensus, but on the level of concrete policy it is often extremely difficult to discover a majoritarian position. As Roger Hilsman has argued in *To Move a Nation*, on most issues there is not one public, but many publics:

Within the general public there is a division of labor—one "attentive public" for agricultural policy, another for Latin American affairs, and perhaps still another for policy towards Asia. Informed and interested groups follow each policy area, but the "general" public [or the majority] becomes involved in a particular policy only rarely.[4]

While Hilsman cited very little data to support his argument, there are a variety of empirical studies substantiating his point. For instance, Gabriel Almond and Sidney Verba find that very few people are interested in a great range of issues. [5] The public consists not of a unified majority but of various individuals who become agitated over a limited range of issues at different points in time. People seem to participate in politics in a cyclical fashion; as soon as an issue appears that troubles them, they become politically active, only to revert back to a role of inactivity once their particular concerns are resolved. Similarly, both David RePass and Philip Converse, whose work was discussed in the previous chapter, note that the political community is fragmented into many diverse and heterogeneous groups interested only in specific policy areas. [6] RePass observes that in 1964 over 86 percent of the population could be classified as members of one of twenty-eight different issue publics. [7] Thus while populists often talk of the necessity of breaking down the influence of special interest groups and maximizing the power of the majority, we can see that on many occasions it is difficult to identify—let alone implement—the majority sentiment on an issue. In place of a conscious majority, we often find a variety of issue publics interested in the outcome of different policy debates.

In light of the above findings, it is interesting to ask what significance should be attached to the results of public referendums. On the basis of our previous discussion, it appears that referendums may not always reflect majoritarian sentiment in the way that populists often assume they do. If members of the public at large are constantly asked to approve or reject proposals that they are not immediately concerned with, we might expect two patterns of behavior to occur. On the one hand, many people may decide to refrain from voting altogether; while on the other hand, people who do vote may select policies for purely whimsical or idiosyncratic reasons.

Although the evidence on referendum voting is often fragmentary, it nonetheless seems to confirm the above propositions. For instance, Duane Lockard argues in his study of state and local politics that the majority of people do not participate in referendums. "Any notion that the referendum turns over to the whole populace, or even to a majority of the adults, the power to legislate is grossly in error," he asserts. "Usually the number of voters participating is a minority of the registered voters, and of those who potentially are eligible voters."[8] Likewise those people who do vote usually come disproportionately from the upper levels of society. A good example of the skewed nature of many referendums can be found in a New London, Connecticut, election in which the residents of the city were asked to vote on a measure instituting nonpartisan elections. In the working-class wards of the city roughly 8 percent of the registered voters went to the polls; in the upper-class wards the turnout was close to 15 percent. But even more interestingly, while working-class districts opposed the measure by 66 percent, it carried by 53 percent of the votes cast. The limited turnout enabled a rather small group of citizens to cast the decisive vote.[9] Ironically enough, although populists often see referendums as an opportunity for the larger public to decide issues, in this case a small minority was able to dictate the final outcome.

However, when referendums are held at the same time as gubernatorial or presidential elections, the turnout of voters is substantially higher. If people come to the polling booth to vote for political officials, they are also likely to vote on referendum issues. Yet even under these favorable conditions a substantial number of people who vote for individual candidates abstain when it comes time to vote on policy questions. In a study of referendum voting in the state of California in the years 1948 to 1954, V. O. Key found that "in about four out of ten elections less than three-quarters of the voters at the polls voted on issues on the ballot."[10] However, in a more recent study of California referendums, John E. Mueller suggests that the rate of voter abstention may be declining over time.[11] Mueller finds a drop in average abstentions of about one percentage point every three years since the time of Key's study. Mueller does not offer any definitive explanation as to why this decline has occurred but he suggests that it can be attributed to a variety of causes, such as higher rates of literacy, wealth, etc. Yet despite this upward trend in the number of people who vote on issues, Mueller notes that the abstention rate on particular items is highly volatile. Voter turnout seems to fluctuate immensely depending on whether there is at least one highly controversial item among the various proposals voters are asked to decide. In the 1965 election, for example, abstentions were two to three times higher than they were a year earlier, when Californians were asked to vote on a very controversial fair housing law. [12]

If, as suggested earlier, the population is split up into a series of issue publics, we should not be surprised at the volatile and generally low rates of voter participation. When voters are asked to decide issues that fall outside of their main concerns, many of them may not vote. However, all uninterested voters do not necessarily stay at home on election day or abstain from voting on certain items. As the authors of *The American Voter* have pointed out, many people may go to the polls because they feel it is their duty to do so even though they are not necessarily concerned about the issues under consideration. But if individuals who go to the polls are really indifferent to the outcome of the election, they may vote for extremely whimsical or idiosyncratic reasons. Similarly, if the majority of citizens are concerned about a particular issue on the ballot, they may vote on other referendum items, which are peripheral to their main concerns, for purely arbitrary reasons.

This arbitrariness can take a variety of forms. For instance, Lockard has argued that if voters are either unconcerned or uncertain about the impact of a particular policy change, they may tend to veto complex legislation. He quoted one advertisement used in a Salt Lake City campaign on home rule: "Confused! Many Are. Play Safe—When in Doubt, Vote No!" [13] Similarly, James Coleman and Robert Crain have noted that the confusion and latent antagonism in the minds of many voters is in large part responsible for the defeat of fluoride legislation. [14] Despite overwhelming evidence that the fluoridation of water is beneficial, many citizens find the issue so baffling that they play safe and vote no.

However, Mueller argues that public indifference will not necessarily result in the rejection of referendum proposals. He believes that voters will act in a consistently informed fashion on hotly debated issues, but finds that voter behavior is highly idiosyncratic and even arbitrary in nature on noncontroversial items. More specifically, when people are asked to vote on many noncontroversial problems that do not directly concern them, they seem to fluctuate between moods of acceptance and moods of rejection:

"It appears that there are good years and bad years for noncontroversial propositions."[15] In some years, such as 1952 and 1960, the voters seem to be in an acceptance mood and approve most of the propositions, while in others, like 1958, they tend to reject most of the noncontroversial items on the ballot. Unfortunately, Mueller notes, it is difficult to determine why political moods arise or why they shift over time. Regression analysis reveals no strong relationships between voter moods of acceptance or rejection and other variables, such as percentage of voter turnout or number of propositions on the ballot.

Interestingly enough, Mueller argues that voting behavior fluctuates both from election to election and from item to item depending on the location of a particular proposition on the ballot. Thus the placement of a measure not only determines whether voters will abstain or not but also influences how they will cast their ballots. In Mueller's words, "on items of low visibility, voters seem to have a tendency to avoid over a long stretch a pattern of behavior which is obviously uniform."[16] That is to say, people are often reluctant to vote uniformly for or against all the propositions on the ballot. One reason state legislatures insist on placing state bond issues at the top of the ballot is that they believe many voters start out voting affirmatively, then switch their votes as the number of propositions increases. An analysis of the data lends support to this belief. Mueller finds that a small, yet significant, number of voters (7 percent) begin voting positively but then vote negatively on items placed lower down on the ballot.[17] However, there appear to be an equal number who follow the opposite course of action, casting negative votes on the initial items but voting positively on succeeding propositions. The outcome of a particular issue may thus be dependent on where it happens to be placed. The results of a referendum could be entirely different if the items on the ballot had appeared in a different order.

There is thus considerable evidence that many voters base their referendum votes on factors completely unrelated to the actual issues at hand. A strong element of arbitrariness is injected into referendum balloting by those who play safe and vote no on issues they do not understand, or vote in accordance with cyclical moods of affirmation or rejection, or vote yes or no depending on the location of the issues on the ballot. In this situation, it is difficult to accept the populist argument that referendums will reflect the true interests of the public at large. While populists often talk as if there were a popular or majoritarian sentiment on most issues, we can see that in many cases such sentiment simply does not exist. Since most people are concerned only with a narrow range of interests, we can understand why they may not participate actively in referendum elections. But if they do participate, we can likewise understand why their behavior may be dictated by such factors as the position of the item on the ballot. If the political system relied extensively on referendums to decide the many issues that it faces, referendums might end up playing a role in society just the opposite of that envisioned by most populists. Instead of identifying an already existing majoritarian position, referendums might artificially create a majority stand out of a large number of whimsical votes. Depending on the prevailing mood of the people or the organization of the ballot, today's majority position could very easily become tomorrow's minority position.

The difficulty in attempting to maximize the power of the majority is that in many cases it simply does not exist. Thus efforts to force a majority stand out of a diverse and heterogeneous set of publics are likely to lead to the problems that Lockard and Mueller have described. While the referendum will mechanically generate a majority opinion on an issue, that opinion may not correspond to any well-defined set of beliefs in the larger population.

The Paradox of Voting Problem

Although referendums often ask people to decide questions they are not interested in, there will always be some issues that will elicit overwhelming public concern and the majority will be interested in the outcome. But we must remember that for populism to work this is not enough: there must also be a majority that share similar standards for resolving the issue in question. If this latter condition is not satisfied, referendums may paradoxically result in collective decisions that do not reflect the individual preferences of the public. While individuals may have consistently ordered preferences, majority rule may result in decisions that are inconsistent with the ordered preferences of the voting public. This phenomenon, which is known as the *Arrow problem* or the *paradox of voting,* can be seen in the following example.[18]

Let us suppose that a national referendum was to be held in the late 1960s on the Viet Nam War. Without too much difficulty we could easily imagine that the population might be roughly divided into three groups of people who favored different courses of action: (A) immediately withdrawing from Viet Nam, (B) maintaining the conventional level of fighting and seeking a negotiated settlement, and (C) dramatically stepping up the fighting to win a complete victory. The preferences of the public would be ordered as in table 2.

Table 2

Doves	*Moderates*	*Hawks*
A immediate withdrawal	B maintain status quo	C step up fighting
B maintain the status quo	C step up fighting	A immediate withdrawal
C step up fighting	A immediate withdrawal	B maintain the status quo

The first group of citizens prefers that the United States withdraw immediately. As an alternative to this policy they desire that the American government maintain the status quo rather than step up the level of warfare. However, the moderates favor maintaining the status quo in the hopes of securing a negotiated settlement. If that course of action fails, they want the government to go all out in an effort to win the war. Immediate withdrawal would thus be seen as the least desirable course of action to follow. The last segment of the population favors an intensification of the war effort in order to secure a complete victory. In case the government is not willing to pursue that option, they support immediate withdrawal, arguing that if the government is not serious about winning, it has no business prolonging American presence in a foreign country. So people in this last category favor stepping up the fighting first, withdrawing second, and maintaining the status quo last.

If we held our referendum on the war, paired the alternative courses of action, and counted the votes, we would discover that a majority of citizens would favor immediate withdrawal over maintaining the status quo, or A over B, and that a majority would favor maintenance of the status quo over stepped up fighting, or B over C. Now if a society prefers policy A over policy B, and policy B over policy C, we would think that to be consistent it must also prefer policy A over policy C. But when we look at our example, such is not the case, for the public favors stepped up fighting over immediate withdrawal, or policy C over policy A. The political system has thus produced an inconsistent or irrational social ordering since A is preferred to B, and B is preferred to C, but C is preferred to A. Given the logic of majoritarian voting, it is possible for people with perfectly consistent individual preferences to arrive at a collective decision that is inconsistent with their own ranking of the alternatives. The transitive, or consistent, individual preferences have been transformed by a majority vote into an intransitive, or inconsistent, social decision. Regardless of which policy is finally adopted, a majority of citizens would prefer an alternative other than the one selected.

When the conditions of the Arrow paradox exist, voting procedures can become highly arbitrary in nature. The alternative that is finally adopted may be determined merely by the order in which the electorate votes on the various policy options. For example, suppose the public voted on each proposition one at a time until a decision was finally reached. Every individual would vote against the Viet Nam option under discussion if he favored another course of action; however, once a proposal had been rejected the electorate could no longer continue to consider it as a real possibility. If, as in our Viet Nam case, there are only three alternative policies to choose from, then there are only six different ways the policies can be voted on, namely ABC, ACB, BAC, BCA, CAB, and CBA. If we hold our elections and eliminate the various possibilities, we find that the following pattern develops. [19]

CASE ONE: Proposition A is voted down because two-thirds of the public favors another course of action. Proposition B wins the referendum since with option A (immediate withdrawal) eliminated, two-thirds of the population favors B to C (stepped up fighting).

CASE TWO: Proposition A is again put before the public and defeated, then followed by proposition C, which is also defeated. Policy B (maintain the status quo) wins.

CASE THREE: Proposition B is now the first proposal presented to the public and is defeated. Option A is then voted on and rejected, leaving proposition C, which wins.

CASE FOUR: By the same electoral mechanism, proposition C wins the referendum.

CASE FIVE: Beginning with proposition C, policy A wins.

CASE SIX: Proposition A wins.

From the above discussion we can see that the alternative favored by the majority of citizens is determined merely by the manner in which the different options are presented. When alternative A (immediate withdrawal) is voted on first, option B (maintain the status quo) wins the election; when proposition B is voted on first, alternative C (stepped up fighting) wins; and when option C is voted on first, proposition A (immediate withdrawal) becomes the first choice. Paradoxical as it may seem, a populist form of democracy can lead to highly irrational forms of decision making; public referendums may be decided merely by the order in which different propositions are presented.

In order to escape this paradox of voting, one of two possibilities must occur. First, individual rank orderings of policy options must exhibit the characteristic that Duncan Black has labeled "single peakedness."[20] That is, all individuals must use the same dimensions or criteria for evaluating a set of policy alternatives. The reason public decisions often do not reflect the rank ordering of different individuals is that people frequently use a variety of standards for assessing the merits or deficiencies of a possible course of action. When individuals try to harmonize their preferences in a referendum vote, the majority position that is generated is likely to reflect the inconsistent standards held by the voting public in a disaggregate form. However, if people can locate their standards for evaluating public policies on a single continuum so that their preference for any alternative declines the further it diverges in either direction from their first choice, no voting paradox results. Whenever individuals with single peaked preferences vote on varied alternatives, the alternative preferred by the median voter always prevails, and the problem of socially intransitive decisions is avoided.

However, it should be pointed out that the position of the median voter does not necessarily reflect the will of the majority. We thus face the anomalous situation that if people's preferences are not single peaked, the collective decision of the referendum will be irrational in the sense that it will not reflect the individual rank ordering of different policies. But if people's values are single peaked, the resulting collective decision will certainly be rational (that is, transitively ordered), but it may not reflect the wishes of the majority. For referendums to yield a majoritarian as well as a nonparadoxical outcome, the public must share single peaked beliefs and a majority must favor the median position. We can thus see that on many occasions, contrary to what populists believe, referendum voting is not an effective means for making known majority preferences.

However, as should be obvious from the above discussion, the indeterminacy problem in majoritarian voting is primarily one of logic. While the paradox of voting is a theoretical possibility that may occur in any referendum, the actual empirical distribution of attitudes in society will determine the frequency of its appearance. Unfortunately, there is very little empirical research on how often the Arrow problem actually occurs since very few polls attempt to determine people's rank ordering of different policy options. Richard Niemi has attempted to describe the conditions under which the Arrow paradox is most likely to occur, and for a variety of reasons he thinks it may not be that prevalent. [21] But a careful examination of Niemi's discussion reveals that his argument is not necessarily supportive of a populist view of politics. Niemi argues that one reason the paradox occurs very infrequently is that the political system operates to standardize the options open to the public. For instance, the Democrats and Republicans either echo one another's proposals, or, if they offer a choice, they usually limit it to two options, which makes it impossible for the paradox to appear in the first place. Similarly, if there are referendums on issues like

Viet Nam, people are allowed to vote only on one course of action. A diversity of opinions is thus never allowed to find expression.

Besides mechanically limiting the options people can vote on, the political system also attempts to standardize values through its various socialization processes. In fact, Niemi thinks the socialization process is most successful in developing a similar outlook among elite groups such as politicians or businessmen.[22] By and large the people recruited into these categories come from relatively homogeneous groups and so are likely to share many of the same beliefs about the political system. Since elites can often define the terms of debate surrounding an issue, they can simplify or standardize the political choices open to the public and thus prevent the Arrow problem from ever arising.

Niemi may be correct in arguing that the above factors help to limit the occurrence of the voting paradox, but his argument raises some troublesome problems for a populist theory of democracy. Niemi suggests that the indeterminacy problem occurs sporadically—not because voters have a well-defined and shared belief system—but because at best they often follow the lead of political elites in favoring certain policies and at worst they are mechanically limited in the number of options from which they can choose. In either case, sentiment on a particular issue may be more problematic than that pictured by the populist. The wishes of the alleged majority that emerge in a referendum may reflect more the options from which the public can choose than the underlying sentiments of large segments of the population. As Niemi himself concedes:

Our findings suggest that intransitivities are most likely to occur in unstructured situations, where there are no common guidelines for judging the alternatives, or in situations involving multiple dimensions. For example, intransitivities might be found relatively often when new issues must be resolved. Similarly, the paradox probably occurs more often in *ad hoc* groups, which are less likely to be influenced by the socialization, selection, and discussion factors which contribute to greater uniformity of judgmental criteria. Such groups might be newly formed ones, groups which meet infrequently and irregularly, or groups which purposely bring together many diverse elements. In elections, the paradox may occur most frequently when parties are absent or when the parties vary along two or more major dimensions.[23]

We can see from Niemi's analysis that populism may face a dual dilemma. If the political system ever decided to increase its reliance on referendums, it would run the risk of having a diverse, heterogeneous set of people decide policy in an unstructured situation. As Niemi notes, the more diverse the portion of the population formulating policy, the more difficult it is for socialization and recruitment procedures to generate a uniform outlook and thus the more likely it is for the voting paradox to arise. However, if the political system attempted to direct public opinion into narrower channels or to limit the policy options placed before the public, the resulting majoritarian sentiment would be open to suspicion. As argued before, a referendum can always mechanically generate a majority position on an issue, but that position may not correspond to any well-defined set of beliefs in the larger population.

Many of these problems can easily be avoided if public policy is made in a pluralistic fashion through bargaining and negotiation. As we have seen, if the electorate is split up into at least three different groups with different rank orderings of various policy options, the problem of indeterminacy will always be present. Unless a populist can empirically show that the public at large actually shares similar values, there is no way he can avoid this difficulty. However, in a pluralistic form of democracy the Arrow problem presents no problem at all. William Baumol and James Coleman, among others, have shown that it is only when various policy options are decided by elections that the issue of indeterminacy occurs.[24] If the members of the political system agree to weight, as well as to count, people's votes, the logical problem of arriving at a transitively ordered collective decision no longer exists. When we account for the intensity as well as the order in which various individuals favor different policy options, it is always possible to reach a determinate, transitively ordered collective decision. If the political system can arrange exchanges between groups who feel intensely about a particular policy and groups who are only mildly concerned with that same policy, it can aggregate individual preferences in such a fashion that the Arrow paradox disappears. Whether the groups in society will actually be responsive to the intensities with which different interests value their preferences is a separate and empirical, rather than logical, question. But if the political system is open and responsive to a diverse array of groups, as public pluralists believe it can be, then a pluralistic form of decision making represents a way of circumventing the paradox of voting.

Normative Objections to Populism

While so far this chapter has stressed the empirical problems likely to plague a populist theory of democracy, it is necessary to point out that pluralism's objections to populism are not confined to empirical considerations alone. Even if it could be demonstrated that there was a genuine majority position on most issues, a pluralist would still have reservations about allowing an unrestrained majority to prevail on every issue. To debate who the people are is as much a normative as an empirical issue. To emphasize this point we shall now assume that the two empirical issues discussed above no longer exist. We shall accept the populist argument that a majority of the public is interested in a particular issue and shares similar values for resolving it. In assuming away the above empirical issues, we are left with two separate, yet related, normative questions. First, we need to decide if the wishes of the majority should always prevail over those of minorities; and secondly, we need to ask how the majority should go about establishing its priorities, whether it should rely on referendums or on some other means like bargaining.

Populists have been inclined to argue that the majority should dictate public policy and that it should do so through the mechanism of referendum voting. In contrast, pluralists not only have wanted to restrain the ability of the majority to dictate policy; they also have suggested that political bargaining rather than referendum voting is the preferable way of arriving at public decisions. The reasons for these sharp differences are many, but in large part they reflect the fact that populists and pluralists attach very different weights to certain key values. On the one hand, as a matter of first principle, populists have stressed the need to maximize the values of political equality and popular sovereignty.[25] All men should be treated equally, they have implied; each man's influence should be the same as any other's. Thus to decide policy issues all the political system needs to do is count the public's preferences and implement those policies which are favored by a majority of the population. While some critics have suggested that such a system of unrestrained majoritarian rule might lead to abuses, populists have tended to minimize the possibility of such an occurrence, arguing that if the political system guarantees the equality of all, then the public will exercise its power in a judicious and responsible fashion.

On the other hand, pluralists not only question the accuracy of populism's view of the public, but also have reservations about the values that populists wish to maximize. As argued earlier, pluralism is a form of liberal democracy that seeks to enhance the opportunities for people to participate in politics at the same time that it protects the basic liberties of the individual. While pluralism certainly wants to insure that the public has some influence over government policy, it does not want to sacrifice other principles, such as equity or individual freedom, in the process. Robert Dahl has argued that political equality and popular sovereignty should not be maximized at the expense of other important values:

For most of us . . . the costs of pursuing any one or two goals at the expense of others are thought to be excessive. Most of us are marginalists. Generally we experience diminishing marginal utility the more we attain any one goal; or in the language of contemporary psychology, goal attainment reduces the drive value of the stimulus. Political equality and popular sovereignty are not absolute goals; we must ask ourselves how much leisure, privacy, consensus, stability, income, security, progress, status, and probably many other goals we are prepared to forego for an additional increment of political equality. [26]

In weighing the advantages and disadvantages of maximizing political equality and popular sovereignty, two conditions would warrant limiting the power of the majority: (1) if majority rule ever threatened to infringe on the rights of minorities, or (2) if an apathetic majority ever adopted a policy that was intensely opposed by a substantial minority.

The Problem of Minority Rights

Traditionally the main reason pluralists have been wary of maximizing majority rule and political equality is the fear that the larger public may abuse the rights of minorities. While the public should have an important voice in politics, this role should not be achieved at the cost of important individual rights, such as free speech or free assembly or the right of all people to receive equal treatment in employment or housing regardless of their racial background.

In addition, apart from the question of individual rights, pluralists believe that the principle of political egalitarianism should govern the allocation of social resources. That is to say, if certain segments of society are outvoted by a majority on one particular issue, they should at least be given the opportunity to influence policy on another issue or on the same issue at a later point in time. Each of the diverse interests that make up society should have its own turn to play an important role in the political process; if an identifiable majority exists and wants to set policy, it should not have the power to permanently exclude other groups from receiving some minimal benefits. However, if one posits political equality and popular sovereignty as the key values to maximize, then one must logically abide by the majoritarian decision in each and every case. Unless the majority willingly agrees to refrain from achieving its wishes on every occasion, it must override the claims of groups that have previously failed to gain a favorable hearing of their views.

Populist views on majority prerogatives and minority rights have been less than uniform. Some populists may be willing to prevent the majority from passing restrictive legislation in the area of civil liberties, but others believe that the only limitations on majority rule should be self-imposed. Austin Ranney and Willmore Kendall have argued that if we try to realize both majority rule and inviolate rights, majority rule is likely to be transformed into minority rule. [27] Unless the public has the sovereign power to decide all issues of importance, and unless the preferences of each man are counted equally, the wishes of the larger public may be superseded by the wishes of various minority groups, thereby violating the spirit of democratic government.

This is not to say, however, that most populists completely ignore the importance of protecting the right to free speech or free assembly. It is essential for a populist to defend a great variety of individual liberties in order to protect the integrity of majority rule. If individuals do not have the opportunity to challenge public officials or contest specific pieces of legislation, their ability to develop a new majoritarian position on a particular issue could be frustrated. The protection of certain fundamental rights is necessary for achieving majority decisions. However, although populists must theoretically defend many basic rights, their defense of civil liberties is limited in two respects. First of all, the civil liberties that a populist must defend in order to guarantee majorities the freedom to form and reform are basically the traditional rights of free speech and assembly. There is no logical reason why a populist who is theoretically committed to these essential liberties must likewise defend the more recently acquired right of minority groups to eat, sleep, and live where they please. The logic of majority rule requires a populist to defend a limited, rather than exhaustive, list of civil liberties. Secondly, while majoritarian democrats like Ranney and Kendall adopt what might be called "liberal principles," they consider them as means rather than ends. Even if majority rule may not be able to operate without them, these freedoms are not viewed as essential liberties. Although the rights of free speech and assembly are necessary to preserve majoritarian democracy, an existing majority always retains the prerogative of terminating majority rule altogether if it exercises the proper procedures in seeking its own demise.

Besides disagreeing over the normative importance of certain key rights, pluralists and populists also differ in their empirical estimate of the public's willingness to respect individual liberties. As mentioned earlier, much of the available evidence does not inspire confidence in the ability of the majority to use its power responsibly. We know from the research of Herbert McClosky that a sizable percentage of the American populace appears willing to deny people the right to advocate unpopular views.[28] However, although the attitudinal evidence suggests that the public is not likely to respect the rights of unpopular minority groups, the actual behavior of the American populace may be less threatening to civil liberties. But our argument has been contingent on the fact that society is organized along pluralistic, rather than populist, lines.

As William Kornhauser has argued, individuals are most likely

to respect liberal values when they are well integrated into a network of group relationships, since interest groups serve as filtering
devices to screen out the periodic anti-civil libertarian demands of
their members.[29] For example, during the 1964 and 1968 presidential elections labor unions played an important role in convincing
their members not to support the candidacy of George Wallace.
Like many other groups, unions provide alternative sources of
information to their members about the dangers of pursuing certain
courses of action, and through a more general process of socialization they moderate the feelings of any members who pose a
threat to the institutions and liberties of the larger society. However, even when a group does not perform this moderating function, as is the case with an association like the Ku Klux Klan, the
existence of other groups in society serves as a restraining influence
on anti-civil libertarian behavior. Under a pluralistic system groups
can check one another and thereby soften the impact of anti-civil
libertarian views, but under a populist system there are no similar
restraints if the majority votes in favor of suppressing individual
rights.

The record of referendums in California bears out the contention
that a populist form of democracy would not be conducive to the
protection of civil liberties. These referendums, which most closely
approximate the kind of majoritarian rule that populists envision,
failed to confirm the argument that the majority will exercise its
power in a responsible fashion. As the late Senator Richard Neuberger commented:

In recent years California, the state where initiative and referendum are
used most frequently, has voted down bills to create a state housing authority, to redistrict the legislature on the basis of present-day population,
to repeal a consumer's sales tax, and to adopt a state FEPC [Fair Employment Practices Committee] forbidding racial discrimination in employment. These setbacks, all by overwhelming margins, have given pause to
liberals and welfare workers.[30]

Moreover, in 1964 California voters went to the polls and repealed
a fair housing law that would have banned racial discrimination in
the sale or purchase of homes. This referendum, which has been

studied extensively by Raymond Wolfinger and Fred Greenstein, was one of the few issues on the 1964 ballot that seemed to interest a majority of citizens.[31] As Mueller notes, only 4 percent of the voters abstained on this issue while 25 to 30 percent abstained on other propositions that happened to be on the ballot. Moreover, as Wolfinger and Greenstein have observed, pre-election surveys indicated that people were aware of the implications of the fair housing proposition despite the fact that it was worded in a very vague and confusing manner. While there was no problem in this case of empirically identifying a genuine majority sentiment on the issue in question, the normative problem of majority power and minority rights was very much in evidence. Even though the legislature, which had passed the fair housing law the year before, was willing to guarantee minority members the right to purchase a house, the majority of citizens were not so inclined. The repeal of the fair housing proposition passed by a better than two-to-one margin. Despite populist insistence that the majority will not empirically misuse its power, we can see that on many occasions this has not been the case. In the past when the majority has had the opportunity to decide issues involving civil liberties, it has often voted to curtail, rather than to expand, the scope of individual rights.

The Problem of Intensity

Another danger in always permitting a numerical majority to prevail is that an apathetic majority may overrule minorities who feel very strongly about a particular policy. But because most populists believe that political equality and popular sovereignty are cardinal values, they insist that all issues should be decided on a one-man one-vote principle. Regardless of how intensely people may feel about a particular issue, populists believe that it is essential to equalize the influence of all citizens.

While political equality and popular sovereignty are important values, pluralists like Dahl argue that in seeking to achieve these principles, we should not sacrifice too many other values that we deem important. In particular, if there are extreme variations in the intensities with which people value different political alternatives, it may be desirable to weight, as well as to count, the preferences of individual voters. The principle of one-man one-vote may be an adequate form of representation when people feel equally intensely about an issue, but the same standard may be inequitable and too costly in terms of alternative values foregone when applied to situations in which individuals' concerns about a particular policy vary considerably. In such a case it may be more fair for the political system to decide in favor of those government policies which are most preferred rather than those programs which are preferred by most.

Ironically enough, while on a normative level populists have minimized the importance of weighting votes, on a practical or empirical level they have often argued that the problem of intensity presents no insurmountable difficulties. Even though theoretically they oppose weighting some people's opinions more heavily than others, they often defend a populistic referendum because in practice it achieves exactly this end. In arguing this point, populists make a twofold argument. On the one hand, they maintain that the public takes account of the intensity of people's concerns before going to the polls. In other words, even though referendums cannot weight people's votes, the individual may let the pattern of public sentiment on a particular issue influence the manner in which he discharges his electoral responsibility. Thus the weighting of preferences takes place even though the voting process per se counts each person's vote equally. While this argument undoubtedly has some merit, it needs to be carefully qualified. To attempt to judge the intensity of different people's preferences requires a concerted amount of effort on the part of the public. Without any meaningful incentives, it is difficult to imagine that the majority would ever try to account for the intensity of other people's beliefs. Moreover, given the communication problems that would be involved in a large political system if every voter tried to assess the depth of other people's preferences, it can be argued that the process is not likely to occur. In fact, Willmore Kendall and George Carey have argued that we can expect people to account for the intensity of other people's beliefs only in small, homogeneous communities.[32] The more homogeneous the community, the easier it becomes for each individual to assume that the wishes of others are similar to his own. However, in a large political system the public is more likely to be unable to gauge the intensity of other people's beliefs as well as indifferent to doing so.

If the problem of intensity is not resolved directly by the voters themselves, then populists often suggest that the issue can be handled indirectly through variations in election turnouts. As we have already seen, not all citizens go to the polls, and of those who do, not all vote on every proposition on the ballot. Although populists admit that referendums theoretically cannot account for intensity of feeling, they argue that in practice this issue presents no real problem since fluctuations in voter turnout reflect the depth of concern with which individuals regard different propositions. There is a considerable degree of evidence to support this argument, but it must also be remembered that citizens often go to the polls even though they are not interested in the issues at hand. Many people cast their ballots because they feel it is their duty as good citizens to participate in all elections and as a result they vote on propositions in which they are only minimally interested. Moreover, the fate of various referendum items is often related more to their position on the ballot than to the intensity of public sentiment for or against the propositions themselves. Thus while it is undoubtedly true that many apathetic people abstain from voting, referendums are still a far from perfect mechanism for recognizing and accommodating intensely, as opposed to nominally, held beliefs.

How Should the Public Express Its Sentiments?

For a variety of reasons we can see that it may be desirable to impose some restraints on the exercise of majority rule. However, even if we are willing to concede that on some occasions the wishes of the public at large should prevail over those of particular interests, we still need to ask if populistic referendums are the most preferable mechanism for deciding issues. Because one insists that the will of the majority should always govern, it does not necessarily follow that the majority should always express its sentiments through public referendums. As pluralists in particular want to argue, political bargaining, compromise, and logrolling may maximize public welfare while referendum voting may generate a set of policies that will achieve only minimal utility. The drawbacks of referendum voting are directly related to the intensity problem discussed earlier. The intensity with which people favor certain policies is to a large extent a reflection of the utility or welfare they would derive from the enactment of these programs. Referendums are generally poor mechanisms for identifying and accommodating intensities of feeling and hence they often tend to be poor decision-making procedures for maximizing public welfare in an aggregate sense. If an apathetic majority prevailed over an intense minority in a public referendum, the final policies that were adopted might restrict, rather than maximize, the total amount of utility in society. Although a certain course of action might greatly hinder the well-being of a minority group, an alternative policy might provide only minimal satisfaction for the majority of people in society. Therefore if policies were decided by referendum vote the final outcome would result in a reduction of the aggregate welfare of all.

To illustrate this point, let us look at table 3 and assume there are three sets of voters who must decide two separate issues. [33] Let us also assume that there are extreme variations in the utility that various citizens would derive from the adoption of certain policies.

Table 3

	Voter X	Voter Y	Voter Z
Issue 1			
Policy A	1	51	60
Policy B	99	49	40
Issue 2			
Policy C	51	52	45
Policy D	49	48	55

If decisions had to be made strictly by referendums and there were legal proscriptions against vote trading or bargaining, policy A and policy C would be chosen. Voters Y and Z prefer policy A to B; voters X and Y prefer policy C to D. However, while voters Y and Z both receive some minimal satisfaction from Policy A, voter

Z incurs a high loss in utility. On policy C, however, voters X and Y both receive some minimal increase in their welfare while voter Z suffers an equally mild loss in utility. If the utilities of all three sets of voters are summed, we find that there would be a net reduction in the total amount of welfare in society. However, if the same decision is made in a pluralistic fashion and the various parties can bargain and trade with one another, the above situation need not occur. Voter X can agree to vote for policy D on issue 2 if voter Z will agree to vote for policy B on issue 1. Both voters X and Z can thus make a net increase in their welfare even though voter Y will suffer a net decrease in his utility on both issues. Because the gains to both voters X and Z are so much greater than the losses to voter Y, there is also a net increase in the collective welfare of the community.

From the above example we can see that whenever a political system relies on referendums to formulate public policy, there is always the possibility that the policies adopted may decrease, rather than increase, the aggregate well-being of society as a whole. This is especially likely to be the case when there is extreme variation in the intensities with which various segments of society prefer alternative courses of action. By and large referendum voting is preferable to political bargaining only if the utilities people attach to particular options are roughly the same.

While political bargaining may increase public welfare, there are two conditions under which it may cease to work effectively. If groups bargain over policy and sincerely state their preferences, the ensuing exchanges will produce the results described above. However, if they overstate or disguise their true preferences, the exchange relationship may fail to maximize public welfare. Our example assumes that the stated preferences are sincere, rather than disguised, preferences. Secondly, the benefits of political bargaining work only if other groups do not incur extensive external costs from the exchanges agreed to by our three parties.[34] A bargaining situation that may increase the aggregate welfare of the parties involved may entail enough offsetting external costs to erase the gains of any political exchange. Obviously, under such circumstances the agreements struck by various groups would not result in optimal decisions. However, this situation is most likely to occur in a political system in which many potential groups fail to become organized or lack access to the policy-making process. If a public form of pluralism can insure that most potential groups are not shut out of the political system, it can minimize, if not contain, the external costs that might result from extensive political bargaining.

Populist Participation: Substantive or Symbolic?

While so far we have looked in great detail at both the empirical and normative problems that are likely to plague a populist theory of democracy, it is also imperative that we critically examine the theoretical suppositions of populist government in order to determine if they are entirely consistent with one another. One of the fundamental assumptions that populists like Harrington have made is that the intensification of public participation and strengthening of government power are entirely compatible objectives. In the opinion of many populists, unless the government has the power to implement the wishes of the public, the effectiveness of participation will be undercut. But it must be pointed out that this relationship between government power and popular participation is a necessary—but by no means sufficient—condition for public involvement to be genuinely meaningful. While the government will need sufficient authority to implement the wishes of the majority, populists must be careful that the state does not misuse its power in interpreting the so-called will of the people. As soon as the problem is defined in these terms it can be seen that a conflict might easily arise between what the public wants and what government officials actually do. When referendums are held on extremely complex problems, they may be stated in such an abstract fashion that they will provide little or no meaningful guidance to the administrator who must actually implement what the majority decides. For example, the public may want the state to enact tough anti-pollution laws, but they may not be willing to accept a slowdown in the rate of economic growth in exchange for clear air. It is difficult to see how the electorate can convey these diverse sentiments in any concrete and specific fashion through the rather unrefined mechanism of a referendum.

The danger thus exists that under a populist form of democracy, government bureaucrats will begin to wield more and more discretionary power in the formulation of policy. While the state will have the power to implement the wishes of the majority, it may increasingly have to rely on its own interpretation of what the public really wants. In the process the very quality of popular participation may become more symbolic than substantive in nature, since instead of actually deciding policy the public may find itself merely authorizing the government to deal with a problem that it considers highly important. As the scope and complexity of the government's activities become enlarged, it stands to reason that the linkage between the public's original wishes and the operations of the state will become more tenuous. While on a theoretical level the majority of citizens may be sanctioning the state to act on a particular issue, the managers of the government may wield the real substance of power by formulating the measures to implement the alleged wishes of the electorate.

NOTES

1. S. E. Finer, "Groups and Political Participation," pp. 58-79.
2. Austin Ranney and Willmore Kendall, *Democracy and the American Party System*, pp. 35-37.
3. Michael Harrington, *Toward a Democratic Left*, p. 266.
4. Roger Hilsman, *To Move a Nation*, p. 542.
5. Gabriel Almond and Sidney Verba, *The Civic Culture*, pp. 337-75.
6. David E. RePass, "Issue Salience and Party Choice," pp. 389-400; Philip E. Converse, "The Nature of Belief Systems in Mass Publics."
7. RePass, "Issue Salience," pp. 392-98.
8. Duane Lockard, *The Politics of State and Local Government*, p. 253.
9. Ibid., p. 237.
10. V. O. Key, *Politics, Parties, and Pressure Groups*, p. 630.
11. John E. Mueller, "Voting on the Propositions," pp. 1197-1212.
12. Ibid., p. 1212.
13. Lockard, *Politics of State and Local Government*, p. 251.
14. James Coleman, *Community Conflict*; Robert L. Crain, Elihu Katz, and Donald Rosenthal, *The Politics of Community Conflict*.
15. Mueller, "Voting on the Propositions," p. 1198.
16. Ibid., p. 1208.
17. Ibid.

18. Kenneth Arrow, *Social Choice and Individual Values.*

19. Robert Paul Wolff, *In Defense of Anarchism*, p. 63.

20. Duncan Black, *The Theory of Committees and Elections*, pp. 39-40.

21. Richard Niemi, "Majority Decision Making with Partial Unidimensionality," pp. 488-97.

22. Ibid., 494.

23. Ibid.

24. William Baumol, *Economic Theory and Operations Research*, pp. 270-74; James Coleman, "The Possibility of a Social Welfare Function," pp. 1105-23.

25. Ranney and Kendall, *Democracy and the American Party System*, pp. 20-35. See Also Robert Dahl, *A Preface to Democratic Theory*, pp. 45, 50.

26. Dahl, *Preface to Democratic Theory*, p. 51.

27. Ranney and Kendall, *Democracy and the American Party System*, p. 24.

28. Herbert McClosky, "Consensus and Ideology in American Politics," pp. 361-82.

29. William Kornhauser, *The Politics of Mass Society*, pp. 60-70.

30. Richard Neuberger, "Government by the People," p. 490.

31. Raymond Wolfinger and Fred Greenstein, "The Repeal of Fair Housing Legislation in California," pp. 753-69.

32. Willmore Kendall and George Carey, "The 'Intensity Problem' and Democratic Theory," pp. 5-24.

33. The example is adapted from Richard Musgrave and Peggy Musgrave, *Public Finance in Theory and Practice*, p. 95.

34. See William H. Riker and Steve J. Brams, "The Paradox of Vote Trading," pp. 1235-47, for a fuller treatment of this issue.

Chapter

5

Pluralism and the
Problem of Group Membership

Pluralists disagree with the populist belief that the public consists of a relatively homogeneous majority with similar interests and concerns, arguing instead that the electorate is fragmented into numerous and diverse issue publics whose interest in politics is often quite limited in scope. However, detractors of pluralism, such as Richard Hamilton and Robert Paul Wolff, claim it is ironic that a doctrine that defines the public in terms of issue publics neglects two facts: many people do not belong to any groups at all, and marginal groups often have difficulty making themselves heard in the determination of public policy.[1] Many important segments of society—for example, the poor or consumers—often lack the financial resources and organizational skills to protect their interests effectively vis-a-vis opposing groups in the political system. While pluralists insist that the citizenry is divided into various issue groups, critics maintain that these interest publics can never become mobilized enough to play a prominent role in formulating policy.

The argument that pluralism ignores the wishes of numerous interests in society raises what are analytically three separate questions. First of all, to determine if most groups are represented in a pluralistic system of decision making, we need to ask if members of issue publics are likely to join either temporary, ad hoc movements or organized groups to achieve their objectives. While some critics accept the fact that society is divided into numerous issue publics, they argue that very few individuals will translate their potential interests into active political behavior. Mancur Olson, for instance, has claimed that it is not rational for individuals to join organizations even though the associations are pursuing objectives they would like to see realized. [2]

Secondly, we need to determine whether the members of issue publics that do join groups represent a cross-section of the population at large. Richard Hamilton has argued that minority-related associations and associations seeking to institute consumer or environmental reforms are likely to experience difficulty in recruiting stable and loyal memberships. Unlike many other types of organizations, consumer or public interest groups are concerned with securing public goods rather than private benefits, and as a consequence, the number of incentives they can use to recruit prospective members is extremely limited. Poverty organizations face equally severe recruitment problems in that they must attempt to attract people who have limited skills in working with organizations and limited expectations that such activities will bring meaningful political change.

Finally, even if individuals are willing to join minority action or consumer associations, we need to ask if they will be able to wield any substantial power in the formulation of public policy. Even if potential groups become activated, the problem of gaining access to important centers of decision making still remains. To meet these criticisms, a pluralist must show how the distinct problems of organizational membership and organizational access can be resolved. In this chapter and the one that follows, I will examine each of the above points in turn.

Potential Groups and Active Members

To defend a pluralistic theory of politics, we need to show that citizens will join or support groups if they feel their interests are threatened. To argue that power should be shared by political elites and the various issue publics in society assumes that these segments of the population can become active in politics when issues of concern to them are being debated. The reason for using the word "can" is that potential groups do not always have to become mobilized in order to wield influence. As Truman has pointed out, the possibility that an issue public will clamor for change may encourage political elites or opposing groups to accommodate the wishes of unorganized citizens despite their lack of overt activity. [3] However, for interest-group politics to be effective over the long run, we also need to demonstrate that potential groups actually become mobilized, rather than merely threaten to do so.

If we look at events in recent American politics, we find repeated examples of issue publics joining temporary, ad hoc associations, or what James Q. Wilson has called "movements," in order to press for political change. [4] Perhaps the most dramatic instances are the civil rights movement and the antiwar movement of the 1960s, which recruited a small yet highly committed number of citizens to support their respective causes. Similarly, there seems to be evidence that the Drug Amendment Act of 1962, the Auto Safety Act, and the various clean air and water bills of the last decade passed Congress because of lobbying by temporary and amorphous issue publics who felt strongly about these issues. [5] In a discussion of these legislative acts, Wilson has noted that each bill "represented not the triumph of an organization, but rather the successful mobilization of a new, usually temporary, political constituency." [6] Members of issue publics do not necessarily become mobilized overnight. In many cases there will have to be a dramatic crisis— such as the thalidomide disaster of the 1960s or a new investigation by Ralph Nader—to galvanize people into pushing for social change. On other occasions mobilization may require "no crisis but only the successful appeal, often through adroit use of the mass media, by a policy entrepreneur," to the relevant issue public. [7] Policy entrepreneurs who can capture the headlines can not only provide issue publics with necessary information, but also goad them into action; e.g., Martin Luther King had a flair for dramatizing the cause of equal rights that stimulated many previously acquiescent black people to actively seek the repeal of segregation laws in the South.

But showing that there are numerous examples of people joining or supporting temporary political associations or movements seeking change still leaves open the question of whether members of issue publics will also be willing to join full-time, permanent groups. For a pluralistic system of politics to function properly, organized groups, as well as more amorphous movements, should have a prominent voice in the policy-making process. The evidence on both the present degree of individual participation and the possibility of increased participation in ongoing group activities is somewhat inconclusive, but at least it provides us with some standards for evaluating the merits or defects of a pluralistic approach to democracy. It also indicates that people's propensity to join groups has changed over time. In 1953, a National Opinion Research Center study of membership in voluntary associations found slightly more than half the population (52 percent) belonged to at least one organization. Similar research in subsequent years showed membership in one or more organizations to fluctuate: 1954 Gallup poll, 55 percent; 1955 NORC, 46 percent; 1960 NORC, 57 percent; 1963 study by Gabriel Almond and Sidney Verba, 57 percent. And a 1972 study by Sidney Verba and Norman Nie found that 62 percent of the public was affiliated with at least one organized group, that 39 percent belonged to more than one organization, and that roughly 40 percent claimed to play an active, rather than nominal, role in their association. [8]

Whether these figures are large or small depends on one's perspective. If one is a participatory democrat and believes that everyone should participate in some form of association or community, then admittedly these statistics will appear inadequate. However, if one compares the number of people who are group members with the number of people who vote in presidential elections, the percentages are roughly comparable. To argue that low membership rates in organized groups undermines a pluralistic theory of democracy raises the issue of how many people need to abstain or support established organizations before pluralism is either undermined or reinforced. We must keep in mind that pluralism has never shared participatory democracy's belief in the beneficial results of highly intensive forms of participation. Because people have diverse and restricted interests, their desire to immerse themselves totally in political and social affairs is likely to be limited. Pluralists believe that if the actual opportunities for individuals to influence the community are enhanced, then participation is apt to increase dramatically. But even though added incentives are likely to stimulate more people to take part in group affairs, many individuals will no doubt always want to restrict both the degree and the scope of their political and social participation.

The above data also indicate that in the last twenty years there has been a sizable increase in the number of people affiliated with organized groups. While the NORC studies of the early 1950s found that from 46 to 52 percent of the public were members of secondary associations, the more recent studies indicate that an additional 10 to 16 percent have become joiners. Why this trend is developing is difficult to say, but it appears that individual membership in organizations is related to a host of environmental variables. Research by Almond and Verba and by Kornhauser indicated that participation in group activities increases as the degree of education and the socioeconomic status of the individual rise.[9] Hence more individuals are likely to join groups as they acquire more education and improve their economic standing. Similarly, structural or political variables seem to explain why people elect to join organizations. The comparative literature on interest groups suggests that individual membership in organizations is directly related to the degree of modernization of a society. Gabriel Almond and Bingham Powell have argued that whereas in the past a few kinship organizations could satisfy most people's demands, a modernized society requires innumerably more organizations to cater to its vastly more numerous and complex needs.[10] By the very nature of a modernized community, the increasing differentiation of tasks fragments society into a large number of groups needed to provide important services for the survival of the political community.[11] In addition to increasing the need for new groups, modernization also makes it easier for groups to become organized. As people become more mobile and the problem of communication declines, it becomes easier for individuals who share common concerns to join organizations seeking political or social change. Finally, the specific actions of the government have spawned the creation of numerous new groups. As David Apter has remarked, the growth of the social welfare state in the last couple of decades has stimulated the development of many new organizations. Or as

H. R. Mahood has observed, the growth of government intervention in the field of labor relations and business regulation has resulted in the proliferation of whole new organizations.[12] While interest-group activity often stimulates government action in the first place, government-sponsored programs often reciprocally stimulate the growth of groups to contest, monitor, or support government action.

In short, the extent to which a nation becomes a nation of joiners may depend on a variety of factors, including the level of income and education of its citizens, the degree of modernity or complexity of its political system, and the scope of its government programs for dealing with important social and economic issues. The higher a nation scores on each of the above factors, the more likely its citizens will engage in some form of interest-group activity. Given the fact that over time our political and economic institutions are becoming increasingly differentiated and complex and our citizens are becoming better educated, it seems likely that more people will join secondary associations in the future.

The Problem of Marginal and Public Interest Groups

While there are a variety of reasons for believing that organizational membership will grow in the future, we need to ask if rising membership levels will also characterize public interest groups and marginal, or poverty, associations. Although group activity might increase, it might very well work to the disadvantage of certain key elements in society. Thus instead of asking whether we are a nation of joiners, we need to ask whether we are a nation that will join reform or so-called promotional interest groups. If only certain kinds of organizations are likely to be successful in attracting members, then the interplay of interest groups in a pluralistic form of democracy may work to the detriment of numerous people in the political system.

Mancur Olson suggests in an extremely insightful and provocative book, *The Logic of Collective Action,* that poverty groups or public interest associations will have considerable difficulty in attracting a sufficient number of supporters.[13] He insists that only certain kinds of interest groups are likely to develop effective organizations: those with limited membership and those which have either the resources to provide selective inducements to their rank and file or the authority to apply legal sanctions against their natural membership.[14] Like many other economists, Olson posits a traditional utilitarian picture of man as a rational, self-interested individual who seeks to minimize the costs while maximizing the benefits associated with his every course of action. Unless a group can provide positive benefits to the individual or invoke negative sanctions against him, the rational, self-interested person will have no incentive to support an association actively even though he may fully agree with its objectives. Borrowing from the terminology of public finance, Olson notes that groups provide their members with "public goods." That is, once a good is created, there is no way of excluding others from obtaining its benefits. While an individual may share with many other people a common interest in acquiring a certain collective benefit, he does not share with them a desire to pay the cost for providing the good. The rational person knows that if the group secures the desired objective, he will receive its benefits regardless of whether he bears any of the cost necessary to realize the objective in the first place. Since the individual is likely to enjoy the benefits of group action whether he contributes or not, he has no incentive to support or join the organization. In addition, the individual may find it irrational to support a group activity if he discerns no perceptible effect of his activities on either the burden or benefit accruing to the other members of the association.

Olson admits that these difficulties are less severe in small groups. The smaller the organization, the easier it becomes for the individual to gauge the impact of his actions on the success or failure of the group's activities. Also, the smaller the organization, the greater the likelihood that the individual "will find that his personal gain from having the collective good exceeds the total cost of providing some amount of the collective good."[15] Therefore in small groups we are apt to find members actively advancing the cause of the organization since each individual is likely to receive a substantial portion of the public good merely because there are so few members with whom he has to share the desired benefits. Ample incentives thus exist for the rank and file to support the cause of the group enthusiastically. But even in small organizations,

Olson argues, the amount of the public good secured by the group may be suboptimal. The optimal amount of a collective good for an individual to obtain occurs when "the rate of gain to the group, multiplied by the fraction of the group gain the individual gets equals the rate of increase of the total cost of the collective good."[16] However, according to Olson's assumptions, the individual's decision to join a group and provide a portion of its public good is determined by the relationship between the marginal costs and benefits associated with his actions. There is no incentive for a person to independently provide any of the collective good once the amount that would be purchased by the individual receiving the largest fraction of group value is available. When the size of the group increases, the willingness of the individual to support the organization's objectives declines even more, for as the group becomes larger, the fraction of benefits that accrues to each member simultaneously becomes smaller.

There are, however, two factors that can offset this tendency of individuals to abstain from supporting organizations whose goals they may happen to agree with. First, Olson points out that an interest group can employ legal sanctions or coercion to force a person to support its activities.[17] Labor unions, for example, often rely on compulsory membership as a means of forcing potential constituents to further the common objectives that most working people supposedly seek to realize. Secondly, Olson argues that an interest group may try to elicit popular support for its activities by providing selective inducements to its constituents that are not necessarily related to the organization's central objectives.[18] For instance, a labor union might offer special privileges to its members—such as cut-rate air fares abroad—as a way of cementing an individual's commitment to the organization. While the central objectives of an interest group may be classified as public goods, the selective inducements that it offers to its members are personal, non-collective goods. Unless an organization provides some individualized benefits to its members, there will be no incentive for people to support an association whose central benefits they would enjoy whether they were members not.

The implications of Olson's argument do not seem to augur well for the success of either public interest groups or poverty associations. He insists that to mobilize a latent or potential group, individuals need to be either legally coerced or provided with non-collective benefits. Since it is obvious that poverty associations or consumer groups cannot legally force anyone to join their organizations, their only possibility of attracting supporters—at least according to Olson's assumptions—is to offer selective inducements to their potential members. However, marginal groups often have negligible resources for providing such kinds of benefits. Their ability to rely on side payments or selective inducements to win supporters may thus be contingent on some form of outside assistance.

Before developing this line of inquiry, we need to ask if Olson's theory of interest groups adequately explains group behavior. The availability of selective inducements may not be the only factor determining how successful reform interests will be in recruiting supporters. Olson is probably correct in arguing that organizations like labor unions have an easier time recruiting new members when they can offer positive benefits or impose negative sanctions on their potential supporters. But as Brian Barry has perceptively pointed out, such an analysis does not account for the significantly different levels of union membership in various countries at different points in time. [19] It is well known that there is a higher level of support for union activity in England than in the United States, but certainly we cannot explain why unions are more successful in attracting followers in England merely by analyzing how many selective inducements they have at their disposal. Similarly, the notion of selective inducements does not seem very successful in explaining why mass unionism in England developed when it did and why it declined precipitously in the late 1920s. [20] On the contrary, to account fully for the success or failure of groups to attract members, we need to include other variables in our analysis. For instance, the reason people might be more willing to join unions in England is that they perceive the prospects for collective action to be better. In contrast, when they experience failure, as occurred during the General Strike of the 1920s, they may decide to abstain from further union activity. In either case, the overall prospects of group action—rather than the portion of the public good or the amount of selective inducements received by the individual—may account for the success or failure of groups to recruit new members. [21]

As a further means of confirming this hypothesis, we might ask why some cities seem to have more group activity than others or why certain marginal groups seem especially active in some regions but not in others. As we have seen, Olson has no way to account for these differences except to refer to the legal sanctions or selective inducements various organizations might offer to their members. However, if we look at the literature on urban politics, an alternative explanation appears. Edward Banfield finds that the structure of city politics, rather than the inducements of groups, accounts for the degree of interest-group activity. Banfield argues that interest groups are active in a city like Chicago because the decision-making process there is extremely fragmented and open. [22] As the prospects of influencing the political process increase, so does a group's ability to attract new members. Another way we might illustrate this same point is to ask why a marginal group like the John Birch Society was more active in southern California in the early 1960s than in other parts of the country. There is no apparent reason for believing that the selective inducements the John Birch Society offered its members were necessarily higher in this area than elsewhere. Indeed, a study of the radical right by Raymond Wolfinger et al. maintained that individuals were encouraged to join extremely conservative organizations in a region like southern California because their activities were likely to succeed. [23] Since California has never had a strong party system, conservative groups have been able to wield significant influence in the political arena, which has meant that such groups have been able to attract even greater support.

If the insights of Barry, Banfield, and Wolfinger are correct, we need to modify Olson's model of group behavior. Regardless of the selective inducements or legal sanctions available to the group, an organization may have no trouble attracting supporters if its chances of political success appear reasonable. An individual may be willing to join an interest group that has some prospects of success even though he would be able to share in the benefits it secured without having to join the organization in the first place. Similarly, if the prospects for collective action are a factor affecting the recruitment efforts of groups, we must realize that our earlier distinction between the problem of organizational membership and that of organizational access is purely an analytic one. The degree to which an organization can wield political influence may determine in part the degree to which it can recruit an active membership. When we discuss in greater detail how the political process can be made more receptive to the demands of reform interests, we need to keep in mind that any such actions may likewise strengthen the internal organization of the reform groups in question. The more effectively a public interest group can make its voice heard in the councils of government, the greater is the possibility that it will recruit more supporters, which in turn will increase its effectiveness.

Besides overlooking the fact that the success of an organization may affect both the number and enthusiasm of its supporters, Olson has also failed to realize that his theory of group behavior rests on an extremely narrow view of human motivation. Olson has carefully constructed his argument around a view of man as a rational, self-interested individual. [24] In contrast, I have pictured man as a more social animal with distinctly limited interests as well as limited rationality and limited knowledge of his own actions. While so far I have refrained from explicitly discussing whether an individual's specific interests and knowledge are used for purely personal or for more inclusive ends, there seems to be ample evidence to indicate that people often join groups for what they consider to be altruistic ends. Olson would no doubt insist that his assumptions of individual self-interest and rationality are responsible for the predictive power of his theory, but these assumptions seem to limit his ability to explain the behavior of groups like Common Cause or Nader's Raiders.

From examining studies of voting behavior as well as from observing the commitment of people in so-called public interest groups, we can argue that political behavior is not solely motivated by self-interest. As mentioned earlier, *The American Voter* found that a significant number of individuals exercise their right to vote because they feel that it is their public duty to do so. For similar reasons many people might join public interest groups because they feel they ought to take an active part in political affairs. Olson himself concedes this very point, but he tries to minimize its importance by arguing that even if individuals were altruistic, rather than self-interested, they would still not support certain kinds of groups out of purely utilitarian calculations. As Olson puts it, "even if the member of a large group were to neglect his own interest entirely, he still would not rationally contribute toward the provision of a collective good or public good since his own contribution would not be perceptible."[25] However, Barry has pointed out that this argument seems fallacious: "If each contribution is literally 'imperceptible,' how can all the contributions together add up to anything?"[26] If the efforts of ten thousand members of Common Cause add up to something, then the contribution of each member must on the average equal one ten-thousandth of the total effort. Furthermore, if all Olson means in the preceding context is that people would not be rational in supporting an organization that has no prospects of being effective, we can certainly agree with him. As hopefully I have shown, individuals are more likely to join an interest group when its prospects for success are enhanced. Regardless of the shifts or alterations in his argument, Olson does not seem very willing to accept the fact that many people are currently supporting organizations like Common Cause for what appear to be altruistic reasons. While it is possible that the consumer-environmental movement may be short-lived, at present many individuals do seem willing to work for groups that seek to realize public, rather than narrowly defined private, interests.

However, even if we insist that a sense of individual duty or altruism may complement or even substitute for the factors Olson focuses on, we must recognize that marginal groups may still have a difficult time recruiting members. The problem of organizational recruitment will probably affect poverty groups more severely than it will more middle-class reform groups. In order to support an organization out of a sense of duty, an individual must be willing to incur certain costs. Whether one contributes his evenings to the activities of the group or merely offers a monetary donation, any kind of organizational membership imposes burdens on the individual. As might be expected, these burdens are likely to weigh more heavily, the lower down on the socioeconomic scale we go. Consumer or environmental groups that recruit members primarily from the relatively affluent layers of the upper middle class are likely to be more successful than poverty or marginal groups in attracting a committed following. Only when people have sufficient resources at their disposal are they able to afford the cost of acting in an altruistic fashion. When organizations of the poor seek to win support for their activities from lower economic neighborhoods, they are likely to find that very few individuals can afford the luxury of public service. Moreover, as Kenneth Clark and other observers of the ghetto have noted, people who live in slums often suffer from feelings of inadequacy and self-hatred. Their ability to widen their horizons and to support group programs that will eventually benefit them is thus likely to be limited. As the cost of engaging in collective action increases, it should be expected that fewer people will elect to spend their time supporting group activities. Regardless of their motives, individuals in marginal groups may find that the cost of supporting organized efforts to secure reforms from the bottom up is prohibitively high.

The obvious problem we must face is how to provide the poor with sufficient incentive so that they can engage in interest-group activity. Left to their own resources, marginal groups are not likely to organize themselves effectively for political action. A laissez-faire version of pluralism, which believes the poor are yet another potential group that will become organized when conditions warrant it, fails to recognize the complexity of the problem. Only when some form of outside assistance is provided to marginal groups will the poor be able to afford the cost of lobbying for collective goods.

Thus a public form of pluralism, which advocates government assistance to poverty organizations, may be essential if marginal groups are ever to become mobilized. Once poverty or Community Action programs are established and funded by government agencies, the poor will be able to afford the luxury of pursuing objectives that will collectively benefit the residents of ghetto areas. While at present there are very few poor people who can altruistically donate their time and energy to group activities, a government-sponsored program of organizing people from the bottom up will significantly reduce the costs such individuals must incur in pursuit of political change. In addition, the resources various government agencies would dispense under a federally financed poverty program could be used by poverty associations as selective inducements to recruit even more supporters. As we all know, old-time political machines often relied on a variety of patronage jobs in order to develop an effective instrument for achieving political objectives. If a sufficient amount of funds can be funneled to poverty groups, there is no reason why such associations cannot provide similar benefits. When adequate resources are available to poverty associations, they too can rely on personal, non-collective rewards as a means of strengthening their internal organizations. Finally, a public form of pluralism may also help to lessen the psychological tendencies of self-hatred that often characterize individuals who live in situations of deprivation.[27] If the federal government assists members of the poor to mobilize themselves, it may help eliminate the psychological, as well as the political and economic, causes of poverty. Unless individuals have the opportunity to wield power, they will always feel powerless. When the poor have assistance in organizing themselves, they are likely to acquire both the confidence and the skills prerequisite for successful political action; but when they must fend for themselves, their psychological and economic dependence may prevent them from collectively pursuing objectives that individually they would no doubt support.

NOTES

1. Robert Paul Wolff, Barrington Moore, Jr. and Herbert Marcuse, *A Critique of Pure Tolerance*, pp. 3-53; Richard Hamilton, *Class and Politics in the United States*, pp. 35-46.

2. Mancur Olson, Jr., *The Logic of Collective Action.*

3. David Truman, *The Governmental Process*, p. 114.

4. James Q. Wilson, *Political Organizations*, p. 7.

5. Ibid., p. 335.

6. Ibid.

7. Ibid.

8. The 1953, 1955, and 1960 studies by the National Opinion Research Center and the 1954 Gallup poll are analyzed in more detail in Hamilton, *Class and Politics in the United States*, pp. 37, 67. See also Gabriel Almond and Sidney Verba, *The Civic Culture*, p. 247; and Sidney Verba and Norman Nie, *Participation in America*, pp. 41-42.

9. Almond and Verba, *Civic Culture*, pp. 186-207; William Kornhauser, *The Politics of Mass Society*, p. 68.

10. Gabriel Almond and Bingham Powell, *Comparative Politics*, pp. 255-98. See also David Apter and Harry Eckstein, *Comparative Politics*, p. 389.

11. Almond and Powell, *Comparative Politics*, pp. 299-333.

12. Apter and Eckstein, *Comparative Politics*, p. 389; H. R. Mahood, ed., *Pressure Groups in American Politics*.

13. Olson, *Logic of Collective Action*.

14. Ibid., pp. 53-76.

15. Ibid., pp. 48-50, 53-76.

16. Ibid., p. 24.

17. Ibid., pp. 66-75.

18. Ibid., pp. 132-33.

19. Brian M. Barry, *Sociologists, Economists and Democracy*, p. 29.

20. Ibid., p. 29.

21. Ibid.

22. Edward C. Banfield, *Political Influence*, pp. 235-306.

23. Raymond E. Wolfinger, Barbara K. Wolfinger, Kenneth Prewitt, and Sheila Rosenhach, "America's Radical Right: Politics and Ideology," pp. 262-93.

24. Olson, *Logic of Collective Action*, p. 64.

25. Ibid.

26. Barry, *Sociologists, Economists and Democracy*, p. 32.

27. Kenneth B. Clark, *Dark Ghetto*, pp. 63-80.

Chapter

6

Pluralism and the
Problem of Group Access

As we have seen in the preceding chapter, individuals like Richard Hamilton have attacked a pluralistic form of democracy because they believe that many persons presently belong to no groups at all. Other commentators, such as Elmer Eric Schattschneider, Peter Bachrach, and Morton Baratz, criticize pluralism for ignoring the fact that many interest groups have difficulty gaining access to important centers of decision making. [1] These critics tend to write off pluralism as an inequitable form of democratic government because they believe it provides relatively few opportunities for the less affluent and less well-educated to defend their interests. The point at issue here is that even if the various issue publics in society do become organized, they are not likely to wield any appreciable degree of influence. "The flaw in the pluralistic heaven," Schattschneider argues, "is that the heavenly chorus sings with a strong upper-class accent." [2] Although he does not cite actual evidence, Schattschneider insists that "probably about 90 percent of the people cannot get into the pressure system." [3] Similarly, Bachrach and Baratz criticize pluralism for overlooking the "important area of what we have called nondecision making, that is, the practice of limiting the scope of actual decision-making to 'safe' issues by manipulating the dominant community values, myths, and political institutions and procedures." They maintain that the "mobilization of bias" in any community, that is, the organization and direction of society's values, often works to the disadvantage of marginal or promotional groups who wish to place their demands on the public agenda.[4] Finally, Robert Paul Wolff insists that even if marginal interests gain access to the bargaining arena, the rules of group competition are likely to frustrate any demands for social change.[5] Wolff believes that the disparities in resources between well-entrenched, established groups and so-called reform groups are so great that the prospects for meaningful bargaining and compromise are slim indeed.

Whether such criticism of pluralism is warranted is the question that will be examined in this chapter. As we shall soon see, it is possible to argue that many of the critics have not been very careful in specifying why they think pluralism has inherently conservative tendencies. First of all, a number of commentators have not specifically stated whether the alleged "conservative bias" of pluralism is primarily a theoretical or practical problem.[6] If one argues that certain key groups are systematically discriminated against under a pluralistic form of democracy, one needs to specify whether the problems are inherent in the theory of pluralism or in the practice of American politics. It is certainly plausible to argue, as do Bachrach and Baratz, that the dominant values in society may limit the range of issues that a political system is willing to consider. But this fact of political life may and probably will hamper the efforts of any theory of democracy—whether it be populism, polyarchy, or pluralism—to respond adequately to demands for reforms that go against prevailing norms. While what Bachrach and Baratz call the mobilization of bias may work to the disadvantage of marginal groups in a pluralistic form of democracy, it may also prevent majorities from voting on "unsafe issues" in populist referendums. Or it may even prevent Lowi's reform-oriented elites from entertaining legislative proposals that threaten to upset well-engrained patterns of behavior. The problem of overcoming cultural norms that reflect and reinforce disparities in power among different elements in society is not a difficulty unique to any one form of democracy, let alone pluralism.

Given the unwillingness of pluralism's detractors to sort out the normative, as opposed to empirical, claims of pluralism, it is all the more essential for us to differentiate carefully between these various kinds of assumptions. As simple as the point may seem, many commentators either ignore it altogether or concede its existence while ignoring its importance in discussing the merits or drawbacks of pluralism. To evaluate pluralism fairly, we must analyze how the doctrine prescriptively responds to the demands of groups that are not necessarily in the mainstream of American politics. This chapter will show that normatively both laissez-faire and public pluralists do not favor restricting any interests, let alone marginal interests, from placing their demands on the public agenda. (As pointed out in chapter 2, only corporate pluralism advocates limiting the number of groups that may participate in the decision-making arena). In addition, I will argue—the claims of critics like Wolff notwithstanding—that the criteria that both laissez-faire and public pluralists believe should govern the settlement of policy issues do not necessarily penalize or favor the demands of any group, including poverty or consumer action groups.

Secondly, this chapter will examine in more detail why pluralists believe that the political system is flexible enough to accommodate the wishes of reform-oriented interest groups. In particular, it will be necessary to determine whether the considerations that laissez-faire and public pluralists believe should determine who prevails in a dispute—such as the intensity of a group's demands—do in fact govern the settlement of issues. If there is some discrepancy between the operations of the political system and the norms pluralism advocates, I will try to show how a public form of pluralism can tilt the partisan give-and-take among groups to the advantage of interests that presently have little or no power. If marginal elements lack access to important centers of power, there is certainly no compelling reason why the resources of those particular groups cannot be altered through federal sponsorship and supervision of interest-group interaction. Finally, instead of simply defending pluralism against the charge that it necessarily excludes marginal groups like the poor, this chapter will make the counter-argument that pluralism may in fact be the only feasible method for such groups to acquire influence over public policy. I will argue that the discrepancies in resources between consumer-environmental groups and large business organizations are likely to be minimized when the two parties can bargain directly with legislative and bureaucratic institutions instead of having to win mass support in public referendums.

The Normative Component of Pluralistic Democracy

Before examining in more detail why some pluralists argue empirically that the political system is open and responsive to the needs of most groups in society, we need to analyze how a pluralist prescriptively believes the political system should react to the demands of previously unorganized or inactive groups. If we may rephrase Schattschneider's comments, there may be nothing wrong in the "pluralistic heaven"; the problems may arise in the more prosaic, empirical earth below. As a way of illustrating this point, it should be noted that pluralism—like any other theory of democracy—must take a normative stand on what are analytically two separate issues. Roger Cobb and Charles Elder have conveniently called the first problem one of *agenda setting;* and for purposes of symmetry we may call the second problem one of *agenda resolution.*[7] By agenda setting, I mean that any theory of democracy must decide how and for what reasons it wishes to let various groups place demands on the political system. Polyarchal democrats like Herbert McClosky and Gabriel Almond have argued that in the interest of stability the government should attempt to restrict the number of demands that the public can place on the political system.[8] Laissez-faire and public pluralists, as we shall soon see, argue otherwise. Besides taking a stand on the issue of agenda setting, a theory of democracy must also articulate a set of principles for resolving disputes over alternative policies. This is the problem that I have chosen to call agenda resolution. Once a proposal is on the public agenda, we need to ask what criteria will be used in either rejecting or accepting its suggestions for some kind of policy alteration.

If we look first at the problem of agenda setting, we can argue that neither laissez-faire nor public pluralism can be accused of normatively justifying the exclusion of any group from the political process. Both laissez-faire and public pluralists believe that the effectiveness of public policy can be greatly enhanced by multiplying, rather than limiting, the number of decision makers. As pointed out in chapter 2, the best made plans often go awry because no one set of policy makers can anticipate—let alone prepare for—all the contingencies that might surround the alteration of an existing policy.[9] Therefore both laissez-faire and public pluralists advocate opening up the process of agenda setting, since by increasing the number of actors who have some say in the formulation of public decisions, the defects in a policy that might be overlooked by one set of decision makers can be pointed out by alternative participants.

In addition, laissez-faire and public pluralists insist that all groups must have some say in the policy-making process if they are to arrive at an accurate assessment of their own needs. As noted in chapter 3, while theories of representative democracy such as polyarchy often assume that political officials can act in the best interests of their constituents without consulting them, pluralism believes there is a subjective side to people's welfare that necessitates public participation in the political process.[10] People's demands cannot always be objectively known in an a priori fashion as individuals often come to a realization of what they wish to accomplish only in the process of negotiating and bargaining with opposing interests. Thus the public agenda cannot be arbitrarily determined by a set of political elites even if they have the most praiseworthy intentions of furthering the welfare of their constituents. In dealing with the problem of agenda setting, the models of pluralism we have been looking at seek to expand, rather than restrict, the opportunities for any group to gain a hearing of its demands. In order both to increase the rationality of public planning and to accurately define the needs of the different interests in society, laissez-faire and public pluralists normatively advocate the creation of a form of decision making in which all groups can easily air their objections to existing policy.

If we now turn to the question of agenda resolution, we can likewise argue that neither of the above two forms of pluralism necessarily benefits nor works to the disadvantage of any particular group in society. Contrary to what critics like Wolff imply, pluralism does not normatively believe that the wealth an interest group can command, nor the amount of raw political power it can mobilize, nor even the number of voters it can attract should be the determining factor in resolving a dispute. While Wolff insists that pluralists advocate a vector-sum theory of decision making, in which decisions are the result of the organized pressure brought to bear on public officials, the situation in reality is far more complex. [11] As indicated earlier, pluralists believe a variety of factors— including the intensity of feeling of a particular group—should determine how an issue is resolved. [12] For example, while chemical companies or oil refineries may be able to mobilize more resources than environmental groups, a pluralist would not necessarily argue that pollution laws should be tailored to business needs. Depending on the intensity of feeling of consumer or environmental interests, government officials should reject the demands of the more powerful business community. Similarly, if blacks feel intensely about integrating certain businesses from which they have previously been excluded, a pluralist would argue that a prima facie case exists for changing present policy. However, in an alternative situation, in which whites feel very intensely about a proposed modification in community living patterns and blacks are indifferent, a pluralist might agree that radical change need not be instituted. The pluralist criterion of group intensity is a standard for resolving agenda disputes that may or may not benefit the interests of environmental or community action groups. The key issue is how seriously the contending parties feel about the particular matter in question. If groups like the Sierra Club or Common Cause or SCLC are intensely interested in preserving or altering certain business or government practices, then the two forms of pluralism we have been discussing would be highly receptive to their demands.

However, if a pluralist encountered a situation in which a variety of parties felt equally intensely about the outcome of a particular policy, he would argue that other criteria—for example, the protection of liberal rights or the egalitarian notion of guaranteeing some minimal benefits to all parties—should be employed to resolve group differences. By minimal benefits to all parties, I mean the standard Lindblom has described: no group should ever be completely shut out of the decision-making process. [13] Both laissez-faire and public pluralists would argue that each group should have "its turn" to influence the shape of public policy. Regardless of how intensely any one specific interest may feel about a particular issue, a pluralist would argue that no group should be given veto power if other groups are similarly concerned about the outcome of the same issue; public policies should guarantee at least some minimal values to interests seeking redress of their grievances. In contrast to a populist form of democracy in which referendums render decisions of a zero-sum nature, laissez-faire and public pluralism seek to resolve disputes between equally intense groups in a nonexclusive manner.

The adequacy of using egalitarian norms to resolve policy disputes, however, may be limited to certain kinds of issues. It is possible to argue that one could settle a disagreement between equally intense groups in an egalitarian fashion only if the dispute involves what Theodore Lowi has called a "distributive" policy, i.e., a policy that is "characterized by the ease with which [it] can be disaggregated and dispensed unit by small unit, each unit more or less in isolation from the other units."[14] In any disagreement over a distributive issue, it is possible for the contending parties never to come directly into conflict with one another in resolving their dispute.[15] For instance, the question of what kind of transportation services a municipality should provide its citizens could be classified as a distributive issue. If two different groups felt intensely about whether public or private transport should be emphasized, each interest could alternate in an egalitarian fashion in deciding how and where the city allocated its resources for transit improvement. In one fiscal year, the city might buy more buses while in another year it might allocate its funds to improve off-street parking for privately operated cars. No one group would dominate the way in which the community utilized its resources; every group would be guaranteed the right to receive some minimal benefits.

However, if two different parties disagree intensely over what is basically a redistributive issue, then the inadequacy of using egalitarian norms to settle disputes becomes readily apparent. For instance, if an issue involved the demand of minority groups to settle in previously all-white areas, a community could not alternately desegregate and then resegregate the same neighborhood. It is impossible to argue that each group should have its chance to determine public policy on the issue in question if the issue itself cannot be disaggregated. By their very nature redistributive policies necessitate substantial compromises from one party or another. [16] But when neither the intensity of a group's demands nor the norm of egalitarianism provides sufficient grounds for resolving all possible political disputes, what other criteria can a laissez-faire or public pluralist espouse? If the problem involves a question of minority rights, a pluralist can be expected to defend the essential liberal freedoms of all groups. Even if both blacks and whites feel equally intensely about a redistributive issue like segregated housing, a pluralist would insist that the protection of certain basic liberties should dictate that the issue be resolved to the benefit of the minority group. However, when issues like civil rights elicit intense reaction from opposing parties, a pluralist would argue that some compensatory rewards should be granted to the party forced to make substantial compromises. While two groups may feel equally intensely about the same issue, they may have different reasons for feeling strongly about the matter, which creates the possibility of developing a compromise settlement that is not completely unpalatable to the losing group. Whites may resist integration of their communities because they may feel that it will lead to the physical deterioration of their neighborhoods; but if a community upholds the right of minorities to live where they please, it can offer to increase the degree of city services to the neighborhood being integrated, or it can offer tax concessions to those property owners who have resisted a change in the status quo. Through a process of logrolling, distributive benefits can be granted to those interests which are forced to make substantial concessions on a redistributive issue. Thus if groups disagree intensely on a redistributive issue that involves civil rights or liberties, it is essential that liberal values be upheld; but by providing some distributive rewards to those groups which are required to compromise their position on the issue in question, the political system can try in an egalitarian fashion to guarantee some minimal benefits to all interests.

On the basis of the above discussion, we can see that the criteria a laissez-faire or public pluralist would normatively use both to define the public agenda and to resolve matters of dispute would not necessarily work to the detriment of any specific group in society. By alternately permitting different parties to decide distributive issues or by granting some minimal level of benefits to groups that lose on redistributive issues, these models of pluralism would attempt to prevent any set of interests from being permanently excluded from the political process.

The Empirical Component of Pluralistic Democracy

While both laissez-faire and public pluralists agree in a normative sense that no set of interests should be denied the opportunity to influence the content of public policy, they disagree empirically on how open or closed the political system presently is to the demands of so-called public interest groups or other marginal elements in society. Even though both models of pluralism espouse criteria for agenda setting and agenda resolution that do not discriminate against the demands of reform interests, they differ as to how often various groups actually have an opportunity to shape public policy. As pointed out in chapter 2, laissez-faire pluralists—like Dahl, Cobb and Elder, Kaufman and Sayre, and Banfield—believe that the political system is basically open and receptive to the demands of a wide array of groups.[17] Dahl, in particular, has described the process of agenda building as a flexible one, "in which there is a high probability that an active and legitimate group in the population can make itself heard effectively at some crucial stage in the process of decision [making]."[18] Sayre and Kaufman have echoed a similar theme in their study of New York, arguing that public decisions are usually made in an open and fragmented fashion:

No part of the city's large and varied population is alienated from participation in the system. The channels of access to the points of decision are numerous, and most of them are open to any group alert to the opportunities offered and persistent in pursuit of its objectives.[19]

However, we noted in chapter 2 that a public pluralist would strike a slightly more pessimistic tone. Even though it is possible to agree in part with many of the observations laissez-faire pluralists have made of urban politics, it should be pointed out that the pattern of pluralistic bargaining on both local and national levels often works hardships on marginal or reform interests. [20] While a great variety of groups do enjoy considerable influence in shaping the content of government policy, the mere appearance of group participation often conceals the unequal distribution of power among various interests.

In order to assess the contention of laissez-faire pluralists that the political system is open, it is necessary to examine how they approach the problem. Since each of the authors cited above relies on very different explanations to account for the flexibility of the decision-making process, we must examine the arguments of each in turn. The next section will deal separately with the laissez-faire pluralists, while later sections will deal with the public pluralist critique of their arguments.

Characteristics of Groups

Interestingly enough, while laissez-faire pluralists like Dahl, Cobb and Elder, and Sayre and Kaufman see a high potential for interest-group success, each relies on a different explanation to account for this phenomenon. [21] Dahl focuses on the characteristics of groups—in particular, the resources various groups have at their disposal—to support his belief that the political system is an open one. In contrast to critics like Wolff, who contend that the discrepancies in power among groups are so great that the prospect of meaningful social change is dim, Dahl argues that the political system contains plenty of slack to accommodate a diverse array of demands for change. [22] Although he accepts the charge made by many of pluralism's critics that the resources available to different groups vary immensely, he tends to minimize its political importance by pointing out that inequalities in resources are usually noncumulative in nature. [23] Dahl insists there is no single asset such as wealth or skill that will enable its possessor to dominate the formulation of public policy. Even though some groups may have more financial assets than others, they also may have considerably less social standing or expertise. In terms of the empirical issue of who wields political power, the important question for Dahl is not whether resources are inequitably distributed but whether they are inequitably distributed in a dispersed or concentrated fashion. If a variety of groups possess a surplus of at least one kind of political asset, as is the case in New Haven, the system may be highly receptive to a great variety of demands. When a group employs its resources in an effort to dominate the political system, opposing interests can tap alternative forms of resources in order to thwart such an attempt.

Besides attacking pluralism's critics for not distinguishing between cumulative, as opposed to dispersed, inequalities in assets, Dahl also points out that the size of a group's resources merely indicates the potential, and not the actual, political power that it wields. [24] While many interests may have more potential power than others to affect the direction of public policy, their actual power to shape political decisions may lag behind groups with far fewer resources. In large part this phenomenon occurs for two very different reasons. First, as Dahl convincingly argues, people with very few resources can often exercise more power than those with considerably more assets if they are skillful in investing the resources they do possess. The effectiveness with which a group uses its assets is certainly as important as the number of assets it can marshal. In addition to the skill with which people employ their resources, Dahl insists that a group's willingness to use all or very little of its resources determines in large part who prevails in most disputes. Although certain groups may possess more assets than others, some interests may be willing to spend a larger percentage of their resources to achieve their objectives. In particular, Dahl claims that groups which feel very intensely about a specific issue may be able to exercise considerable power if they are willing to pay a high enough price. [25] In *Who Governs?* he notes that a few hundred enraged members of an Italian working-class neighborhood were able to prevent a group of wealthy businessmen from building a low-cost housing project in the community. While the businessmen, who had close ties with the incumbent mayor, seemed to possess more potential power, the neighborhood, which spent more of its resources to persuade the city council to reject the plans of the developers, wielded more actual power. [26]

The considerations that laissez-faire and public pluralists believe should determine who prevails on a disputed issue—particularly the intensity of a group's demands—may thus on numerous occasions actually decide issues of policy. If a group feels more intensely about a matter than a contending party, it may, as Dahl's example illustrates, be able to use resources more thoroughly to block the requests of a potentially more powerful adversary. Once we recognize that potential power is not the same as actual power, we can argue that the normative and empirical aspects of a laissez-faire theory of pluralism complement one another. When decisions are made in a bargaining fashion, those groups which feel most intensely about a particular issue can translate all of their potential assets into actual political influence. The size or the number of assets a group possesses may be less important than the manner in which it employs them.

The Nature of Group Demands

While Dahl focuses on the characteristics of groups to account for the alleged openness of the political system, Cobb and Elder show how the manner in which a group defines its objectives may be a crucial factor in affecting its success or failure. By drawing heavily on the work of Schattschneider, they argue that the success of an interest may depend less on its own resources than on the influence of the allies it can enlist. [27] Even if resources are noncumulatively distributed, and even if some groups are more willing than others to expend their assets, they may not succeed in placing their demands on the public agenda unless their requests are supported by other elements in society. Thus the manner in which a group articulates its objectives may have a significant bearing on its ability to disarm its opponents and attract potential supporters. For an interest to achieve its objectives, it must try to associate its policies with the symbols of legitimacy in the larger political system, while conversely demonstrating that the wishes of its adversaries fall outside the boundaries of the key values espoused by the political community. [28] Cobb and Elder point out that when a group's demands are seen as legitimate in terms of the symbols prevailing in the political system, the ability of the group to form alliances with other strategically placed elements in society is facilitated, while the flexibility of its opponents is diminished. [29] Depending on how an interest identifies its goals, it may either galvanize its adversaries into open opposition or confuse and divide its opponents while strengthening its own ties with like-minded groups.

For example, if a group finds itself unable to place its demands on the public agenda, it should try to reformulate its objectives in order to widen the arena of conflict and draw more participants into the dispute. Conversely, if an interest finds the political system amenable to its suggestions, it should try to confine any challenge to its power by monopolizing the symbols of legitimacy. While the weaker group wishes to widen the nature of the dispute in the hopes of attracting more allies, the dominant group wants to narrow the definition of the political issue to limit the entry of new parties. If a well-established group can no longer succeed in defining the issues facing the polity, it may be confronted by an array of opposing interests that it can no longer defeat. The leverage an interest group can exercise in society may in large part be dependent on its skill in defining and redefining its objectives as political circumstances change.

Although Cobb and Elder do not explicitly deal with the issue, their work implicitly represents a rejoinder to the neo-elitist critique of pluralism by Bachrach and Baratz.[30] The latter attack pluralistic theories of power for defining the determinants of interest-group success too narrowly. In particular, they severely criticize pluralists like Dahl for focusing on actual decision making and on the resources interests employ to secure their ends while ignoring other characteristics—or, as they prefer to call it, "other faces of power"—that determine the success or failure of groups. As noted earlier, Bachrach and Baratz insist that the mobilization of bias within a community is a second face of power that greatly influences the way in which a society allocates its values.[31]

However, while Bachrach and Baratz repeatedly use the phrase mobilization of bias, they often seem to employ a variety of definitions to explain the term. On the one hand, they argue that mobilization of bias refers to "a set of predominant values, beliefs, and rituals, and institutional procedures ('rules of the game') that operate systematically and consistently to the benefit of certain persons and groups at the expense of others."[32] They seem to be arguing that the general cultural values of a society will undermine the acceptability of some demands while enhancing and legitimizing others; they imply that any group trying to implement changes that go against the grain of these well-entrenched values is not likely to enjoy much political success. As pointed out earlier, mobilization of bias in this sense suggests that the possibility of achieving any radical social change will be minimal indeed. Regardless of what form of democracy society embraces, the political system is bound to be hostile to unconventional ideas that threaten to undo well-established patterns of behavior.

But Bachrach and Baratz often seem to use the phrase mobilization of bias in a much more limited sense to refer to a group's ability to monopolize community symbols in such a way as to exclude the demands of potential opponents. They note that a form of nondecision making occurs when a group "invokes an existing bias of the political system—a norm, precedent, rule or procedure—to squelch a threatening demand or incipient issue."[33] In this sense Bachrach's and Baratz's argument, like that of Cobb and Elder, can be seen as a reformulation of Schattschneider's observation that the group that defines the nature of the debate will usually emerge victorious. If a group succeeds in monopolistically defining the stakes involved in a dispute, it may be able to drive a wedge between its adversaries while consolidating its own ties with other strategically placed interests. The important question is whether this tactic can be used only to the advantage of conservatively oriented groups.

While Bachrach and Baratz seem to argue that status quo groups will try to use the symbols of the larger society to prevent marginal interests from placing their demands on the public agenda, Cobb and Elder suggest that this tactic may not always succeed. Unlike Bachrach and Baratz, Cobb and Elder contend that there is plenty of slack in the political system to accommodate a diverse array of demands if groups only learn how to dramatize their requests properly.[34] If marginal interests challenge established political norms, they are likely to fail; but if they attempt to couch their demands in terms of more conventional political symbolism, they may be able to achieve a considerable degree of success. For example, in their study of the grape strike, Cobb and Elder note that once Cesar Chavez tried to identify the cause of migrant workers with the goals of organized labor as well as with the civil rights movement, he began to receive considerable moral and financial support from such diverse groups as the AFL-CIO, the Catholic church, and the liberal wing of the Democratic party. By carefully articulating his objectives and expanding the nature of his goals, Chavez was able to enlist the efforts of more established reform interests, which provided the margin of influence his union needed to negotiate successfully with the grape growers. While the symbols of the larger political system may be used by status quo groups to prevent social change, they may—as Cobb and Elder have shown— also be used by marginal interests to institute reform.

The Influence of Government Structure

If laissez-faire pluralists like Dahl stress the noncumulative nature of resources while others like Cobb and Elder focus on the manner in which groups articulate their goals, still others—like Sayre and Kaufman and, to a lesser extent, Banfield—emphasize the structure of government decision making to account for the behavior of the political system. [35] In their study of New York City, Sayre and Kaufman argue that the decentralized nature of the city's decision-making process explains its receptivity to a diverse array of demands. They insist that since there are so many stages at which key decisions are made, no groups can easily be shut out of the political process. If an interest is denied access at one center of decision making, it has numerous other points at which it may try to place its demands on the public agenda. [36] Regardless of how many resources a group possesses, it is likely to be more active in the political process if it perceives numerous opportunities to influence the formulation of public policy. Banfield makes a similar argument in his classic study of Chicago to account for the widespread participation by interest groups in the affairs of Cook County. [37] Banfield notes that despite the attempts of the city machine to centralize power, there are numerous points at which various interests can intervene in the political process. Thus the price a group must pay to publicize its wishes is anything but prohibitive. Because a decentralized style of decision making reduces the costs an interest must incur to participate in the policy-making process, a group is always likely to find some forum to dramatize its requests even though it possesses minimal political or economic resources.

Conversely, as Sayre and Kaufman point out, when the formal authority of a political system is decentralized, it becomes prohibitively costly for any one group to try to shut out the demands of competing interests. In the case of New York City, Sayre and Kaufman observe that at every stage of the policy-making process a variety of "core" and "satellite" groups seem to share responsibility for making public decisions. Depending on the particular issue at hand, different core or government groups bargain and negotiate with a wide assortment of satellite, or private interest groups. In place of one centrally directed political system, there are a whole series of decision-making points at which various core and satellite interests share in the formulation of specific and limited policy issues. [38]

Sayre and Kaufman also argue that a decentralized pattern of decision making tends to facilitate a style of resolving disputes that guarantees at least some minimal benefits to all interests. They note that when power is fragmented, it is often easier for groups to veto proposals than to initiate change. [39] To enact a modification in existing policy, a group must try to form coalitions of similar interests in order to overcome its opponents, or it must be willing to grant some concessions and side payments to those groups which will be affected by the change. The more decentralized the structure of decision making, the greater the chances that the group that wants to satisfy its demands will be willing to grant compensatory benefits to aggrieved interests. As Sayre and Kaufman point out, every decision of importance in New York must be the product of mutual accommodation. Even though interest groups can put together coalitions strong enough to override the wishes of their opposition, the fragmentation of governmental authority provides the losing interest with enough residual power to extract some minimal compensation from the victorious party.

The Limitations of Laissez-faire Pluralism

Laissez-faire pluralists thus insist that whether one focuses on (1) the resources of groups, (2) the symbols they employ to justify their requests, or (3) the actual structure of government decision making, there seems to be sufficient reason for believing that a variety of interests have both the opportunity and the inclination to exercise influence over the shape of public policy.

However, even though laissez-faire pluralists cite numerous examples to substantiate their claim that the political system is receptive to many diverse demands, their findings are open to criticism. First of all, it is necessary to keep in mind that pluralists like Dahl or Sayre and Kaufman have primarily shown that no single elite influences all public decisions. But to demonstrate that multiple parties have some power to influence crucial policy issues is not the same as to prove that marginal groups like the poor or so-called public interest groups can likewise play an important role in the political arena. If one can find several examples of numerous groups participating in the formulation of public decisions, one can easily argue the negative case that the political system is not a closed entity catering only to the needs of a particular few. But to argue in a positive vein that marginal interests do in fact wield influence is a slightly more difficult task. If we wish to maintain that the polity is receptive to the needs of many groups, we need to recognize that there are varying degrees of openness and receptivity. A system that is open to the demands of labor unions and business organizations may not be equally open to the demands of the poor or consumers who wish to complain about the behavior of more established interests. Except for Cobb and Elder, most of the pluralists we have looked at have cited very few examples of groups like poverty or consumer-related associations that actually exercise any degree of influence.

In order to account for the discrepancies between the conclusions of the laissez-faire pluralists and their actual findings, we need to examine their studies in more detail. In many cases, by using the tools of analysis developed by the laissez-faire pluralists, we can show why marginal groups may have trouble gaining access to the political arena. For instance, Dahl argues that because resources are noncumulatively distributed, every major interest is likely to have some bargaining power. Likewise he points out that because potential power is not the same as actual power, groups that feel intensely enough about an issue can often override the wishes of adversaries who are potentially much more influential. While Dahl's observations about how people use their political resources may be correct, it is possible that they are correct only up to a certain point. If we are talking about unions, for example, we can certainly agree that the sheer number of workers was an effective form of political power that labor employed at the polls to curb the actions of the business community. If, in contrast, we attempt to enumerate the noncumulative resources available to the poor, we have a harder time identifying some countervailing assets they can use to defend their interests. The poor possess neither social standing, nor numerous financial assets, nor great numbers of people. It is true that the ability to disrupt the rest of society is in some sense a form of political power. But it is a type of power that I suspect most laissez-faire pluralists would consider unacceptable as a means of securing one's goals. Riots in most cases reflect a breakdown in the bargaining process rather than an alternative form of interest-group give-and-take. In addition, the ability to disrupt society is a form of power that may have only short-run consequences. Even if the poor can dramatize their needs through periodic riots, they may not be able to secure what Murray Edelman has called "tangible benefits" until they acquire more conventional and dependable political resources. [40] By themselves riots are too diffuse a means for any group to obtain benefits from the rest of society.

Similarly, Dahl may be correct in implying that groups which feel very intensely about a specific issue and commit most of their potential resources to it may wield a considerable amount of actual power. Naturally, if the discrepancies in resources between groups are not immense, the party most willing to use its assets is likely to be victorious. However, when marginal groups, which possess only minimal resources to begin with, expend most of their resources to secure their objectives, they still may not be able to exercise a significant degree of political power. Regardless of how totally a group may commit itself to securing its objectives, it may fail to overcome the advantages of its potentially more powerful adversaries if it has very few assets to draw on in the first place.

We can illustrate yet additional shortcomings in the laissez-faire model by analyzing how the structure of government decision making affects the distribution of political power. Sayre and Kaufman argue that because the political system is fragmented into many separate policy-making centers, no group is ever permanently alienated from the political process. Since no one core group dominates all points of decision making and since interests denied access at one point can choose to go elsewhere, a variety of groups can make their voices heard. While Sayre and Kaufman's analysis merits our serious attention, it is possible that they greatly overstate their case. Whether we confine ourselves to New York, or take a more inclusive look at national politics, there is ample evidence that numerous, as well as fragmented, centers of decision making often tend to shield powerful established interests from the demands of competing groups. For instance, as Marilyn Gittell notes, the school bureaucracy in New York achieved a striking degree of success in insulating itself from the pressures of the mayor's office, the various neighborhoods, civic educational groups, and the then poorly organized teachers' union. [41] By demanding that educational issues be taken out of politics, by eliminating the mayor's right to appoint the new superintendent of schools, and by securing a "lump sum" appropriation from the Board of Estimates, school administrators were able to screen out all demands for educational reform that did not conform to their liking. Gittell's findings do not appear to be an isolated case. Gittell suggests, and even Sayre and Kaufman concede at one point in their book, that other policy areas in New York might be equally closed off from outside pressure. [42] In the various studies of corporate pluralism cited in chapter 2, we find additional examples on the state and national levels of groups successfully fragmenting the policy-making process in order to insulate themselves from external competition.

Although Sayre and Kaufman may be correct in pointing out that no single group makes all the decisions in New York, they overlook the fact that the fragmentation of the decision-making process greatly enhances the ability of core and satellite groups in each separate policy area to disregard the wishes of a great number of interests. The argument that multiple centers of decision making facilitate interest-group participation rests on the assumption that the various decision-making points overlap on certain key policy issues. If, as Gittell shows, the reality of policy making violates this assumption, then it may be easy for key groups to frustrate the wishes of numerous other interests in society. First, when the policy that various groups seek to change is formulated at only one highly specialized and contained decision-making center, there are no incentives for groups denied access at that location to go elsewhere. Secondly, when policies are formulated at separate decision-making points, established interests have the advantage in defining the parameters of any possible disagreement. As we saw in chapter 2, when the decision-making process becomes increasingly specialized, the dominant interest in a field like education or transportation can refuse to consider certain demands that ostensibly fall outside the narrow boundaries of professional education or transit policy.

While Cobb and Elder believe that any group can learn to employ the symbols of the larger political system to advance its own objectives, it is apparent that the structure of government selectively benefits some interests while working to the disadvantage of others. By its very nature a fragmented style of decision making hinders reform groups from enlarging the number of participants in any specific policy domain and upsetting the existing distribution of power. As issues become narrowed and depoliticized, the power of specialists to decide policy grows progressively greater. Thus instead of opening up the political system, a decentralized form of policy making facilitates the growth of numerous, semiclosed decision-making centers.

Public Pluralism: The Revision of Laissez-Faire Pluralism

If, for the various reasons cited above, the existing political system is not as open as laissez-faire pluralists would have us believe, we need to ask how we can remove some of the obstacles that hinder group participation in the political arena. On the one hand, some groups like poverty or consumer-environmental associations seem to possess inadequate resources to bargain with their adversaries, while on the other hand, the decentralized, fragmented style of much public decision-making tends to maximize the assets at the disposal of more established interests. The various reform programs which I have called public pluralism represent one attempt to open the political system to groups that have previously been denied access. Many of the obstacles to group participation can be minimized by fostering competition and bargaining among units of government. Instead of assuming, as do Sayre and Kaufman, that decentralized centers of policy making will interact with one another, the federal government can consciously try to expand the decision-making arena by building duplication and overlap into the jurisdiction of various governmental bodies. When the responsibilities of public officials crisscross one another, groups denied access at one government forum will have meaningful opportunities to seek redress of grievances from alternative decision-making centers. Only such a system of policy making, which actively seeks to build checks and balances into the deliberative process, will afford marginal or consumer groups a reasonable chance of competing with more powerful adversaries. As James Madison noted years ago, the larger the political arena and the more numerous the points at which groups can make themselves heard, the harder it becomes for any one element in society to monopolize the decision-making process.

Secondly, and even more importantly, the federal government must also offer direct assistance to marginal or reform interests that possess only minimal resources of their own. There are a variety of institutional measures that can be undertaken to improve the bargaining position of reform-oriented associations that presently enjoy little or no power. For instance, the federal government has recently established a Consumer Product Safety Commission to test products that consumer groups feel are defective. Such an agency can significantly reduce the expenses imposed on consumers for investigating questionable practices of business organizations. Similarly, Congress could seek to institute changes in the legal code so that private organizations like Ralph Nader's could more easily bring class action suits against firms they suspect of engaging in dubious practices. Likewise, the federal government can try to help poverty associations and public interest groups gain entry into the political arena by continuing to stipulate that there be participation by a cross-section of the larger population in the planning and implementation of all federal programs. By altering the legal rules that regulate the interaction among different kinds of interest publics, government officials could go a long way toward reducing the discrepancies in resources that various groups now enjoy.

Finally, the federal government can also act as a direct advocate for potential groups like the poor through the continued support of organizations such as Vista and OEO. If the government provides low-income citizens with the resources to become organized and the legal right to participate in the planning and implementation of federal policies, it can make sure that the bargaining process is more representative of the diverse interests in society.

A logical question to ask, however, is whether such a policy is ever likely to succeed. As pointed out earlier, there is a long tradition of federal assistance to associations such as labor unions and farm groups, which at one time or another have been excluded from the decision-making process. Commentators like Grant McConnell and Theodore Lowi, who have closely studied public efforts to increase the influence of the above groups, believe that such government activities have been quite effective in achieving their objectives. Indeed, in *Private Power and American Democracy,* McConnell asserts that the federal government has been and can be a powerful advocate for potential groups if it decides to throw its financial and legal resources behind them. Nevertheless, despite impressive evidence that the government has enjoyed considerable success in increasing the political clout of many groups, a number of critics continue to doubt whether public efforts to mobilize indigents will result in any significant social change.

This is not to say that all observers believe programs like OEO will be unable to enhance the power of the poor. Patrick Moynihan and, to a lesser extent, James Sundquist insist that agencies like OEO were almost too successful in helping the poor to mobilize and gain access to the decision-making table. [43] Ironically enough, while some critics believe that pluralism is too status quo oriented to bring about any degree of social reform, Moynihan argues just the opposite about a public form of pluralism. Reviewing the early Community Action Programs, or CAPs, he notes that in several cities intense factional battles broke out when the government attempted to organize the poor in self-help projects. In contrast to those who assert that OEO programs have been too conservative, Moynihan implies that they have been far too radical and disruptive in their attempt to redistribute power and resources to the poor. Quoting Arthur Schlesinger's observation that John Kennedy had "an acute and anguished sense of the fragility of the membranes of civilization, stretched so thin over a nation so disparate in its composition," he maintains that government efforts to mobilize the poor jeopardized the political health of the country by attempting to alter existing social relationships too drastically and too rapidly. [44]

Although Moynihan's pronouncements reflect a genuine concern for the stability of the political system, his assessment of OEO appears premature since his evidence is based on only a few cases that occurred in the formative years of OEO. He overlooks the fact that the politics of pluralism in providing access to a new interest may be very different from the politics of pluralism once a new group is firmly established in the political arena. As James Sundquist notes in his study *Making Federalism Work*, many cities often felt overwhelmed by the demands of OEO in its earliest years but much of their hostility to Community Action Programs soon dissipated, as the poor became incorporated into the decision-making arena as just another interest group. [45] In fact, as Moynihan even admits, many mayors had concluded by 1967 that if community action agencies did not exist, they would have to be invented, since OEO played an important liaison role in linking together the mayor's office and the often tense inner city. [46] Thus to properly assess public pluralism's ability to institute social and political change, we need to evaluate it both before and after new groups have gained access to the bargaining table.

While Moynihan argues that OEO has been too successful in enhancing the power of the poor, other critics like Lowi maintain that OEO's accomplishments have been more symbolic than substantive in nature. Lowi criticizes government efforts to organize the poor on the grounds that such programs result in the cooptation of community leaders in the ghetto. The problem according to Lowi is that the masses of poor will be the recipients of only minor policy changes because the leaders of Community Action Programs will use their position to enhance their own careers rather than to ameliorate the economic and political situation of their followers. He implies that the officials of poverty programs will tend to es-

chew radical proposals since the continued existence of their position in Community Action Programs is dependent on maintaining
favorable ties with political higher-ups.

In spite of Lowi's cynicism about the willingness of poverty
leaders to fight for improved conditions for the poor, it is debatable
how many leaders in the poverty program were coopted by their
political adversaries. J. David Greenstone and Paul E. Peterson
have found in one of the most detailed and exhaustive studies of
Community Action Programs that leaders were often genuinely
concerned with advancing the interests of their constituents. They
note that

> the elites can win mass support necessary for success only if the institutions
> they build serve some of the economic, political, or cultural needs which
> prove appealing to the black community. And significantly enough, in
> Detroit and New York, where participation was greatest, black leaders
> focused their attention on bringing additional institutions—Model Cities
> programs, schools, housing bureaucracies, and the welfare system—under
> greater client and community influence. [47]

Similarly, Ralph Kramer finds little evidence in his study of five
CAPs in the San Francisco Bay area to indicate that poverty leaders
sought to advance their own interests rather than those of their
constituents. He notes that "although the belief was widespread in
many Oakland advisory committees that their representatives to
the OEDC (Oakland Economic Development Council) had 'sold
out,' there were surprisingly few instances where cooptation was
clearly evident." Kramer admits that "the target area representatives were 'different' from their membership in being among the
more able, ambitious, and articulate persons in these groups" and
that "their experience . . . [in CAP] often enhanced their organizational skills." But he goes on to argue that "whether they were
selected on a rather casual basis, as in Oakland, or by means of
a series of 'elections,' as in Santa Clara, the target area representatives . . . did not seem to separate themselves in any substantial
way from their members." [48] Sar Levitan and Robert Taggart make
the same point in their review of Johnson's poverty programs.
They maintain that "community participation was not substantial
in terms of election turnouts or influence on the boards of com-

munity-based organizations," yet they insist that "these organizations generally did represent their constituencies."[49]

If Lowi believes that Community Action Programs were designed to pacify the leaders of OEO—a charge that is not completely substantiated by the evidence—other critics maintain that government efforts to mobilize low-income individuals were designed to induce quiescence among the majority of the poor. Peter Marris and Martin Rein, as well as Frances Fox Piven and Richard Cloward, suggest that government efforts to organize indigents were intended to appease the poor rather than to institute significant reforms that would substantially improve their well-being. As a result, OEO's accomplishments were more symbolic than substantive in nature. By bringing the poor into the policy-making arena, the political system could socialize them into the necessity of making incremental changes and thus defuse any radical proposals for altering social relationships.[50]

This is not to suggest, however, that the poor were not able to squeeze some tangible benefits out of the polity. Piven and Cloward note that OEO was instrumental in securing more welfare benefits for thousands of people in the black ghetto. By providing the poor with the financial assets they needed to organize themselves, the federal government enabled ghetto residents to bargain and negotiate with local welfare boards over the decisions they perceived to be detrimental to their interests. Similarly, Piven and Cloward would no doubt agree with Sundquist's findings that Community Action Programs were often highly successful in forcing state employment agencies to launch outreach programs to identify potentially employable people in the ghetto.[51] Prior to the establishment of the poverty program, most state agencies had played a passive role, merely passing on information from business firms to unemployed persons who happened to visit their offices. When Community Action groups were established, pressure was placed on employment bureaus to play a more positive role in reducing the ranks of the unemployed poor. As the federal government began to finance the operations of thousands of Community Action centers across the nation, the poor acquired an advocate agency that would bargain on their behalf with other government bureaus.

The important question, however, is whether these reforms significantly advanced or retarded other efforts to bring about major political and economic changes. Piven and Cloward maintain that these policies were merely minor tactical concessions the government agreed to in order to shore up the political order and undermine the need for more far-reaching social change. In their provocative book *Regulating the Poor* they argue that in politically unstable times the government expands its welfare activities in order to mollify the demands of restive citizens in large urban ghettos. [52] The poverty program of the late 1960s played its part in stabilizing the political system by speeding up the expansion of the welfare rolls and inducing quiescence among the poor. Likewise, by stressing the participation of indigents in the decision-making process, OEO provided low-income citizens with a symbolic stake in the political system, which undoubtedly had a moderating effect on their demands for further economic and social reform. According to Piven and Cloward, the inclusion of marginal groups in the bargaining process is an effective strategy through which the political system consciously or unconsciously maintains the existing distribution of power. Granting access to the bargaining table serves as a means of forestalling, rather than furthering, a significant reallocation of society's scarce resources.

While Piven and Cloward are extremely critical of government efforts to organize the poor, it is questionable whether the record of OEO completely substantiates all of their conclusions. We must recognize that in an organization as large as OEO, which had thousands of community action agencies, there were numerous successes as well as failures. We must also keep in mind that until recently, most of the studies of OEO focused on Community Action Programs in their first year or two of operation, when they inevitably experienced the troublesome birth pangs of any newly established organization. Despite the mixed nature of much of the data, there is considerable evidence to indicate that in many communities OEO significantly advanced the interests of lower-income individuals. After reviewing the relevant literature on the topic, Levitan and Taggart conclude that

the products of the Great Society's community-based programs are significant. A variety of clearly useful services were provided: child care, preschool education, vocational training, health care, narcotics treatment, and on and on. The innovations and institutional changes resulting from community participation and control were of lasting significance. CAP and Model Cities were the precursors of the contemporary movement for greater governmental responsiveness, more direct forms of citizen involvement in local public affairs, and the decentralization of municipal government. [53]

They also point out that CAPs and Model Cities had high "target efficiencies." [54] Services were focused on the poor and near poor or were restricted to poverty neighborhoods. In contrast to the critics, they insist, "if employment services, schools, or other established agencies had initiated similar operations, it is doubtful that minorities and the poor would have fared as well." [55] Levitan and Taggart also argue that OEO had other benefits such as identifying and developing leaders, like Kenneth Gibson, the black mayor of Newark, who are now active in minority communities. Moreover, Levitan and Taggart stress the fact that "community action must be credited with increasing the responsiveness of delivery agents to client needs." While they concede that "there may be less than 'maximum feasible participation' in decision making," they point out that the poor "have a much greater voice than in the past." [56]

Not surprisingly, however, assessments of OEO vary from city to city as well as from author to author. Walter Grove and Herbert Costner maintain that OEO's efforts to build an association of the poor have been a failure in Seattle; [57] while in contrast, Bachrach and Baratz conclude that "federal programs and federal funds have been the main means, directly or indirectly, by which the black poor have gained a foothold" in Baltimore. [58] Greenstone and Peterson argue that in the cities of New York and Detroit "some power redistribution occurred as low-income and minority groups gained representation on city and neighborhood poverty councils and managed to influence the operations of various governmental bureaus." [59] Likewise, Kramer concludes that the five California CAPs that he analyzed "demonstrated some ability to bring about minor adjustments and modifications in environmental conditions." [60] He finds that OEO displayed the highest degree of effectiveness in Santa Clara County, where the local Community Action Program "became another center of power . . . largely representative of the interests of Mexican-Americans and some of the poor."[61] The Santa Clara poverty groups engaged in mild forms of social action and were particularly successful in influencing major policies in public housing. Among other things they "persuaded the San Jose City Council to adopt a rent subsidy program . . . and also influenced the County Board of Supervisors to establish a public housing authority."[62]

In yet another study of CAPs in fifty cities, Barss, Rietzel, and Associates conclude that "changes directly credited to CAP have tended to be auxiliary in nature," but they add that "these changes may be meaningful first steps towards a basic reordering of these institutions to provide more substantial satisfaction to the needs of the poor."[63] Kenneth Clark and Jeannette Hopkins likewise find a mixed picture of success and failure in their study of ten CAPs, concluding that three programs are definite failures, three others are still in an unclear state of evolution, and four appear to be relatively effective.[64] Finally, an internal analysis of CAPs by OEO substantiates Sundquist's early findings that poverty groups have significantly changed the employment practices of state and local governments and of private employers and have also made many government services more accessible to the poor.[65]

However, the nagging issue still remains as to whether the above successes of OEO are purely symbolic in content. We can certainly argue that numerous Community Action Programs initiated a variety of important structural reforms that have materially benefitted lower-class citizens. The alterations OEO secured in such diverse fields as welfare, housing, and government employment practices are substantial reforms in the sense that they not only have improved the well-being of the poor in the short run but also have increased the long-range opportunities for lower-income individuals to climb out of the ranks of the poor. Why, then, do critics such as Piven and Cloward insist that such benefits are merely symbolic reforms that do not actually enhance the overall conditions of the poor?

Perhaps one reason is that the manner in which they have formulated their point precludes any meaningful test of their thesis. Piven's and Cloward's argument is seductive in that it can explain every government response in simple, unequivocal terms regardless of the scope of the government's activities or the intentions of its planners. Nowhere, it should be stressed, do Piven and Cloward explicitly state the standards for determining when a program such as OEO has achieved a purely symbolic, as opposed to meaningful, reform. To use Karl Popper's terminology, they have formulated a hypothesis about the government's poverty program that seems difficult to falsify.[66] If there is a criterion implicit in Piven's and Cloward's argument for gauging to what extent a poverty program is symbolic, it is perhaps whether or not such public efforts have had a pacifying effect on the poor. Piven and Cloward suggest that the federal government mobilized the poor and undertook temporary ameliorative action in order to induce quiescence among a restive population. But if the presence or absence of vocal dissent is the standard they wish to use, it is not a very good indicator of whether or not a particular program is symbolic. The evidence indicating that the turmoil surrounding CAPs eventually died down may reflect the fact that in many communities the poor had finally become vested as another participant in the bargaining process with a claim to a certain share of the community's resources. As noted earlier, the actions of a group seeking to become incorporated into the polity may be very different from the actions of a group that has already secured a role within the political system. The absence of strife in the late 1960s—which Piven and Cloward believe is a sign of the government's success in temporarily buying off the poor—may instead reflect the success that indigents and minority members achieved in acquiring membership in various local communities.

Secondly, Piven and Cloward often seem guilty of failing to distinguish between the pace at which CAPs have sought to bring about social change and the goals which they have attempted to realize. Greenstone and Peterson, Levitan and Taggart, and Kramer note that many poverty associations have tried to greatly expand opportunities afforded their constituents in the areas of employment, housing, and education. Greenstone and Peterson stress the fact that in the cities of Detroit and New York, black leaders have focused their attention on bringing numerous public services, such as housing and schools, under greater client and community influence. If programs like OEO were designed to coopt the poor, they seem to have had little success in dissuading low-income individuals from seeking significant changes in the services they receive. Admittedly, Community Action Programs have often sought to achieve these objectives in an incremental fashion, but we must not confuse the pace at which they have tried to facilitate change with the content of the goals they wish to achieve.

Even in those cases in which the poor have secured only the formal right to be consulted by public officials, we must refrain from glibly concluding that the victory of Community Action Programs is meaningless. All too often Piven and Cloward fail to see that even symbolic victories may have long-range, beneficial consequences for the poor. As noted earlier, Bachrach and Baratz suggest that the political symbols of a community may in part determine which grievances of the population become the subject of public debate and which are ignored or neglected. It is possible that even in cases where CAPs did not result in immediate or significant benefits for lower-income individuals, they were still effective in altering the bureaucratic view of the poor as passive subjects who need to be catered to in a paternalistic fashion. By the end of the 1960s, it certainly seemed apparent that OEO had helped change the mobilization of bias previously prevalent in many communities by sanctioning and legitimizing the right of the poor to have a say in the formulation and implementation of government services. Even when public officials were opposed to transferring power or resources to indigents, they increasingly had to operate in a political system that legally and culturally sanctioned more intensive citizen participation—including that of the poor—in a wide assortment of government activities. OEO had definitely helped move the issue of poverty from the status of a nondecision to that of a central issue facing American communities. While not all CAPs have immediately improved the well-being of the poor, they nonetheless have insured that the invisible poor of the 1950s, whom Michael Harrington dubbed "the other Americans," are now a very visible part of the political scene.

But even more importantly, we should recognize that Piven's and Cloward's assessment of OEO's success is colored by their normative belief concerning the proper share of the nation's resources that the poor ought to receive. While the issue of whether government assistance can help the poor gain a meaningful voice in policy deliberations is an empirical one, Piven's and Cloward's normative values are bound to influence their view of whether the poor are securing an adequate, and therefore nonsymbolic, share of society's benefits. Although we have no definite statement of their theory of social justice, it can be surmised that they favor an extensive redistribution of power and wealth among various segments of the population. Implicit in their writing is the belief that a more egalitarian society with few if any differentials in wealth is inherently more just. Piven and Cloward have a tendency to minimize the accomplishments of poverty programs that do not bring the political system substantially closer to this egalitarian ideal. However, if one believes that the poor are entitled to a decent, rather than exactly equal, share of society's resources, then one must be inclined to view OEO's achievements in a more favorable light. In too many cases OEO's critics have had such high normative expectations of what government efforts to mobilize the poor should accomplish that they have often needlessly deprecated the results of Community Action Programs.

Finally, Piven's and Cloward's attacks on OEO can be criticized on simple tactical and strategic grounds. Their work raises the important issue of whether low-income individuals would have fared better if there had been no government efforts to mobilize the poor. Inherent in their argument is the assumption that if minority members had been left to their own accord, they would have militantly fought for more significant changes in the present make-up of society.[67] But as pointed out in the previous chapter, without some outside assistance, low-income people are likely to experience difficulty in organizing and in gaining access to important centers of decision making. It is difficult to see how the poor without the help of Community Action Programs could ever become active members of a militant coalition that would seek radical changes. And even if they were able to become organized, it is also debatable whether any such coalition would have much success in influencing important policy decisions. As Moynihan has pointed out, severe attacks on existing groups or existing forms of decision making are bound to elicit intense and hostile reaction from those interests that feel threatened. In contrast, if the poor can be established as a legitimate group in the bargaining process, they can seek reforms in a fashion that will not threaten opposing interests and therefore not jeopardize their long-range chances of success. The initial problem, however, is to make sure that blacks and low-income citizens are duly represented in the pluralistic process of group bargaining.

Thus instead of debating whether low-income people will disrupt the political system or be coopted by it once they achieve access to the bargaining table, we must ask what conditions will facilitate the incorporation of the poor into the bargaining process as a legitimate interest group. One of the best studies to look at in accounting for the uneven impact of Community Action Programs is Greenstone's and Peterson's description of the poverty programs in New York, Detroit, Philadelphia, Los Angeles, and Chicago.[68] In a rather complicated analysis they insist that a variety of factors, including local elite attitudes toward OEO, were of crucial importance in determining the relative success of different poverty programs. Greenstone and Peterson maintain that the inclinations of political officials, and especially the attitude of the mayor, were a significant factor in deciding whether the poor actually wielded power in Community Action Programs. In New York and Detroit, the two cities in which CAP was judged most successful, Mayors Lindsay and Cavanagh were strong supporters of OEO efforts to mobilize the poor. In contrast, in Chicago, where Mayor Daley was determined to see that OEO did not stir up black neighborhoods, the municipal administration succeeded in imposing its will on the activities of the local poverty program. According to Greenstone and Peterson, unless the poor can establish a mutually supportive coalition with public officials at the top, they are not likely to become permanently vested as legitimate members of the decision-making process.[69]

However, as Greenstone and Peterson also argue, the lack of executive support need not always be fatal. Depending on the allies CAPs can enlist to help fight their battles or on the tactics they use, they may still be able to secure important concessions for their constituents. In addition, Greenstone and Peterson insist that the mechanism by which Community Action Programs relied to choose representatives of the poor had a significant impact on their subsequent behavior. Representatives of the poor who decided the policy of local OEO councils were chosen in one of three ways: (1) appointment by local city administrators, (2) selection by the poor in special elections, or (3) appointment by local neighborhood groups in poverty districts. As should be expected, representatives chosen by municipal officials were often reluctant to pursue policies that might antagonize the existing city administration. However, representatives of the poor who had won special elections often sought very particularistic goals for their neighborhoods and avoided more universal goals that might have benefited all poor or minority members. In elections that lacked well-organized groups, candidates tended to run on a "friends and neighbors" platform. Thus if any local poverty leaders were likely to be coopted or satisfied by the acquisition of limited and parochial objectives, they were the ones chosen through special elections. In contrast, Community Action representatives who were selected by neighborhood groups tended to seek more universalistic goals that affected whole categories of people. Greenstone and Peterson observe that Community Action personnel in New York, who were appointed by local groups, "tried to organize the local population on behalf of causes which might benefit all neighborhood residents."[70]

The reasons for the differences in behavior are difficult to specify, but Greenstone and Peterson suggest that when various groups in the ghetto could appoint members to poverty councils, the members often competed with one another for larger community support. "Competition for power within the community forced the competing leaderships to justify the appeal for community support by representing broad community interests."[71] Even though the constellation of forces supportive of or opposed to an active Community Action Program initially determined the manner in which representatives of the poor were selected, the selection process itself also seems to have had an independent impact on the success or failure of subsequent OEO activities. Thus if the supporters of OEO had drafted their legislation more carefully to stipulate how the representatives of the poor were to be chosen, Community Action Programs might have been even more successful in overcoming the intransigence of those city mayors opposed to increased participation by low-income citizens. As Greenstone and Peterson point out, had Mayor Daley been forced to allow community organizations to control the appointments to local poverty councils, he might not have been as successful in hindering their organizational activities.

While the above findings are based on a detailed study of Community Action Programs in only five cities, they are nonetheless significant in that they suggest that under the proper conditions the federal government can help marginal groups to gain access to important centers of decision making and to secure tangible benefits for themselves. This is not to say that public efforts to mobilize the poor will be easy. Altering the political system by institutionalizing the poor as another group in the decision-making process is bound to be a difficult and time-consuming task. But as was the case with many other groups (like the Farm Bureau and the CIO) that received government assistance, the poor appear to have made important strides in gaining access to the bargaining table as a legitimate interest group.

The Alternatives Reevaluated

On the basis of the above discussion we can argue that a pluralistic form of decision making need not work to the disadvantage of either marginal or consumer-environmental groups. By the government's undertaking certain institutional changes in the way present policies are made, it is possible that marginal interests may acquire a significant voice in the political system. But even if none of the above measures were instituted, there are other reasons for believing that a pluralistic sysem offers more opportunities for reform groups to secure their objectives than do alternative forms of democracy. Instead of simply defending pluralism against the charge that it necessarily excludes marginal interests like the poor, we can make the counterargument that pluralism may in fact be the most feasible method for marginal groups to acquire influence over public policy.

First of all, it should be pointed out that polyarchists are interested in restricting, rather than enlarging, public access to the decision-making process. Even among reform polyarchists like Lowi, there is a belief that elites, perhaps imbued with a sense of

noblesse oblige, will maximize the resources that accrue to environmental or poverty elements, provided they are given a free hand in
setting public policy. However, there are enormous pitfalls in
allowing elites to enact reforms on behalf of their constituents
without consulting them.[72] While polyarchists have sought to
insulate government officials from outside pressure, participatory
democrats have been very concerned with increasing public access
to the decision-making process. But in order to maximize opportunities for public participation, they have called for the creation of
small political units that make it considerably more difficult for
environmental or poverty groups to gain a redress of their grievances. For by reducing the size of the polity, participatory democrats reduce the amount of resources a community can draw on to
solve problems, such as pollution or poverty, that by their very
nature require a massive commitment of effort and funds. Since
this issue will be dealt with in more detail in chapter 8, the bulk of
this section will be devoted to the third and final alternative, that
of populism.

As mentioned earlier, populists like Harrington believe it is
possible to organize a majoritarian form of democracy that will
support substantial changes in the present economic and political
system. However, while Harrington insists that a sizable portion of
the population will support liberal programs, it remains to be seen
whether such will be the case. As less and less people find themselves below the poverty line, we are likely to find diminished
popular support for programs that are basically redistributive in
nature. For similar reasons we are likely to find only limited popular sentiment for programs that radically alter existing racial balances. Consequently, if decisions are made in a populist fashion,
we might expect minority groups to receive considerably fewer
benefits than they would under a pluralistic form of interest-group
bargaining. As a case in point, we can look once again at Wolfinger's and Greenstein's study of fair housing legislation in California.[73] In 1963 the California legislature passed a fair housing law,
but the majority of citizens nullified this law in a public referendum. Although the legislature was willing to take into account the
intensity of feeling of different segments of society and to strike
compromises among various elements in the community, the larger

population was not of a similar mind. Wolfinger and Greenstein state that in a legislative or administrative arena, where decisions are made in a bargaining fashion, considerations other than the mere quantitative distribution of attitudes are relevant, but in a referendum "compromise is impossible once the issue has been formally posed."[74]

Even if reform groups like the Sierra Club do not elicit popular resistance, they may still fail to achieve their objectives in populist referendums because of their minimal financial resources. When consumer or environmental interests and large business organizations must compete with one another in legislative and bureaucratic arenas, the discrepancy in resources between the two groups can be minimized. However, while any well-organized interest like the Sierra Club can match the lobbying efforts of oil companies, it may not have sufficient funds to inform the public about the necessity of voting in favor of referendum items that will advance environmental causes. An excellent example of this phenomenon can be found in the 1972 California referendum on financing mass transit from the highway trust fund. Through intensive lobbying, environmental interests were initially successful in convincing the legislature to underwrite mass transit with the revenues in the highway trust fund. However, in a statewide referendum, the powerful highway lobby prevailed. Because there was no crystallized majority sentiment on the issue, the public was susceptible to the media campaigns of the two contending parties. Since the highway lobby and the oil companies had more money to publicize their position than the environmentalists, their mass media appeal eventually won over a majority of the populace. What had initially been a victory for the environmental groups in the pluralistic give-and-take of the legislative arena turned into a defeat once the results of the state's populist referendum were tabulated. While lack of funds had not crippled a well-organized environmental interest in a legislative setting, it had proven fatal in a campaign to persuade the public at large.

Finally, even if it were possible to persuade a majority of citizens to support environmental propositions on referendums, their votes might prove to be highly ineffective in stopping pollution, while the demands of smaller and more tightly organized groups, like

Nader's Raiders, might produce greater results. The reason for this possible difference in impact is related to the way government programs are administered. As Edelman has convincingly argued in *The Symbolic Uses of Politics*, bureaucrats usually engage in mutual role taking vis-a-vis the various parties with which they constantly have to deal. [75] Officials are not likely to be sensitized to the demands of the public, since the groups they bargain with are a constant reality while the general public is much more remote. Thus if voters make diffuse demands on bureaucrats for tightening up pollution standards, they are likely to receive symbolic, rather than tangible, benefits. Similarly, as Raymond Bauer, Ithiel de Sola Pool, and Lewis Dexter have noted in their study of tariff policy, government officials often have difficulty knowing how to implement diffuse calls for reform. [76] When bureaucrats face amorphous appeals for lowering tariffs as opposed to specific demands for raising duties on certain hard-hit commodities, they are likely to accede to the latter. If consumer oriented groups want to achieve specific, tangible gains, they need to bargain on a semipermanent basis with the relevant public officials. Until the consumer-environmental movement becomes a consistent participant in the concrete deliberations of the FTC and EPA, these agencies are likely to lack the information—as well as the incentives—to view problems from the viewpoint of the consumer. Regardless of how many people support referendums to protect consumer interests, their efforts are likely to be frustrated at the administrative level unless they pursue their objectives in a concrete, pluralistic fashion.

Thus pluralism's critics insist that "the pluralistic heaven . . . sings with a strong upper-class accent," but in reality it may contain a variety of melodies. Even though certain groups may face a difficult time gaining access to the bargaining table in a laissez-faire model of pluralism, they will have a greater opportunity to air their grievances under a system of public pluralism. With government assistance, any chorus can come to reflect the diverse accents prevalent in the larger society.

NOTES

1. Elmer Eric Schattschneider, *The Semi-Sovereign People;* Peter Bachrach and Morton S. Baratz, *Power and Poverty;* Peter Bachrach and

Morton S. Baratz, "Decisions and Nondecisions," pp. 641-51; Peter Bachrach and Morton S. Baratz, "Two Faces of Power," pp. 947-52.

2. Schattschneider, *Semi-Sovereign People*, p. 35.

3. Ibid.

4. Bachrach and Baratz, *Power and Poverty*, p. 18.

5. Robert Paul Wolff, Barrington Moore, Jr., and Herbert Marcuse, *A Critique of Pure Tolerance*, pp. 3-53.

6. Wolff in particular fails to make this distinction; see ibid., pp. 3-53. See also Donald Hanson, "What Is Living and What Is Dead in Liberalism," p. 25.

7. Roger W. Cobb and Charles Elder, *Participation in American Politics*, pp. 1-36.

8. Herbert McClosky, "Consensus and Ideology in American Politics," pp. 361-382; Gabriel Almond and Sidney Verba, *The Civic Culture*, pp. 337-74.

9. Charles Lindblom, *The Intelligence of Democracy*, pp. 165-81.

10. See Hanna F. Pitkin, *The Concept of Representation*, for an alternative view.

11. Wolff, Moore, and Marcuse, *Critique of Pure Tolerance*, p. 46.

12. Lindblom, *Intelligence of Democracy*, pp. 226-65; Robert Dahl, *A Preface to Democratic Theory*, pp. 34-62.

13. Lindblom, *Intelligence of Democracy*, pp. 246-65.

14. Theodore J. Lowi, "American Business, Public Policy, Case Studies, and Political Theory," p. 690.

15. Ibid., p. 690.

16. Ibid., p. 691.

17. Robert Dahl, *Who Governs?*; Cobb and Elder, *Participation in American Politics*; Wallace Sayre and Herbert Kaufman, *Governing New York City*; Edward C. Banfield, *Political Influence*.

18. Dahl, *Preface to Democratic Theory*, p. 145.

19. Sayre and Kaufman, *Governing New York City*, p. 720.

20. See Grant McConnell, *Private Power and American Democracy*; Theodore J. Lowi, *The End of Liberalism*; Martha Derthick, *The Influence of Federal Grants*.

21. In particular see Harry Eckstein, *Pressure Group Politics*, pp. 15-39.

22. Dahl, *Who Governs?*, p. 305.

23. Ibid., pp. 85-88.

24. Ibid., pp. 270-75.

25. Ibid., pp. 270-75.

26. Ibid., pp. 192-99.

27. Schattschneider, *Semi-Sovereign People*, pp. 1-40.

28. Cobb and Elder, *Participation in American Politics*, pp. 82-110.

29. Ibid., pp. 94-110.

30. Bachrach and Baratz, *Power and Poverty*.

31. Ibid., p. 43.

32. Ibid., p. 43.

33. Ibid., p. 45.

34. Cobb and Elder, *Participation in American Politics*, pp. 67-71.

35. Sayre and Kaufman, *Governing New York City;* Banfield, *Political Influence.*

36. Sayre and Kaufman, *Governing New York City*, p. 712.

37. Banfield, *Political Influence*, pp. 235-85.

38. Sayre and Kaufman, *Governing New York City*, pp. 710-14.

39. Ibid., p. 714.

40. Murray Edelman, *The Symbolic Uses of Politics.*

41. Marilyn Gittell, *Participants and Participation.*

42. Ibid., pp. 24-100; Sayre and Kaufman, *Governing New York City,* pp. 714-16.

43. Daniel P. Moynihan, *Maximum Feasible Misunderstanding,* p. 70; James L. Sundquist, *Making Federalism Work,* pp. 32-60.

44. Moynihan, *Maximum Feasible Misunderstanding,* p. 193.

45. Sundquist, *Making Federalism Work*, pp. 60-80.

46. Moynihan, *Maximum Feasible Misunderstanding*, pp. 156-57.

47. J. David Greenstone, and Paul E. Peterson, *Race and Authority in Urban Politics,* p. 309.

48. Ralph M. Kramer, *Participation of the Poor*, p. 208.

49. Sar A Levitan and Robert Taggart, *The Promise of Greatness,* p. 187.

50. Peter Marris and Martin Rein, *Dilemmas of Social Reform;* Frances Fox Piven and Richard Cloward, *Regulating the Poor.*

51. Sundquist, *Making Federalism Work*, pp. 49-54.

52. Piven and Cloward, *Regulating the Poor.*

53. Levitan and Taggart, *Promise of Greatness,* pp. 185-86.

54. Ibid., p. 173.

55. Ibid., p. 173.

56. Ibid., p. 186.

57. Walter Grove and Herbert Costner, "Organizing the Poor," p. 654.

58. Bachrach and Baratz, *Power and Poverty*, p. 69.

59. Greenstone and Peterson, *Race and Authority in Urban Politics,* p. 5.

60. R. M. Kramer, *Participation of the Poor,* p. 238.

61. Ibid., p. 107.

62. Ibid., p. 102.

63. Barss, Rietzel, and Associates, "Community Action and Institutional Changes," pp. 16-17.

64. Kenneth B. Clark and Jeannette Hopkins, *A Relevant War Against Poverty*, pp. 205-30.

65. Office of Economic Opportunity, Office of Operations, "Utilization Test Survey Data for 591 CAA's."

66. Karl Popper, *The Logic of Scientific Discovery*, pp. 78-92.

67. Greenstone and Peterson, *Race and Authority in Urban Politics*, pp. 304-15.

68. Ibid., pp. 304-15.

69. Ibid., pp. 229-60.

70. Ibid., p. 181.

71. Ibid., p. 183.

72. See chapter 3 above, pp. 52-53.

73. Raymond Wolfinger and Fred Greenstein, "The Repeal of Fair Housing Legislation in California," pp. 753-69.

74. Ibid., p. 768.

75. Edelman, *Symbolic Uses of Politics*, pp. 44-73.

76. Raymond A. Bauer, Ithiel de Sola Pool, and Lewis Anthony Dexter, *American Business and Public Policy*, pp. 320-30.

Chapter

7

Pluralism and the
Problem of Elitist Groups

Another common criticism of pluralist theory is that groups are dominated by small elites, or *oligarchies*. Disagreeing with David Truman, who claims that groups serve to protect the interests of their members, many observers argue that private associations often enhance the well-being of their officials rather than the rank and file. Henry Kariel maintains there is an internal contradiction within pluralism, for "the voluntary organizations which the early theorists of pluralism relied upon to sustain the individual against a unified government have themselves become oligarchically governed hierarchies."[1] In a similar vein, Grant McConnell criticizes pluralists for disregarding the implications of Robert Michels's famous "iron law of oligarchy." If private associations are to play an important role in politics, we need to ask how they have governed themselves, and in McConnell's eyes, they have not governed themselves well at all.[2]

Because of the frequency of these attacks, it is essential to determine if such harsh criticism of the internal activities of interest groups is actually justified. Before rejecting a pluralistic style of decision making, we need to examine in a more critical fashion the claims of pluralism's detractors. In particular, the argument that an iron law of oligarchy exists raises questions that call for analytic clarification as well as normative and empirical verification. First, in order to assess the contention that interest groups are oligarchical in nature, it is imperative to define analytically what one means by the word *oligarchy.* When scholars like Kariel and McConnell argue that groups are elitist in nature, we need to know whether that means that officials misuse their power to advance their own interests or whether it merely signifies that power is unequally distributed within various organizations. Secondly, when critics maintain that the oligarchical tendency of groups creates an internal contradiction within pluralism, it is essential to stipulate in exactly what way the allegedly elitist nature of groups compromises pluralism or poses a threat to its central tenets. As a normative doctrine, pluralism is adamantly opposed to the leadership of a group abusing the rights of its members, but it does not necessarily see anything wrong with members of a group voluntarily playing a passive role. Thirdly, once we have determined in exactly what sense the oligarchical nature of groups violates pluralistic norms, we need to know whether the alleged iron law of oligarchy of Michels applies to all organizations or whether it applies merely to certain kinds of groups in particular. Finally, we need to ask how any elitist abuses of power that we may find might be curtailed. In particular, it is important to know if a pluralistic form of democracy can contain the misuse of power by group officials without violating its own principles. While Kariel maintains that a pluralistic system of politics is inherently incapable of controlling elite power, this chapter will suggest that his argument stems from a failure to realize that there are different types of pluralism.

Oligarchical Organizations: Variations on a Theme

Analytically it is possible to identify three different conceptions of oligarchical leadership.[3] First, the assertion that groups are run by small elites may mean only that power is differentially, rather than evenly, distributed within an organization. In this sense the charge that groups are run by oligarchies may be a rather mild statement. It indicates merely that whenever organizations develop, so will positions of leadership. This definition of oligarchy does not imply that the leaders of a group are necessarily unresponsive or insensitive to the wishes of the larger membership. On the contrary, an organization may at times concentrate power in the hands of its officials in order to pursue its objectives more effectively vis-a-vis other groups in society.

The word oligarchy is often used in a second sense to suggest that the power of officials is uncontrolled or unchecked. In this case, the presence of elites means not only that power is unevenly distributed but also that it is unrestrained by other elements within the group. In essence the members of the organization have no effective means for directing or blocking the activities of their leaders. But the fact that the leaders of a group may not be accountable to their constituents does not necessarily mean that they will misuse their power; group officials may still look after the interests of their members even though they are relatively immune from rank-and-file pressure.

Finally, a third way in which critics argue that groups are elitist in orientation is to suggest that the leaders use the resources of the group to advance their own interests rather than those of the rank and file. In this case a select few not only (1) wield more power than most members of the organization, but also (2) exercise power unencumbered by the wishes of the rank and file, and most importantly, (3) pursue objectives that often disproportionately benefit the leadership at the expense of the membership. This third conception of oligarchy assumes that the leaders will develop interests distinct from the goals of the larger organization and that they will deliberately choose to exploit the goodwill of the rank and file to further their own objectives.

Unfortunately, when critics like Kariel or McConnell argue that groups are elitist in nature, they often fail to distinguish clearly among these three different definitions of oligarchy. Kariel asserts that the organizations that the early pluralists relied upon to shield the public from arbitrary or capricious government action "have themselves become oligarchically governed hierarchies," yet nowhere does he systematically explicate what he means by this phrase. [4] As a result, his critique of pluralism is not always clearly stated or rigorously developed. At times he seems to be talking about unequal—as opposed to unchecked or misused—power, particularly when he deals with the kinds of large-scale bureaucracies that characterize modern industrial life. Kariel argues that the imperatives of technology have forced organizations to become more centralized and impersonal: "To operate harmoniously and continuously the fully rationalized system of mass production demands . . . a hierarchical apparatus of control which can encompass the continually proliferating parts of the system."[5] In this case the presence of oligarchical leadership results from "seemingly irresistible bureaucratic tendencies in the modern organization."[6] However, this first form of oligarchy is a rather benign form of elitism. To state that an organization is oligarchical in this sense is simply to indicate that the leaders wield disproportionately more power than those who occupy the lower rungs of the hierarchy.

On other occasions, Kariel uses the term oligarchy to signify power that is unchecked as well as unequal. In his description of labor unions, for example, he argues that "the power to make decisions has come to reside in well-protected, self-perpetuating incumbents whose prestige and skill—backed by an extensive staff of professional attorneys, economists, statisticians, writers, and administrators—is such that the rank and file, perhaps gratefully unconcerned, only rarely challenges their word."[7] In this case, the leadership has evolved into our second form of oligarchy, that is, an elite that enjoys a completely free hand in running the affairs of the organization. Kariel notes that elite predominance is facilitated by rank-and-file apathy but in many instances it is also reinforced by institutional arrangements that render mass participation virtually meaningless. In any case, the end result is the same: the membership is transformed into "little more than a massive organ of assent and affirmation."[8]

However, Kariel is somewhat ambiguous when it comes to assessing the consequences of this type of uncontrolled leadership, particularly when he deals with the case of labor unions. On the one hand, he suggests that union officials who are unaccountable to the rank and file inevitably utilize their authority to further their own personal ends; while on the other hand, he implies that these very same leaders often seek to promote the best interests of their constituents. At one point he argues that labor officials have selfish reasons for perpetuating their immunity from rank-and-file control since union leadership provides them with a unique avenue for personal advancement. "The union leader finds himself in a peculiar situation," Kariel asserts. "His stake in office is doubly great since, unlike his counterpart in the business corporation, the loss of his office is likely to be a serious matter for him . . . Unless he has cultivated nonunion business, he must remain attached."[9] Thus "what began as a movement to protect individual members from outsiders [has] generally ended as one to protect the leadership from insiders."[10] However, a short while later, in a slightly different context, Kariel goes on to suggest that labor leaders "are beginning to be exhilarated by the prospects of securing not only readily calculable economic benefits but of guaranteeing the worker self-realization in all phases of his life."[11] Here Kariel clearly implies that union officials do not seek to betray the rank and file for their own self-serving purposes but, on the contrary, seek to further the best interests of their constituents. In short, Kariel fails to make a clear-cut distinction between unchecked power (oligarchy two) and misused power (oligarchy three). While he speaks of oligarchies "interested in advancing their own welfare," nowhere does he systematically distinguish between this kind of elite, which abuses its position for self-seeking ends, and the type that exercises unchecked power but nonetheless acts to promote the well-being of its followers.[12]

Kariel's rather vague usage of the term oligarchy is shared by another prominent critic of pluralism, Grant McConnell. Like Kariel, McConnell rejects a pluralistic theory of democracy on the grounds that groups are elitist in nature, but as is the case with Kariel, he often jumps back and forth between very different conceptions of elitism. McConnell recognizes that power will be unevenly distributed within any large organization "since as a matter of technical necessity direct government by the membership is 'mechanically' impossible" (oligarchy one).[13] But he suggests that the real implication of the term oligarchy is that elites come to wield power for their own particular ends (oligarchy three). Because leaders "engage in different activities and come to enjoy a different status," they will pursue goals that diverge from those of the rank and file. "Leaders tend to identify their own interests with those of the organization and seek to preserve the foundations of their own position, thus laying the foundation for conflict of interests between leaders and led."[14] However, at other times McConnell suggests that oligarchy involves unchecked, rather than misused, power (oligarchy two). "Public governments have a long tradition of grappling with the problem of controlling and limiting power," McConnell argues. "With private associations, however, this tradition has not applied."[15] Here the issue is not whether leaders misuse their authority for private gain but whether there are any institutional restraints on the exercise of that authority. Moreover, the implication is that even though there may not be any meaningful checks and balances governing the internal politics of voluntary associations, such bodies have nonetheless addressed themselves to obtaining benefits for their rank and file.[16]

In his analysis of oligarchy, McConnell relies quite heavily on the work of Michels. "The weight of available evidence on private associations is overwhelmingly on the side of Michels' 'law' of oligarchy," he declares and argues that those who seek to defend an interest-group theory of democracy must come to grips with the implications of this "law."[17] However, it should be noted that Michels himself was often somewhat unclear as to what the phenomenon of oligarchy involved. In his study of the German Social Democratic Party, which has long been cited as the classic work on organizational elitism, Michels utilized the term oligarchy to describe several very different kinds of leadership. On the one hand, he argued that the SPD was oligarchical in nature simply because it was made up of leaders and led (oligarchy one): "organization implies the tendency to oligarchy," he asserted. "As a result of organization, every party or professional union becomes divided into a minority of directors and a majority of directed."[18] On the other hand, he often implied that the SPD was elitist in the sense that the rank and file was incapable of monitoring or checking the activities of its leaders (oligarchy two). Since the working class was made up of apathetic and uninformed individuals who were "incapable of looking after their own interests," the leaders of the SPD were able to run the party as they saw fit.[19] However, on other occasions Michels maintained that the SPD was oligarchical in the sense that its officials had developed goals distinctly different from those of the rank and file (oligarchy three). Many leaders "regarded their position . . . simply as a means for personal advancement" and were more interested in pursuing a conservative policy line that would not jeopardize their status as party officials than they were in fighting for increased benefits for the membership.[20] In arguing that the interests of the leaders of the SPD and their rank and file often diverged, Michels acted on the assumption that the workers were militant revolutionaries whose goals were being thwarted by conservative leadership. This view of the working class departed significantly from his earlier picture of the rank and file as basically inert and apathetic.

To account for this discrepancy, several scholars have argued that Michels often entertained yet another and even more contradictory view of the SPD leadership. In particular, Philip Cook and John May assert that Michels was critical of the SPD because it catered to the expressed wishes of its conservative membership rather than adhering to the Marxian path of militant revolution.[21] Cook insists that Michels wanted party officials to be more responsive to the "true" interests of workers, as defined by the Marxian revolutionary tradition, and less concerned about the actual conscious wishes of the rank and file. Since workers often achieved nothing more than trade union consciousness, it was only natural that leaders who were attuned to their wishes would pursue moderate and conciliatory policies. Ironically enough, Cook implies that Michels's displeasure with the SPD was less a result of the fact that it had developed a closed and self-serving elite than of the fact that it had created an elite responsive to the sentiments of its membership.[22]

The manner in which Kariel, McConnell, and even Michels often unconsciously jump back and forth between very different conceptions of organizational elites suggests the need for caution in glibly attacking the allegedly elitist tendencies of groups. While some groups have elected officials who systematically use the organization for their own benefit, many other so-called elitist groups have not. If we are not careful, however, we may inadvertently place possibly autocratic associations under the same rubric with highly centralized yet responsive interest groups. Even though the term oligarchy can and has been applied to the leadership of many different organizations, it is a word that often conceals more than it reveals.

The Alleged Conflict Within Pluralism

Once we realize that the word oligarchy has various meanings, it is essential to ask in what manner these different forms of elitism constitute a threat to pluralism. While critics like Kariel sometimes appear to suggest that the mere presence of any oligarchical tendencies within groups creates an internal dilemma for pluralism, the question we need to ask is whether the doctrine is prescriptively opposed to all forms of organizational elitism or merely to certain varieties. Obviously, pluralism is normatively opposed to group elites abusing the rights of their members for self-seeking purposes (oligarchy three). If secondary associations are to serve as a mechanism for protecting the interests of the individual, group officials must not be allowed to exploit their rank and file for private gain. However, there is nothing wrong with a set of officials wielding a considerable amount of power within an interest group (oligarchy one). While participatory democrats envision a communal group life in which there is intensive and equal participation by all in the affairs of the organization, pluralists have a much more limited conception of what participation should involve. Pluralists look upon organizations in utilitarian terms as vehicles through which the individual can satisfy certain of his basic personal and political needs. Groups not only can protect individual liberties from unjustified government interference; they also can serve as positive instruments for bringing about changes in existing legislation. But groups need not be *gemeinschaft* organizations in which people participate as an end in and of itself. If the members of a group either are satisfied with the activities of their organization or have competing commitments, it is only natural that they will be willing to grant a considerable degree of latitude to their officers.

While a pluralist would not be opposed to organizational elites in our first sense of the word, he would insist that restrants be placed on the power of group officials. However, pluralism seeks to check the action of group leaders in two different and often antagonistic ways. First of all, provisions must be made for the rank and file to influence the content of a group's policies. As an obvious example, the membership—rather than the officials of a union— should have the final say in deciding whether a union should go on strike, stay on the job, or accept a proposed settlement from management. However, it can also be argued that other groups in society should be able to externally pressure or limit the actions of an association's leadership. The rank and file of any particular group should not have a monopoly on those issues that happen to concern it; the demands of any one group must always be weighed by the demands of competing interests in society. By insisting that the leaders of every interest group be checked in a dual fashion, internally by the association's own membership as well as externally by other organizations, a pluralist recognizes that group officials will often have to play a crucial yet precarious role. The leaders of a group cannot become so committed to the wishes of their members that they refuse to seek out compromises or to bargain in good faith with other groups. Conversely, they must not be so amenable to the wishes of other interests in society that they ignore the needs of their own rank and file. If the officials of organized groups are not significantly influenced by their own membership, the danger of organizations developing oligarchies in either our second or third sense of the word is very real. But if organizational elites do not periodically attempt to influence as well as be influenced by their own membership, they may disrupt the give-and-take of a pluralistic form of bargaining. Rather than being a threat to pluralistic tenets, the presence of an independent set of officials (oligarchy one) may be essential to the smooth functioning of a pluralistic form of democracy.

The Empirical Problem of Oligarchy

While we can thus see that certain kinds of elitism are inimical to pluralism, we must recognize that other varieties are not. Unfortunately, critics of pluralism have often failed to make this distinction and, further, have made assertions about the existence of group elitism without providing substantiating evidence for their claims. In order to make a case against an interest-group theory of politics on the grounds of organizational elitism, pluralism's detractors need (1) to show that the diverse array of groups in society—from labor unions and business associations to public interest groups like Common Cause—are dominated by either our second or third form of oligarchy and (2) to argue convincingly that these kinds of elitism are inevitable and not merely transitional forms of leadership. However, the critics have failed to offer impressive empirical or theoretical reasons for believing that these two conditions are widespread. Many rely more on fragmentary incidents, scattered anecdotes, or appeals to personal knowledge than they do on systematic studies of interest-group behavior. McConnell, for instance, merely asserts that those who are familiar with Michels have "found disturbing corroboration [of the iron law of oligarchy] from their personal experience with many modern American associations."[23] And although he declares that virtually all private associations that "have been made the subject of careful study have to some degree substantiated that 'law,'" he fails to provide any documentation for this assertion.[24] Similarly, Kariel states that the policy-making process is dominated by a "plurality of entrenched oligarchies," but he offers very little empirical evidence to back up this contention.[25] We are merely told that oligarchies have come to prevail in all types of groups. "It would not seem to matter whether an organization is composed of businessmen, industrial workers, farmers, attorneys, or morticians," Kariel alleges, "provided only it is large in scale, complex in its interests, and heterogeneous in its membership. The rights of members to dissent, and to make their dissent effective, are not being habitually exercised."[26]

Kariel and McConnell are not alone in regarding Michels's law of oligarchy as a self-evident proposition. Although a vast body of literature has grown up around the topic of interest groups, very few studies explicitly address the task of testing the validity of this iron law. One of the few exceptions is a study by Seymour Martin Lipset, Martin Trow, and James Coleman of the International Typographical Union, in which they make a systematic attempt to deal with the question of the self-government of trade unions.[27] Generally, however, the major focus of the research on interest groups revolves around their role in the larger political system and their impact on the policy-making process.[28] In a good deal of the literature, Michels's pronouncements concerning the inevitability of oligarchical leadership are simply mentioned in passing or treated as axioms needing no further verification.

Nevertheless, even though many studies of voluntary associations do not systematically deal with the question of oligarchical leadership, it is possible to find data—albeit fragmentary in nature —that suggests the rise of unchecked or misused power is by no means a universal occurrence. The existing body of literature on interest groups provides a good deal of evidence that most organizational leaders do not abuse their positions for their own gain. The same data also indicate that many group officials are often quite responsive to the wishes of their membership and usually advance positions favored by the rank and file. For example, Raymond Bauer, Ithiel de Sola Pool, and Lewis Dexter have observed that the officials of groups like the Chamber of Commerce and the National Association of Manufacturers are usually very solicitous of their members and generally attempt to pursue policies acceptable to all elements in the organization: "Since such organizations represent a wide range of interests in a wide range of businesses, special efforts are taken to avoid generating any avoidable internal conflict. Cautious procedures are employed for reaching a policy position and spokesmen are confined to stating that position without elaboration." They also pointed out that the chamber polls its members on controversial issues. The stand advocated by the chamber is usually that position favored by a majority, "but there is a general understanding that no stand will be taken if opinion is sharply divided."[29] This practice of consulting the rank and file is by no means limited to the Chamber of Commerce. John Bunzel has found in his study of the National Federation of Independent Businesses that the organization polls "the members to learn their opinions on a variety of domestic and international issues." The federation then uses the published reports of its internal referendums to lobby for those government programs that its constituents believe will benefit them.[30]

The desire to represent and advance the interests of the rank and file is not limited to business associations alone. Ironically enough, while McConnell argues in *Private Power and American Democracy* that organizational elites often pursue their own interests to the detriment of the membership, he does not find any evidence of such behavior in his study of the American Farm Bureau.[31] On the contrary, he observes that the leadership of the bureau is conscious of the fact that its members have diverse goals and is eager to harmonize these differences. "The outstanding achievement of the Farm Bureau," he declares, "has been to weld the dominant economic interests of the Middle West and the South" together.[32] The Farm Bureau, like the NAM, "must reconcile the different claims of various producing groups within its own ranks; this necessarily results in compromise and a greater degree of temperateness in its own demands."[33] However, while the members of the Farm Bureau who grow different crops have different objectives, the organization has enjoyed a certain degree of unity because it is primarily oriented toward the more affluent members of the farm community. Although McConnell deplores the narrow class outlook of this organization, he seems to imply that the leadership has faithfully represented its constituents' wishes. He notes that "the Farm Bureau, in the words of its own publication, is an 'organization of superior farmers.' Moreover, the record of its actions shows that it has served as the spokesman of these 'superior farmers.'"[34]

The same pattern of responsiveness seems to characterize yet other organizations. In particular, several researchers have observed that there is often widespread participation and competition in political parties and clubs. Seymour Martin Lipset's study of the Cooperative Commonwealth Federation in Saskatchewan does not find an organization dominated by either our second or third variety of oligarchy. On the contrary, Lipset argues:

> Though the forces making for bureaucratic control of the farmer's movement exist in Saskatchewan as they do elsewhere, the structural conditions for rank-and-file participation and for resistance to such control are stronger there than in most other areas. . . . The secondary leaders of all the farm groups are working farmers who are just as much affected by economic pressures and general currents of opinion as are the rank and file. Unless these leaders express the feelings of their neighbors, who have chosen them, they will be replaced by others who do. The extent of direct participation means that the farmers' movement must always be receptive to the needs of the members.[35]

In a similar vein, James Q. Wilson finds in his study of amateur democrats and socialist parties that organizations based on ideology—as opposed to patronage—tend to have very responsible leaders.[36] "Political amateurs in this country and perhaps generally," he notes, "are vitally interested in mechanisms to ensure the intraparty accountability of office holders and party leaders."[37] This concern is reflected in the fact that "ideological parties and amateur clubs are alike in their reluctance to vest discretionary authority in their leaders."[38]

But even nonideological parties that vest more authority in the hands of their officials are not free of all internal checks and balances. In his study of the Detroit Republican and Democratic parties, Samuel Eldersveld has stressed the high degree of factionalism that exists in both parties.[39] On the basis of such studies, Wilson observes that "few parties, and indeed few large organizations of any kind, are monolithic structures free of disagreement and faction." "Indeed," he argues, "parties, being voluntary associations, are especially likely to be a coalition of subgroups that operate in uneasy alliance with one another."[40] This observation can be easily confirmed by anyone who witnessed the chaotic proceedings of the 1972 Democratic convention. It would be difficult to argue that the national Democratic party was ruled by an autocratic or unchecked elite since such notable party officials as Mayor Daley were defeated on the convention floor by insurgent groups led by the McGovern forces.

In other groups as diverse as Common Cause, state teachers' associations, or the American Medical Association, we likewise find evidence that the leadership is representative of its members. Common Cause, for instance, establishes its legislative priorities on the basis of a referendum it conducts among its members each year. In order to maintain and expand its membership, the association tries to focus its energy on those issues that most trouble its rank and file. Among educational groups there is often a similar desire to reflect the needs of constituents. Nicholas Masters's, Robert Salisbury's, and Thomas Eliot's study, "The School Men in Missouri," notes that the Missouri State Teachers' Association "takes great care to avoid actions that will result in divisions in the education lobby." MSTA believes that the educational lobby will be most effective if it can present a united front to the state legislature. "Nothing would be more damaging to MSTA's standing as an expert than to have rival experts on the legislative scene."[41] Rather than acting as an imperious, self-serving bureaucracy, MSTA tries to be a broker, reconciling and exhorting divergent groups to support a unified legislative program.

And finally, even in the American Medical Association there is evidence that the organization's officials are highly responsive to membership wishes. However, in contrast to the other associations we have looked at, the AMA leadership does not seem to be informally checked by the need to reconcile diverse interests nor formally checked by genuinely meaningful electoral mechanisms. Despite the absence of these constraints, the organization's leadership still appears not to have misused its authority for its self-enrichment. On the contrary, many critics would no doubt willingly agree that the AMA has vigorously defended the economic interests of the profession. Elton Rayack, for instance, maintains in his study of the medical profession that "evidence leads to the general conclusion that the American Medical Association, on socio-economic issues related to medical care, does in fact truly reflect the will of the overwhelming majority of physicians in private medical practice." Rayack concludes:

> Revolts against the leadership of the AMA are not indicative of general discontent with organized medicine's policies. The "revolts" have been sporadic, rather widely spaced in time, short-lived, and generally ineffective. Furthermore, except on the relatively minor issue of social security coverage for physicians, the dissidents have been unable to muster any widespread support. For the most part, the opposition has come from physicians outside private practice—from physicians in medical schools, in research organizations, in large hospitals, and in government service. There is no significant evidence to indicate any meaningful opposition to the AMA leadership among the private practitioners who make up 75 percent of the medical profession and probably about 90 percent of the AMA membership. On the contrary, whatever evidence is available points to the conclusion that the policies of the leadership are consistent with the wishes of the vast majority of AMA membership. [42]

Contrary to what pluralism's critics claim, we can see that there are numerous organizations that are not served by officials solely interested in their own self-aggrandizement (oligarchy three). In addition, the preceding examples demonstrate that many groups have leaders who are either informally checked by the need to harmonize heterogeneous interests in their organizations or more formally checked by referendums and other electoral constraints (oligarchy two).

Besides asserting that organizational elites pursue goals that diverge from those of the rank and file, critics like Kariel and

McConnell at times imply that such tendencies are inherent or inevitable in all large organizations. However, as we shall soon see, the explanation they offer to account for the rise of our more pernicious varieties of oligarchy seems more relevant to certain kinds of organizations than to others.

Inquiries into the origins of our second form of elitism usually focus on certain external and internal characteristics of the group in question. For instance, the nature of an organization's external environment seems to play an important role in influencing how the association is internally governed. Richard Simpson and William Gulley have shown that if an organization must constantly bargain with other groups to realize its objectives, it will tend to involve its members more fully in the decision-making process.[43] In a study of 211 different organizations they found that the more an organization is dependent on other parties in the community, the more it is "relatively decentralized with initiation of activity concentrated at the local level and with a strong concern for grass roots membership involvement and internal communications."[44] The reasons for such a relationship are relatively self-evident. Simpson and Gulley argue that when an organization needs the consent of other groups to realize its goals, the leadership feels it is essential to communicate with the rank and file about the obstacles facing the organization. In addition, in order to enhance their bargaining position with other elements in society, the leaders need to have the full support of their membership. The officials of such a group thus have a tendency to involve the grass roots as fully as they can in the activities of the organization. The more knowledgeable and supportive the membership is, the more effective the leadership can be in pursuit of the group's objectives. Simpson and Gulley's findings also suggest that the more competitive the political system becomes, the greater the probability that organizational leaders will keep in touch with the wishes of the rank and file. In a society based on partisan mutual adjustment, an organization that appears not to speak for its members will wield little or no influence with opposing interests.

If organizations that need to strike bargains with other groups to achieve their ends are often run by leaders who are solicitous of the rank and file, organizations that feel severely threatened by the larger society tend to be governed by officials who are hostile to any kind of internal checks and balances. Kariel suggests that one reason many labor unions have been run by unchecked elites is that they initially faced a tremendous degree of hostility from the business and political community. "Unions were inevitably forced to develop tactics and organizational arrangements that would assure their survival," Kariel notes. "Somehow they had to respond to the potent antagonistic forces in their environment: to ideology, public law, and the sheer violence of business."[45] Since unions encountered a great deal of antagonism from other groups in society, it was only natural that their leaders became adamant about maintaining internal unity. Likewise William Leiserson has observed that labor leaders who had to fight for the very survival of their organizations have often regarded internal opposition as a threat to the existence of the labor movement.[46] In times of stress these officials believe that the course of action they themselves prefer is the only conceivable policy the organization can follow, and they therefore tend to resist any rank-and-file attempts to set limits on their power. However, if Kariel and Leiserson are correct, then we can expect groups that do not feel their survival is jeopardized by the counterclaims of other organizations to have leaders who are more willing to debate the group's goals and strategies. In fact, most of Kariel's references are to labor unions, which historically have encountered bitter opposition from other interests in society. In contrast, most of the groups cited above, which are more tolerant of internal opposition, have not been forced to contend with such hostile opposition.

While the external pressures confronting an organization are highly important in shaping the attitudes of its leadership, the inclinations of its membership also tend to have a bearing on whether an organization has a checked or unchecked elite. For example, the reasons people choose to join a group and the diversity of their demands seem to affect the discretionary power exercised by group officials. As mentioned before, Wilson finds in *The Amateur Democrats* that individuals who join a group for ideological or purposive reasons are very insistent that they be involved in the deliberations of the organization.[47] In contrast, people who join an interest group or support a political machine because they expect patronage or tangible economic rewards may be relatively indifferent to how the organization is internally governed. As long as the association satisfies the rank-and-file's desire for material rewards, the membership may not care whether there are formal checks on the leadership's authority. When the rank and file are concerned only with the goods or services an organization can provide, it stands to reason that they may be unconcerned how the leadership goes about delivering those goods. However, the lack of formal checks does not mean that officials have a completely free hand in running the association. The quiescence of the membership may not last if the organization is no longer able to meet the expectations of the rank and file.

These informal restraints on group elites are likely to be more apparent in associations made up of diverse elements. If a group has a heterogeneous membership with multiple and, in some cases, divergent goals, the leadership will be under more pressure to negotiate with the rank and file. Unlike an organization that has a homogeneous membership and a limited number of objectives, a diverse organization with multiple goals will have a more difficult time satisfying its members' preferences. Such associations are likely to go to greater lengths to consult with their members and to avoid taking stands on issues that might divide their rank and file. The behavior of the Chamber of Commerce, the NAM, and the Farm Bureau clearly illustrates this point. As noted earlier, Bauer, Pool, and Dexter as well as McConnell have shown that these groups have often tempered their proposals and avoided issues they felt might disrupt the unity of the organization. Similarly, Simpson's and Gulley's study found that organizations that seek to achieve multiple goals as well as organizations that must deal with numerous external parties tend to "stress loyal, active involvement of rank and file members in their activities."[48] The more faction-ridden an association is, the harder it is for the leadership to govern in a centralized, autocratic fashion.

However, as should be obvious, merely because the rank and file want to influence their leaders is no guarantee that they will always succeed. Even if an association has members who have joined for purposive reasons or has members who wish to achieve divergent goals, we cannot necessarily conclude that the rank and file will be able to restrain the actions of their officials. Besides analyzing the intentions of group members, we must also look at the opportunities they have to challenge their leaders and at their ability to do so.

According to Albert Hirschman, individuals who are dissatisfied with an organization's activities have two different options open to them, "exit" or "voice."[49] That is, if people are dissatisfied, they can either withdraw from the association or they can stay and actively voice their opposition to the group's existing policy. As should be expected, the more options or resources an organization's rank and file possess, the easier it is for them to hold their officials accountable if they so desire. For instance, an organization that has a heterogeneous rank and file who are not unwilling to terminate their association with the group would be likely to have leaders who are solicitous of membership wishes. And if we may refer to the Farm Bureau and the NAM again, such seems to be the case. McConnell points out that the Farm Bureau must constantly face the prospect that wealthy growers who produce specialized crops may quit and join narrower commodity associations. Since the 1930s the bureau has been "alive to the dangers of commodity-ism"[50] and has fought such tendencies by attempting to represent the wishes of its constituents in a forceful manner.[51]

Similarly, Richard Gable has observed in his study of the NAM that the organization has been apprehensive about its fluctuating membership and has tried to focus on issues, like labor relations, about which it believes its supporters are most concerned.[52] "As a voluntary organization the Association must formulate policies that are acceptable to the members and are felt essential to their well-being and [to] achieving group objectives. If it does not, the members may withdraw." He goes on to note the "the fluctuations of membership indicate that the NAM's labor policies have been essentially reflective of members' desires, because membership has swollen during campaigns of union opposition."[53] The threat of exit thus appears especially potent as an informal check on the leadership when the organization relies on a heterogeneous and somewhat volatile constituency. Officials who blatantly ignore the sentiments of the membership may find that they have few resources to command and even fewer followers to lead.

However, as Hirschman points out, not all individuals exit when they become dissatisfied with existing programs. Either because of necessity or loyalty, many elect to stay in an organization and protest actions they deem undesirable. But the success with which the rank and file can oppose their leaders is again dependent on a variety of factors. For instance, Michels suggested that the unique background of workers has a bearing on whether union leaders can insulate themselves from membership pressure. Michels argued that the leaders of the SPD were able to acquire uncontested power because the great majority of the rank and file lacked the political skills to monitor the decisions of their officials. Both the manner of their educational training and the nature of their work prevented them from acquiring the talents necessary to play an active role in the affairs of the party. [54] Even if they became agitated over an issue or disagreed with the direction the organization was pursuing, they lacked the ability to make their objections effectively known. Lipset, Trow, and Coleman provide confirming evidence of this point, noting that those unions such as the ITU or the Actors' Guild which draw from the best-educated segments of the working class are internally the least oligarchically structured. [55] Untrained and uneducated members often seem to go hand in hand with unchecked organizational power. If such is the case, then working-class groups like labor unions, which have constituents who often lack both verbal and organizational skills necessary to oppose their leaders, are more likely to be run by unchecked elites than are associations dominated by a more educated and articulate membership. The success with which an association's officials can develop into our second form of oligarchy is in part dependent upon the abilities of the rank and file.

However, even if the rank and file have the ability to challenge their leaders, the success of their efforts may also be influenced by the structure of the organization, in particular, by the number and kind of subunits within the organization and by the way in which the parent body formally or informally interacts with its subunits. David Truman suggests that a useful distinction that "can be applied to political organizations in the United States is that between federated and unitary forms." [56] The first type of structure formally divides power between its subunits and the larger, more inclusive body, as in a national organization that has relatively separate and independent state or even county associations. In many cases membership in the larger organization is indirect in the sense that the individual joins the parent body via his participation in the smaller subunit. In contrast, a unitary association is a "single organization that may, and usually does, have subdivisions to carry on various functions."[57] In this type of association, individuals usually belong directly to the parent organization and participate in the activities of local affiliates only if their needs or preferences so dictate.

This variation in types of organizational structure can often be important to dissident groups wishing to oppose the leaders of the parent group. Obviously, a federated structure offers any parties who might wish to challenge the larger organization a more secure and independent base from which to launch their attack. When state or county units are formally independent of the parent organization, they can criticize the association with only minimal fear of punishment. The record of many federated interest groups indicates that state associations have often opposed the leaders of the national organization. Truman notes that even in the AMA various state societies and even some county societies have on occasion opposed the policies of the parent organization. And he remarks that "the national organization once was reduced to petulant complaints that it was not permitted to state its position in the pages of the California Medical Association's journal."[58] The Farm Bureau has also experienced similar internal disputes. John Heinz has observed that "state bureaus of the AFBF often appear at Congressional hearings to oppose the position of the national organization when it conflicts with the interests of crops in their own states."[59] Similarly, McConnell has pointed out that the Ohio and Vermont federations came to the support of the Farm Security Administration at a time when the national organization was severely attacking it.[60]

Even in more unitary organizations we find that a tradition of local independence facilitates internal diversity and dissent. For instance, in the 1960s a group of so-called young Turks challenged the leadership of the NAACP, arguing that the organization should place more emphasis on protest activities and less stress on legal action in order to bring about social change. While this insurgent group gained some support, it was never able to dominate the organization, at the height of its power controlling only twelve of the sixty seats on the NAACP's board of directors.[61] However, even though these more impatient reformers never succeeded in altering the official objectives of the organization, they did succeed in controlling a number of the association's branch offices. In Milwaukee, for example, Father Groppi led NAACP youth councils in mass protest activities against that city's segregated housing patterns, while in Mississippi Charles Evers organized local campaigns against the practice of Jim Crow. The autonomy of the NAACP's branch offices enabled the insurgents to pursue policies on a local level that the parent organization and its leadership refused to advocate on a national level.

While the preceding discussion is not meant to be an exhaustive treatment of the topic or a definitive survey of the existing literature, it nonetheless reveals that (1) the nature of a group's environment, (2) the inclinations of its rank and file, and (3) the capabilities of its membership to exit or voice are crucial in determining whether or not an organization's elites are restrained. This is not to deny, of course, that leaders and led come to possess differences in outlook by virtue of their differing roles in the organization. However, as noted above, there is a good deal of evidence suggesting that such a gap does not necessarily lead to the emergence of unchecked leadership. Institutionalized opposition such as that found in the two-party system of the ITU seems to be relatively rare (incidentally, such a system seems to be evolving in the American Political Science Association, of which McConnell and Kariel have been members) but nonetheless there are a number of other formal and informal restraints operating in many interest groups to prevent the rise of unchecked power.

In addition, we must also remember that even if an association's leaders do come to wield unchecked power (oligarchy two), there is no reason for assuming that they will automatically utilize their authority to advance their own private objectives (oligarchy three). Kariel, McConnell, and even Michels imply that leaders who wield unchecked power may at times scrupulously attempt to act in the best interests of their rank and file. If that is the case, then we need to ask what conditions give rise to our third form of elitism. Unfortunately, the situation is not all that clear. In large part, because so few studies find organizational leaders who advance their welfare at the expense of the membership, there are few insights into why such a phenomenon might arise. However, both Kariel and Michels at times insist that elites do misuse their power, and they account for its occurrence in such a fashion that we cannot believe it happens very frequently. In fact, their explanation of our third form of elitism focuses on factors that are likely to trouble primarily lower-class organizations. Kariel observes that misused power is most likely to occur in working-class organizations, like labor unions, where the status differences that separate the leaders of a group from their members are great. When individuals who become officials in an organization acquire wealth and prestige that they never could enjoy as members of the rank and file, they are often reluctant to surrender their power since it would entail a dramatic alteration in their life style. Similarly, Michels stresses the fact that SPD officials who were of working-class origins were not eager to be thrown back into the factories from which they had just escaped. After enjoying the perquisites associated with being union or party officials, they knew it would be a major readjustment to take up the life of a factory worker again. Instead of struggling unremittingly to advance the interests of their followers, the leaders often behaved in a conciliatory fashion toward business and the state for fear of jeopardizing the status of the organization and their own position within it. [62]

However, the very reasons Kariel and Michels use to explain the rise of our third form of oligarchy should give us reason to believe that it is not a very prevalent form of organizational elitism. The stark differences Kariel and Michels paint between the status of a union official and the life of an average factory worker are not to be found in most interest groups today. In many of the associations that are dominated by middle-class people, the salary and life style of the officials are not likely to diverge much from the patterns of the rank and file. Whereas the leaders of the SPD had no separate skills by which they might earn an income or enjoy the status they knew as union leaders, the officials of business associations or reform groups like Common Cause or the Sierra Club are usually lawyers or professionals of some type who could easily find lucrative employment elsewhere. They thus lack the incentives to misuse power that Kariel and Michels have attributed to working-class leaders.

Furthermore, even among organizations like labor unions, which are most likely to be subject to our third form of elitism, there are reasons for believing that the worst forms of oligarchy may be less prevalent in the future. First of all, in contrast to workers at the beginning of the twentieth century, present-day union members have dramatically increased their level of education and are thus less likely to be apathetic, uninformed, or unable to monitor or override the decisions of their leadership. Secondly, in many unions, college-educated or professionally trained individuals are replacing former factory workers in positions of leadership. This new core of industrial leaders lacks the incentive its predecessors might have had to abuse power for fear of being thrown back into the factory if displaced from office.

Pluralism's Remedies for Oligarchy

Even if the more pernicious forms of oligarchy are not extensive, we must still ask how pluralism would deal with those situations in which group officials have in fact misused their power. When individuals within groups feel they have come to be dominated by our second or third form of oligarchy, we need to know what options are open to them. Logically, there are two positions that have been espoused. First, laissez-faire pluralists have usually suggested that the option of exiting is sufficient to protect an individual's rights. As soon as a person feels the leadership of an organization he is affiliated with ignores his interests or pursues policies detrimental to his wishes, he can always voluntarily choose to terminate his relationship with the group in question. Voluntary associations are qualitatively different from the state—they exercise no sovereign authority over the individual. While the state will legally expect a certain degree of compliance with its directives and impose penalties on those who seek to sever their ties with the polity, most private associations are not in a comparable position to levy sanctions against departing members. Interest groups are concerned with far fewer aspects of an individual's life than is the state, and it is thus far easier for a person to disassociate himself from a group than from the state and to suffer no serious consequences. If a substantial number of people terminate their ties to a particular interest group, the ability of that group to wield power in society at large is bound to suffer. And in fact, as noted earlier, the very possibility that members might withdraw has made many organizations like the NAM, the Chamber of Commerce, and Common Cause more sensitive to the wishes of the rank and file.

However, if the option of severing one's relationship with an interest group may be a viable one for many people, it must be admitted that it is less than a totally satisfactory solution to the problem of organizational elitism. On some occasions membership in an organization is not a mere luxury an individual can indulge in to satisfy his personal needs or to achieve a particular social goal; on the contrary, it may be a prerequisite for a person to earn his very livelihood. A doctor who loses his right to practice in a hospital because of AMA sanctions has no meaningful option to leave the organization and go elsewhere. Similarly, with the rise of the union shop, individuals who voluntarily terminate their association with the union simultaneously terminate their prospects for gainful employment in that field.

If the individual option of leaving the group is not a completely satisfactory answer to our worst form of organizational oligarchy, a second and perhaps more effective solution is to have the government oversee or regulate the internal affairs of particular interest groups. For instance, when private associations have the legal right to limit or deny people's access to certain occupations or professions, the state can certainly insure that the officials of these organizations do not abuse their power or abridge the prerogatives of the rank and file. Thus doctors denied the use of hospital facilities should have the right to appeal that decision to a court of law. In order to guarantee that valid professional reasons, as opposed to political or personal considerations, are invoked, the state should be able to regulate a group like the AMA, which itself exercises quasi-regulatory power. Similarly, labor dissidents should be able to count on government supervision of union elections if the threat of fraud is a genuine possibility.

If, as a public pluralist would point out, the distinction between public and many so-called private associations is at best a tenuous one, there is ample justification for government regulation of the internal as well as the external affairs of many organizations. Especially when groups purport to regulate their members for reasons of public safety or when groups have used the power and authority of the state to advance their own interests, it is difficult for these same associations to claim immunity from some degree of public scrutiny. This is especially true of the types of organizations most likely to develop our third form of oligarchy, namely, unions and Community Action groups or poverty associations. In return for government assistance during the initial organizing stage, the government should have the right to require that the officials of these associations not misuse their positions of power.

In fact, over the past several decades there have been several attempts to pass legislation that would give the government the authority to oversee the activities of various private groups. OEO, for instance, has the power to stipulate when and how poverty officials are elected as well as the authority to oversee the spending of money by local Community Action groups. Likewise, the two major postwar pieces of labor legislation, the Taft-Hartley Law and the Landrum-Griffin Act, authorize the Departments of Justice and Labor to intervene in union affairs if it appears that the rights of the rank and file are being violated. While the Taft-Hartley Law insures that the members, rather than the officials, of a union have the final say on whether a union strikes or stays on the job, the Landrum-Griffin Act goes even further by (1) granting to union members a bill of rights comparable to that of the federal Constitution, (2) regulating the timing as well as the manner in which elections are held, and, finally, (3) requiring union officials to make extensive reports on their financial activities. [63]

However, the impact of such legislation has been uneven. As pointed out in the previous chapter, Greenstone and Peterson generally have praised the operation of the OEO poverty programs. Rather than finding a self-serving elite, they note that poverty leaders in Detroit and New York attempted to "increase community control over social welfare institutions."[64] They also insist that even in those cities where poverty officials were less than vigorous in pursuing community goals, the problem was not inevitable and might have been easily avoided if OEO had insisted on different methods of recruiting and selecting staff to run the local organizations.

Government efforts to limit the abuse of power by union officials have met with more mixed results. But in many cases the failure of public officials to check the abuses of labor leaders has been a result more of their lack of concern and motivation than of insufficient legal power. This point is dramatically illustrated by the attempt of dissident forces to oust Tony Boyle from the presidency of the United Mine Workers. In the initial campaign between Boyle and Chip Yablonski, the Yablonski-led insurgents repeatedly asked the Department of Labor to invoke its authority under the Landrum-Griffin Act to supervise the union's election; either because of indifference or political considerations, the Nixon administration decided not to intervene. Unfortunately, it was not until the murder of Yablonski that the Department of Labor did take action to guarantee that the election between Boyle and Arnold Miller was an honest one. As this case graphically illustrates, once political elites are willing to implement the laws presently on the books, it is possible for flagrant abuses of power in private associations to be contained.

Interestingly enough, critics of pluralism like Kariel recognize that such government intervention in the internal affairs of many organizations can be successful in preventing the misuse of elite power, but they tend to see such action as a denial—rather than merely an extension—of pluralistic doctrine. [65] This error stems in large part from a failure to recognize that there are a variety of forms of pluralism. Historically most laissez-faire pluralists have seen the concentration of power in the hands of public officials as the chief threat to the liberties of the individual. But if today we recognize, as a public pluralist would, that private groups may at times likewise pose a threat to the interests of their members, we can easily argue that government checks on groups may be needed to supplement associational restraints on government. If the government can limit the misuse of power within associations without at the same time hindering the ability of interest groups to challenge government activities, the vitality of the pluralistic process can be maintained. This is especially the case if, as in the Landrum-Griffin Act, the government regulates the internal procedures of an organization but refrains from dictating the goals or the policy objectives of the association it supervises. It is the presence of checks and balances on concentrated forms of power rather than the protection of what are in many cases only semiprivate groups that constitutes the essence of public pluralism. On those few occasions when either our second or third forms of oligarchy have appeared, judicious public regulation of the internal affairs of troublesome organizations may be necessary to curtail the misuse of a group's trust. If the more pernicious forms of organizational elitism do not succumb to the increasing skills and education of the constituents who make up most interest groups, or to the growing acceptance of most groups in the political system, or to the changes in the composition of most organizational elites, then government assistance may provide the members of a group with one more means of checking their elected officials.

NOTES

1, Henry S. Kariel, *The Decline of American Pluralism*, pp. 3-4.
2. Grant McConnell, *Private Power and American Democracy*, p. 120.
3. See Juan Linz, "Robert Michels," p. 268, for an alternative attempt to clarify what the word oligarchy means.
4. Kariel, *Decline of American Pluralism*, p. 4.
5. Ibid., p. 20.
6. Ibid., p. 33.
7. Ibid., pp. 51-52.
8. Ibid., p. 55.
9. Ibid., p. 52.
10. Ibid., p. 51.
11. Ibid., p. 64.
12. Ibid.
13. McConnell, *Private Power and American Democracy*, p. 122.
14. Ibid., p. 122.
15. Ibid., p. 153.
16. For example, see ibid., pp. 148-49.
17. Ibid., p. 152.
18. Robert Michels, *Political Parties*, p. 70.
19. Ibid., p. 111.

20. Ibid., p. 288.
21. Philip J. Cook, "Robert Michels' "Political Parties in Perspective," pp. 773-96; John May, "Democracy, Organizations, Michels," pp. 417-29.
22. P. J. Cook, "Robert Michels' *Political Parties*," pp. 792-94.
23. McConnell, *Private Power and American Democracy*, p. 121.
24. Ibid., p. 151.
25. Kariel, *Decline of American Pluralism*, p. 68.
26. Ibid.
27. Seymour Martin Lipset, Martin A. Trow, and James S. Coleman, *Union Democracy*.
28. See for example, Harmon Zeigler, *Interest Groups in American Society*; H. R. Mahood, ed., *Pressure Groups in American Politics*; Raymond A. Bauer, Ithiel de Sola Pool, and Lewis Anthony Dexter, *American Business and Public Policy*.
29. Bauer, Pool, and Dexter, *American Business and Public Policy*, p. 333.
30. John H. Bunzel, "The National Federation of Independent Business," p. 113.
31. Grant McConnell, *The Decline of Agrarian Democracy*.
32. Ibid., p. 140.
33. Ibid., p. 148.
34. Ibid., p. 170.
35. Seymour Martin Lipset, *Agrarian Socialism*, p. 204.
36. James Q. Wilson, *The Amateur Democrat*. See also *Political Organizations*.
37. Wilson, *Political Organizations*, p. 107.
38. Ibid., p. 108.
39. Samuel J. Eldersveld, *Political Parties*.
40. Wilson, *Political Organizations*, p. 114.
41. Nicholas A. Masters, Robert H. Salisbury, and Thomas H. Eliot, "The School Men in Missouri," p. 223.
42. Elton Rayack, *Professional Power and American Medicine*, p. 17.
43. Richard Simpson and William Gulley, "Goals, Environmental Pressures, and Organizational Characteristics," pp. 344-50.
44. Ibid., p. 345.
45. Kariel, *Decline of American Pluralism*, p. 51.
46. William Leiserson, *American Trade Union Democracy*, p. 55.
47. Wilson, *Amateur Democrat*, pp. 180-87.
48. Simpson and Gulley, "Goals, Environmental Pressures, and Organizational Characteristics," p. 345.
49. Albert Hirschman, *Exit, Voice, and Loyalty*.

50. McConnell, *Decline of Agrarian Democracy*, p. 76.

51. Ibid., p. 80-91.

52. Richard Gable, "NAM, Influential Lobby or Kiss of Death?" pp. 250-66.

53. Ibid., p. 260.

54. Michels, *Political Parties*, pp. 85-98.

55. Lipset, Trow, and Coleman, *Union Democracy*, p. 320.

56. David Truman, *The Governmental Process*, p. 115.

57. Ibid., p. 116.

58. Ibid., p. 117.

59. John Heinz, "The Political Impasse in Farm Support Legislation," p. 195.

60. McConnell, *Decline of Agrarian Democracy*, p. 157.

61. Wilson, *Political Organizations*, p. 179.

62. Michels, *Political Parties*, pp. 172-88.

63. Sanford Cohen, *Labor Law*, p. 265.

64. J. David Greenstone and Paul E. Peterson, *Race and Authority in Urban Politics*, p. 309.

65. Kariel, *Decline of American Pluralism*, pp. 252-72.

Chapter

8

Pluralism Vs.
Participatory Democracy:
The Purpose of Participation

In the preceding chapters I have tried to show that alternative theories of democracy have very different notions of what role the citizenry should play in the political arena as well as very different conceptions of who constitutes the relevant public. While polyarchal democrats have argued that the public's role should be limited to choosing among competing elites, both populists and pluralists have insisted that the electorate should have some say in the formulation of government policy. However, populists and pluralists have often vigorously disagreed with one another over who constitutes the relevant citizenry. Populists have envisaged the people as the majority of citizens and have insisted that they should express their views through referendums, while pluralists have usually argued that the numerous issue publics in society should be the relevant public to decide important issues, and they have argued that these interests should exercise their say primarily through the give-and-take of political bargaining.

Because it has been argued that many people do not belong to any groups, or that marginal or public interest groups have difficulty gaining access to the bargaining table, or that groups are dominated by a handful of elites, a number of academicians have often voiced reservations about pluralism's conception of the public. Yet, we have seen in the last several chapters that many of these criticisms seem unfounded. Through a policy of public regulation of interest-group activity, it is possible to insure that the members of all issue publics have some meaningful say in the formulation of government programs.

In this chapter it is necessary to analyze one final alternative to pluralism, that of participatory democracy. The term participatory democracy has been applied to several different variants of democratic theory, all of which share the belief that devolution of power to smaller units of government will maximize opportunities for public participation. In the following chapter I shall examine in more detail the assumptions of community control, a variety of participatory democracy that has gained widespread support among those who seek to make governmental institutions more responsive to minority interests. In this chapter, however, I wish to look at what I have chosen to call *communitarian democracy*, a variant of participatory doctrine that is concerned less with governmental responsiveness to local needs than with the broader functions of participation in a communal setting.

Communitarian democracy's commitment to widespread participation is reflected in its criticism of pluralism. Participatory democrats like Robert Paul Wolff, Peter Bachrach, and David Ellerman believe that pluralism, like most other theories of democracy, fails to appreciate the inherent benefits of public participation as an end in and of itself.[1] While pluralists have tended to view political involvement as a means by which the individual might secure certain tangible benefits, communitarian democrats argue that the very act of participation leads to individual moral growth and development and thus is desirable apart from any instrumental benefits it may provide.

Examples and Assumptions of Communitarian Democracy

Although communitarian forms of democracy have enjoyed great popularity in recent years, the doctrine is rooted in a long and venerable tradition. Examples of communal participation have varied greatly in time and place, ranging from the New England town meeting to the utopian settlement of nineteenth-century

America, from the Israeli kibbutz movement to the experiments in industrial democracy in Yugoslavia. Likewise, spokesmen for participatory democracy range from eighteenth-century political philosophers like Rousseau to more recent advocates like Wolff, Ellerman, and Bachrach. Beneath these variations, however, it is possible to discern certain common values implicitly shared by all communitarian democrats.

First of all, the advocates of communitarian forms of democracy usually insist that the overwhelming majority of individuals want to play a more active role in guiding and shaping their own lives. They argue that intermittent political participation is inadequate if individuals are to exercise control over their own destiny and fulfill their basic human need for social interaction. According to this line of reasoning, instead of merely holding elites accountable at election time or influencing policy indirectly via group bargaining, members of the public should partake in the actual deliberations of the community. However, communitarian democrats often express varying degrees of optimism about man's present degree of readiness to take this kind of an active part in the political process. While some like Wolff write as if the citizenry is currently prepared to assume a more prominent role, others like Carole Pateman concede that people may presently be apathetic about political matters but insist that this apathy stems from the realities of the political situation today.[2] That is, people are indifferent to politics because they know they have no real opportunities to influence the outcome of most issues; but if institutional changes were made to facilitate participation, then they would chose to involve themselves more actively. Still other communitarian democrats like Ellerman argue that the citizenry's unwillingness to participate actively in politics is an outgrowth of a false consciousness created and sustained by our capitalist economic system.[3] Like Ellerman, many participatory democrats are socialists who maintain in Marxian fashion that economic changes are necessary for the complete realization of communitarian democracy. In their view, only an egalitarian society in which the means of production are publicly owned is likely to instill in individuals the proclivities necessary to make a political system based on intensive participation a genuine possibility.

Secondly, most participatory democrats insist that it is only in small communities that individuals will have the opportunity to deliberate matters of social importance. In the eighteenth century Rousseau argued that the city-state rather than the nation-state was the best vehicle to maximize citizen involvement. Today, in a similar vein, Wolff calls for the creation of small communities where people can share in the common political life, and Bachrach advocates the development of new centers of participation within factories and other places of work. Likewise, communitarian democrats with socialist leanings insist that centralized state planning must be replaced by decentralized forms of decision making that will allow individuals to assume control over their own lives. Participatory democrats, whether socialist or not, view large-scale units of government as too remote to allow for the kind of intensive individual involvement they deem desirable.

Thirdly, most communitarian democrats believe that once people are given the opportunity to become involved in politics, the quality of public life will improve dramatically. They insist that the issues that divide men are not fundamental in nature or incapable of resolution; on the contrary, they believe that if people are given the chance to meaningfully debate the problems that trouble them, they will be able to resolve their differences peacefully and harmoniously. Through the give-and-take of communal assemblies individuals can search for the common interests that unite them and upon this basis forge an affective sense of community.

Finally, as noted above, communitarian democrats tend to view the fact of participation as a desirable end in and of itself. Advocates of participatory democracy like Wolff and Pateman believe that the individual will be likely to develop his capabilities to their fullest only when he has an opportunity to share in the deliberation of important social issues. Individual fulfillment and public involvement are thus seen as inextricably linked. Regardless of the instrumental gains to be secured, participatory democrats believe that a person will emotionally and morally benefit from immersing himself in the social affairs of his community. Rousseau, for example, thought participating in a democratic state "could elevate men and turn them into moral and intelligent human beings."[4] Similarly, as Terrence Cook and Patrick Morgan point out, many participatory democrats believe that public involvement will make people both more knowledgeable about important events and less selfish in their attitudes toward others. [5] Rather than being a necessary burden an individual must bear in order to accomplish other substantive goals, participation in the life of the community is seen as a beneficial objective in and of itself.

Assumptions and Reality

The four points outlined above constitute the cornerstone of the participatory argument, yet it is interesting to note that communitarian democrats by and large neglect to demonstrate whether these assumptions are in fact valid. Many participatory democrats muster very little data in support of their arguments, and those who do attempt to offer empirical evidence often end up citing data that undermine their own position. In order to determine the workability of the communitarian model, an analysis of relevant empirical evidence needs to be undertaken. However, it should be pointed out that the data to be examined in this chapter are diverse and heterogeneous in nature, ranging from studies of participation in American politics to analyses of Yugoslavian factories, Israeli kibbutzim, and other experiments in participatory democracy. While some might argue that experiments like the kibbutzim are not always identical with the communities they would like to see built, we must recognize that such sources represent the best and in fact only evidence available. All too often, people like Bachrach or Wolff who favor communal experiments have neither participated in building such communities nor cited examples of communities that they think were successful. Unless we are willing to argue that there is no way of ever empirically determining whether the assumptions of participatory democracy are valid, we must look at those cases that most clearly approximate the participatory/communal model.

As we shall soon see, an examination of these kinds of sources, which modern participatory democrats have all too often ignored, reveals that communitarian forms of government are not necessarily as workable as advocates like Pateman et al. would like to believe. First of all, while participatory democrats like Wolff have insisted that people are intensely interested in political matters, much of the recent empirical evidence on participation in American politics suggests otherwise. Instead of being eager to immerse themselves in community affairs, most individuals appear to want to participate in a narrow and segmented fashion. As mentioned earlier, students of public opinion and voting behavior have shown that the vast majority of people are concerned about only a limited range of issues. Philip Converse, Sidney Verba, Norman Nie, and David RePass, among others, have found that instead of constituting a single cohesive body, the electorate is fragmented into numerous issue publics whose interest and involvement in politics seem to fluctuate back and forth between peaks of activity and inactivity.[6] When issues of importance to particular individuals are in the news or elicit government reaction, certain segments of the populace become highly involved in politics, but as old disputes recede and new ones come to the fore, different issue publics become activated.[7]

Perhaps even more damaging to the participatory cause is the fact that even within these rather narrow issue publics, many individuals choose not to play an active role in advancing their own interests. While people may be willing to join and financially support an interest group, they often want the officers of the association to assume most of the responsibility for the day-to-day operations of the group. In this way individuals can pursue the policies they deem desirable without incurring too many demands on their scarce time or energy. By participating in only a limited fashion in a group's activities, an individual can receive the psychological benefits of supporting a cause he believes in, as well as the tangible benefits the organization may happen to secure, without having to exhaust his own spare time. Thus, many groups become elitist in nature because the rank and file want to consolidate power in the hands of their leadership. Even though people may be willing to join interest groups and may want to play a more active role in public affairs, they often have very clear reservations about becoming too absorbed in the give-and-take of political life. Rather than viewing intensive participation as an ennobling process, many individuals simply see it as too great a burden to shoulder. In place of a *gemeinschaft* community where all directly partake in the deliberations of the group, people often prefer a centrally run association that places fewer demands on their leisure time.

However, as noted earlier, some participatory democrats like Pateman argue that people are indifferent to community affairs because the present structure of the political system does not provide any meaningful opportunities for expanded participation. Once people become socialized into accepting a passive political life, they will inevitably show little concern with public affairs. But Pateman maintains that if institutional changes were made to facilitate more public involvement, attitudes toward participation would likewise change.[8] Individuals as diverse as David Ellerman, Charles Hampden-Turner, and the authors of the Port Huron Manifesto of SDS take Pateman's argument one step further, insisting that the economic realities underlying our present political system also work to the detriment of greater public concern with political affairs.[9] They contend that the traditional voting studies of academic political scientists are so parochial in their design and execution that they provide us with few insights into the ultimate capabilities or interests of the average citizen. According to communitarian democrats of a socialist bent, altering the capitalist nature of our economy will do away with the conditions that have led the individual to become politically apathetic.

While this argument has a certain degree of plausibility, we must be careful to interpret it in the proper context. By undertaking certain institutional changes we may very well encourage more people to participate in politics, but the individuals who are stimulated to participate may choose to involve themselves in a limited, rather than an all-encompassing, fashion. The record of a variety of experiments that best seem to approximate the participatory model—including communal movements in the United States in the nineteenth and twentieth centuries, Israeli kibbutzim, worker councils in industrial societies, and self-managed factories in Yugoslavia—indicates that the overwhelming majority of people are not enamored with intensive participation over a prolonged period of time. In many respects, these experiments are appropriate subjects of study, for they all have attempted to develop a cooperative, communal environment on a small scale. In addition, many of the American communes, most of the Israeli kibbutzim, and certainly all of the Yugoslavian factories are institutions that are not based on capitalist assumptions. If participatory democrats of a socialist inclination are correct in insisting that the present economic make-up of American society either prevents or discourages people from wanting to participate actively in a communal setting, we should expect these alternative forms of political life based on different economic principles to enjoy considerable success in recruiting people to participate in their affairs.

However, such is not the case. If we look first at the evidence on the utopian communities established in the United States between 1820 and 1870, we cannot fail to note that most of them lasted for only a relatively short period of time. In a fundamentally sympathetic examination of American utopian movements, Rosabeth Kanter has studied over ninety-one communal ventures that left some kind of historical record and finds that "less than a dozen of the ninety-one known groups lasted more than sixteen years; for the majority, the average life-span was less than four years." Furthermore, she admits, "such well known communes as New Harmony and Brook Farm were among the short-lived groups. . . . Brook Farm ended after six years despite support from leading intellectuals of the time." On the basis of this data Kanter notes that "building viable utopian communities has proven to be difficult: translating the utopian dream into reality is fraught with issues that in time may even distort the original vision." [10]

If these communes supposedly tapped a deep-seated human desire to participate intensely in the affairs of a *gemeinschaft* community, one must ask why they were unable to sustain themselves over a longer period of time. Institutionally the opportunities existed for individuals to participate more actively in a communal setting, but very few persons seemed to have taken advantage of them. Moreover, even when people did decide to join a commune, their commitment was often halfhearted. As Kanter points out, most of the utopian settlements had to worry constantly that the lure of the larger, impersonal world outside the confines of the group would lead their members to lose interest in sustaining new forms of communal living. In fact, many communes frequently acted under the assumption that people would not voluntarily choose to remain in *gemeinschaft* organizations. The settlements that were most successful depended on a series of "commitment mechanisms" to promote a sense of communal solidarity. These included renunciation, sacrifices, mortification, the application of sanctions, mutual criticism sessions, and the institutionalization of the power and authority of the leader. [11] Kanter observes that many groups required people to relinquish "relationships that . . . [were] potentially disruptive to group cohesion, thereby heightening the relationship of individual to group." [12] The communities that were most successful usually formulated elaborate sets of rules to minimize the contact between their members and the outside world. Even personal relationships between two individuals within the commune were often viewed in a less than favorable light for fear that they might detract from the individual's commitment to the larger group.

Besides isolating their members from outside contact, many utopian settlements also undertook systematic efforts to break down or transform the values of their recruits. Kanter notes that a number of communes relied on the commitment mechanism of mortification to maintain the allegiance of their followers. The essence of mortification was to "strip away aspects of an individual's previous identity, to make him dependent on authority for direction, and to place him in a position of uncertainty . . . until he learns and comes to accept the norms of the group." [13] To achieve this goal the successful communes usually forced their members to undergo extensive periods of self-criticism or they applied direct sanctions to deviant members in order to make them uncertain about their status in the larger community. Kanter remarks that in successful nineteenth-century communities

the individual "bared his soul" to social control, admitting weaknesses, failings, and imperfections. The individual humbled himself before the group. . . . No part of his life was left unexamined and uncriticized, since all belonged to the system. The group might probe and pry into the most intimate matters, indicating its right to be a significant presence in the internal life of the individual. These mortification practices thus indicated to members that even their innermost "selves" were being "watched" by others. [14]

When mutual criticism failed to work, the community often used sanctions designed to "embarrass the member before the community and indicate to him that his membership status in the organization is always in question."[15]

Rather than proving that people will automatically choose the benefits of an affective, communal form of life if only they have the opportunity to experience them, the record of most nineteenth-century communes seems to indicate otherwise. By limiting the group's relations with outsiders and relying on a variety of often harsh conversion mechanisms, many utopian communities sought to resocialize people so that they would want to participate more intensely in the group's activities. Yet even these efforts proved to be unsuccessful in the great majority of communal experiments. If intensive socialization could have remolded people to accept the dictates of communal existence, as participatory democrats have often argued, one would have expected the second generation to remain with the utopian settlements. However, Kanter points out that even in those few communes, such as the Shakers' settlement, that lasted for any length of time, "most of the children . . . did not remain in the community when [they were] old enough to leave."[16] Ironically, most offspring of the original founders chose not to support the communal form of life in which they had been raised, despite the fact that they had experienced only minimal contact with the outside world.

David and Elena French have pointed out that support for communal life underwent several modifications during the nineteenth century. They argue that there were two distinct periods in the communal movement, one lasting from 1824 to 1846 and the other spanning the period from 1847 to 1866.[17] The first period, which they label the *Owenite era*, witnessed a basic concern with building a very intensive form of communal life in which all shared equally their possessions, ideas, and emotions. But the people who participated in these early experiments were ultimately to discover that the "interpersonal demands of communal life were more than they were prepared to accept," and "in the exhaustion and disillusionment that followed, people became more cautious, approaching social organization with sharply limited assumptions as to what it could offer them."[18] As a result, French and French argue, the second period of communal building, which they call the *Fourieristic era*, was more limited in its scope and more individualistic in its outlook: "In the flight from 'communes' with their overtones of total sharing and familial bonds, people were moving towards looser 'communities,' in which relationships were to be more partial and contractual."[19] Interestingly enough, French and French, who themselves are advocates of communal forms of living, recognize that the same shift away from all-encompassing to more limited communities has characterized the American "alternative" movement of the last fifteen years. This shift in emphasis is epitomized in the swing from the "commune" of the 1960s to the "community" of the 1970s as the basic social unit. "At least symbolically, the commune had been a place for total, intimate experience within a relatively small group of people." However, they note, "in the communities of the 1970s . . . relationships were to be segmented and muted. . . . The structure of life was increasingly reminiscent of American society prior to the convulsions of the 1960s."[20]

If the record of communal societies in the United States provides little, if any, evidence in support of the participatory argument, it does not necessarily mean that the communal ideal cannot be realized in other countries with different economic and political traditions. For example, a participatory democrat could argue that communitarian patterns of democracy seem to be flourishing in the kibbutz movement in Israel. Some of the earliest settlements trace their origins back to 1910, even though a majority of the existing 230 kibbutzim were founded in the early 1950s during the birth of the Israeli state.[21] While most of the communal settlements are relatively small, averaging around 400 members, their population has grown by about 1 percent during the decade of the 1960s.

Despite the longevity of some of the kibbutzim, it is questionable whether the evolution of these settlements would completely satisfy the expectations of a communitarian democrat. It must be kept in mind that many of the kibbutzim were founded by long-time Zionists and Jewish socialists who were extremely hostile to what they perceived to be the commercialism and crass individualism of modern capitalist society. In establishing enclaves in which all individuals could directly participate in building and running a communal enterprise, the founders of the kibbutzim felt that they were developing an alternative pattern of living that would be quickly emulated throughout the state of Israel. [22] These aspirations have by no means been fulfilled. At its high point, over 7.5 percent of the total Israeli population was tied to the kibbutz movement, with 50 percent of the rural population living in a settlement; today less than 3.5 percent of the overall population and less than 25 percent of rural inhabitants belong to a kibbutz.

In fact, in contrast to the late 1940s, when a whole series of new kibbutzim were created, the last several years have seen the creation of only a handful of communes. Contrary to the hope of its Zionist and socialist founders that the kibbutz would be a form of political existence appealing to a great majority of Jews, such appears not to be the case. Only a very small minority of the Israeli population have found the intense atmosphere of the kibbutz to their liking, and even the many defenders of the kibbutz recognize that the attractiveness of their movement is based as much upon the role the kibbutz has played in Israeli history as it is upon the organnization's political and social principles. Dan Leon argues that "there can be little doubt that the rapid development of all the major kibbutzim . . . can only be explained in terms of the pioneering role which the kibbutzim played in the upbuilding and defense of Jewish Palestine." He acknowledges that "the Israeli commune would have gone the way of other communal experiments . . . were it not for the fact that . . . the kibbutzim played a vanguard role in the Jewish national and social revival in Israel." The kibbutz was constantly in the "forefront of every phase of the struggle for political independence against the . . . Arabs." [23] As substantiating evidence, it is interesting to note that the few additional kibbutzim that have been created in recent years have generally been established in the land the Israelis won in the 1967 Arab war.

If the relatively small number of people who presently belong to a kibbutz raises the question of whether the great majority of individuals could ever be induced to embrace participatory ideals, the lack of participatory fervor within the kibbutz itself raises even more nagging doubts on this subject. The major institution in the kibbutz for making decisions is the general assembly, which usually convenes on a weekly basis. In addition to this meeting, where the majority of members have the power to set policy, there are within the kibbutz numerous committees and elected officials whose job it is to attend to specialized problems facing the commune. While the kibbutz is thus theoretically a pure form of participatory democracy, the practice of kibbutz democracy often falls far short of the communitarian ideal. In the general meeting, for instance, participation is often halfhearted and limited in nature. Avraham Ben-Yosef notes:

> The one serious weakness in the practical application of kibbutz organization is the sporadic attendance of most members at general meetings. There is a tendency for the general meeting to fall, all too fixedly, into the hands of a certain body of stalwarts who almost always attend. . . . It is clear that these phenomena detract not a little from the reality of kibbutz democracy, and although they may be natural enough, they are none the less deplorable. It may well be contended that a member who does not attend the general meeting fairly regularly has no real conception of the kibbutz as a framework for life. [24]

Ben-Yosef adds that "an average attendance of three-quarters of the total membership . . . certainly seems to be desirable, instead of the mere one-third or one-half which usually forms the actual quorum." [25] A small percentage of people who choose to live in a kibbutz—who in turn are a small portion of the Israeli population—indicate a desire to participate fully in the affairs of the commune.

The lack of attendance at the general assembly is only one indication of membership apathy in the kibbutz. Ben-Yosef observes it is often extremely difficult to get people to serve on the various committees within the kibbutz settlement, remarking that the nominating committee, which has the task of choosing people to do service work, "has one of the hardest tasks of all in the kibbutz, for members by no means rush to offer their services." [26] Even with expanded opportunities to become involved in the deliberations of their community, many people elect not to take advantage of them. For supporters of kibbutz democracy such as Ben-Yosef, this lack of public interest raises many problems. He points out that "the kibbutzim insist that their democracy be all embracing," yet he notes that "there is a tendency for a rather narrow leadership group to rotate the many posts among themselves most of the time. . . . These members . . . undoubtedly form a kind of elite."[27] H. Darin-Drabkin has argued that this tendency has become more pronounced over time: "The most conspicuous development has been the shift in the field of policy making from the general assembly to the secretariat and its committees. . . . If we compare the present relationships in the kibbutz with the situation in the 1920s, we find that the general assembly's scope has considerably diminished." In contrast, he notes that the power of the secretariat, the committees, and other executive institutions has been augmented and cautioned that "the strengthening of the centralist forces in the kibbutz and the shift of power to executive institutions contain some inherent dangers to kibbutz democracy which cannot be ignored."[28]

The problems facing the kibbutz are not only political but also social in nature. Besides attempting to build an organization in which all individuals share in the exercise of political power, the kibbutz has tried to develop communal living and educational arrangements. But in recent years the membership's desire to forego their own private lives in order to participate in such communal activities seems to be waning. French and French note that parents increasingly choose to take their meals in their own apartments rather than in the communal dining rooms. Moreover, in contrast "to the established tradition of communal child rearing, many parents are taking their children home for the night rather than leaving them in the communal children's house."[29] In other cases people complain about the joint purchases of goods and services and insist that there be more individualized consumption. When the kibbutzim were relatively unmechanized and poor, people were more willing to adopt a standardized, communal pattern of living. But as French and French remark, "with greater wealth comes increasing opportunity for individualized consumption, and the kibbutz experience indicates that this can be damaging to communal solidarity."[30] Presently the kibbutzim are toying with the idea of allowing personal budgets, but Haim Barkai has observed that this proposal has become the subject of "one of the most heated debates the kibbutz movement has ever come on."[31] Many people perhaps rightly feel that the movement towards more personalized comsumption will jeopardize the very basis of kibbutz solidarity. To observers like Leon, the kibbutz has begun to yield to the dangerous tendency "for the centrifugal forces . . . to grow and for the individual to be so occupied with his own work, his own family, his own social circle and his own interests that he loses sight of the organic totality of kibbutz life."[32] In the opinion of many commentators, the kibbutzim are gradually evolving towards a less collective form of living. French and French even conclude that "the future of collective settlements in Israel would seem to be unclear. The kibbutzim remain alive and well today; it remains to be seen how long this will continue to be true."[33]

If the Israeli kibbutz represents an attempt, however flawed, to build the kind of community that participatory democrats often seem to advocate, it by no means exhausts the possibilities for enhanced individual participation. Many communitarian democrats, including Bachrach, Pateman, and Ellerman, suggest that the most feasible way of building participatory communities in the United States or in any industrial country, for that matter, is through worker control of industry. This is especially true of participatory democrats with socialist leanings, who believe that economic changes need to precede or accompany attempts at increasing individual participation. In fact, the idea of worker participation has gained such popularity that even pluralists like Robert Dahl have affirmed the importance of experimenting with new forms of worker involvement in factories.[34] Yet Dahl has recognized, as many communitarian democrats have not, that perhaps the greatest obstacle to more participation in the work place may be the relative indifference of the average wage earner.

In discussing worker participation, we must distinguish between worker interest in lower-level, or job-centered, issues and in higher-level, or managerial, decisions. Lower-level activities refer "broadly to those management decisions relating to control of day-to-day shop floor activities, while the higher level refers to decisions on investment, marketing and so forth."[35] As Paul Blumberg has shown in a survey of the literature on industrial relations, most workers are interested in having some say in industrial decisions that directly affect them in the shop.[36] As is to be expected, workers appear to prefer democratic managers who treat them with respect to authoritarian supervisors who preside over the shop by fiat. But merely because workers are interested in job-centered problems does not necessarily mean that they want to participate in higher-level, managerial decisions. There is considerable evidence from experiments in a variety of countries indicating that workers are apathetic about such forms of participation.

For example, since 1951 the West German government has attempted to increase worker participation in the operation of the steel and mining industries. By law the government has required firms in these industries to set up workers' councils in which labor shares equally with management the right to make decisions governing vacations, work rules, the administration of plant welfare facilities, and the time and method of wage payments. These same councils also have some say in the determination of pay scales and in the hiring and firing of employees. Most observers of the German workers' councils, including Daniel Kramer and Hardy Wagner, find that the authority of the councils is substantial and that they vigorously exercise the statutory powers granted to them.[37] However, despite the apparent presence of an effective vehicle to govern their factories, most workers appear indifferent to the councils. On a visit to one firm Kramer found that only 15 percent of the work force attended a plant personnel meeting of the workers' council. "It does appear," he notes, "that the reaction of the ordinary employee to the doings of the councils is one of almost total unconcern." Kramer quotes the chairman of another workers' council as saying that "the workers in our place are really not interested in their works councils. They come to us quickly enough if they have a pay question or a dispute about hours with management. They are concerned only with what they can get out of it."[38]

Efforts in other countries to involve workers more fully in industrial decisions have repeatedly fallen short of their objectives. In Israel the attempt to provide for more worker participation in factories has met with even less success than in Germany. The Israeli case is interesting because the enterprises that have attempted to introduce more worker participation are owned by the General Federation of Labor (the Histadrut), an organization that officially describes itself as committed to socialist principles. Between 1945 and 1967 the Histadrut leadership made three major attempts, all of which proved to be unsuccessful, to institutionalize worker participation in the industrial sector.[39] This failure cannot be attributed to any single cause, but worker apathy seems to have been a contributing factor blocking implementation of the program. Keitha Fina concludes that the program failed to work because of "managerial resistance . . . worker reluctance to vary well established norms without drastic technological changes in evidence, and worker apathy towards activities other than those related to setting norms and premiums."[40] In a similar vein, Pateman cites a survey of Norwegian workers by H. Holter that found that only "16% of blue collar and 11% of white collar workers wished they had more participation in decisions concerning the management of the whole firm."[41]

On the basis of a series of instances such as those described above, Paul Blumberg, who is himself an advocate of workers' control, has admitted:

Workers' indifference cannot be overcome simply by involving them directly. And here we must take note of the record of joint consultation bodies, miscellaneous plant committees, and other advisory councils in England, France, Belgium, Sweden, . . . Israel and elsewhere. While these have involved workers directly or through representatives close to home, they have generally proved very disappointing and have failed to arouse workers' sustained interest. . . . In Britain, France, Israel, and India these bodies have achieved the most meager results, at best, and discussions of these forms sound like nothing so much as funeral orations.[42]

The repeated failure of so many efforts to involve labor more fully in the work place thus seems to raise numerous doubts about the feasibility of Pateman's and Bachrach's calls for more worker control.

However, participatory democrats who are also socialists insist that the data we have looked at by no means definitively prove that individuals cannot become interested in the running of their factories. They argue that in a profit-oriented, capitalist system, workers become so socialized into being passive tools of management that they are never likely to want a larger voice in running their own lives. In the view of Ellerman et al., the trouble with

Pateman's argument is that merely expanding political opportunities is insufficient to change the attitudes of the public. The very economic base underlying the political system must also be altered if we expect workers to embrace the goals of participatory democracy. The assumption of Ellerman et al. is that unless the structure of large-scale capitalism is replaced by small-scale political and economic institutions, individuals will lack the incentives necessary to exercise a greater role in shaping the forces that govern them. The inability to grasp this point, a participatory democrat might argue, even accounts for the mistaken belief that the problems we have identified in American communes or Israeli kibbutzim are likely to recur in all communal experiments. Even if communes or factories are based on socialist principles, they are not likely to survive if they exist in a larger capitalist economy.

While this argument has a certain degree of appeal, it is a rather difficult proposition to test. All too often, radical communitarian socialists seem inclined to suggest ad infinitum that if only an additional political or economic change were made, the public would respond as participatory democrats believe they should. Since the prospect of creating a decentralized socialist system in the U.S. is not very promising, it is difficult to predict how people would behave under changed economic conditions. Fortunately, however, the fact that Yugoslavia has adopted a highly decentralized socialist system of government does provide us with some means of examining the thesis of the more radical participatory democrats.

In 1950 Yugoslavia established an economic system that has sought to avoid both the pattern of large-scale capitalism found in the West and the pattern of state socialism practiced by the Soviet Union. In place of a command economy, in which a few elites make decisions, Tito has attempted to create a decentralized system in which a great deal of economic and political power is devolved to individual factories. Up until 1970 the state required every economic enterprise to set up a workers' council to be elected by the employees. While workers' councils, which usually consisted of twenty members, were theoretically to retain primary responsibility for running the enterprise, most elected a smaller management board and appointed a director to assume operating responsibility for the factory. Since the Yugoslavian model seems to satisfy the conditions stipulated by communitarian socialists, we should expect to find more workers displaying interest and participating in the operation of the factories. However, as in many nonsocialist countries, the data on Yugoslavian worker participation are not very encouraging. First of all, it should be pointed out that worker control of factories is a highly indirect, formalistic process. To alter conditions in their enterprises, employees must work through their elected representatives on the workers' councils. But as Kramer has noted, many workers' councils often ignore the demands of their own constituents: "A questionnaire circulated by . . . [the journal] *Borba* showed that only fifty-six per cent of the workers who completed the form said that their work council had disclosed to them what it was trying to accomplish."[43] Secondly, even when the councils do stay in closer contact with workers, it is an open question whether they actually exercise much power. Opinion on this subject is split. Fred Neal has argued "that the meaningfulness of worker management varied from enterprise to enterprise."[44] In some plants he found workers' councils that were in control of factory operations, while in other cases he encountered councils that were not coming to grips with any important managerial problems. In contrast, in several studies of worker perceptions of influence within their factories, Josip Zupanov and Arnold Tannenbaum have observed that the director, rather than the workers' council, wields the most power.[45] Similarly, Jiri Kolaja conducted content analysis of numerous council meetings and has concluded that the plant director and not the workers' council is the key figure in the Yugoslavian factory.[46] In one plant, for instance, he found that in the course of a year the director seemed responsible for initiating over sixty-six decisions while the councils seemed responsible for only nine.

Even if workers' councils were more active in running their factories than the present evidence indicates, we still need to know (1) whether workers think self-management is an important goal to strive for and (2) whether they as individuals are willing to spend their time participating in such self-management councils. Until recently, most observers have found that workers said it was important to strengthen the power of workers' councils—or at least paid lip service to such a goal. However, Veljko Rus has pointed out that in recent years public support for all-powerful councils has abated. By 1968, he noted, most workers argued that the managers should have about the same amount of power as that exercised by the councils. [47] Likewise, Gerry Hunnius has observed that after a constitutional amendment was passed in 1970, relaxing the standards for worker participation in factories, many firms became more centralized in their operations. [48] The Yugoslavian government undertook the constitutional revision in order to enhance the flexibility of individual factories, allowing the amount of power that enterprises parcel out to workers' councils to be a matter of their own choosing. In order to maximize the plant's efficiency and productivity, many workers have taken advantage of the new constitutional provisions to concede more power to their own corps of professionally trained managers and to deemphasize the importance of the workers' councils.

When we inquire whether most workers themselves are eager to participate in the operations of the councils, the evidence is negative. In 1965 Josip Obradovic undertook an extensive survey of worker attitudes in Yugoslavia, interviewing over 537 workers in twenty different plants. [49] On the basis of his survey he "concluded that participation in self-management should not be overemphasized as a source of satisfaction." [50] He noted that workers mentioned wages, working conditions, and possibilities for advancement highest in their list of desired job characteristics. In contrast, participation on workers' councils rated fifth with participants and sixth with nonparticipants. Many other observers of Yugoslavian factories have often remarked that the average worker is indifferent to participation in self-management. Ichak Adizes relates the conversation of one worker, who told him, "Let someone else manage; I want good pay." He observes that instead of eagerly participating in the affairs of their council, many individuals complain of the constant round of meetings and political activities as a drain on their time. [51]

Sharon Zukin arrives at a similar conclusion in her study of public attitudes in Yugoslavia, noting that "Yugoslavians tend to see self-management more in terms of economic benefits than ideological goals." [52] In an extensive set of discussions with numerous Yugoslavians, she finds that "self-management as an ideological goal has little relevance to people's everyday lives" and that most "appear preoccupied with the standard of living. . . . The two decades of self-management are perceived as a given institution, a formalism from which the ordinary Yugoslav derives only such benefits as he can see and spend."[53] Similarly, Kolaja observed that Yugoslavian workers are often highly selective in their participation, displaying little or no concern about many of the general industrial problems facing their factories but great interest in more personal questions, such as how many apartments their plants will build and who will be assigned to them.[54] In fact, on the basis of studies such as Kolaja's, Pateman admits that among average Yugoslavian factory workers "there is evidence of a more general lack of knowledge of, and interest in, the basic working of the system."[55] However, later she tries to argue that "the Yugoslav experience gives us no good reason to suppose that the democratization of industrial authority structure is impossible, difficult and complicated though it may be."[56] Whether the evidence she herself cites warrants such optimism is another question.

As has been true of experiments with worker control in Germany and elsewhere, the Yugoslavian effort to increase participation has not met with complete success. While communitarian socialists claim that changes in the economic structure will precipitate alterations in worker attitudes and behavior, the record seems to indicate otherwise. Over a quarter of a century of decentralized socialism in Yugoslavia appears to have had no appreciable impact on the willingness of its citizenry to participate actively in industrial affairs. A few Yugoslavian socialists like Dragan Markovic argue that the "consciousness of workers formed in capitalist relations of production—when the means of production have been separated from producers—is changing very slowly,"[57] but they overlook the fact that workers appear to be becoming less, rather than more, concerned with self-management, the longer socialism exists in Yugoslavia. Even when there are ample opportunities to become involved, people seem unable to sustain any long-term interest in inclusive forms of communal or industrial participation, preferring instead to restrict their involvement to matters of more direct and personal concern.

If workers often choose not to participate more fully in communal activities, participatory democrats of a socialist persuasion always have the convenient argument of claiming that the public is still suffering from "false consciousness." Many communal socialists seem to fall into the trap of insisting that there is a one-to-one relationship between a country's economic system and its political institutions. But as anyone knows after even a cursory look at the diverse array of governments in various countries where the means of production are publicly owned, the link between politics and economics is not always that apparent. Moreover, it should be stressed that even if we accept the participatory socialist critique as valid, it would still be possible to question the feasibility of implementing the communitarian model. If the creation of a more decentralized, egalitarian socialist community would change public attitudes towards community involvement, one must ask how participatory socialists expect to build a socialist society in a country they believe to be dominated by capitalist interests. The socialist variety of participatory democracy seems flawed in that it lacks a meaningful theory of social change. While communitarian democrats have a vision of the kind of society they would like to build, they provide few if any viable suggestions as to how that vision will finally be attained. To insist that people will change only if certain economic or political reforms are instituted begs the question of how those alterations are to be implemented in the first place.

The Nature of Communal Life

There are still other difficulties that plague a participatory form of democracy. It is certainly not clear from the record of previous experiments in communal living whether small communities are the most suitable form of government for encouraging meaningful public debate. Nevertheless, most communitarian democrats have insisted that small political units provide the individual with more opportunities for meaningful participation than do larger bodies of government. Through the vehicle of the town meeting or communal gathering, scaled-down units of government supposedly afford every citizen the chance to discuss the whole range of issues facing the community. Unfortunately, however, the practice of small, face-to-face communities often falls short of their promise. Indeed, there seems to be considerable evidence that such communities tend to inhibit public debate rather than to facilitate it. Edward Banfield, James Q. Wilson, Arthur Vidich, Joseph Bensman and A. H. Birch have observed that people in small communities usually go out of their way to avoid discussing controversial issues.[58] City councils in small towns are often noted for their ability to ramble on indefinitely without ever coming to grips with the issues before them. Instead of directly confronting potentially troublesome problems, most seek to avoid dealing with the issues as long as possible, and when they finally do make decisions, they usually formulate proposals in such a way as to gain the support of every member of the council. Vidich and Bensman reported that in the two years they observed a small town government at work, "all decisions brought to a vote were passed unanimously. The dissent, disagreement, and factionalism which existed in the community [were] not expressed at board meetings."[59]

In a similar vein, utopian communities and kibbutz settlements often develop norms that lead to the repression, rather than the expression, of alternative points of view. Kanter has noted that many of the utopian experiments of the nineteenth century went out of their way to ostracize persons who deviated in the slightest way from the established norms of the community.[60] Rather than encouraging individuals to question the prevailing style of life, most communes sought to resocialize their members to conform to existing patterns of behavior. Even when communities held assemblies to formulate policy, their purpose was often less to hear and act upon the grievances of their members than to instill the kinds of attitudes that would prevent them from complaining in the first place. Robert Hine has observed in his study of utopian colonies in California over the last hundred years that those communes that lasted for any length of time were often extremely authoritarian, requiring "unquestioning obedience to leadership."[61] Similarly, Bruno Bettelheim has pointed out that there are well-defined restraints on meaningful debate in the Israeli kibbutz. Bettelheim argues that kibbutz children are trained not to deviate from the norms of the community and that while they can criticize certain practices of the settlement, they come to realize that there are clearly defined limits beyond which they should not venture.[62]

Likewise Melford Spiro claims that "although the regimentation that certain critics of socialism regard as intrinsic to a planned society is not characteristic [of the kibbutz] there can be no doubt that one's choices are restricted in a social system of this type."[63] He points out that "group censure, informal though it is, is highly effective in a small community" in dampening the expression of unpopular ideas.[64]

There are a variety of possible explanations that may account for the restricted political life in these types of communities. Kanter at times suggests that the lack of genuine debate and participation in many of the nineteenth-century utopian settlements was an accident of their precarious situation.[65] Since many communities faced an uncertain existence, they went to great lengths to reinforce the commitment of their followers by limiting the influx of new ideas and by pressuring members to internalize the prevailing norms of the group. This explanation suggests that the very scarcity of people who wanted to belong to an affective community may in part account for the fact that many communes chose to restrict, rather than expand, the scope of public debate.

However, at other times Kanter, as well as scholars like Bettelheim and Boris Stern, have implied that the hostility of communal settlements to internal debate was inherent in their very conception of community and public participation.[66] Stern has remarked that the socialist founders of the kibbutz considered "the movement to represent the highest form of social organization as yet devised by human beings. As such the kibbutz community cannot tolerate deviations, revisionism, or internal revolutionary changes." "All educational and cultural activities of the kibbutz," he noted, "are designed to transmit to the children the importance of preserving the kibbutz and its social and moral values."[67] Communal movements like the kibbutz have been founded on the belief that public participation will lead to individual moral growth and self-development since it will allow the individual to identify with the higher moral purposes embodied in the community. Participation is not simply a mechanism for achieving compromises among competing private interests; on the contrary, it is a means for the individual to overcome his selfish concerns by involving himself with the welfare of the community as a whole.

However, in specifying the ways in which men should benefit

from participation, many communal movements have ended up restricting the scope of public debate. If participation should lead to individual moral development, as they have believed, then participation cannot be a completely open-end process. Utopian communities and kibbutz settlements have had no reason to tolerate—let alone encourage—a diversity of opinions since they have believed they know how men should develop in the first place. If people will morally grow only when they become less concerned with their own private affairs, there seems to be little justification for tolerating what has often been interpreted as self-serving criticism on the part of individual participants. When people have argued over the goals of the group, it is only natural that participatory settlements have seen it as a failure of communal spirit. Because utopian communities and kibbutz settlements have believed that citizen involvement is a means of making people more public minded, it is perhaps inevitable that they have insisted participation reinforce, not challenge, the norms of the group. In the process these communities have inverted the purpose of participation by insisting that individuals involve themselves in community affairs, not to debate the objectives of the group, but to internalize community goals that have already been formulated.

This conception of participation was summed up well by Rousseau's notion of the "general will."[68] Rousseau believed that the individual could attain moral self-development through participation in the life of the community, but he shared with many modern participatory democrats some definite notions about which forms of citizen involvement were permissible and which were not. Although at times he suggested that people should be free to participate as they wished, he also insisted that they ought to "will the general will," that they should affirm the standards best suited to the larger community.[69] Since Rousseau believed that an individual would not morally grow or develop unless he chose what was in the common interest of all, he did not believe that public participation could be a process of totally unrestricted give-and-take. Like the members of the utopian settlements and kibbutzim, Rousseau regarded popular participation less as a means for identifying and resolving public differences than as a vehicle for realizing higher moral purposes.

Although many participatory democrats have espoused very limited conceptions of participation, other advocates of communal forms of democracy entertain less restrictive views on this subject. For instance, unlike many of his predecessors, Wolff repeatedly stresses the need for communities to develop elaborate procedures to guarantee full and complete discussion.[70] Wolff is eager to build a theory of participatory democracy that does not specify in a priori fashion the benefits that will accrue to individuals from participating in public affairs. In contrast to Rousseau and the builders of the utopian communities and kibbutz settlements, he envisions the creation of a polity that normatively will tolerate the expression of a diversity of opinions. The question we need to ask, however, is whether empirically it is possible to have much meaningful debate in a small community. Even if the founders of participatory settlements do not equate individual development with the internalization of group standards, strong pressures may inevitably develop within the community to choke off debate.

The avoidance of controversy in small towns is instructive in this respect. Students of urban politics have often argued that the reluctance of small communities to tolerate dissent may reflect their fear of public conflict. As the unit of government in which people interact becomes smaller, the problem of dealing with discord becomes more acute. This observation raises troublesome problems for one of participatory democracy's most cherished beliefs, that the differences that divide men are not serious in nature. In contrast to pluralists, who insist that there are always likely to be disagreements between individuals that can be compromised but never completely eliminated, participatory democrats have been much more sanguine about the possibility of eliminating conflict. They have argued that by scaling down the size of the political community it will be possible for people to resolve their differences amicably and decide upon mutually satisfactory policies. But ironically enough, many observers, including George Simmel, Lewis Coser, and Banfield and Wilson, suggest that the opposite relationship may be true: the closer the ties between people become, the more likely intense conflict will occur.[71] Thus when the unit of government becomes smaller, the danger that disagreement will become intense and uncontainable increases rather than diminishes. In small communities there is no way to segment or isolate differences between individuals. As Simmel notes:

> The more we have in common with another as a whole person, the more easily will our totality be involved in every single relation to him. Therefore if a quarrel arises between persons in an internal relationship, it often . . . will be . . . passionately expansive. [72]

Similarly, as Coser points out, if people constantly interact with one another, the possibility exists "that conflict would mobilize the entire affect of [an individual's] personality" and totally disrupt his personal relations. [73] Banfield and Wilson observe that when conflict does arise in small communities, it is often difficult to contain since by their very nature small localities have no formal structure for dealing with dissension in an impersonal manner. It is precisely because of this danger that small communities have a tendency either to avoid or to suppress situations of potential conflict. The generally accepted rule of unanimity and the rambling, pointless style of discourse characteristic of many small towns are effective ways of insuring that individuals are not put on the spot or forced to clearly examine their differences with others. [74] Besides tacitly agreeing not to disagree, the only other option is for communities to pressure their members into internalizing certain common standards of behavior.

While many of the utopian settlements or kibbutzim may have restricted public debate because they had a particular conception of the benefits of participation, their policies also helped to prevent potentially dangerous disagreements from breaking out. Hine has noted in his study of California communes that the most democratic organizations were the ones least likely to last. In those organizations that established general assemblies to foster debate, "tremendous conflicts" arose "which usually proved quickly fatal." [75] Perhaps inevitably, then, most participatory experiments have attempted to avoid or suppress debate and conflict, for when they occur, their impact on the group is difficult to limit. If issues ever do break through these social restraints, they are apt, as Banfield and Wilson note, "to polarize the community into hostile camps." [76]

The Internal Dilemma of Participatory Democracy

Even if participatory communities did encourage more internal debate, there are additional reasons for being skeptical about their ability to foster meaningful citizen involvement. As a basic tenet, participatory democrats have wanted to increase both the individual's ability to participate and his power to control the events that trouble him. However, as Dahl has pointed out, a conflict may exist between maximizing opportunities for individual involvement and maximizing the ability to actually implement one's wishes. [77] If we want to expand individual participation, we must, as most communitarian democrats have long recognized, limit the size and population of the political unit. Naturally, as the number of members in a community begins to grow, the ability of each individual to influence the shaping of policy must decline correspondingly.

As a way of illustrating this point, we might try to estimate how many people could be expected to play a moderate to active role in the deliberations of a community. If we take as our model the New England town meeting, which two or three hundred persons might attend, we would soon see that the limits of time would severely restrict the actual number of participants who could voice their opinions. If the community held a meeting once a week for four hours, and if the time allotted to each individual was ten minutes, only twenty-four people would be able to state their views. These individuals would represent less than one-tenth of the total number of people gathered in the assembly. As the community became smaller, the percentage of people who could play a direct role would naturally begin to grow. Thus the size of the political unit and the degree of citizen involvement are inversely related. However, as the size of the community diminishes, so do the resources and power it can draw on to cope with problems that are regional or national in nature. The smaller the jurisdiction of the political unit, the less its "government can regulate aspects of the environment that its citizens want to regulate, from air and water pollution and racial justice to the dissemination of nuclear weapons." [78] In their quest for effective or meaningful participation, communitarian democrats thus seem to confront an unresolvable paradox. By reducing the size of the polity, they increase the opportunities for individuals to participate; but by increasing the opportunities for citizen involvement, they run the risk of trivializing its importance. The smaller the unit of government, the less significant become the issues that the individuals within the political community can effectively influence.

This dilemma is best seen in the work of Wolff, one of the most articulate defenders of communitarian democracy. In "Beyond Tolerance" Wolff talks of the need for developing policies that will deal with pressing collective problems such as poverty, public order, and pollution.[79] However, his solution to these problems is not to centralize power but to fragment it among many independent communities. While these units may afford numerous opportunities for the individual to participate in politics, Wolff provides no hint as to how they will be able to deal effectively with the social ills that alarm him. Since most of the issues he mentions transcend narrow political units, any established participatory government would lack jurisdiction for effectively alleviating these problems. Likewise, if independent communes were not subject to the authority of a larger political entity, the danger might arise that one unit's answer to an issue like pollution would be unacceptable to other localities.

The Costs and Benefits of Intensive Participation

It is also possible to argue that the psychological costs of intensive communal participation often outweigh their assumed benefits. Nevertheless, communitarian democrats have frequently defended active citizen involvement for just the opposite reason. They insist that pluralism, like most other theories of democracy, fails to appreciate the value of participation as an end in and of itself. In their view, public involvement itself is a means of realizing man's fullest moral and emotional potential and is thus desirable apart from any instrumental benefits it might provide.

However, most participatory democrats have mustered very little evidence in support of their contention that communal life has a beneficial effect on the individual personality. Indeed, if we look at analyses of the impact of communal life in the Israeli kibbutz on the psychological makeup of its members, we find evidence which, although fragmentary in nature, suggests that intensive forms of participation may entail very high costs. Scholars like Murray Weingarten, Yonina Talmon, Bruno Bettelheim, A. I. Rabin, and Melford Spiro—who are by no means unsympathetic observers of the kibbutz—have found that communal forms of life often stifle, rather than enhance, an individual's sense of freedom and self-fulfillment. [80] Even though the kibbutz may envelop the individual in an affective community and successfully socialize him to look after the interests of the larger whole, it appears to impoverish his outlook on life. Bettelheim has noted that

in . . . striving to undo social alienation on the one hand and too much family closeness on the other [members of the kibbutz] have gone way out in seeking a solidarity of equals. But having enjoyed collective closeness for a while now, they seem to find it hard to bear at times.

Precisely because they share so much of daily life with each other, they have a great need, like turtles, to withdraw into their shells. Though they greet each other with a "Shalom!" or "How's things?" twenty times or more each day, they really have little to talk about, since everyone knows everything about everyone else—good reason to withhold the really important things for oneself and to share them with no one. [81]

In a similar vein, Murray Weingarten has pointed out that the word *matzuv raah* ("depression") is very popular in a number of kibbutzim. Because life in a communal setting places heavy demands on a person's time and energy, many individuals consciously or subconsciously feel overburdened by community affairs. Rather than being fulfilled by the intensity of their affective ties with other members of the settlement, they become depressed by their inability to have a life apart from the kibbutz. Weingarten notes that in recognition of this problem, some kibbutzim have formulated an individual bill of rights in order to provide people with a private outlet for the expression of their own needs. [82]

Likewise, Yonina Talmon has observed that most members of the second generation are very ambivalent about the continuity of the kibbutz movement. While they believe that they have an obligation to their parents and to the kibbutz that raised them to stay and help the movement survive, they often see communal activities as restricting, rather than enlarging or enriching, their lives. Regardless of the sense of security that the closely knit community provides, many feel a sense of claustrophobia within the kibbutz settlement. Talmon notes that the decision to remain a part of the community is often a difficult one.

The duty to stay on in the native village engenders a deep fear of closure because it implies blocked mobility and a curtailment of life chances. It imposes a drastic limitation on free choice of domicile, of career or associates, and of friends. The cultivation of external contact and the period of service outside the kibbutz mitigate local closure but at the same time accentuate the problems involved in local continuity. Many second generation members are loath to sever their external ties and to forego the more variegated opportunities offered by life outside their kibbutz. They feel cut off and hemmed in. [83]

In addition to limiting the individual's freedom to act as he pleases, the closeness of the kibbutz also seems to retard the creativity of its members. Because children are taught to be concerned about the welfare of the community, they are often discouraged from entertaining ideas that challenge well-engrained attitudes. The spirit of loyalty and commitment that the kibbutz attempts to instill in its members frequently tends to kill off any spark of originality or uniqueness in its children. A. I. Rabin has observed that "the kibbutz subject's own goals are rather short range, characterized by a short future time perspective." [84] He maintains that "this trend is primarily due to the fact that the kibbutz does not hold out the freedom of vocational and occupational choice to its membership; individual goals of a long range are determined by the collectivity." [85] In a similar vein, Bettelheim argues that the "personality of the kibbutz-born generation seems depleted compared to the complexity and richness in some of the first generation." [86] To further confirm this point, we may note that soldiers from the kibbutz often seem to lack the ability to make flexible and spontaneous adjustments to ever changing situations. In the opinion of many Israeli officers, children of the kibbutz are committed and courageous fighters who will endure countless hardships to protect their country, but they are unable to adapt effectively to situations with which they have had no prior experience.[87] The environment from which they come seems to have provided them with limited capacity to deal with the vagaries of new and complex developments.[88]

Even though life in a kibbutz often seems to result in a sense of claustrophobia, lack of a private life, and diminished creativity, it still is possible to argue that the friendship and warm, supportive environment of the commune more than compensate for any of these deficiencies. In an intensive, affective organization we would expect few members to suffer from human isolation or lack of close personal ties. However, in an important study, *Children of the Kibbutz,* Melford Spiro raises serious doubts about the veracity of this claim. On the basis of his examination of kibbutz children, he notes:

> Very few *sabras* [those born and raised in a kibbutz] have intimate friends. Even in the high school the "chum" or "buddy"—the inseparable same sex friend that is so characteristic of American adolescent behavior—is all but nonexistent. Moreover, the ordinary close friend is also infrequent. . . . The situation is no different from the adult *sabras.* . . . The *sabras* not only avoid deep emotional relationships with a few, but they maintain an attitude of psychological distance with the many.[89]

Spiro insists that these traits are not endemic in Israeli culture nor found among Jews in general, for he claims that "since this syndrome is not characteristic of the *sabra's* parents, we may further assume that such experiences are a function of kibbutz socialization."[90]

Ironically enough, many communitarian democrats advocate the creation of a collective form of politics because they believe that the atomistic nature of early liberalism has had damaging psychological consequences for the individual. They argue that because the highly individualistic outlook of liberalism ignores man's social needs, it has led to the alienation, rather than the fulfillment, of the individual. What participatory democrats have failed to see is that their own proposals to create a tightly knit community can likewise have serious psychological repercussions. While extreme individualism seems to lead to social isolation or anomic behavior, a small, cohesive political and social organization seems to restrict a person's opportunities to develop his own personality. Even though children in a participatory setting may be more community minded than individuals raised on the outside, they frequently end up paying a relatively high price. In exchange for the alleged benefits of affective ties with others, they often must curtail their imagination and control their creative instincts. Instead of being ennobling, participation in a communal form of politics seems to be a restricting experience that limits the overall development of the individual. While communitarian democrats claim that pluralism fails to appreciate the beneficial effects of participation as an end in and of itself, the actual record of participation in the types of communities described above shows that involvement in such communities frequently has its offsetting psychological costs.

A Reassessment of the Data

Despite the critical implications of the empirical studies cited above, a variety of commentators have questioned whether it is valid to evaluate the prospects for participatory democracy on the basis of past historical examples. Some proponents of communitarian participation maintain that empirical data can never undermine or refute what is basically a normative theory of democracy. Graeme Duncan and Steven Lukes insist that "to claim that sociological findings can show these . . . political theories to be demonstrably invalid is seriously to misunderstand the most basic features of much political theory, which often touches reality only at the edges."[91] They maintain that participatory democrats are not so much proposing an empirical theory of government that is readily attainable as offering a normative ideal that they hope people will eventually aspire to fulfill. Advocates of communitarian democracy regard their theory as a critique of the status quo and look upon intensive participation as a goal that men should constantly try to attain. While they recognize that people fail to live up to the assumptions of the communitarian model, they see no need to abandon the goal itself. On the contrary, because intensive participation is an ideal, communitarian forms of democracy are valid as a standard for measuring and evaluating the worthiness of our present political institutions. The gap between the assumptions of the participatory model and the behavior of the public is thus less an indication of the model's failure than a sign of the need for political reform. The theories of communitarian democracy "are a critique of reality in terms of a vision of human nature and possibilities, and for this reason cannot simply be refuted on the grounds that people do not satisfy the required standards."[92]

While the above line of reasoning may seem persuasive, it is flawed in two respects. First of all, even if we accept the participatory argument as a radical critique of the status quo and a statement of a more egalitarian ideal, it is still important to ask if the vision of communitarian democracy can ever be achieved. Unless advocates of communal politics such as Duncan and Lukes are willing to agree that their conception of democracy is merely a utopian goal with no chance of ever being realized, it is important to empirically assess the feasibility of building a participatory community. All social critics must eventually decide if their proposals are merely wistful propositions that perhaps only "true believers" may find interesting, or if they are serious calls for reform that will one day become a reality. Secondly, and even more importantly, Duncan's and Luke's argument seems to be based on a misunderstanding of what the empirical evidence actually shows. They suggest that merely because the data indicate that it is not presently feasible to implement the goal of communitarian democracy, we should not jettison the participatory ideal. But an important question to ask is whether the ideals of communitarian democracy are worth achieving regardless of whether or not they are feasible to implement. To make that assessment we need to know if the achievement of certain values, such as a sense of community, compromises other important values, such as individuality or creativity. While studies such as Bettelheim's or Weingarten's cannot tell us how to rank order different sets of objectives, they can certainly provide some insight into the costs of realizing alternative sets of values. The dichotomy that Duncan and Lukes implicitly make between a feasible and a normative argument does not undermine the relevance of empirical data for evaluating the claims of communitarian democrats. In this sense, the collection of empirical data is central to a proper assessment of the benefits and drawbacks of participatory democracy.

It should also be pointed out that even if we accept the proposition that the empirical data on participation are unfavorable, other critics have suggested that evidence from past experiments in communitarian democracy does not necessarily imply anything about the future. Merely because some attempts at achieving more intensive participation have been flawed does not logically mean that all future attempts must likewise fail. However, even though the thrust of this argument is basically correct, it seems somewhat beside the point. The possibility exists that in certain cases people might be able to sustain an interest in a participatory settlement that provided its members with a satisfying, rather than restrictive, communal existence. The limitations of other experiments do not rule out that eventuality. But it is necessary to stress that the available data indicate that the outlook for building such communal forms of democracy on a widespread scale is not very promising.

NOTES

1. Robert Paul Wolff, *In Defense of Anarchism;* Robert Paul Wolff, *The Poverty of Liberalism;* Peter Bachrach, *The Theory of Democratic Elitism;* David Ellerman, "Capitalism and Workers' Self-Management," pp. 3-20.

2. Wolff, *Poverty of Liberalism,* pp. 185-95; Carole Pateman, *Participation and Democratic Theory,* pp. 79-101. See also Arnold S. Kaufman, "Human Nature and Participatory Democracy," pp. 178-201.

3. Ellerman, "Capitalism and Workers' Self-Management," pp. 3-20.

4. Jean Jacques Rousseau, *The Social Contract,* p. 20.

5. Terrence Cook and Patrick Morgan, *Participatory Democracy,* p. 10.

6. Philip Converse, "The Nature of Belief Systems in Mass Publics," pp. 206-61; Sidney Verba and Norman Nie, *Participation in America,* p. 106; David E. RePass, "Issue Salience and Party Choice," pp. 389-400.

7. Gabriel Almond and Sidney Verba, *The Civic Culture,* pp. 337-75.

8. Pateman, *Participation and Democratic Theory,* pp. 79-101.

9. Ellerman, "Capitalism and Workers' Self-Management"; Charles Hampden-Turner, "The Factory as an Oppressive and Non-Emancipatory Environment," pp. 30-45; Paul Jacobs and Saul Landau, eds., *The New Radicals,* p. 154.

10. Rosabeth Moss Kanter, *Commitment and Community,* p. 63.

11. Ibid., pp. 75-125.

12. Ibid., p. 82.

13. Ibid., p. 103.

14. Ibid., p. 106.
15. Ibid., p. 107.
16. Ibid., p. 146.
17. David French and Elena French, *Working Communally*, pp. 65-67.
18. Ibid., p. 67.
19. Ibid., p. 69.
20. Ibid., p. 103.
21. Dan Leon, *The Kibbutz*, pp. 1-24.
22. Ibid., pp. 1-24.
23. Ibid., p. 15.
24. Avraham Ben-Yosef, *The Purest Democracy in the World*, pp. 33-34.
25. Ibid., p. 34.
26. Ibid., p. 29.
27. Ibid., p. 32.
28. H. Darin-Drabkin, *The Other Society*, p. 109.
29. French and French, *Working Communally*, p. 135.
30. Ibid., p. 137.
31. Haim Barkai, *The Kibbutz*, p. 40.
32. Leon, *The Kibbutz*, p. 73.
33. French and French, *Working Communally*, p. 135.
34. Robert Dahl, *After the Revolution*, pp. 120-40.
35. Pateman, *Participation and Democratic Theory*, p. 70.
36. Paul Blumberg, *Industrial Democracy*, pp. 70-138.
37. Daniel Kramer, *Participatory Democracy*, p. 78; Hardy Wagner, *Erfahr ungen mit dem Betriebsverfassungsgesetz*, pp. 82-90.
38. D. Kramer, *Participatory Democracy*, p. 82.
39. Keitha Sapsin Fine, "Worker Participation in Israel," pp. 226-67.
40. Ibid., p. 238.
41. Pateman, *Participation and Democratic Theory*, p. 85.
42. Blumberg, *Industrial Democracy*, p. 3.
43. D. Kramer, *Participatory Democracy*, p. 81.
44. Fred Neal, *Titoism in Action*, p. 138.
45. Josip Zupanov and Arnold S. Tannenbaum, "The Distribution of Control in Some Yugoslav Industrial Organizations as Perceived by Members," pp. 98-99.
46. Jiri Kolaja, *Workers' Councils*, p. 34.
47. Veljko Rus, "Influence Structure in Yugoslav Enterprise," p. 150.
48. Gerry Hunnius, "Yugoslavia," p. 267.
49. Josip Obradovic, "Participation and Work Attitudes in Yugoslavia," pp. 161-69.

50. Josip Obradovic, as summarized by Gerry Hunnius, "Workers' Self-Management in Yugoslavia," p. 303.

51. Ichak Adizes, *Industrial Democracy*, p. 219.

52. Sharon Zukin, *Beyond Marx and Tito*, p. 97.

53. Ibid., p. 98.

54. Kolaja, *Workers' Councils*, pp. 45-50.

55. Pateman, *Participation and Democratic Theory*, p. 99.

56. Ibid., p. 102.

57. Dragan Markovic et al., *Factories to Their Workers*, p. 18.

58. Edward C. Banfield and James Q. Wilson, *City Politics*, p. 25; Arthur J. Vidich and Joseph Bensman, *Small Town in Mass Society*, pp. 111-15; A. H. Birch, *Small Town Politics*.

59. Vidich and Bensman, *Small Town in Mass Society*, p. 112.

60. Kanter, *Commitment and Community*, pp. 75-126.

61. Robert Hine, *California's Utopian Colonies*, p. 170.

62. Bruno Bettelheim, *Children of the Dream*.

63. Melford Spiro, *Kibbutz*, p. 204.

64. Ibid., p. 99.

65. Kanter, *Commitment and Community*, pp. 71, 75-90.

66. Bettelheim, *Children of the Dream*, pp. 13-28, 303-17; Boris Stern, *The Kibbutz That Was*, p. 117.

67. Stern, *The Kibbutz that Was*, p. 117.

68. J. L. Talmon, *The Origins of Totalitarian Democracy*.

69. See also Patrick Riley, "A Possible Explanation of Rousseau's General Will."

70. Wolff, *Poverty of Liberalism*, pp. 3-51.

71. Banfield and Wilson, *City Politics*; Lewis Coser, *The Functions of Social Conflict*.

72. George Simmel, quoted in Coser, *Functions of Social Conflict*, p. 67.

73. Coser, *Functions of Social Conflict*, p. 69.

74. Banfield and Wilson, *City Politics*, p. 25.

75. Hine, *California's Utopian Colonies*, p. 170.

76. Banfield and Wilson, *City Politics*, p. 25.

77. Robert Dahl, "Democracy and the Chinese Boxes," p. 374.

78. Ibid.

79. Robert Paul Wolff, Barrington Moore, Jr., and Herbert Marcuse, *A Critique of Pure Tolerance*, pp. 49-53.

80. Murray Weingarten, "The Individual and the Community"; Yonina Talmon, *Family and Community in the Kibbutz*; Bettelheim, *Children*

of the Dream; A. I. Rabin, *Growing Up in the Kibbutz;* Melford Spiro, *Children of the Kibbutz.*

81. Bettelheim, *Children of the Dream,* p. 251.
82. Weingarten, "The Individual and the Community," p. 519.
83. Y. Talmon, *Family and Community in the Kibbutz,* p. 160.
84. Rabin, *Growing Up in the Kibbutz,* p. 209.
85. Ibid., p. 294.
86. Bettelheim, *Children of the Dream,* p. 294.
87. Ibid., p. 294.
88. Ibid., p. 264.
89. Spiro, *Children of the Kibbutz,* p. 424.
90. Ibid., p. 429.
91. Graeme Duncan and Steven Lukes, "Democracy Restated," p. 197.
92. Ibid., p. 199.

PART III

The Issue of Decision Making

The previous section of this book has analyzed in considerable detail how various theories of democracy have viewed the problem of public participation. In this third and final section, we need to deal with one remaining issue in democratic theory, the problem of decision making. The reason for focusing on this issue is undoubtedly obvious since most people choose to participate in politics in order to affect the outcome of public decisions. For analytic reasons we have separated the problem of decision making from that of participation, but we must recognize that for all practical purposes the two issues are intimately linked. The scope of popular participation is bound to affect the content of any publicly made decision. As we shall see, most theories of democracy implicitly—if not explicitly—contain a theory of decision making that complements and reinforces its theory of participation. The alternative approaches to democracy that we have considered disagree not only on the capabilities of the individual to participate in politics but also on the consequences of public involvement for governmental decision making.

To explore these differences in a more systematic fashion, chapter 9 will examine the proposals various democratic theorists have advanced for altering the decision-making process. While pluralists want to share power between government officials and the numerous interest groups in society, polyarchists want to concentrate authority in the hands of elected officials and participatory democrats want to disperse power among smaller communities and neighborhoods. These theories of democracy often rely on radically different arguments for justifying the restructuring of the decision-making process. By analyzing a variety of studies of community decision making, I hope to demonstrate that the proposals of participatory and polyarchal democracy fail to achieve their stated objectives even when judged by the criteria they themselves suggest are important. In contrast, I hope to show how a pluralistic form of decision making, involving mutual adjustment among numerous parties, can yield many of the benefits that more centralized or decentralized decision-making procedures are purportedly capable of achieving.

Finally, chapter 10 will focus on the problem of policy implementation, or public administration. Not only do alternative approaches to democratic theory have radically different assessments of what kinds of decision-making procedures are apt to be effective; they also disagree with one another over what kinds of institutional or administrative procedures are apt to be successful in translating publicly determined goals into workable policy. Polyarchal and populist democrats believe it is possible to prevent public policies from being distorted or altered at the administrative stage if the goals of government agencies are clearly defined and their discretionary powers are strictly limited. While these versions of democracy tend to view organizations in Weberian terms as rational, neutral instruments for achieving externally determined goals, pluralist democrats recognize that administrative bodies are highly political and on occasion even pathological in their behavior, and they argue that a process of partisan mutual adjustment is necessary to limit and neutralize these organizational tendencies. In the pluralist view, the give-and-take of interest-group bargaining can improve the implementation of public decisions as well as contribute to their formulation.

Chapter
9

Pluralism and the
Problem of Decision Making

Because most theories of democracy have different estimates of people's ability to participate in politics, it is important to know how public involvement affects the content of government policies. Besides determining to what extent people are capable of participating in politics, a normative theory of democracy must decide to what extent popular participation has beneficial or deleterious effects on the output of the political system. Some scholars believe a tradeoff exists between participation and effective policy making, while others insist that the two complement and reinforce one another. In part, this chapter will attempt to determine which of these claims is the more accurate and defensible position.

Community control advocates like Alan Altshuler or Milton Kotler—who represent a variety of participatory democracy differing from the one considered in the preceding chapter—argue that the decision-making process should be decentralized to allow for greater popular involvement on the local level.[1] They insist that politicians elected in city, state, or national elections are too remote to understand the needs of localized neighborhoods and that as a result many people no longer feel they can trust in the honesty or impartiality of their officials.[2] In the participatory view, political power will never be wielded in an equitable fashion unless local neighborhoods gain effective control over important institutions, like the police or schools. In contrast, polyarchal democrats like Theodore Lowi and Robert Crain maintain that popular participation leads to an excessive fragmentation of political power. [3] They contend that the crisis facing the political system stems less from the public's mistrust of high officials than from the government's inability to develop effective solutions for complex social problems like pollution, transportation, or poverty. In their opinion, power must be concentrated in the hands of political elites if the state is to engage in the kind of long-range, comprehensive planning necessary to solve these troublesome social issues. In contrast to both polyarchists and participatory democrats, pluralists argue that the decision-making process should be neither highly centralized nor highly decentralized. They advocate a mixed form of policy making in which power is divided among political elites and the myriad number of interest publics that make up society. Rather than devolve power to autonomous units of government or centralize authority in the hands of a few officials, they favor a middle course that incorporates the benefits of popular participation but avoids the pitfalls of excessive fragmentation. *

---

*Like polyarchists, many populists—Michael Harrington, for one—seem sympathetic with efforts to engage in long-range planning. But in comparison with the other forms of democracy that we have examined, populism's theory of decision making is not always clearly stated. While populists insist that the public should play an important role in the decision-making process, they never clearly spell out the relationship between comprehensive planning by the state and public involvement in policy making. In Harrington's book *Toward a Democratic Left*, we are never certain whether the public is merely to have the final say over options that a political elite may formulate or whether the majority is actually to be involved in the formulation as well as the final selection of policy (pp. 63-88). In either case, populism's theory of decision making cannot be considered unique. If it favors centralized elites developing comprehensive plans, its view of decision making does not radically differ from that of polyarchy. If, in contrast, it wants the public to have some say in the formulation and the ratification of decisions, it is apt to accept many of pluralism's assumptions about the desirability of numerous policy makers. In evaluating populism, we must stress that its main contribution to democratic theory seems to lie in its theory of participation. Regardless of how decisions are made, populism has insisted that the majority should express its approval in periodic referendums. As should be obvious, this theory of participation is logically compatible with either a centralized or a decentralized style of decision making.

Before attempting to evaluate the relative merits of these competing theories of decision making, we must recall that the proponents of various approaches to democracy often suggest radically different criteria for measuring success. Because commentators cannot always agree on the main problems confronting the political system, they naturally tend to stress the importance of realizing different values. This very wealth of standards makes it difficult to compare alternative patterns of decision making since there is no commonly accepted criterion of accomplishment or failure. As we shall soon see, some authors think the poverty-race issue is of such importance that decision-making procedures should be evaluated primarily by their ability to alleviate the worst consequences of ghetto life. Other critics stress criteria that are broader in nature, focusing on values that are not necessarily beneficial to any one particular group in society.

Among the criteria that have been cited, the following seem to have received the most attention. First, many authors, including Altshuler, claim that decision-making procedures should be evaluated primarily in terms of their ability to generate a sense of confidence and trust among the public.[4] Advocates of community control insist that this issue is an especially troublesome problem in the inner city, where many residents no longer see the exercise of political power as legitimate and noncoercive in nature.

A second type of criterion by which to compare various forms of decision making is to ask which pattern can most effectively achieve a sense of efficacy among presently disorganized segments of the population. Again, this is a criterion that focuses primarily on the problems of the ghetto. As many commentators have noted, the sense of despair that accompanies poverty often leads people to inaction, which in turn feeds on and reinforces their initial despair.[5] Using this criterion of efficacy, we might ask to what extent a pattern of decision making can help people to break out of this vicious cycle and gain a sense of mastery over their own lives.

A third standard, which has somewhat broader consequences than our first two, is to determine to what extent a decision-making pattern can increase government responsiveness to public demands. This criterion, as should be obvious by now, raises the issue discussed in part II of this book: determining who constitutes the relevant public.

A fourth criterion is to ask which pattern of decision making is most likely to minimize spill-over effects among different units of government. In many cases the costs and benefits of public services may accrue to people who live outside a political unit's boundaries. This issue is an important one because when benefits spill over beyond a government's boundaries, an insufficient quantity of a good may be provided; but when costs spill over, the level of services may be carried on at too high a level. [6]

A fifth alternative is to evaluate different forms of policy making on the basis of their ability to achieve significant economies of scale. As we shall see, the price that residents of a community must pay in order to obtain certain basic public amenities may depend on the size of the unit providing the service. [7]

A sixth criterion, which critics like Robert Crain think is important, might be labeled the standard of social justice. [8] That is, to what degree can a pattern of decision making implement needed social programs or achieve a more equitable redistribution of goods and services among the various segments of society? In large metropolitan areas, there is often a mismatch between the financial needs of the inner city, where the poor and minorities have congregated, and the economic resources of suburban neighborhoods, where white middle-class professionals have taken up residence. The key issue is how to design a decision-making procedure for linking together these needs and assets.

Finally, a seventh alternative is to judge a form of policy making by its ability to generate innovative as well as effective solutions to pressing social problems. Using this criterion we might ask what forms of decision making have been most successful in developing new policies. In contrast to our sixth criterion, we are less concerned with whether the solution restructures or redistributes resources than with how quickly and creatively it can act. [9]

Although all democratic theories would no doubt agree that the above mentioned criteria are important, they would rank these values in a different fashion. Participatory democrats often seem to deemphasize the importance of economies of scale or innovative policy making (criteria five and seven) in order to maximize the legitimacy, efficacy, and responsiveness of the political system (criteria one, two and three). Elitist democrats have appeared more interested in developing a form of decision making that will minimize spill-over effects and promote social justice and innovative policy making (criteria four, six, and seven). Polyarchists like Lowi seem willing to sacrifice some of the values that participatory democrats stress in order to build a political system that can act decisively to meet the country's social problems. In contrast, pluralists seek to strike a balance among our various criteria. They believe that the political system faces a serious legitimacy problem that requires more intensive citizen involvement in the policy-making arena; but at the same time they feel that the polity needs to develop more innovative policies for dealing with problems like pollution, energy conservation, and urban deterioration.

In order to assess these rival models of decision making, it will be necessary to examine how each would handle the criteria that alternative theories cite as being important. Even if a certain style of policy making achieves the objectives it hopes to realize, we must know what the price of that success is in terms of alternative values foregone. It will also be necessary to evaluate each theory by the standards it chooses to stress. If a model of democracy gives up certain values in order to realize others but cannot achieve the objectives that it regards as important, then we must judge it as deficient.

The Participatory Option

Proponents of community control—including scholars interested in the problems of the ghetto, advocates for the poor, and black civil rights leaders—are primarily concerned with overcoming the alienation of the inner city. As Altshuler has convincingly argued, a large part of the urban problem in the United States stems from the unfortunate fact that many poor and black residents of large cities feel powerless to exercise any control over their own lives.[10] Ghetto dwellers believe that the government is insensitive to their needs and that as a result their life situation can never be altered for the better. This problem of trust and responsiveness is intimately related to the paucity of power enjoyed by most communities. Many residents of the inner city have no faith in the bureaucrats they come in contact with precisely because they know they do not have any control over the institutions to which these bureaucrats are answerable.

The participatory solution for this crisis of authority is to devolve political power to the local level. Participatory democrats believe confidence in public authority can be restored if neighborhoods within large cities are allowed to assume control of institutions like the schools or police that are important in shaping the lives of urban residents. Advocates of community control also contend that the dispersal of power to local neighborhoods will help to instill a greater sense of self-esteem in low-income people. While many individuals in the inner city presently suffer from a low sense of efficacy, the acquisition of controlling power over key institutions is likely to alter their perceptions of themselves. As advocates of participatory democracy have noted, granting power to the powerless is one of the most obvious ways to break people's sense of dependency. This shift in attitudes, in turn, is likely to result in the development of a new set of local leaders who will possess the confidence necessary to seek further improvements in community institutions. Likewise, the enhanced sense of efficacy that is apt to grow out of community control efforts is bound to lead to an increased sense of self-regulation within local neighborhoods. A well-organized community that actively participates in the running of its own institutions is more likely to discourage deviant behavior than an atomized neighborhood debilitated by the psychological consequences of poverty and powerlessness.

Although these arguments merit serious consideration, they also raise some significant doubts. There is no denying that the problems cited by participatory democrats are real and must eventually be dealt with, but the question is whether the proliferation of numerous independent government entities is either the proper or the complete solution. Regardless of whether participatory democracy is a success by the criteria it wishes to be judged by, it is a form of decision making that may entail some very high costs. In looking at our criteria for evaluating policy making, a strong case can be made that a very decentralized manner of formulating decisions will be relatively unsuccessful in developing policies that promote social justice (criterion six), foster innovative and effective decision making (criterion seven), limit spill-over effects (criterion four), or minimize the unit costs of delivering services (criterion five).

The most glaring weakness in the decentralization effort—particularly in the movement for community control of schools—is its apparent inability to achieve an equitable distribution of goods and services in society as a whole (criterion six). Neighborhood management of institutions like the school system might make the personnel of those organizations more sensitive to the needs of their constituents, but it is difficult to see how devolving more power to local school boards will guarantee that inner city schools receive an equitable distribution of funds in the first place. Given their limited resources, many ghetto schools will undoubtedly be hard pressed to provide adequate compensation to their faculty or adequate facilities to their students without some kind of outside assistance. To achieve a just distribution of goods within the larger society, policy decisions must be made on a macro rather than a micro level. In dispersing more power to neighborhoods, all the advocates of community control can ever hope to accomplish is to give local residents the opportunity to revise the way resources in their neighborhoods have traditionally been allocated. In contrast to a pluralistic or polyarchal form of decision making, community control will not provide inner city residents with any means of increasing the benefits that they receive from the larger political system. By its very nature, participatory democracy is more suited to altering the internal allocation of benefits within a single community than to altering the distribution of resources within society as a whole.

Similarly, community control may have the unintended consequence of eroding the basic rights of many minority groups. Even if local management of institutions like schools, police, or welfare departments will make these bureaucracies more responsive to the needs of the ghetto, where blacks or the poor constitute a majority, it may very well have adverse consequences for minority members who live in predominantly white areas. A police force that is sensitive to the needs of blacks in a ghetto might in another context just as easily be sensitive to the wishes of whites who want to halt the advance of civil rights. It is perhaps ironic that a doctrine related so long to calls for white separatism is now advanced as a radically new proposal for improving the situation of minority groups. While community control may provide some tangible benefits for blacks who live in the ghetto, it may very well hinder the efforts of minority members to secure nonprejudicial treatment outside the inner city. And even within minority neighborhoods, there is the danger that white ethnic groups might find themselves the victims of a reverse form of racism, as occurred with the anti-Semitism that often surfaced in the Ocean Hill-Brownsville controversy.

Aside from problems in protecting minority rights or in achieving a redistribution of social resources, a decentralized form of decision making might also encounter difficulties in formulating innovative policies (criterion seven). On the basis of a variety of studies, it appears that the development of independent communities inhibits, rather than fosters, the adoption of new policy options. In a survey of the literature on organizational innovation, James Q. Wilson has noted that the number of innovations generated is directly related to the diversity of an organization (i.e., to the complexity of its tasks and its incentive systems), while the number of innovations implemented is inversely related to these factors.[11] Although Wilson's observations refer to individual organizations, they can easily be applied to the political system as a whole, as Samuel Huntington has argued, if we equate organizational diversity with the dispersion of political power.[12] That is, the more political power is dispersed, the more likely we are to see a variety of proposals for policy innovations, but conversely, the less likely we are to see many new policy adoptions. Similarly, when power is highly centralized, we are apt to see few new policy suggestions but quite a few adoptions of the proposals that are put forth. Thus whenever power is either highly dispersed or highly concentrated, the rate of innovation will tend to be low. It is only when a political system contains both a diversity of groups and a sufficient concentration of power to implement new ideas that the policy-making process is bound to be receptive to program innovations.

However, this conclusion needs to be qualified in one important respect. As will be argued in more detail later on, there are theoretical as well as empirical reasons for believing that the number of innovations generated is related not only to how many decision-making parties there are but also to how often these parties interact with one another. Charles Lindblom and Michael Aiken, among others, have pointed out that the interaction among groups serves both to stimulate the creation of new ideas and to encourage their diffusion. [13] The optimal form of decision making for encouraging new policy options is thus one that contains both (1) a multiplicity of parties interacting with one another to generate new ideas and (2) adequate power to implement the policies that happen to be formulated.

Participatory democracy is deficient in both these respects. Since the very notion of community control entails the concentration of power in the hands of locally elected officials rather than the sharing of power among different levels of government, there is likely to be little interaction among political units. While it is possible that locally controlled communities might attempt radically different kinds of programs when they first acquire power, the process would probably be short-lived. Without suitable interaction with groups or other units of government, community control experiments would lack the necessary degree of interchange to compel further policy innovation. Moreover, even if neighborhoods did generate new proposals for dealing with issues that transcend their own boundaries, they would have neither the power nor the jurisdiction to implement their decisions. In terms of Wilson's argument, community control definitely occupies that end of the continuum where organizations lack the capability to adopt any policy innovations that might conceivably be developed.

In addition, a segmented form of decision making runs the risk of undermining the effectiveness of any form of policy making regardless of its degree of creativity. Whenever local communities attempt to deal with problems that are regional in nature, their solutions may turn into someone else's problems. As the decision-making process becomes more fragmented, individual neighborhoods will have few incentives to weigh the spill-over effects or external costs that accompany the implementation of a particular policy (criterion four). It is thus possible that community control could result in a rather inequitable system of decision making in which individual localities would pass on part of the costs of their decisions to other units of government. If every decision of a community affected only that community, there would naturally be no objection to autonomous units of government. However, since problems often cross politically determined boundaries, independent localities might easily ignore the costs and gains to other communities and produce too much or too little of a certain service or good. If a local government builds and maintains an extensive park system, residents from other districts who have not borne the cost of the parks through taxation may nonetheless come and use them. Or if a community takes a lax attitude towards the prosecution of crime, its actions may adversely affect surrounding neighborhoods. Similarly, if a municipality decides to alter its zoning laws in order to attract heavy industry, it may result in polluting the air in the whole region. Given a system of autonomous units of government each with its own zoning power, there would be no way either of prohibiting such actions or of extracting benefits from the offending community.

Finally, the creation of multiple, autonomous units of government has the added drawback that it may entail unnecessarily high costs for the performance of certain functions (criterion five). In the production of government services it is often possible to realize noticeable economies of scale; i.e., the average cost of producing a good or service may decline as the output of that good or service is increased. On the basis of a number of economic studies undertaken in the 1950s and 1960s, Werner Hirsch has argued that air pollution control, sewage disposal, public transportation, power, water, public health services, and hospitals are likely to enjoy major economies of scale.[14] If separate neighborhoods try to operate their own transportation departments or run their own public health programs, they may have to pay more than they would if a larger unit of government provided the same service. Whether the possible economic costs of such fragmentation are more or less important than the psychological benefits received from running one's own neighborhood is a separate question that cannot be dealt with here. But it must be kept in mind that regardless of the extent to which community control restores a sense of trust or efficacy among residents of a community, it has its definite costs.

In recent years, however, some economists have insisted that there are no economies of scale to be realized in municipal services that are labor intensive. Unlike transportation, air pollution, or utilities, which involve large amounts of capital investment, many municipal services, such as education, fire or police protection, require little or no capital. In fact, in a recent study of the Indianapolis police department and surrounding law enforcement units, Elinor Ostrum has indicated that there may be large-scale diseconomies when service organizations become too large.[15] Unfortunately, as Robert Bish and Hugh Nourse have argued, studies such as Ostrum's are "plagued with the difficulties of output measurement and thus cannot be used to indicate whether or not the governments analyzed were producing efficiently."[16] Unless there is an adequate measure of outputs, it is difficult to control for the quality of services provided by various units of government. Also, as will be shown in the next chapter, in order to minimize the costs in running a large organization facing heterogeneous tasks, it is imperative that the organization decentralize its operations and grant considerable discretion to lower-level administrators. Thus to adequately compare the costs of running police departments, it is necessary to compare an efficiently run, large unit that has administratively decentralized its operations and an efficiently run, smaller department. Unfortunately, most of the present cost comparisons of municipal departments fail to control for such variables.

It should also be pointed out that research by Peter Blau, Richard Schoenherr, and S.R. Klatzky indicates that as an organization gets larger, its staff personnel and administrative overhead decline regardless of whether the organization is capital or labor intensive.[17] If these findings are reliable, the costs of providing a unit of service could conceivably be lower for large labor-intensive organizations like police departments. Given the present difficulties in much of the literature and the fact that some of the data are internally inconsistent, it is still an open question whether or not there are diseconomies of scale in labor-intensive organizations.

On the basis of the above discussion, we can thus argue that community control is an incomplete solution to the problems that face the political system. In fact, it is interesting to note that some proponents of community control, such as Altshuler, seem willing to concede this very point. Altshuler has modified his advocacy of community control in two important respects. First, in order to promote the redistribution of resources from wealthier to poorer areas and to prevent communities from passing on part of the costs associated with their decisions to other localities, he appears willing to accept a federated system of decision making. Altshuler calls for the creation of a two- or three-tier system of government, in which local communities would formulate policies dealing with institutions like the schools while larger units of government would decide policies that had redistributive consequences or spill-over effects on other communities.[18]

Secondly, in addition to espousing community control, Altshuler implicitly endorses a variant of public pluralism as a strategy for improving conditions in the inner city. Besides calling for neighborhood self-government, Altshuler talks of the necessity of mobilizing the poor so that they can deal more effectively with city hall.[19] He argues that organizing the poor will serve a dual purpose: not only will it enable them to take charge of neighborhood government, but it will also allow them to bargain more effectively with other interests in the city. While Altshuler groups both these activities under the rubric of community control, it is questionable to what extent the notion of political bargaining remains true to the kind of local autonomy envisioned by most participatory democrats. More importantly, in making the distinction between self-government on the neighborhood level and interest-group pressure within the larger political system, Altshuler implies that community control is only a partial, and not a complete, solution to the urban problem. In order to supplement the deficiencies of neighborhood self-government, he falls back on the kind of interest-group politics that public pluralists advocate.

Although Altshuler's eclectic approach to decision making answers many of the objections raised earlier about community control, it leaves yet other issues unresolved. To be fair to community control, we must evaluate it by a variety of standards, including the criteria its advocates think are important. If participatory democrats like Altshuler implicitly admit that community control is only a partial solution to the urban crisis, they nonetheless argue that it constitutes a necessary complement to other forms of decision making. The issue at hand, then, is not whether community control fails to take other costs or values into account but whether it is capable of realizing the values that participatory democrats themselves have deemed important. As pointed out previously, most proponents of community control believe it is essential to make government officials more responsive to the wishes of the public (criterion three). The question is whether community control is either the only way or necessarily the best way to achieve this objective.

Contrary to the claims of its proponents, it can be argued that community control might inhibit government responsiveness to a diverse array of groups. To argue that decentralization will make the government more responsive to the public necessitates defining who constitutes the public. As pointed out in chapter 6, whenever there are separate decision-making points for different policy areas, such as education or law enforcement, it becomes much easier for the dominant interest in the field to limit the scope of conflict and the array of forces opposing it. Instead of doing away with isolated and segmented decision-making centers, the establishment of community control would probably lead to their proliferation. As a result, the ability of one particular group to monopolize the formulation of policy would be enhanced rather than curtailed. In the case of education, it would be members of the various communities who would have the dominant voice, to the detriment of other groups such as teachers' unions. Whether the decision-making process is divided into isolated segments by function (as is presently the case with school policy) or by territory (as the proponents of participatory democracy suggest), the number of groups that can participate in the political system will be limited. To argue that decentralization will make the government more responsive to the public is to argue that the government should be responsive to a different segment of the citizenry. Community control will undoubtedly increase the receptivity of certain institutions to the needs of the neighborhood community, but in the process it will make the same institutions less responsive to other elements in society.

However, many economists argue that this fragmented and isolated pattern of decision making is desirable because it allows individual political units to cater to the needs of specialized groups. Charles Tiebout, Robert Bish, and Hugh Nourse insist that autonomous communities are necessary both in the inner city and in suburban areas in order to adequately satisfy individual preferences for public goods.[20] They maintain that large units of government must cater to the demands of a relatively heterogeneous public. In a large jurisdiction "we would expect public good provision to approximate that preferred by the median voter."[21] Either through a process of voting or bargaining, the political system would produce an array of goods and services that not all members would individually like to see provided. However, when the metropolitan area is fragmented into numerous, smaller units of government, municipalities can cater to more homogeneous populations with similar tastes. Citizens are likely to achieve a higher level of welfare since they no longer have to pay for goods and services they do not want. The more homogeneous the preferences of the population, the more likely it is that individuals who fit the local norms will find all of their wants amply satisfied.

Despite the apparent attractiveness of these proposals, there are certain empirical and normative questions that need to be faced. First, given the high degree of daily mobility in the metropolitan area and the fact that most people work, live, and shop in a variety of different jurisdictions, it seems questionable whether individuals would maximize their preferences by participating in only one governmental unit. Usually people consume public services in a variety of places but have the opportunity to express their political preferences in only one jurisdiction.[22] Secondly, it should be pointed out that the creation of autonomous, homogeneous communities is not solely the result of like-minded individuals voluntarily clustering together. Through restrictive zoning and subdivision regulation, many suburban communities have made it legally and financially difficult for people of heterogeneous backgrounds to settle within their boundaries. Rather than maximizing the opportunities for people to live in the jurisdiction that best satisfies their preferences, the proliferation of suburban townships has often resulted in a diminution of life chances for many persons. Unquestionably there are numerous individuals of modest income in the inner city who prefer the mixture of public goods and services provided by suburban neighborhoods. But they recognize, as Tiebout, Bish, and Nourse often do not, that their place of residence has more to do with the legal and financial barriers that the suburbs have placed in their path than with their own preferences for public goods. Instead of assuming, as many urban economists do, that the growth of numerous municipalities will result in "better performance satisfaction" for all citizens, we must recognize that it may lead to the maximization of satisfaction for only the more affluent residents of suburban communities.

Besides arguing that community control will lead to greater responsiveness, critics like Altshuler have maintained that devolution of power to local units of government will create an enhanced sense of trust and efficacy within the inner city (criteria one and two). If local management of institutions like schools or police can provide better service to neighborhoods, then public trust in government will be restored. Likewise, if power is turned over to the inner city, there will likely develop a new corps of leaders who feel efficacious enough to seek additional changes that will alter the status of the inner city for the better. Unfortunately, however, the available evidence suggests the need for caution in accepting these claims. In a study of experiments in decentralization in the cities of New York and New Haven, Douglas Yates has found that an inverse relationship exists between the extent of power a community exercises and the degree of success it enjoys in either improving local services or in building a sense of efficiacy among its members. [23] While his terminology is different from that used in this book, Yates has arranged the experiments he observed along a continuum with highly specific (what we would call pluralistic) groups at one end and more diffuse (what we would call community control) projects at the other end. The pluralistic experiments were designed to provide a very limited service to the neighborhood or to monitor or bargain with a specific government agency over its programs in the community. In contrast, the experiments at the opposite end of the continuum entailed local neighborhoods actually governing complex institutions like the school system. When Yates attempted to determine which approach fostered the greatest sense of efficacy among local residents, he found that community control experiments had the lowest ratings, while more pluralistic and functionally specific efforts had the highest ratings. [24] A similar pattern emerged when he attempted to see which approach most improved services to the neighborhood. Contrary to what the advocates of community control had argued, he found that as the power of the neighborhood increased to the point where it was actually governing local institutions, its ability to improve services did not increase correspondingly. However, when neighborhoods were organized into advocate groups to secure tangible benefits from city-wide bureaucracies, their record was substantially better. The explanation for this discrepancy reflects the nature of the tasks confronting the two different kinds of experiments. As soon as members of a community attempted to govern institutions like the local schools, they became overwhelmed by the number and the complexity of problems facing them. In some cases they were not certain what they wanted to do with their grant of power once they had acquired it. As a result, community-controlled school boards often undertook very few initiatives and had very little impact on the institutions they ostensibly administered. For similar reasons, many of the participants on locally controlled school boards became so disillusioned and discouraged about what they had accomplished that their sense of political efficacy did not significantly improve. However, when groups were organized to achieve more limited and specific goals, they were more likely to achieve their objectives, and this fact in turn reinforced the confidence they had in their ability to influence the decision-making process.[25] If a group was interested in applying pressure on a city agency to improve the delivery of municipal services to its neighborhood, its goals were clearly focused and its task was minimal in comparison to the burdens borne by organizations that had day-to-day administrative duties. It was thus much easier for advocate groups to build a record of success than it was for their community control counterparts.

Yates's study is highly significant in that it is one of the first efforts to determine whether the claims of participatory democrats are supported by the evidence. Yates suggested that if we want to promote a sense of efficacy or trust among inner city residents, a pluralistic, rather than a community control, approach may be the most feasible alternative. By organizing the poor for political action, pluralism can greatly increase the ability of ghetto residents to influence the conditions that govern their lives. But if people are expected to assume responsibility for running institutions with which they have little experience, it should not be surprising that they easily become frustrated and disillusioned. The problem with the program of participatory democrats is that merely turning power over to the poor will not automatically guarantee that they will be able to use it either wisely or effectively.

The Polyarchal Option

While participatory democrats have called for the dispersal of power to local neighborhoods, polyarchal democrats have argued that authority should be concentrated in the hands of elected officials. Polyarchists like Lowi maintain that the major problems facing the United States stem less from inner city alienation than from the government's inability to implement comprehensive plans for dealing with issues like pollution, mass transportation, or poverty. They insist that the problems of the inner city reflect the inability of the larger city to deliver effective services to individual neighborhoods rather than a shortage of power within local communities themselves. In the polyarchal view, authority is so fragmented that the political system is forced to pursue a strategy of muddling through, of dealing with troublesome issues in a piecemeal, rather than a comprehensive and innovative, fashion. [26]

To remedy this situation, polyarchists insist that the institutional power of publicly elected officials should be strengthened so that they can deal quickly and effectively with the myriad problems that face the nation. [27] On a national level, elitist democrats usually favor an active president who possesses the authority to override the veto power wielded by agencies and interest groups. The need for a vigilant judicial branch is also seen by many, especially Lowi, who insists that the Supreme Court must restrain Congress's propensity to parcel out its authority to administrative agencies and to special interests. On a local level, polyarchists have endorsed efforts to consolidate metropolitan governments and to eliminate the present fragmentation of political units. In place of multiple, overlapping lines of authority, they favor the simplification of the decision-making process and the concentration of official responsibility at the top. In the polyarchist view, if political elites can be insulated from the direct pressure of interest groups, they will be able to engage in systematic as well as effective long-range planning. "Planning requires law, choice, priorities, moralities," Lowi has argued.[28] Public involvement, or more specifically, public bargaining over policies, is seen as the antithesis of this orderly process. Like many other elitist democrats, Lowi maintains that the compromises and logrolling of pluralism are a corruption of, rather than an aid to, the rational process of establishing priorities and formulating options.

Although polyarchists have often vigorously stated their case, it is debatable whether the available evidence supports their call for more centralized policy making. Before determining the extent to which elitist patterns of democracy can actually realize the values polyarchists stress as being important, we must see how this form of decision making deals with alternative standards of performance. Even if concentrating power in the hands of elected officials can minimize spill-over effects (criterion four) or lead to more equitable social programs (criterion six) or more innovative policies (criterion seven), we also need to know whether it can offer any answer to the kinds of problems Altshuler and other participatory democrats have so graphically described. It is possible that polyarchy, like community control, is at best only a partial solution to the numerous difficulties confronting the political system.

For instance, it can be argued that the treatment of the poverty problem in a book like *The End of Liberalism* raises serious doubts about polyarchy's solution to the urban crisis. Lowi in particular seems to have overlooked the gravity of the situation Altshuler has described, for nowhere in his study does he address the problem of alienation and apathy that many commentators claim is widespread among residents of the inner city. Perhaps because of this oversight, Lowi fails to show how concentrating power could ever restore a sense of legitimacy (criterion one) among the poor. In fact, there are reasons for believing that the polyarchal call for centralized authority might very well exacerbate the prevalent attitude of alienation found in the ghetto. As Altshuler has argued, residents of the inner city often reject the legitimacy of the political system because they feel that they have little or no influence over its actions. Thus concentrating power in the hands of a few elected officials would make the poor feel even more estranged from the decision-making process. However, Lowi insists that consolidation of power could strengthen respect for authority if it were coupled with stricter enforcement of the law.

While Lowi does not specifically address the problem of alienation among the poor, he does confront the larger issue of cynicism about government among the general population. Lowi concedes that the public has grown increasingly cynical about political institutions in recent years, and he contends that it is the capriciousness of a discretionary system of administration, rather than the remoteness of centralized institutions, that is responsible for this crisis of legitimacy. Because lower-level bureaucrats have been given considerable leeway in interpreting the intent of officially made laws, the administration of justice has become less than evenhanded.[29] In Lowi's opinion, public confidence in government will be restored only when this discretionary pattern of administration is replaced by stricter enforcement of the law. While this line of reasoning at first appears persuasive, it seems somewhat beside the point. Many residents of the inner city seem to be complaining less about the administration of the law than about the content of the law itself. The decline of public authority is as much a problem of people feeling excluded from the policy-making process as it is of the law being unevenly applied. Even if centralization of power were accompanied by more stringent enforcement of the law, it might very well contribute to, rather than alleviate, the problem of public distrust. In making the decision-making process more remote from the residents of the inner city, polyarchy makes it difficult for local citizens to have any say over the decisions that affect their daily lives.

If consolidating power in the hands of elected officials is not likely to restore a sense of trust among lower-income residents, it is likely to encounter even more difficulties in reviving dormant neighborhoods and in instituting a sense of efficacy (criterion two) among the poor. Polyarchal democrats like Lowi often overlook the importance of helping the poor to become more active in helping themselves. Lowi maintains that poverty is essentially a problem of limited work opportunities and inadequate welfare funds; and to cope with this issue, he repeatedly praises what he calls the

"old system of welfare," in which the government doles out monthly payments to the indigent.[30] Rejecting the "new system of welfare," which tries to organize the poor for political action, he argues
that the old system meets the needs of the poor at the same time
that it preserves the rule of law.[31]

However, this whole approach seems to stem from a mispercep-
tion on Lowi's part of the nature of urban social problems. He fails
to take account of the work of scholars like Dorothy James, Kenneth Clark, and Milton Greenblatt, among others, who argue that
poverty is as much a psychological as an economic problem.[32]
These studies have shown that prolonged exposure to ghetto conditions seem to have a corrosive effect on the personalities of the
poor; when people are unable to escape from the restraints of
poverty, they often experience a pervasive sense of hopelessness
and depression, which in turn makes it more difficult for them to
break out of the cycle of poverty. When the effects of racial discrimination reinforce the conditions of economic want, the damage
to the psychology of the individual becomes magnified even more.
Centralized attempts to increase employment opportunities or to
increase the size of welfare handouts can thus be considered only
partial solutions to the problem. If individuals suffer from a low
sense of efficacy, they are often unable to take advantage of economic opportunities even when these are present in large numbers.
Similarly, if people feel they are unable to control their own lives,
strengthening the old system of welfare will tend to reinforce, not
change, that attitude. A sense of self-respect is not likely to be
generated within an individual by treating him as an object of a
centralized welfare program; on the contrary, such measures will
serve only to reinforce his feelings of dependence. Indeed, the
centralized, dole-oriented system of welfare that Lowi praises was
widely criticized in the early 1960s for precisely this reason. Its
most glaring fault, as critics pointed out, lies in the fact that it
attacks the surface manifestations of poverty rather than its underlying causes.[33]

Despite the claim by Lowi and other polyarchists that concentrating power in the hands of political elites is necessary to deal
with the country's social problems, we can argue, then, that at best
it is only an incomplete solution. Polyarchists like Lowi seem to

misread the problems of the inner city, in particular, and the problems of poverty, in general. While centralized planning may be desirable in some policy areas, it seems inadequate as a method of restoring a sense of efficacy or trust among lower-income residents.

But as was the case with participatory democracy, we must also judge polyarchy by the criteria that its supporters stress as being important. To be fair, we must keep in mind that advocates have defended centralization of political power on the grounds that it will minimize externalities (criterion four) and lead to more socially just (criterion six) as well as more innovative policy making (criterion seven). A polyarchist would point out that political elites could prevent local units of government from passing on part of the costs of their decisions to neighboring communities if they had the power to engage in comprehensive planning. Similarly, elitist democrats like Lowi insist that the political system would be able to deal effectively with redistributive problems by limiting the proliferation of government units and concentrating power in the hands of a few elected officials. Only a centralized form of government would have the authority to transfer payments from one segment of society to another when an inequitable distribution of resources had occurred. In contrast to the decentralized, participatory model, a polyarchal form of decision making would never lack the power to equalize the funds that suburban and inner city schools could spend on education. As the power and jurisdiction of a unit of government were increased, its ability to affect the allocation of resources in society as a whole would likewise increase. Similarly, expanding the policy-making arena would insure that basic civil rights were protected in a uniform fashion. A centralized administration would have sufficient power to insist that every community guarantee certain essential liberties to all individuals regardless of their ethnic background. Finally, by concentrating authority in the hands of a few, the political system would be able to experiment with the adoption of novel approaches to traditional social problems and to thwart the efforts of veto groups seeking to stall needed social change. Only a centralized form of decision making, freed from the endless process of interest-group bargaining, would have the time to develop innovative social policies.

Merely because a centralized form of policy making could theoretically achieve these objectives does not mean that it necessarily will accomplish them in practice. Even if we assume that most political elites are eager to limit externalities, promote redistributive goals, and introduce innovative social programs, there are a variety of structural reasons for believing that centralized decision making will retard, rather than advance, these objectives.[34] The polyarchal view of decision making seems to be based on an exaggerated view of man's information-gathering and problem-solving abilities. If this were a world of costless information, it is conceivable that a few political elites might be able to detect any inefficient or inequitable distribution of social services. However, since most decision makers have limited cognitive abilities, it is not surprising that centralized elites often encounter serious difficulties in identifying and creatively resolving these kinds of problems. If there are externalities associated with a program, the parties that are affected are not necessarily in a position to alert public officials to the need for change. Similarly, when power is centralized at the top and direct involvement of the public is minimized, political elites cut themselves off from a great deal of information about the distribution of a program's costs and benefits. Those individuals who are most affected by an inequitable distribution of resources or a breakdown in the protection of civil liberties may not have an avenue for airing their grievances. Once power is concentrated, it becomes more difficult for dissenting views, which might expose these social costs, to get through to key decision makers.

Likewise, centralization of authority may retard the development of new ideas in that it alters the incentives for proposing radically new policies. In delegating more power to upper levels of government, polyarchal democrats would dramatically change the costs and rewards for innovative behavior facing personnel at lower levels. If decisions were made exclusively at the top, subordinates would not find it very rewarding to consider alternative ways of solving problems because they would not have any say over the final decision. No agency or interest group would consider wasting its resources developing new ideas if it had no real influence in the policy-making process. Similarly, interest groups and agencies would be less inclined to criticize the proposals of other groups since their suggestions would not carry much weight with decision makers at the top. Moreover, the lack of competition and interaction among agencies and interest groups would reinforce the propensity of agencies to play a cautious, rather than creative, role in the policy-making process. As Roland McKean has noted, bureaus with a relatively high degree of centralization probably face fewer threats of innovation by rival groups and greater reprimands for making mistakes. [35] If major decisions were made on a centralized level, agencies would no longer have to fear competitive bureaus instituting overlapping programs to rival or threaten their domains.

Although we may not fully appreciate this fact, the possibility that one agency might preempt the activities of another and infringe on its jurisdiction has been one of the greatest spurs to innovative policy making. The development of the Polaris missile by the navy probably played a bigger role in stimulating the army to reduce the vulnerability of its Minuteman than did any comprehensive, rational planning. Similarly, competition between the EPA and the AEC (and, later, its successor, the Nuclear Regulatory Commission), has done more to insure the safe disposal of radioactive material than any degree of centralized, long-range planning. If the influence of various lower- or middle-level bureaus were dramatically curbed, the bargaining and competition among agencies would likewise decrease. Bureaus would be rewarded for complying with, rather than challenging, major policy decisions. Such a state of affairs would not be likely to stimulate the development of either innovative or socially just programs.

The impact of centralization may just as significantly affect the creative capacities of upper-level officials as that of interest groups and lower- and middle-level bureaucrats. Polyarchal democrats have often overlooked the fact that the bargaining and interaction of private and public groups serve to lighten the load confronting government officials. Once political power becomes concentrated, public officials acquire responsibility for devising policies that were previously decided by private groups. The attempt to limit the influence of interest groups may impose such immense demands on the cognitive abilities of a few decision makers that it will eventually prove to be self-defeating. As McKean has argued, when there is a dramatic escalation in the number of decisions that must be made, political officials will "find it advantageous—indeed imperative—to screen alternatives rapidly, apply crude rules of thumb and quick judgments, and in general simplify the decision making process, because they would have to make a thousand instead of a hundred decisions per day."[36] As the authority for making decisions becomes increasingly concentrated, elites have no choice but to minimize the attention they give to each problem before them. Given the limited time and ability of most decision makers, the only way they can handle an increased work load is to speed up the consideration of various policy options.

The resulting simplification of the decision-making process is likely to have two adverse consequences. First, rather than surveying all possible options and rationally weighing the alternatives, centralized political elites will tend to neglect important social values. As pointed out earlier, when government officials are not subject to the pressures of the bargaining table, they are less likely to perceive the objectives and needs of people other than themselves. Even if they have the best of intentions, they are apt to fall back on simple decision-making rules in generating their proposals. Secondly, the centralization of the decision-making process is likely to result in a loss of flexibility. If the number of demands facing political officials forces them to adopt crude rules of thumb, policies may be formulated arbitrarily instead of being tailored to meet local conditions. However, if political elites attempt to correct this problem by spending an inordinate amount of time on any one particular issue, the decision-making process as a whole could very well grind to a halt. This is especially likely to be the case if, as Lowi suggests, political elites grant only limited discretion to lower-level officials.[37] Instead of risking the wrath of their superiors by exercising their own judgment, lower-level bureaucrats will play it safe and refer more and more matters to their superiors for final consideration. But the inevitable consequence of referring more and more issues to the top is that the decision-making process will be troubled by additional delays and slowdowns. Regardless of what polyarchists say about centralized planning, it is a form of policy making that could result in a loss of flexibility and quickness.

Finally, the advocates of centralized planning have often over-

looked the fact that small groups of decision makers can fall victim
to what Irving Janis has called the problem of "groupthink." Whenever small numbers of officials have sole responsibility for making
important decisions, the danger exists that they may develop informal norms that effectively suppress the expression of dissenting
opinions and the examination of conflicting evidence.[38] This danger
is especially likely to emerge when political officials have responsibility for making vital decisions that pose threats of social disap-
proval and self-disapproval, such as committing the nation to a
course of war.[39] As Janis has shown in several case studies of foreign policy making, political elites often do not have completely
accurate information about the problems under study, nor do they
necessarily want to be exposed to such information.

For instance, in making the Bay of Pigs decision, Kennedy believed that there were widespread pockets of opposition to Castro,
and as a consequence he assumed that the Cuban army was ill
prepared to repulse an armed attack. Intelligence experts in both the
State Department and CIA knew that these assumptions were
totally inaccurate. Unfortunately, however, they were never consulted. In fact, when the head of the State Department's intelligence
section asked Dean Rusk if his experts could scrutinize the invasion
plan, he was turned down.[40] Once the decision to attack Cuba
gained momentum, no one in Kennedy's inner circle of decision
makers seemed eager to question its wisdom. As Janis has argued,
given the controversial nature of the plan, Kennedy's aides did not
want to disturb their self-confidence by raising policy alternatives
or by examining troublesome evidence. However, if the various
government bureaus concerned with foreign policy had been able
to criticize and contest the assumptions of Kennedy's advisors, it
is possible that the Bay of Pigs fiasco could have been avoided.

We can thus see that for a variety of reasons consolidation of
power in the hands of a few officials may not always be desirable.
If we want the political system to act in a creative fashion, centralized planning may actually hinder the accomplishment of that goal.
So far we have primarily relied on theoretical arguments to support
this contention, but there are a number of empirical studies of
organizational behavior and comparative city government that
likewise indicate that multiple, rather than centralized, decision

makers tend to foster innovative policy making. As mentioned earlier, Wilson has found in a survey of the literature on organizational innovation that an inverse relationship exists between the degree of centralization and the number of new policy ideas generated.[41] Similarly, in a series of studies on community decision making, several authors, including Robert Lineberry, Edmund Fowler, Terry Clark, Michael Aiken, and Robert Alford, have discovered that as the number of decision makers increases, so does the number of policies enacted. Instead of simply asking whether cities are ruled by an elite or by a plurality of groups, these authors have attempted to determine what effect various patterns of decision making might have on the outputs of a city. Generally, they have found that cities with centralized decision making are apt to be less active and innovative than municipalities with more pluralistic or diffuse patterns of government.

Lineberry and Fowler have compared the performance of reformed city governments, which tend to be highly centralized, with non-reformed city governments, which tend to be more open and responsive to group demands, and have discovered that centralized municipalities are more likely to have low levels of taxation and expenditures.[42] Contrary to the polyarchal argument, centralized reform cities seem to provide fewer services to their citizens. Similarly, Clark hypothesized that centralized policy making will lead to more program outputs, but in a comparative study of 51 cities he found just the opposite.[43] Considering public participation in the three policy areas of urban renewal, air pollution, and poverty, Clark discovered that as the number of groups involved increases, the city's level of expenditures also increases. Instead of hindering the city's ability to get anything done, group involvement seems to stimulate the city to become more involved in public-related activities. In another study, Aiken characterized the power structure of 31 cities as being either pyramidal, factional, or amorphous and compared the impact of these various power structures on the policy areas of poverty, urban renewal, and low-rent housing. Like Clark and Lineberry and Fowler, he found that as more groups participate in city politics, the municipality is more likely to initiate programs in these policy areas.[44] Finally, in two separate studies, Aiken and Alford compared 675 cities for the degree of innovation in the areas of poverty and public housing. They discovered that two variables are especially important in predicting whether a city will attempt to develop a program in these areas: the number of power centers in the city and the degree of interaction among these various power coalitions.[45] Once again, cities that have pluralistic, rather than centralized, decision-making arrangements are more likely to implement innovative programs.

In the comparative literature on urban government, the only study that finds that centralized communities are more likely to implement innovative policies is Robert Crain's, Elihu Katz's, and Donald Rosenthal's examination of the fluoridation issue.[46] Why their data are so at odds with the work of Aiken and Alford, Clark, and Lineberry and Fowler is not readily apparent. Clark has suggested that the type of issue might have some bearing on the success of different forms of decision making: "For less fragile decisions, the more centralized the decision making structure, the lower the level of outputs."[47] In contrast, when a municipality deals with a highly controversial issue, like fluoridation, a more centralized political system may be necessary to implement new programs. However, one would certainly be hard pressed to explain why the issue of fluoridation is more of a "fragile decision" than public housing, welfare, or tax levels. An alternative explanation would focus on the types of public participation involved in each issue. On close examination it is evident that the findings of Crain et al. do not contradict our previous studies because they compare elitism with referendums, or populistic forms of decision making. In contrast, Aiken et al. looked at group-oriented forms of participation, focusing on the number of actors involved in each issue and the scope and extent of their interaction with one another. Instead of simply asking whether centralized or noncentralized cities are most likely to be receptive to new ideas and programs, we must also distinguish between the behavior of different types of noncentralized communities. When centralized communities are contrasted with municipalities that rely on multiple actors to make decisions, the evidence still indicates that a participatory style of policy making results in higher levels of outputs.

Thus even if we use the criteria polyarchal democrats themselves have stressed as being important, the performance of centralized decision making is less impressive than advocates have led us to believe. Although polyarchists like Lowi often insist that pluralistic interest groups serve as veto groups that limit and frustrate efforts of the political system to provide more outputs, the record seems to indicate otherwise. It is centralized cities—not pluralistically oriented municipalities—that have difficulty generating and adopting new programs. In implying that a trade-off exists between rational planning and public participation, polyarchists fail to see that public participation can simplify the tasks confronting political elites as well as stimulate elected officials to engage in more creative social planning. The process of partisan mutual adjustment among groups is not antithetical to long-range, innovative planning; on the contrary, it is essential to the success of any form of decision making.

The Pluralistic Option

The difficulties with both the participatory and polyarchal forms of decision making serve only to illustrate in greater detail the benefits of a pluralistic style of government. Critics of pluralism have failed to see that the troubles confronting the present political system stem both from a feeling of alienation and mistrust in the ghetto and from a lack of innovative and creative planning. Besides restoring a sense of legitimacy and confidence in its operations, the political system needs to offer more guidance to various groups seeking to shape the outcome of policy deliberations. Unfortunately, the participatory and polyarchal alternatives seem incapable of simultaneously providing for inner city involvement and effective, long-range planning. The defenders of community control, who claim their style of resolving issues can handle the problems of trust, self-esteem, and responsiveness, seem to have difficulty dealing with larger problems such as economies of scale, spill-over effects, social justice, and innovative policy making. Conversely, the advocates of centralized decision making, who claim their form of planning can achieve more innovative and more equitable policy, often seem oblivious to the problems cited by participatory democrats as well as ill prepared to cope with them.

In contrast, the doctrine of public pluralism, which advocates a dual policy of organizing the poor from the bottom up and regulating the interplay of interests from the top down, seems to have the potential for dealing with both sets of issues. On a national level, the decision-making process can be vastly improved if the chief executive shares his power more fully with Congress and the various federal agencies and their clientele groups. If for one reason or another there is minimal interaction among these institutions, the executive branch must play the divergent roles of advocate, custodian, and manager of the political arena, fostering competition among these parties. On a local or metropolitan level, it is necessary to foster the development of a federated or multi-tier system of government with multiple, overlapping units. Rather than devolving more power to autonomous political entities in the suburban ring and in the inner city, or concentrating authority in a single, hierarchically structured metropolitan government, it would be preferable to develop a more diverse and complex political structure that would:

(1) Assist the formation of neighborhood organizations, especially among residents of the ghetto;
(2) Tolerate the development of multiple government units with varying jurisdictions and responsibilities;
(3) Arrange the above units of government in an overlapping, federated fashion so that the ability of communities to isolate themselves from neighboring communities would be limited;
(4) Provide some government body such as the Councils of Government, which came into being as a result of federal prodding in the late 1960s, with the power to review and veto the actions of smaller government authorities.

The reasons for advocating such a system of decision making are by now readily apparent. If the government encourages and assists the poor to organize themselves, it is possible to restore a sense of trust among inner city residents as well as to increase their ability to help themselves (criteria one and two). When the poor attempt to manage large and unwieldy organizations like the school system, they are less likely to realize their objectives than when they participate in a more limited and segmented fashion. Especially for political novices, the running of an institution with which they have little or no experience can actually serve to retard a sense of personal efficacy. But as Yates has shown, when the residents of ghetto neighborhoods join specific, functionally oriented groups, they are apt to feel a heightened sense of confidence both in their own ability and in the political system's ability to improve the condition of their lives. [48] Moreover, the organization of neighborhood residents is likely to improve the delivery of services to the public and thus increase the responsiveness of government institutions to citizen demands (criterion three).

Similarly, by allowing a variety of jurisdictions within a metropolitan area to maintain a certain degree of autonomy, it will be possible to enable citizens with relatively homogeneous preferences to purchase varying amounts of goods according to their priorities. In this fashion the production of government amenities will be more in accordance with the diverse array of citizen wants found in an urban community. And if additional research should show more convincingly than do the present data that there are no large economies of scale in the provision of those municipal services which are labor intensive, resources can be saved by allowing the existence of a variety of different-sized jurisdictions. Large units can provide services in which economies of scale are realizable, while smaller jurisdictions can perform any functions that are more economical when carried out by smaller administrative bodies (criterion five). However, to minimize the possibility of any one community passing on part of its costs to other districts, it is necessary to include smaller political units in a larger, federated metropolitan government that can check or veto the decisions made by its constituent parts. The existence of extensive overlap in political boundaries and the ability of communities to seek redress of grievances at more inclusive levels of government would provide a favorable environment for the resolution of spill-over effects among different units of decision making (criterion four). The larger units of government could impose levies on communities that fail to pay their fair share for combatting an external cost like pollution. And conversely, they could compensate those segments of the urban environment which have provided the larger community with external benefits, like recreational facilities, but have received no compensation.

Similarly, by developing a complex federal, as well as metropolitan, form of government in which one unit presides over a diverse array of smaller, overlapping jurisdictions, the political system can maximize its ability to deal with redistributive problems (criterion six). As pointed out earlier, there is often a geographical mismatch between the economic needs of our traditional municipal centers and the financial wealth of the surrounding suburban communities. As the middle classes have fled from urban centers, their place has usually been taken by the poor and minorities, who are most in need of social services. Because the more affluent classes have often isolated themselves in autonomous, satellite communities, they not only have escaped paying taxes to traditional urban centers that would support programs for lower-income individuals; they also have directly added to the costs that core cities must bear. Through the passage of exclusionary housing and land-use policies, most suburban communities have deliberately sought to prevent lower- and lower-middle-class families from moving to the outskirts. This attempt at self-isolation has reduced the financial burdens on the suburban resident at the expense of those remaining in the core city.

While economists like Bish and Nourse favor the proliferation of small communities, which can cater to the special preferences of different groups, they fail to see that such a policy has definite social consequences unless certain restraints are placed on suburban autonomy. In order to implement programs that would reduce the problems of poverty and inequality, it is necessary to create a federated urban structure that would have both the fiscal ability to levy taxes on those individuals living in the suburban fringe and the legal power to veto discriminatory housing or zoning laws. As indicated in chapter 2, the federal government presently requires all municipalities to submit applications for federal funds to area-wide review boards charged with the responsibility of harmonizing the requests of individual communities. To carry out such directives most cities have joined Councils of Government. Because these institutions are still in a state of evolution, it is difficult to tell whether they will undertake redistributive policies or assume responsibility for compensating municipalities that are the recipients of negative spill-over effects. The eventual power wielded by these area-wide units of government will depend on how strongly the executive branch insists that municipalities practice some form of regional planning. Left to themselves, local communities are not likely to pick up the tab for costs they can easily pass on to other communities. But if the president and the executive branch vigorously use the financial leverage of federal assistance to develop a multilevel form of regional government with veto power over the subunits within its jurisdiction, there is a genuine possibility that the spill-over and redistributive problems that plague local units of government can be minimized.

Finally, by using COGs to develop a centrally guided form of pluralistic decision making, it may be possible to stimulate the development of creative and innovative policy making (criterion seven). In an expanded, overlapping form of decision making, there will be plenty of incentives, as well as opportunities, for interest groups and local units of government to voice their opinions on policies that directly bear on them. The possibility of public officials succumbing to groupthink or ignoring important information is thus likely to be minimized. And if the president or the OMB on the national level and Councils of Government on the local level acquire enough power to supervise the interaction of these multiple participants—as public pluralists hope will eventually be the case—the political system will be able to implement the policies generated by a diverse number of groups. Unlike a polyarchal form of decision making, where power is concentrated in the hands of a few officials, or participatory democracy, where it is fragmented among numerous autonomous units, a supervised form of pluralism seeks to realize that middle ground which Wilson believes is most conducive to innovative policy making.

Whether we compare alternative forms of decision making by their ability to promote a sense of public trust, efficacy, and responsiveness, or by their capacity to achieve economies of scale or minimize spill-over effects, or by their success in stimulating social reform and innovative policy making, a public form of pluralism seems to have many advantages. Pluralism has been criticized by the advocates of centralized and decentralized power for opposite reasons, but in many cases these criticisms do not seem justified. According to the numerous criteria we have looked at, a pluralistic system of decision making often seems preferable to its competitors. That is no mean achievement when we consider that pluralism's detractors suggested many of the criteria in the first place.

NOTES

1. Alan Altshuler, *Community Control;* Milton Kotler, *Neighborhood Government.*
2. Altshuler, *Community Control,* p. 16.
3. Theodore J. Lowi, *The End of Liberalism;* Robert L. Crain, Elihu Katz, and Donald Rosenthal, *The Politics of Community Conflict.*
4. Altshuler, *Community Control,* p. 15.
5. Douglas Yates, *Neighborhood Democracy,* p. 26.
6. Robert L. Bish and Hugh O. Nourse, *Urban Economics and Policy Analysis,* pp. 111-13.
7. Ibid., pp. 107-11.
8. Crain, Katz, and Rosenthal, *Politics of Community Conflict.*
9. James Q. Wilson, "Innovation in Organizations," pp. 193-218.
10. Altshuler, *Community Control,* pp. 13-65.
11. Wilson, "Innovation in Organizations," pp. 193-218.
12. Samuel P. Huntington, *Political Order in Changing Societies.*
13. Charles Lindblom, *The Intelligence of Democracy,* pp. 165-274; Michael Aiken and Robert Alford, "Community Structure and Mobilization," p. 63.
14. Werner Hirsch, *The Economics of State and Local Government,* pp. 189, 178-83.
15. Elinor Ostrom et al., *Community Organization and the Provision of Police Services.*
16. Bish and Nourse, *Urban Economics,* p. 133.
17. Peter Blau and Richard Schoenherr, *The Structure of Organizations;* S. R. Klatzky, "Relationship of Organizational Size to Complexity and Coordination."
18. Altshuler, *Community Control,* pp. 123-90.
19. Ibid.
20. Bish and Nourse, *Urban Economics,* pp. 129-31; Charles Tiebout, "A Pure Theory of Local Expenditures," pp. 416-24.

21. Bish and Nourse, *Urban Economics*, p. 129.
22. James Heilbrun, *Urban Economics and Public Policy*, p. 345.
23. Yates, *Neighborhood Democracy*, p. 66.
24. Ibid., p. 105.
25. Ibid., p. 67.
26. Lowi, *End of Liberalism*, p. 101.
27. Crain, Katz, and Rosenthal, *Politics of Community Conflict*, p. 13.
28. Lowi, *End of Liberalism*, p. 101.
29. Ibid., p. 127.
30. Ibid., pp. 217-26.
31. Ibid., pp. 226-39.
32. Kenneth B. Clark, *Dark Ghetto*, pp. 63-80; Milton Greenblatt, ed., *Poverty and Mental Health*; Dorothy B. James, *Poverty, Politics, and Change*.
33. James, *Poverty, Politics, and Change*, pp. 148-58.
34. Herbert A. Simon and James G. March, *Organizations*; Lindblom, *Intelligence of Democracy*.
35. Roland McKean, *Public Spending*, p. 149.
36. Ibid.
37. Lowi, *End of Liberalism*, p. 302.
38. Irving L. Janis, *Victims of Groupthink*.
39. Ibid., pp. 196-97.
40. Ibid., pp. 14-50.
41. Wilson, "Innovation in Organizations," pp. 193-218.
42. Robert L. Lineberry and Edmund P. Fowler, "Reformism and Public Policies in American Cities," pp. 707-09.
43. Terry Clark, "Community Structure, Decision Making, Budget Expenditures, and Urban Renewal in Fifty-one American Cities," p. 594.
44. Michael Aiken, "The Distribution of Community Power: Structural Bases and Social Consequences."
45. Aiken and Alford, "Community Structure and Mobilization"; Michael Aiken and Robert Alford, "Community Structure and Innovation," pp. 843-64.
46. Crain, Katz, and Rosenthal, *Politics of Community Conflict*.
47. T. Clark, "Community Structure, in Fifty-one American Cities," p. 587.
48. Yates, *Neighborhood Democracy*, p. 65.

Chapter

10

Pluralism and the
Problem of Public Administration

In this chapter we need to deal with one final problem facing every theory of democracy, that of public administration. Besides determining how decisions should be made, the advocates of various theories of democracy must decide how agreed-upon policies should be implemented. Even though a form of democracy may be successful in generating new ideas, its public record will be less than impressive if it cannot successfully translate its decisions into operating programs.

Any discussion of public administration is often a confusing task in American politics because government agencies perform a multitude of functions. Many play an input role in the political system, organizing clientele groups and mobilizing support for new or existing policies. In fact, some agencies—OEO, the Departments of Commerce and Labor—perform an almost exclusively representative function, for their main task is to look after the interests of their various constituencies. Others—such as HUD, HEW, or the Defense Department—play both input and output roles, lobbying for new policies as well as implementing existing programs. While earlier we discussed the role that government bureaus should play in the policy-making process, in this chapter we need to analyze how they should perform their administrative tasks. In particular, it is necessary to determine what organizational patterns are most likely to be successful in translating public policies into operating programs.

In the quest for the optimal administrative arrangements, the proponents of competing theories of democracy must often pursue conflicting objectives. On the one hand they must try to insure that the administrative arm of the executive branch has the organizational capabilities and resources necessary to achieve its objectives, while on the other they must try to prevent agencies with administrative duties from abusing their grants of public authority. The optimal administrative arrangements must strike a balance between (1) promoting organizational effectiveness and (2) achieving organizational control. Although agencies must be given sufficient authority to carry out their stated functions, at the same time measures must be taken to insure that the goals of a policy are not consciously or unconsciously subverted in the very act of implementation.

To cope with these difficulties, the advocates of various theories of democracy must decide two separate yet crucially related issues. First, they must determine how individual agencies should be administered. Should they be highly centralized with only limited discretion granted to field offices, or should they have the option of delegating considerable authority to subunits? Secondly, the proponents of different theories of democracy must decide how they wish to organize the executive branch as a whole. Should they try as Franklin Roosevelt did to build creative disorder and duplication into the structure of the federal bureaucracy, or should they follow the suggestions of the Hoover and Ash Commissions and streamline the executive branch by functionally grouping related agencies into similar departments?[1]

Advocates of community control have argued that considerable leeway and discretion should be allowed on the individual agency level. Unless lower-level bureaucrats have the flexibility to respond to immediate community problems and the discretion to tailor the substance of programs to local demands, the delivery of public services may be ineffectual in meeting constituent needs. However, because they wish to parcel out the power of the federal government to smaller political units, most participatory democrats have paid very little attention to the problems of organizing the federal bureaucracy as a whole.

In contrast, polyarchists and populists have implicitly, if not always explicitly, called for a more centralized administration of programs on both individual agency and executive levels of government. Lowi has argued that individual agencies will lack any degree of effectiveness unless they avoid dispersing their power among various subunits. In a similar vein, polyarchists and populists have sought to consolidate and streamline the organization of the executive branch as a whole, insisting that the haphazard, overlapping nature of administrative jurisdictions constitutes an inherently wasteful and inefficient manner of implementing policy.[2] Like the members of the Hoover and Ash Commissions, who have studied the makeup of the executive branch on three separate occasions since World War II, they have concluded that (1) agencies with related duties should be consolidated and the proliferation of new agencies should be held to a minimum, (2) bureaus with functionally related tasks should be grouped together in larger departments, and (3) the jurisdictions and responsibilities of agencies should be clearly defined and delineated. In Lowi's opinion, a pluralistic system of overlapping jurisdictions so weakens and fragments the administrative process that it renders the government incapable of achieving its objectives. Likewise, the granting of any appreciable degree of flexibility to lower-level officials in the interpretation of their duties leads to widespread misuse of government power. He has maintained that under a system of administration in which rules and responsibilities are not clearly delineated, lower-level bureaucrats have too many opportunities to bargain and logroll with the clientele groups that they serve. In Lowi's view, this process of interest-group bargaining leads to the displacement of agency goals and to a corruption of the whole notion of strict implementation of the law.

Because participatory democrats have failed to develop a comprehensive approach to organizational problems, this chapter will primarily focus on polyarchy's and populism's proposals for administrative reorganization. As will be explained in greater detail later on, pluralism rejects the recommendations of its polyarchal and populist counterparts, arguing that the administrative process will be enhanced by allowing for more flexibility and duplication. While pluralists share the belief in the need for effective and efficient administration, they question whether polyarchy's measures will be capable of achieving these objectives.

The Problem of Organizational Effectiveness

If we wish to maximize an organization's effectiveness, we can argue that polyarchal-populist prescriptions for administrative reform might hamper the performance of individual agencies. Like Max Weber and Luther Gulick, polyarchists and populists seem to believe that there are certain universal administrative principles that can be applied to all organizations, e. g., straight lines of authority, unity of command, and authority commensurate with responsibility.[3] They often insist that the most effective, efficient agencies are hierarchically organized with limited discretion granted to lower-level bureaucrats. In recent years, however, this attitude has been attacked by a group of scholars who have sought to replace universalistic administrative theories with contingency models of organizational structure. Starting in the late 1960s, sociologists engaged in the comparative study of organizations began to notice that a relationship exists between an agency's size, tasks, and structure. Instead of finding that certain principles of administration are suitable for all kinds of organizations, they have observed that the most appropriate arrangements are contingent upon the volume and complexity of problems facing an organization. In an important study of state employment agencies, Peter Blau has shown that as the amount of work increases, an agency finds itself under greater pressure to decentralize its operations.[4] As an organization grows in size, it becomes increasingly difficult for the agency to administer its programs in a highly centralized fashion. However, in related studies, Paul Lawrence, Jay Lorsch, Charles Perrow, and James Thompson find that the optimal administrative arrangements are as dependent on the variability in an agency's tasks as on the amount of work actually performed.[5] While these studies often differ in terminology and emphasis, they share the conclusion that a centralized, rule-oriented organization is suitable for performing only certain kinds of tasks.

Perrow in particular finds that the most desirable administrative arrangements are contingent upon two factors: the degree of variability in the problems confronting an agency and the degree to which an agency has reliable and established techniques for solving the problems facing it. By combining these two variables, Perrow has developed a typology of four different kinds of organizations, each with very different types of administrative needs (see table 4).[6]

Table 4

Technology available to agency	Nature of tasks	
	UNIFORM	COMPLEX
Solutions to problems clear	Passport Bureau Box 1	Voice of America Box 2
Solutions to problems unclear	Bureau of Education Box 4	HUD Box 3

Box one represents an organization like the Passport Bureau of the U. S. Department of State, which faces very routine tasks and has a fairly clear conception of how best to deal with its administrative duties. In box two we find an agency like the Voice of America, whose broadcasts must explain a great variety of phenomena but can rely on a clear idea of how to handle the issues. Box three represents an administrative body like HUD, which not only faces the complex task of revitalizing the nation's decaying cities but also must rely on a body of knowledge that as yet cannot reliably specify which programs would be most effective in furthering the agency's goals. Finally, in box four we find an organization like the Office of Education in HEW, which has a more homogeneous task than HUD yet may not be quite certain what mixture of policies will be most effective in achieving its goals.

The identification of different types of agencies can tell us in turn what kinds of organizational arrangements are most likely to lead to effective administration. Perrow argues that the centralized, rule-oriented model of organization that Lowi advocates would be appropriate only for an agency administering relatively simple, straightforward programs, such as those found in box one. While an organization that reacted in a consistent fashion to every problem would perform more than adequately if its tasks never varied, it would prove to be inordinately inept, as Lawrence and Lorsch have shown, once its administrative duties lacked uniformity. [7] As the tasks confronting an agency become more heterogeneous and the solutions to its problems become more uncertain, it will have to grant greater discretion to middle- and lower-level officials, as do the agencies in boxes three and four. When exceptions arise or unusual problems develop, a centralized organization lacks the flexibility necessary to deal with administrative problems that deviate from the usual tasks at hand. Similarly, if the state of knowledge in policy areas such as education or crime is rather undeveloped, agencies in those fields will have to forego reliance on detailed plans in order to experiment with a variety of approaches in their search for appropriate solutions. Unless lower-level bureaucrats can exercise discretion in implementing policy, their agencies will be unable to launch any creative attacks on their respective problems. The lack of certainty about how best to run a particular program rules out centralized administration.

Unfortunately, however, polyarchal and populist democrats like Lowi and Harrington seem oblivious to these findings. Like the members of the Hoover and Ash Commissions, who have insisted that centralized and well-disciplined organizations are necessarily the most effective, polyarchists and populists have fallen into the mistake of believing that there are universal principles of good management that apply to all organizations. From the recent literature on contingency models of organizational theory, we now know that when the problems bureaucracies deal with are neither standardized nor easily understood, centralized agencies may be the least effective form of administration.

For similar reasons the desire of polyarchists and populists to rationalize and streamline the executive branch as a whole may in the long run prove to be self-defeating. While polyarchists and populists have often seen the duplication and overlap of federal programs as an inherently inefficient, ineffectual way of implementing policy, it can be argued that the most effective structuring of the executive branch may be contingent on the nature of the issues that must be handled. If it is possible to isolate a relatively self-contained problem, a single agency can conceivably take sole responsibility for dealing with it. But when issues cut across the boundaries of traditional government agencies, as is becoming increasingly true in many policy areas, some blurring of agency responsibilities may be desirable.[8] As policy planners began to realize in the 1960s, programs dealing with poverty, housing, manpower training, health, education, and welfare are all intimately linked. The Johnson administration's war on poverty could not focus on a series of separate and unrelated problems, for the issue involved the activities of a variety of government agencies.

In fact, on the basis of recent administrative experience, Warren Bennis has gone so far as to suggest that established, traditional bureaucracies may be ill equipped to deal with the complexities of modern-day social issues.[9] In a similar vein, Harold Seidman has argued that because of the interdependent, overlapping nature of so many social problems, the executive branch will eventually be composed of "adaptive, rapidly changing temporary systems" organized around problem areas.[10] Although Bennis and Seidman may have overstated their case, it can nonetheless be argued that a blurring of agency jurisdictions is essential for problems that resist simple categorization. The most appropriate organizational arrangements for maximizing agency effectiveness are contingent on the issues they face. Since so many government bureaus deal with problems that are (1) heterogeneous in nature, (2) not fully understood by experts in the field, and (3) not conterminous with traditional agency boundaries, efforts to consolidate operations on the executive level may have the unintended consequence of impairing administrative effectiveness.

The Problem of Organizational Control

Regardless of the impact that centralized administration of individual agencies or consolidation of the executive branch as a whole may have on the effectiveness of various government agencies, we still need to ask if these measures will insure organizational control. While every theory of democracy must attempt to provide sufficient resources and flexibility to the administrative arm of the executive branch, it must simultaneously try to prevent agencies from consciously or unconsciously altering the goals of their respective programs. Merely because an agency has the proper administrative structure to match its tasks is no guarantee that it will faithfully and vigorously execute its responsibilities. The question that thus needs to be asked is whether polyarchal-populist suggestions for controlling individual agencies would stimulate government bureaus to remain faithful to their initial goals. While polyarchists like Lowi often insist that it is the constant bargaining an agency must undertake in a pluralistic system that leads to the displacement of goals, they fail to realize that informal norms within an organization may be just as important in accounting for an agency's failure to achieve its objectives. Polyarchists argue that by doing away with discretion and the bargaining associated with it and by instituting centralized, rule-oriented methods of organizational control, it will be possible to insure that an agency remains faithful to its original goals.

However, it can be argued that this approach to administration places too much reliance on formalized, rule-oriented modes of control. On the basis of the work of Robert Merton and the early Peter Blau, students of organizational theory have increasingly come to reject the view held by Weber and others that organizations are rational instruments that can be scientifically programmed to achieve specified objectives.[11] Merton et al. pointed out that agencies, especially centralized, rule-oriented agencies, often develop their own informal norms of behavior that sometimes act to undermine the organization's original objectives. In a study of state welfare agencies Merton has described how the top hierarchy attempted to increase the reliability of behavior within the organization by instituting a wide variety of rules. By closely regulating the conduct of its personnel, the agency believed it could provide better service to its clientele, but in fact, Merton noted, the opposite situation developed. Once the agency formulated an elaborate set of rules, its case workers became wary that they might violate some organizational regulation and thereby jeopardize their careers. To counter these feelings, employees developed their own informal norms for dealing with clients, including a reduction in the amount of personal relations between case workers and their clients and an extreme reliance on organizational rules for making decisions. One such rule was that families not be broken up, and it was enforced to the point where "a social worker in violation of his own judgment as to what would be most beneficial for the clients" would recommend that mentally disturbed children remain with their families even though the brothers and sisters would suffer as a result. [12] Ironically enough, an agency that attempted to insure better service to its clients inadvertently ended up providing worse service. The informal norms that the organization's personnel had developed in response to the internal directives of the top hierarchy resulted in the subtle yet significant displacement of the agency's original objectives. The employees became more intent on routinely applying the rules of the organization than on meeting the needs of their clients.

Peter Blau's analysis of a state employment bureau offers another illustration of the same type of phenomenon. [13] The bureau, which had the official task of helping people find employment, developed a simple and, at first glance, highly effective procedure for guaranteeing that its personnel actually attempted to find jobs for their clients. Each month placement officers were evaluated by the percentage of people they found employment for out of the total number of individuals they interviewed. Unfortunately, these rules, which were meant to make the employment agency more productive, often served to limit the usefulness of the agency to the job hunters it was supposed to assist. As was the case of the welfare bureau, employees developed informal norms of behavior to mitigate the severity of the organization's evaluation scheme. For instance, when employment officials heard of new job openings they refused to share that information with other personnel. Each placement worker would attempt to hoard as many job notices as he could until he happened to interview individuals who qualified for the positions. But even more importantly, since it was difficult to place minority members with limited education or skills, employees sought to reduce the possibility of receiving low evaluation scores by deliberately discouraging such individuals from utilizing the services of the agency. The rules the organization established to achieve its goals had the unintended consequence of impairing the ability of the agency to meet its objectives. Instead of attempting to help the people most in need of their services, i.e., indigent minority members, the personnel of the employment agency attempted to dissuade them from calling on state help in the first place. The informal norms that the employees had developed in response to evaluation procedures worked at cross-purposes to the original objectives of the agency.

Both the Blau and Merton studies indicate that internal procedures are important in explaining why agencies often fail to achieve their objectives. But even more importantly, they show that the informal norms of a bureau are most likely to subvert the original objectives of the organization when it is run in a highly centralized, formalistic fashion. While Lowi believes that limiting the discretion of lower-level bureaucrats will insure their faithful adherence to agency goals, such procedures will often have the opposite result. If bureaucratic personnel are governed by an elaborate set of rules, they may lose sight of their original objectives, as Merton has demonstrated, or subvert the intent of the established procedures, as Blau has demonstrated.

The failure of polyarchists and populists to see that their efforts to control individual agencies may have certain unintended consequences is symptomatic of a much larger problem. While informal groups within an agency can intentionally or unintentionally lead to the alteration of an organization's goals, an agency's political ties with outside clientele groups can also affect its commitment to its official objectives. Recognition of this fact is essential if we wish to properly evaluate recommendations for rearranging the structure of the federal bureaucracy. As noted earlier, polyarchal-populist suggestions for organizing the executive branch as a whole include (1) holding to a minimum the proliferation of new agencies, (2) grouping functionally related agencies together into larger departments, and (3) carefully delineating each agency's duties and responsibilities in order to eliminate overlapping programs. As we have already seen, the delineation of each agency's duties and responsibilities may not always be desirable when problems cut across traditional agency boundaries. But even more importantly, we can argue that if all of the polyarchal-populist proposals were ever fully implemented, they would restrict rather than facilitate public control of the bureaucracy. Proponents of consolidating and streamlining the executive branch often seem naive in their assumption that reorganization efforts will have little or no adverse impact on the way in which government programs are administered. As Francis Rourke, Mathew Holden, Philip Selznick, and Richard Neustadt have pointed out, agencies often acquire a political stake in the continuation of their programs.[14] This phenomenon belies the polyarchal-populist assumption, derived from Weber, that organizations are neutral administrators of the programs they oversee. Either through selective recruitment or internal socialization, most of the personnel of various government bureaus become highly committed to the policies they administer. To preserve the essential parts of their programs, agencies will generally seek out clientele groups or constituencies in order to protect themselves from the claims of competing agencies. Every bureau wishes to generate enough potential support in the larger political community so that it can fight off legislative attacks that might jeopardize the existence of its programs.

While these observations may at first seem rather obvious, they provide us with some guidelines that may be more realistic than Lowi's administrative prescriptions for guaranteeing that government agencies vigorously pursue their stated objectives. First of all, Lowi's call for limiting the proliferation of new agencies could be a serious political mistake, for, as Holden has shown, it is not advisable to ask an established bureau to administer new or controversial programs. Holden has pointed out that once an agency develops its clientele groups, it is likely to be hostile to acquiring new programs that may jeopardize its existing network of relationships.[15] If a well-established agency is forced to operate a program that may alienate its supporters, it is likely to drag its feet in implementing the new policy. In the process the original objectives of the program may very will be altered or displaced.

A prime example of this phenomenon can be found in the administration of the food stamp program, which Congress delegated to the Department of Agriculture in the late 1960s when it expanded its relief-in-kind programs. Since the Department of Agriculture is primarily oriented toward the Farm Bureau and corporate farmers rather than the urban or rural poor, its administration of the program has been less than vigorous. [16] Because Congress failed to consider the implementation of its policies carefully, it employed an organizational strategy that worked at cross-purposes to its policy objectives. It would have been more advisable to create a separate agency, since new organizations will tend to vigorously implement their assigned programs in order to overcome the precarious political position they occupy as newly established bodies. A recently created bureau without any established power base will naturally try to build a following by making sure that its policies are successfully administered. To ward off attacks from competing agencies or from hostile legislators, it must provide enough tangible or symbolic benefits to its potential supporters that they will be willing to come to the aid of the bureau in times of trouble. In order to build a viable political following, an agency will implement those policies which will earn it the consistent support of at least one constituency group.

The argument that applies to the placement of individual programs likewise applies to the placement of agencies as a whole. As Selznick has pointed out, if government programs are violently opposed by other interests in society, it may be necessary to shield them organizationally from their opponents so that they can survive politically. [17] If two separate agencies have functionally similar jobs but different and conflicting goals, it may not be advisable to place both of them in one large department since the agency that is weakest will then be much more vulnerable to interests that oppose its activities. For example, in the late 1940s the Hoover Commission called for the consolidation of the Farm Home Administration, the Farm Credit Administration, and the Agricultural Extension Service on the grounds that all these agencies were concerned with the same function of extending credit to farmers. What seemed like a logical move to end administrative duplication would in reality have worked a hardship on marginal farmers. [18] The Farm Credit Administration and the Agricultural Extension Service, which were both created at the request of the Farm Bureau, are primarily concerned with serving the needs of moderate and well-to-do farmers, while the Farm Home Administration seeks to provide special assistance to marginal farmers who might not otherwise receive any kind of credit. If the various agencies had been combined, the resulting bureau would have sought to cultivate the undivided support of at least one clientele group. Since the Farm Bureau is better organized than marginal farmers, an agency that had the responsibility for extending loans to both constituencies would probably cater to the wishes of the more organized group. In the process the goal of Congress to provide needed financial aid to marginal farmers would be attenuated, if not displaced altogether.

On the basis of the above examples, we can see why the attempts of polyarchal and populist democrats to control the federal bureaucracy not only may prove to be ineffective but also may contribute to the very practices they wish to avoid in the first place. Regardless of how centralized a bureau may be or how much discretion an agency happens to wield, its political ties to outside groups will significantly influence its ultimate behavior. While Lowi might deplore this tendency of organizations to develop political links with outside groups, he fails to see that it is possible to utilize a knowledge of this phenomenon to safeguard the implementation of government policies. If the structure of the federal bureaucracy were ever reorganized along more centralized lines, as Lowi and the Hoover and Ash Commissions have suggested, the danger of organizations displacing their goals would be heightened rather than lessened. Since established departments tend to have their personnel and programs coopted by outside constituencies, an important way to provide new or controversial programs with a chance of survival is to allow for the proliferation of new agencies. Similarly, because new or controversial bureaus are politically more vulnerable when they are placed next to bureaus that oppose their objectives, it may not always be desirable to rationalize the administrative process by grouping functionally related agencies together into larger departments. The attempts of polyarchal democrats to consolidate the executive branch would effectively foreclose reliance on these administrative strategies. Ironically enough, while Lowi often sees the profusion of government agencies and the untidy nature of the bureaucratic system as a sign of administrative weakness, it may in fact be a sign of administrative vitality. While the efforts of populists and polyarchists to operate individual bureaus in a more centralized, nondiscretionary fashion may make it more difficult to insure that agencies remain committed to their programs, their desire to streamline the executive branch as a whole may also have the same unintended consequence.

The Pluralistic Alternative

The difficulties with a centrally operated bureaucracy only cast in greater relief the benefits of a more pluralistic pattern of administration. We noted earler that pluralists are not adverse to agencies' either decentralizing their operations or exercising discretion in the administration of their programs. As Perrow convincingly argues, when the responsibilities of organizations are heterogeneous in nature and the methodology they must employ to deal with their problems is not well established, it is essential that agencies decentralize their operations. When government bureaus must respond to a series of diverse demands, centralized, formalistically run organizations may be both too slow and too rigid to provide adequate services to their clients. If the residents of large cities come to play a more active role in government, it will be imperative that city, state, and federal agencies have the flexibility to meet their demands promptly. The sense of public mistrust that is found in many communities may be difficult to overcome if centralized, rule-oriented bureaus are unable to respond quickly to local needs.

While Lowi suggests that the discretionary manner in which many laws are enforced has led to a breakdown in respect for public authority, in reality the situation may be much more complex. Residents of the inner city may not be opposed to lower-level bureaucrats exercising discretion per se so much as they are opposed to the manner in which officials have exercised that discretion in the past. Even though residents of urban areas feel that public officials have utilized their discretionary power to the disadvantage of the inner city, they may hope that bureaucrats will eventually use such authority to be more sensitive to the wishes of local neighborhoods. For example, it may be appropriate for the police to strictly enforce an ordinance against loitering or disorderly conduct in a suburban community, but it may be necessary to interpret that ordinance more leniently in an inner city neighborhood. If a residential area lacks adequate back yards or parks, it will be natural for citizens to spend more of their leisure time in the streets. As a result, behavior that a suburban neighborhood might see as undesirable might appear very differently to residents of an inner city community. If a police department attempts to enforce an ordinance uniformly in these two contrasting situations, it may alienate, rather than win the support of, the local community. How officials use their power of discretion—not whether they should have it—is the key administrative problem that needs to be confronted.

The best way to prevent agencies from abusing their discretion is to build some degree of organizational duplication and planned disorder into the structure of the executive branch as a whole. While pluralists argue that on a micro-level the decentralization of individual agencies can lead to greater administrative effectiveness, they insist that on a macro-level, agency and group competition can limit any misuse of government power that may arise. It is not discretion or bargaining per se—but the political proclivities cited by Holden et al. or the presence of informal groups trying to protect their interests in the larger organization—that causes agencies to displace their goals. To control these tendencies, a carefully designed system of organizational checks and balances is preferable to a system of rigid internal procedures and limited discretion.

First of all, when some degree of creative disorder exists in the arrangement of federal agencies, crucial programs can be more easily protected from opposing interests. Both the Roosevelt and Johnson administrations provide excellent illustrations of this point. According to the orthodox polyarchal theory of administration, Roosevelt should have assigned his programs to alleviate the depression to established departments such as Agriculture, Labor, Commerce, and Treasury. But he recognized, as many commentators in public administration have not, that even with new chiefs, the old-line agencies would not be likely to generate the enthusiasm and vigor that the gravity of the situation warranted. [19] To circumvent the power of established groups and agencies, Roosevelt made it part of his strategy to create new administrative bodies when he wanted creative attacks on the problems at hand. He was determined not to lose in the process of administration what he had previously won in the legislative arena. Similarly, Johnson deliberately refrained from asking the traditional-line agencies to administer his war on poverty. Not only did he insist that OEO be established as an independent agency, he also sought to shield it from hostile interests by locating it in the executive office of the president. The war on poverty might have turned out very differently if he had succumbed to the wishes of big city mayors and placed OEO in the Department of Housing and Urban Development, which has been oriented primarily to the needs of metropolitian government. If HUD had been given responsibility for administering OEO programs, OEO might never have become an advocate agency seeking to challenge the actions of municipal governments. [20] Even though polyarchists and populists often argue that an untidy, pluralistic administrative system is wasteful and inefficient, they fail to realize that it may serve other important purposes. Some degree of creative disorder in the overall organization of the federal bureaucracy may be necessary to protect new programs against hostile interests.

For related reasons, pluralists believe that administrative overlap is important in fostering interagency competition in the implementation of federal programs. While a degree of organizational disorder is necessary to protect the establishment of new or controversial programs, it also serves to guarantee that bureaus do not abuse their powers of discretion in carrying out their tasks. As indicated earlier, the fact that many present-day political problems cut across traditional boundaries is in large part responsible for the blurring of agency jurisdictions, but the granting of overlapping jurisdictions may have an added virtue. If agencies like OEO, HUD, HEW, or the Department of Labor have related responsibilities, each can scrutinize the others' activities that might have some impact on its own constituents. In the process they can make certain that policies designed to benefit certain groups are not subtly altered in the process of administration. For instance, as James Sundquist had noted, once OEO was established, it successfully put pressure on state employment agencies to launch outreach programs to find work for the urban poor. [21] While the internal norms of the state employment agencies that Blau studied often led them to discourage residents of the inner city from seeking their help, the external pressure of OEO stimulated other employment agencies to redouble their efforts to assist the poor.

Finally, if government bureaus are given only incomplete grants of authority and overlapping jurisdictions in the running of their programs, they cannot conceal their operations from the scrutiny of outside interests. In the same manner that group competition can insure more rational policy making, interest-group as well as interagency competition can insure that government agencies do not alter the original objectives of a policy in the process of administering it. When agencies do not have a monopoly over any particular issue or program, they face greater pressure to justify their activities and to improve the performance of their tasks. While the report of the Ash Commission testifies to the lack of popularity of this view, the record of the Roosevelt administration indicates that it can work. More than any other president, Roosevelt attempted to administer his policies in a pluralistic, competitive, overlapping fashion. As Arthur Schlesinger has noted, jurisdictional overlap "was sloppy and caused much trouble," but at the same time he recognized that the resulting administrative competition helped to keep the bureaucracy "forever on its toes."[22]

NOTES

1. See Arthur M. Schlesinger, Jr., *The Age of Roosevelt,* Vol. II: *The Coming of the New Deal,* pp. 535-52, for a description of Roosevelt's view of administration; and Harold Seidman, *Politics, Position, and Power,* pp. 3-37, for an analysis of the Hoover Commission's administrative proposals.

2. Theodore J. Lowi, *The End of Liberalism,* pp. 101-57; Michael Harrington, *Toward a Democratic Left,* pp. 3-56.

3. Max Weber, *From Max Weber;* Luther H. Gulick and L. Urwick, eds., *Papers on the Science of Administration.*

4. Peter Blau and Richard Schoenherr, *The Structure of Organizations.*

5. Paul R. Lawrence and Jay W. Lorsch, *Organization and Environment;* Charles Perrow, *Complex Organizations;* Charles Perrow, "A Framework for the Comparative Analysis of Organizations," pp. 194-208; James D. Thompson, *Organizations in Action.*

6. Charles Perrow, *Organizational Analysis*, p. 81.

7. Lawrence and Lorsch, *Organizations and Environment*.

8. James L. Sundquist, *Making Federalism Work*, pp. 1-32.

9. Warren Bennis, *Changing Organizations*.

10. Seidman, *Politics, Position, and Power*, p. 281.

11. Robert K. Merton, *Social Theory and Social Structure*; Peter Blau, *The Dynamics of Bureaucracy*.

12. Merton, *Social Theory and Social Structure*, p. 197. See also Amitai Etzioni, *Modern Organizations*, p. 12.

13. Blau, *Dynamics of Bureaucracy*, pp. 1-100.

14. Francis E. Rourke, *Bureaucracy, Politics, and Public Policy*; Mathew Holden, "Imperialism in Bureaucracy," pp. 943-51; Philip Selznick, *Leadership in Administration*; Richard Neustadt, *Presidential Power*.

15. Holden, "Imperialism in Bureaucracy," p. 945.

16. Seidman, *Politics, Position, and Power*, p. 16.

17. Selznick, *Leadership in Administration*, pp. 119-30.

18. Seidman, *Politics, Position, and Power*, p. 15.

19. Schlesinger, *The Age of Roosevelt*, Vol. II: *The Coming of the New Deal*, p. 534.

20. Seidman, *Politics, Position, and Power*, p. 19.

21. Sundquist, *Making Federalism Work*, pp. 49-54.

22. Schlesinger, *The Age of Roosevelt*, Vol. II, p. 535.

Chapter

11

Conclusion

The preceding chapters have suggested that the literature on democratic theory suffers from two serious problems. First, much of the commentary lacks a comparative focus. Instead of systematically weighing the advantages and disadvantages of alternative models of democratic government, many studies have examined the weaknesses or strengths of only one or two approaches. Such a circumspect and partial view can often lead to incomplete and distorted assessments; the merits of a particular variety of democratic government can never be fully appreciated or discounted until we know the costs and benefits associated with deciding policy in an alternative fashion.

Moreover, very few studies have made any serious effort to deal with criticism that is hostile to their own position. In *The End of Liberalism*, Lowi devotes over three hundred pages to the alleged defects of pluralism, yet he spends a scant thirteen pages discussing his own suggestions for reform. [1] Bachrach devotes 90 percent of his book, *The Theory of Democratic Elitism*, to a critique of polyarchy and pluralism while he defends a participatory form of democracy in a brief fourteen pages. [2] Likewise, Wolff spends roughly fifty pages in his article "Beyond Tolerance" criticizing pluralism but only one or two pages detailing his plans for small, intensive communities. [3] Many participatory democrats have argued that because the pluralistic interplay of groups fails to provide a sense of community, it is inherently inferior to more decentralized forms of democracy. But unfortunately, the same participatory democrats have merely assumed—rather than proven—that communal forms of participation are always desirable. Before we can make any statements about the need to go "beyond tolerance" and pluralistic democracy, we must carefully consider whether the participatory option is actually superior to a pluralistic form of government. Participatory democrats like Wolff and Bachrach often do not provide us with that kind of balanced assessment. With a similar lack of systematic analysis, many polyarchists have assumed that by showing how an allegedly pluralistic form of decision making failed to work adequately in a particular instance, they have thereby proved the opposite case for centralized planning. Such reasoning is both bad logic as well as bad political science. Before we can argue that a pluralistic form of government cannot get anything done, we need to compare the performance of pluralism with more centralized patterns of decision making. The recent literature on democratic government, whether it is written from a polyarchal, populist, or participatory perspective, seems better as political criticism than as positive political philosophy. While Lowi or Bachrach or Wolff have written subtle, sustained critiques of pluralism, their suggestions for reform neither confront nor convincingly refute the arguments against both more centralized and more decentralized patterns of democracy.

The second major shortcoming of the literature on democratic theory lies in its failure to distinguish among different types of pluralism. Many commentators have assumed that there is a single type of interest-group democracy and have therefore failed to see that the criticisms they have made of pluralism often apply to only one particular form of the doctrine. Similarly, because the critics have not distinguished among various types of pluralism, they have failed to realize that their proposed reforms can often be easily incorporated within a pluralistic framework. Many of the reforms proposed by commentators like Kariel constitute modifications of a laissez-faire version of pluralism rather than radical alternatives to pluralism in general. For instance, Kariel argues that it is necessary for the federal government to regulate the internal affairs of groups dominated by self-serving elites, but he believes that such policies constitute an attack on pluralism rather than simply a modification of one form of the doctrine. [4] A public pluralist would argue that if the government refrains from dictating policy objectives to an organization but insures that the rank and file have the final say over the group's goals, the integrity of a pluralistic system need not be compromised.

The failure to distinguish among different varieties of pluralism has led Lowi and McConnell to insist that the problems that plague a laissez-faire form of economics are analogous to those that trouble a pluralistic form of decision making. Both Lowi and McConnell attack pluralism for failing to see that competition between groups can break down and that the equilibrium point established by the interplay of groups—even if competition is maintained— may not necessarily be the optimal decision-making point. "One of the major Keynesian criticisms of market theory," Lowi points out, "is that even if pure competition among factors of supply and demand did yield an equilibrium, the equilibrium could be at something far less than the ideal of full employment." [5] By analogy, Lowi argues that even if a pluralistic system were competitive, the resulting policies might not necessarily be desirable from the viewpoint of society as a whole. While Lowi and McConnell may be correct in drawing a comparison between laissez-faire economics and certain varieties of pluralistic democracy, they fail to see that their arguments do not readily apply to all forms of pluralism, especially public pluralism. By organizing marginal interests from the bottom up, by expanding the size of the decision-making arena, and by fostering competition among government agencies, a public form of pluralism attempts to prevent any set of groups or agencies from establishing semi-monopolies. Likewise, by having political elites supervise the give-and-take of group bargaining, public pluralism seeks to insure that the equilibrium point established between interest groups and agencies is also the optimal decision-making point.

Because Lowi fails to distinguish among several different types of pluralism, he overlooks the fact that the reforms of laissez-faire economics in the twentieth century have more in common with public pluralism's recommendations for change than with his own calls for more centralized planning. Many economists, like Keynes, who were critical of the laissez-faire model of the economy nonetheless felt that the market system would work well if it were properly stimulated and regulated. Even though they had limited faith in the invisible hand of Adam Smith, they were equally wary of a completely controlled economy. They believed that the market system was basically an effective mechanism for deciding economic issues and that active state intervention was necessary only when monopolies appeared or when the economy failed to achieve full employment. In place of a command system, they favored a dual structure in which the government intervened in the workings of the market system only when the latter failed to work effectively by itself.

In a similar vein, a public pluralist would insist that it is unnecessary to restrict the participation of interest groups merely because in the past certain interests have established semi-monopolies or because the decisions reached through group bargaining have not necessarily been socially desirable. If, as Lowi argues, the workings of a laissez-faire economy and the operations of pluralism are comparable, then the reforms of Keynesian economics and the proposals of public pluralism are likewise analogous. Just as Keynesian economists do not wish to substitute government planning for the operations of the market system, so public pluralists do not wish to see the curtailment of pluralistic bargaining. Like a market economy, which can function well if the state regulates the workings of the price system, a pluralistic system of government can function well if the state guides and supervises the process of interest-group bargaining. The pluralistic interplay of groups may not be self-sustaining, but if it is properly regulated, it may be far superior to the alternatives from which we have to choose.

NOTES

1. Theodore J. Lowi, *The End of Liberalism*, pp. 297-309.
2. Peter Bachrach, *The Theory of Democratic Elitism*, pp. 93-106.
3. Robert Paul Wolff, Barrington Moore, Jr., and Herbert Marcuse, *A Critique of Pure Tolerance*, pp. 51-52.
4. Henry S. Kariel, *The Decline of American Pluralism*, pp. 179-87.
5. Lowi, *End of Liberalism*, pp. 294-95.

Bibliography

Aberbach, Joel, and Walker, Jack. "The Meaning of Black Power: A Comparison of White and Black Interpretations of a Political Slogan." *American Political Science Review* 64, no. 2 (June 1970): 367-88.

Adizes, Ichak. *Industrial Democracy: Yugoslav Style.* New York: Free Press, 1971.

Aiken, Michael. "The Distribution of Community Power: Structural Bases and Social Consequences." In *The Structure of Community Power,* edited by Michael Aiken and Paul Mott, pp. 487-525. New York: Random House, 1970.

Aiken, Michael, and Alford, Robert. "Community Structure and Innovation: The Case of Public Housing." *American Political Science Review* 64, No. 3 (September 1970): 843-64.

———. "Community Structure and Mobilization: The Case of the War on Poverty." Discussion Paper, Institute for Research on Poverty, Madison: University of Wisconsin, October 1968.

Almond, Gabriel, and Powell, Bingham. *Comparative Politics.* Boston: Little, Brown & Co., 1966.

Almond, Gabriel, and Verba, Sidney. *The Civic Culture.* Boston: Little Brown & Co., 1963.

Altshuler, Alan A. *Community Control.* New York: Pegasus, 1970.

Anderson, Martin. *The Federal Bulldozer: A Critical Analysis of Urban Renewal, 1949-1962.* Cambridge, Mass.: M.I.T. Press, 1964.

Apple, R. W., Jr. "The GOP Fears November Will Be No Grand Old Picnic." *New York Times,* the Week in Review, 3 March, 1974, p. 1.

Apter, David, and Eckstein, Harry, eds. *Comparative Politics.* New York: Free Press, 1963.

Arrow, Kenneth. *Social Choice and Individual Values.* New York: John Wiley & Sons, 1951.

Bachrach, Peter. *The Theory of Democratic Elitism.* Boston: Little, Brown & Co., 1967.

Bachrach, Peter, and Baratz, Morton S. "Decisions and Nondecisions."
    American Political Science Review 57, no.3 (September 1963): 641-51.
————. *Power and Poverty: Theory and Practice*. New York: Oxford
    University Press, 1970.
————. "Two Faces of Power." *American Political Science Review* 56, no. 4
    (December 1962): 947-52.
Banfield, Edward C. *Political Influence: A New Theory of Urban Politics*.
    New York: Free Press, 1965.
Banfield, Edward C. and Wilson, James Q. *City Politics*. New York:
    Random House, 1963.
Barkai, Haim. *The Kibbutz: An Experience in Microsocialism*. Jerusalem:
    Hebrew University Press, 1971.
Barry, Brian M. *Political Argument*. London: Routledge & Kegan Paul,
    1965.
————. *Sociologists, Economists and Democracy*. London: Collier-Mac-
    millan, 1970.
Barss, Rietzel, and Associates. "Community Action and Institutional
    Changes." Unpublished report to OEO, July 1969.
Baskin, Darryl. *American Pluralistic Democracy: A Critique*. New York:
    Van Nostrand Reinhold Co., 1971.
Bauer, Raymond A.; Pool, Ithiel de Sola; and Dexter, Lewis Anthony.
    American Business and Public Policy. New York: Atherton Press, 1963.
Baumol, William J. *Economic Theory and Operations Research*. Engle-
    wood Cliffs, N. J.: Prentice-Hall, 1961.
————. *Welfare Economics and the Theory of the State*. London: G. Bell
    & Sons, 1965.
Ben-Yosef, Avraham. *The Purest Democracy in the World*. New York:
    Herzel Press, 1963.
Bennis, Warren. *Changing Organizations: Essays on the Development and
    Evolution of Human Organizations*. New York: McGraw-Hill, 1966.
Bentley, Arthur F. *The Process of Government*. Chicago: University of
    Chicago Press, 1908.
Berelson, Bernard; Lazarsfeld, Paul F.; and McPhee, William N. *Voting:
    A Study of Opinion Formation in a Presidential Campaign*. Chicago:
    University of Chicago Press, 1954.
Berlin, Isaiah. *Four Essays on Liberty*. London: Oxford University Press,
    1966.
Bettelheim, Bruno. *Children of the Dream*. London: Collier-Macmillan,
    1969.
Birch, Anthony Harold. *Small Town Politics*. London: Oxford University
    Press, 1959.

Bish, Robert L., and Nourse, Hugh O. *Urban Economics and Policy Analysis.* New York: McGraw-Hill, 1975.

Black, Duncan. *The Theory of Committees and Elections.* Cambridge: At the University Press, 1958.

Blau, Peter M. *Bureaucracy in Modern Society.* New York: Random House, 1956.

―――. *The Dynamics of Bureaucracy.* Chicago: University of Chicago Press, 1955.

Blau, Peter M., and Meyer, Marshall W. *Bureaucracy in Modern Society.* 2d ed. New York: Random House, 1971.

Blau, Peter M., and Schoenherr, Richard. *The Structure of Organizations.* New York: Basic Books, 1971.

Blumberg, Paul. *Industrial Democracy.* Cambridge, Mass.: Schenkman Publishing Co., 1972.

Boyd, Richard W. "Popular Control of Public Policy: A Normal Vote Analysis of the 1968 Election." *American Political Science Review* 66, no. 2 (June 1972): 429-49.

Braybrooke, David, and Lindblom, Charles. *A Strategy of Decision Making.* New York: Free Press, 1963.

Brody, Richard A., and Page, Benjamin I. "Comment: The Assessment of Policy Voting." *American Political Science Review* 66, no.2 (June 1972): 451-58.

Brown, Steve R., and Taylor, Richard W. "Objectivity and Subjectivity in Concept Formation: Problems of Perspective, Partition, and Frames of Reference." Paper delivered at the 66th annual meeting of the American Political Science Association, Los Angeles, September 1970.

Buchanan, James, and Tullock, Gordon. *The Calculus of Consent.* Ann Arbor: University of Michigan Press, 1969.

Bunzel, John H. "The National Federation of Independent Business." In *Interest Group Politics in America,* edited by Robert Salisbury, pp. 106-19. New York: Harper & Row, 1970.

Burtt, Everett Johnson, Jr. *Labor Markets, Unions, and Government Policies.* New York: St. Martin's Press, 1963.

Campbell, Angus; Converse, Philip E.; Miller, Warren E.; and Stokes, Donald E. *The American Voter.* New York: John Wiley & Sons, 1960.

―――. *Elections and the Political Order.* New York: John Wiley & Sons, 1966.

Campbell, Angus; Gurin, Gerald; and Miller, Warren E. *The Voter Decides.* Evanston, Ill.: Row & Peterson, 1954.

Cassinelli, C. W. "The Law of Oligarchy." *American Political Science Review* 47, no. 3 (September 1953): 773-84.

Clark, Kenneth B. *Dark Ghetto.* New York: Harper & Row, 1965.

Clark, Kenneth B., and Hopkins, Jeannette. *A Relevant War Against Poverty.* New York: Harper & Row, 1968.

Clark, Terry. "Community Structure, Decision Making, Budget Expenditures, and Urban Renewal in Fifty-one American Cities." *American Sociological Review* 33, no. 3 (August 1968): 576-91.

Cobb, Roger W., and Elder, Charles. *Participation in American Politics: The Dynamics of Agenda Building.* Boston: Allyn & Bacon, 1972.

Cohen, Sanford. *Labor Law.* Columbus, Ohio: C. F. Merrill Books, 1964.

Coleman, James. *Community Conflict.* New York: Free Press, 1957.

———. "The Possibility of a Social Welfare Function." *American Economic Review* 56, no. 5 (December 1966): 1105-23.

Connolly, William E., ed. *The Bias of Pluralism.* New York: Atherton Press, 1969.

Converse, Philip E. "The Nature of Belief Systems in Mass Publics." In *Ideology and Discontent,* edited by David E. Apter, pp. 206-61. New York: Free Press, 1964.

Cook Philip J. "Robert Michels' *Political Parties* in Perspective." *Journal of Politics* 33, no. 3 (August 1971): 773-96.

Cook, Terrence, and Morgan, Patrick. *Participatory Democracy.* San Francisco: Canfield Press, 1971.

Coser, Lewis. *The Functions of Social Conflict.* New York: Free Press, 1956.

Crain, Robert L. *The Politics of School Desegregation.* New York: Aldine, 1968.

Crain, Robert L.; Katz, Elihu; and Rosenthal, Donald. *The Politics of Community Conflict: The Fluoridation Decision.* Indianapolis: Bobbs-Merrill Co., 1969.

Crick, Bernard. *In Defense of Politics.* Baltimore: Penguin Books, 1964.

Dahl, Robert A. *After the Revolution.* New Haven: Yale University Press, 1970.

———. "Democracy and the Chinese Boxes." In *Frontiers in Democratic Theory,* edited by Henry S. Kariel, pp. 370-74. New York: Random House, 1970.

———. *Pluralistic Democracy in the United States: Conflict and Consensus.* Chicago: Rand McNally & Co., 1967.

———. *A Preface to Democratic Theory.* Chicago: University of Chicago Press, 1956.

———. *Who Governs?* New Haven: Yale University Press, 1961.

Dahl, Robert A., and Lindblom, Charles E. *Politics, Economics, and Welfare.* New York: Harper Torchbooks, 1963.

Darin-Drabkin, H. *The Other Society*. London: Victor Gollancz, 1962.

Derthick, Martha. *The Influence of Federal Grants: Public Assistance in Massachusetts*. Cambridge, Mass.: Harvard University Press, 1970.

——. *Between State and Nation: Regional Organizations of the United States*. Washington, D.C.: The Brookings Institution, 1974.

Downs, Anthony. *An Economic Theory of Democracy*. New York: Harper & Row, 1957.

Duncan, Graeme, and Lukes, Steven. "Democracy Restated." In *Frontiers in Democratic Theory*, edited by Henry S. Kariel, pp. 188-213. New York: Random House, 1970.

Dye, Thomas R., and Zeigler, L. Harmon. *The Irony of Democracy: An Uncommon Introduction to American Politics*. Belmont, Calif.: Wadsworth Publishing Co., 1970.

Eckstein, Harry. *Pressure Group Politics*. Stanford: Stanford University Press, 1960.

Edelman, Murray. *The Symbolic Uses of Politics*. Urbana: University of Illinois Press, 1967.

Eldersveld, Samuel V. *Political Parties*. Chicago: Rand McNally & Co., 1964.

Ellerman, David. "Capitalism and Workers' Self Management." In *Workers' Control*, edited by Gerry Hunnius et al., pp. 3-20. New York: Random House, 1973.

Elliot, W. Y. *The Pragmatic Revolt in Politics*. New York: Macmillan Co., 1928.

Etzioni, Amitai. *Modern Organizations*. Englewood Cliffs, N. J.: Prentice-Hall, 1964.

Fenno, Richard. *Congressmen in Committee*. Boston: Little, Brown & Co., 1973.

Field, John O., and Anderson, Ronald E. "Ideology in the Public's Conceptualization of the 1964 Election." *Public Opinion Quarterly* 33, no. 3 (Fall 1969): 380-93.

Fine, Keitha Sapsin. "Worker Participation in Israel." In *Workers' Control*, edited by Gerry Hunnius et al., pp. 226-67. New York: Random House, 1973.

Finer, S. E. "Groups and Political Participation." In *Participation in Politics*, edited by Geraint Parry, pp. 58-79. Manchester: Manchester University Press. 1972.

French, David, and French, Elena. *Working Communally*. New York: Russell Sage Foundation, 1975.

Gable, Richard. "NAM, Influential Lobby or Kiss of Death?" *Journal of Politics* 15, no. 2 (May 1953): 250-66.

Galbraith, John Kenneth. *American Capitalism.* Boston: Houghton Mifflin Co., 1956.

Gans, Herbert J. *The Urban Villagers.* New York: Free Press, 1962.

George, Alexander L. "The Case for Multiple Advocacy in Making Foreign Policy." *American Political Science Review* 66, no. 3 (September 1972): 751-86.

Gittell, Marilyn. *Participants and Participation: A Study of School Policy in New York City.* New York: Praeger, 1967.

Greenblatt, Milton, ed. *Poverty and Mental Health.* Psychiatric Research Reports, no. 21. New York: American Psychiatric Association, January 1967.

Greenstone, J. David, and Peterson, Paul E. *Race and Authority in Urban Politics.* New York: Russell Sage Foundation, 1973.

Grove, Walter, and Costner, Herbert. "Organizing the Poor: An Evaluation of a Strategy." *Social Science Quarterly* 50, no. 3 (December 1969): 643-56.

Gulick, Luther H., and Urwick, L., eds. *Papers on the Science of Administration.* New York: Institute of Public Administration, Columbia University, 1937.

Hamilton, Richard. *Class and Politics in the United States.* New York: John Wiley & Sons, 1972.

Hampden-Turner, Charles. "The Factory as an Oppressive and Non-Emancipatory Environment." In *Workers' Control,* edited by Gerry Hunnius et al., New York: Random House, 1973, pp. 30-45.

Hanson, Donald. "What is Living and What is Dead in Liberalism." *American Politics Quarterly* 2, no. 1 (January 1974): 3-37.

Harrington, Michael. *Toward a Democratic Left.* New York: Harper & Row, 1970.

Hastings, Philip K. "The Nonvoter in 1952: A Study of Pittsfield, Massachusetts." *Journal of Psychology,* 38 (October 1954): 301-12.

———. "The Voter and Nonvoter." *American Journal of Sociology* 62, no. 3 (November 1956): 302-307.

Hawley, Amos H. "Community Power Structure and Urban Renewal Success." *American Journal of Sociology* 68, no. 4 (January 1963): 422-31.

Heilbrun, James. *Urban Economics and Public Policy.* New York: St. Martin's Press, 1974.

Heinz, John. "The Political Impasse in Farm Support Legislation." In *Interest Group Politics in America,* edited by Robert Salisbury, pp. 186-98. New York: Harper & Row, 1970.

Hilsman, Roger. *To Move a Nation.* Garden City, N. Y.: Doubleday & Co., 1967.

Hine, Robert. *California's Utopian Colonies.* San Marino, Calif.: Huntington Library, 1953.

Hirsch, Werner. *The Economics of State and Local Government.* New York: McGraw-Hill, 1970.

Hirschman, Albert O. *Exit, Voice, and Loyalty: Responses to Decline in Firms, Organizations, and States.* Cambridge, Mass.: Harvard University Press, 1970.

Holden, Mathew. "Imperialism in Bureaucracy." *American Political Science Review* 60, no. 4 (December 1966): 943-51.

Hunnius, Gerry. "Workers' Self Management in Yugoslavia." In *Workers' Control,* edited by Gerry Hunnius et al., pp. 268-324. New York: Random House, 1973.

———. "Yugoslavia." In *Workers' Control,* edited by Gerry Hunnius et al., pp. 265-67. New York: Random House, 1973.

Huntington, Samuel P. *Political Order in Changing Societies.* New Haven: Yale University Press, 1968.

Jacobs, Paul and Landau, Saul, eds. *The New Radicals.* New York: Random House, 1966.

James, Dorothy B. *Poverty, Politics, and Change.* Englewood Cliffs, N. J.: Prentice-Hall, 1972.

Janis, Irving L. *Victims of Groupthink.* Boston: Houghton Mifflin Co., 1972.

Johnson, Hugh. *The Blue Eagle.* New York: Alfred A. Knopf, 1935.

Kanter, Rosabeth Moss. *Commitment and Community.* Cambridge, Mass.: Harvard University Press, 1972.

Kariel, Henry S. *The Decline of American Pluralism.* Stanford: Stanford University Press, 1961.

———, ed. *Frontiers of Democratic Theory.* New York: Random House, 1970.

Kaufman, Arnold S. "Human Nature and Participatory Democracy." In *The Bias of Pluralism,* edited by William E. Connolly, pp. 178-201. New York: Atherton Press, 1969.

Kendall, Willmore, and Carey, George W. "The 'Intensity Problem' and Democratic Theory." *American Political Science Review* 62, no. 1 (March 1968): 5-24.

Key, V. O. *Politics, Parties, and Pressure Groups.* 4th ed. New York: Thomas Y. Crowell Co., 1958.

———. *Public Opinion and American Democracy.* New York: Alfred A. Knopf, 1961.

———. *The Responsible Electorate.* Cambridge, Mass.: Harvard University Press, 1966.

Klatzky, S. R. "Relationship of Organizational Size to Complexity and

Coordination." *Administrative Science Quarterly* 15, no. 4 (December 1970): 428-38.

Kolaja, Jiri. *Workers' Councils: The Yugoslav Experience.* New York: Praeger, 1965.

Kornhauser, William. *The Politics of Mass Society.* Glencoe, Ill.: Free Press, 1959.

Kotler, Milton. *Neighborhood Government.* Indianapolis: Bobbs-Merrill Co., 1967.

Kramer, Daniel. *Participatory Democracy.* Cambridge, Mass.: Schenkman Publishing Co., 1972.

Kramer, Ralph M. *Participation of the Poor.* Englewood Cliffs, N. J.: Prentice-Hall, 1969.

Lane, Robert E., and Sears, David O. *Public Opinion.* Englewood Cliffs, N. J.: Prentice-Hall, 1964.

Laski, Harold J. *The State in Theory and Practice.* New York: Viking Press, 1935.

Lasswell, Harold; Lerner, Daniel; and Rothwell, C. Easton. *The Comparative Study of Elites.* Stanford: Stanford University Press, 1952.

Lawrence, Paul R., and Lorsch, Jay W. *Organization and Environment.* Cambridge, Mass.: Harvard University Press, 1967.

Lazarsfeld, Paul F.; Berelson, Bernard; and Gaudet, Hazel. *The People's Choice: How the Voter Makes up his Mind in a Presidential Campaign.* 2d ed. New York: Columbia University Press, 1948.

Leiserson, William M. *American Trade Union Democracy.* New York: Columbia University Press, 1959.

Leon, Don. *The Kibbutz.* London: Pergamon Press, 1969.

Leuthold, David. *Electioneering in a Democracy.* New York: John Wiley & Sons, 1968.

Levitan, Sar A., and Taggart, Robert. *The Promise of Greatness.* Cambridge, Mass.: Harvard University Press, 1976.

Lindblom, Charles E. *The Intelligence of Democracy.* New York: Free Press, 1965.

———. "Policy Analysis." *American Economic Review* 48, no. 3 (June 1958): 288-312.

———. "The Science of Muddling Through." *Public Administration Review* 19, no. 4 (Spring 1959): 79-88.

Lineberry, Robert L., and Fowler, Edmund P. "Reformism and Public Policies in American Cities." *American Political Science Review* 61, no. 3 (September 1967): 707-709.

Linz, Juan. "Robert Michels." *International Encyclopedia of the Social Sciences,* vol. 10, pp. 264-71, 1968.

Lipset, Seymour Martin. *Agrarian Socialism.* Berkeley and Los Angeles: University of California Press, 1959.

———. Lipset, Seymour Martin; Trow, Martin A.; and Coleman, James S. *Union Democracy: The Internal Politics of the International Typographical Union.* Glencoe, Ill.: Free Press, 1956.

Lockard, Duane. *The Politics of State and Local Government.* New York: Macmillan Co., 1969.

Lowi, Theodore J. "American Business, Public Policy, Case Studies, and Political Theory." *World Politics* 16, no. 4 (July 1964): 677-715.

———. *The End of Liberalism.* New York: W. W. Norton & Co., 1969.

———. "The Public Philosophy: Interest Group Liberalism." *American Political Science Review* 61, no. 1 (March 1967): 5-24.

Luttbeg, Norman. "The Structure of Beliefs Among Leaders and the Public." *Public Opinion Quarterly* 32, no. 3 (Fall 1968): 398-409.

McClosky, Herbert. "Consensus and Ideology in American Politics." *American Political Science Review* 58, no. 2 (June 1964): 361-82.

McConnell, Grant. *The Decline of Agrarian Democracy.* Berkeley and Los Angeles: University of California Press, 1953.

———. *Private Power and American Democracy.* New York: Alfred A. Knopf, 1966.

McFarland, Andrew S. *Power and Leadership in Pluralistic Systems.* Stanford: Stanford University Press, 1969.

McKean, Roland. *Public Spending.* New York: McGraw-Hill, 1968.

MacPhearson, C. B. *The Real World of Democracy.* New York: Oxford University Press, 1966.

Madison, James. "Federalist 10." In *The Federalist Papers,* by Alexander Hamilton, James Madison, and John Jay. New York: New American Library, 1961.

Mahood, H. R., ed. *Pressure Groups in American Politics.* New York: Charles Scribner's Sons, 1967.

Markovic, Dragan, et al. *Factories to Their Workers.* Belgrade; Prirredni Pregled, 1965.

Marris, Peter, and Rein, Martin. *Dilemmas of Social Reform.* New York: Atherton Press, 1967.

Masters, Nicholas A.; Salisbury, Robert H.; and Eliot, Thomas H. "The School Men in Missouri." In *Interest Group Politics in America,* edited by Robert Salisbury, pp. 216-43. New York: Harper & Row, 1970.

Matthews, Donald. *U.S. Senators and Their World.* New York: Vintage Books, 1960.

May, John. "Democracy, Organizations, Michels." *American Political Science Review* 59, no. 2 (June 1965): 417-29.

Mayo, H. B. *An Introduction to Democratic Theory.* New York: Oxford University Press, 1960.

Merton, Robert K. *Social Theory and Social Structure.* Glencoe, Ill.: Free Press, 1957.

Michels, Robert. *Political Parties: A Sociological Study of the Oligarchical Tendencies of Modern Democracy.* Translated by Eden Paul and Cedar Paul. 1915. Reprint. Glencoe, Ill.: Free Press, 1958.

Miller, Warren E., and Stokes, Donald E. "Constituency Influence in Congress." *American Political Science Review* 57, no. 1 (March 1963): 45-56.

Miner, Horace. *St. Denis, A French Canadian Parish.* Chicago: University of Chicago Press, 1963.

Moley, Raymond. *The First New Deal.* New York: Harcourt, Brace & World, 1966.

Moynihan, Daniel Patrick. *Maximum Feasible Misunderstanding.* New York: Free Press, 1969.

Mueller, John E. "Voting on the Propositions: Ballot Patterns and Historical Trends in California." *American Political Science Review* 63, no. 4 (December 1969): 1197-1212.

Musgrave, Richard A., and Musgrave, Peggy B. *Public Finance in Theory and Practice.* New York: McGraw-Hill, 1973.

Neal, Fred. *Titoism in Action.* Berkeley and Los Angeles: University of California Press, 1958.

Neuberger, Richard. "Governments by the People." *Survey* 86, no. 11 (November 1950): 490-93.

Neustadt, Richard. *Presidential Power.* New York: John Wiley & Sons, 1960.

Newfield, Jack, and Greenfield, Jeff. *A Populist Manifesto.* New York: Praeger, 1972.

Nie, Norman; Verba, Sidney; and Petrocik, John. *The Changing American Voter.* Cambridge, Mass.: Harvard University Press, 1976.

Niemi, Richard. "Majority Decision Making with Partial Unidimensionality." *American Political Science Review* 63, no. 2 (June 1969): 488-97.

Obradovic, Josip. "Participation and Work Attitudes in Yugoslavia." *Industrial Relations* 9, no. 2 (February 1970): 161-69.

Office of Economic Opportunity, Office of Operations. "Utilization Test Survey Data for 591 CAA's."

Olson, Mancur, Jr., *The Logic of Collective Action.* New York: Schocken Books, 1968.

Ostrom, Elinor, et al. *Community Organization and the Provision of Police Services.* Beverly Hills, Calif.: Sage Professional Papers in Administration and Policy Studies, 1973.

Page, Benjamin I., and Brody, Richard A. "Policy Voting and the Electoral Process: The View Nam War Issue." *American Political Science Review* 66, no. 3 (September 1972): pp. 979-96.

Parry, Geraint, ed. *Participation in Politics.* Manchester: Manchester University Press, 1972.

———. *Political Elites.* London: George Allen and Unwin, 1969.

Pateman, Carole. *Participation and Democratic Theory.* Cambridge: At the University Press, 1970.

Perrow, Charles. *Complex Organizations.* Glenview, Ill.: Scott, Foresman & Co., 1972.

———. "A Framework for the Comparative Analysis of Organizations." *American Sociological Review* 32, no. 2 (April 1967): 194-208.

———. *Organizational Analysis: A Sociological Review.* Belmont, Calif.: Brooks/Cole Publishing, 1970.

———. "Technology and Organizational Structure." In *Proceedings of the Nineteenth Annual Meeting of the Industrial Relations Research Association,* pp. 156-63, Madison, Wis., 1967.

Pitkin, Hanna F. *The Concept of Representation.* Berkeley and Los Angeles: University of California Press, 1967.

Piven, Frances Fox, and Cloward, Richard. *Regulating the Poor.* New York: Vintage Books, 1971.

Polsby, Nelson. *Community Power and Political Theory.* New Haven: Yale University Press, 1963.

Pomper, Gerald M. *Elections in America: Control and Influence in Democratic Politics.* New York: Dodd, Mead & Co., 1974.

Popper, Karl. *The Logic of Scientific Discovery.* New York: Harper & Row, 1968.

Prewitt, Kenneth. "Political Ambitions, Volunteerism, and Electoral Accountability." *American Political Science Review* 64, no. 1 (March 1970): 5-18.

Rabin, A. I. *Growing Up in the Kibbutz.* New York: Springer Publishing Co., 1965.

Ranney, Austin, and Kendall, Willmore. *Democracy and the American Party System.* New York: Harcourt, Brace & Co., 1956.

Rayack, Elton. *Professional Power and American Medicine.* New York: World Publishing Co., 1967.

RePass, David E. "Issue Salience and Party Choice." *American Political Science Review* 65, no. 2 (June 1971): 389-400

Ricci, David M., and Keynes, Edward. *Political Power, Community and Democracy.* Chicago: Rand McNally & Co., 1970.

Riker, William H., and Brams, Steve J. "The Paradox of Vote Trading." *American Political Science Review* 67, no. 4 (December 1973): 1235-47.

Riley, Patrick, "A Possible Explanation of Rousseau's General Will." *American Political Science Review* 64, no. 1 (March 1970): 86-93.

Rourke, Francis E. *Bureaucracy, Politics, and Public Policy.* Boston: Little, Brown & Co., 1969.

Rousseau, Jean Jacques. *The Social Contract.* In *Political Writings.* Translated by F. Watkins. Edinburgh: Thomas Nelson & Sons, 1953.

Rus, Veljko. "Influence Structure in Yugoslav Enterprise." *Industrial Relations* 9, no. 2 (February 1970): 148-60.

Sartori, Giovanni. *Democratic Theory.* New York: Praeger, 1958.

Sayre, Wallace S., and Kaufman, Herbert. *Governing New York City: Politics in the Metropolis.* New York: Russell Sage Foundation, 1960.

Schattschneider, Elmer Eric. *The Semi-Sovereign People.* New York: Holt Rinehart & Winston, 1960.

Schlesinger, Arthur M., Jr. *The Coming of the New Deal.* Vol II of *The Age of Roosevelt.* Boston: Houghton Mifflin Co., 1958.

Schumpeter, Joseph A. *Capitalism, Socialism and Democracy.* New York: Harper & Brothers, 1950.

Seidman, Harold. *Politics, Position, and Power.* New York: Oxford University Press, 1970.

Selznick, Philip. *Leadership in Administration: A Sociological Interpretation.* New York: Harper and Row, 1957.

———. *TVA and the Grass Roots.* Berkeley and Los Angeles: University of California Press, 1949.

Simon, Herbert A., and March, James G. *Organizations.* New York: John Wiley & Sons, 1958.

Simpson, Richard, and Gulley, William. "Goals, Environmental Pressures, and Organizational Characteristics." *American Sociological Review* 27, no. 3 (June 1962): 344-50.

Spiro, Melford. *Children of the Kibbutz.* New York: Schocken Books, 1965.

———. *Kibbutz: Ventures in Utopia.* Cambridge, Mass.: Harvard University Press, 1956.

Stern, Boris. *The Kibbutz That Was.* Washington, D. C.: Public Affairs Press, 1965.

Sullivan, John L., and O'Connor, Robert E. "Electoral Choice and Popular Control of Public Policy: The Case of the 1966 House Elections." *American Political Science Review* 66, no. 4 (December 1972): 1256-68.

Sundquist, James L. *Making Federalism Work.* Washington, D.C.: The Brookings Institution, 1969.

Talmon, J. L. *The Origins of Totalitarian Democracy.* New York: Praeger, 1960.

Talmon, Yonina. *Family and Community in the Kibbutz.* Cambridge, Mass.: Harvard University Press, 1972.

Thompson, James D. *Organizations in Action.* New York: McGraw-Hill, 1967.

Tiebout, Charles. "A Pure Theory of Local Expenditures." *Journal of Political Economy* 64 (October 1956): 416-24.

Tornquist, David. *Look East, Look West: The Socialist Adventure in Yugoslavia.* New York: Macmillan Co., 1966.

Truman, David. *The Governmental Process.* New York: Alfred A. Knopf, 1951.

U. S. Department of Commerce. *Annual Report of the Secretary.* Washington, D.C.: Government Printing Office, 1922.

Verba, Sidney, and Nie, Horman H. *Participation in America.* New York: Harper & Row, 1972.

Vidich, Arthur J., and Bensman, Joseph. *Small Town in Mass Society: Class, Power and Religion in a Rural Community.* Garden City, N.Y.: Doubleday & Co., 1960.

Wagner, Hardy. *Erfahr ungen mit dem Betriebsverfassungsgesetz.* Cologne: Bund-Verlag, 1960.

Walker, Jack L. "A Critique of the Elitist Theory of Democracy." *American Political Science Review* 60, no. 2 (June 1966): 285-95.

Weber, Max. *From Max Weber: Essays in Sociology.* Translated and edited by H. H. Gerth and C. Wright Mills. London: Oxford University Press, 1946.

Weingarten, Murray. "The Individual and the Community." In *Man Alone,* edited by Eric Josephson and Mary Josephson, pp. 516-32. New York: Dell Publishing Co., 1962.

Wilson, James Q. *The Amateur Democrat.* Chicago: University of Chicago Press, 1962.

―――. "Innovation in Organizations: Notes towards a Theory." In *Approaches to Organizational Design,* edited by James D. Thompson, pp. 193-218. Pittsburgh: University of Pittsburgh Press, 1966.

―――. *Political Organizations.* New York: Basic Books, 1973.

Wolff, Robert Paul. *In Defense of Anarchism.* New York: Harper & Row, 1970.

―――. *The Poverty of Liberalism.* Boston: Beacon Press, 1968.

Wolff, Robert Paul; Moore, Barrington, Jr.,; and Marcuse, Herbert. *A Critique of Pure Tolerance.* Boston: Beacon Press, 1965.

Wolfinger, Raymond E., and Greenstein, Fred I. "The Repeal of Fair Housing Legislation in California: An Analysis of Referendum Voting." *American Political Science Review* 62, no. 3 (September 1968): 753-69.

Wolfinger, Raymond E.; Wolfinger, Barbara Kay; Prewitt, Kenneth; and Rosenhach, Sheilah. "America's Radical Right: Politics and Ideology." In *Ideology and Discontent*, edited by David E. Apter, pp. 262-93. New York: Free Press, 1964.

Yates, Douglas. *Neighborhood Democracy*. Lexington, Mass.: D. C. Heath & Co., 1973.

Zeigler, Harmon. *Interest Groups in American Society*. Englewood Cliffs, N.J.: Prentice-Hall, 1964.

Zukin, Sharon. *Beyond Marx and Tito*. London: Cambridge University Press, 1975.

Zupanov, Josip, and Tannenbaum, Arnold S. "The Distribution of Control in Some Yugoslav Industrial Organizations as Perceived by Members." In *Control in Organizations*, edited by Arnold Tannenbaum, pp. 91-109. New York: McGraw-Hill, 1958.

Index

About the Author

William Kelso, assistant professor of political science at the University of Florida, has specialized in American political theory and public administration. His articles have appeared in *The Bureaucrat, Midwest Review of Public Administration,* and other journals.